Unarmed Forces

The Transnational Movement to End the Cold War

MATTHEW EVANGELISTA

Cornell University Press

ITHACA AND LONDON

To Clara and Marielle
and to their grandparents

THIS BOOK HAS BEEN PUBLISHED WITH THE AID OF A GRANT FROM THE
HULL MEMORIAL PUBLICATION FUND OF CORNELL UNIVERSITY

First published 1999 by Cornell University Press
First printing, Cornell Paperbacks, 2002

Printed in the United States of America

Library of Congress Cataloging-in-Publication Data

Evangelista, Matthew, 1958–
  Unarmed forces : the transnational movement to end the
Cold War / Matthew Evangelista.
    p. cm.
  Includes index.
  ISBN-13: 978-0-8014-3628-4 (cloth : alk. paper)
  ISBN-10: 0-8014-3628-1 (cloth : alk. paper)
  ISBN-13: 978-0-8014-8784-2 (pbk. : alk. paper)
  ISBN-10: 0-8014-8784-6 (pbk. : alk. paper)
    1. World politics—1989– 2. Cold War. I. Title.
D860.E93 1999
327.1'74'09045—dc21   98-51376

Cornell University Press strives to use environmentally responsible
suppliers and materials to the fullest extent possible in the publishing
of its books. Such materials include vegetable-based, low-VOC inks
and acid-free papers that are recycled, totally chlorine-free, or partly
composed of nonwood fibers. For further information, visit our website at
www.cornellpress.cornell.edu.

Cloth printing   10 9 8 7 6 5 4 3 2 1
Paperback printing 10 9 8 7 6 5 4 3 2

Contents

Preface

I began work on this book in the second half of the 1980s, at a time when the United States and the Soviet Union were engaged in an expensive and dangerous arms race and a major debate was raging over what to do about it. In those days, many people around the world had come to believe that the Soviet and U.S. governments were incapable of ending the arms race and the Cold War on their own. Citizens began to form transnational networks across the Iron Curtain to promote ideas and policies that would lessen the danger of superpower conflict. Particularly active were scientists and physicians, many of whom had engaged in similar transnational activity back in the 1950s and 1960s.

When I began to study the influence of transnational activism on the military policies of the United States and the Soviet Union, the topic was of immediate policy relevance. People wondered whether such efforts made any difference. What was the likelihood that Soviet participants in such transnational efforts were doing anything other than mouthing the official policies of their governments? Would not a surer route to ending the Cold War lie in support for the U.S. government's official policy of "peace through strength"? The literature in political science on transnational relations was not of much help in answering these questions. It dealt neither with military policy nor with the Soviet Union.

Much has changed since then. The Cold War and the arms race are over. My questions about the impact of U.S.-Soviet transnational networks shifted from the realm of policy debate to the realm of historical debate—a very contentious and lively debate about how the Cold War ended. At the same time, a new opportunity has arisen to conduct historical research using primary sources from the Soviet era. To be sure, these newly available memoirs, interviews, and archival documents do not tell us all we want to know. The *New*

York Times has aptly characterized the Russian archives as "a half-open, dirty window on the past." Access to materials on many sensitive military issues is still limited. Nevertheless, getting hold of the documents now available was unimaginable when I first began research for this book.

The combination of advances in the literature on transnationalism and possibilities for original historical research has led me to emphasize history over theory. This book presents a rich, theoretically informed history of key developments in the Soviet-American arms race and a reinterpretation of the course of the Cold War and how it ended.

A number of institutions have supported this project by providing funds for research and travel: the Center for Russian and East European Studies, the Program on International Peace and Security Research, and the Memorial-Phoenix Project at the University of Michigan; Harvard University's Center for Science and International Affairs; the United States Institute of Peace; the National Council for Soviet and East European Research; the American Council of Learned Societies; the Council on Economic Priorities; the Cold War International History Project; and Cornell University's Peace Studies Program. I thank the Hull Fund for supporting the book's publication.

I am grateful to the staffs at several archives and libraries where I conducted research: the Center for the Storage of Contemporary Documentation (the former Communist Party Central Committee archive), the archive of the Foreign Ministry of the Russian Federation, and the archive of the Russian Academy of Sciences in Moscow; the document center at Harvard University's Lamont Library, where I consulted Soviet archival materials on microfilm; the Hoover Institution Library at Stanford University, where I benefited from listening to some of the many hours of interviews conducted by Michael McFaul and Sergei Markov with former Soviet officials in the early 1990s; the Public Record Office in London; and the Dwight D. Eisenhower Library in Abilene, Kansas. Over the years I have benefited from the excellent research assistance of Marc Bennett, Paul Passavant, Yury Polsky, and Sharon Werning.

Many scholars, activists, and policymakers have assisted this project by agreeing to interviews, reading drafts, sharing documents, photographs, and information, and generally offering encouragement. I would particularly like to thank Aleksei Arbatov, Valerie Bunce, Anne Cahn, Jeffrey Checkel, Anatolii Cherniaev, Walter Clemens, Thomas Cochran, Jonathan Dean, Paul Doty, Randall Forsberg, Raymond Garthoff, Charles Glaser, Lisbeth Gronlund, David Holloway, Martin Kaplan, Peter Katzenstein, Stuart Kaufman, Sergei Khrushchev, Andrei Kokoshin, Georgii Kornienko, Mark Kramer, Bernd Kubbig, Milton Leitenberg, James Lerager, Bernard Lown, Katherine Magraw, Sarah Mendelson, Tom Milne, Christopher Paine, Robert Pape, Bruce Parrott, Pavel Podvig, Yale Richmond, Thomas Risse, Joseph Rotblat, Roald Sagdeev, Evgenii Shaposhnikov, Stephen Shenfield, Joanna Spear, Jeremy Stone, Boris Surikov, Sidney Tarrow, Aleksei Titkov, Evgenii Velikhov, Frank von Hippel, Kimberly Zisk, Vladislav Zubok, and Mikhail Zuev. I am grateful to Charles

Naef for arranging for me to meet Mikhail Gorbachev for the first time; to John LeRoy for copyediting; to Sandra Kisner for proofreading and help in preparing the index; and to Roger Haydon of Cornell University Press for his unstinting support throughout the preparation of this book.

I owe a special debt of gratitude to David Wright for several discussions on the topic of U.S.-Soviet scientific cooperation on arms control, and particularly for sharing the results of his research into the archives of the American Academy of Arts and Sciences Committee on International Studies of Arms Control and his notes on interviews with key participants. David's commitment to dealing with the still persistent problems of arms control, in his work with Lisbeth Gronlund and others (including training a new generation of transnational scientists), has left him little time to pursue his own study of the history of transnational efforts to end the Soviet-American arms race. I hope he finds that I have done justice to the subject.

In the acknowledgments to my first book I neglected to thank Joshua Epstein, who had loaned me one of the key documents I had used in writing it. If I have committed any comparably egregious error of omission this time, I apologize in advance.

Parts of this book were written in Moscow in May and June 1997 as I waited for archivists to find materials for me (or excuses not to give me any). I am grateful to the Institute of Economic Problems of the Transition Period and Harvard's Davis Center in Moscow for arranging my invitation and to Stefan Zhurek for loaning me his apartment. I thank Barry Strauss and Judith Reppy for providing a Peace Studies travel grant to fund the trip. I thank the members of my family for their indulgence while I was gone and during my "virtual" absence (even though I write at home) for the month following my return as I worked like an *udarnik* to finish the manuscript.

Despite the difficult conditions for research in the former Soviet Union, I enjoyed my many trips there thanks especially to the hospitality of Mikhail Selikhov and his family: Olia, Mikhail *mladshii*, and Mitia. I first met Misha near the nuclear test site in Kazakhstan, where he was filming a documentary for Soviet television; he has been a source of friendship and support throughout the project.

Much of my interest in the role of scientists in the arms race stems from the time during the early 1980s I spent as a graduate student affiliated with Cornell University's Peace Studies Program. There I learned a great deal from the veterans of many transnational campaigns for arms control and disarmament—Hans Bethe, Kurt Gottfried, Franklin Long, and Peter Stein most prominent among them—from the directors of the Program, Judith Reppy and Richard Ned Lebow, and from other students, many of them representing a younger generation of physicists involved in the disarmament work of the November 11th Committee. Nothing has pleased me more than to find myself completing this book back at Cornell.

MATTHEW EVANGELISTA

Ithaca, New York

The President said that he would like to see some social scientists brought into our security planning to study how long civilization can take these weapons developments.

—Report of President Dwight D. Eisenhower's comments at a National Security Council meeting, 1955

Why are so many social scientists so anxious to give advice to policymakers when there is nothing in their theories that would suggest that it would do any good?

—Stephen D. Krasner, 1978

History is not a variable to be neatly reduced to international structure or international situation; nor is it an infinite set of possibilities that actors can explore at their own will. A historically oriented social science makes contingent generalizations in periods when important parameters are reasonably stable. In the absence of a social-science version of chaos theory, it describes political conflicts and policy choices when they are unstable, hoping to capture how norms shape the definition of actor interests and thus the politics of state security.

—Peter Katzenstein, 1996

PART I

Transnational Relations and the Cold War

[1]

Taming the Bear

It is characteristic of the Pugwash movement that it has always combined ideals and long-term aims with concrete work aimed at more immediate targets. It has not sought public and media attention, and it is not tied into the political decision-making process. What it has been able to make the most of is the fact that scientists have a shared frame of reference and speak the same language across ideological, religious or national dividing lines.

—FRANCIS SEJERSTED, 1995

In 1995 the Norwegian Nobel Committee, chaired by Francis Sejersted, awarded its Peace Prize to the original transnational antinuclear movement—the Pugwash Conferences on Science and World Affairs—and to its president and founder, Joseph Rotblat. Most people had barely heard of the organization or its accomplishments. For many of those who did know Pugwash, the Nobel Prize seemed a welcome, if belated, acknowledgment of the role that the transnational movement had played in seeking to halt the Soviet-American arms race.

For its supporters Pugwash achieved its greatest success in helping Soviet leader Mikhail Gorbachev in his effort to end the Cold War.[1] The very expression associated with Gorbachev's foreign policy—the "new thinking"—comes from the founding document of the Pugwash movement, a statement drafted by Bertrand Russell and endorsed by Albert Einstein in 1955.[2] Eduard Shevardnadze, the foreign minister who carried out Gorbachev's epochal reforms, paid tribute to the Russell-Einstein manifesto in his memoirs as "the key to the most complex and troublesome riddles of the age."[3]

Despite such praise for Pugwash and its ideals, the Nobel award generated some harsh criticism in the United States. The *Wall Street Journal* published an

1. Metta Spencer, "'Political' Scientists," *Bulletin of the Atomic Scientists* 51, 4 (July/August 1995): 62–68.
2. The document is reprinted as Appendix 1 in Joseph Rotblat, *Scientists in the Quest for Peace: A History of the Pugwash Conferences* (Cambridge, Mass., 1972).
3. Eduard Shevardnadze, *The Future Belongs to Freedom*, trans. Catherine Fitzpatrick (New York, 1991), 46–47.

Bertrand Russell's 1955 manifesto launched the Pugwash movement of scientists and provided some of the inspiration for the "new thinking" that motivated Mikhail Gorbachev's foreign policy thirty years later. Here Russell is congratulated on his ninetieth birthday in 1962 by Joseph Rotblat, Pugwash secretary-general and the leading force behind the movement for decades. Photo courtesy of Pugwash and Professor Rotblat, used by permission.

opinion piece denouncing Pugwash, and the *New York Times*, in its news story, devoted three paragraphs to quoting the views of a former official in President Ronald Reagan's administration that the organization could not "be seen as anything other than, at the very least, an unwitting tool of the Kremlin, if not worse." At best the official offered to give Pugwash participants "the benefit of the doubt and think they were simply dupes."[4] In 1996 a respected *New York Times* science reporter repeated the Reagan official's criticism of the scientists and went a step beyond. Joseph Rotblat was the only participant in the Manhattan Project, the wartime program to develop the U.S. atomic bomb, to have resigned on ethical grounds. When it became apparent that Nazi Germany would be defeated before it could build the bomb, Rotblat could find no moral justification for continuing his participation. Rather than credit this explanation for Rotblat's return to civilian work in England, the reporter insinuated that the scientist might have been a spy for the Soviet Union.[5]

The negative reaction to the Nobel Committee's decision to award its Peace Prize to Pugwash was hardly unprecedented. A decade earlier, another transnational disarmament movement, the International Physicians for the Prevention of Nuclear War (IPPNW), had received the prize for its efforts to increase public awareness of the dangers of nuclear weapons. Dr. Evgenii Chazov, IPPNW's Soviet co-president, came under harsh criticism when it was revealed that he had once signed a letter denouncing the human rights activist Andrei Sakharov, himself a Nobel laureate, and that his Soviet chapter of IPPNW included psychiatrists who were implicated in the repression of Soviet dissidents by confining them in mental hospitals. The American co-president of IPPNW, Dr. Bernard Lown, was criticized as naive or worse.[6] He was in good company, though. During the 1950s, Nobel laureate Dr. Albert Schweitzer, widely revered for his humanitarian work in Africa, was denounced within the U.S. State Department and in some U.S. newspapers as a communist dupe for his advocacy of a nuclear test ban.[7]

Given the degree of ignorance and controversy that surrounds the transnational disarmament movement, a study of its activities during the Cold War is important just to set the historical record straight. That is the first goal of this book: to elucidate the role that such actors as Pugwash and the international physicians movement played in East-West relations during the four decades following the death of the Soviet dictator Iosif Stalin. My main focus is how transnational actors sought to moderate Soviet and U.S. military

4. Frank J. Gaffney, Jr., quoted in Richard W. Stevenson, "Peace Prize Goes to A-Bomb Scientist Who Turned Critic," *New York Times*, 14 October 1995; George Melloan, "Oslo's Nobel Peace Message Is Mostly Static," *Wall Street Journal*, 16 October 1995.

5. William J. Broad, "Still Battling the Nuclear Menace 50 Years after Manhattan Project," *New York Times*, 21 May 1996. For a more fair-minded discussion of Rotblat, see Susan Landau, "Joseph Rotblat: The Road Less Traveled," *Bulletin of the Atomic Scientists* 52, 1 (January/February 1996): 47–54.

6. See Peter Hübner, *E. Čazov—ein "ganz integrer Mann"?* Report No. 48/1985 of the Bundesinstituts für ostwissenschaftliche und internationale Studien, Cologne, 1985; and Allan Wynn and Peter Reddaway, "What Sort of Peace Do These Men Want?" *The Times* (London), 3 December 1985. I am grateful to Professor Reddaway for lending me his copy of the report.

7. Lawrence S. Wittner, "Blacklisting Schweitzer," *Bulletin of the Atomic Scientists* 51, 3 (May/June 1995): 55–61.

policies in order to bring about some accommodation through arms control and disarmament—and what factors influenced their successes and failures. I also explore why, given the achievements of the transnational peace activists in influencing Soviet policy during the 1980s, they fared far worse in Boris Yeltsin's postcommunist Russia.

In addition to its contribution to answering the crucial historical questions of how the Cold War ended and whether it could have ended sooner, this book also seeks to address an emerging debate about the role of transnational relations. Transnational relations have been defined as "regular interactions across national boundaries when at least one actor is a non-state agent or does not operate on behalf of a national government or an intergovernmental organization."[8] The concept is intended to capture a phenomenon that many have observed: ordinary citizens involving themselves in issues that used to be the exclusive preserve of governments, or promoting new issues, such as the environment or human rights, onto the agenda of interstate relations.[9] Such citizen-activists formed networks across borders, established sister-city relationships, and engaged in "track-two diplomacy" as an alternative to the official negotiations of government diplomats.[10]

The end of the Cold War and the changes in Soviet foreign policy that precipitated it constitute a hard case for demonstrating the importance of transnational relations. International security policy is already an area where state-centered explanations predominate. The early literature on transnationalism tended to neglect it.[11] Moreover, the prevailing explanations for changes in Soviet policy leave no room for transnationalism. By emphasizing the pressures of economic decline and U.S. assertiveness they obscure the importance of domestic disagreements about how to interpret and respond to internal and external constraints. In the absence of internal debates over policy, there is no point of entry for transnational actors. But we know that the Soviet Union during the Cold War, despite its facade of unity, was rife with debates about foreign policy.

8. Thomas Risse-Kappen, ed., *Bringing Transnational Relations Back In: Non-State Actors, Domestic Structures and International Institutions* (Cambridge, U.K., 1995), 3.

9. Margaret Keck and Kathryn Sikkink, *Activists beyond Borders: Advocacy Networks in International Politics* (Ithaca, N.Y., 1998); Jackie Smith, Charles Chatfield, and Ron Pagnucco, eds., *Transnational Social Movements: Solidarity beyond the State* (Syracuse, N.Y., 1997); Sidney Tarrow, *Power in Movement: Social Movements and Contentious Politics*, 2d ed. (Cambridge, U.K., 1998).

10. These activities were so widespread by the late 1980s that the Center for Innovative Diplomacy in California began publishing a quarterly *Bulletin of Municipal Foreign Policy* to report on them. On the Soviet case, see David D. Newsom, ed., *Private Diplomacy with the Soviet Union* (Lanham, Md., 1987); and Gale Warner and Michael Shuman, *Citizen Diplomats* (New York, 1987).

11. Robert O. Keohane and Joseph S. Nye, Jr., eds., *Transnational Relations and World Politics* (Cambridge, Mass., 1972). Keohane and Nye, "Transgovernmental Relations and International Organizations," *World Politics*, 27, 1 (October 1974): 39–62.

THE ARGUMENT: STRUCTURE AND OPPORTUNITY

Thus, in exploring the history of the Cold War, we have no excuse for treating the Soviet Union as a "black box," whose internal workings cannot be understood or need not be understood because the constraints of the international system tell us all we need to know. One way to understand how the external environment affected the making of Soviet and Russian foreign policy requires examining the country's domestic structure—the relative strengths of the state apparatus and societal forces and the policy networks that link them. We also seek to identify the opportunities that arose for what political scientists call "policy entrepreneurs" to promote their preferred solutions to Soviet security problems.

Recently, documents from the Russian archives, interviews, and memoir accounts have yielded an abundance of information concerning Soviet foreign policy. These sources make clear that conventional explanations err in treating such phenomena as economic decline, U.S. pressure, and the failures and inadequacies of existing policy as objective factors that influenced the Soviet Union in a straightforward way. The new evidence shows, instead, that the interpretation of the external environment and the choice of appropriate responses were frequently subject to dispute between rival Soviet political leaders and coalitions contending for influence. Policy entrepreneurs from within government and the Soviet scholarly and scientific communities sought to promote their favored policies to leaders. They often took advantage of crises, policy failures, and changes in leadership as opportunities to introduce new policy ideas, some of which came from abroad.[12]

Since the 1950s many of those policy entrepreneurs were members of transnational networks such as the Pugwash movement. The main role of Western transnational activists was to provide resources to their "allies" within the Soviet Union to influence internal Soviet debates over foreign policy. These resources typically consisted of information, arguments, ideas, and a certain legitimacy conferred by association with eminent international figures. The Soviet members of transnational networks sometimes sought to influence their government's policy by appealing to internationally accepted norms that resonated within Soviet society—such as the commitment to nuclear disarmament.

To understand how transnational organizations managed to influence such a closed and secretive society as the former Soviet Union, we must look not only to opportunity but to structure as well. I argue that certain aspects of the

12. On policy entrepreneurs, see Jeffrey T. Checkel, *Ideas and International Political Change: Soviet/Russian Behavior and the End of the Cold War* (New Haven, Conn., 1997); and Sarah Mendelson, *Changing Course: Ideas, Politics, and the Soviet Withdrawal from Afghanistan* (Princeton, N.J., 1998). On leadership change, see Valerie Bunce, *Do New Leaders Make a Difference? Executive Succession and Public Policy under Capitalism and Socialism* (Princeton, N.J., 1981).

domestic structure of the Soviet Union—in particular the domination of a weak, fragmented society by a strong, hierarchical party-state apparatus—made it difficult for new ideas to find their way to the top of the policy process. Once a window of opportunity provided policy entrepreneurs with access to the leadership, however, such ideas were often implemented quickly. The role of the leader in such hierarchical states is crucial. That is why figures such as Nikita Khrushchev, Leonid Brezhnev, and Mikhail Gorbachev cut such a high profile in our account.

In contrast to the Soviet Union, the domestic structure of the United States—an open, decentralized, fragmented state, easily influenced by strong societal and bureaucratic forces—posed no barriers to transnational activity. But transnational entrepreneurs typically found it difficult to compete with well-established and better-funded domestic interest groups and government bureaucracies in trying to get their preferred policies accepted and carried out.

Thus, differences in domestic structure help explain why it was the Soviet Union rather than the United States that led the way in winding down the Cold War, largely by implementing ideas and norms promoted by the transnational disarmament movement. Western peace activists found, surprisingly, that they often had greater impact on Soviet policies than on U.S. ones. Seeking to reduce the degree of militarization in both countries, they hoped that taming the Russian bear would eventually produce a calming effect on the American eagle as well.

THE CASES

A promising way to explore the interaction of structure and opportunity is through a close, comparative analysis of historical cases. The partial opening of the Soviet-era archives, the flood of memoir accounts by top policymakers and their aides, and the possibility to interview key figures have only recently made such an analysis possible. The story told here depends heavily on such new sources, along with U.S. and British archival documents and secondary accounts, and most of it has not been told before.[13]

This book examines Soviet, and later Russian, policy in three areas: nuclear testing, antiballistic missile defense, and conventional forces. All three of these issues were central to the Cold War military competition between the United States and the Soviet Union from the mid-1950s on, and they remained relevant in the new era of Russian-American relations. The cases are of intrinsic, historical interest—important both for explaining the Cold War and the U.S.-Soviet arms race and how they ended and for investigating the

13. For a broader historical overview, drawing on a rich array of sources, see R. Craig Nation, *Black Earth, Red Star: A History of Soviet Security Policy, 1917–1991* (Ithaca, N.Y., 1992).

role of transnational actors. From a methodological standpoint, the three cases vary along several dimensions. The balance of relevant military capabilities, the economic situation, and the role of the United States varied from period to period or case to case. In some cases, Soviet/Russian policy exhibited restraint or moderation, in others not. The level of transnational activity also varied.

Nuclear Testing

The debate over nuclear testing in the mid-1950s, which first cast attention on the international scientists' movement, allows us to examine the origins of the scientists' transnational collaboration and how well it fared in its first task. The main goal of the scientists' efforts was a comprehensive ban on nuclear tests—"the longest-sought, hardest-fought prize in the history of arms control," according to President Bill Clinton.[14]

The results of the scientists' activities in the 1950s and 1960s were mixed. The USSR for a time maintained a moratorium on testing, sometimes unilaterally, sometimes with U.S. participation. But it also dramatically broke the moratorium, despite the protests of some of its own leading scientists and their international colleagues, and exploded the world's largest nuclear device in 1961. A couple of years later, however, nuclear testing became the subject of the first major U.S.-Soviet arms control agreement: the 1963 treaty banning nuclear tests in the atmosphere, in space, and under water. This Limited Test Ban Treaty, by eliminating popular concerns about radioactive fallout, helped to demobilize the mass movement for a test ban. It was followed in the 1970s by other treaties that added moderate restrictions to the two sides' testing programs.

Then, in 1985, Mikhail Gorbachev chose nuclear testing as the first area to introduce a major unilateral Soviet initiative of restraint—a test moratorium that lasted over a year and a half, despite U.S. refusal to go along. Finally, nuclear testing was the issue that mobilized the largest popular antinuclear activity in Soviet history: The Nevada-Semipalatinsk movement, with its potent mix of ecological nationalism and transnational peace activism, brought tens of thousands of protesters into the streets and eventually shut down the main Soviet nuclear test range in Kazakhstan, thereby providing a key prerequisite for the United States, Britain, France, and China to cease their tests.

Strategic Defense

Strategic defenses have played a prominent role in the history of the U.S.-Soviet arms race and the Cold War. The Soviet Union actively pursued

---

14. James Bennet, "Clinton, at U.N., Says He'll Press Senate on Test Ban Pact," *New York Times*, 23 September 1997.

antiballistic missile (ABM) defenses in the 1960s, helping to justify U.S. pursuit of offensive, multiple-warhead missiles and its own ABM defense. At the same time, ABM became the focus of a sustained discussion between Soviet and Western scientists, many of whom came to the conclusion that the system was of dubious technical feasibility, an enormous waste of economic resources, potentially destabilizing, and a spur to the competition in offensive weapons. A large popular movement in the United States arose to protest the deployment of ABM systems around major U.S. cities. The United States and the USSR eventually agreed to limit their strategic defenses in the 1972 ABM Treaty, perhaps the most significant achievement of U.S.-Soviet arms control, and considered —by the transnational coalition of Soviet and U.S. scientists—the high point of their influence on the superpowers' security policy.

Strategic defenses burst into public consciousness again in 1983 when President Ronald Reagan announced his Strategic Defense Initiative (SDI), dubbed "Star Wars" by its critics. The impact of SDI on Soviet policy is a subject of great dispute. Supporters of Reagan's policy of "peace through strength" credit Star Wars with providing the impetus to Soviet political and economic reforms and thus constituting a major cause of the end of the Cold War. Critics argue that it actually delayed the onset of reforms and unnecessarily heightened East-West tensions. In any case, the Soviet reaction to SDI, and the role of scientists in shaping it, are essential parts of the story of how the Cold War ended.

Conventional Forces

Many historians of the Cold War argue that its main symbol, and perhaps its main cause, was the armed division of Europe that emerged in the wake of the Second World War. Efforts at easing East-West tensions through disarmament often included schemes for limiting, redeploying, or restructuring the armies that faced each other across the inter-German border. A number of proposals during the 1950s focused on the establishment of nuclear-free zones or inspection zones in central Europe, but they made little headway. The Soviet side substantially reduced its armed forces in the late 1950s and early 1960s, effectively cutting them in half. But in the late 1960s, the USSR began building up its army and improving its capability for conventional warfare in Europe. During the early 1970s formal East-West negotiations on conventional forces in Europe began, but they had little to show for themselves when they concluded a decade and a half later.

The most dramatic breakthrough in the negotiations on conventional forces in Europe came with Mikhail Gorbachev's announcement in December 1988 of a substantial unilateral reduction in the Soviet Army. This initiative was combined with a commitment to a new, defensive orientation of Soviet conventional forces and a repudiation of the previous Soviet practice of military intervention in member-states of the Warsaw Pact. All three actions—the unilateral disarmament initiative, the shift to "nonoffensive defense," and the new policy toward Eastern Europe represented in part by the notion of "common security"—had been consistently promoted by transnational activists, sometimes in personal meetings with Gorbachev and his advisers during the months before his speech.

The implications of the transnational initiatives that the USSR embraced went well beyond the sphere of disarmament. By signaling Soviet military restraint in the face of anticommunist demonstrations in east-central Europe, Gorbachev gave the green light to the dismantling of the Berlin Wall, the peaceful overthrow of communist regimes, and the reunification of Germany. Soviet concessions at the negotiating table, along with the prior unilateral reductions, finally led to the conclusion of a major treaty limiting conventional forces in Europe (CFE). Leaders of NATO, the Warsaw Pact, and a dozen nonaligned European countries emphasized the direct link between the Cold War and the armed standoff in Europe when they met in Paris in November 1990 to sign the CFE Treaty. They declared a formal end to the Cold War, stated that they were "no longer adversaries," and pledged to "build new partnerships and extend to each other the hand of friendship." [15]

The Post-Soviet Era

The expectation of harmonious relations between the former Cold War adversaries was, unfortunately, short lived. As Gorbachev dismantled the legacy of highly centralized Communist Party discipline, he left first the Soviet Union and then post-Soviet Russia with little capacity to control the still powerful members of the national-security apparatus. In competition with the Ministry of Defense, the nuclear weapons establishment, and the military-industrial sector, the transnational coalition of scientists and arms control activists found many of their goals threatened with reversal. As I describe in a chapter on the post-Soviet era, the Yeltsin administration came close to resuming its nuclear testing program in the early 1990s; elements from the Russian military and space industries sought to promote development of strategic defenses, in collaboration with Star Wars advocates in the United States; and the Russian Defense Ministry demanded a revision of the CFE Treaty to allow deployment of more forces in southern Russia, where Moscow waged a brutal war against the secessionist republic of Chechnya.

Clearly many other factors, besides the weakening of transnational influence, contributed to the deterioration in relations between Russia and the West. Russia's interference in the affairs of its neighbors, along with its efforts to sell weapons abroad and to foster relations with states antagonistic to

15. William Drozdiak, "East and West Declare the End of Cold War at Paris Conference," *International Herald Tribune,* 20 November 1990.

the United States, caused some unease in the U.S. government. From the Russian perspective, the mid-1990s saw the United States strongly advocating—against clear Russian opposition—the expansion of NATO to include former allies of the Soviet Union and perhaps even former constituent republics of the USSR that now border on Russia. Undoubtedly the promise of friendship and partnership between Russia and the West was oversold. Despite the setbacks, however, transnational relations between Russia and the United States in the security field are likely to continue, especially concerning conversion of the former Soviet military industry to civilian production and the dismantling of the nuclear complex.

Thus the study of the transnational disarmament community during the Cold War is not only of historical interest. It is a story both of missed opportunities and of surprising successes against great odds—and it holds lessons for the post-Cold War era as well. The new era is unlikely to witness the unusual combination of state structure and political opportunity that characterized the Soviet Union of the late 1980s. Instead, the lessons that one should draw from the successes and failures of transnational organizations relate mainly to their methods of persuasion and political strategy. How transnational groups share information and ideas, appeal to norms, and coordinate policy initiatives in order to achieve their ends is the topic of the final chapter.

[2]

Structure, Opportunity, and Change

It's not only a country's military potential that matters. Its economic potential plays a part too. And, in questions of economics, even bourgeois propaganda cannot assert that we took advantage of détente or anything else to achieve superiority. Quite the contrary. In adhering to a peaceful foreign policy, our country has from its very inception steadily, irreversibly, and single-mindedly been reducing its economic potential, whereas the capitalist countries have been increasing theirs. . . . We have caught up with and overtaken the United States many times already. Now you try to catch up with us. Bring your economy down to our level, so that we will have equality in armaments and in everything else as well.

—VLADIMIR VOINOVICH, 1985

Since the demise of the Soviet Union, two interrelated explanations for Soviet retrenchment have come to the fore. One emphasizes Soviet economic decline; the other focuses on the role of U.S. behavior, particularly the policies of containment and "peace through strength." The explanations are often linked, as in the argument that U.S. military policy exacerbated Soviet economic woes by forcing the USSR to compete in a high-technology arms race. Eventually the Soviet leadership recognized the futility of the effort and began enacting reforms—in both domestic and foreign policy. But these reforms could not stave off the collapse of the system and the breakup of the country in 1991.

This interpretation of the sources of Soviet retrenchment and reform is not merely a product of the end of the Cold War and the demise of the USSR. It has been one of the explanations most frequently offered for periods of Soviet moderation dating back to the 1950s, and it was particularly favored within various branches of the U.S. government. Throughout the Cold War, observers sought to account for changes in Soviet policy by appealing to the impact of economic conditions and U.S. behavior.

A related explanation—one that has not survived the demise of the USSR quite so well—argues, in effect, that moderation in Soviet security policy was not really moderation at all. In this view, instances of apparent Soviet restraint in the security sphere were actually dictated by military requirements. Given a limited military budget, the argument goes, the Soviet Union could not accord the same priority to all of its military programs at once. One should expect to see restraint in certain programs (for example, strategic nuclear weapons) at times when other programs (say, conventional forces) were receiving higher priority. At its extreme, this explanation can account even for absolute decreases in Soviet military budgets and substantial reductions in forces (either unilaterally or through disarmament agreements). These actions would be described as "breathing spaces," necessary to prepare the USSR for future military competition.

Although the breakup of the Soviet Union would appear to render the "breathing space" argument irrelevant for understanding the dramatic retrenchment of the last years of the USSR, some alarmist predictions about future Russian policy depend on the same logic: once Russia recovers economically it will again be ready and willing to engage the West in conflict.[1] As one observer put it, "Russia is down but far from out; with its literate population and unlimited resources, now unstultified by Communism, it will regain superpower status soon."[2] So an evaluation of even this explanation could be of policy relevance as well as historical interest.

All three of these interrelated explanations—economic stringency, U.S. behavior, and military requirements—share a common feature. They underestimate the contingent nature of Soviet policy decisions and the role of internal debates about the country's security policy.

The most popular version of the explanation that focuses on U.S. behavior holds that external pressure induced Soviet moderation—specifically, that Soviet restraint resulted from a U.S. practice of negotiation from strength. In some variants, the notion was narrowly defined to mean that threats of Western military deployments could be used as "bargaining chips" to secure reductions or limitations in Soviet forces.[3] More extreme versions of "negotiation from strength" or "peace through strength" focused on strength more than on negotiation. Their proponents often opposed negotiations on principle. They maintained that Soviet change could be induced only by external Western pressure, in the form of both military programs and economic warfare, until the Soviet leadership saw no alternative but to reform.[4] In this view, an unwavering policy of U.S. "strength" would contribute to that end, even without formal negotiations.

The peace-through-strength explanation is consistent with George Kennan's predictions about the consequences of a U.S. policy of "containment" of the USSR: In 1947 he argued that the Kremlin could not "face frustration

1. See, e.g., Mark Helprin, "The Power of Russia Alone," *Wall Street Journal*, 27 December 1991.

2. William Safire, "The End of Yalta," *New York Times*, 9 July 1997.

3. For sophisticated analyses of the sources of successful bargaining on arms control, see George Bunn, *Arms Control by Committee: Managing Negotiations with the Russians* (Stanford, Calif., 1992); and April Carter, *Success and Failure in Arms Control Negotiations* (Oxford, U.K., 1989).

4. Richard Pipes, "Can the Soviet Union Reform?" *Foreign Affairs* 63, 1 (1984): 47–61.

indefinitely without eventually adjusting itself in one way or another to the logic of that state of affairs." Such adjustment would entail either the "break-up or the gradual mellowing of Soviet power."[5] From the perspective of the late twentieth century, Kennan's words seemed quite prophetic. The irony, however, is that Kennan believed that Soviet power had mellowed already by the middle 1950s, following the death of Stalin, and that U.S. insistence on a policy of militarized containment actually prolonged the Cold War unnecessarily for decades. Debates about how the Cold War ended become, in this respect, debates about whether it could have ended far sooner.

Proponents of "strength" typically argued that domestic political disagreements within the Soviet leadership were nonexistent or of little consequence. A conception of a monolithic Soviet decision-making system was implicit in arguments, such as the one made by a prominent historian of the Cold War, that U.S. military pressure could put such a strain on the Soviet economy "that the Soviet leadership would have little choice but to make substantial concessions on arms control."[6] For some observers, it mattered little even who held the top office in the Soviet Union—that of general secretary of the Communist Party—because any Soviet leader was expected to respond appropriately to U.S. positions of strength. Thus, on the eve of the Gorbachev revolution, Richard Pipes, a Harvard professor who worked for the Reagan administration, claimed that "it is really not so important who succeeds Chernenko" as general secretary (it was Gorbachev).[7]

Many explanations based on economic stringency have a mechanistic, even deterministic, quality. They take little account of possible internal Soviet disagreements about the nature of the external threat and the state of the economy. The typical argument maintained that the Soviet Union was compelled by economic circumstances to limit its military forces by negotiated agreement or unilateral action and to retrench in its strategic commitments. When the growth rate declined, when competition for resources between the civilian and military sectors became particularly severe, when major bottlenecks occurred, the Soviets would be compelled to slacken their military efforts, even without a formal agreement.

More sophisticated accounts recognize that assessments of relative economic and military strength are matters of perception.[8] There are two ways

5. George F. Kennan [under pseudonym "X"], "The Sources of Soviet Conduct," *Foreign Affairs* 25 (1947): 566–582; Jerry F. Hough, "The 'X' Article and Contemporary Sources of Soviet Conduct," in Terry L. Deibel and John Lewis Gaddis, eds., *Containing the Soviet Union* (London, 1987).

6. John Lewis Gaddis, "Hanging Tough Paid Off," *Bulletin of the Atomic Scientists* 45, 1 (January 1989): 13.

7. Richard Pipes, "Intelligence in the Formation of Foreign Policy," in Roy Godson, ed., *Intelligence Requirements for the 1980's* (Lexington, Mass., 1986), 43.

8. Aaron L. Friedberg, *The Weary Titan: Britain and the Experience of Relative Decline, 1895–1905* (Princeton, N.J., 1988); William Wohlforth, *The Elusive Balance: Power and Perceptions during the Cold War* (Ithaca, N.Y., 1993); Thomas J. Christensen, *Useful Adversaries: Grand Strategy, Domestic Mobilization, and Sino-American Conflict, 1947–1958* (Princeton, N.J., 1996).

that a state could come to moderate its security policy in response to apparent economic and military constraints. First, the leadership could reach a consensus that moderation is the best course. If consensus is easily and often achieved, one could justifiably model the state as a unitary actor. The second way would be for proponents of moderation to outmaneuver or overpower their domestic opponents politically in order to secure a policy of moderation. In practice, absent a quick and easy consensus, proponents of moderation could use a combination of persuasion and political maneuvering to achieve their preferred policies.[9]

The case studies that follow this chapter are organized in such a way as to evaluate the most parsimonious explanations for Soviet moderation first— those that model the state as a unitary actor. If, however, we find situations where there is no consensus within the Soviet leadership about the implications of U.S. behavior or the economic and military capabilities of the USSR, then we open the way for a more subtle analysis of the internal politics of Soviet security policy, the patterns of domestic-international linkages, and the possibility that transnational relations affect Soviet policy.

TRANSNATIONAL RELATIONS AND SECURITY POLICY

Before evaluating whether transnational relations made a difference to Soviet security policy, we should explore more carefully why we might expect that they *could* have made any difference. There are many rival explanations for what caused shifts toward moderation and retrenchment in Soviet policy.[10] To claim a role for transnational relations would require indicating where existing explanations are inadequate or incorrect. Moreover, the literature on transnational relations, at least until recently, would prejudice us against expecting any transnational influence on Soviet security policy.

The present study of the effect of transnational actors on Soviet and Russian security policy addresses a country and subject that were assumed out of the original theorizing about transnational relations in the 1970s. That literature, and the related work on interdependence, argued that transnational relations would predominate in issues outside the realm of "high politics" (security policy) and in countries where democratic polities would permit penetration of government policymaking by transnational as well as domestic actors.[11] According to this perspective, the centralized, secretive, and au-

9. For the theoretical basis of this argument, with some evidence, see Matthew Evangelista, "Internal and External Constraints on Grand Strategy: The Soviet Case," in Richard Rosecrance and Arthur Stein, eds., *The Domestic Bases of Grand Strategy* (Ithaca, N.Y., 1993), 154–178.

10. For an overview, see Matthew Evangelista, "Sources of Moderation in Soviet Security Policy," in P. Tetlock et al., eds., *Behavior, Society, and Nuclear War* 2 (New York, 1991), 254–354.

11. Robert O. Keohane and Joseph S. Nye, Jr., eds., *Transnational Relations and World Politics* (Cambridge, Mass., 1972). Keohane and Nye, "Transgovernmental Relations and International Organizations," *World Politics* 27, 1 (October 1974): 39–62.

thoritarian regime that prevailed in the Soviet Union until the end of the 1980s was the archetypal "strong state" and, therefore, one of the least likely candidates for transnational influence. By the same token, security policy in the USSR would have been the most immune to such influence.

Some prominent recent work on linkages between domestic and international politics reiterates the conventional wisdom on transnational relations and security policy. For example, a summary of the findings of a collaborative project on "two-level games" notes the "sharp contrast between the security cases and the economically oriented cases on the issue of transnational alliances" and states unequivocally: "Issues of sovereignty and national security generate few transnational alliances." [12] The study's one chapter on the Soviet Union finds little evidence of transnational influence.[13]

The theoretical reasons not to expect transnational influence on Soviet security policy are straightforward. In a political system dominated by a strong party-state apparatus, such as the Soviet one, societal forces, including transnational actors, should exert little influence on policy. Moreover, in the security realm, as Jack Snyder hypothesizes, the systemic constraints of international anarchy should hinder transnational activity because countries' "fear of mutual exploitation will make cooperative security coalitions across international borders hard to form." Any transnational coalitions that do form should fare poorly in competition with domestic ones because "networks that facilitate the formation of political coalitions are thicker within countries and blocs than between them." [14]

In a pathbreaking study of relations between the United States and its European NATO allies, Thomas Risse has challenged the conventional wisdom on transnational relations and security policy. He found that transnational coalitions of societal actors and transgovernmental networks of officials were able to shift U.S. policy toward the preferences of its European allies even on such core security issues as the Korean War, nuclear weapons, and the Cuban missile crisis. In their policy preferences, transnational actors often found more in common with their counterparts in the allied country than with their own government.[15]

A number of recent studies have tried to make a similar case for the Soviet Union. They argue that transnational actors did play a role in Soviet security policy, especially during the 1980s, and that their efforts contributed to the

12. Peter B. Evans, "Building an Integrative Approach to International and Domestic Politics: Reflections and Projections," in Peter B. Evans, Harold K. Jacobson, and Robert D. Putnam, eds., *Double-Edged Diplomacy: International Bargaining and Domestic Politics* (Berkeley, Calif., 1993), 418, 424.

13. Jack Snyder, "East-West Bargaining over Germany: The Search for Synergy in a Two-Level Game," in Evans et al., *Double-Edged Diplomacy*.

14. Snyder, "East-West Bargaining," 115–116.

15. Thomas Risse-Kappen, *Cooperation among Democracies: The European Influence on U.S. Foreign Policy* (Princeton, N.J., 1995).

end of the Cold War.[16] The existing work consists mainly of article-length studies that did not benefit from access to Soviet archival sources or memoirs and were generally limited to the Gorbachev period.[17] But they do point in the direction this book takes.

TRANSNATIONAL INFLUENCE IN THEORY

Despite strong theoretical arguments against the expectation of transnational influence on Soviet security policy, then, there are compelling theoretical reasons to anticipate it. Many studies from diverse subfields of political science provide remarkably similar insights of relevance to the question of transnational influence. That literature has been extensively reviewed elsewhere.[18] Here I simply present the basic theoretical model that underlies my historical discussion. The historical accounts themselves serve to evaluate its plausibility.

Most studies of transnational activism call into question the core assumption of much of the traditional scholarship on international relations, especially in the "realist" school of political science—namely, that countries can be accurately modeled as unitary actors responding to the constraints of the international system. In much of the relevant empirical work—including the historical cases I present here—scholars test this assumption, either implicitly or explicitly, as a kind of "null hypothesis," rather than reject it a priori. In other words, if transnational actors are shown to have little influence on a country's foreign policies, and if those policies are little affected by internal, domestic politics, then perhaps states in the international system can be represented as "billiard balls," as the common metaphor puts it. That would certainly save a lot of effort in learning foreign languages and researching the actual politics of particular countries.

But scholars of transnationalism typically find another set of assumptions more useful than that of the state as a unitary, rational actor. They maintain

16. David S. Meyer, "How We Helped End the Cold War (and Let Someone Else Take All the Credit)," *Nuclear Times* (Winter 1990–91), 9–14; Gloria Duffy, "Track-Two Diplomacy and the Revolution in the Soviet Union," *Nuclear Times* 10, 2–3 (Autumn/Winter 1992): 48–51; David Cortright, *Peace Works: The Citizen's Role in Ending the Cold War* (Boulder, Colo., 1993), 209–210; Thomas Risse-Kappen, "Ideas Do Not Float Freely: Transnational Coalitions, Domestic Structures, and the End of the Cold War," *International Organization* 48, 2 (Spring 1994).

17. One important study did, however, address an earlier period of U.S.-Soviet relations: Emanuel Adler, "The Emergence of Cooperation: National Epistemic Communities and the International Evolution of the Idea of Nuclear Arms Control," *International Organization* 46, 1 (Winter 1992): 101–145.

18. See, in particular, Jeffrey T. Checkel, *Ideas and International Political Change: Soviet/Russian Behavior and the End of the Cold War* (New Haven, Conn., 1997); and Matthew Evangelista, "The Paradox of State Strength: Transnational Relations, Domestic Structures, and Security Policy in Russia and the Soviet Union," *International Organization* 49, 1 (Winter 1995): 1–38.

that within a given country, rival political coalitions often disagree over both the interpretation of the external environment (such as other states' behavior and intentions) and the appropriate foreign policies that should follow. Policy entrepreneurs seek to promote their preferred policies to leaders. Ideas and norms, as well as material interests, make a difference in determining which foreign policies a state pursues. Crises, policy failures, and changes in leadership provide "windows of opportunity" for policy entrepreneurs to introduce their new policy ideas.

In this model the transnational allies of domestic political actors provide resources to influence internal debates over foreign policy. Resources come in a number of forms. In the realm of security policy, even basic data on the relative balance of U.S. and Soviet military forces were so closely held that Soviet moderates depended on their transnational contacts to provide such information. They also drew on such resources as the ideas and arguments they heard from their foreign colleagues. Sometimes they could appeal to the reputation and views of a prominent international expert to make the case for a particular policy at home. Introducing transnational actors and their ideas into a policy debate can change the dynamics of the domestic political scene. In some cases, for example, scholars have argued that ideas promoted by transnational actors helped facilitate the formation of new domestic political coalitions by identifying previously unrecognized common interests among disparate groups. In this respect, ideas serve as a kind of coalitional "glue."[19] In the final chapter I explain why this metaphor does not capture well the experience of transnational actors in the Soviet context.

A key distinction in the study of transnational politics is between the ability of policy entrepreneurs to gain access to government decision makers and their ability to achieve implementation of their preferred policies. Variation in both appears to be associated with differences in countries' domestic structures. Decentralized, fragmented states provide multiple points of access to policy entrepreneurs and their innovative ideas, but they have difficulty implementing the new policies. Centralized, hierarchical, bureaucratized states may be resistant to new ideas at first but are able to implement relevant policies effectively, once adopted.[20] In such hierarchical states the top leadership plays a key role.

---

19. The expression comes from Judith Goldstein and Robert O. Keohane, "Ideas and Foreign Policy: An Analytical Framework," in Goldstein and Keohane, eds., *Ideas and Foreign Policy: Beliefs, Institutions, and Political Change* (Ithaca, N.Y., 1993), 17–18. They also provide a more technical definition: ideas may serve "to alleviate coordination problems arising from the absence of unique equilibrium solutions."

20. This argument parallels somewhat the one made for another issue-area—technological innovation and weapons production—in Matthew Evangelista, *Innovation and the Arms Race: How the Soviet Union and the United States Develop New Military Technologies* (Ithaca, N.Y., 1988); it, in turn, drew on Zbigniew Brzezinski and Samuel P. Huntington, *Political Power: USA/USSR* (New York, 1963).

Transnational Influence in Practice

Here we see how the Soviet system, despite our initial expectations, could under certain conditions be quite susceptible to transnational influence—especially if the policies promoted by a transnational network appeal to the top leader. But that does not mean that we should expect to find transnational influence behind every Soviet policy innovation. After all, the role of policy entrepreneur and conveyor of new ideas could be played solely by domestic actors. Indeed, at least a couple of scholarly accounts of key aspects of the "new thinking" in Soviet foreign policy after 1985 provide persuasive explanations for Soviet change, based on the role of ideas and policy entrepreneurs, but without according any great role to transnational actors.[21] The challenge for my account, then, is not only to show that a unitary-actor approach fails to explain the changes in Soviet and Russian security policy that I describe. I also have to show that by taking into consideration transnational relations I can account for the formation and content of key Soviet policy initiatives better than by focusing only on domestic political actors.

In fact I do not find that transnational networks were influential in every instance; there was considerable variation between issues and between leadership periods. Soviet leaders typically held scientists in high regard—perhaps owing to the pervasive emphasis in Soviet culture and society on engineering and technical progress. The views of a transnational network of scientists working on an arms control issue with high technical content might be expected to get a respectful hearing, especially if the network included some Nobel laureates, as Pugwash did.

But not all Soviet leaders were equally receptive to the scientists' influence. Nikita Khrushchev and Mikhail Gorbachev were more open to the scientists' views, for example, than Leonid Brezhnev, Iurii Andropov, or Konstantin Chernenko were. Khrushchev and Gorbachev seemed to welcome the opportunity to hear alternative civilian analyses of the nuclear arms race—an area that was monopolized in the USSR by professional military officers. The Brezhnev-era leaders, by contrast, seemed more comfortable conceding much of this sphere to military control. On the other hand, Brezhnev, Andropov, and Chernenko gave a sometimes sympathetic ear to the international movement of physicians who were raising alarm about the threat of nuclear war—not least because one of the movement's leaders was the personal physician on whom their fragile health depended. Undoubtedly such idiosyncratic factors played a part in many of the decisions I recount in the following chapters.

21. Sarah Mendelson, *Changing Course: Ideas, Politics, and the Soviet Withdrawal from Afghanistan* (Princeton, N.J., 1998); Jeff Checkel, "Ideas, Institutions, and the Gorbachev Foreign Policy Revolution," *World Politics* 45, 2 (January 1993): 271–300.

Perhaps most intriguing is the role of Mikhail Gorbachev. Much like Khrushchev, he seemed to welcome transnational contacts—and not only on technical issues of nuclear arms control. He paved the way for transnational activists to challenge the Soviet military's competence within their core domain of planning for conventional warfare in Europe. The influence of foreign scientists and peace activists in preparing the intellectual ground for ending the East-West military standoff in central Europe contributed much to the peaceful demise of the Cold War. Gorbachev's interest in transnational political and cultural exchanges dates to his student days in the mid-1950s—the beginning of the Khrushchev "thaw" period following Stalin's death. That time marked the birth of transnationalism in the postwar period—the topic of the next chapter.

PART II

The Khrushchev Era

[3]

The Birth of Transnationalism

It is difficult to imagine the climate of mistrust and fear that existed at the time [of the first Pugwash meeting in 1957]. It required a great deal of civic courage to come. Anyone in the West who came to such a meeting, who talked peace with the Russians, was condemned as a Communist dupe.

—Joseph Rotblat, 1996

We scientists have become like gypsies. . . . We wander from conference to conference, trying to find roads to peace, acting as voluntary advisers to our political leaders. We know better than anyone else what there is to be concerned about, so it is possible that, without trying to, we have become the most peaceful people in the world.

—Academician Lev Artsimovich, 1963

In my opinion the more frequently and broadly representatives of science, culture and the public of various countries meet with each other to discuss urgent international problems and the more concern they display for the fate of peace, the greater the guarantee that peoples' struggle for complete and universal disarmament, for final removal of war from human life and for peaceful coexistence will be crowned with success.

—Nikita Khrushchev, 1960

Iosif Stalin's death in March 1953 made possible both a relaxation of internal repression in the USSR and an improvement in the international climate. Among many other profound changes in Soviet society, the "thaw" initiated by Nikita Khrushchev and Stalin's other successors permitted greater contact with the outside world. For scientists, the new atmosphere provided opportunities to engage foreign colleagues not only on professional matters but on issues of common concern—among which the nuclear arms race was paramount. Although contacts between Soviet and Western scientists were strictly supervised by communist authorities, they still allowed for meaningful exchanges of information and ideas. Nikita Khrushchev himself endorsed direct discussions between U.S. and Soviet scientists whose access to their governments promised at least a hearing for any innovative solutions that might emerge. The Khrushchev era thus witnessed the birth of transnational efforts at disarmament, with the change in Soviet leadership representing a crucial "window of opportunity."

Transnational contacts between scientists were part of a broader phenomenon of the post-Stalin period—an opening up to the rest of the world and a renunciation of the Stalinist legacy of isolation. Two events of the mid-1950s symbolized the changes especially well; they are consistently mentioned in the reminiscences of the *shestidesiatniki*, the "children of the sixties" inspired by Khrushchev-era reformist politics. The first was a visit to Moscow State University in June 1955 by Jawaharlal Nehru, prime minister of India. Nehru's visit made a lasting impression on many people he met there, including a young law student named Mikhail Gorbachev. The Indian leader's discussions, as Gorbachev later recalled in his memoirs, "linked the question of peace to the preservation and progress of all human civilization"—themes that Gorbachev would embrace when he took control of Soviet foreign policy three decades later. As Gorbachev wrote: "For people raised on the 'class approach'" to international relations, Nehru's "words sounded at the very least unusual—they stimulated our consciousness."[1]

The second event was the World Festival of Youth, held in Moscow during the summer of 1957. In the words of Aleksei Adzhubei, Khrushchev's son-in-law and then editor of *Komsomol'skaia pravda*, the newspaper of the Young Communist League, "if the first of these" events—the visit of Nehru—"personified the new, 'open' diplomacy, the second was a step toward an open society, a manifestation of the faith *of* youth in a better future and the faith *in* youth" on the part of the authorities.[2] Another Russian observer explained that the festival "was significant in that it allowed Muscovites to see and even speak with foreigners for the first time in decades."[3] In fact, wrote the historian Roi Medvedev, it was the first time "in the history of the USSR that so many guests from other countries had come to Moscow," and the event left a strong impression in the memories of the city's residents.[4] The visit to Moscow of thousands of young men and women from around the world helped undermine the Stalinist "myth of enemy encirclement."[5]

FAILED TRANSNATIONALISM OF THE STALIN YEARS

For many Soviet scientists, and especially some older physicists, the opportunity to interact with foreigners was not the novelty it was for the young people at the Moscow festival. Rather, it was, as they saw it, a right and a pro-

1. Mikhail Gorbachev, *Zhizn' i reformy* (Moscow, 1995), 1:73.
2. Aleksei Adzhubei, *Te desiat' let* (Moscow, 1989), 119; emphasis added for clarity.
3. Vladimir Shlapentokh, *Soviet Intellectuals and Political Power: The Post-Stalin Era* (Princeton, N.J., 1990), 140.
4. R. Medvedev, "N. S. Khrushchev, god 1957-i—ukreplenie pozitsii," originally published in *Argumenty i fakty*, 1988, no. 25, reprinted in Iu. V. Aksiutin, ed., *Nikita Sergeevich Khrushchev: materialy k biografii* (Moscow, 1989), 43–47.
5. Adzhubei, *Te desiat' let*, photo caption opposite p. 192.

fessional necessity that had been taken away from them during the dark Stalin years. As David Holloway puts it, "no field better exemplified the international character of science than nuclear physics in the 1920s and 1930s."[6] Soviet physicists had been active participants in international research until the mid-1930s, spending long periods abroad, as Petr Kapitsa did at Cambridge, and inviting Western colleagues for extended stays at Soviet institutions.[7] Thereafter, increasing repression at home and the deteriorating situation abroad put an end to their collaborative efforts. The Cold War and the nuclear arms race further limited contact between Soviet and Western physicists.

The gravity of the postwar political situation led some Western scientists to attempt to forge or renew links with Soviet counterparts even under Stalin. A group of scientists who had participated in the Manhattan Project to build the first U.S. atomic weapons formed the Federation of Atomic Scientists (soon renamed the Federation of American Scientists or FAS) in order to educate the public and promote efforts at international control of atomic energy for peaceful purposes. In late 1945, the FAS established a Committee for Foreign Correspondence to enlist support from international colleagues. The following year, with funding solicited by an Emergency Committee of Atomic Scientists chaired by Albert Einstein, its members sent packets of information to three thousand foreign scientists, including many in the Soviet Union, and a questionnaire asking for their views on how to improve scientific exchanges, enhance the prospects for international control, and ensure peace.[8]

One of the most active advocates of transnational dialogue was Leo Szilard, a prominent physicist, a pioneer of nuclear fission, and, in the writer Norman Cousins's words, a "free-lance peace advocate."[9] It was Szilard who had drafted the letter that Albert Einstein sent to President Franklin Roosevelt in 1939, alerting him to the dangerous prospect of atomic weapons and setting in motion the U.S. bomb program.[10] Already in the mid-1940s Szilard was keen on the idea of bringing together Western and Soviet-bloc scientists—in what could have been an early version of the Pugwash conferences—to figure out how to prevent a nuclear arms race. After hearing similar proposals from some of Szilard's colleagues in 1946, the U.S. State

6. David Holloway, *Stalin and the Bomb: The Soviet Union and Atomic Energy, 1939–1956* (New Haven, Conn., 1994), 5.

7. For example, Victor Weisskopf (later a member of the Manhattan Project) spent eight months at the Kharkov Physical-Technical Institute in 1932. See his memoir, *The Joy of Insight: Passions of a Physicist* (New York, 1991), 52–58.

8. Alice Kimball Smith, *A Peril and a Hope: The Scientists' Movement in America, 1945–47*, rev. ed. (Cambridge, Mass., 1971), 298–299; Lawrence S. Wittner, *One World or None: A History of the World Nuclear Disarmament Movement through 1953* (Stanford, Calif., 1993), 59–61.

9. Cousins's characterization of Szilard is found in his foreword to Helen S. Hawkins, G. Allen Greb, and Gertrud Weiss Szilard, eds., *Toward a Livable World: Leo Szilard and the Crusade for Nuclear Arms Control* (Cambridge, Mass., 1987), xi.

10. For a discussion, see Barton J. Bernstein's introduction in ibid., esp. xxviii–xxx; and William Lanouette, *Genius in the Shadows: A Biography of Leo Szilard, The Man Behind the Bomb* (Chicago, 1992), chap. 15.

Department official George Kennan commented caustically that the physicists had "an unshakeable faith that if they could only get some Soviet scientists by the buttonhole and enlighten them about the nature of atomic weapons, all would be well. . . . Politically, these people are as innocent as six-year old maidens."[11]

During 1947, at Szilard's suggestion, representatives of the Emergency Committee met twice with Andrei Gromyko, then Soviet delegate to the United Nations Security Council, to propose a meeting of Soviet-bloc and Western scientists to discuss international control. At the second meeting, Gromyko conveyed Moscow's rejection of the proposal.[12] In December 1947 Szilard took his ideas directly to Stalin by writing an open letter to the Soviet dictator and publishing it in the *Bulletin of the Atomic Scientists*. He received no response.[13]

A few Soviet scientists apparently reacted positively to the initiatives undertaken by the FAS Committee for Foreign Correspondence when they met with a couple of Western visitors who still managed to travel to the USSR after the war. But the official response from the Soviet side was worse than discouraging.[14] In December 1946, the Soviet authorities instructed their scientists, if they were to respond at all, merely to echo the positions of the Soviet government—and they did so.[15] Worse still, the Soviet press, under the direction of Politburo ideologue Andrei Zhdanov, launched a vicious attack against the Western scientists. Zhdanov personally denounced the "Kantian vagaries of modern bourgeois atomic physicists," and Soviet newspapers and magazine articles criticized such prominent figures as Einstein, Niels Bohr, and Linus Pauling in the crudest manner. As Lawrence Wittner has argued, the campaign seemed "designed to sever the connections of Soviet scientists with a Western scientific community that was promoting nuclear disarmament," and it succeeded for nearly a decade.[16] The scurrilous attacks on internationally minded scholars also fit with Stalin's anti-Semitic campaign against "cosmopolitanism."

The attitude of the U.S. government did not help promote the cause of transnational scientific contacts either. On Kennan's recommendation, the State Department blocked the meeting the scientists had planned for 1946.[17] Even purely professional conferences were difficult to arrange because of the political criteria the U.S. government established for issuing visas to foreign (not only Soviet-bloc) scholars.[18] The government made a special point of ha-

11. Wittner, *One World or None*, 264.
12. Hawkins, Greb, and Szilard, *Toward a Livable World*, 111–113.
13. Originally published in December 1947, it is reprinted in Hawkins, Greb, and Szilard, *Toward a Livable World*, 26–33.
14. Smith, *A Peril and a Hope*, 299.
15. Holloway, *Stalin and the Bomb*, 407 n. 96.
16. Wittner, *One World or None*, 291–292, includes the quotation from Zhdanov and others.
17. Wittner, *One World or None*, 264.
18. Weisskopf, *Joy of Insight*, 192–193.

rassing politically active American scientists. In 1947, for example, the U.S. attorney general refused to respond to Leo Szilard's request for advice on the legality of writing to Stalin. When Szilard went ahead and published his open letter, the Justice Department considered prosecuting him for violating the Logan Act of 1799, which "prohibited private citizens' correspondence with a foreign government on a subject of dispute between it and the United States."[19] In 1950, the FBI opened an investigation of Albert Einstein to find out whether he might be a communist or a Soviet agent. That same year, Senator Joseph McCarthy, the notorious anticommunist demagogue, denounced the Federation of American Scientists as "heavily infiltrated with communist fellow-travellers."[20]

Although many in the U.S. government, even during the Kennedy administration, opposed the transnational political activity of the scientists, the change in Soviet policy following Stalin's death allowed for a resumption of international scientific contacts, and these soon included discussion of crucial issues of war and peace.

TRANSNATIONAL SCIENCE AND POLITICS

In 1953 U.S. scientists renewed their efforts to work with Soviet colleagues. Their first success was the Conference on the Peaceful Uses of Atomic Energy, convened in Geneva in August 1955. In David Holloway's words, "the most significant aspect of the conference," which brought together scientists from East and West, was that "the international scientific community was being reconstituted after a twenty-year interval caused by repression in the Soviet Union and Germany in the 1930s, by World War II, and by the nuclear arms race." Participants praised the conference as "helping to reestablish the worldwide community and communion of scientists" (I. I. Rabi) and "the normal pattern of communication in the scientific world" (James Cockroft).[21]

Many of the advocates of professional meetings such as the Geneva conference were also proponents of establishing a transnational dialogue to discuss political issues related to the threat of nuclear war. Victor Weisskopf, for example, one of the first American physicists invited to visit the Soviet physics center at Dubna in 1955, had been a founding member of the Emergency Committee of Atomic Scientists. Throughout the 1950s he and others sought to ease the barriers for Soviet scientists to attend physics conferences in the United States. At the same time, he continued to pursue opportunities

19. Hawkins, Greb, and Szilard, *Toward a Livable World*, 262 n. 4; Wittner, *One World or None*, 398 n. 65.
20. Wittner, *One World or None*, 267.
21. Holloway, *Stalin and the Bomb*, 353.

to engage his Soviet colleagues on questions of the arms race and became an early leader of the Pugwash movement.[22]

Some observers date the intellectual origins of Pugwash not to the mid-1950s but to the ill-fated proposals for international cooperation that the renowned physicist Niels Bohr promoted a decade earlier. In 1944, Bohr, a refugee from Nazi-occupied Denmark, spent some months at Los Alamos working on the Manhattan Project and became alarmed at the prospect of a postwar nuclear arms race. He appealed—unsuccessfully—to Winston Churchill and Franklin Roosevelt to let Stalin know about the allies' secret atomic research, so that the Soviet leader could be persuaded of the need for international control. In Bohr's conception, as Holloway summarizes it, although political leaders would be ultimately responsible for decisions on controlling nuclear power, the scientists could play an important role: "personal connections between scientists from different countries might offer a means of establishing contact and working out a common approach to security."[23]

Bohr's views about the international role of scientists were well known to his colleagues and were shared by many of them, including some in the Soviet Union. Petr Kapitsa, who had unsuccessfully invited Bohr to seek refuge in the Soviet Union after his escape from Denmark in 1943, gave a speech the next year in which he expressed very similar sentiments to Bohr's. Addressing the third Anti-Fascist Meeting of Soviet Scientists in June 1944, Kapitsa argued that after the war "our task, the task of all scientists, must not be limited to gaining a knowledge of nature in order to harness it for the benefit of mankind in peaceful construction. It is my opinion that scientists must also take an active part in the establishment of a sound and lasting peace."[24]

Although the politicians rejected such an active political role for scientists—and led their countries into an arms race just as Bohr had feared—the ideas expressed by Bohr and Kapitsa continued to inspire groups such as the Federation of American Scientists. Particularly influenced by Bohr's concerns about a postwar arms race and his vision of an international solution was Joseph Rotblat, a refugee from Nazi-occupied Poland and a Manhattan Project physicist. Rotblat had many conversations with Bohr on their long walks through the woods around Los Alamos.[25] Bohr's idea of using the common language of science to address the threat of nuclear war finally bore fruit in the 1950s when Rotblat helped found the Pugwash movement.[26]

22. Weisskopf, *Joy of Insight*, 193–198, 205–209.

23. Holloway, *Stalin and the Bomb*, 118–119.

24. Quoted in Holloway, *Stalin and the Bomb*, 113.

25. Susan Landau, "Joseph Rotblat: The Road Less Traveled," *Bulletin of the Atomic Scientists* 52, 1 (January/February 1996), 50.

26. For a summary of Pugwash's history, see the *F.A.S. Public Interest Report* 40, 8 (October 1987); for more detail, see Joseph Rotblat, *Scientists in the Quest for Peace: A History of the Pugwash Conferences* (Cambridge, Mass., 1972).

Origins of Pugwash

If the post-Stalin thaw provided the political preconditions for a transnational dialogue of scientists, developments in nuclear technology provided the stimulus. By 1954 both the United States and the Soviet Union had developed and tested thermonuclear weapons (hydrogen bombs or "H-bombs"), with the potential for explosive power thousands of times greater than the bombs that destroyed Hiroshima and Nagasaki. Responding to the alarm caused by radioactive fallout from nuclear tests, Nehru "called for the setting up of a committee of scientists to explain to the world the effect a nuclear war would have on humanity."[27] At the same time, Bertrand Russell, the British philosopher and mathematician, began to speak out on the danger of nuclear war. He drafted a document echoing Nehru's call for a conference of scientists "to appraise the perils that have arisen as a result of the development of weapons of mass destruction." Russell urged governments "to realize, and to acknowledge publicly, that their purposes cannot be furthered by a world war." He insisted that "we have to learn to think in a new way."[28]

Russell sought endorsement of his statement from prominent fellow scientists, starting with Albert Einstein, who signed it two days before his death. The Russell-Einstein Manifesto, as it became known, attracted a great deal of attention when Russell read it at a press conference in London in July 1955, with Rotblat at his side. The original signatories from Britain, France, Germany, Japan, Poland, and the United States appealed "as human beings, to human beings: remember your humanity, and forget the rest." A month later the London-based Association of Parliamentarians for World Government, in collaboration with the Federation of American Scientists and the British Atomic Scientists' Association, sponsored an international conference, whose members included nonscientists as well as scientists. The conference delegates, including four Soviet scientists led by Academician Aleksandr Topchiev, formally endorsed the Russell-Einstein Manifesto.[29]

Back in the USSR, Petr Kapitsa was invited by the editors of a Soviet weekly magazine to respond to Russell's views. Kapitsa wrote that Russell's "activities appeal to my deepest sympathies," and he reiterated his position of twelve years earlier that "scientists should not confine themselves to the scientific aspect of the problem [of averting war], but should also interfere in its social and political aspects."[30] This time Kapitsa's views were shared by the Soviet government, which gave its scientists permission to participate in the international scientists' movement.

27. Rotblat, *Quest for Peace*, 1.
28. The document is reprinted as appendix 1 in Rotblat, *Quest for Peace*, 137–140.
29. Rotblat, *Quest for Peace*, 1. For a short biography of Topchiev see V. M. Buzuev and V. P. Pavlichenko, *Uchenye predostergaiut* (Moscow, 1964), 89.
30. Petr Kapitsa, "The Paramount Task," *New Times*, 1956, no. 39:10.

After initial plans to convene a scientists' meeting in New Delhi fell through, the first Conference on Science and World Affairs took place from 7 to 10 July 1957 at the estate of Cyrus Eaton in Pugwash, Nova Scotia—whence the movement's name. Twenty-two scientists from ten countries participated, including three from the USSR, again led by Academician Topchiev.[31] Thereafter, Pugwash conferences were held once or twice a year. The thirteenth convened in Czechoslovakia just a month before Nikita Khrushchev was ousted from power.

Eventually Pugwash came to sponsor, in addition to the major conferences, specialized symposia, study groups, and other informal groupings, including one that brought together U.S. and Soviet scientists for direct, private discussions. In the late 1950s, President Dwight Eisenhower asked Norman Cousins, then editor of the *Saturday Review,* to establish a similar forum for "off-the-record, informal talks between leading citizens" of the two countries to discuss issues relating to U.S.-Soviet relations and world peace. The first meeting was held at Dartmouth College in New Hampshire in 1960, and the sixteen that followed between then and 1990 came to be known as the Dartmouth Conferences, even though many were held in the Soviet Union.[32] These transnational activities—especially Pugwash—were the only way for Soviet scientists to participate in unofficial discussions of disarmament and security with their foreign colleagues.

THE SOVIET PARTY-STATE AND THE SCIENTISTS

The Soviet government supported participation by Soviet scientists in the Pugwash meetings, but sought, with mixed success, to maintain a tight leash over their activities. Although the formal system for official approval of Soviet Pugwash delegations remained consistent well into the Gorbachev era, there seems to have been a trend on the part of some of the Soviet authorities toward greater confidence in the foreign scientists' goodwill and less concern that Pugwash would undermine Soviet foreign policy goals. In any case, be-

31. Rotblat, *Quest for Peace,* 4–5. Among Soviet archival documents, a letter to the Central Committee of the Communist Party from V. Tereshkin, deputy head of the International Department, describes the international scientists' movement and the first Pugwash meeting. Storage Center for Contemporary Documentation [Tsentr khraneniia sovremennoi dokumentatsii] (hereafter TsKhSD), CPSU Central Committee, 20th convocation, from protocol no. 45, Secretariat sesssion of 2 August 1957, item 24: "On the call for an international conference of scientists for the cessation of nuclear tests" [in Russian].

32. The quote is from p. 2 of the preface to "Soviet-American Security Relations: Toward the Year 2000," a report by the Dartmouth Conference Task Force on Security and Arms Control on a conference in Moscow, 16–18 January 1989. On Eisenhower's role, see Norman Cousins, *The Pathology of Power* (New York, 1987), 74–75. James Voorhees is preparing a comprehensive history of the Dartmouth Conference. See his "The Dartmouth Conference: The Influence of a Transnational Community on US-Soviet Relations, 1960–1991," paper prepared for the 39th Annual Convention of the International Studies Association, Minneapolis, March 1998.

fore they could attend a meeting, the members of each delegation had to be approved in advance by the Central Committee of the Communist Party and sometimes the Politburo (called the Presidium during the Khrushchev years) as well.

Controlling the Arms Controllers

This formal authorization procedure violated one of the basic tenets of the Pugwash movement—that the scientists participate as individuals and not represent anybody but themselves. Nevertheless, even allowing Soviet scientists to attend the international meetings constituted a major concession for the Soviet authorities. Western Pugwash participants were aware of the conditions imposed by Soviet-bloc governments, but chose to look on the bright side. As Victor Weisskopf observed, "the Communist participants could join the meetings only if they were approved by and closely connected to their governments. For once, the USSR's restrictive policies worked in our favor by putting us in contact with very highly placed people." Weisskopf argued that "through Pugwash we had a rather direct line of communication with the Soviet government"—a contention supported by many of the cases described in this book.[33]

At first the Soviet government was reluctant to become involved in transnational efforts that it would have difficulty controlling. In April 1955, for example, Leo Szilard revived his proposal for a direct U.S.-Soviet dialogue. He discussed with the Soviet ambassador to Washington the idea of creating a commission of five to ten people who would "objectively study" the sources of Soviet-American disagreements on nuclear weapons and propose recommendations for avoiding war. Szilard hoped to obtain financial backing from the Soviet government as well as private U.S. foundations. The U.S. department in the Soviet Foreign Ministry recommended against the proposal. It considered "inexpedient" (*netselesoobraznym*) Soviet participation in the financing of the commission's work or the work itself, because the commission would be privately created and "it is doubtful that we would be able to exert any influence" on its conclusions.[34]

Although Soviet scientists soon became active participants in the Pugwash movement, Soviet leaders initially preferred to promote their disarmament objectives through international meetings more directly under their control. Just two weeks after the first Pugwash meeting, on 20 July 1957, Andrei Gromyko, the Soviet foreign minister, sent a letter to the Central Committee proposing Soviet sponsorship of a larger international scientific conference

33. Weisskopf, *Joy of Insight*, 206.
34. V. Bazykin to A. A. Gromyko, memorandum, 25 May 1955, Archive of the Foreign Policy of the Russian Federation [Arkhiv Vneshnei Politiki Rossiiskoi Federatsii], Fond: Ref. po SShA, op. 39, por. 31, pap. 289, no. 194/112.

dedicated specifically to the question of nuclear testing. In his words, "the conference of scientists would be a significant support to the position of the Soviet Union in this question and would help in exposing the position of the western powers blocking a solution to the question of the tests."[35] Mikhail Suslov, secretary of the Central Committee, instructed his deputies to prepare a proposal for the Secretariat. The proposal adopted the format and wording of Gromyko's letter almost entirely. On 5 August 1957 the Central Committee issued a resolution instructing the USSR Academy of Sciences, in cooperation with the Foreign Ministry, to prepare within five days a statement from a group of Soviet scientists "widely known abroad" inviting their colleagues to an international conference and urging them to support a halt in testing of nuclear weapons. At the same time, the Central Committee directed the Communist Party organizations in the union republics and major cities, such as Moscow, Leningrad, and Sverdlovsk, to organize meetings of scientists "to discuss the question of banning the use of atomic energy for military purposes." The three Soviet participants at the first Pugwash meeting—A. V. Topchiev, D. V. Skobel'tsyn, and A. M. Kuzin—were instructed to cooperate with the committee organizing the international conference, and the newspapers *Pravda* and *Izvestiia* were ordered to publish articles about it. It was hoped that the conference could be organized by September or October so that its results could be used to support the Soviet position at the forthcoming meeting of the United Nations General Assembly.[36]

Gromyko's letter proposing a Soviet-sponsored conference apparently came not at his own initiative but in response to Khrushchev's suggestion. A top-secret (*strogo sekretno*) directive from the Presidium instructing the Secretariat to consider Gromyko's proposal was issued nearly three weeks before the foreign minister actually sent his letter to the Central Committee.[37]

The Soviet government was not alone is seeking close supervision of its Pugwash delegates. Especially during the Kennedy administration, when several members of the President's Science Advisory Committee attended Pugwash meetings, the U.S. government kept tabs on their activities. The State Department, for example, received what were in effect intelligence reports from delegates attending the 1961 Pugwash meetings in Stowe, Vermont. On occasion, participants who anticipated working in the U.S. government in the future would seek official approval of their conference papers

35. A. A. Gromyko to Central Committee, 20 July 1957, "On the call for an international conference of scientists," TsKhSD.

36. Ibid.

37. TsKhSD, CPSU, TsK, No. p103/X1X, order from protocol no. 103, session of the Central Committee Presidium of 4 July 1957, to comrades Aristov, Beliaev, Brezhnev, Kuusinen, Pospelov, Suslov, Furtseva, and the CPSU Secretariat, "On the conduct of a broad international conference of scientists for the cessation of tests of atomic and hydrogen weaponry" [in Russian].

before presenting them—in Soviet-like violation of the Pugwash norms of independence.[38]

The Origins of Bilateral Contacts

Within a few years after the first Pugwash conference, Khrushchev came to view the transnational scientists' dialogue as more than just a propaganda opportunity. We can trace the evolution of his thinking indirectly through his relationship to Leo Szilard—one of the earliest and most persistent advocates of bilateral discussions between Soviet and U.S. scientists. We also observe that barriers to direct contacts had to be overcome, not only on the Soviet side but on the U.S. side as well.

Szilard first wrote to Khrushchev personally in September 1959. He sent the Soviet leader a copy of a recent paper he had presented at a Pugwash meeting, but he received no reply. Later the next year, while Szilard was being treated for cancer in a New York hospital, he received a visit from a Soviet colleague and was inspired to write again to Khrushchev. In his letter of June 1960, Szilard reviewed the history of unsuccessful attempts at bilateral meetings of scientists and proposed a new opportunity: that U.S. participants in the forthcoming Pugwash conference in Moscow stay on beyond the end of the meeting to meet informally with their Soviet counterparts.[39] Khrushchev wrote back at the end of August: "Giving credit to your noble efforts aimed at the improvement of the mutual understanding and relations between the United States and the Soviet Union, I welcome your new initiative."[40]

Encouraged by this reply, Szilard made plans to meet Khrushchev when the Soviet leader visited New York in September 1960. Initially invited to the Soviet embassy at the United Nations for a fifteen-minute meeting, Szilard ended up spending a full two hours with Khrushchev, discussing various proposals for resolving East-West differences over issues ranging from the threat of surprise attack to the situation in Berlin. The two seemed to get along well, and Khrushchev evidently appreciated Szilard's offbeat sense of humor. On his arrival at the embassy, for example, Szilard presented Khrushchev a gift of a new Schick injector razor and a supply of blades to last six months.

---

38. On these points, see Bernd W. Kubbig, "Communicators in the Cold War: The Pugwash Conferences, the U.S.-Soviet Study Group and the ABM Treaty," PRIF Reports No. 44, Peace Research Institute Frankfurt (Frankfurt am Main, 1996), 10. He gives the example of W. W. Rostow, who cleared his paper with the U.S. ambassador to the Soviet Union before presenting it at a Pugwash meeting in Moscow in December 1960. Rostow entered the government with the Kennedy administration the next month.

39. See the summary of these events in Hawkins, Greb, and Szilard, *Toward a Livable World*, 254.

40. Szilard to Khrushchev (27 June 1960) and Khrushchev to Szilard (30 August 1960), in Hawkins, Greb, and Szilard, *Toward a Livable World*, 46–48.

He promised to replenish the supply "only as long as there is no war." As Szilard later recalled, Khrushchev replied that "if there is a war he will stop shaving, and he thinks that most other people will stop shaving also."[41] Most important, Khrushchev endorsed Szilard's proposals for direct contacts between Soviet and U.S. scientists.

Szilard had been in contact with Academician Topchiev, a senior official in the Soviet Academy of Sciences and then head of the Soviet Pugwash Committee, about organizing a bilateral U.S.-Soviet discussion. In their September meeting Khrushchev promised Szilard that Topchiev would make all the necessary arrangements. Szilard's illness prevented him from taking an active role at this point beyond securing Khrushchev's blessing, so he recommended that Topchiev deal with a group of scientists led by Paul Doty, a Harvard chemistry professor, who had also taken an interest in the idea of direct bilateral contacts. Their efforts were supported by the American Academy of Arts and Sciences in Cambridge, Massachusetts. Much of the Academy's early work was carried out by Doty and Donald Brennan of the Massachusetts Institute of Technology. It was Brennan, for example, who followed through on Szilard's initiative to meet with Soviet colleagues after the Moscow Pugwash meeting in December 1960 to plan for the bilateral discussions.[42]

Although they were not precisely what Szilard had proposed to Khrushchev, the U.S.-Soviet discussions in Moscow went well, and there was some progress toward establishing a study group of Soviet and U.S. scientists to meet on a regular basis. On the U.S. side, the American Academy established a Committee on International Studies of Arms Control in March 1961. It became the main vehicle for promoting the bilateral discussions that became known, among the U.S. organizers, as the Soviet-American Disarmament Study Group or SADS. Doty, Brennan, and others met on several occasions during 1961 with Topchiev and other Soviet Pugwash members to promote the project. In August, the Academy sent a proposal to the Ford Foundation to fund the U.S.-Soviet exchanges. In late November 1961 Topchiev sent a cable to Doty conveying Soviet acceptance of the SADS project.[43]

In the meantime the bilateral project nearly foundered for lack of support

41. Szilard, "Conversation with K on October 5, 1960," memorandum recorded four days later and reprinted in Hawkins, Greb, and Szilard, *Toward a Livable World*, 279–287; Lanouette, *Genius in the Shadows*, chap. 27.

42. Chronology of the activities of the Soviet-American Disarmament Study (SADS) group, compiled by Anne Cahn and located in the archives of the American Academy of Arts and Sciences, Cambridge, Mass. (hereafter, the Cahn chronology); and "Report on Informal Arms Control Meetings with the Soviets," Committee on International Studies of Arms Control, AAAS, n.d. (probably between June 1964 and March 1965). I am grateful to David Wright for providing these and other materials from his research in the American Academy archives. See also Hawkins, Greb, and Szilard, *Toward a Livable World*, 255.

43. Cahn chronology; and "Report on Informal Arms Control Meetings."

on the U.S. side.[44] The Ford Foundation had begun to get cold feet. It made financial support for the Cambridge-based SADS project contingent on written approval from the Kennedy administration. The likely source of such approval was the newly created Arms Control and Disarmament Agency (ACDA). But William Foster, the ACDA director, was initially hostile to the idea of a bilateral study group, ostensibly for fear that sensitive information would leak. After two discussions with Doty, he offered to endorse the project only if ACDA were given veto power over selection of the U.S. participants. Doty and his colleagues were not willing to go that far. Foster eventually signed a statement, drafted essentially by Doty's committee, that fell short of an endorsement; it expressed confidence that the group would "act as responsible private citizens and scientists" but were "not official spokesmen in any sense whatever."[45] Nevertheless, the Ford Foundation finally awarded the grant to fund the project in April 1963.

Thus, ironically, the bilateral discussions between Soviet and U.S. scientists—initially proposed by the Americans—received full endorsement for Soviet participation nearly two years before the U.S. side was financially or politically prepared to make concrete arrangements for a first meeting. Documents from the Soviet archives indicate that a Central Committee decision of 22 August 1961 initially gave the Soviet Pugwash Committee permission to participate in direct discussions with U.S. scientists for a period of one year.[46] Because the discussions did not get off the ground for so long—owing in part to Topchiev's death in December 1962, as well as to the delays on the U.S. side—the permission was extended as further plans were worked out. In February 1963, Doty met with three senior Soviet Pugwash representatives at a session of the Pugwash Continuing Committee meeting in London. In June, following approval of the Ford grant, Doty and Sovietologist Marshall Shulman traveled to Moscow to negotiate the terms for the SADS meetings with Vladimir Kirillin, a vice president of the Soviet Academy of Sciences who had taken over as chair of the Soviet Pugwash Committee from the deceased Topchiev.[47]

In a September 1963 letter to the Central Committee, Kirillin requested permission to send a delegation to the United States for the first SADS workshop and proposed several names. In support of his proposal he traced the background of plans for direct U.S.-Soviet discussions, from the 1960 Pugwash

44. This history was originally pieced together by David Wright, from his research in the American Academy archives, and presented as "Scientists and Diplomacy in the 1960's: The Soviet American Defense Study Group," notes for a talk in Budapest, May 1990.

45. Foster's letter of 25 April 1962 is quoted in ibid.

46. Decision no. P-342/36 of 22 August 1961 is mentioned in "On the participation of Soviet scientists in the work of the joint Soviet-American group for the study of disarmament and international security," document on microfilm at TsKhSD, CPSU Central Committee, 22nd convocation, from protocol no. 96, Secretariat session, 4 April 1964, item 186g [in Russian].

47. Cahn chronology.

meeting in Moscow, through the Central Committee approval of August 1961, and up to the recent June visit of Shulman and Doty. Kirillin mentioned that the U.S. side had now received three hundred thousand dollars from a foundation to fund the project and that many prominent scientists had expressed interest, including I. I. Rabi, Hans Bethe, George Kistiakowsky, Wolfgang Panofsky, and Freeman Dyson. He explained that scholarly work on disarmament problems was being undertaken by two Soviet working groups—one at the Institute of History and the other at the Institute of the World Economy and International Relations (IMEMO in its Russian acronym).

Kirillin's letter was followed two months later by a very similar one under the signature of Mstislav Keldysh, president of the Academy of Sciences, and was approved by the deputy heads of the ideology and international relations departments of the Central Committee and then formulated as a formal decree and approved by the Secretariat. The Communist authorities also granted the Soviet Academy permission to invite nine U.S. scientists for a three-week return visit to the USSR in the second half of the year. The final document approving Soviet participation in the SADS workshops was issued 4 April 1964, and the first meeting was finally held that June near Boston.[48]

Four years had passed since Leo Szilard had first written to Khrushchev to propose the direct U.S.-Soviet meetings. It had been more than three years since the Americans had established an institution—the Committee on International Studies of Arms Control—to support the workshops, and over a year since the Ford grant had been approved. In the face of so many delays, and resistance from their own government, the Americans considered abandoning the project; but they decided to remain patient, viewing it "as a long-term educational effort."[49] Years later, when Paul Doty was asked how he could account for Soviet participation in the Boston meeting after so much hesitation, he gave particular credit to Mikhail Millionshchikov. Academician Millionshchikov, argued Doty, infused new energy into the Soviet Pugwash group and brought his high-level contacts to bear in facilitating cooperation with the U.S. colleagues.[50] It is true that Millionshchikov, a vice president of the Academy, first got involved in Pugwash at the January 1964 meeting in India. And the main difference between the Central Committee documents from 1961–63 and the decree of April 1964 that finally got the Soviet delegation over to Boston is that Millionshchikov's name appears as a proposed member only in the latter.[51]

Millionshchikov became the leader of the Soviet delegations to the SADS workshops, as well as chair of the Soviet Pugwash Committee from 1964. He was clearly the driving force behind Soviet participation in transnational sci-

48. "On the participation of Soviet scientists"; and appended documents on microfilm.
49. "Report on Informal Arms Control Meetings with the Soviets," 1.
50. Paul Doty, interview by David Wright, Cambridge, Mass., 17 July 1990.
51. "On the participation of Soviet scientists."

entists' discussions of disarmament until his death in 1973. For many of the U.S. participants, the period of Millionshchikov's leadership marked the heyday of transnational contacts—when real progress was made particularly on questions relating to stability of the nuclear balance and the relationship between offense and defense. Although the most fruitful of these contacts took place after Khrushchev's removal from office, the seeds were planted during the Khrushchev years, and their successful growth owes a great deal to the Soviet leader's personal interest.

Tacit Transnationalism

The Pugwash movement and the bilateral contacts of the Soviet-American Disarmament Study Group were the visible manifestations of transnational relations between Soviet and Western scientists. Another important source of East-West contact was less visible and, in fact, little known until recently. It turns out that many Soviet scientists were aware of their Western colleagues' views on the paramount issues of war and peace, without ever having left Soviet soil or attended any international meetings. Instead, they read the journals in which the Western debates about the nuclear arms race were conducted. Particularly important was the *Bulletin of the Atomic Scientists,* which, despite its title, focused less on technical issues than on political concerns and proposals for resolving international problems such as the arms race. By reading the *Bulletin,* Soviet nuclear weapons designers became among the best-informed people in the USSR on international and military affairs. They established a tacit transnational connection with like-minded colleagues abroad.

How was such a connection established? David Holloway has called attention to the paradoxical situation whereby Soviet physicists working in the nuclear weapons field became an "embryonic civil society," even under Stalin. It was the bomb itself, he argues—the high priority assigned to development of nuclear weapons—that "helped to protect a small element of civil society in a state that strove for totalitarian control."[52] The more information that comes out of the secret world of the Soviet nuclear complex, the more Holloway's point is reinforced, particularly for the post-Stalin period. Viktor Adamskii, a theoretical physicist who worked under Andrei Sakharov at the nuclear weapons laboratory at Arzamas-16, has written that "the privileged position of nuclear weapon scientists gave them a certain freedom from the censorship that was a reality for other Soviet citizens. . . . We nuclear scientists felt free to have broad discussions on international and domestic issues."

52. Holloway, *Stalin and the Bomb,* 367, 363. Also Holloway, "Science, the Bomb, and Civil Society in the Soviet Union," the Nordlander Lecture, given at Cornell University, 5 October 1995.

Adamskii attributes the scientists' discussions in part to the fact that the library at Arzamas-16 received a subscription to the *Bulletin of the Atomic Scientists:* "When we read the *Bulletin,* we began to comprehend what free debate truly meant. . . . Our exposure to the debates among U.S. scientists helped nurture a certain freedom of thought and expression among us." Soviet nuclear scientists came to realize that some of their U.S. counterparts "considered it their moral duty to understand the situation and to try to influence their government in the direction of reason on nuclear issues."[53] During the Khrushchev era, some Soviet scientists, most famously Andrei Sakharov, began to act on their moral convictions, and to do so in tacit concert with U.S. colleagues whom they had never met. Although such activity does not typically receive much attention from scholars of transnational relations, it was clearly important in several of the cases discussed in the following chapters. The transfer of ideas through professional journals contributed to the growth of a transnational scientific ethos during the Khrushchev years.

KHRUSHCHEV AND THE "ANGELS"

Many individuals were important to the revival of transnational scientific contacts during the 1950s, but none more than the reformist Soviet leader Nikita Khrushchev. Khrushchev believed strongly, as he described in an interview with the U.S. broadcasting company CBS in May 1957, that questions of war and peace depended on forging agreements between the United States and the Soviet Union, and he came to see informal contacts as useful for that goal. This view was heretical for Marxist-Leninist ideology because it ascribed such importance to intergovernmental relations between the two major powers. The traditional thinking saw the prospects for peace as fully contingent on the strength of the working class, represented by the Soviet Union and its communist allies abroad: To elevate the importance of state-to-state relations, let alone transnational contacts, was ideologically suspect.

In contrast to other leading figures in the Soviet leadership, Khrushchev evinced, in James Richter's words, "a greater willingness to rely on progressive forces within the capitalist societies as a powerful social force independent of the governments of those countries." Khrushchev sought "to expand the circle of potential allies" to include "both the newly independent nationalist countries and the members of the bourgeoisie in all countries who hoped

53. Viktor Adamskii, "Dear Mr. Khrushchev," *Bulletin of the Atomic Scientists* 51, 6 (November/December 1995): 28–31. Similar points are made in a fundraising letter from Roald Sagdeev to subscribers to the *Bulletin of the Atomic Scientists,* September 1993, p. 2; and, regarding contacts with the outside world and the relative "freedom of discussion and of opinion," by Evgenii Velikhov in Stephen F. Cohen and Katrina vanden Heuvel, eds., *Voices of Glasnost: Interviews with Gorbachev's Reformers* (New York, 1989), 163.

to avoid nuclear war."[54] Thus it was natural for Khrushchev to endorse such proposals as Nehru's nuclear test moratorium and Szilard's idea of bringing together noncommunist scientists from the West to meet with their Soviet counterparts.

Khrushchev's approach obviously differed from Stalin's postwar foreign policy, but it also met resistance from members of his own leadership circle. When Khrushchev's colleagues in the so-called anti-Party group attempted to remove him from power in June 1957, for example, they justified their actions in part as a response to the Soviet leader's erroneous foreign policy views (although most of the criticism focused on domestic policy mistakes). One of his critics cited in particular the CBS interview as evidence of Khrushchev's incorrect approach.[55]

Khrushchev came to attach particular importance to the role of nongovernmental actors in mediating East-West relations, and here much of the credit should go to Szilard and the other founders of the Pugwash movement. Again the contrast with Stalin could hardly be greater. Although Stalin and some of his like-minded successors were willing to take advantage of foreigners whom they could control (as with the Moscow-influenced peace movement of the early 1950s), Khrushchev's approach was different.[56] Perhaps most symbolic of the difference was the two leaders' attitude to Szilard. Szilard was a maverick by any standard, fiercely independent and iconoclastic. Typical of the behavior of this lifelong advocate of international scientific cooperation, this intellectual progenitor of the Pugwash movement, was his refusal to sign the common statements drafted with great effort at the end of Pugwash conferences—or any other petitions—if he disagreed even with minor aspects of them.[57] Stalin's reaction to such an independent-mindedness was predictable. When Szilard wrote to the Soviet dictator in 1947, Stalin's "answer"—he never formally responded—was the Soviet press campaign of vilification against all such internationally oriented scientists.

Szilard was nobody's puppet, and his political views were manifestly unsympathetic to communism. Yet Khrushchev, unlike Stalin, acknowledged Szilard's goodwill. He not only answered Szilard's letters (either directly or

54. James Richter, *Khrushchev's Double Bind: International Pressures and Domestic Coalition Politics* (Baltimore, Md., 1994), 57, 58.

55. See the remarks of Georgii Malenkov in the transcript of the June 1957 Plenum of the Communist Party Central Committee (where the anti-Party group's efforts to overthrow Khrushchev were turned back), printed in *Istoricheskii arkhiv*, no. 3, 1993, 30. I am grateful to Mark Kramer for lending me his copy. Ironically, Malenkov's own worldview emphasized state-to-state relations, before he was discredited by a temporary alliance between Molotov and Khrushchev and an inhospitable external environment. See Richter, *Khrushchev's Double Bind*, chap. 2.

56. On Soviet involvement with the peace movement, see Marshall D. Shulman, *Stalin's Foreign Policy Reappraised* (Cambridge, Mass., 1963).

57. Szilard once refused to sign a Pugwash statement that was drafted at his initiative. See Hawkins, Greb, and Szilard, *Toward a Livable World*, 164–165; Lanouette, *Genius in the Shadows*, 371.

through his ambassadors), but he took the time to read some of his proposals and even parts of his work of science fiction, *Voice of the Dolphins*, that were translated into Russian. Following his two-hour conversation with Szilard in September 1960, Khrushchev ordered a detailed report of their meeting circulated among Soviet participants in the Pugwash conference held in Moscow later that autumn.

Many of Szilard's ideas seemed to appeal to Khrushchev, particularly his projects for direct contacts between Soviet and Western scientists to work out solutions to the arms race. One particular proposal that never got off the ground, however, was something Szilard dubbed the "Angels-Project." As he wrote in a letter to Khrushchev in early October 1962, Szilard believed that there were many people close to the administration of John F. Kennedy who were "on the side of the angels" and opposed an endless arms race with the Soviet Union. Szilard told Khrushchev that they "have consistently taken the position that the United States should be prepared to give up certain temporary advantages it holds, for the sake of attaining an agreement with the Soviet Union that would stop the arms race."[58] It was Szilard's hope that such people—many of whom were "consultants to the Department of State, Department of Defense and the White House"—would be involved in direct, long-term discussions with like-minded Soviet scientists and mid-level government officials: "Because of their special relationship to the US government they could be very effective in fighting for specific disarmament proposals."[59]

Written in the immediate aftermath of the Cuban missile crisis, Khrushchev's response to Szilard's proposal was his warmest and most enthusiastic yet. He invited Szilard to Moscow to discuss the Angels-Project in more detail.[60] But Szilard had misjudged the Kennedy administration: it was not as angelic as he had supposed. Instead, it pursued a policy consistent with that of its predecessors and was generally—with the exception of a couple of individuals—unsupportive of Szilard's initiatives. The previous administration had deliberately discouraged Szilard's approaches to Khrushchev. Charles Bohlen, Eisenhower's State Department specialist on the Soviet Union, for example, threatened Szilard with the specter of the Logan Act for writing to Khrushchev, just as the Truman administration had done when Szilard wrote to Stalin.[61] Christian Herter, successor to John Foster Dulles as Eisenhower's secretary of state, warned Szilard, when he traveled to Moscow in late 1960, not to "undermine" the U.S. position on disarmament in his talks with Soviet scientists.[62]

58. Letter to N. S. Khrushchev (9 October 1962), in Hawkins, Greb, and Szilard, *Toward a Livable World*, 300.
59. Letter to N. S. Khrushchev (15 November 1962), in Hawkins, Greb, and Szilard, *Toward a Livable World*, 307.
60. Translation of a letter from N. S. Khrushchev (4 November 1962), in Hawkins, Greb, and Szilard, *Toward a Livable World*, 305–306.
61. Ibid., 254–255.
62. Letter from Secretary of State Christian A. Herter (10 November 1960), in ibid., 290.

Szilard expected the Kennedy administration to take a more favorable attitude toward his efforts, but he was disappointed. First, on the eve of Szilard's visit to Moscow in November 1962, McGeorge Bundy, President Kennedy's national security advisor, expressed strong objections to the Angels-Project, leading Szilard to cancel his trip.[63] Then, in July 1963, ACDA director William Foster forbade any of his employees or any members of his advisory committee to attend Szilard's Soviet-American meetings.[64] Foster's action eliminated precisely that group of people Szilard considered most likely to possess the rare combination of independent thinking and access to and respect from the government.

On 15 July 1963, Szilard informed Khrushchev of Foster's decision, accepting that the absence of well-connected U.S. officials would diminish the value of an informal U.S.-Soviet meeting. He reminded Khrushchev that the American Academy continued to support the Doty-Brennan (SADS) project for bilateral discussions and expressed the hope that it "may perhaps fulfill some of the functions which I had in mind when I proposed the 'Angels-Project' to you last October."[65] The Soviet response marked the end of Khrushchev's direct involvement in supporting unofficial transnational contacts. Indeed the response itself did not come, as it had in the past, in the form of a personal letter from Khrushchev but rather as a formal reply on his behalf ("I am instructed to inform you that your letter . . . has been received," etc.). The Soviet side acknowledged "certain difficulties which you have encountered in implementing your plan," implicitly accepting the demise of the Angels-Project. It endorsed direct U.S.-Soviet contacts under the auspices of Pugwash as an alternative.[66]

Thus, for most of the Khrushchev period, the main vehicles for promoting a transnational dialogue on problems of war and peace were the Pugwash movement and, in the last months of Khrushchev's tenure, the Soviet-American Disarmament Study Group. As the next three chapters reveal, these groups made substantial contributions to curbing the nuclear arms race. It is an open question whether a more supportive attitude on the part of the Eisenhower and Kennedy administrations would have made for a more effective transnational effort. One Soviet scientist implied as much, when Leo Szilard described the Angels-Project to him at a Pugwash meeting in August 1962. As Szilard recounted, "What struck me was his insistence that we do in a hurry whatever we intended to do. He said that Khrushchev had expected to reach an accommodation with the Kennedy Administration and that as long as he

63. Hawkins, Greb, and Szilard, eds., *Toward a Livable World*, 259; Lanouette, *Genius in the Shadows*, 459.
64. Hawkins, Greb, and Szilard, *Toward a Livable World*, 260.
65. Letter to N. S. Khrushchev with appendix and memorandum (15 July 1963), in ibid., 321–322.
66. Soviet reply to letter of 15 July 1963 (undated), in Hawkins, Greb, and Szilard, *Toward a Livable World*, 328–329.

had hoped that this would be possible, he had kept the lid on the arms race, but that with this hope virtually gone now, the lid was now off."[67]

In Chapter 2 I argued that the relationship between structure and opportunity is key to the prospects for successful transnational influence. In the highly centralized and hierarchical Soviet system, access to government decision makers could be difficult for transnational actors to achieve. Once they did gain access, however, their proposals could be implemented effectively if they received a favorable hearing from the top leaders. In this case, the international prestige of U.S. scientists—and the sheer persistence of Leo Szilard, in particular—attracted the attention of Nikita Khrushchev. The widespread fear of nuclear testing and Khrushchev's concerns about the economic costs of an arms race, among other factors, made him open to proposals for bilateral discussions among scientists. My argument would lead one to expect that the more Khrushchev became directly involved in support of the bilateral contacts, the more likely such contacts would achieve their objective of producing innovative solutions to the arms race.

Certainly Khrushchev also deserves some of the blame for hindering progress in arms control. His threats over Berlin and his reckless behavior in secretly installing missiles in Cuba poisoned the international atmosphere and complicated U.S.-Soviet relations on other issues. As Walt Rostow, a Kennedy administration adviser, once explained to a Soviet Foreign Ministry official, "We are a country that can't work on a two-track policy very well. If we have a Berlin crisis, we are not going to be able to talk very seriously about arms control."[68] All the same, however, it may be that the Kennedy administration (and its predecessors) forfeited an opportunity to make progress on arms control by their opposition to informal discussions among the "angels"—the Soviet and U.S. proponents of restraint in the arms race.

67. Confidential memorandum (8 January 1963), in Hawkins, Greb, and Szilard, *Toward a Livable World*, 314.
68. His comments to Vasilii Kuznetsov, Soviet deputy foreign minister, are quoted in Michael Beschloss, *The Crisis Years: Kennedy and Khrushchev, 1960–1963* (New York, 1991), 41.

[4]

"A Battle on Two Fronts": Khrushchev's Test Ban

Working in the White House and the Office of the Secretary of Defense, I was then [1958] in close touch with those in the intelligence community charged with analyzing Soviet nuclear and other technological developments. I never heard a single suggestion that there might be people inside the Soviet nuclear establishment who were pressing for moderation. In retrospect this seems astonishing, but the picture of the Soviet Union as being, in effect, a vast prison camp simply did not allow room for such an idea. Of course, one swallow does not make a summer, but we might have made slightly different and perhaps better policy decisions had we known about even one such voice.

—Herbert York, 1987

I would be a slob, and not chairman of the Council of Ministers, if I listened to the likes of Sakharov.

—Nikita Khrushchev, 1961

The case of nuclear testing represented the first effort of a new international movement of scientists to influence the security policies of the nuclear powers. In a sense the test ban debate played to the scientists' strengths. It entailed consideration of technical issues ranging from the health and environmental effects of atmospheric test explosions of nuclear weapons to the prospects for reliable verification of a test ban agreement using seismic monitoring and other techniques. Scientists were involved in discussions of the merits of a test ban at many levels, and some of them were of course engaged in the actual development and testing of the nuclear weapons themselves. Finally, gathered under the umbrella of the Pugwash movement, a number of leading scientists formed a transnational alliance of test ban proponents, seeking to influence the U.S. and Soviet governments mainly through the force of their technical arguments.

The transnational movement for a test ban failed in its main objective—to end nuclear testing by getting the nuclear powers, initially the United States, Soviet Union, and Britain, to sign a comprehensive test ban treaty. It does deserve some credit, however, for the compromise agreement that put an end to radioactive pollution of the atmosphere but allowed the nuclear arms race to continue: The Limited Test Ban Treaty of 1963 (known in Russia as the "Moscow agreement") was the only major arms control accord successfully negotiated during Khrushchev's tenure in office, and it was furthermore the first significant agreement of the nuclear age. The period between the initial public outcry against nuclear testing in 1954 and the signing of the Moscow agreement nine years later witnessed a number of significant developments and missed opportunities. To what extent did the transnational movement of scientists and peace activists influence Soviet government policy on nuclear testing? In order to show that they had any influence, we would have, at the very least, to demonstrate that other, more common, explanations for Soviet behavior do not tell the whole story.

In this chapter and the ones that follow, I identify particular Soviet initiatives and examine the various explanations that could be put forward to account for them. The questions I examine here include: Why did the Soviet Union put a nuclear test ban on the disarmament agenda in the first place? What led the government to consider a test ban as a distinct "first step" toward disarmament rather than as an inseparable part of a comprehensive agreement, as it had previously maintained? Why did the Soviet government initiate a unilateral moratorium on nuclear testing in March 1958? Why did it break the trilateral (U.S., Britain, USSR) moratorium in September 1961? What accounts for the fluctuations in the Soviet position on on-site monitoring and inspection of possible test ban violations—an initial reluctance and then a final acceptance of a partial test ban that allowed continued underground testing?

PUTTING THE TEST BAN ON THE AGENDA

The USSR first proposed a nuclear test ban as part of its sweeping disarmament proposal of 10 May 1955.[1] It continued to pursue a comprehensive test ban throughout Khrushchev's tenure until the Limited Test Ban Treaty of 1963 was signed. Test cessation was clearly Khrushchev's personal initiative. His enthusiasm for the measure, although it waxed and waned, was hardly shared by his fellow leaders or by his successors—until Gorbachev. Thus, the case of the test ban emphasizes the importance of the structure of the centralized Soviet political system to the pursuit of arms control. The top leader enjoyed considerable autonomy in initiating policies, both internal and external.

1. For further discussion of the proposal, see the next chapter and Matthew Evangelista, "Cooperation Theory and Disarmament Negotiations in the 1950s," *World Politics* 42, 4 (July 1990): 502–528.

The test ban also shows how particular opportunities can enhance the role of transnational actors in the arms control process. Khrushchev sought initiatives that would distinguish him from his rivals in the Soviet leadership. He chose to distance himself particularly from much of the Stalinist legacy. His embrace, starting in the mid-1950s, of noncommunist supporters of disarmament and of the movement of nonaligned countries was intended to contrast with the approach of the then Foreign Minister Viacheslav Molotov, who preferred (especially after the disastrous pact he signed with Nazi Germany in 1939) to deal with orthodox communists under Moscow's control.[2] The test ban offered Khrushchev an ideal opportunity to reject Molotov's orthodoxy because the leading opponents of nuclear testing were the very groups Molotov most distrusted and Khrushchev supported—noncommunist peace activists, including prominent scientists, and the nonaligned nations, led by India.

In an important respect scientists deserve most credit for bringing the problem of nuclear testing to the attention of the international public and governments. The event that mobilized the scientists and subsequently world opinion to promote a test ban was the U.S. explosion of a hydrogen bomb, code-named BRAVO, at the Bikini Atoll in the Pacific Ocean on 1 March 1954. Radioactive fallout from the test doused a Japanese fishing boat, the Lucky Dragon, causing severe symptoms of radiation sickness and one death among the crew, and setting off a panic in Japan over the risk of radioactive tuna.[3]

In response to the BRAVO test, a public campaign for a halt to nuclear testing was organized by groups such as the Federation of American Scientists and Norman Cousins's Committee for a SANE Nuclear Policy. The campaign took off so quickly that by April 1954 more than a hundred letters, telegrams, and postcards were arriving at the White House every day protesting the explosions.[4] Respected international figures—scientists, politicians, and religious leaders—began to speak out against the tests. They included Dr. Albert Schweitzer and Prime Minister Jawaharlal Nehru of India, representing countries that had not chosen sides in the Cold War between East and West.[5] Scientists such as Ralph Lapp in the United States and Joseph Rotblat in Britain—both participants in the Manhattan Project—provided the first public information on the health and environmental effects of radioactive fallout.[6]

The Soviet government and Communist Party followed closely the growth of international public concern about nuclear testing. In January 1955 an

2. For Molotov's comments on his negotiations with foreign minister von Ribbentrop and other Nazi leaders, see Feliks Chuev, *Sto sorok besed s Molotovym* (Moscow, 1991), 17–29.

3. Robert A. Divine, *The Nuclear Test Ban Debate, 1954–1960* (New York, 1978), chap. 1.

4. Ibid., 18–19. Also, Milton S. Katz, *Ban the Bomb: A History of SANE, the Committee for a Sane Nuclear Policy, 1957–1985* (New York, 1986), chaps. 1–2.

5. Divine, *Nuclear Test Ban Debate*, 20–21.

6. Ibid., 37–38; Katz, *Ban the Bomb*, 14–20.

official at the Soviet embassy in Washington, D.C., compiled a short history of the movement for a nuclear test ban. It stressed the activities of parliamentarians, the labor movement, and peace activists in countries closely allied to the United States, such as England and Japan, and mentioned Prime Minister Nehru's call in April 1954 for the United Nations to secure a halt to nuclear testing. The report reviewed the main arguments in favor of a test ban, culled largely from TASS, the Soviet press agency, but also from Western sources such as the *New York Times*. The secret report was sent to the American department of the Foreign Ministry.[7]

The May 1955 Disarmament Plan

What prompted the Soviet Union to include a nuclear test ban as part of its comprehensive disarmament plan submitted to the United Nations in May 1955? The most apparent answer, given the widespread public alarm about nuclear testing, is that the Soviet leaders sought to score propaganda points with international public opinion at U.S. expense. Certainly this was an important Soviet objective. But it is also clear that the May disarmament plan was a genuine one: It incorporated many previous proposals from the Western side, and Soviet officials viewed it as a starting point for serious negotiations.[8] Thus, we need to consider why the Soviet side saw a test ban as in its interests in 1955.

Negotiation from Strength? Explanations that focus on the role of U.S. negotiation from strength would account for Soviet interest in a test ban by pointing to the impact of U.S. military programs and bargaining positions on Soviet policy. Yet U.S. actions could often be interpreted in conflicting ways. Soviet proponents of moderation sought to depict U.S. behavior, or the over-

7. P. Fedosimov, "International Movement for a Cessation of Testing of Hydrogen Weapons (brief information)" [in Russian], 22 January 1955, Archive of the Foreign Policy of the Russian Federation [Arkhiv Vneshnei Politiki Rossiiskoi Federatsii] (hereafter AVP), Fond: Ref. po SShA, op. 39, por. 31, pap. 289, no. 194/112—USA.

8. For accounts by a key Soviet participant, see A. A. Roshchin, "Gody obnovleniia, nadezhd i razocharovanii (1953–1959 gg.)," *Novaia i noveishaia istoriia*, 1988, no.5:127–147; and Roshchin, *Mezhdunarodnaia bezopasnost' i iadernoe oruzhie* (Moscow, 1980), 119–132. The Soviet proposal is reprinted in *Documents on Disarmament, 1945–1959*, vol. 1, 1945–1956 (Washington, D.C., 1960), 456–467, and is discussed in a declassified official document: "Progress Report, Proposed Policy of the United States on the Question of Disarmament," vol. 1, 26 May 1955, Special Staff Study for the President, NSC Action No. 1328, by Harold E. Stassen. This document is located in papers of the Office of the Special Assistant for National Security Affairs (hereafter osANSA), NSC Series, Policy Papers Subseries, Box 2, Folder: "NSC 112/1 Disarmament (3)," Dwight D. Eisenhower Library, Abilene, Kansas (hereafter DDEL). For additional evidence of Soviet intentions, see Vladislav Zubok, "SSSR-SShA: put' k peregovoram po razoruzheniiu v iadernyi vek (1953–1955 gg.)," paper presented at a conference at Ohio University, Athens, Ohio, October 1988; O. Grinevskii, "Na Smolenskoi ploshchadi v 1950-kh godakh," *Mezhdunarodnaia zhizn'*, 1994, no. 11:120–126; Oleg Troyanovsky, "Nikita Khrushchev and the Making of Soviet Foreign Policy," paper prepared for a conference on the centenary of Nikita Khrushchev's birth held at Brown University, Providence, R.I., 1–3 December 1994.

all international situation, as congenial to negotiating mutual restraint in the arms race. Opponents of moderation sought to portray U.S. actions as unremittingly sinister and the international atmosphere as inhospitable. The impact of U.S. behavior then is often indeterminate. In particular instances, however, we can identify U.S. actions that influenced Soviet behavior. As a rule, U.S. "positions of strength" typically produced a like Soviet counterreaction, whereas U.S. openness to compromise provided the possibility for Soviet initiatives of restraint.

Some sense of the conflicting interpretations of U.S. policies comes from archival materials from the period just before the USSR proposed a nuclear test ban as part of its May 1955 disarmament plan. In February of that year, representatives of the Soviet embassy in Washington reported back to Moscow that the U.S. government was basically uninterested in dealing with the problem of nuclear weapons by coming to an agreement with the Soviet Union.[9] Embassy officials did, however, point to the growing pressure from U.S. allies and public opinion concerned about the threat of nuclear war.[10] Overall, they argued, the international atmosphere had improved during the course of the previous year and had opened the possibility for negotiated solutions to major East-West conflicts. They cited the Geneva agreement on Indochina as having disproved the U.S. claim that it is impossible to negotiate with communists, and showed "that the most complicated international questions can be resolved on a mutually acceptable basis."[11]

Back in Moscow, the hard-line foreign minister Molotov sought to interpret the embassy's reports in such a way as to present the prospects for fruitful negotiation with the West as negligible. In his personal copy of the February 1955 report, for example, Molotov marked in red the passage indicating U.S. lack of interest in an agreement.[12] At the time the Soviet government was preparing to present its May 1955 disarmament proposal, the embassy in Washington, in its quarterly report, described a mood of optimism in the United States about the economic situation there. The foreign minister marked that passage in red as well.[13] In the traditional Marxist-Leninist thinking that characterized Molotov's worldview, a strong economy would provide no incentive for the United States to bargain. He also marked an extensive discussion of the recent nuclearization of U.S. military forces, including a list of new

9. AVP, Fond: Ref. po SShA, Op. 38, por. 15, pap. 276, "Political Report of the Embassy of the USSR in the USA for 1954" [in Russian], written on 25 February 1955 and received in the Foreign Ministry on 3 March.

10. AVP, Fond: Ref. po SShA, op. 38, por. 14, pap. 14, second quarterly report (Zarubin), 16 July 1954, p. 62; third quarterly report, 8 October 1954, p. 27.

11. AVP, Fond: Ref. po SShA, op. 38, por. 14, pap. 14, third quarterly report, 8 October 1954, p. 26.

12. "Political Report of the Embassy of the USSR in the USA for 1954," written on 25 February 1955, sent to Molotov (this is his copy), received in the Foreign Ministry on 3 March 1955 and classified top secret, note appended from Molotov to Soldatov, 9 April 1955, to prepare for the Foreign Ministry collegium to discuss the report at the end of April. AVP, op. 38, por. 15, pap. 276, p. 92.

13. Ibid. The discussion of the atmosphere on the economy in the United States is on p. 21.

nuclear-capable weapons.[14] For Molotov, a U.S. nuclear buildup was incompatible with any intention to negotiate a test ban.

Molotov's views were reinforced by the Eisenhower administration's penchant for bargaining "from positions of strength." The evidence suggests that this approach was not very effective in eliciting Soviet moderation. The 1954 embassy report equated negotiation from strength with U.S. intransigence and saw the policy as an indication that the Eisenhower administration was not serious about wanting to reduce international tensions. As the report described, the State Department consistently reacted to Soviet disarmament initiatives and proposals by arguing that they were "nothing new" or that they were proposed "for propaganda reasons."[15] Overall, the report argued, the year 1954 demonstrated the failure of the U.S. policy of positions of strength. World opinion forced the United States to attend the Berlin meeting of foreign ministers, for example. Moreover, in the words of the report, measures of the Soviet government to maintain and strengthen peace were meeting with greater and greater support throughout the world among various circles concerned about preventing a new war.[16] Khrushchev was able to use such indications of international support, especially from the emerging nonaligned movement, to bolster his case for taking Soviet disarmament initiatives against Molotov's hard-line opposition. In this case, however, Molotov's interpretation of U.S. motives was more accurate than Khrushchev's: the United States rejected the May 1955 disarmament proposals, including the test ban.[17]

Relative Capabilities. Even before the May 1955 initiative, the U.S. government had considered the issue of which side would benefit most from a test ban. In April 1954, in response to Nehru's proposal for a worldwide moratorium, the Eisenhower administration solicited the views of the various relevant agencies. The Atomic Energy Commission—in charge of production of U.S. nuclear weapons—put the United States far ahead: "It is believed that the United States has, at present, an indeterminate advantage over the USSR with respect to the technical status of thermonuclear weapons development." At the same time, however, the Atomic Energy Commission opposed a test ban for fear that the USSR could pursue theoretical studies of nuclear weapons technology during a ban and then resume testing in a much better position to catch up to the United States.[18]

The Central Intelligence Agency put forward a carefully and redundantly qualified argument that a test ban could, on balance, possibly benefit Soviet military interests: "The Kremlin probably believes that, in general, numerous

14. Ibid., 43.
15. Ibid., 84.
16. Ibid., 86–88.
17. Evangelista, "Cooperation Theory and Disarmament."
18. Chair of the Joint Chiefs of Staff to the Secretary of Defense, memorandum, 30 April 1954, White House Office, OSANSA, Box 2, NSC 112/1 Disarmament (6), DDEL, p. 2.

weapons tests are more important for the U.S. nuclear program than they are for the Soviet program. . . . Provided the USSR completes its next series of tests, which may well occur this summer [1954], the Kremlin would probably estimate that a moratorium on weapons tests would not for the time being impair Soviet capabilities more than it would those of the U.S."[19] Eisenhower found little support within his government for a test moratorium, even from those agencies that viewed the United States as far head of the Soviets in nuclear technology. Thus he did not seek to negotiate from strength, or negotiate at all, toward a test ban at this point.

Soviet Scientists Speak Up

One cannot understand the motives for Soviet interest in a test ban simply by looking at U.S. negotiating behavior or the relative strengths of the two sides' nuclear weapons programs. Soviet scientists played a role in informing Soviet leaders about the dangers of nuclear war and in making some of them see a test ban as a way to reduce those dangers.

In the West, organizations such as the Federation of American Scientists and SANE were important in disseminating information about the dangers of fallout from nuclear tests—and Soviet officials kept track of their activities. But the Soviet government was already aware of those dangers well before the March 1954 BRAVO test, thanks to its own scientists. As Andrei Sakharov reported in his memoirs, officals involved in the Soviet nuclear program (in which he played a major role) took account of the risks of radioactive fallout when planning their nuclear tests. In July 1953, for example, concern about the effects of fallout on the local population caused the Soviet military authorities to evacuate some ten thousand people near the nuclear test site in Kazakhstan. Residents of the settlement at Karaul were not allowed to return home for eight months.[20]

Although Soviet nuclear specialists were already aware of the risks of fallout, the public campaign in the West against nuclear testing stimulated them to do something about it. In late March 1954, a group of four Soviet physicists, led by Igor' Kurchatov, the scientific director of the Soviet atomic project since 1943, drafted a classified report on the dangers of nuclear weapons.[21]

19. Director, Central Intelligence Agency to the Executive Secretary, National Security Council, memorandum, 25 May 1954, on "Indian Proposal for a World-Wide Moratorium on Nuclear Weapons Tests," Box 2, NSC 112/1 Disarmament (5), OSANSA, DDEL, p. 3.

20. Andrei Sakharov, *Memoirs*, trans. Richard Lourie (New York, 1990), 170–173.

21. I. V. Kurchatov, A. I. Alikhanov, I. K. Kikoin, A. P. Vinogradov, "Opasnosti atomnoi voiny i predlozhenie prezidenta Eizekhauera," Storage Center for Contemporary Documentation [Tsentr khraneniia sovremennoi dokumentatsii] (hereafter TsKhSD), fond 5, opis 30, delo 126, 38ff. This document is discussed in Yuri Smirnov and Vladislav Zubok, "Nuclear Weapons after Stalin's Death: Moscow Enters the H-Bomb Age," *Cold War International History Project Bulletin*, no. 4 (Fall 1994): 1, 14–18. I am grateful to Vlad Zubok for sharing his notes from this document with me.

They mentioned the ongoing U.S. test program, including the BRAVO shot that showered radioactive fallout on the Lucky Dragon. "The world commmunity is concerned," wrote the scientists, and "such concern is entirely under-standable." The scientists argued that "it is clear that the use of atomic weapons on a mass scale will lead to the devastation of the warring coun-tries. . . . In just a few years the stockpiles of atomic explosives will be sufficient to create conditions under which the existence of life over the whole globe will be impossible. . . . We cannot but admit that humanity faces an enormous threat of the end of all life on Earth."[22]

The scientists' views contrasted sharply with the Soviet ideological ortho-doxy of the time, which insisted on the inevitable victory of "socialism" in any military conflict with "imperialism." When Georgii Malenkov, then So-viet prime minister, adopted the scientists' position and declared that war be-tween the United States and the USSR "would mean the end of world civi-lization," Nikita Khrushchev denounced his views as "theoretically mistaken and politically harmful."[23] Khrushchev later came to adopt such views him-self, after he had secured Malenkov's political defeat, and after he himself had become better informed about the consequences of nuclear war.[24]

To make such information available to the Soviet public, Kurchatov and his colleagues had originally hoped to publish a version of their secret report as an article in the popular press. V. A. Malyshev, head of the Ministry of Medium-Machine Building (the euphemistic name for the nuclear weapons complex) proposed to Khrushchev that the article be published, not under the names of the authors themselves—whose identities could not be revealed because of the sensitivity of their work—but under those of other Soviet sci-entists "well known abroad and not related to our field" [i.e., building nuclear weapons]. One of the proposed "authors," Dmitrii Skobel'tsyn, had represented the Soviet Union at the United Nations in 1946, in fruitless dis-cussions on international control of atomic energy. He later led the Soviet delegation to the 1955 Geneva conference on peaceful uses of nuclear energy and became an active participant in Pugwash.[25] But in the still highly suspi-cious climate of 1954—and in the midst of a tense struggle for political power among the top Soviet leaders—such heterodox views on the threat of nuclear war could not be published even pseudonymously.

The draft article remained buried in the Soviet archives for nearly three

22. Kurchatov et al., "Opasnosti atomnoi voiny," 40–41, from Zubok's notes. See also the discussion in David Holloway, *Stalin and the Bomb: The Soviet Union and Atomic Energy, 1939–1956* (New Haven, Conn., 1994), 337–339.

23. Smirnov and Zubok, "Nuclear Weapons after Stalin's Death," 14–15.

24. James Richter, *Khrushchev's Double Bind: International Pressures and Domestic Coalition Pol-itics* (Baltimore, Md., 1994), esp. chap. 2.

25. V. Malyshev to N. Khrushchev, memorandum, 1 April 1954, TsKhSD, fond 5, opis 30, delo 126, p. 38, from Zubok's notes. On Skobel'tsyn's activities, see Holloway, *Stalin and the Bomb*, 163–166, 351–353; and Joseph Rotblat, *Scientists in the Quest for Peace: A History of the Pug-wash Conferences* (Cambridge, Mass., 1972).

decades. It provides strong evidence that despite the years of Stalinist isolation, Soviet scientists were well informed about the threat of nuclear war and shared the concerns of their Western colleagues. But it was mainly the combination of public protests against nuclear tests, the international scientific condemnation, and the demands for a test moratorium by the nonaligned states that provided the opportunity for Khrushchev to put a test ban on the disarmament agenda. There it languished for nearly three years, as opponents of a test ban within the Eisenhower administration ruled out any constructive response to Khrushchev's initiative, and much of the administration's effort was focused on trying not to lose the battle for world public opinion.[26]

THE UNILATERAL MORATORIUM: "LIKE THUNDER IN A CLEAR SKY"

Khrushchev's next opportunity to promote a test ban came nearly three years later. It was one he seized himself. In late March 1958, Khrushchev consolidated his position in the Soviet leadership by becoming chair of the Council of Ministers. Thus, in addition to his role as top Party leader, Khrushchev became, in effect, Soviet "prime minister" and head of government. Just a few days later, on 31 March 1958, the USSR Supreme Soviet, the nominal parliament, issued a decree announcing a unilateral suspension of Soviet nuclear tests. The moratorium would continue as long as other countries refrained from testing as well.

The Role of Military Programs

One analysis describes the timing of the move as "transparently cynical—they had just completed a major series of tests and the U.S. was just about to start one."[27] In fact, however, Khrushchev seems not to have consulted his nuclear scientists about the state of the Soviet test program when he made his decision to suspend testing. Andrei Sakharov, who was then working at the nuclear complex Arzamas-16 (the "Installation"), learned about it in January 1958 when Central Committee Secretary Mikhail Suslov showed him the text of the Presidium's decision to announce the moratorium in March at the Supreme Soviet. Sakharov recalls the reaction of the nuclear scientists: "My colleagues at the Installation could not believe their ears when they learned of the forthcoming halt in testing." Although Sakharov was pleased by the decision in principle, he was concerned about its disruptive impact on the Soviet nuclear weapons program. As he told Suslov, "we should have been informed of such a major decision beforehand so that we could tie up loose

26. Jeffrey W. Knopf, *Domestic Society and International Cooperation: The Impact of Protest on U.S. Arms Control Policy* (Cambridge, U.K., 1998), chap. 5.

27. Glenn T. Seaborg and Benjamin S. Loeb, *Kennedy, Khrushchev, and the Test Ban* (Berkeley, Calif., 1981), 11.

ends at the Installation."[28] Sakharov makes clear that the West was mistaken in its claim "that the USSR had prepared itself for the halt in testing while the U.S. and Britain were caught by surprise, before they'd been able to carry out the scheduled programs" of nuclear tests. Soviet nuclear scientists were surprised as well.[29]

Khrushchev's son Sergei, in his two-volume memoir of the period, claims that even top officials in charge of nuclear and military programs were kept unaware of Khrushchev's plans for a moratorium: "They found out about it at the last minute, virtually from the newspapers." The news took them by surprise, bursting out "like thunder in a clear sky."[30]

Khrushchev's announcement of a test ban in 1958 runs contrary to arguments that Soviet moderation resulted from U.S. negotiation from strength in the face of Soviet weakness. On the contrary, Khrushchev appears to have been encouraged by Soviet progress in the field of military technology to undertake a gesture of restraint. It was not the specific achievements of the nuclear testing program, because, as Sakharov reports, Khrushchev apparently did not seek to inform himself about it before announcing the moratorium. Instead, such events as the launching of the world's first artificial satellite, Sputnik, in October 1957, and the related advances in the ballistic missile program appear to have given Khrushchev the confidence to pursue restraint in the nuclear weapons area.[31]

Indeed, at this point the Soviet notion of "positions of strength" seemed to undergo a curious role reversal. Some Soviet officials expressed concern that the United States might consider itself in a position of relative weakness vis-à-vis the USSR and could be reluctant to negotiate on disarmament and nuclear testing until it had regained its strength. In his letter of 8 January 1958 to President Eisenhower, for example, Marshal Nikolai Bulganin, then Soviet prime minister, sought to persuade the president to enter negotiations despite Soviet gains in missile and space technology. Gaining a position of strength was never our policy, he argued. We will negotiate fairly even though we are strong.[32] At about the same time, an official in the Soviet Foreign Ministry, in a memorandum to the minister, made a similar interpretation of U.S. reluctance to negotiate from a position of weakness. He backed

28. Sakharov, *Memoirs*, 206.

29. Sakharov, *Memoirs*, 207.

30. Sergei Khrushchev, *Nikita Khrushchev: Krizisy i rakety* (Moscow, 1994), 1:358.

31. Khrushchev offered a similar explanation to his colleagues during the following year when President Eisenhower invited him to the United States: "Who would have guessed, twenty years ago, that the most powerful capitalist country would invite a Communist to visit? This is incredible. Today they *have* to take us into account. It's our strength that led to this— they have to recognize our existence and our power." Quoted in Sergei Khrushchev, *Khrushchev on Khrushchev: An Inside Account of the Man and His Era*, ed. and trans. William Taubman (Boston, Mass., 1990), 356.

32. Bulganin to Eisenhower, 8 January 1958, AVP, Fond: Ref. po SShA, op. 44, por. 20, pap. 89, Department of American Countries, 102-USA, "Exchange of messages between Bulganin, N. S. Khrushchev and D. Eisenhower, 8 January–2 June 1958" [in Russian], p. 8.

up his interpretation with quotations from U.S. analysts, and he pointed to the failure of a recent U.S. missile test as contributing to the overall malaise.[33]

In fact, within the Eisenhower administration, the president's top experts conveyed a very different interpretation of relative U.S. and Soviet strengths than the one suggested by popular alarm about Sputnik. By the time the Soviets initiated the unilateral moratorium in March 1958, Dr. James Killian and his colleagues on the President's Scientific Advisory Committee were convinced that a test ban would be of greater value to the United States than to the Soviet Union because it would lock in a substantial U.S. advantage. The scientists' views, in combination with his own concern about international public opinion, led Secretary of State John Foster Dulles to reverse his earlier view and favor a moratorium: "Dr. Killian makes a persuasive case that continued testing will help the Soviet weapons program more than it will ours. . . . I believe that the time is now ripe for a decision that we will agree to a contingent nuclear test suspension after completion of the testing program now under way."[34]

Although Khrushchev's optimism about Soviet military programs led him to halt nuclear testing, the views of his weapons designers and military officials on the balance of U.S. and Soviet nuclear technology were closer to those of President Eisenhower's advisers. By the summer of 1958, members of the Soviet military establishment began to express doubts that the Soviet side would maintain a position of strength during the forthcoming negotiations on a test ban. Unlike political leaders such as Khrushchev and Bulganin, or Foreign Ministry diplomats, the military technologists were less confident about the *impressions* of Soviet strength created by Sputnik and the missile tests and more worried about the actual balance of military-technical capabilities.[35]

Thus, in launching the unilateral initiative, Khrushchev became embroiled in what his son called "a hard and long period of battle on two fronts." On one front were the Americans, whom Khrushchev had to convince of the merits of a test ban—that it would slow the arms race, reduce the danger of war, and provide greater security for both sides. On the other front were

33. G. Saksin to A. Gromyko, memorandum, 25 January 1958, AVP, Fond: Ref. po SShA, Department of American Countries, op. 44, por. 36, pap. 92, folder 194/III-USA, "Problems of disarmament, on a halt to testing of atomic and hydrogen weapons, 29 January–29 October 1958" [in Russian]. On the atmosphere in the United States, see Divine, *Nuclear Test Ban Debate*, 169–170.

34. John Foster Dulles to the President, memorandum, 30 April 1958, Eisenhower, Dwight D.: Papers as President of the United States, 1953–61, Dulles-Herter Series, Box 8: Dulles, John Foster, April 1958 (1), 1–2, DDEL. See also Donald A. Quarles, deputy secretary of defense, to the Chairman, Ad Hoc Panel on Nuclear Test Cessation, memorandum, 21 March 1958, "The Effects of a Total Suspension or Cessation of Nuclear Testing," White House Office, Office of the Special Assistant for National Security Affairs: Records, 1952–61, NSC Series, Briefing Notes Subseries, Box 2: [Atomic Testing] Killian Report—Technical Feasibility of Cessation of Nuclear Testing [1958], p. 1, DDEL.

35. Khrushchev, *Krizisy i rakety*, 1:398–399, 410–411.

Khrushchev's internal critics, who were not by and large persuaded by those arguments and who often had their own parochial reasons for wanting to continue nuclear testing. As Sergei Khrushchev explains, by rejecting calls to join the March 1958 moratorium, "the Americans were strengthening the arguments of our opponents of the moratorium."[36]

The Public Campaign against Nuclear Testing

It is now certain that the March 1958 moratorium was not the result of a plan by the Soviet nuclear establishment to take advantage of a temporary lead over the U.S. program. The idea of a unilateral Soviet nuclear test moratorium originated from several other sources but was mainly Khrushchev's personal initiative.

As with the first Soviet decision to include a test ban in its 1955 disarmament proposal, this time as well the Soviet government was particularly attentive to international public opinion and the opportunity for a propaganda coup. The United States had consistently rejected Soviet offers to negotiate a test ban as a first step toward a wider disarmament agreement. The inability of the nuclear powers to make progress at the negotiating table, coupled with their ongoing programs of atmospheric nuclear test explosions, fueled a worldwide popular movement of opposition to the tests. The Soviet government took advantage of the widespread sentiment against tesing to make frequent public offers to join a multilateral test moratorium with the United States and Britain, the other two nuclear powers.

In 1957 the Nobel laureate biochemist Linus Pauling had launched an international campaign to gather signatures of prominent scientists opposed to further nuclear testing. Pauling's campaign complemented the mass demonstrations and acts of civil disobedience organized by SANE and the affiliated Committee for Non-Violent Action in the United States, and the Campaign for Nuclear Disarmament in England. In June 1957 Pauling collected 2,000 signatures of fellow scientists in the United States. In January 1958 he submitted a list of more than 9,200 scientists from around the world to Dag Hammarskjold, the secretary-general of the United Nations.[37] Earlier that month, the Soviet government had made an unsuccessful appeal for all three nuclear powers to stop testing for a period of two or three years.[38] The proposal for a mutual moratorium marked a response to the many well-publicized international demands for a halt to testing, but the United States rebuffed it.

36. Ibid., 1:359.

37. Katz, *Ban the Bomb*, 17–18; Divine, *Nuclear Test Ban Debate*, 182.

38. Discussed in the document "Seven statements of the Soviet government about a summit meeting" [in Russian], in AVP, Fond: Ref. po SShA, op. 44, por. 36, pap. 92, folder 194/III-USA, "Problems of disarmament, on a halt to testing of atomic and hydrogen weapons, 29 January–29 October 1958" [in Russian].

The proposal for a unilateral Soviet test suspension was discussed within the Soviet Foreign Ministry in late 1957 and early 1958, as the popular protest movement gathered steam. One former Foreign Ministry official, citing Foreign Minister Andrei Gromyko as his authority, claims that the unilateral moratorium was mainly Khrushchev's personal initiative, and that the Soviet leader directed Gromyko to prepare some proposals.[39]

In any case, in January 1958 a member of Gromyko's staff sent the foreign minister a memorandum discussing the conditions under which it would be desirable for the USSR to initiate a unilateral test moratorium.[40] Such an initiative, he argued, would serve the "goal of increasing pressure on the USA and England" by mobilizing international public opinion in favor of a test ban. The memomorandum proposed that the Soviet Union issue the following statement: "The government of the USSR has decided to halt from 1 February 1958 all tests of atomic and hydrogen weapons. The Soviet government declares that it is ready to adhere to this decision for any period if the USA and England agree not to conduct tests of their weaponry. If the USA and England are the first to undertake during this time the production of new tests, the USSR will be forced to review its decision."[41] This document contains the gist of the actual March announcement, and the timing of the memorandum is about right to coincide with Sakharov's recollection of a Presidium decision in January.[42]

Soviet Attempts at Manipulating the Peace Movement

Not surprisingly, Soviet support for international efforts to ban nuclear tests was strongest in the wake of the announcement of a unilateral moratorium in March 1958. The Central Committee stepped up its activities during the summer of 1958 to promote a broadscale international campaign. Much of its attention focused on an international meeting of scientists in Tokyo on 15 August, at which, it was expected, information on the health hazards of radioactive fallout would be discussed. The Central Committee wanted Soviet scientists to see to it that the conference would help launch a major public

39. Arkady N. Shevchenko, *Breaking with Moscow* (New York, 1985), 86–87. Another official makes the same claim, without attribution, but he could be repeating the account in Shevchenko's book, which is listed in his bibliography. See Oleg Grinevskij, *Tauwetter: Entspannung, Krisen und neue Eiszeit* (Berlin, 1996), 83, 98.

40. G. Saksin to A. Gromyko, memorandum, 25 January 1958, AVP, Fond: Ref. po SShA, Department of American Countries, op. 44, por. 36, pap. 92, folder 194/III-USA, "Problems of disarmament, on a halt to testing of atomic and hydrogen weapons, 29 January–29 October 1958" [in Russian]. The memorandum mentions a previous note by A. E. Bogomolov from 28 December 1957 with other related proposals.

41. Ibid.

42. For the text of the announcement, see "Decree of the USSR Supreme Soviet Concerning the Discontinuance of Soviet Atomic and Hydrogen Weapons Tests, March 31, 1958," Document No. 21, in (Col.) V. Morozov, ed., *The Last Nuclear Explosion: A Historical Survey* (Moscow, 1986), 135–137.

campaign against nuclear testing, one that emphasized a test ban as a first step toward banning nuclear weapons, a step that could be taken independently of a more comprehensive disarmament agreement.[43] The directive instructed the Academy of Sciences and several departments of the Central Committee "to prepare and carry out in a two-month period measures for the dissemination abroad of scientific materials about the danger for life and health of people of the continuing tests of atomic and hydrogen weaponry."[44] The campaign was clearly oriented toward raising the issue of fallout with the foreign public, but not at home. As Boris Ponomarev of the Central Committee International Department put it, "we have in mind that these measures should be directed above all at the capitalist countries in order not to allow the populations in the socialist states to become frightened."[45]

Andrei Sakharov recalls participating in a Soviet campaign to disseminate information about the dangers of nuclear tests in 1957 and 1958, when he was asked by Igor' Kurchatov (or volunteered—he did not remember which) to write an article for the Soviet journal *Atomnaia energiia*. The article appeared in 1958 in the wake of Khrushchev's announcement of the unilateral moratorium. It was later translated into English, and, in a more popularized and politicized version, was translated into several languages and widely distributed in Soviet publications abroad. Sakharov reported that Kurchatov discussed the articles with Khrushchev on two occasions and that Khrushchev personally authorized their publication.[46] The main point of Sakharov's article was to estimate the number of deaths that would be caused in the future by genetic mutations produced by fallout of radioactive Carbon 14.[47] These estimates prompted his later intense concern to prevent further Soviet atmospheric nuclear explosions.

The Limits of Scientists' Influence

The highest levels of the Soviet leadership were kept informed of the activities of the international peace movement, not least because Western ac-

43. TsKhSD, CPSU Central Committee, from protocol no. 75, Secretariat session of 14 August 1958, item 141g.: "On the conduct of an international campaign for a halt to the testing of nuclear weaponry" [in Russian].
44. Ibid.
45. TsKhSD, letter from Ponomarev to Central Committee, 7 August 1958, p. 2, on microfilm role 3340.
46. A. D. Sakharov, "Radioactive Carbon from Nuclear Explosions and Nonthreshold Biological Effects." This article, originally published in 1958 in *Atomnaia energiia*, later appeared in A. V. Lebedinskii, *Sovetskie uchenye ob opasnosti ispytanii iadernogo oruzhiia* (Moscow, 1959), and has been translated as *What Russian Scientists Say about Fallout* (New York, 1962). For discussion of the popular versions, see Sakharov, *Memoirs*, 203–204.
47. In 1990, Frank von Hippel reprinted Sakharov's original article along with his own review of Sakharov's estimates in light of more recent information and more accurate assumptions. See von Hippel, "Appendix: Revisiting Sakharov's Assumptions," *Science and Global Security* 1, 3–4 (1990): 185–186.

tivists frequently appealed directly to Soviet leaders on the question of nuclear testing. But there were clearly limits to what such an approach could achieve. In April 1958, for example, the Central Committee Secretariat took up the issue of a letter from Linus Pauling proposing to bring to trial the individuals responsible for the continuation of nuclear testing in the United States, Britain, and the Soviet Union on the grounds that they were endangering the lives and health of the world's people.[48] The Central Committee officials were not very enthusiastic about the idea, even though at that point the USSR had instituted its unilateral moratorium.

When the United States and Britain refused to halt their own nuclear tests, Khrushchev threatened to resume Soviet testing. At this point we have solid information about the efforts made by Soviet scientists to moderate Soviet policy by forestalling the resumption of the tests—and they failed. Andrei Sakharov has described how he tried in September 1958 to persuade Nikita Khrushchev not to break the unilateral Soviet moratorium. He enlisted the aid of Kurchatov, who flew to Yalta, where Khrushchev was on vacation, to talk to him. The Soviet leader rejected the arguments of Sakharov and Kurchatov, which were partly political (resumption of testing would destroy trust in the USSR and set back chances for a negotiated test ban), but mostly technical (nuclear weapons could be produced using simulations and calculations without full-scale testing).[49]

Despite Sakharov and Kurchatov, many leading figures in the Soviet nuclear establishment wanted to resume testing, especially given that the United States was unwilling to agree to a mutual test moratorium.[50] As an alternative, President Eisenhower suggested convening a panel of experts to investigate the potential for monitoring a test ban. The proposal for a technical conference had originally been suggested to Eisenhower by the British, who were playing for time as they completed tests on their own hydrogen bombs.[51]

On 22 August 1958 the United States and Britain changed their positions on the test moratorium. President Eisenhower and Prime Minister Harold Macmillan issued a joint statement offering to begin negotiations with the Soviet Union on a test ban starting in late October, and at that point to implement a

---

48. TsKhSD, CPSU Central Committee, 20th convocation, Commission on questions of ideology, culture, and international party contacts, from protocol no. 7, commission session of 7 April 1958, item 18: "On the letter from the American scientist L. Pauling, to Comrades Tereshkin, Romanov, Rumiantsev, Furtseva, Suslov" [in Russian].

49. Sakharov, *Memoirs*, 207–209.

50. For speculation about Khrushchev's internal opposition, see Christer Jönsson, *Soviet Bargaining Behavior: The Nuclear Test Ban Case* (New York, 1979), esp. part 4. His analysis has stood up well in light of subsequent archival and memoir material. See, for example, Khrushchev, *Krizisy i rakety*, 1:398–399.

51. Thomas Risse-Kappen, *Cooperation among Democracies: The European Influence on U.S. Foreign Policy* (Princeton, N.J., 1995), 114.

one-year moratorium on testing. The proposal for a moratorium led to "a last-minute rash of testing by all three nuclear powers."[52] The United States completed its tests the day before the negotiations opened; the USSR broke its unilateral moratorium on 30 September—after observing that the United States had conducted over fifty tests since the Soviet moratorium began—and continued testing until 3 November. At that point it renewed its moratorium. The temporary resumption of Soviet testing took some of the pressure off Khrushchev from his internal test ban opponents. Even Sakharov, who had adamantly opposed the new tests, had to admit that they "were indeed a great success and important from a technical point of view."[53]

THE TRILATERAL MORATORIUM

What accounts for the reversal in U.S. and British policy to join the Soviet Union in a test moratorium? The scientists deserve much of the credit. The Geneva conference, convened to study methods of verifying a test ban, was a surprising success. Scientists from East and West managed to come to agreement on the components of an arms control verification scheme—including, for the first time, on-site inspection of Soviet territory.[54] The achievements of the scientists generated momentum for the politicians in England and the United States to agree to something they had been resisting—a multilateral test moratorium.[55]

The Geneva Conferences

When President Eisenhower proposed a conference of experts in 1958 to discuss the possibilities for a scheme to verify a nuclear test ban, he opened the door to extensive participation of scientists in the arms control process. As Robert Gilpin writes, "the Conference of Experts was unique in the annals of diplomacy. For, while the responsibility of the scientists was ostensibly solely technical in nature, in reality these men had been assigned a political task of the highest order." The United States "had entrusted to a group of untrained private citizens the serious diplomatic responsiblity of negotiating the broad outlines of an arms control agreement."[56]

As Gilpin points out, the U.S. delegation consisted of experts from univer-

52. Divine, *Nuclear Test Ban Debate*, 231.
53. Sakharov, *Memoirs*, 208.
54. The standard sources are Harold K. Jacobson and Eric Stein, *Diplomats, Scientists, and Politicians: The United States and the Nuclear Test Ban Negotiations* (Ann Arbor, Mich., 1966); and Robert Gilpin, *American Scientists and Nuclear Weapons Policy* (Princeton, N.J., 1962). For the wording of the apparent commitment to on-site inspections, see Jacobson and Stein, *Diplomats, Scientists, and Politicians*, 78–79.
55. This is not to argue that the scientists were the main or only cause for the shift in the Western position. For a discussion, see Gilpin, *American Scientists*, 196–200.
56. Gilpin, *American Scientists*, 202.

sities and the private sector, rather than government officials or diplomats (although some junior officials served as advisers). The Eisenhower administration chose the members to represent a range of views on the merits of a test ban, assuming that a diverse group would best produce an objective, technical evaluation of a verification system. The president issued the group no political guidelines. The British scientific experts, by contrast, held official government positions as representatives of their country's Atomic Energy Authority and were instructed to strive for an agreement that would facilitate a test ban treaty. The Soviet delegation consisted mainly of prominent academic specialists, some of whom had worked on military applications of nuclear technology. As members of the Soviet Academy of Sciences and of the Communist Party of the Soviet Union, none of the delegates could be considered strictly private citizens; they were in some respect all "officials," although one delegate, Igor' Tamm, was not a Party member. Unlike the British and U.S. delegations, the Soviet one included an experienced diplomat from the Foreign Ministry, Semen Tsarapkin. Although the Soviet delegation engaged in hard bargaining, it was also, like the British one, intent on coming to an agreement. At the close of the Geneva conference the Soviet delegation took responsibility for drafting the final communiqué, which was then endorsed by the Western delegates.[57]

Although the Geneva participants were formally representatives of their governments, they can still be considered part of a transnational effort to achieve a measure of international cooperation that would not have been possible under normal state-to-state relations.[58] In some respects the formal negotiations in Geneva paralleled informal discussions within the Pugwash movement, with some overlap of participants, especially on the Soviet side. The atmosphere, in any case, was similar. Professor Hans Bethe of Cornell University, one of the leading U.S. participants, described it as "highly professional and oriented toward problem-solving based on consensual scientific knowledge."[59] One former Soviet diplomat recounts how on meeting each other in Geneva, the Soviet and U.S. scientists revealed the extent to which they were already acquainted even with colleagues they had never met: "'My name is Igor' Tamm. I . . .' 'Oh, yes, I know you well. You are a brilliant physicist, Nobel prize winner, academician, mountain climber, and an extremely witty conversationalist. Yes, there are entire legends about you going around. And my name is Hans Bethe. I . . .' 'Speak no further. You are an eminent atomic physicist, member of the President's Science Advisory Council, participant in the building of the atomic bomb.'"[60]

57. Gilpin, *American Scientists*, 194. On the makeup of the delegations, see Jacobson and Stein, *Diplomats, Scientists, and Politicians*, 54–58. For an account of the conference from a former Soviet diplomat, see Grinevskij, *Tauwetter*, chaps. 4, 5.
58. Risse-Kappen makes this case in *Cooperation among Democracies*, 115 n. 30.
59. Quoted in Risse-Kappen, *Cooperation among Democracies*, 115.
60. Grinevskij, *Tauwetter*, 103.

The main task of the Geneva conference was to devise a system of seismic monitoring of suspicious explosions, including some number of control stations, run by teams of technicians. The U.S. delegation initially proposed a system of 650 stations. The Soviet side preferred one with 100–110 stations. The two sides compromised on a British proposal for 170 land-based stations, supplemented by sea-based posts.[61]

In one respect the conference of experts was only a short-lived success. The scientists were able to agree on the parameters of a verification system for monitoring a test ban, but their conclusions were soon undermined on technical and political grounds by the revelation of new data from U.S. nuclear explosions that challenged some of the working assumptions of the conference.[62] As the political barriers to an accord mounted and each side mobilized its opposition, these ostensibly technical disagreements fueled political animosity and diminished the chances for an accord.

Transnational Interventions and Manipulations

In the autumn of 1958 the scientists were replaced in Geneva by the diplomats as the United States, Britain, and the Soviet Union opened formal negotiations on a test ban and concurrently suspended their nuclear test programs. The negotiations continued for several years but got bogged down mainly over disputes about the relevance of the verification system agreed by the scientists during the summer of 1958 and what improvements to it were necessary, given the U.S. reevaluation of the difficulties of seismic monitoring. Probably the major point of dispute concerned Soviet ambivalence about allowing on-site inspections.

During the years of negotiations, transnational actors regularly tried to break the impasse. The nuclear powers, for their part, often sought to manipulate these transnational interventions to bolster their own positions. As a rule, the Soviet government and Communist Party sought to control all communication between Soviet citizens and foreigners on issues of national security, including a nuclear test ban. On one occasion, the Foreign Ministry went so far as to prevent the delivery of letters from James Wadsworth, the head of the U.S. delegation to the UN negotiations on a test ban, to some Soviet citizens who had written to him about the U.S. position.[63]

At other points, when transnational interventions would appear to support their case, the Soviet authorities would welcome them. On 30 January 1959, for example, several prominent U.S. citizens, including Norman Cousins, Norman Thomas, and Eleanor Roosevelt, addressed a letter to Khrushchev,

61. Risse-Kappen, *Cooperation among Democracies*, 116.

62. Jacobson and Stein, *Diplomats, Scientists, and Politicians*, chap. 5.

63. Soldatov to Kuznetsov, 12 March 1959, AVP, Fond: Ref. po SShA, op. 47, por. 34, pap. 133, Department of American Countries, folder 194/IIIUSA, "Problem of disarmament, on the ban of atomic and hydrogen weaponry, 8 February–18 December 1959" [in Russian].

Eisenhower, and Macmillan urging them to conduct serious negotiations toward a test ban, despite the U.S. revelation of new scientific results purporting to make verification more difficult.[64] Khrushchev sent a response on 20 March in which he blamed the United States for coming up with "new seismic data" that proved problematic for the agreed inspection system: "It is not difficult to see that this step of the U.S. government is intended to destroy the basis which was built as a result of patient work by competent specialists from a range of countries and on which a system of verification of tests should be built."[65]

Clearly many officials in the Soviet government and Communist Party tried to use Soviet scientists and their transnational colleagues as an instrument of Soviet foreign policy and negotiating strategy. In early 1960, for example, Semen Tsarapkin, the head of the Soviet delegation to the Geneva talks on a nuclear test ban, communicated to the Foreign Ministry his sense from the course of the negotiations that there had been a decrease in public pressure on the Western governments to agree to a test ban. Officials from the Foreign Ministry and the Central Committee's International Department drafted a proposal "to carry out measures through international organizations to strengthen the campaign for a test ban agreement."[66] The Central Committee sent out instructions to Soviet representatives in "international democratic organizations," including Pugwash and various Soviet-backed groups such as the World Peace Council, the World Federation of Trade Unions, and the International Democratic Federation of Women. The wording closely followed the joint proposal from the Foreign Ministry and International Department. The Soviet representatives were directed to help mobilize the international movement for a test ban. Once the international campaign was successfully reinvigorated, the Soviet representatives would send letters and petitions to the negotiators in Geneva urging them to conclude an agreement.[67]

Tsarapkin subsequently reported to an American journalist that he was receiving a great deal of mail from Soviet citizens concerned about the test ban

64. Katz, *Ban the Bomb*, 66.

65. Cousins et al. to Khrushchev, 30 January 1959; Khrushchev to Cousins et al., 20 March 1959, in AVP, Fond: Ref. po SShA, op. 47, por. 34, pap. 133, Department of American Countries, folder 194/IIIUSA, "Problem of disarmament, on the ban of atomic and hydrogen weaponry, 8 February–18 December 1959" [in Russian].

66. Letter to the Central Committee from V. Kuznetsov and V. Tereshkin, 10 February 1960, TsKhSD, CPSU Central Committee, Commission on questions of ideology, culture, and international party contacts, fond 11, op. 1, ed. khr. 482, 20th convocation, materials to protocol no. 43, session of 18 February 1960. "On the strengthening of the public campaign for conclusion of an agreement on halting tests of nuclear weaponry" [in Russian].

67. Instructions and supplement k p.22go, pr. 44, TsKhSD, CPSU Central Committee, Commission on questions of ideology, culture, and international party contacts, fond 11, op. 1, ed. khr. 482, 20th convocation, materials to protocol no. 43, session of 18 February 1960. "On the strengthening of the public campaign for conclusion of an agreement on halting tests of nuclear weaponry."

conference.[68] In June 1961, however, after the trilateral moratorium on testing had been in effect for more than two and a half years, Tsarapkin complained of a decrease in public interest in the negotiations: "The letters are not so much now," he told an American writer. "Perhaps people have become used to no more explosions. Perhaps they have begun to think that such things cannot happen again."[69]

The cynical attitude of the Soviet authorities toward Western peace activists does not necessarily mean that the USSR was uninterested in the goal of a test ban. On the contrary, the Soviet leaders seemed to try to generate public pressure for a test ban at times when they were hoping to be able to negotiate an agreement with the West. When they appeared to be having second thoughts about a test ban, or had given it lower priority in their disarmament and security objectives, they tended to mute their support for the international test ban movement.

At various points in the course of the negotiations, the Pugwash movement sought to address some of the contentious issues that remained unresolved in Geneva. On 5 January 1960, for example, Joseph Rotblat, the secretary-general of Pugwash, wrote to Academician Topchiev to propose a Pugwash meeting to help resolve the technical disagreements on verification in the three-power negotiations on a test ban.[70] Two top officials of the Soviet Academy of Sciences, A. N. Nesmeianov and E. K. Fedorov (the latter led the Soviet delegation to the original conference of experts), then wrote to the Central Committee asking permission to send a delegation including, among others Topchiev, Fedorov, and Kurchatov.[71] The proposal was endorsed by the relevant Central Commitee officials, but ultimately had to be approved at the highest level—by Khrushchev and his colleagues on the Presidium.[72] In the meantime Kurchatov died of a heart attack on 7 February 1960, at the age of fifty-seven.[73] One of his last public acts was his speech at a session of the Supreme Soviet in mid-January, when he was the only participant, besides Khrushchev himself, to make a strong case for a test ban.[74]

On 9 March 1960, after soliciting the views of Efim Slavskii, then minister of Medium Machine Building (nuclear weapons), and V. V. Kuznetsov of the Foreign Ministry, the Central Committee instructed Topchiev to accept Rot-

68. Daniel Lang, *An Inquiry into Enoughness: Of Bombs and Men and Staying Alive* (New York, 1965), 48–49.

69. Ibid., 58–59.

70. Rotblat to Topchiev, 5 January 1960, TsKhSD, CPSU Central Committee, 20th Convocation, from protocol no. 138, Secretariat session of 23 February 1960, item 16: "On the participation of Soviet scientists in an International Pugwash conference on the question of halting nuclear tests" [in Russian].

71. Nesmeianov and Fedorov to Central Committee, 26 January 1960, in ibid.

72. Letter from V. Kirillin and V. Tereshkin, 12 February 1960, in ibid.

73. A. P. Aleksandrov, ed., *Vospominaniia ob Igore Vasil'eviche Kurchatove* (Moscow, 1988), 467. Kurchatov's name was subsequently crossed out in the letter from Nesmianov and Fedorov.

74. Jönsson, *Soviet Bargaining Behavior*, 151.

blat's invitation "agreeing to the call for a meeting in the second half of March in Geneva."[75] It was impossible to call the meeting on such short notice, however. Pugwash next met in Moscow in late November 1960, following the failed Paris summit in May and the U.S. presidential election.[76]

"Real Agreement between Intelligent People"

The main achievements of the transnational scientists' movement by the end of the 1950s were to place the test ban on the disarmament agenda, to get the three nuclear powers to agree to a multilateral test moratorium, and to demonstrate that experts from the three countries could devise a mutually acceptable system of verification. Although the last achievement proved ephemeral, it nevertheless created a process that ultimately contributed to the agreement signed in Moscow in 1963 to ban tests in the atmosphere, in space, and under water. As President Eisenhower explained following the conclusion of the conference of experts in August 1958, "any step like this that proves that you have a real agreement between intelligent people of both sides, gives grounds to hope that you can go another step, and every step that you go means you can go another one."[77] Not all subsequent steps were in the same direction—the Soviet side notably retreated in its commitment to on-site verification, for example—but the scientists' efforts were nevertheless crucial in generating momentum toward a test ban.

Internal and External Challenges to the Moratorium

During the first year of the trilateral moratorium, Khrushchev came under intense pressure from his missile designers and military-industrial officials to resume testing. Tests were particularly needed, they argued, to provide warheads for the new ballistic missiles about to be produced. In particular, according to his son's account, Khrushchev had to decide whether the R-16 rocket, under development by the Iangel' design bureau, should go into production with an old-model warhead, or whether some nuclear tests could be conducted to develop a new, lighter, more powerful and efficient model.[78]

Against the advice of leading figures in the military-industrial sector—notably, Leonid Brezhnev and Dmitrii Ustinov—Khrushchev maintained the moratorium and chose the outmoded warhead for the new missile. He felt

75. TsKhSD, CPSU Central Committee, 20th Convocation, from protocol no. 140, Secretariat session of 9 March 1960, item 26: "Concerning the call for a special Pugwash conference of scientists on the question of technical aspects of a halt to tests of nuclear weapons" [in Russian].
76. Rotblat, *Quest for Peace*, 166.
77. Press conference, reported in the *New York Times*, 22 August 1958, quoted in Gilpin, *American Scientists*, 195.
78. Grinevskij, *Tauwetter*, 110–112.

vindicated when on 26 August the U.S. government announced that it would extend the one-year moratorium, scheduled to expire at the end of October, until the end of the year. As Sergei Khrushchev reports, the U.S. initiative was a small step, just an extension of two months, but "father interpreted the announcement as a good sign." It helped him fend off calls for resuming tests. The Soviet government announced that it would maintain its moratorium as long as the Western powers refrained from testing.[79]

The mutual moratorium almost broke down in December 1959 when the Eisenhower administration announced that the U.S. was formally ending its obligation to refrain from testing. It promised, however, to give advanced notice of any future tests. At that point, Slavskii, the minister in charge of the Soviet nuclear establishment, made a concerted effort to persuade Khrushchev to resume testing. In a meeting with Khrushchev and top military officials, Slavskii argued that the U.S. was preparing for new tests that would put the Soviet side "not a step behind, but two, if not more." Sergei Khrushchev, who was present at the meeting, reports that Slavskii's arguments made a big impression on his father.[80] Khrushchev nevertheless argued that it would be foolish to be the first to break the moratorium, and that the Soviet side would look bad if it resumed testing before the forthcoming four-power summit meeting, scheduled for May 1960 in Paris.

Some Soviet scientists weighed in, at least indirectly, in support of Khrushchev's position. For example, E. K. Fedorov, head of the Soviet delegation to the 1958 conference of experts and a consultant to the Soviet nuclear establishment, appears to have seen himself as responsible for mobilizing Soviet scientific opinion in favor of a test ban. He argued at the annual meeting of the Soviet Academy of Sciences in February 1959 that "our scientists have to appear more often in the Soviet and foreign press on the most important political issues, for example disarmament, the cessation of atomic weapons tests, and so forth."[81] Leading by his own example, he published an article in the Soviet press in support of a test ban at the end of 1959, a time when Khrushchev was apparently the only top leader who strongly endorsed the measure. Fedorov's article had originally been presented at a Pugwash meeting, and it seemed designed to bolster Khrushchev.[82]

Khrushchev had barely overcome one challenge to his test moratorium when he faced another. In February 1960, France became a nuclear power by testing its first atomic weapon in the Sahara desert; at the United Nations, the

---

79. Khrushchev, *Krizisy i rakety*, 1:471.

80. Ibid., 48.

81. *Vestnik Akademii Nauk SSSR*, 1959, no. 4:50, quoted in Jönsson, *Soviet Bargaining Behavior*, 149. On Fedorov's status as consultant, see B. I. Ogorodnikov, ed., *Iadernyi arkhipelag* (Moscow, 1995), 43. I thank Pavel Podvig for calling this book to my attention.

82. E. K. Fedorov, "Soglashenie o prekrashchenii ispytanii iadernogo oruzhiia dolzhno byt' zakliucheno bezotlagatel'no," *Vestnik Akademii Nauk SSSR*, 1959, no. 10:11–16. For a discussion, see Jönsson, *Soviet Bargaining Behavior*, 149–151.

U.S. delegate supported the French right to nuclear testing, even though the Soviets had warned that they considered a test by France, a NATO member, as equivalent to one by the U.S. or Britain. Allen Dulles, head of the CIA, predicted that Khrushchev might use an anticipated French test as a pretext to resume Soviet tests.[83] Khrushchev was on a state visit to India, accompanied by his son Sergei, when the news of the French test was reported. Back in Moscow his colleagues argued for following through on the Soviet pledge to respond in kind to what they saw as the West's violation of the moratorium. Slavskii argued that a Soviet test series could be completed in time for the Paris summit, with no harm done to the country's international standing. Khrushchev again insisted on maintaining the Soviet moratorium until after the summit.[84]

MISSED OPPORTUNITIES

The transnational scientists' movement against nuclear testing achieved several successes during the first years of the Khrushchev period. It helped to make the public aware of the dangers of fallout and to get a test ban on the international agenda. It persuaded the nuclear powers to convene the conference of experts, to impose a temporary test moratorium, and to begin tripartite negotiations on a permanent ban.

Thereafter, however, from the start of the trilateral moratorium in 1958 until the signing of the Limited Test Ban Treaty in 1963, the history of test ban negotiations can be understood as a series of missed opportunities. The major opportunity foregone was the achievement of a permanent halt to all nuclear tests—the original goal of the opponents of nuclear testing. A comprehensive test ban was not successfully negotiated until 1996, many years after the end of the Cold War, indeed five years after the demise of the Soviet Union itself. During the Khrushchev years, a comprehensive ban seemed within reach at several points. That it was not achieved attests to the ultimate failure of the transnational test ban movement during this period.

Yet we can still understand something about the impact of transnational activity on the test ban issue by studying examples of near misses, as well as clear successes. What role did scientists and popular movements play in removing the various objections to a comprehensive test ban put forward by the nuclear powers?

83. Memorandum of Conversation, 19 January 1960, "Threshold Proposal for Nuclear Test Negotiations," White House Office, Office of the Special Assistant for National Security Affairs: Records, 1952–61, NSC Series, Briefing Notes Subseries, Box 2: [Atomic Testing] Suspension of Nuclear Testing, and Surprise Attack (3), DDEL.
84. Khrushchev, *Krizisy i rakety*, 1:471–472.

The Paris Summit

Many advocates of a test ban viewed the summit meeting scheduled for mid-May 1960 in Paris as a key opportunity to resolve the differences among the nuclear powers and advance the prospects for a treaty. We still do not know to what extent Khrushchev thought it possible to work out an agreement on nuclear testing at the Paris summit. His U.S. experts in the Foreign Ministry carefully scrutinized the translations of Eisenhower's correspondence for evidence of any change in the American negotiating position and his delegation to the Geneva conference appeared to be making progress toward compromise in the days leading up to the meeting.

Eisenhower's letter of 13 March 1960 expressed the hope that progress could be made on narrowing differences on a test ban before the May summit—specifically by agreeing to ban tests that could be reliably verified while working to improve the seismic verification system to include all tests.[85] A couple of weeks later, meeting with Prime Minister Macmillan at Camp David, Eisenhower agreed to overrule the Pentagon and the U.S. Atomic Energy Commission and offer the Soviets a "threshold" test ban treaty. It would have banned all tests registering above a seismic magnitude of 4.75 and included a moratorium on all tests below that threshold for a period of one to two years, while a coordinated East-West seismic research program was conducted to identify the means for bringing the threshold further down.[86] Eisenhower's decision represented a victory for the transgovernmental coalition of British and U.S. test ban supporters, including members of the President's Science Advisory Committee, that sought to influence internal U.S. deliberations on the test ban.[87]

As the date for the four-power summit meeting in Paris neared, there seemed to be some progress on the crucial question of on-site inspections as well. At Camp David, U.S. secretary of state Christian Herter suggested to Eisenhower and Macmillan that "it may be necessary to leave the number of inspections blank in the treaty and have that number settled at the Summit." The president agreed, leading his science adviser to note approvingly in his diary that "in a simple quick way, he conceded to the Soviets one of their main contentions, namely that the number of on-site inspections is a political rather than a technical issue."[88]

On 31 March, the Eisenhower-Macmillan proposal for a threshold treaty was formally submitted to the Geneva conference. The next day, Eisenhower

---

85. Eisenhower to Khrushchev, 13 March 1960, AVP, Fond: Ref. po SShA, op. 46, por. 27, pap. 120, Department of American Countries, 102-USA, "Exchange of messages between N. S. Khrushchev and D. Eisenhower, 14 January–1 September 1960" [in Russian].

86. Risse-Kappen, *Cooperation among Democracies*, 124–125. George Kistiakowsky, *A Scientist at the White House: The Private Diary of President Eisenhower's Special Assistant for Science and Technology* (Cambridge, Mass., 1976), 286–287.

87. Risse-Kappen, *Cooperation among Democracies*, 122.

88. Kistiakowsky, *A Scientist at the White House*, 288.

sent a letter to Khrushchev arguing that the two countries' positions had moved closer together. One copy (perhaps Ambassador Anatolii Dobrynin's) of the Russian translation of Eisenhower's letter has several of the president's more hopeful remarks underlined: "*now we have an agreed basis for approaching the problem of concluding* an agreement. . . . I instructed my representatives in Geneva to carry out negotiations in the most active way in order to *clarify the possiblity for working out a mutually agreed decision.*" The Soviet official also took note of Eisenhower's assurance, unreliable as it later turned out, that by excluding underground tests from the proposed agreement the United States did not intend that testing be renewed in that sphere. Finally, Eisenhower outlined the remaining points of disagreement between the two sides, all of which were underlined in the Russian translation. They included the Soviet proposal for an (unmonitored) underground test moratorium for four to five years, questions about the number of annual inspections the Soviet side would actually accept, the composition of the staff of the control commission, voting procedures, peaceful nuclear explosions, the geographic distribution of the monitoring system, and the production of fissionable material.[89]

The Soviet delegation to Paris had apparently prepared compromise positions on some of these issues and several of its members anticipated agreement on at least a partial test ban.[90] In any case, Khrushchev scuttled the summit in reaction to the downing of an American U-2 spy plane over Soviet territory.[91] It may be that he considered a compromise allowing for continued nuclear testing to be an insufficiently successful achievement for such a high-level meeting anyhow, especially when it became clear—well before the summit—that the West would not budge on the question of a divided Germany that really preoccupied the Soviet leader. Coming home from Paris with merely an agreement on a threshold test ban, after the humiliation of the spy flights, Eisenhower's refusal to apologize for them, and continued Western intransigence on Berlin, Khrushchev would have appeared even more vulnerable to his hawkish critics than he did in the event.[92]

The Berlin crisis undoubtedly complicated Khrushchev's efforts to improve relations with the West, and, in particular, to negotiate a test ban treaty.

---

89. Eisenhower to Khrushchev, 1 April 1960, Russian translations, 2–3, AVP, Fond: Ref. po SShA, op. 46, por. 27, pap. 120, Department of American Countries, 102-USA, "Exchange of messages between N. S. Khrushchev and D. Eisenhower, 14 January–1 September 1960."

90. Oleg Troyanovsky, "Nikita Khrushchev and the Making of Soviet Foreign Policy," paper prepared for a conference on the centenary of Nikita Khrushchev's birth held at Brown University, Providence, R.I., 1–3 December 1994, p. 22; Fedor Burlatsky, *Khrushchev and the First Russian Spring: The Era of Khrushchev through the Eyes of His Adviser*, trans. Daphne Skillen (New York, 1991), 155–156; Anatoly Dobrynin, *In Confidence: Moscow's Ambassador to Six Cold War Presidents* (New York, 1995), 42.

91. On the Paris summit, see Michael R. Beschloss, *Mayday: The U-2 Affair* (New York, 1986).

92. Richter, *Khrushchev's Double Bind*, 129–132; Vladislav Zubok, "Khrushchev and the Berlin Crisis (1958–1962)," Working Paper No. 6, Cold War International History Project, 1993; Troyanovsky, "Khrushchev and Soviet Foreign Policy," 22; Jönsson, *Soviet Bargaining Behavior*, 166–168.

Khrushchev was under pressure from the East German communist regime to normalize the situation of a divided Berlin and two German states. In his view, there were two options: the West could recognize the legitimacy of the German Democratic Republic and permit West Berlin to be transformed from an outpost of the West, located deep within the commmunist bloc, into a "free city;" or the Soviet Union could sign a peace treaty with the GDR, thereby ceding it control over West Berlin. Neither option was acceptable to the West, and therein lay the conflict over Berlin that lasted from 1958 through much of 1961.[93] Finally, the building of the Berlin wall in August 1961 relieved pressure on the East German regime by stemming the flow of refugees to the West. It eventually allowed for the crisis to subside, but not in time to rescue the Paris summit.

In the wake of the failed summit meeting, Khrushchev came under renewed pressure from military officials and weapons designers to resume testing.[94] He nevertheless argued for maintaining the moratorium at least until after the end of Eisenhower's term in office to demonstrate to the new president Soviet "peaceful intentions, not in words, but in deeds."[95] Eisenhower, by contrast, had given up on achieving a test ban. Had his vice president, Richard Nixon, won the presidential election in November 1960, Eisenhower would have resumed U.S. nuclear testing shortly thereafter. Instead, he urged President-elect John F. Kennedy to begin testing as soon as possible.[96]

The Kennedy Administration and the End of the Moratorium

Kennedy was unreceptive to his predecessor's advice. On the contrary, he was keen on achieving a nuclear test ban agreement early in his administration.[97] Unfortunately, the disastrous Bay of Pigs invasion of Cuba, plans for which Kennedy inherited from Eisenhower, coupled with Khrushchev's own domestic problems, made it difficult for the two leaders to summon the necessary political will to make the negotiations bear fruit. Nevertheless, despite the setbacks, both leaders kept returning to the topic of a test ban. In a letter of 18 April 1961 criticizing the U.S. aggression against Cuba, Khrushchev called for steps to improve the international atmosphere.[98] In his response,

93. For recent archival evidence on the Berlin crisis, see Hope M. Harrison, "Ulbricht and the Concrete 'Rose': New Archival Evidence on the Dynamics of Soviet-East German Relations and the Berlin Crisis, 1958–1961," Working Paper No. 5, Cold War International History Project, May 1993; and Zubok, "Khrushchev and the Berlin Crisis."
94. Transcript of Khrushchev's tape-recorded reminiscences, Harriman Institute, Columbia University, 940–941.
95. Khrushchev, *Krizisy i rakety*, 2:47–48.
96. Seaborg, *Kennedy, Khrushchev, and the Test Ban*, 24–25.
97. Michael R. Beschloss, *The Crisis Years: Kennedy and Khrushchev, 1960–1963* (New York, 1991), 84–85.
98. Khrushchev to Kennedy, 18 April 1961, AVP, Fond: Ref. po SShA, op. 47, por. 23, pap. 132, Department of American Countries, 102-USA, "Exchange of messages, 18 April–6 October 1961" [in Russian].

Kennedy specifically advocated "a speedy conclusion of an acceptable treaty for the banning of nuclear tests."[99]

But the talks between Britain, the United States, and the USSR in Geneva dragged on with little apparent progress. Meanwhile, the French refused to join the moratorium and continued to develop and test their nuclear weapons. On 1 September 1961, the Soviet side broke the trilateral moratorium and began a series of atmospheric nuclear tests. Two weeks later the U.S. followed suit, first with underground tests, then with atmospheric ones.[100]

The resumption of nuclear testing marked a clear failure of the transnational movement for a test ban treaty. Recent memoir accounts and archival documents shed light on the internal decisionmaking on the Soviet side, but they essentially reinforce the standard interpretation of the reversal in Soviet policy: In autumn 1961 Khrushchev was more influenced by the arguments of Soviet weapons designers and by his own broader foreign-policy goals than by the views of Soviet test ban advocates and their transnational allies.

The Balance of Military Technology, Politics, and Morality. On 10 July 1961 Khrushchev convened a meeting in the Kremlin with military officials, weapons designers, and nuclear scientists to announce his intention to resume testing in the fall. At the meeting, Andrei Sakharov recalls having "volunteered the opinion that we had little to gain from a resumption of testing at this juncture in our program" of nuclear weapons development. Sakharov was apparently the only participant to express objections to breaking the moratorium.[101]

He followed up his remarks with a letter to the Soviet leader, which Sakharov quotes in full from memory in his memoirs:[102]

To Comrade N. S. Khrushchev:

I am convinced that a resumption of testing at this time would only favor the USA. Prompted by the success of our Sputniks, they could use tests to improve their devices. They have underestimated us in the past, whereas our program has been based on a realistic appraisal of the situation. [Here Sakharov "omitted a sentence for reasons of security."] Don't you think that new tests will seriously jeopardize the test ban negotiations, the cause of disarmament, and world peace?

A. Sakharov

99. Kennedy to Khrushchev, 18 April 1961, ibid.

100. The most comprehensive published list of known Soviet nuclear tests is found in P. L. Podvig, ed., *Strategicheskoe iadernoe vooruzhenie Rossii* (Moscow, 1998). For an English-language list, broken down by year and type of test (underground versus atmospheric), see Robert Norris and William Arkin, "Known Nuclear Tests Worldwide, 1945–1995," *Bulletin of the Atomic Scientists* 52, 3 (May/June 1996): 61–63. For the U.S. reaction to the Soviet test resumption, see Seaborg, *Kennedy, Khrushchev, and the Test Ban,* chap. 6.

101. Khrushchev, *Krizisy i rakety,* 2:120–121. Sakharov reports that after the meeting one other scientist came over to express support for his position; see *Memoirs,* 217.

102. Sakharov, *Memoirs,* 215–216.

Sakharov's was evidently a minority position. Most participants in the Soviet weapons establishment viewed nuclear tests as essential for further development of key programs.

Sakharov did manage, however, to enlist Iulii Khariton, the scientific director of Arzamas-16 and a leading figure in the Soviet nuclear program, to make the case for cancelling the large-yield tests. Khariton went to see Leonid Brezhnev, the Party secretary in charge of military industry, in mid-August, but, as Sakharov recalled, "from the little he told me, it sounded as if his arguments were too narrow and technical to make any real difference, given the political context of the decision."[103]

On 31 August 1961 the Soviet government publicly announced its withdrawal from the multilateral moratorium, but it did not at first announce the actual tests as they were conducted. The first nuclear test took place the following day.[104] Subsequent tests fulfilled a number of military objectives. Soviet military specialists were particularly interested in understanding the effects of high-altitude atmospheric explosions useful for anti-ballistic missile defense. They also used the 1961 test series to narrow the gap with the U.S. in large-yield warhead technology.[105]

On 17 October 1961, the Soviet Union took the unprecedented step of announcing and describing one of its nuclear tests in advance. Khrushchev made the announcement at the opening session of the 22d Congress of the Soviet Communist Party, clearly to maximize its impact. The bomb would be the biggest ever exploded, he said, with an expected explosive yield of fifty megatons. The actual yield was later estimated at fifty-seven megatons. According to a recent account by participants in the test, the explosion, which took place on 30 October 1961, was of a "one-of-a-kind device, whose design allowed it to achieve a yield of up to 100 megatons when fully loaded with nuclear fuel."[106]

The work on the massive weapon had begun in mid-July 1961, immediately after the meeting in the Kremlin where Khrushchev announced the impending end of the moratorium.[107] Unlike the September tests, which had clear

---

103. Sakharov, *Memoirs*, 217–218.

104. Khrushchev (*Krizisy i rakety*, 2:137) claims that this was a thermonuclear device, the long-awaited new warhead for the R-16 missile, but the most comprehensive review of the Soviet nuclear test program calls this claim into question. Warheads suitable for the R-16 were apparently not included among the first tests of the series. See Podvig, *Strategicheskoe iadernoe vooruzhenie Rossii*, 431–432. I thank Pavel Podvig for calling this discrepancy to my attention.

105. Douglas Franklin Garthoff, "The Domestic Dimension of Soviet Foreign Policy: The Kremlin Debate on the Test Ban, October 1962 to October 1963" (Ph.D. diss., Johns Hopkins University, 1972), 187–190; Jönsson, *Soviet Bargaining Behavior*, 37; Seaborg, *Kennedy, Khrushchev, and the Test Ban*, 119–123.

106. Viktor Adamsky and Yuri Smirnov, "Moscow's Biggest Bomb: The 50-Megaton Test of October 1961," *Cold War International History Project Bulletin*, no. 4 (Fall 1994): 19.

107. Ibid., 20; Ogorodnikov, *Iadernyi arkhipelag*, 45.

military goals that had been delayed by the moratorium (notably the R-16 warhead), the fifty-megaton bomb had no obvious military purpose. Only after the device was tested did Soviet weapons-design bureaus begin to consider what delivery vehicles (for example, rockets or airplanes) might be able to carry it.

Here Andrei Sakharov played a peculiar role. He had passionately opposed the "Big Bomb," as he called it. "During the 1950s," he later wrote, "I had come to regard testing in the atmosphere as a crime against humanity, no different from secretly pouring disease-producing microbes into a city's water supply." [108] But once his advice was rejected and the tests scheduled anyhow, Sakharov tried to be as helpful as possible: "After the test of the Big Bomb, I was concerned that the military couldn't use it without an effective carrier (a bomber would be too easy to shoot down). I dreamed up the idea of a giant torpedo, launched from a submarine and fitted with an atomic-powered jet engine that would convert the water to steam. The targets would be enemy ports several hundred miles away. . . . When they reached their targets, the 100-megaton charges would explode both underwater and in the air, causing heavy casualties."

Sakharov reports that when he proposed his idea to a senior naval officer, an admiral, the officer "was shocked and disgusted by the idea of merciless mass slaughter, and remarked that the officers and sailors of the fleet were accustomed to fighting only armed adversaries, in open battle." [109] The admiral seemed better acquainted than the scientist with the just-war tradition of protecting civilians in warfare.

Sakharov was rewarded for his work on the 1961 test series with his third Hero of Socialist Labor medal. Some Soviet officials wanted to deny Sakharov his medal because of the scientist's outspoken opposition to the test series. Yet Khrushchev correctly pointed out that both Khariton and Sakharov, despite their opposition, "had been doing excellent work" on the new super-bombs. [110] Yet, unlike Sakharov, Khrushchev never anticipated using such horror weapons. As he put it in his speech at the Party congress, "in exploding the 50-megaton bomb we are testing the device for triggering a 100-megaton bomb. But may God grant, as they used to say, that we are never called upon to explode these bombs over anybody's territory. This is the greatest wish of our lives." [111] Khrushchev denied requests from Slavskii and the nuclear establishment to test the hundred-megaton bomb. As his son reports, "the superpowerful charge was retained only as a means of exerting pressure in political disputes." [112]

108. Sakharov, *Memoirs*, 225.
109. Ibid., 221.
110. Ibid., 224; Khrushchev, *Krizisy i rakety*, 2:215.
111. Quoted in Adamsky and Smirnov, "Moscow's Biggest Bomb," 20.
112. Khrushchev, *Krizisy i rakety*, 2:215.

Conflicting Foreign-Policy Objectives. The high-yield bombs exploded during the autumn of 1961 did seem intended mainly to intimidate the West, as part of Khrushchev's war of nerves over the status of Berlin.[113] The Berlin crisis contributed to the missed opportunity of negotiating a test ban or even maintaining the moratorium. It also helped undermine several of Khrushchev's other initiatives. Khrushchev, for example, publicly suspended a previously announced troop reduction at about the same time as he announced the resumption of nuclear testing. He sought to justify his actions as a response to President Kennedy's announcement of increases in the U.S. military budget as well as to the tense situation in Berlin, which he himself had caused.[114]

Despite his attempt to use the test resumption to bolster an assertive foreign policy, Khrushchev clearly broke the moratorium with considerable reluctance.[115] It is an open question whether a stronger U.S. commitment to the moratorium, a willingness to restrain its own military buildup, and a more flexible negotiating stance on Berlin might have strengthened Khrushchev's hand against opponents of a test ban. Sergei Khrushchev's metaphor of the "battle on two fronts" does imply as much.

Transnational Efforts Betrayed. Western peace activists and representatives of nonaligned states were deeply disappointed by the resumption of Soviet nuclear testing. They reacted immediately. The Russian archives contain evidence of a flood of letters and telegrams to the Kremlin and to Soviet embassies abroad, denouncing the Soviet action and urging a return to the moratorium.[116] Emissaries from the nonaligned movement traveled to Moscow to try to persuade Khrushchev to reverse his decision.

Soviet participants in the Pugwash movement were put in an especially awkward position because several of them were attending a conference in Stowe, Vermont, from 11 to 16 September as the Soviet test explosions were poisoning the atmosphere with radioactive fallout.[117] Khrushchev had sent a

113. Ibid., 2:147–148; Andrei D. Sakharov, *Sakharov Speaks* (New York: Knopf, 1974), 32.
114. Khrushchev, *Krizisy i rakety*, 2:132–133.
115. Khrushchev, *Krizisy i rakety*, 2:137. Also Robert M. Slusser, *The Berlin Crisis of 1961: Soviet-American Relations and the Struggle for Power in the Kremlin* (Baltimore, Md., 1973), chap. 8; and Carl A. Linden, *Khrushchev and the Soviet Leadership, 1957–1964* (Baltimore, Md., 1966), 113–116.
116. For example, Linus Pauling, telegram to Khrushchev, 2 September 1961, calling on USSR to cease atmospheric testing; Eleanor Roosevelt et al., telegram, 27 October 1961, criticizing Soviet resumption of tests, AVP, Fond: Ref. po SShA, op. 47, por. 33, pap. 133, Department of American Countries, 194/III, "Problem of disarmament. On the ban on atomic and hydrogen weaponry, 19 February–21 December 1961" [in Russian]. See also the materials in op. 48, por. 40, pap. 143, Department of the USA, 194/III, "Questions of disarmament, 4 January–23 August 1962" [in Russian], including another telegram from Norman Cousins, a copy of petition signed by Linus Pauling and others to the Soviet Supreme Court filing a complaint against Soviet defense ministry and other ministries involved in nuclear testing; a letter from Ambassador Anatolii Dobrynin conveying his decision not to issue a visa to an American peace activist who requested to visit Moscow to deliver Pauling's petition. See also Katz, *Ban the Bomb*, 68–69.
117. Rotblat, *Quest for Peace*, 185–187.

two-page letter, dated 5 September 1961, to the Pugwash participants, seeking to justify the resumption of Soviet testing. He argued that German revanchists and militarists and U.S. cold warriors were trying to exacerbate tensions over Berlin and that "under this circumstance the Soviet Union has recently undertaken a range of measures to strengthen the security of our country . . . among these measures the decision of the Soviet government to renew tests of nuclear weaponry occupies an important place." Khrushchev maintained that "the Soviet government took this step with a heavy heart and profound regret. But it is certain that this serious measure will serve the task of preventing a new world war."[118]

The Soviet test resumption of September 1961 coincided not only with a Pugwash conference but also with a meeting of the leaders of nonaligned states in Belgrade, Yugoslavia. The conference adopted a resolution urging the United States and the USSR to resume negotiations, and it sent representatives to both countries to present the case. Prime Minister Nehru of India flew directly from Belgrade to Moscow on 6 September. He held discussions with Khrushchev, as well as with a group of Soviet scientists, but he failed to persuade the Soviet leader to reinstate the test moratorium.[119]

The "Internationalization" of Soviet Domestic Debates. The resumption of nuclear testing clearly damaged Khrushchev's standing among his two key international audiences: the transnational disarmament movement and the nonaligned states. The timing of the announcements and the tests themselves have led some Sovietologists to view the test resumption as a product of an internal Kremlin power struggle, an effort to embarrass Khrushchev.[120] Recent archival and memoir evidence undermines this interpretation somewhat.[121] Nevertheless, without discounting the pressures from weapons designers or Khrushchev's own preoccupation with foreign-policy concerns such as the situation in Berlin, we can identify some developments concerning the test ban that represent a kind of "internationalization" of the Soviet domestic political competition.

Khrushchev's opponents in the leadership—whether they planned it that way or not—were undoubtedly pleased with the effect of test resumption on

118. Khrushchev to Pugwash scientists, 5 September 1961, sent by Soviet embassy in Washington to Professor Harrison Brown. AVP, Fond: Ref. po SShA, op. 47, por. 23, pap. 132, Department of American Countries, 102-USA, "Exchange of messages, 18 April–6 October 1961."

119. Slusser, *Berlin Crisis of 1961*, 187–190, 387–391.

120. In particular Slusser, *Berlin Crisis of 1961*, chap. 8; Linden, *Khrushchev and the Soviet Leadership*, 113–116; and David Burg and Peter Wiles, "Khrushchev's Power Position—Polycentrism within the Soviet Ruling Group," in Sidney I. Ploss, ed., *The Soviet Political Process: Aims, Techniques, and Examples of Analysis* (Waltham, Mass., 1971).

121. For example, what we now know about the timing of the decisions and Khrushchev's direct role in them contradicts some of Slusser's suppositions. The key role assigned by Slusser, Linden, and others to fellow Presidium member Frol Koslov as leader of Khrushchev's political opposition has come into question in the light of the memoirs of Sergei Khrushchev and others who were close to the Soviet leadership. See, e.g., his *Khrushchev on Khrushchev*, 28–29.

the transnational scientists movement and on the nonaligned states. Khrushchev, for his part, sought immediately to recoup his position with these groups. Two weeks after resumption of tests, in a rare gesture of openness, the Soviet authorities allowed a group of thirty Western peace marchers to travel to the USSR and argue for a test ban before a Moscow University audience. In fact it was through the peace activists' anti-nuclear demonstrations that the Soviet public first became aware of the Soviet Union's resumption of nuclear testing. The Soviet press had publicized the government's statement announcing the end of its commitment to maintain the moratorium, but it did not announce any tests until after the Western activists had criticized them.

Good circumstantial evidence suggests that Khrushchev himself wanted to use the peace movement's criticism to build support for further efforts toward a test ban, despite the Soviet resumption of testing. First, the unprecedented nature of the peace march suggests that approval had to be secured at the top. As one account put it, "in the international situation at this time, permission for the peace march was truly fantastic liberalism. Indeed, while the Soviet atomic tests were taking place, an open foreign rally against these tests was allowed to be held on Soviet territory."[122] The peace marchers stayed in the Soviet Union more than three weeks. The group met with Nina Petrovna Khrushcheva, the Soviet leader's wife. She expressed some sympathy for their position: "I shall certainly tell my husband of the concern of the demonstrators over the Soviet atomic tests. We, too, are concerned about these dangers."[123] Meanwhile, on 10 September at a transnational disarmament conference in London, two prominent Soviet writers known to be close to Khrushchev signed a petition which "appealed to the governments engaged in carrying out atomic tests to stop these tests immediately"—even though the Soviet government clearly had no intention of doing so. Khrushchev may have hoped to use international public opinion, as he had done in the past, to bolster his case among his fellow leaders for pursuing a test ban more vigorously.

Yet there were limits to how much even Soviet proponents of a test ban would accommodate the transnational activists. In 1962, a few months after the USSR broke the moratorium, Linus Pauling launched a new petition campaign, gathering signatures to file a complaint at the Soviet Supreme Court against the Soviet Defense Mininstry and other ministries involved in nuclear testing; when an American peace activist requested to visit Moscow to deliver Pauling's petition, Anatolii Dobrynin, the Soviet ambassador to Washington, refused to issue him a visa.[124]

---

122. Burg and Wiles, "Khrushchev's Power Position," 224.

123. *New York Times*, 7 October 1961, quoted in Burg and Wiles, "Khrushchev's Power Position," 223–224; Jönsson, *Soviet Bargaining Behavior*, 172.

124. AVP, op. 48, por. 40, pap. 143, Department of the USA, 194/III, "Questions of disarmament, 4 January–23 August 1962" [in Russian].

Last Attempts at Bridging the Verification Gap

Lack of trust in Soviet willingness to abide by nuclear test restrictions posed the ultimate obstacle to gaining U.S. support for a comprehensive test ban treaty, even if other objections of the military and nuclear establishments could be overcome. The transnational scientists movement remained active on the test ban issue by focusing on technical aspects of the problem of verification.

The "Black Box" Solution. The Soviet Pugwash scientists, undoubtedly discomfited by the resumption of Soviet testing, had a chance to redeem themselves when the Tenth Pugwash Conference convened in London in September 1962, just a year after the Soviets had ended their moratorium. At the meeting three Soviet scientists and three American scientists worked out a proposal for monitoring seismic activity to help verify a test ban through the use of sealed, automatic, seismic recording stations. The Pugwash scientists argued that these "black boxes"—as they were dubbed by the physicist Lev Artsimovich—would limit the need for on-site inspections.[125] A smaller, follow-up meeting of Pugwash experts on seismology explored the remaining technical issues and concluded that "the clarity now attained in the scientific and technical aspects of the problem provide a sufficient basis for the governments to arrive at an agreement for the conclusion of a test ban treaty in the near future."[126] The black box proposal was subsequently pursued in correspondence between Kennedy and Khrushchev, and the technical discussions of test ban monitoring within Pugwash are considered by some to have contributed to the signing of the Moscow agreement banning nuclear tests in the atmosphere, in outer space, and under water.[127] If the political will to achieve a comprehensive ban had been present in 1963, the black-box solution could have played an important role in any verification program.

"Hold Out a Finger to Them—They Chop Off Your Whole Hand." One of the key stumbling blocks on the path to a comprehensive ban was the question of how many, if any, on-site inspections the Soviet side would allow. The British had long been active in trying to come up with a compromise between the long-standing U.S. insistence on unlimited inspections of suspicious seismic events and the Soviet preference for none. They frequently employed transgovernmental contacts between scientists and officials. The earliest example

125. S. P. Kapitsa, "Diapason lichnosti," in *Vospominaniia ob akademike L. A. Artsimoviche*, 2d ed. (Moscow, 1988), 140; Jacobson and Stein, *Diplomats, Scientists, and Politicians*, 425. The idea of using such seismic stations apparently originated in 1959 in the work of the U.S. Panel on Seismic Improvement, called the Berkner Panel after its head, Lloyd V. Berkner. See Seaborg, *Kennedy, Khrushchev, and the Test Ban*, 18–19.

126. Quoted in Joseph Rotblat, "Movements of Scientists against the Arms Race," in Rotblat, ed., *Scientists, the Arms Race, and Disarmament* (London, 1982), 139.

127. Rotblat, *Quest for Peace*, 33.

involved Evgenii Fedorov, a scientist and Pugwash participant who had led the Soviet delegation to the Geneva conference on verification in 1958 and then stayed on as part of the Soviet test ban negotiating team. In January 1959 Fedorov proposed to David Ormsby-Gore, the British delegate, that any test ban treaty establish a quota for inspections rather than a provision for un-limited numbers. He suggested that an annual quota of anywhere from three to twenty inspections might be acceptable to the Soviet side. The next month Prime Minister Macmillan traveled to Moscow and, without U.S. approval, repeated the proposal back to Khrushchev, who reacted positively but made no formal agreement. Despite the official and consistent U.S. opposition to any figure as low as three, this British initiative seems to have put the idea in Khrushchev's head that he might get the United States to sign a comprehensive test ban if he could secure support in the USSR for an annual quota of three inspections.[128]

Transnational and transgovernmental efforts continued into the Kennedy administration to try to gain agreement on a number of annual inspections. In May 1961 the president himself had tried, through a "back-channel" contact between his brother Robert and a Soviet intelligence officer, to come to some compromise settlement at about fifteen inspections. Khrushchev re-buffed the approach.[129] Subsequent probes from the Western side went forward without prior official authorization. In October 1962, for example, Ambassador Arthur Dean, U.S. representative to the Geneva disarmament talks, discussed the subject of quotas with V. V. Kuznetsov, Soviet first deputy foreign minister. Two months later, Jerome Wiesner, Kennedy's science advisor and another Pugwash alumnus, met in Washington with Fedorov—a key source of continuity in these informal discussions of quotas. These two discussions, like the one initiated by Robert Kennedy, were reported by the Soviet participants back to Khrushchev in Moscow.

There is some confusion about what figures were actually discussed in these meetings. Robert Kennedy was reported by Georgii Bolshakov, his Soviet contact, to have suggested that the figure of ten inspections would be acceptable if it came in the form of a proposal from the Soviet side.[130] In the other two cases, the Soviet interlocutors believed that their U.S. counterparts had mentioned a low number of three inspections. Dean later claimed that he had suggested nothing lower than eight or ten. Wiesner explained that his proposal to Fedorov was more complicated: He suggested that if Khrushchev proposed a number of three to four inspections, and if Kennedy came back

128. "Memorandum of conversation with Soviets at dinner party," 28 January 1959, PRO:FO 371/140483; "Memorandum by Ormsby-Gore," 3 February 1959, PRO:FO 371/140435, cited in Risse-Kappen, *Cooperation among Democracies*, 119. See also Jacobson and Stein, *Diplomats, Scientists, and Politicians*, 167.

129. Aleksandr Fursenko and Timothy Naftali, *"One Hell of a Gamble": Khrushchev, Castro, and Kennedy, 1958–1964* (New York, 1997), 108–118.

130. Ibid., 113.

with a counterproposal of seven or eight, then a compromise might be worked out at an intermediate figure of five.[131] In any event, Khrushchev apparently got the impression that the United States would be willing to sign a treaty providing for only three annual inspections. He wrote to President Kennedy on 19 December 1962, citing the meeting between Dean and Kuznetsov and claiming that "Ambassador Dean said that in the opinion of the United States Government two to four onsite inspections a year in the territory of the Soviet Union would be sufficient." Khrushchev indicated, on behalf of the Soviet government, and in the interest of "overcoming the deadlock and reaching a mutually acceptable agreement at last," that "we would be prepared to agree to two to three inspections a year."[132]

Khrushchev evidently expended considerable political capital in getting his colleagues' approval to extend the offer of three annual inspections. Even Khrushchev himself had a hard time thinking of arms control verification as anything other than an excuse for espionage. The other Soviet leaders were even less interested in taking risks for the sake of East-West rapprochement and reducing the danger of nuclear war. None was committed to a test ban. Thus, Khrushchev was crushed and angered when Kennedy responded to his letter on 28 December by rejecting what Khrushchev had considered a major concession.

Kennedy had made a counterproposal of eight to ten annual inspections. Formally, this could be considered a major concession because the Anglo-American draft test ban treaty tabled in Geneva in April 1961—the last official statement on the number of annual inspections—had stipulated twenty.[133] But, in fact, we know now that Kennedy's counterproposal was little better than what his brother had offered Bolshakov in May 1961. The president nevertheless expected that Khrushchev would now be willing to negotiate, perhaps to split the difference between three and eight. Khrushchev had rejected out of hand the offer conveyed by Bolshakov a year and a half earlier. Now, having persuaded himself and then his colleagues that three was a number acceptable to the United States, the Soviet leader could go no further. He angrily complained to his son that making concessions to the Americans was a thankless task: you "hold out a finger to them—they chop off your whole hand."[134]

Kennedy eventually realized that a misunderstanding lay behind Khrushchev's anger. In April 1963, he attempted to use a well-known transnational

131. Seaborg, *Kennedy, Khrushchev, and the Test Ban*, 179–181.
132. An extensive quotation from Khrushchev's letter is found in Seaborg, *Kennedy, Khrushchev, and the Test Ban*, 179.
133. For a report from the Soviet delegation to the disarmament talks that highlights the conflict over inspections, see "Otchet delegatsii SSSR v komitete 18 gosudarstv po razoruzheniiu za period s 16 iiuliia po 7 sentiabria 1962 goda: obshchaia obstanovka," 24 September 1962, No. 2874/gs, Ministry of Defense archives. I have put a copy of this document on file at the National Security Archive in Washington, D.C.
134. Khrushchev, *Krizisy i rakety*, 2:456.

activist—Norman Cousins—to convey to Khrushchev his sincere interest in achieving a test ban treaty. Khrushchev was familiar with Cousins's efforts at improving Soviet-American relations. He had received, through the KGB, direct reports from Soviet participants at transnational conferences that Cousins had sponsored.[135] The Soviet leader invited Cousins to visit him while on vacation at the Black Sea. A year after Kennedy's assassination Cousins published "Notes on a 1963 Visit with Khrushchev" in his *Saturday Review*, presenting Khrushchev's side of the test ban story.[136] Khrushchev revealed for the first time that the discussion between Wiesner and Fedorov had served as one of the sources of his expectation that the United States would welcome a Soviet concession of three annual inspections. He told Cousins of how he argued to his Council of Ministers that "we can have an agreement with the United States to stop nuclear tests if we agree to three inspections. . . . Finally I persuaded them." Then "back came the American rejection. They now wanted—not three inspections or even six. They wanted eight. And so once again I was made to look foolish. But I can tell you this: it won't happen again."[137]

We now know that Kennedy was in fact willing to go down to six annual inspections on Soviet territory.[138] Thus, with good reason Thomas Risse calls this ill-fated incident of miscommunication "the major lost opportunity for the Kennedy administration to achieve a comprehensive test ban."[139] In this case, transnational and transgovernmental contacts played an ambiguous role. On the one hand, one could argue that the discussions initiated by Fedorov deserve credit as the source of Khrushchev's unprecedented achievement of convincing the Soviet government to agree to any on-site inspections. On the other hand, had Fedorov and Kuznetsov been more careful to elicit an accurate portrayal of the U.S. position from their American interlocutors (i.e., that three was an impossibly low number), Khrushchev might have succeeded in extracting a higher number from the other Soviet leaders— one that would have brought the two sides' positions within reach of compromise.

THE MOSCOW AGREEMENT

The United States and Britain had on several occasions proposed to the USSR a treaty that would ban nuclear tests in the atmosphere and not require such stringent measures of verification as a comprehensive ban would do.

---

135. Fursenko and Naftali, *"One Hell of a Gamble,"* 126–127.
136. Norman Cousins, "Notes on a 1963 Visit with Khrushchev," *Saturday Review*, 7 November 1964, 16–21, 58–60.
137. Ibid.
138. Seaborg, *Kennedy, Khrushchev, and the Test Ban*, 187–188.
139. Risse-Kappen, *Cooperation among Democracies*, 134.

Khrushchev had long resisted signing any agreement that would appear to endorse the continued testing of nuclear weapons underground and would have little effect in slowing the development of new weapons. On 3 September 1961, two days after the Soviet Union broke the three-power moratorium with a major nuclear test, President Kennedy and Prime Minister Macmillan again raised the issue of a partial test ban. Their appeal—"that their three governments agree, effective immediately, not to conduct nuclear tests which take place in the atmosphere and produce radioactive fall-out,"—was clearly intended to embarrass Khrushchev, coming as it did at the beginning of a series of Soviet atmospheric tests. But the proposal did include a new feature— a Western willingness "to rely upon existing means of detection" of atmospheric explosions, rather than insist on intrusive measures of inspection.[140]

Military and Economic Considerations

In addition to his commitment to a comprehensive test ban as a means of curbing the nuclear arms race, Khrushchev had a couple of good reasons for resisting a partial ban. By the end of 1962, the Soviet Union had conducted only two underground explosions—one in 1961 and one in 1962. By comparison, the United States had first tested underground in 1951 and by the end of 1962 had conducted eighty-nine underground tests—fifty-seven of them in 1962 alone.[141] Eventually Khrushchev came to believe that a U.S. advantage in underground testing could not affect the basic ability of the USSR to destroy the United States in a retaliatory strike if the U.S. launched a nuclear war. But many of Khrushchev's weapons designers, including his son, felt otherwise—that the United States would take advantage of its "rich experience of underground tests" to surge forward in nuclear weapons technology.[142] Indeed in the two decades between the signing of the Limited Test Ban Treaty and Mikhail Gorbachev's launching of a new series of Soviet test ban initiatives, the Soviet Union never came close to matching the pace of the U.S. underground nuclear test program. Such concerns about a nuclear testing "gap" evidently hindered early Soviet acceptance of a limited test ban— an observation that runs contrary to expectations about negotiation from strength.

One reason the Soviet side lagged in the technology of underground testing is that the top nuclear weapons designers were skeptical about conducting such tests. They were mainly interested in large-yield tests, and they had constructed the relevant equipment for carrying them out above ground. Typical of the Soviet process of developing weapons, the designers showed no enthusiasm for taking risks for the sake of innovation, and were only

---

140. Quoted in Slusser, *Berlin Crisis of 1961*, 183.
141. Norris and Arkin, "Known Nuclear Tests Worldwide," 62.
142. Khrushchev, *Krizisy i rakety*, 2: 458.

prompted to do so once the Americans had paved the way.[143] Indeed, as one weapons designer later wrote, the Soviet nuclear establishment learned about underground testing "only from American sources. We ourselves made very timid steps in the technology for carrying them out."[144]

Finally, underground nuclear testing was enormously expensive. Khrushchev was always preoccupied with the cost of the arms race, and he often made a point of complaining about the expense of the nuclear test program, even when the Soviets were conducting only atmospheric tests. In March 1960, for example, Khrushchev was visiting France as the guest of President Charles de Gaulle when news of the second French atomic test became known. The Soviet leader congratulated his host: "I understand your joy . . . but, you know it's very expensive!"[145] In an interview with the New York Times held just after the resumption of Soviet nuclear testing in September 1961 Khrushchev again complained about the costs—particularly the opportunity costs for the civilian sector—of nuclear testing: "What the hell do we want with tests? You cannot put a bomb in soup or make an overcoat out of it. Nevertheless we are compelled to test."[146] These comments might be dismissed as disingenuous propaganda were it not for the firsthand evidence from Sergei Khrushchev that the cost of the nuclear test program was of genuine concern to his father and that even the officials of the nuclear weapons establishment itself found the expense of underground testing prohibitive.[147]

Transnationalism: Tacit and Explicit

Given Khrushchev's reluctance to accept a limited test ban treaty, he needed some external impetus to push him toward one. The sobering impact of the Cuban missile crisis by his own admission prompted Khrushchev to redouble his efforts to curb the nuclear arms race, as it did Kennedy. But the initial goal was still a comprehensive test ban. Still, Khrushchev appears to have wanted to achieve a breakthrough in disarmament in order to have something to show in the wake of the Cuban fiasco.[148]

Part of the impetus for pursuing a limited test ban came from scientists within the Soviet nuclear establishment. When I first reviewed the evidence

143. Ibid., 119–120. For the general argument, see Matthew Evangelista, *Innovation and the Arms Race: How the Soviet Union and the United States Develop New Military Technologies* (Ithaca, N.Y., 1988).

144. V. N. Mikhailov, *Ia—"Iastreb"* (Moscow, 1993), 22. For a description of the first efforts at underground testing, see Ogorodnikov, *Iadernyi arkhipelag*, 69–70.

145. Beschloss, *Mayday*, 276, quoting De Gaulle's memoirs.

146. C. L. Sulzberger, interview with Khrushchev, *New York Times*, 8 September 1961, quoted in Slusser, *Berlin Crisis of 1961*, 203.

147. Khrushchev, *Krizisy i rakety*, 2:119–120, 208, 456. When Khrushchev ordered preparations for an atmospheric test series to begin in September 1961, for example, all preparations for underground testing as Novaia Zemlia ceased. See Ogorodnikov, *Iadernyi arkhipelag*, 133.

148. Jönsson, *Soviet Bargaining Behavior*, 195.

from new Soviet archival and memoir sources on the test ban several years ago, I evaluated the role of Soviet scientists. I argued then that leading nuclear physicists such as Sakharov, Kurchatov, and Khariton, even though they had from time to time come out against Soviet nuclear testing, should not be described as part of a transnational movement of scientists. Overall, I argued, in their impact on Soviet nuclear testing scientists were more important in their capacity as national advisers on weapons policy than as members of a transnational organization such as Pugwash.[149]

This distinction, although useful, should not be overdrawn. We now understand that even those nuclear scientists who had no direct contact with foreign colleagues and never traveled abroad considered themselves part of an international community.[150] During the Cold War, these scientists constituted what could be called a "tacit" or, as we might say these days, a "virtual" transnational alliance, for they often worked in parallel to promote certain policies that could reduce East-West tensions and slow the arms race. This is not to say that all nuclear scientists thought alike. In fact there were hawks and doves in the Soviet nuclear establishment just as in the U.S. one.[151] The point is that Soviet scientists who favored arms control believed that they were working on a common project with like-minded colleagues in the West—and, in fact, they were.

The campaign to secure a limited test ban treaty constitutes a key example of this phenomenon of tacit transnationalism. It concerns scientists at the main Soviet nuclear weapons design facility, Arzamas-16, and their effort to persuade Khrushchev to accept a treaty that allowed continuing underground tests. In the summer of 1962, Viktor Adamskii suggested to his colleague Andrei Sakharov that, given the lack of progress in negotiations on a comprehensive test ban, the time might be ripe for the Soviet authorities to promote the idea of a partial test ban. Adamskii had drafted a letter to Khrushchev making the case on both political and technical grounds. Sakharov agreed with the letter but told Adamskii that it might be better to get the support of Efim Slavskii, head of the nuclear weapons program, and let him deal with the government.[152]

149. Matthew Evangelista, "Soviet Scientists and Nuclear Testing, 1954–1963: The New Archival Evidence and its Limitations," Report to the National Council for Soviet and East European Research, August 1993.

150. This is one of the themes of Holloway's *Stalin and the Bomb,* and it has influenced my thinking quite a lot.

151. Consider the aptly titled memoir by V. N. Mikhailov, then Boris Yeltsin's minister in charge of the nuclear industry and a lifelong member of the nuclear weapons establishment: *Ia—"Iastreb"* [I'm a "hawk"] (Moscow, 1993). Mikhailov's only interest in his U.S. colleagues was a burning curiousity about their material and working conditions, especially at the Nevada test site (see 39, 42), and, during the post-Soviet period, a desire for U.S. financial aid to rescue the Russian nuclear industry.

152. Viktor Adamskii, "Dear Mr. Khrushchev," *Bulletin of the Atomic Scientists* 51, 6 (November/December 1995): 28–31. I thank David Holloway for calling my attention to Adamskii's role.

According to Sakharov, when he raised the issue with Slavskii, the minister "seemed sympathetic" and promised to talk to Iakov Malik, the deputy minister of foreign affairs: "Of course, the boss himself [i.e., Khrushchev] will have to decide." A couple of months later Slavskii telephoned Sakharov to report that "there's a great deal of interest at the top in your proposal, and in all probability some steps will shortly be taken by our side."[153]

Why should scientists in the secretive world of Soviet nuclear weapons technology be considered part of a transnational effort to achieve a test ban? The most basic answer is because they considered themselves so. Adamskii and Sakharov felt part of an international community of scientists whose concerns extended well beyond their own fields of technical expertise. One source of such beliefs, as I mentioned in the last chapter, was the U.S. *Bulletin of the Atomic Scientists*. As Adamskii wrote, "that magazine gave coverage of social and moral problems encountered by the American scientists who worked in the same field as us, which made them our overseas colleagues, if you can put it this way."[154] Adamskii was particularly drawn to Leo Szilard, one of the original sponsors of the *Bulletin,* whom he later called "the brightest figure among the more politically active American scientists."[155] Sakharov had given Adamskii a copy of Szilard's *Voice of the Dolphins*—the futuristic novel that Szilard had earlier presented to Khrushchev. Adamskii was struck by how Szilard's work highlighted a moral conflict that faced the designers of nuclear weapons on both sides of the Iron Curtain, no matter how justified they believed their cause to be.[156]

The evolution of Sakharov's own interest in the test ban reflects the tension between state goals and transnational norms and values. In 1957, in the early years of the test ban debate, Igor' Kurchatov wanted Sakharov to write an article criticizing U.S. proposals (associated mainly with Edward Teller) to develop "clean" bombs that supposedly limited radioactive fallout. Sakharov began his research by "reading through the extensive humanistic, political, and scientific literature on the subject" of nuclear testing and found that he did not want to limit his article to a propagandistic critique of the U.S. position. Sakharov was particularly influenced by the work of Albert Schweitzer, the Swiss physician, musician, philosopher, and Nobel laureate who had been converted by Norman Cousins to the cause of the test ban in 1956.[157] "Among the writers with a philosophical and humanist perspective," wrote Sakharov, "Albert Schweitzer left a lasting impression on me: eighteen years later, as I drafted my Nobel lecture, I would recall his words . . . his opposition to nuclear tests was a spur to my own activity in the 1950s."[158] Clearly

---

153. Sakharov, *Memoirs*, 230–231.
154. V. B. Adamskii, "Becoming a Citizen," in L. V. Keldysh et al., eds., *Andrei Sakharov: Facets of a Life* (Gif-sur-Yvette, France, 1991), 29.
155. Adamskii, "Dear Mr. Khrushchev," 30.
156. Adamskii, "Becoming a Citizen," 37.
157. Divine, *Nuclear Test Ban Debate*, 121–122.
158. Sakharov, *Memoirs*, 200–201, 433.

Sakharov considered himself part of the transnational movement for a test ban, even if he had never attended a Pugwash meeting or met Szilard, Schweitzer, or Cousins.

Norman Cousins, the founder of the SANE antinuclear organization and a prominent writer, represented that segment of U.S. public opinion critical of the arms race and supportive of a test ban. His visit to Khrushchev in April 1963 was particularly important in paving the way to the limited test ban treaty. In this instance Cousins was not only the representative of a transnational movement but also the personal emissary of President Kennedy. His visit served two functions. He sought, evidently with success, to persuade Khrushchev that despite the rejection of the Soviet offer of two or three inspections, Kennedy was still interested in a test ban. But he also needed to make clear that Kennedy did not feel strong enough politically to accept Khrushchev's position. Therefore if a test ban were to be negotiated without the number of inspections that Kennedy required, it could not be a comprehensive one. Khrushchev complained, "Why am I always the one who must understand the difficulties of the other fellow? Maybe it's time for the other fellow to understand my position."[159] But he eventually accommodated his American counterpart.

Khrushchev learned of Kennedy's political problems with the test ban from various other unofficial U.S. sources as well. In response to a visiting U.S. farmer who described the political and military opposition Kennedy faced on the test ban issue, Khrushchev drew a sharp contrast—and a rather prescient one, as it turned out—between the implications of such opposition in the U.S. system compared to the Soviet one: "Well you tell Mr. Kennedy that if he's not president anymore, he'll still be a rich man. But if I'm not Soviet leader anymore I'll just have this suit I'm wearing."[160] Despite his complaints, Khrushchev does seem to have got the message from his transnational contacts that Kennedy had not given up on achieving some restraints on nuclear testing.

In July 1963, Khrushchev announced his willingness to endorse a treaty banning only nuclear tests in the atmosphere, under water, and in outer space. The treaty was negotiated by Averell Harriman on the U.S. side and signed in Moscow on 5 August 1963.[161]

To get support from the U.S. Joint Chiefs of Staff in pursuing the test ban treaty, Kennedy had to commit to a vigorous program of underground nuclear testing. In the decade after the treaty was signed (1963–72) the United States conducted 385 nuclear tests (plus 23 "peaceful nuclear explosions"—PNEs—for civilian purposes), compared to a total of 268, plus 3 PNEs, for the

159. Norman Cousins, *The Improbable Triumvirate: John F. Kennedy, Pope John, Nikita Khrushchev* (New York, 1972), 95–110, quoted in Beschloss, *The Crisis Years*, 587.

160. John Crystal, the farmer who talked to Khrushchev, recalled the conversation in an interview on the U.S. National Public Radio program, "Weekend Edition," 4 April 1993.

161. Seaborg, *Kennedy, Khrushchev, and the Test Ban*, 227–231.

preceding decade (1953–62).[162] Even with these concessions, Kennedy feared that the U.S. military might undermine support for ratification in the Senate.[163] As in the United States, the fact that the Moscow treaty allowed continued underground testing reduced resistance to the agreement from the USSR's nuclear establishment, but the Soviet military were by no means happy about the treaty.[164] The Soviet program of underground tests got off to a slow start after the treaty was signed (ten tests in 1964 compared to forty-five for the United States) and never reached the magnitude of the U.S. one. In the decade after the Moscow treaty, the USSR conducted 124 nuclear tests for military purposes, plus 33 PNEs, compared to 218 atmospheric and underground tests in the previous decade.[165] The health and environmental concerns that had sparked international opposition to nuclear testing had been alleviated, but the nuclear arms race continued apace.

TRANSNATIONAL INFLUENCE IN RETROSPECT

The military balance, economic constraints, and the behavior of the adversary: these are the explanations typically offered to account for the success and failure of arms control initiatives during the Cold War. They all played a role in the test ban debate and all had an influence on Soviet policy. But all these factors were subject to differing interpretations that were influenced in turn by various actors' prior views on the merits of a test ban. When leaders made decisions, unless they were faced with a rare consensus, they had to decide which interpretations to accept. In the case of the test ban, external influences often pushed them toward accommodation. Particularly important were the pressures of international public opinion and the expert advice of a transnational movement of scientists opposed to nuclear testing.

Assessing the relevant balance of nuclear weapons technology was a difficult endeavor in the 1950s and 1960s.[166] Moreover, the assessments them-

162. Calculated from Norris and Arkin, "Known Nuclear Tests Worldwide," 62.

163. "Winning Senate Support for the Nuclear Test Ban Treaty, 1963," Presidential Recordings Transcripts, Papers of John F. Kennedy, Presidential Papers, President's Office Files, John F. Kennedy Library; and Seaborg, *Kennedy, Khrushchev, and the Test Ban*, 269–271.

164. See Jönsson, *Soviet Bargaining Behavior*, 199.

165. Calculated from Norris and Arkin, "Known Nuclear Tests Worldwide," 62.

166. Perhaps the most illustrative of this problem on the U.S. side is the transcript of the President's Science Advisory Committee, Meeting of the Ad Hoc Panel on Nuclear Test Limitations, Washington, D.C., 15 March 1958, White House Office, Office of the Special Assistant for Science and Technology: Records, 1957–61, Box 3: President's Science Advisory Committee (5), DDEL. Much of it is still classified, but one can nevertheless get a good feel for the nature of the arguments and how much they hinge on particular assumptions. The same is true of subsequent reports prepared for the Kennedy administration. See, e.g., "Report of the Ad Hoc Panel on Nuclear Testing," 21 July 1961, the so-called Panofsky report, in Theodore Sorenson Papers, classified subject files, box #53, folder: Nuclear test ban, report of the Ad Hoc Panel, John F. Kennedy Library. I am grateful to Paul Passavant for tracking down this document and others from the Kennedy Library.

selves did not bear a determinate relationship to either side's policy preferences. The side that was behind might have wanted to freeze the competition for fear of falling further behind, or it might have wanted to continue the competition in hopes of catching up. The same applied for the leading side.

Sergei Khrushchev has argued that at certain points his father was particularly sensitive to the gap between U.S. and Soviet nuclear weapons technology, but that ultimately he came to believe that a preoccupation with the nuclear balance was counterproductive.[167] When he agreed to sign the Limited Test Ban Treaty in 1963, for example, Khrushchev was aware that the United States possessed an advantage in the ability to test nuclear weapons underground—indeed, exploiting that advantage was a condition that U.S. military leaders imposed on President Kennedy in return for their support of the treaty. But Khrushchev by this time was convinced that whatever technical benefits the U.S. might enjoy, they would not negate the ability of the Soviet Union to inflict massive damage on the United States in the event of war. And the threat of such damage, in Khrushchev's view, would provide an adequate deterrent to a U.S. attack.[168]

Many of his advisers on military-technical matters, including even his own son, disagreed with Khrushchev's position. For them, and for their counterparts in the United States, relative differences in the level of nuclear technology were crucial to their evaluation of the merits of a test moratorium. Many contemporary observers assumed that Soviet interpretations of the relative state of nuclear weapons technology in the United States and the USSR played an important role in Soviet decisions about when to suspend testing, how seriously to negotiate, what kind of agreement to favor, and so forth. The evidence reviewed here, however, suggests that comparisons of relative strength played an inconsistent and episodic role in both U.S. and Soviet decisions. Perhaps the best generalization one can make is that the U.S. tended to pass up opportunities to negotiate from strength, especially during the mid-1950s, when the test ban first emerged on the international agenda.[169] The Soviets, for their part, were never really in a position to negotiate from strength. Khrushchev and his colleagues sometimes seem to have been encouraged by successes in Soviet military developments and showed a willingness to countenance mutual restraint or even risk unilateral initiatives. Times of relative weakness, however, typically found them withdrawing from previous commitments to negotiation or unilateral restraint. This behavior confounds expectations of U.S. advocates of "peace through strength," who argued that agreements favorable to U.S. interests would result from negotiations undertaken during periods of relative Soviet weakness and U.S. strength.

167. Khrushchev, *Krizisy i rakety*, 2:208.
168. Ibid., 2:458.
169. Knopf, *Domestic Society and International Cooperation*, chap. 5.

Economic constraints clearly motivated Khrushchev in his desire to curb the nuclear arms race, as well as in his other military reforms—most notably the reduction in conventional forces. But his specific concerns about the cost of "climbing underground" to conduct nuclear tests, as his son colorfully put it, hindered the compromise solution of a limited test ban: Khrushchev preferred to do away with the expense of testing altogether.[170]

Scientists played key roles in many aspects of the nuclear test ban debates of the 1950s and 1960s: as creators of the nuclear weapons themselves; as experts warning about the dangers of radioactive fallout; as activists mobilizing public support for a test moratorium; as government advisers assessing the relative impact of a test ban on the nuclear technology of the two sides; as negotiators working out the details of a verification scheme; and finally, as a transnational alliance of test ban proponents acting through the Pugwash movement or in tacit cooperation with like-minded colleagues on the other side.

In many respects the tacit transnational movement was more important than the explicit one. Pugwash, for example, seems to have played a relatively insignificant role in inducing the Soviet government to suspend nuclear tests in 1958 or to join the moratorium from 1958 to 1961. Pugwash support for a continued moratorium and the anticipated negative reaction from the world scientific community were not enough to prevent the resumption of Soviet nuclear testing in September 1961. Nor, apparently, did Pugwash figure prominently in the Soviet decision to embrace the limited test ban treaty in 1963.

On the U.S. side, the scientists who supported a test ban would probably not have succeeded in the absence of an active public campaign against the tests. Particularly important was the mobilization of thousands of women from some one hundred communities in the United States in the "Women Strike for Peace" in the early 1960s. This movement of housewives and mothers emerged in reaction to the hierarchical structures and conventional lobbying efforts of organizations such as SANE. The women's campaign bolstered the efforts of the "insiders" in the Kennedy administration, and, according to Jerome Wiesner, the president's science adviser at the time, such popular movements deserve the most credit for pushing the government toward a test ban.[171]

Yet one should not underestimate the importance of the transnational scientists' efforts. Indirectly, through their influence on international public opinion, the scientists undoubtedly had an effect on government policy in the United States and the Soviet Union. The activities of Pugwash concerning nuclear testing provided an important precedent for the organization's future

170. Khrushchev, *Krizisy i rakety*, 2:456.
171. Amy Swerdlow, *Women Strike for Peace: Traditional Motherhood and Radical Politics in the 1960s* (Chicago, 1993), 81.

work. The smaller meetings and the groups that evolved out of Pugwash to provide direct Soviet-American contacts proved especially valuable in promoting mutual understanding and restraint between the nuclear superpowers. The Soviet government came to value such contacts and repeatedly gave its endorsement to them. Independent-minded Soviet scientists took advantage of their relationship with Western counterparts to gain new information that was useful in internal Soviet debates about disarmament and security policy. Soviet scientists did not bloom into full-fledged participants in the making of security policy until the second half of the 1980s, but the seeds were first planted during the test ban debates of three decades earlier.

[5]

"Why Keep Such An Army?"
Khrushchev's Troop Reductions

Until we stop pushing the Kremlin against a closed door, we shall never learn whether it would be prepared to go through an open one.

— GEORGE F. KENNAN, 1957

[If] we carry out a further reduction of our armed forces, then such a step would encourage those forces in bourgeois countries, those liberal bourgeois, capitalist circles who seek to improve the international situation. . . . This would strengthen them and weaken the arguments of aggressive, militarist circles.

— NIKITA KHRUSHCHEV, 1959

Following the death of Stalin, the Soviet Union undertook initiatives seemingly intended to reduce international tensions and improve the prospects for arms control. Perhaps the most significant was the reduction in Soviet conventional forces by nearly half from 1953 to 1961. The Eisenhower administration publicly denigrated the Soviet gesture, maintaining that it was forced on the USSR by economic conditions, was militarily insignificant in an age of nuclear weapons, and was not intended to serve the goal of détente. This chapter examines the motives for the Soviet troop reductions and evaluates the explanations typically given to account for them.[1]

Unlike many of the other cases discussed in this book, Khrushchev's troop reductions reveal little evidence of the influence of transnational actors. This case demonstrates that transnational activity was surely not a necessary condition for Soviet moderation. But because Khrushchev's reforms were short-lived and were reversed by his successors, we should consider whether the absence of transnational influence played any role in their lack of durability.

---

1. A longer version of this chapter, with more detail on economic aspects of the troop reductions, has been published under the same title as Occasional Paper No. 19 of the Cold War International History Project (Washington, D.C., 1997). Thanks to James Hershberg for his comments.

Evidence for Soviet moderation in conventional forces during the Khrushchev period consists mainly in the unilateral troop reductions and in Soviet disarmament proposals that were compromises intended to meet Western demands. The following sections consider whether these initiatives should be seen as forced by economic conditions, desired as militarily expedient, or intended to signal interest in further restraint and in negotiated disarmament accords.

Arms Control

East-West disarmament negotiations began soon after the end of World War II and included discussion of conventional as well as nuclear forces.[2] The talks, held for many years under the auspices of the United Nations, made little progress while Stalin was alive. A number of observers and participants, including former Soviet officials, have argued that a major change in the USSR's approach to arms negotiations took place after his death. For example, a Soviet defector who had specialized in disarmament at the Foreign Ministry quotes his superior as revealing that "we're starting a new policy that will mean serious negotiating on disarmament."[3] He dates the change in policy to 1954.[4] A Yugoslav diplomat, whom Khrushchev treated somewhat as a confidant, presents further evidence of the new leader's interest in the issue.[5] The new, cooperative approach to arms control coincided with concessions in other areas, such as the status of Austria.[6]

The change in Soviet policy first became evident in the spring of 1955. On 10 May, the USSR put forward a proposal that incorporated the main features of an earlier Anglo-French memorandum that was intended to form the basis for the future work of the UN Disarmament Subcommittee. The United States

2. This section draws on my article "Cooperation Theory and Disarmament Negotiations in the 1950s," *World Politics* 42, 4 (July 1990). For a recent discussion of the early negotiations, see McGeorge Bundy, *Danger and Survival: Choices about the Bomb in the First Fifty Years* (New York, 1988), chap. 4. For a more comprehensive account: Bernhard G. Bechhoefer, *Postwar Negotiations for Arms Control* (Washington, D.C., 1961).

3. Arkady N. Shevchenko, *Breaking with Moscow* (New York, 1985), 78.

4. Shevchenko, personal communication, 23 September 1987.

5. Veljko Micunovic, *Moscow Diary*, trans. David Floyd (New York, 1980), 157, 166.

6. Vladislav Zubok, "SSSR-SShA: put' k peregovoram po razoruzheniiu v iadernyi vek (1953–1955 gg.)," paper presented at a conference at Ohio University, Athens, Ohio, October 1988; O. Grinevskii, "Na Smolenskoi ploshchadi v 1950-kh godakh," *Mezhdunarodnaia zhizn'*, 1994, no. 11:120–126; Oleg Troyanovsky, "Nikita Khrushchev and the Making of Soviet Foreign Policy," paper prepared for a conference on the centenary of Nikita Khrushchev's birth held at Brown University, Providence, Rhode Island, 1–3 December 1994; Vojtech Mastny, "Kremlin Politics and the Austrian Settlement," *Problems of Communism* 31 (July–August 1982): 37–51; Deborah Welch Larson, "Crisis Prevention and the Austrian State Treaty," *International Organization* 41, 1 (Winter 1987): 27–60. See also Lincoln P. Bloomfield, Walter C. Clemens, Jr., and Franklyn Griffiths, *Khrushchev and the Arms Race: Soviet Interest in Arms Control and Disarmament, 1954–1964* (Cambridge, Mass., 1966).

had already expressed support for the goals of the memorandum, which included major reductions in all armed forces and conventional armaments, in addition to prohibition of the use and manufacture of nuclear weapons and the establishment of adequate organs of control and inspection. The USSR's adherence to the plan would have entailed cutting back the Soviet armed forces from nearly 5 million soldiers to between 1 and 1.5 million. These figures, proposed originally by the Western powers, would have constituted a significantly disproportionate reduction in Soviet forces, compared to those of France, Britain, or the United States. In return the Soviets would benefit from the eventual destruction of stocks of American nuclear weapons, but their own would have to be destroyed as well. The USSR seemed willing to accept such a deal, yet, in response to the Soviet concessions, the United States withdrew its support for the Western position, and no agreement was reached.[7]

We know now that the May 1955 proposal was a serious one, deliberately formulated as a "new approach" that would help to fulfill Khrushchev's directive to the Foreign Ministry to seek an improvement in the international atmosphere by "decisively clearing away the 'barriers' in international affairs," as one retired official recalled in 1988.[8] Because the proposal came so close to the Western position, the wholesale U.S. rejection of the Soviet initiative surprised its authors: "For us who had worked out the proposal of May 10th, all this was inconceivable."[9] When Khrushchev met President Eisenhower at a summit meeting in Geneva in July 1955, he made a point of reminding him of the U.S. reversal. As Secretary of State John Foster Dulles recounted in a cable back to Washington, "Khrushchev jokingly said sometimes people made far-reaching proposals expecting other persons not to accept them and, when [the] other person did accept them [the] proposer hardly knew what to do." When Eisenhower failed to get the reference, Marshal Georgii Zhukov, the Soviet defense minister, explained that Khrushchev "was referring to Soviet disarmament proposals."[10]

7. The classic account of these negotiations is Philip Noel-Baker, *The Arms Race: A Programme for World Disarmament* (New York, 1958), 12–30. For accounts by a key Soviet participant, see A. A. Roshchin, "Gody obnovleniia, nadezhd i razocharovanii (1953–1959 gg.)," *Novaia i noveishaia istoriia*, 1988, no. 5:127–147; and Roshchin, *Mezhdunarodnaia bezopasnost' i iadernoe oruzhie* (Moscow, 1980), 119–132. The Soviet proposal is reprinted in *Documents on Disarmament, 1945–1959*, vol. 1, *1945–1956* (Washington, D.C., 1960), 456–467, and is discussed in a declassified official document: "Progress Report, Proposed Policy of the United States on the Question of Disarmament," Volume I, 26 May 1955, Special Staff Study for the President, NSC Action No. 1328, by Harold E. Stassen. This document is located in papers of the Office of the Special Assistant for National Security Affairs, NSC Series, Policy Papers Subseries, Box 2, Folder: "NSC 112/1 Disarmament (3)," Dwight D. Eisenhower Library, Abilene, Kansas (hereafter DDEL). A detailed analysis of Soviet objectives is found in Bloomfield, Clemens, and Griffiths, *Khrushchev and the Arms Race*.

8. Roshchin, "Gody obnovleniia," 127–129.

9. Ibid., 129.

10. Secret (declassified) cable from Geneva to secretary of state, 23 July 1955, p. 2, White House Office, Office of the Staff Secretary: Records, 1952–61, International Trips and Meetings Series, Box 2: Memoranda of President's Conversations—Geneva 1955, DDEL.

Variations on the May 1955 proposal continued to form the basis for subsequent Soviet negotiating positions until the Soviets left the UN Disarmament Subcommittee in December 1957. In addition to these overall plans, the Soviets supported various partial measures, including establishment of demilitarized and denuclearized zones in Central Europe. The USSR supported the so-called Eden Plan in 1954 and 1955 (proposed by the British foreign minister Anthony Eden), as well as the various versions of the Rapacki Plan put forward by the Polish foreign minister Adam Rapacki in 1957 and 1958.[11]

The Troop Reductions

Reductions in Soviet troop strength in the 1950s and early 1960s were carried out in several stages. Declassified Soviet military documents indicate that the reductions did not correspond precisely to the official Soviet announcements at the time, which had formed the basis for all previous Western analyses. Most observers, for example, accepted Khrushchev's figure of 5.763 million troops as an accurate description of the size of the Soviet armed forces in 1955.[12] In fact, the documents reveal that the authorized strength of the armed forces in that year was about 4.8 million, with the actual strength somewhat less.[13] The high point of postwar Soviet troop strength evidently came in 1953, when the authorized forces numbered about 5.4 million. Thus, the first major reductions were not the ones that Khrushchev announced with much fanfare in August 1955 but those that took place unannounced following Stalin's death in March 1953. The authorized strength of the armed forces was reduced by about 600,000 troops between then and Khrushchev's August announcement.[14]

The August 1955 announcement promised a reduction of 640,000 troops to be completed by mid-December of the same year. The declassified documents indicate that only 340,000 troops were actually demobilized, producing a force of 4.4 million by January 1956, some 300,000 more than would have resulted from the full, announced reduction. Those "missing" 300,000 troops were not demobilized but rather assigned to inactive, low-strength units (*nekomplekt*).[15] In May 1956 a further demobilization of 1,200,000 troops was

11. Bloomfield, Clemens, and Griffiths, *Khrushchev and the Arms Race*, 147–151.
12. Thomas W. Wolfe, *Soviet Power and Europe, 1945–1970* (Baltimore, Md., 1970), 164–166; Raymond L. Garthoff, "Estimating Soviet Military Force Levels: Some Light from the Past," *International Security* 14, 4 (Spring 1990): 93–109.
13. "Spravka-doklad [G. K. Zhukova o sokrashchenii Vooruzhennykh Sil, 12 avgusta 1955 g.]," Originally classified as "strictly secret, of special importance," reprinted in the collection entitled "Sokrashchenie Vooruzhennykh Sil SSSR v seredine 50-kh godov," *Voennye arkhivy Rossii*, 1993, no. 1:80.
14. "Zapiska G. Zhukova i V. Sokolovskogo v TsK KPSS o khode vypolneniia postanovleniia Soveta Ministrov SSSR ot 12 avgusta 1956 g. o sokrashchenii chislennosti Sovetskoi Armii i s predlozheniiami po dalneishemu sokrasheniiu Vooruzhennykh Sil SSSR, 9 fevralia 1956 g.," *Voennye arkhivy Rossii*, 1993, no. 1:271–309.
15. "O Sokrashchenii chislennosti Vooruzhennykh Sil" [On the reduction of the strength of the armed forces], resolution of the Council of Ministers, No. 1481–825ss, 12 August 1955, *Voennye arkhivy Rossii*, 1993, no. 1:273.

Table 1. Khrushchev's Announced Troop Reductions

Date	Amount
August 1955	640,000
May 1956	1,200,000
January 1958	300,000
January 1960	1,200,000[a]

Source: Thomas W. Wolfe, Soviet Power and Europe, 1945–1970 (Baltimore, Md., 1970), 164–166.
[a]Not completed.

Table 2. Personnel Strength of Soviet Armed Forces, 1953–56

Date	Authorized	Actual
March 1953	5,396,038	—
August 1955	4,815,870	4,637,523
January 1956	4,406,216	4,147,496

Source: "Zapiska G. Zhukova i V. Sokolovskogo v TsK KPSS o khode vypolneniia postanovleniia Soveta Ministrov SSSR ot 12 avgusta 1956 g. o sokrashchenii chislennosti Sovet-skoi Armii i s predlozheniiami po dalneishemu sokrashcheniiu Vooruzhennykh Sil SSSR, 9 fevralia 1956 g.," Voennye arkhivy Rossii, 1993, no. 1:283.

announced. In November 1957, Marshal Rodion Malinovskii, the Soviet defense minister, revealed in conversation with three American journalists that the Soviet armed forces had been reduced by 1.4 million "over the last couple of years" [za poslednye gody].[16] In January 1958, a month after breaking up the UN Disarmament Subcommittee, the Soviets announced a unilateral reduction of 300,000 troops; it was completed a year later.[17] In January 1960, Khrushchev announced a reduction of another 1,200,000 troops, including 250,000 officers. It was scheduled to be completed by the following winter, but was suspended during the Berlin crisis (see Tables 1 and 2).[18]

The following sections explore the extent to which the Soviet initiatives—disarmament proposals and unilateral measures—were the result of changes in military requirements, internal economic pressures, or U.S. behavior.

16. V. S. Golubovich, Marshal Malinovskii (Kiev, 1988), 212. For the journalists' account, see William Randolph Hearst, Jr., Bob Considine, and Frank Conniff, Ask Me Anything: Our Adventures with Khrushchev (New York, 1960), 148–155. It does not include that remark, but other details coincide.

17. The actual reduction was somewhat less: 289,668. See "Zapiska R. Malinovskogo v TsK KPSS o rabote po sokrashcheniiu Vooruzhennykh Sil, 8 ianvaria 1959 g.," Voennye arkhivy Rossii, 1993, no. 1:305–307.

18. Krasnaia zvezda, 20 January 1960; Wolfe, Soviet Power and Europe, 1945–1970, 164–166; Garthoff, "Estimating Soviet Military Force Levels"; George F. Minde II and Michael Hennessey, "Reform of the Soviet Military under Khrushchev and the Role of America's Strategic Modernization," in Robert O. Crummey, ed., Reform in Russia and the U.S.S.R. (Urbana, Ill., 1989), 182–206.

Military Requirements

One common explanation holds that Khrushchev's reductions were not a sign of moderation in security policy at all but merely a product of changing military requirements. In this view, mass armies of the traditional type were no longer necessary in an age of battlefield nuclear warfare: the extensive demobilization of ground and tactical air forces was a sensible means to "modernize" the Soviet armed forces. From this perspective, the troop reductions were entirely in the Soviet interest and should not be considered as concessions intended to demonstrate a new cooperative attitude toward disarmament. Some observers have argued that the change in the Soviet attitude toward Western disarmament plans, for example, was a bluff. Walt W. Rostow has suggested that the USSR's proposals were designed "to encourage complacency in the West." The Soviets' intention, in his view, was not to signal a willingness to restrict their armaments but rather "to induce the West to diminish the attention and outlays devoted to the arms race," while they continued "to close the gap in weapons of mass destruction and to modernize their ground forces."[19]

More Rubble for the Ruble. The interpretation that the reductions did not hurt but rather benefited Soviet military capabilities apparently stems from the belief that nuclear weapons—especially tactical nuclear weapons—compensated for cuts in conventional forces. The "more bang for the buck" argument was widely promoted in the United States by the Eisenhower administration to support nuclearization of NATO forces on grounds of cost effectiveness. Khrushchev put forward his own version—often dubbed "more rubble for the ruble"—to justify his disarmament proposals and his unilateral troop cuts.

Yet it would be inaccurate to imply that reduction of conventional forces on military grounds was a consensus position, within either the United States or the USSR. In the United States, for example, the Army chief of staff himself disagreed with the president's policy. In 1954, General Matthew Ridgway claimed that the deployment of tactical nuclear weapons "does not warrant the assumption that the need for soldiers will become less. On the contrary," he argued, "there are indications that the trend will be in the opposite direction." He cited several reasons for needing more forces: the increased depth of the battlefield, the need for greater dispersion of forces, and the multi-

19. W. W. Rostow, *Open Skies: Eisenhower's Proposal of July 21, 1955* (Austin, Texas, 1982), 20.

plication of maintenance and support facilities to supply large numbers of small, mobile combat units.[20]

On the Soviet side, many prominent military officers agreed with their American counterparts. They cited arguments by U.S. Generals Bradley, Collins, Ridgway, Taylor, and others to support a case for maintaining mass armies.[21] Lt. Gen. Krasil'nikov of the General Staff, for example, argued that the prospect of a nuclear battlefield "calls not for the reduction of the numbers of combatants, but for their logical further increase, since the threat of wiping out divisions grows, and large reserves will be needed for their replacement."[22] Marshal Rodion Malinovskii, who, as defense minister, oversaw Khrushchev's troop reductions from 1957 to 1964, maintained a thoroughly traditional view of the role of tanks and armored vehicles. Despite the nuclear revolution, his evaluation reflected his wartime experience: "The more machines on the battlefield, he thought, the fewer the losses, the more certain the successes."[23]

Marshal Zhukov's Role. Significantly, Marshal Georgii Zhukov—Malinovskii's predecessor as defense minister from 1955 to 1957—appears not to have opposed the initial cuts. None of the reminiscences about Zhukov suggests that the troop reductions were a source of conflict between him and Khrushchev.[24] On the contrary, Khrushchev, in his tape-recorded reminiscences, claims that Zhukov initiated many of the proposals for reductions in personnel and military spending. Whether or not that is an overstatement, Zhukov does seem to have been a reliable executor of Khrushchev's policies. It was Zhukov, for example, who in 1956 dismissed Admiral Nikolai Kuznetsov as commander of the navy ("in an exceptionally rude manner," as the admiral later recalled), when the latter came into conflict with

20. Ridgway's remarks come from a speech delivered on 9 September 1954, quoted in Memorandum for Admiral Radford, Subject: Differing Philosophies, Generals Ridgway and Gruenther, 11 September 1954, p. 3, CJCS 092.2 North Atlantic Treaty, Modern Military Branch, National Archives (MMB NA). I am grateful to Charles Naef for calling this document to my attention. Ridgway expressed similar views in Congressional testimony, in an undated document, "Notes for Questions or Comment," Office of the Staff Secretary, Subject Series, Alphabetical Subseries, Box 3, Folder: "Army—Testimony [by Gen. Ridgway] re Strength," DDEL. See also his biography, Matthew Ridgway, *Soldier* (New York: Harper & Bros., 1956). For similar views from other Army officers, see Maxwell Taylor, *The Uncertain Trumpet* (New York, 1960); and James Gavin, *War and Peace in the Space Age* (New York, 1958), 139, 151, 229.

21. See the discussion in Raymond L. Garthoff, *Soviet Strategy in the Nuclear Age* (New York, 1958), 124–125.

22. S. Krasil'nikov, *Marksizm-Leninizm o voine i armii* (Moscow, 1956), 148, 150–151, discussed in ibid.

23. Golubovich, *Marshal Malinovskii*, 218–219.

24. See, e.g., Iu. V. Aksiutin, ed., *Nikita Sergeevich Khrushchev: materialy k biografii* (Moscow, 1989). Also, Sergei Khrushchev, *Nikita Khrushchev: Krizisy i rakety*, 2 vols. (Moscow: Novosti, 1994); and his "Nikita Khrushchev i voennoe stroitel'stvo v 1953–64 godakh," paper prepared for the Khrushchev centenary conference, Brown University, 1–3 December 1994.

Khrushchev over the scope and nature of the Soviet naval program.[25] And Zhukov's support was apparently crucial in helping Khrushchev overcome the opposition of the "anti-Party group" in June 1957.[26] Khrushchev does not seem to have been motivated by Zhukov's attitude toward the military reforms when he decided to fire the marshal in October 1957.[27]

Zhukov was evidently instrumental in promoting the nuclearization of the Soviet armed forces and was apparently willing to go along with Khrushchev's desire for cuts in order to be able to do so.[28] Furthermore, the 1955 reductions coincided with a reorganization of the ground forces that included reductions in personnel levels of individual units in the overall structure.[29] In this regard, the cuts made military sense, although presumably the Soviets could have formed additional units with the excess personnel if their goal were only to streamline the force structure.

From Reluctance to Resistance. If the troop reductions were dictated by Soviet security requirements one might expect to find that the military high command had initiated them or at least had gone willingly along with the political leadership's directive. This may be the case for the early reductions through 1955. The subsequent cuts, however, engendered considerable unease and resistance from the armed forces, as the archival materials and memoir accounts now reveal.

In implementing the reductions, the high command sought to minimize their impact on combat capability. In early 1956, Marshal Zhukov, the defense minister, and Marshal Sokolovskii, chief of the General Staff, informed the Central Committee of the progress of demobilization so far. In addition to the 340,000 troops demobilized in response to August 1955 order, the Defense Ministry had reduced the army by a further 65,400 troops, including nearly 17,000 troops withdrawn when the Soviet base at Porkkala-Udd was returned to Finland.[30] Apparently under political pressure to do more, the military leaders expressed willingness to cut the army by a further 420,000 troops during 1956. Many of the cuts were to come from noncombat formations, such as the proposed reduction of 126,000 construction troops. Reductions were to be

25. (Capt.) O. Odnokolenko, "Narkom Kuznetsov," *Krasnaia zvezda*, 21 May 1988, p. 4. Also, Khrushchev, "Nikita Khrushchev i voennoe stroitel'stvo," 9–14.

26. Fedor Burlatskii, "Khrushchev: Shtrikhi k politicheskomu portretu," *Literaturnaia gazeta*, 24 February 1988, p. 14.

27. For Zhukov's own interpretation of the reasons for his firing, see A. D. Mirkina and V. S. Iarovikov, eds., *Marshal Zhukov: polkovodets i chelovek* (Moscow, 1988), 2:70–71.

28. Vladimir Karpov, *Polkovodets* (Moscow, 1985), esp. 524; Igor' Itskov and Marina Babak, "Marshal Zhukov," part 3, *Ogonek*, 1986, no. 51:27; Matthew Evangelista, *Innovation and the Arms Race: How the United States and the Soviet Union Develop New Military Technologies* (Ithaca, N.Y., 1988), 236–239.

29. Minde and Hennessey, "Reform of the Soviet Military," 183–184. "Spravka-Doklad G. K. Zhukova o sokrashchenii Vooruzhennykh Sil, 12 avgusta 1955 g.," *Voennye arkhivy Rossii*, 1993, no. 1:280–281.

30. "Zapiska G. Zhukova i V. Sokolovskogo," 283.

implemented by such actions as transferring officers' dining facilities and stores to civilian control and closing or transforming many of the army's educational facilities, such as its military law academy and its 15 music schools.[31]

The Central Committee approved the military's proposals for reducing the army by 420,000 in March 1956, but that was apparently not enough for Khrushchev. Less than two months later, the Soviet government announced that the army would be cut by 1.2 million over the next year. We have known for some time from open sources that this announcement caused considerable unhappiness within the armed forces. In 1982, for example, a former commander of an air defense division wrote in his memoirs that the late 1950s were "a difficult time for us military people. We still hadn't managed to survive the first unilateral reduction of the Soviet armed forces when a second began. Some of us didn't take the so-called reforms very cheerfully. Sometimes it seemed that everything we had done up until then was now unnecessary."[32] In early 1988 a senior Soviet military officer recalled the 1956 reduction in a thinly disguised warning against any further such unilateral initiatives: "As a professional military man, I'll tell you that the step was a rash one, it dealt a terrible blow at our defence capacity, and at our officer personnel. At the time skilled personnel, with tremendous combat know-how, left the army. The army officer lost prestige in the eyes of young people. To be honest, we are still feeling this."[33]

The new archival materials reveal that Khrushchev and the political leadership were apprised of the army's negative reaction to the cuts already in 1956. In a report to the Central Committee, two senior officials revealed that "some of our officers express doubts about the expediency of a unilateral reduction." The report provides several evocative quotes from disgruntled commanders warning about German remilitarization and U.S. intentions, and recalling the Nazi invasion of the USSR in 1941. The authors describe a "mood of nervousness and uncertainty" among officers who were demobilized without guarantees of adequate housing or work, or even a pension. Some were driven to contemplate suicide ("If it weren't for the children, it would be a bullet in the forehead"). These detailed examples undermine the report's obligatory reference to "an overwhelming majority" of the troops who supposedly supported the reductions and looked upon them as "a great step along the path of alleviating international tension and improving the welfare of the Soviet people."[34]

31. Ibid., 283–288.
32. Vladimir Lavrinenkov, *Bez voiny* (Kiev, 1982), 225.
33. (General of the Army) Ivan Tret'iak, "Reliable Defense First and Foremost," interview by Iurii Tepliakov, *Moscow News*, 28 February–6 March 1988, p. 12.
34. "Zapiska I. Koneva i A. Zheltova v TsK KPSS ob otnoshenii v armii k Zaiavleniiu Sovetskogo pravitel'stva po voprosu o razoruzhenii, 1 iiunia 1956 g.," *Voennye arkhivy Rossii*, 1993, no. 1:292–293.

Despite the evidence of unease among the troops, the political leadership continued reducing the army with a demobilization of 300,000 forces announced in January 1958. The KGB and the Communist Party monitored the army's reaction to the new cuts and found much cause for concern. Two formerly top-secret reports from March 1958 not only provide evidence of demoralization and unhappiness among the troops slated for demobilization but also suggest that the military authorities were carrying out the reductions in such a way as to exacerbate such problems. In particular, the Defense Ministry was discharging officers without the right to a pension, even though they were within a year or two of eligibility (normally after twenty years of service). During five days in February 1958 the KGB read the mail of troops stationed in the Transbaikal military district and turned up "more than a hundred letters in which officers of the Soviet Army express dissatisfaction with the organizational measures connected with the reduction" and fear about their own futures. One officer wrote of being "thrown overboard a half year before the end" of his service. Another described "demobilizing officers who have 2 to 3 children, no clothing, no money, nothing, who are being dismissed without pension, lacking only 1.5–2 years [to qualify]. Everyone is in a terrible mood."[35]

Less than a week after receiving the KGB report, two senior Central Committee officials involved in military affairs presented a general overview of the status of the demobilization. Their report pointed out that the government's original demobilization order stipulated the officers to be dismissed as those who had completed their terms of service and were therefore eligible for pensions, those who were ill, and those who lacked "the required military and specialist training." The report described how the Ministry of Defense "complied" with the 1958 reduction order by dismissing 72,000 officers, of whom nearly 35,000 would receive no pension, even though 8,000 of them had served for seventeen or more years. The majority of the demobilized officers from military districts in the eastern part of the country and from abroad were provided no housing.[36] One infers from the report that the military authorities, either deliberately or through incompetence, were sabotaging the demobilization efforts and creating fear and resentment among the troops and the officer corps.

It is not surprising, then, that in reporting the completion of the demobilization, Defense Minister Rodion Malinovskii found that "as a rule" the demobilized career officers "left the army with great unwillingness." Dismissal was "extremely painful" for "officers with families, who had no civilian

35. "Zapiska I. Serova v TsK KPSS o nedovol'stve nekotorykh ofitserov zabaikal'skogo voennogo okruga organizatsionnymi meropriatiami po sokrashcheniiu Vooruzhennykh Sil," 1 March 1958, report from the head of the KGB, originally classified top secret, *osobaia papka* (special file), *Voennye arkhivy Rossii*, 1993, no. 1:301–302.

36. "Zapiska I. Shikina i V. Zolotukhina v TsK KPSS, 6 marta 1987 [*sic:* 1958] g.," *Voennye arkhivy Rossii*, 1993, no. 1:303–304.

profession, no right to a pension or housing." Tens of thousands of officers had still received no living space.[37] Whereas the Central Committee report seemed to accuse the Defense Ministry of poor handling of the demobilization, Malinovskii placed the blame on local political and economic authorities for inadequate support of the demobilized soldiers.

Undoubtedly, Malinovskii also considered Khrushchev responsible for the widespread demoralization, especially among the officer corps. In March 1959, the defense minister wrote Khrushchev a long, detailed letter quoting from some of the nine thousand letters of complaint he had received about the effects of the demobilizations ("I curse the day I first wanted to become an officer").[38] As late as 1964 Malinovskii reported to Khrushchev that nearly two hundred thousand family members associated with Ministry of Defense personnel still had either nowhere to live or were living in substandard conditions (e.g., in basements).[39]

Even though Nikita Khrushchev publicly justified his demobilizations on military grounds, and many Western observers have described them as simply a means to "modernize" the armed forces, the troop reductions did not receive the approval or support of the military command or the rank-and-file troops. In fact, the more Khrushchev sought military justification for the cuts, the more the army's attitude shifted from reluctance to outright resistance.[40]

Radical Doctrinal Changes. Khrushchev's most dramatic announcement of force reductions came in a major speech in January 1960 when he explicitly associated the cuts with a new military doctrine that emphasized nuclear deterrence by a strategic missile force. The new policy was clearly the Soviet leader's personal initiative. He first revealed it to his fellow members of the Presidium (the name for the Politburo at that time) in a secret memorandum of 8 December 1959, probably dictated while on vacation at the Black Sea.[41]

37. "Zapiska R. Malinovskogo v TsK KPSS o rabote po sokrashcheniiu Vooruzhennykh Sil, 8 ianvaria 1959 g.," *Voennye arkhivy Rossii,* 1993, no. 1:305–306. The report also presents a detailed account of numbers of officers discharged and for what reason.

38. Malinovskii to Khrushchev, 13 March 1959, f. 5, op. 30, d. 289 (microfilm roll 4615), Storage Center for Contemporary Documentation [Tsentr khraneniia sovremennoi dokumentatsii] (hereafter TsKhSD), the former Central Committee archive. It should be noted that this particular letter was, according to Malinovskii, intended to respond to a resolution of the Central Committee of 5 August 1958, urging all Soviet institutions to do a better job of handling letters of complaint from citizens.

39. Malinovskii to Khrushchev, 25 April 1964, f. 5, op. 30, d. 458 (microfilm roll 4654), TsKhSD.

40. For firsthand accounts of military criticisms, see Troyanovsky, "Nikita Khrushchev"; and Khrushchev, "Nikita Khrushchev i voennoe stroitel'stvo."

41. The document and other related ones are translated and reprinted following an article by the person who discovered them, Vladislav M. Zubok, "Khrushchev's 1960 Troop Cut: New Russian Evidence," *Cold War International History Project Bulletin,* Issues 8–9 (Winter 1996/97), 416–420. The archival source is the TsKhSD, f. 2, op. 1, d. 416, pp. 1–11.

The Presidium approved the memo on 14 December. Four days later a conference of top military officials convened to work out a practical plan of implementation. The plenum of the Communist Party Central Committee approved the proposal on 26 December 1959, and Khrushchev made his historic announcement to the Supreme Soviet on 14 January 1960.[42]

Four days later, the Central Committee addressed a "closed" letter (*zakrytoe pis'mo*) to the armed forces justifying the reductions on economic, political, and military grounds—and making exaggerated claims about the "serial production" of missiles.[43] The development of nuclear and missile technology meant, in Khrushchev's estimation, that a state's military capabilities depended more on nuclear "firepower" than on "how many soldiers we have under arms, how many people are wearing soldiers' greatcoats."[44] Thus, in his view, changing military conditions permitted a further reduction of Soviet troop strength by 1.2 million. Some time later he posed the question during a meeting with his military commanders, neither expecting nor receiving an answer: "If missiles are capable of defending us, then why do we need to keep such an army?"[45] He used virtually the same words to justify the reductions in his original memo to his Presidium colleagues a month earlier.[46]

Some observers have identified a further link between military requirements and the troop reductions. They have drawn the conclusion that, in keeping with Khrushchev's new military doctrine, the savings from reducing conventional forces were used to finance the buildup of strategic weapons. This explanation is valid in a limited sense. Archival documents indicate, for example, that the pseudonymous Ministry of Medium-Machine Building—responsible for nuclear weapons development—hired 3,600 soldiers, including 600 officers, demobilized in 1960. In fact, however, the context suggests that the initiative did not come from the ministry but from the political leaders as they sought to alleviate employment problems associated with the demobilization. The ministry's offer, in April 1960, responded to an official decree of four months earlier concerning the work and living conditions of the demobilized troops. This decree, in turn, followed Khrushchev's announcement of the troop cut. Finally, several other nonmilitary ministries—including those in charge of civil aviation and the merchant marine—made similar

42. The speech is reprinted in *Pravda*, 15 January 1960.
43. The letter, dated 18 January 1960, is addressed "To the Soldiers of the Valiant Armed Forces of the USSR" and is found with the original decision to draft it in 20th Convocation of the Central Committee Secretariat, from protocol no. 132, Secretariat session of 16 January 1960, located in a card file (*kartoteka*) N 3, TsKhSD. The claims about missile production are on page 5. On the actual state of missile production during this time, see Khrushchev, "Nikita Khrushchev i voennoe stroitel'stvo."
44. *Pravda*, 15 January 1960.
45. Khrushchev, *Krizisy i rakety*, 2:427, and his "Nikita Khrushchev i voennoe stroitel'stvo," 48.
46. Zubok, "Khrushchev's 1960 Troop Cut," 418–419.

offers to hire demobilized troops, in what was clearly a coordinated campaign to find employment for the soldiers and officers released from service.[47]

During the period of major troop reductions there does seem to have been an increase in Soviet efforts in advanced-technology military fields, such as nuclear weapons and rocketry. For example, some scholars have identified a major growth (23 percent) in employment of personnel in research and development institutions from mid-1955 to the end of 1956.[48] But, strictly speaking, the conventional-force reductions did not compensate for the major cost of Soviet strategic weapons programs—the actual mass production of missiles—simply because that buildup occurred long after the troop cuts, indeed after Khrushchev was removed from office.[49] The Brezhnev era witnessed both a strategic nuclear buildup and an expensive modernization and increase in conventional forces.

With the exception of those in the newly created Strategic Rocket Forces, much of the military high command disagreed with Khrushchev's formulation of a new military doctrine that denigrated the traditional role of ground, air, and naval forces. So even though both Khrushchev's public pronouncements and the Party's closed letter to the troops justified the cuts on military grounds, the army did not accept that rationale.[50] Moreover, whereas the closed letter emphasized the economic benefits of demobilization, military leaders were concerned about problems of morale and dislocation, as hundreds of thousands of soldiers and officers were forced to reintegrate themselves into the civilian workforce. Marshal Malinovskii, the defense minister, made this point himself only a few days after Khrushchev announced his

47. This account is based on several Defense Ministry documents, all classified "secret," copies of which I have deposited at the National Security Archive, Washington, D.C. A report to the Central Committee and Council of Ministers from R. Malinovskii and P. Ivanov, 24 May 1960, describes the program to place demobilized officers and soldiers with civilian ministries and gives details on its results. The remaining documents are letters from the individuals listed to the Council of Ministers: from E. Slavskii, minister of medium machine-building, 27 April 1960; from V. Bakaev, minister of the maritime fleet, 27 April 1960; from B. Butoma, chair, State Committee for Shipbuilding, 27 April 1960; from P. Dement'ev, chair, State Committee for Aviation Technology, 10 May 1960; from G. Schetchikov, head, main administration of the civil air fleet (Aeroflot), 5 May 1960.

48. Bloomfield et al., *Khrushchev and the Arms Race*, 42.

49. Jutta and Stephan Tiedtke, "The Soviet Union's Internal Problems and the Development of the Warsaw Treaty Organization," in Egbert Jahn, ed., *Soviet Foreign Policy: Its Social and Economic Conditions* (London, 1978), 126–127. Also, Minde and Hennessey, "Reform of the Soviet Military," 185.

50. The best recent discussion of military opposition to Khrushchev's doctrinal changes is Thomas M. Nichols, *The Sacred Cause: Civil-Military Conflict over Soviet National Security, 1917–1992* (Ithaca, N.Y., 1993), esp. 71–84. Nichols points out that even the Strategic Rocket Forces, after March 1963, were headed by a combined-arms officer—Marshal Ivan Krylov—who opposed the excessive emphasis on nuclear weapons at the expense of traditional forces. He argues, on 78–79, that Marshal Malinovskii insisted on Krylov's appointment particularly for that reason. For a Russian account, see Il'ia Dragan, *Nikolai Krylov* (Moscow, 1988), 298–303. Retrospective accounts of Malinovskii's views on the importance of conventional forces would appear to support Nichols's interpretation. See, e.g., Golubovich, *Marshal Malinovskii*, esp. 210–220.

1960 round of cuts.[51] Military criticism of Khrushchev's reductions became particularly vocal from that point on.[52]

Even though Khrushchev felt obliged to suspend the 1960 troop reductions during a particularly tense period of confrontation with the United States over the status of Berlin in 1961, his commitment to military reform was not diminished. During the last years of his tenure, he made increasingly radical proposals for reducing the military forces, and his views about the best means of insuring national security increasingly diverged from those of the military leadership. In private discussions with his top commanders in 1963 and 1964, Khrushchev argued that the Soviet Army should consist primarily of strategic rocket troops commanding a nuclear deterrent force of two or three hundred missiles and ground forces of no more than three to five hundred thousand troops. As his son Sergei—who was present at several of these meetings—recalled, the commanders viewed reductions to that level as heralding the "ultimate ruin of the army. The military did not want to, and could not, reconcile themselves with this."[53] Yet Khrushchev went even further. Drawing on his experience in Ukraine during the 1920s, following the Bolshevik victory in the Civil War, he advocated creation of locally based militia forces to replace the enormous standing army of conscripts.[54] Khrushchev had actually broached this subject in his December 1959 memo to his colleagues in the leadership, but it was not an idea that found its way into the military's plans to implement the troop reductions. As Khrushchev insistently denigrated traditional weapons such as tanks and artillery, the military equally insistently extolled them. The high command was not interested in Khrushchev's radical reforms.

Khrushchev's interest in demilitarized zones in central Europe, while also plausibly explicable on military grounds, did not receive support from the army. According to Aleksei Adzhubei, Khrushchev's son-in-law and political ally (he edited the newspapers *Komsomol'skaia pravda* and then *Izvestiia* during Khrushchev's tenure), Khrushchev wanted for international political reasons to withdraw Soviet forces from central Europe. In 1959, Khrushchev reportedly asked János Kádár, the Hungarian leader put in office as a result of

51. See Malinovskii's report in *Krasnaia zvezda*, 20 January 1960; for an extensive discussion see Jutta Tiedtke, *Abrüstung in der Sowjetunion: Wirtschaftliche Bedingungen und soziale Folgen der Truppenreduzierung von 1960* (Frankfurt am Main, 1985), 157–179.

52. Matthew Gallagher, "Military Manpower: A Case Study," *Problems of Communism* 13 (May–June 1964), 53–62; Thomas W. Wolfe, *Soviet Strategy at the Crossroads* (Cambridge, Mass., 1965), 238–242; Tiedtke, *Abrüstung in der Sowjetunion*, 54–62; Herbert Ritvo, "Internal Divisions on Disarmament in the USSR," in Seymour Melman, ed., *Disarmament: Its Politics and Economics* (Boston, 1962), 212–237; Roman Kolkowicz, *The Soviet Military and the Communist Party* (Princeton, N.J., 1967), 150–173.

53. Khrushchev, "Nikita Khrushchev i voennoe stroitel'stvo," 50–52.

54. Ibid., and Khrushchev, *Krizisy i rakety*, 2:488–489. For detailed consideration of the public discussion of such issues, see Walter C. Clemens, Jr., "Soviet Disarmament Proposals and the Cadre-Territorial Army," *Orbis* 7, 4 (Winter 1964): 778–799; Clemens, "The Soviet Militia in the Missile Age," *Orbis* 8, 1 (Spring 1964): 84–105.

the 1956 Soviet invasion, if it were not time to remove Soviet troops from that country. Kádár demurred. At about the same time, Khrushchev evidently discussed with Polish leader Wladislaw Gomulka the possibility of withdrawing Soviet troops from Poland.[55] Khrushchev's son Sergei also mentions his father's desire to withdraw troops from those countries—for a mix of military, political, and economic reasons. The Soviet leader was convinced that security now depended on nuclear deterrence and that traditional armies were largely irrelevant. His son quotes him to that effect: "From a strategic viewpoint the presence of Soviet ground forces on the western borders is useless, and their withdrawal will give us enormous political and economic advantages." According to Sergei Khrushchev, the military leaders disagreed. The high command "did not want to withdraw from the borders won in the Second World War. Their defense, in the generals' opinion, served as the guarantor of Soviet Union's security."[56]

Economic Conditions

That Khrushchev's military reforms were motivated by economic concerns is evident from many sources. In the transcript of his tape-recorded memoirs, for example, his remarks about the troop reductions come directly after he expresses his belief that the United States was using the arms race to destroy the Soviet economy, "and by that means to obtain its goals even without war."[57] Looking at gross indicators of economic performance, however, would not lead one to identify economic motives as preeminent in Khrushchev's decision to cut the armed forces. Western estimates of Soviet gross national product, for example, show that the highest GNP growth of the postwar period occurred in the 1950s, averaging 5.7 percent per year. Soviet figures are higher. The serious decline in growth rates began only in the Brezhnev period (see Table 3).

Internal Soviet reports during the Khrushchev era were often quite optimistic about the economy. Consider, for example, a report prepared by the Foreign Ministry, "On the Question of Economic Competition between the USSR and USA"—one of Khrushchev's favorite themes. Completed in mid-1961, during the course of the fifth round of major troop reductions, the report stressed that "for the past seven years the increase in industrial productivity in the USSR averaged 11.1 percent per year versus 2.5 percent for the

55. Aleksei Adzhubei, *Te desiat' let* (Moscow, 1989), 155–156; *Khrushchev Remembers: The Glasnost Tapes*, trans. J. L. Schecter and V. V. Luchkov, (Boston, 1990), 119–120; Khrushchev, *Krizisy i rakety*, 1:240–241.

56. Khrushchev, "Nikita Khrushchev i voennoe stroitel'stvo," 39.

57. Nikita Khrushchev, transcript of tape-recorded reminiscences, Harriman Institute Library, Columbia University, New York, 403.

Table 3. Soviet Economic Growth, 1951–87

Year	GNP (%)[a]	National Income Produced (%)[b]
1951–58	6.0	11.4
1958–61	5.8	9.1
1961–65	4.8	6.5
1966–70	5.0	7.8
1971–75	3.1	5.7
1976–80	2.2	4.3
1981–85	1.8	3.6
1986–87	2.2	3.2

Sources: For 1951–61, Philip Hanson, "Economic Constraints on Soviet Policies in the 1980s," *International Affairs* 57, 1 (Winter 1980–81): 22; for 1961–87, "Revisiting Soviet Economic Performance under *Glasnost*: Implications for CIA Estimates," CIA report SOV 88–10068, September 1988, p. 9.

[a]CIA estimated Gross National Product, in keeping with Soviet practice, to exclude services that do not contribute directly to material output.

[b]Official Soviet figures for national income produced exclude depreciation and services that do not contribute directly to material product, and include some double counting of transactions between wholesale producers.

United States, 4 to 5 times faster." A Foreign Ministry official who read the report underlined the last phrase.[58]

Despite the overall picture of strong economic growth, one can—by looking in more detail at annual growth rates, indicators of growth in labor productivity, performance in the agricultural sector, and the nature of the labor pool—find economic and demographic incentives for the reductions, but they vary from year to year (see Table 4).

The initial troop reductions of the mid-1950s came at a time of impressive economic growth. As one study points out, "in the years 1954–1956 Soviet industry appears to have grown at the most rapid pace seen in the 1952–1962 decade." Growth of civilian machinery output increased from 7.5 percent in 1951–53 to 16 percent in 1954–56. Labor productivity increased in 1954 and 1955 at about twice the rate of the previous three years.[59] It could be that the desire for such high levels of growth called the leaders' attention to the value of the troop reductions. Certainly the influx of labor from the army contributed to growth.

58. Archive of the Foreign Policy of the Russian Federation [Arkhiv Vneshnei Politiki Rossiiskoi Federatsii] (hereafter AVP), fond: Referentura po SShA, op. 47–6, por. 3, papka 158, Otdel SSha, 24 June 1961, No. 1317, "K voprosu ob ekonomicheskom sorevnovanii mezhdu SSSR i SShA (spravka)," by Iu. Vasil'ev.

59. Bloomfield et al., *Khrushchev and the Arms Race*, chap. 3, esp. 51–53.

Table 4. Growth of National Income and Labor
Productivity (Soviet Estimates), 1955–62

Year	National Income Produced (%)	Labor Productivity (%)
1955	11.9	9.5
1956	11.3	7.0
1957	7.0	6.6
1958	12.4	6.2
1959	7.5	7.4
1960	7.7	5.4
1961	6.8	4.4
1962	5.7	5.5

Source: Tsentral'noe statisticheskoe upravlenie SSSR, Narodnoe khoziastvo SSSR v 1967 g.: Statisticheskii ezhegodnik (Moscow, 1968), 59, cited in Ed A. Hewett, Reforming the Soviet Economy: Equality versus Efficiency (Washington, D.C., 1988), 226.

Both preceding and following the August 1955 announcement of a Soviet troop cut, various references appeared in the Soviet press to the need for demobilized soldiers in the civilian economy. At a meeting of the Central Committee plenum on 4 July 1955, Marshal Nikolai Bulganin, the Soviet prime minister, referred to the labor shortage in the Soviet economy.[60] Following the demobilization announcement, Soviet sources identified agriculture as one of the sectors with the most pressing need for labor. Members of the British embassy in Moscow also drew that conclusion from their contacts, as a formerly secret report details: "An officer of the Soviet armed forces in civilian clothes told a member of this Embassy the other day that he had spent three days studying at the agricultural exhibition. When asked why, he said that the Army was being cut down and they had to prepare themselves. He had evidently been sent to Moscow on leave from Brest for this purpose."[61]

Later, Soviet press accounts mentioned that demobilized forces would be especially needed in the coal-mining and timber industries as well as agriculture.[62]

Yet demographic considerations did not necessitate the troop reductions of 1953–55. The growth rate of the workforce was declining, and the amount of

60. Bulganin's remarks are quoted and analyzed in several reports from the British embassy in Moscow from August 1955, in Foreign Office records, FO 371/113453–118673, 1955 General Correspondence: Political, File 116729, Folder NS1202/19, Public Record Office, London [hereafter PRO].

61. Report from Moscow Embassy, 13 August 1955, Foreign Office records, Foreign Office, FO 371/113453–118673, 1955 General Correspondence: Political, File 116729, Folder NS1202/11, PRO.

62. [Lt. Gen.] Kuleshov, "To Peaceful Labor," Pravda, 12 November 1955, quoted along with several other contemporaneous press accounts in Foreign Office records, FO 371/113453–118673, 1955 General Correspondence: Political, File 116729, Folder NS1202/23, PRO.

Table 5. Average Annual Growth of Workforce, 1946–58

Year	Percent Growth
1946–50	11.45
1951–53	8.67
1954–58	4.70

Source: Jutta Tiedtke, *Abrüstung in der Sowjetunion: Wirtschaftliche Bedingungen und soziale Folgen der Truppenreduzierung von 1960* (Frankfurt am Main, 1985), 77.

new entrants to the workforce each year was decreasing in absolute terms (see Tables 5 and 6). But the crunch was still a couple of years away (1957–58), and there were numerous other means to increase the workforce besides demobilizing soldiers. In 1955, for example, most of the political prisoners from Stalin's labor camps were released to rejoin the workforce.[63] If the Soviet leaders had wanted to maintain the army at its present size, they could have increased the workforce further by providing incentives to bring more women and students into it—as they did later—and they could have refrained from initiatives such as those undertaken in 1956 to shorten the workweek (although this was justified on the grounds of increasing labor productivity).[64] Finally, they could have made more use of soldiers in the civilian economy without demobilizing them, through the practice of *shefstvo* (lending soldiers to local industrial and agricultural enterprises), as they resumed doing in 1957.[65]

The decision to demobilize an additional 1,200,000 troops starting in mid-1956 was evidently linked to the targets of the new (sixth) Five-Year Plan (1956–60). According to one British government analysis, the demobilized soldiers were expected to make up for shortfalls in the nonstate (mainly, collective farm) sectors of the economy, either by returning to collective farms or by contributing to an increase in labor at state-owned enterprises.[66]

If the political leaders intended the demobilizations to serve as a "quick fix" for Soviet economic deficiencies, they were surely disappointed. Archival materials reveal that the demobilized soldiers and officers frequently did not receive a warm welcome or much support from the communities supposedly in need of their labor. The military leadership had already called attention to this problem in 1956.[67] In May 1957, the Party leaders instructed the

63. Alec Nove, *An Economic History of the U.S.S.R.*, 2d ed. (London, 1989), 319.
64. Ibid., 339.
65. R. Kolkowicz, *The Use of Soviet Military Labor in the Civilian Economy: A Study of Military "Shefstvo,"* Rand Corporation Memorandum RM-3360-PR (Santa Monica, Calif., 1962).
66. Report to Brig. C. H. Tarver of the War Office, 1 August 1957, in the records of the Foreign Office, FO 371/124918–131174, 1957 General Correspondence: Political, File 129055, Folder NS 1192/8, PRO.
67. "Zapiska I. Koneva i A. Zheltova."

Table 6. Increase in New Entrants to Workforce

Year	Increase (in millions)
1953	2.6
1954	2.5
1955	2.4
1956	2.1
1957	1.8
1958	0.8
1959	0.3
1960	0.3

Source: Tiedtke, Abrüstung in der Sowjetunion, 79.

Central Committee and the Defense Ministry to address the issue of demobilization by means of a letter to local party organizations, military units, and ministries. In August 1957, the Central Committee distributed nine thousand copies of the "closed letter."[68]

The letter makes perfunctory reference to the "great joy" and "fatherly concern" with which the Soviet people welcome the demobilized soldiers. It points out, however, that some of the soldiers "have experienced difficulties" in adjusting to civilian life and "don't everywhere meet with the necessary concern and attention from local party and soviet organizations and the leaders of enterprises and institutions." In some of the larger towns and industrial centers, demobilized military personnel often found themselves without jobs or places to live and in poor material circumstances. The Central Committee called on local political and economic authorities to provide work for the ex-soldiers "no later than a month" after their arrival and "not at a lower level than the work they did before being called to military service."[69]

The letter points out that dealing with the demobilized soldiers in the large cities in the European parts of the USSR is particularly difficult because "there are already people looking for work as a result of the reduction of the state apparatus and also young men and women finishing school." It advocates sending the ex-soldiers to areas of labor shortage: "In the interests of the state it is necessary by every means to support the patriotic striving of demobilized soldiers to go to the new construction areas of the eastern and northern regions of the country, to mines and virgin lands." It encourages soldiers who originally came from rural areas to return there rather than move to the cities.[70]

Possible economic motives for the January 1958 reduction of three hundred thousand troops are not difficult to identify. As Table 6 indicates, the year

68. The letter and supporting material are found in fond 4, opis' 16, ed. khr. 318, Materialy k protokolu No. 45 zasedaniia Sekretariata TsK KPSS ot 2 Avgusta 1957 g., 20th convocation of the Central Committee Secretariat, KPSS, TsK, No. p93/1u, TsKhSD. The initial decision was taken by the Presidium at its 93rd session, 4 May 1957.
69. Ibid.
70. Ibid.

1958 saw a decline of one million in the pool of new entrants to the workforce, the most dramatic shortfall of the decade.

The economic motivations for the 1960 demobilization are thoroughly explored in a study by Jutta Tiedtke.[71] She links the troop reductions to shortfalls in the Seven-Year Plan (1959–65), especially in the newly developing industrial and agricultural regions in the Far East and Kazakhstan. According to Tiedtke, Soviet planners were well aware of the forthcoming slowdown in the growth of the labor pool—a consequence of the low birth rate during the war (see Tables 5 and 6). They originally expected to compensate for it by increasing labor productivity mainly through advanced technology and mechanization in agriculture—the much-touted switch from "extensive" to "intensive" development. Labor productivity failed to increase as expected, however, and key plan indicators went unmet. At the same time, the drive to expand agricultural and industrial production east of the Urals was not attracting the necessary numbers of workers, owing mainly to insufficient material incentives and poor quality of life. As Tiedtke explains it, the troop demobilization promised to solve both problems at once: An influx of new workers would help fulfill the plan, albeit by traditional extensive methods. A major recruitment and propaganda campaign would draw the new workers to the developing areas where they were most needed. Moreover, the discipline and *esprit de corps* associated with the newly released soldiers, in addition to their proven ability to tolerate relatively harsh living conditions, would make them ideal migrants to the new regions. The archival evidence that has become available since the publication of Tiedtke's book supports much of her argument.[72]

Economic concerns certainly influenced Khrushchev's decisions to reduce Soviet troop strength. They also played an important role in the decision to withdraw forces from Eastern Europe as part of the demobilization campaigns, and contributed as well to his interest in proposals such as the Eden and Rapacki Plans.[73] Both in his memoir accounts and in his son's recollection Khrushchev frequently stressed the high cost of maintaining troops abroad compared to keeping them at home.[74]

In acknowledging the important economic motives behind the troop reductions, one should not, however, neglect the other goals of Khrushchev's initiatives—in particular his desire to influence Western policy and improve the international atmosphere.

71. Tiedtke, *Abrüstung in der Sowjetunion*.
72. Documents reveal that the Party and the Soviet government issued numerous directives between December 1959 and March 1960 intended to promote migration of demobilized soldiers to areas of labor shortage. The directives are mentioned in a Defense Ministry report by R. Malinovskii and F. Golikov to the main military commands and districts, 2 April 1960. A copy of the report has been deposited at the National Security Archive.
73. For details on the troops withdrawn from various Warsaw Pact countries as part of the demobilizations, see the materials published in *Voennye arkhivy Rossii*, 1993, no. 1:271–309.
74. Khrushchev, "Nikita Khrushchev i voennoe stroitel'stvo," 39.

U.S. Behavior

It is now apparent that Khrushchev did not view the reductions merely as a means to modernize the Soviet armed forces. Such a limited objective would hardly seem worth the risk of alienating important segments of the military. In addition to his economic motives, Khrushchev does appear to have hoped that the United States would view the reductions as a concession that would improve the prospects for wide-ranging disarmament agreements. In his memoirs, Khrushchev justified the cuts by associating them with his broader disarmament proposals: "to fight for disarmament or arms reductions at the time the Soviet Union had such an enormous army—no one would believe it."[75]

Soviet disarmament diplomacy stressed the importance of the unilateral reductions. In January 1958, following the previous month's announcement of a cut of three hundred thousand troops, Bulganin sent a sixteen-page letter to President Eisenhower. He urged Eisenhower to recognize the USSR's "good intentions" as witnessed by the "reduction in recent years by almost 2 million of the strength of the armed forces of the Soviet Union, including more than 50 thousand Soviet troops in the German Democratic Republic." He promised that the current round of cuts would include withdrawal of more than 41,000 troops from East Germany and 17,000 from Hungary.[76] Archival documents indicate that these forces were, in fact, withdrawn.[77] Bulganin argued that "if the Western powers would make similar steps, then that would be a big contribution to the beginning of the liquidation of the 'cold war,'" to the reduction of the armed forces of all countries, and to disarmament.[78] Khrushchev, in his personal memorandum to the his colleagues of 8 December 1959, specifically argues that the announcement of a unilateral troop reduction should be made in time to create a favorable impression at forthcoming disarmament talks, to demonstrate peaceful Soviet intentions, and to encourage reciprocation by the West.[79]

Given the importance of the West, and the United States, in particular, to Soviet considerations, a number of questions arise: To what extent did the Soviet reductions represent a reaction to U.S. policy? In particular, did the United States induce Soviet restraint by pursuing a policy of "negotiation

75. Khrushchev, transcript of tape-recorded reminiscences, 403–404.
76. Bulganin to Eisenhower, 8 January 1958, in AVP, fond: Ref. po SShA, op. 44, por. 20, papka 89, Otdel stran Ameriki, 102-ssha, "Exchange of correspondence between Bulganin, N. S. Khrushchev, and D. Eisenhower, 8 January–2 June 1958" [in Russian].
77. "Zapiska R. Malinovskogo i V. Sokolovskogo v TsK KPSS s predlozheniiami po dal'neishemu sokrashcheniiu Vooruzhennnykh Sil SSSR, 3 ianvaria 1956 [*sic*: 1958] g.," *Voennye arkhivy Rossii*, 1993, no. 1:297.
78. Bulganin to Eisenhower, 8 January 1958.
79. Zubok, "Khrushchev's 1960 Troop Cut," 419. In a similar fashion, senior Soviet diplomats, as well as military officials, sought to convey to the West that the troop reductions demonstrated the USSR's peaceful intentions. See, e.g., Marshal Malinovskii's comments to journalists, quoted at length in Golubovich, *Marshal Malinovskii*, esp. 218–219.

from strength," or did the United States encourage Soviet moderation by reducing its own military threat to the USSR? Did Western reactions to the Soviet initiatives play any role in determining whether Khrushchev would be able to continue his policy of restraining military growth? The picture is somewhat mixed.

Negotiation from Strength. A consideration of the overall context of Soviet military policy at the time provides some background for understanding the interaction of U.S. and Soviet behavior. The death of Stalin in March 1953 left his successors to deal with a number of pressing issues in the military sphere. During the next couple of years the Soviet leadership faced crucial decisions, for example, concerning the character and scope of the strategic nuclear weapons program. Khrushchev and his allies appear to have wanted to use a disarmament agreement as a substitute for expensive new weapons that would undercut his domestic economic plans.

In the mid-1950s Khrushchev seems to have been motivated by both a sense of confidence in Soviet military capabilities and a foreboding about ominous developments in Western policy. In the nuclear sphere, Khrushchev apparently felt some relief that the USSR had finally matched the United States in the development of a hydrogen bomb. In August 1953, the Soviets had tested their first nuclear weapon that involved thermonuclear reactions, but they had not yet developed a true "superbomb," capable in principle of unlimited explosive force. Only in November 1955 did the USSR test such a weapon, with a yield of 1.6 megatons. The United States, by contrast, had already tested a 10-megaton device in October 1952, and a 15-megaton bomb in February 1954. On the one hand, the Soviets were encouraged by the imminent approach of some rudimentary form of strategic parity; on the other, they were concerned that the U.S. advantage in nuclear technology would nevertheless persist and perhaps increase.[80]

In August 1955, Harold Stassen, President Eisenhower's special assistant for disarmament, argued at a meeting of the National Security Council that the premise of his work "was that the Soviets would be more amenable during the period when they had, and knew that they had, a lesser power position, than they would be later." The president replied that "he assumed that what was intended here was the same thing that we meant when we talked about negotiation from strength," and he seemed to express his approval of the approach.[81]

---

80. David Holloway, *Stalin and the Bomb: The Soviet Union and Atomic Energy, 1939–1956* (New Haven, Conn., 1994). Chapter 15 deals with the foreign policy of Stalin's successors, under the shadow of the nuclear arms race.

81. Harold Stassen, memorandum, 5 August 1955, "Discussion at the 257th Meeting of the National Security Council, Thursday, August 4, 1955," DDEL, Ann Whitman File [NLE case 78–145 #19], p. 5.

It does seem that one of the motives for the initial Soviet interest in disarmament and in a general relaxation in tensions was the prospect of a deteriorating military balance and especially concern about the evolving military situation in Europe. In a speech delivered in February 1955, three months before the USSR presented its UN disarmament plan, Marshal Zhukov, the Soviet defense minister, called attention to worrisome developments there. He expressed particular concern over the rearmament of West Germany and its entry into NATO, over the deployment of U.S. tactical nuclear weapons with NATO forces, and over the expansion of U.S. military bases.[82]

Viacheslav Molotov, the foreign minister, also followed developments in the West's military policy in considerable detail. The Soviet embassy in Washington, for example, sent quarterly and annual reports back to Moscow with extensive information on trends in U.S. economic and military power. In one report from February 1955, Molotov underlined in red pencil the sections describing the nuclearization of U.S. army units, including discussion of the new tactical nuclear systems, such as the "atomic cannon," being introduced.[83] Some analysts believe that the Soviets sought specifically to trade their numerical strength in conventional forces for the growing U.S. advantages in tactical nuclear weaponry, and to weaken the drive for German rearmament by unilateral concessions.[84]

Khrushchev was actually quite candid about using unilateral measures of restraint to undermine NATO by reducing the perception of a Soviet threat. As the Soviet leader explained to the Danish prime minister when he visited Moscow in March 1956, "NATO was created as a result of a big military psychosis, when some people painted the Soviet Union in a very unfavorable militarist light before the peoples of the European countries. On our side we also gave a pretext for that." Now, he argued, as a result of reducing the Soviet army, "we have already proved rather convincingly our peacefulness, and will prove it further. That way we will loosen up NATO. We will proceed unilaterally to reduce the armed forces so that everyone will see our peacefulness, and then it would be hard for you to preserve NATO in the face of public opinion."[85]

There is little doubt that some of Khrushchev's initiatives were intended to

82. "Rech' tovarishcha G.K. Zhukova," *Krasnaia zvezda*, 21 February 1955.
83. "Politicheskii otchet posol'stva SSSR v SShA za 1954 god," written on 25 February 1955, sent to Molotov (this is his copy), received and classified "top secret," 3 March 1955. AVP, fond: Ref. po SShA, op. 38, por. 15, papka 276, The discussion of NATO military developments on 42–49 and 107.
84. Bloomfield et al., *Khrushchev and the Arms Race*, esp. 85–86.
85. "Zapis besedy Bulganina, Khrushcheva, Mikoiana, Molotova, s prem'er-ministrom i ministrom inostrannykh del Danii Khansenom," TsKhSD, fond 5, op. 30, d. 163, p. 33, quoted in Vladislav Zubok, "Khrushchev and the Divided Germany, 1953–1964," paper presented at the Khrushchev centenary conference, Brown University, 1–3 December 1994, 18–19. I have revised the translation somewhat. On a May 1997 visit to this archive I discovered that this file (*delo*) and many others have been reclassified secret and are now unavailable to researchers.

induce the United States to restrain its military programs so that he in turn could curb Soviet military expenditures. Indeed, that is one of the purposes of pursuing arms agreements. New U.S. weapons might have served as bargaining chips to achieve further Soviet concessions if the Pentagon had been willing to give them up. Does that mean we can attribute Soviet moderation to a U.S. policy of negotiation from strength?

There are two problems with the negotiation-from-strength interpretation. First, in the realm where the Soviets made the greatest concessions—troop reductions and a willingness to reduce in a disarmament agreement down to an equal level to the United States—they were the ones negotiating from strength. U.S. conventional forces were always fewer than Soviet ones. It is reasonable, however, to consider that the Soviets were influenced by other aspects of Western military programs that did represent "strength"—nuclearization of NATO ground and air forces, plans for rearmament of West Germany, U.S. strategic nuclear superiority.

The second problem with the negotiation-from-strength explanation, however, is that the United States was not pursuing that policy. Although U.S. policymakers, including the president and secretary of state, made reference to Soviet weakness and U.S. negotiation from strength—for example, in the weeks preceding the Geneva summit of July 1955—the United States was not prepared to take advantage of Soviet concessions in order to come to an agreement. Furthermore, such talk of U.S. negotiation from strength appears to have hardened Soviet positions in the disarmament talks.[86] As one of Khrushchev's aides observed: "Khrushchev, as the prime mover of the policy of relaxation of international tensions, was finding himself in political difficulties for not being able to show anything for all the moves he had initiated to meet the Western position. Such hard-liners in the leadership group as Vyacheslav Molotov were insisting that Khrushchev was giving away the whole game to Washington. On one occasion I heard him say that naiveté in foreign policy is tantamount to a crime."[87]

Finally, archival documents from the Eisenhower period indicate that the U.S. government—divided internally, but dominated by opponents of arms control—was not at this point interested in a negotiated outcome.[88]

Conciliation and Reciprocity. What about the alternative explanation—that U.S. concessions induced Soviet moderation? If we look at certain U.S. military programs, we could get a superficial impression that U.S. *weakness*, or, let us say, restraint, encouraged the Soviets to adopt restraint themselves. If we consider, for example, the area of conventional forces, we see that reductions

86. Coral Bell, *Negotiation from Strength: A Study in the Politics of Power* (London, 1962), 116–121.
87. Troyanovsky, "Nikita Khrushchev," 8–9.
88. Evangelista, "Cooperation Theory and Disarmament."

Table 7. U.S. Military Personnel in Europe, 1950–64

Year	Personnel (thousands)
1950	145
1951	346
1952	405
1953	427
1954	404
1955	405
1956	398
1957	393
1958	380
1959	380
1960	379
1961	417
1962	416
1963	380
1964	374

Source: Richard D. Lawrence and Jeffrey Record, *U.S. Force Structure in NATO: An Alternative* (Washington, D.C., 1974), 93.

in U.S.—and British—forces actually preceded the "unilateral" Soviet reductions announced in 1955 (although perhaps not the unannounced reductions of the previous two years). In this sense calling the Soviet cuts "unilateral" is a misnomer. During 1954 U.S. Army personnel was reduced by 150,000, from 1,480,000 to 1,330,000 and the Marines were cut by 23,000 to a force of 220,000. By the fall of 1956 the U.S. Army was down to 1,000,000 and the Marines about 200,000.[89] Overall, from the time Eisenhower took office in 1953 until the beginning of the Kennedy administration in 1961, Army personnel declined from 1,533,000 to 856,000.[90]

Yet, initial appearances in this case are deceiving. The United States in 1953, when the Eisenhower administration came into office, was still at war in Korea. Much of the reduction in 1954 actually represents demobilization of troops involved in the war, following the armistice the previous year. If we look at the area of apparently greatest concern to the Soviets—deployment of U.S. troops in Europe—the decline is much less dramatic (Table 7). The minor U.S. reductions in Europe did, however, coincide with decisions of several NATO allies—on domestic economic and political grounds—to pare down the ambitious plans for a conventional buildup (the so-called Lisbon force goals). But they also coincided with plans for the creation of a 500,000-

89. Samuel P. Huntington, *The Common Defense: Strategic Programs in National Politics* (New York, 1961, paperback ed., 1966), 79.
90. Bell, *Negotiation from Strength*, 138.

strong *Bundeswehr* and the nuclearization of NATO forces—prospects that the Soviet viewed with trepidation.[91]

From a strictly military standpoint, these developments were not likely to have convinced the Soviets unambiguously that the threat from the West had declined sufficiently to reduce their own forces. Yet Soviet leaders were clearly aware of U.S. developments. Reports from the Soviet embassy in Washington to the Foreign Ministry in 1954 reported a reduction in the U.S. Army of two hundred thousand troops scheduled to be completed by the beginning of 1955, with further reductions down to a total military force of 2.85 million toward the middle of 1956. They also noted the *growth* of personnel in the air force by some 50,000, with a goal of 975,000 by mid-1956. They reported that NATO armed forces consisted of one hundred divisions, half of which were combat ready, and gave details—largely culled from the *New York Times*—of the alliance's plans to expand its ground and air forces and its system of air bases. Foreign Minister Molotov underlined several of these points in red, including the argument that the U.S. conventional-force reductions would not harm combat effectiveness because they came mainly from service and administrative units and because the troops were receiving nuclear weapons.[92]

Molotov was never a proponent of Soviet moderation.[93] He was particularly drawn to the report's conclusion that the United States "is not interested in solving the problem of atomic weapons by agreement with the USSR" (underlined in red) and that one should not expect any improvement in U.S.-Soviet relations any time soon (marked twice with red).[94] Other leaders could, however, have used information about the reduction of the U.S. armed forces—even if they were just routine adjustments to the end of the Korean War—to argue for similar Soviet measures.

Other events, however, do seem to have convinced at least some of the Soviet leadership that the international environment was not as threatening in the mid-1950s as it had been a few years earlier. The end of the Korean War in 1953, the willingness of Western leaders to meet the new Soviet leadership in Geneva in 1955, the Western decision to take into account Soviet security concerns by guaranteeing Austrian neutrality in the 1955 settlement, all combined with the Soviet achievement of a rudimentary thermonuclear capability, made Khrushchev and some of his colleagues willing to risk some unilateral gestures of restraint.[95]

91. Robert E. Osgood, *NATO: The Entangling Alliance* (Chicago, 1962), chap. 4.
92. "Politicheskii otchet posol'stva SSSR v SShA za 1954 god," 42–49, 107. For the details of NATO's planned expansion, see the first quarterly report for 1954, drafted by Anatolii Dobrynin, in AVP, Ref. po SShA, op. 38, por. 14, papka 276, 15 April 1954, 25–26.
93. F. Chuev, *Sto sorok besed s Molotovym* (Moscow, 1991); Troyanovsky, "Nikita Khrushchev."
94. "Politicheskii otchet posol'stva SSSR v SShA za 1954 god," 92.
95. James Richter, *Khrushchev's Double Bind: International Pressures and Domestic Coalition Politics* (Baltimore, Md., 1994), esp. 68–73; Troyanovsky, "Nikita Khrushchev."

COULD U.S. POLICY HAVE HELPED KHRUSHCHEV?

Unfortunately, however, Western policy did not encourage the continuation of such restraint. Military and political leaders did not represent the reduction in Western conventional forces in the 1950s as an inducement or a reciprocation for Soviet gestures. Rather, they stressed the arming of the remaining forces with nuclear weapons, which, they boasted, would provide "more bang for the buck." Khrushchev later adopted a similar tack in justifying Soviet reductions. This approach was counterproductive for both sides, since it portrayed the cutbacks as a function of military expediency rather than as gestures of restraint. Later, during the Kennedy administration, U.S. policy explicitly favored a conventional-force buildup (in addition to a nuclear one), at a time when Khrushchev was pushing for increasingly radical reforms and reductions in Soviet forces.

The Eisenhower Years

During the second half of the 1950s both the United States and Britain were intent on minimizing the significance of the Soviet troop reductions. Following the August 1955 reductions, for example, officials at the British Foreign Office expressed concern that the Soviets would seek a quid pro quo at the upcoming UN disarmament negotiations: "The answer to any tactic of this kind should be that the Western powers demobilised their troops in 1945, and that many of the men since recalled as the result of the Korean War have already been released without any fuss."[96] In the United States, Harold Stassen's staff proposed a similar response to potential Soviet initiatives to reduce conventional forces: The United States should point out that its troops had already demobilized after World War II, had maintained an army of only a half million men until the Korean War broke out, and—unlike the USSR—made public the annual size of its armed forces: "This record demonstrates the willingness of the United States to reduce arms when circumstances are propitious for world peace."[97]

In the wake of the Soviet announcement in May 1956, Stassen prepared a position paper for President Eisenhower and relevant departments and agencies with his suggestions for responses to the Soviet initiatives. Some of the responses Stassen proposed were cautiously positive and intended to encourage further progress in arms control, but ultimately only the negative recommendations found expression in U.S. policy. Stassen suggested, for ex-

96. Comments on cover of Folder NS 1202/9, File 116729, in FO 371/113453–118673, 1955 General Correspondence: Political, Public Record Office, London.

97. Position Paper on Probable Soviet Positions and Proposed US Responses, Special Staff Study for the President—NSC Action No. 1328, DCS/12-R.1, 29 February 1956, White House Office, Office of the Special Assistant for Disarmament (Harold Stassen): Records, 1955–58, Box 3: DCS Position Papers (8), p. 4, DDEL.

ample, that the United States should both welcome the Soviet gesture and press for acceptance of preferred U.S. arms control measures—mainly concerning aerial inspection. He also recommended that if the Soviet reduction were substantial, the United States should review its own force levels and military aid to its allies, but he did not request the president to approve such measures at the time.

Stassen's suggestions for positive responses were overshadowed by recommendations for how to prevent the USSR from gaining a propaganda coup for its initiative. In particular, he sought to "deflate any exaggerated Soviet claims" about "the true extent and real significance" of the reductions and "to minimize [the] impression that [the] reduction is solely motivated by [a] Soviet desire to reduce tension." He went so far as to argue that in the nuclear age it was more dangerous to have small armies than large ones if that meant that the demobilized soldiers were at work building nuclear weapons, missiles, and bombers.[98] This line of argument was taken up by Secretary of State Dulles as well. At a press conference the day after the Soviet announcement of reductions Dulles consistently deprecated the Soviet initiative as insignificant. When one exasperated reporter suggested that Dulles would prefer that the Soviets not demobilize their soldiers, he answered that in fact he would "rather have them standing around doing guard duty than making atomic bombs." Some analysts have described this response as indicating Dulles's inherent distrust of Soviet motives and have contrasted it to Stassen's more positive reception.[99] It seems, however, that this too-clever dismissal of the Soviet initiative originated with Stassen himself.

Six weeks after the announcement of the reductions, Stassen did try to take advantage of the Soviet initiative to promote his disarmament proposals to the president.[100] By this time, however, it was too late. The administration had already dismissed the Soviet gesture as a propaganda stunt—an action not likely to encourage further Soviet moderation or even indicate any serious U.S. interest in negotiations.[101]

Western policymakers appear not to have taken into consideration that

98. Stassen to Eisenhower and departments and agencies concerned, memorandum, 14 May 1956, "Recommended Guidelines for Anticipation of and Response to Probable Soviet Reduction of Armed Force Levels," White House Office, Office of the Special Assistant for Disarmament (Harold Stassen): Records, 1955–58, Box 1: D[isarmament] P[roblems] C[ommittee] Notes [64–99] (1), p. 3, DDEL.

99. Ole R. Holsti, "Cognitive Dynamics and Images of the Enemy: Dulles and Russia," in David J. Finlay, Ole R. Holsti, and Richard R. Fagen, *Enemies in Politics* (Chicago, 1967), 61–62.

100. Stassen to Eisenhower, memorandum, 29 June 1956, Subject: Report Pursuant to NSC Action 1553, White House Office, Office of the Staff Secretary: Records, 1952–61, Subject Series, Alphabetical Subseries, Box 11: Disarmament [vol. 1] (7), DDEL.

101. See, for example, the background press statement prepared by the President's Special Committee on Disarmament Problems, Joseph S. Toner, executive secretary, in response to the May 1956 announcement, in Office of the Staff Secretary, Subject Series, Alphabetical Subseries, Box 11, Folder: "Disarmament [vol. 1] (6) [May–June 1956]," DDEL.

their countries' behavior could have any influence on the continuation of Soviet restraint. In particular, they found it hard to believe that the Soviets could
perceive a threat from the West, the alleviation of which would induce them
to reduce their own military efforts. In July 1955, Secretary Dulles, for example, reported to the National Security Council his conviction that the Soviets were not concerned about Western military plans. His evidence? At the
summit meeting earlier that month, according to Dulles, members of the U.S.
delegation had tried unsuccessfully to get the Soviet representatives to explain their concern about possible German reunification—"did they fear the
twelve German divisions now planned, or did they fear NATO armies on a
Soviet frontier?" The U.S. representatives evidently told their Soviet counterparts "that the West was prepared to reassure the Soviets if they were fearful
of German aggression or the revival of German militarism." When the Soviets declined to pursue the issue, Dulles "concluded that the Russians did not
really fear German rearmament or German military power," but were concerned mainly about the effect that the loss of East Germany would have on
the remaining communist regimes in the Soviet bloc.[102] Following the first
publicly announced Soviet troop reductions in August 1955, Dulles stated in
a press conference that the Soviet action demonstrated the USSR's recognition that the United States would not be an aggressor.[103] Thus, Dulles and
other Western policymakers indicated that they did not think concessions on
German rearmament or U.S. military programs would contribute to further
Soviet restraint.

Ironically, many of the policies that President Eisenhower—if not his administration—favored could have supported Khrushchev's efforts. It is generally agreed now that, especially in comparison with his immediate predecessor and successors, Khrushchev advocated a relatively modest nuclear
force as well as sharply reduced conventional forces. On the requirements for
nuclear missiles Khrushchev expressed his opinion in typically colorful fashion: "Missiles are not cucumbers, one cannot eat them and one does not
require more than a certain number in order to ward off an attack."[104]
Eisenhower, who oversaw an unprecedented buildup of nuclear weapons
production facilities, weapons, and delivery vehicles, seems at times to have
been inclined toward notions of "minimum deterrence" compatible with
Khrushchev's—and sometimes expressed with equal color: In August 1955,
he told the members of his National Security Council that "he thought we
should develop a few of these missiles as a threat, but not 1000 or more . . . if
the Russians can fire 1000 a day at us and we can fire 1000 a day at them, then

---

102. Memorandum, 29 July 1955, "Discussion at the 256th Meeting of the National Security
Council, Thursday, July 28, 1955," Ann Whitman File, DDEL, pp. 4–5.

103. Press conference, 16 August 1955.

104. N. S. Khrushchev, *Pravda*, 29 May 1960. Sergei Khrushchev provides similar evidence of
his father's views in "Nikita Khrushchev i voennoe stroitel'stvo"; and throughout *Krizisy i
rakety*, e.g., 1:358, 2:173, 426, 458.

he personally would want to take off for the Argentine."[105] The Soviet leaders made comparable statements about the suicidal consequences of using nuclear weapons.

Concerning conventional forces, there seems to have been considerable similarity in the positions of Khrushchev and Eisenhower. Toward the end of his tenure in office, the Soviet leader became increasingly critical of large ground forces. In September 1964 he abolished the position of commander of ground forces, subordinating these forces directly to the General Staff, and he spoke favorably of a territorial militia system.[106] Eisenhower cut back U.S. army strength considerably, and evidently wanted to do more. In August 1959 he told General Lauris Norstad, NATO supreme commander, "that he felt there is strong reason for the United States to start pulling some of its forces out of Europe," without, as General Norstad proposed, waiting for a disarmament agreement.[107]

Eisenhower's view on zonal disarmament arrangements, such as the Eden Plan, was initially sympathetic, and he seemed to think there might be some common ground with the Soviets, especially if the Soviet plan for ground control posts could be combined with Eisenhower's preference for aerial inspection.[108] As he wrote to General Alfred Gruenther, "Anthony's proposal and mine, far from being mutually antagonistic, were intended to be complimentary [sic]."[109] Yet, as with most aspects of disarmament policy, the Eisenhower administration was sharply divided. At the Geneva summit in July 1955, Eden pressed the president privately—after Secretary Dulles left the room—to agree with the Soviets on a disarmament zone in central Europe.[110] But Dulles was skeptical. He instructed U.S. representatives not even to discuss such proposals at the UN Disarmament Subcommittee; in his view, the subject was too closely linked to political issues concerning the status of Germany and should be discussed only at the level of foreign ministers.[111] Even Dulles's skepticism paled in comparison to the resistance of Admiral

105. Memorandum, 5 August 1955, Discussion at the 257th Meeting of the National Security Council, Thursday, August 4, 1955, Eisenhower Papers, 1953–1961, Ann Whitman File, DDEL, pp. 11–12.

106. Clemens, "Soviet Disarmament Proposals"; Clemens, "The Soviet Militia"; Wolfe, *Soviet Power and Europe*, 464.

107. "Memorandum of Conference with the President, August 24, 1959," 25 August 1959, White House Office, Office of the Staff Secretary: Records, 1952–61, Box 5: NATO (2), p. 3, DDEL.

108. See, e.g., the discussions at the NSC meetings on 13 October 1955, pp. 5–11 and 22 December 1955, pp. 10–13, in memoranda dated 14 October 1955 and 23 December 1955 respectively, Ann Whitman File, DDEL.

109. Eisenhower to Gruenther, 25 July 1955, DDE Diary #11, DDEL. Thanks to Bart Bernstein for this document.

110. Memorandum of Conversation at Breakfast, 20 July 1955, Ann Whitman File, International Series, Box 1: Geneva Conference July 18–23, 1955 [#1] (3), DDEL.

111. Dulles to Lodge and Stassen, telegram, 30 August 1955, Dulles, John Foster: Papers, 1952–59, John Foster Dulles Chronological Series, Box 12: John Foster Dulles Chronological August 1955 (1), DDEL.

Radford and the military.[112] Finally, in addition to these obstacles, the Eden Plan, the Rapacki Plan, and related proposals for European disarmament zones, foundered on West German opposition: Konrad Adenauer's government feared that formal disarmament measures in central Europe would give Western sanction to the status quo of a divided Germany and Soviet occupation of Eastern Europe.[113]

Despite an apparent accord in the views of their top leaders, the United States and the USSR never came to agreement on limiting nuclear or conventional forces during the Eisenhower years.

The Kennedy Administration

Even though the actions of the Eisenhower administration were not particularly helpful in advancing Khrushchev's agenda of restraining the Soviet military, those of the Kennedy administration were even worse. Kennedy's "whiz kids" came into office with a mandate to correct what they had criticized as the deficiencies in Eisenhower's military policies: namely, inadequate attention to, and overreliance on, the nuclear deterrent. The first criticism was reflected in the spurious "missile gap" controversy and the Kennedy administration's acceleration of the Eisenhower nuclear buildup. The second was the critique of "massive retaliation" and the subsequent program for increasing conventional forces and enhancing capabilities for "flexible response" in Europe and "limited war" elsewhere.[114]

From Khrushchev's standpoint, the timing of the Kennedy military buildup could not have been worse. It is certainly plausible that a more moderate U.S. approach, one that recognized the battle that Khrushchev was waging against the Soviet "military-industrial complex," could have given the Soviet leader more time to carry out his foundering domestic reforms.[115] Of course, Khrushchev bears some of the blame himself for his aggressively blustering behavior over Suez, the Soviet invasion of Hungary, and perhaps especially his threats and ultimata over Berlin.[116] In retrospect, one can un-

112. See, especially, the memorandum of the NSC meeting on 13 October 1955, cited above.

113. Bruce to Dulles, telegram, 24 July 1957, reporting a conversation with the German ambassador to London, [MR 85–465 #5], DDEL; Harold Stassen to the Secretary of State for the President, memorandum, 7 October 1957, "Report and Recommendations," Ann Whitman File, ACW Diary Series, Administration Series, Box 35: Stassen, Harold E. 1957 (1), p. 3, DDEL; *Current Foreign Relations*, Department of State Policy Report, Issue No. 45, 12 November 1958 (originally classified "secret"), Staff Secretary Records, 1952–61, Subject Series, State Department Subseries, Folder: State Department—September 1958–January 1959 (3), pp. 5–8, DDEL.

114. For a forceful statement of this critique from a disgruntled member of the Eisenhower adminstration, see Taylor, *Uncertain Trumpet*.

115. The strongest expression of this view is Alexander Yanov, "In the Grip of the Adversarial Paradigm: The Case of Nikita Sergeevich Khrushchev in Retrospect," in Crummey, *Reform in Russia*, 156–181; for supporting argumentation about the Kennedy military buildup, Minde and Hennessey, "Reform of the Soviet Military," 182–206.

116. For an account that stresses this argument, see William Taubman, "Khrushchev and Detente: Reform in the International Context," in Crummey, *Reform in Russia*, 143–155.

derstand this behavior as part of Khrushchev's internal political maneuvering, ultimately geared toward a relaxation and demilitarization of Soviet domestic and international politics.[117] At the time, however, such actions appeared quite threatening to Kennedy administration officials, who in any case were already predisposed for political and economic reasons toward a military buildup.[118]

In his last year in office, Khrushchev revealed ever more clearly his intentions vis-à-vis the Soviet military, and he seized every opportunity to promote his program of military reform.[119] The signing of the Limited Test Ban Treaty in 1963, for example, gave Khrushchev a chance to press for further reductions of armed forces and military spending, in the wake of what he consistently sought to portray as a major improvement in the international atmosphere. By the time the Kennedy administration began to take the prospect of cooperation with Khrushchev seriously, it was too late.[120]

Transnational Inactivity and Its Consequences

The measures of unilateral disarmament undertaken by Khrushchev in the field of conventional armed forces owe little to transnational influence. Issues related to European security and conventional forces were not, however, entirely absent from transnational discussions during the Khrushchev era. Indeed, some concepts that received great attention during the Gorbachev period date to this time.

In 1957, after retiring from government service, George Kennan delivered a series of radio lectures on the BBC, some of which were later published by *Harper's* magazine and then as a book.[121] His discussions of nuclear disengagement and national defense by means of territorial militia forces received considerable attention and resemble many of the ideas that became popular in the 1980s. In Germany, during the early 1950s, Colonel Bogislaw von Bonin promoted concepts of militia-based, territorial defense intended to provide for German security without posing an offensive threat to the USSR. He was in many respects the intellectual forebear of the European peace researchers who advocated "nonoffensive defense" in the 1980s. But von Bonin's defense-dominant proposals were at odds with the prevailing plans to integrate a new

117. See, especially, Richter, *Khrushchev's Double Bind*; and Khrushchev, *Krizisy i rakety*; and his "Nikita Khrushchev i voennoe stroitel'stvo."

118. Desmond Ball, *Politics and Force Levels: The Strategic Missile Program of the Kennedy Administration* (Berkeley, 1980).

119. Matthew P. Gallagher, "Military Manpower: A Case Study," *Problems of Communism* 13, 3 (May/June 1964): 53–62; Minde and Hennessey, "Reform of the Soviet Military."

120. Glenn T. Seaborg with Benjamin S. Loeb, *Kennedy, Khrushchev, and the Test Ban* (Berkeley, Calif., 1981); Christer Jönsson, *Soviet Bargaining Behavior: The Nuclear Test Ban Case* (New York, 1979).

121. George F. Kennan, *Russia, the Atom, and the West* (New York, 1958).

German army into a NATO force structure that emphasized tanks, artillery, and offensive aircraft. Von Bonin's plans were rejected and he lost his job.[122]

Finally, the Pugwash movement spent considerable time discussing issues of European security, but it never came up with a compelling proposal around which to mobilize popular opinion—as it did during this same period with the nuclear test ban.

The striking thing about Khrushchev's troop reductions is how short-lived they were. The Brezhnev leadership reversed the personnel cuts, adding nearly a million soldiers to the armed forces, and began massive serial production of the full range of conventional weapons. Khrushchev's tentative advocacy of "minimum deterrence" was also declared a failure as Brezhnev sponsored a major expansion of Soviet nuclear capabilities. In retrospect, Khrushchev made two particularly serious mistakes that undercut his attempts at restraining the arms race. First, his reliance on nuclear deterrence and denigration of conventional forces made it easy for skeptical Western politicians to argue that the troop reductions constituted not a conciliatory gesture but a purely self-interested expedient. Second, his attempts to demonstrate that Soviet nuclear power could compensate for the neglect of conventional air, ground, and naval forces led him to exaggerate Soviet capabilities. By brandishing nuclear missiles—even ones that did not yet exist—Khrushchev expected to kill two birds with one stone: He thought he could achieve deterrence of the West on the cheap, and perhaps some diplomatic victories into the bargain; and he thought he could quiet the criticisms of the opponents of his troop reductions by stressing the preeminence of nuclear weapons. What he failed to realize is how counterproductive his missile diplomacy would be—that it would provoke a U.S. missile buildup well beyond any conception of "minimum deterrence" and that it would undermine the sincerity of his troop cuts.

A comparison to the more successful and durable troop reductions of the Gorbachev era, discussed in Chapter 14, is instructive. In that case, transnational groups promoted nonoffensive defense as a means of reducing conventional forces and enhancing security—without increasing reliance on nuclear weapons. One might speculate that if transnational actors of the 1950s had promoted an intellectual construct as attractive as nonoffensive defense they might have given Khrushchev some arguments to bolster the case for the security-enhancing benefits of his troop reductions. They might thereby have exerted a moderating influence on Khrushchev's pronuclear stance, decreasing the West's perception of a Soviet threat and improving the possibilities for some reciprocal restraint on the Western side.

122. For a discussion, see Jonathan Dean, *Meeting Gorbachev's Challenge: How to Build Down the NATO-Warsaw Pact Confrontation* (New York, 1989), 69–70.

[6]

"Hitting a Fly in Outer Space": Khrushchev and Missile Defenses

So significant was the progress of the USSR in the field of ABM that the Americans were compelled to look for the possibility of concluding a Treaty limiting antiballistic missile defenses.

—Soviet ABM designer G. V. Kisun'ko, 1990

Theoretically it's possible to shoot down a rocket, and science permits this to be done, but in my time I came forward and said that we had created antiballistic missiles that could attack a fly. Well, this was just an expression.

—Nikita Khrushchev, 1971

After Jack [Ruina]'s presentation [at a 1964 Pugwash meeting] the head of the Soviet delegation approached him and said there must have been something wrong with the translation. He explained that he actually heard the interpreter say Jack proposed to limit *defensive* weapons!

—Herbert York, 1987

The Khrushchev period, 1953–64, saw the development of the first Soviet antiballistic missile (ABM) systems and the start of a concerted effort on the part of Western scientists to convince their Soviet colleagues that an ABM race would be a bad idea. This chapter considers how well Soviet behavior can be explained on the basis of economic, military, and technological factors, the role of the United States, and the influence of transnational actors. It begins with a summary of the various criticisms of ABM that were eventually raised to advocate mutual limitations or were used later to explain U.S. and Soviet decisions to sign the ABM Treaty in 1972. It then reviews Soviet developments in ABM technology during the Khrushchev period and evaluates the effect of military requirements, U.S. programs, and economic constraints on Soviet ABM programs.

The Critique of ABM

Forswearing defense of one's country in the interest of national security is a counterintuitive idea and one that many people still find difficult to accept. Thus it is worth reviewing the arguments in favor of mutual limitations on ballistic missile defense (BMD) as they emerged during the 1960s. Two of the main arguments for restricting ABM are clearly articulated in the preamble to the 1972 ABM Treaty itself: The two parties consider "that effective measures to limit anti-ballistic missile systems would be a substantial factor curbing the race in strategic offensive arms and would lead to a decrease in the risk of outbreak of war involving nuclear weapons."[1] In the jargon of security studies, these arguments concern "arms-race stability" and "crisis stability."[2]

Deployment of ballistic missile defenses by one side was considered to stimulate procurement of offensive nuclear weapons by the opposing side, causing arms-race instability. Each side viewed its security as dependent on the deterrent effect of maintaining an ability to launch a devastating attack in retaliation for the other side's aggression. If one side attempted to weaken that retaliatory capability by deploying defenses, the other side would seek to overcome those defenses through development of further offensive measures. Thus, ABMs were considered a major factor contributing to an arms race in offensive as well as defensive weapons.

The implications of ABM for crisis stability depend on the fact that defenses were likely to be less effective against a first strike than against a ragged, retaliatory strike by the side that has been attacked first. Thus, deployment of ABMs on both sides could create the impression that the side striking first would gain a considerable advantage and that—with a combination of highly accurate and powerful offensive weapons and a moderately effective defensive system—it might even be able to prevent a devastating retaliation from the other side. In times of crisis, it was argued, when war seemed imminent, each side would feel under pressure to strike first or risk having its retaliatory forces destroyed. In the absence of defenses, when each side possessed secure, relatively invulnerable retaliatory forces, crisis stability would be bolstered. There would be less pressure for crises to escalate into war.

A third category of argument against ABM was economic. At the most basic level, ABM systems are enormously expensive, and both sides could readily perceive benefits to spending the money elsewhere. A second variant of the economic argument was related to arms-race stability. ABM systems are not considered "cost effective at the margin." Not only are they expensive,

---

1. Treaty reprinted as Appendix A in Matthew Bunn, *Foundation for the Future: The ABM Treaty and National Security* (Washington, D.C., 1990), 162.
2. The most thorough analysis of this question is the work of Charles Glaser. See, e.g., his "Why Even Good Defenses May Be Bad," *International Security* 9, 2 (Fall 1984): 92–123.

but they are more expensive for one side to build than they are for the other side to defeat by deploying more offensive forces.

Opposition to ABM also stemmed from the view that it was technologically infeasible. Again, this argument was closely related to the economic issues. Even if a relatively reliable BMD system could be built with existing technologies, the fact that it could be defeated more cheaply with existing and potential offensive technologies would mean that the level of defensive technology was never adequate. The argument was also made that even though neither side could rely on existing technology to provide ABM defenses, the technologically inferior side would be worse off if both sides tried to deploy ABMs than if neither did. This argument has been offered to account for Soviet acceptance of ABM limitations.

A final argument—again related to the previous ones—was essentially a military one. Given the state of ABM technology, the relative level of technology on each side, and the relative cost of offense versus defense, certain military requirements could be fulfilled more reliably if defenses were banned on each side. This was considered the case for an "assured destruction" requirement—the ability of one side to inflict a certain level of damage on the other side even after suffering a first strike; such a requirement would be easier to fulfill if defenses, especially of population centers, were banned. It may also be the case that a counterforce, damage-limiting strategy—one that tries to destroy as much of the opposing side's offensive military forces in order to limit the damage to one's own homeland—would be easier to carry out in the absence of defenses that protect each side's strategic weapons. Thus, the argument was often made that by accepting bilateral restrictions on ABM, the USSR enhanced its counterforce capabilities to a greater extent, or at least acquired them less expensively, than if it had pursued an unconstrained arms race in defensive and offensive systems. By the same token, when Robert McNamara, U.S. secretary of defense, embraced a damage-limitation strategy in 1962, he eschewed ABM as less cost-effective than the deployment of offensive counterforce weapons combined with nationwide civil defense shelters.

The task of this chapter, and subsequent ones on ABM debates during the Brezhnev and Gorbachev eras, is to identify which of these arguments figured in decisions on ABM development in Moscow, who made the arguments, and when. But first we must review the basic history of Soviet and U.S. ballistic missile defense programs.

"THE WORLD'S FIRST ABM SYSTEM"

Soviet interest in ballistic missile defense followed naturally from work on air defense against nuclear-armed aircraft and coincided temporally with the

[125]

development of offensive missile technology.[3] By the mid-1950s development of specific BMD technologies was under way and a test range was constructed near the village of Sary Shagan in 1956. In April 1960, U.S. intelligence analysts received their first photographs of the test site from a U-2 reconnaissance flight. Seven months later, the Soviets for the first time launched an ABM rocket against a real target—a warhead from a test-fired ballistic missile. That test failed, but a similar one conducted in March 1961 succeeded: a Soviet ABM rocket destroyed a warhead in flight. These successes prompted Nikita Khrushchev and his defense minister Rodion Malinovskii to boast about the achievements of Soviet BMD efforts, including Khrushchev's famous remark that now the Soviet Union had the capability to "hit a fly in outer space."[4]

By 1962, a system was being deployed near Leningrad that U.S. intelligence analysts considered to have potential BMD capability. During the annual parade celebrating the Bolshevik revolution in November 1963, the Soviets displayed a missile associated with the Leningrad system; it was designated "Griffon" in the West. We now know that even as the missile was paraded across Red Square, the Soviet authorities had already decided to discontinue development of the Leningrad system on technical grounds. The missile's participation in the parade was a deliberate—and successful—act of "disinformation," intended to deceive the West into thinking that Soviet ABM capabilities were more advanced than they actually were.[5]

In November 1964, less than a month after Khrushchev's removal from office, the Soviet Union displayed another missile—called "Galosh" in the West, and A-350 by its designer, P. D. Grushin—that was part of a BMD system being constructed around Moscow. The Moscow system (Soviet designation: A-35) was originally expected to consist of eight complexes with a total of 128 interceptor missiles. Work on A-35 apparently accelerated during 1966 and 1967, but only six of the eight complexes were under active con-

3. Two valuable, if partisan, primary sources on Soviet ABM development are Grigorii Vasil'evich Kisun'ko, *Sekretnaia zona: Ispoved' general'nogo konstruktora* (Moscow, 1996), a memoir by a radar specialist who was in charge of the overall ABM development project during much of the Khrushchev period; and O. V. Golubev et al., "Proshloe i nastoiashchee Rossiiskikh sistem protivoraketnoi oborony (vzgliad iznutri)" (Moscow, 1992), a history written by several ABM designers. I am grateful to Sergei Khrushchev for providing me a copy of Kisun'ko's memoir and to David Holloway for a copy of the designers' report. This section also draws on Sayre Stevens, "The Soviet BMD Program," in Ashton B. Carter and David N. Schwartz, eds., *Ballistic Missile Defense* (Washington, D.C., 1984), 182–220; Johan J. Holst, "Missile Defense, the Soviet Union, and the Arms Race," in Holst and William Schneider, Jr., eds., *Why ABM? Policy Issues in the Missile Defense Controversy* (New York, 1969), 145–186; David S. Yost, *Soviet Ballistic Missile Defense and the Western Alliance* (Cambridge, Mass., 1988), 24–29; and various declassified National Intelligence Estimates prepared by the U.S. Central Intelligence Agency and cited below.

4. Golubev et al., "Proshloe i nastoiashchee," 10–11.

5. Kisun'ko, *Sekretnaia zona*, 407. For an account of the U.S. debate on this system, see Lawrence Freedman, *U.S. Intelligence and the Soviet Strategic Threat*, 2d ed. (Princeton, N.J., 1986), 91–96.

struction. In 1968, construction on two of the six ceased, leaving a system of four complexes with a total of sixty-four missiles. U.S. intelligence believed that the system was operational by 1970 or 1971, the year Khrushchev died. In fact, the Moscow system did not achieve that status until 1977, five years after the ABM Treaty was signed.[6]

EXPLAINING SOVIET ABM DEVELOPMENTS

To what extent do the economic, political, and military factors we examine in other cases help explain development of ABM systems during the Khrushchev years? What accounts for the failure to consider limiting ABM deployments until long after Khrushchev's removal from office?

Military Requirements and U.S. Behavior

The demand for defense against ballistic missiles arose naturally in the years following World War II. Starting in 1948, Soviet research on ABM defenses was conducted at the same research institutes that developed ballistic missiles. An ABM system seemed a logical and necessary complement to the nationwide air defense system then undergoing construction. In September 1953, six months after Stalin's death, on the petition of seven top military leaders (bearing the rank of Marshal of the Soviet Union) the Communist Party Central Committee approved a proposal for pursuing a national ABM system.[7]

Much of the Soviet research into ballistic missiles and BMD was stimulated by the wartime efforts of Nazi Germany in the rocket field and the anticipation that the United States, where many of the German rocket scientists were now working, would develop such weapons. Indeed, interest in ballistic missile defense arose in the United States immediately after the war, with the initiation of two U.S. Air Force programs, Thumper and Wizard, in 1946.[8] In the mid-1950s, the U.S. Army began to explore the possibility of expanding its Nike series of air-defense missile programs to include ballistic missile defense. At that point the Army's Nike-Zeus ABM system came into competition with the Air Force's Wizard project. Soviet ABM scientists followed developments in U.S. ABM programs quite closely at the time.[9]

In 1958, the U.S. Army's program received authorization to proceed to operational development, while the Wizard program was scaled down. At the

6. Golubev et al., "Proshloe i nastoiashchee," 14, 21.
7. Kisun'ko, *Sekretnaia zona*, 292–293; Golubev et al., "Proshloe i nastoiashchee," 5–6.
8. This section follows very closely the account in David N. Schwartz, "Past and Present: The Historical Legacy," in Carter and Schwartz, *Ballistic Missile Defense*, 330–349.
9. Kisun'ko, *Sekretnaia zona*; Golubev et al., "Proshloe i nastoiashchee."

same time, the Pentagon's Advanced Research Projects Agency was established to study potential future military technologies, including BMD. Although the Army pressed for funding to deploy the Nike-Zeus system, its requests were rejected, mainly owing to technical criticism of the system from Pentagon scientists. By going directly to Congress, however, the Army managed to get funding for fiscal year 1961, but the president refused to spend it.

During the Kennedy administration Secretary of Defense McNamara continued to oppose Nike-Zeus on technical grounds. He also argued that the system was not a cost-effective means of implementing current U.S. nuclear strategy, one that at that time favored damage limitation. McNamara argued that BMD would make no sense in the absence of a nationwide civil-defense shelter program. Finally, the defense secretary and his civilian aides, particularly Jack Ruina, director of the Advanced Research Projects Agency, were able to eliminate Nike-Zeus altogether in favor of developing an advanced system called Nike-X.[10] The new system was considered much more promising technically.

As pressure built to authorize production of the Nike-X system, McNamara and his colleagues developed a new rationale to oppose ABMs. Beginning in about 1962, some civilian scientists in the Pentagon and the White House came to believe that deployment of a U.S. ABM system would stimulate increases in Soviet offensive weapons intended to compensate.[11] Academic analysts appear to have reached that conclusion somewhat earlier.[12] Once the Soviets had increased their offensive capabilities in response to a U.S. ABM system, they argued, the United States would have to improve its defenses further to provide the previous level of protection. The Soviets would again improve their offensive forces to insure their previous level of destructive capability. Thus, even a technically feasible ABM system would not gain the United States any advantage because of such arms-race instability.

By far the aspect of the American ABM debate most scrupulously followed in Soviet military circles during the Khrushchev era concerned the technical capabilities of various proposed systems and components. By contrast, the motives of American ABM opponents tended to be misrepresented or, at best, ignored. An August 1964 article in the restricted General Staff journal *Military Thought*, for example, examined the technical prospects for ballistic mis-

10. Ruina briefed President Kennedy on ABM in November 1962 in Washington just before the Thanksgiving holiday, but was interrupted when the president had to leave for Hyannis Port. Kennedy invited Ruina to join him there the next day, by which time Ruina believes the president had come to oppose ABM on technical grounds. Jack Ruina, interview by David Wright, Cambridge, Mass., 6 July 1990.

11. Jack Ruina first developed the critique of ABM in 1962 when he followed up on a half-joking remark about ABM by President Kennedy's science adviser, Jerome Wiesner. Herbert F. York, *Making Weapons, Talking Peace: A Physicist's Odyssey from Hiroshima to Geneva* (New York, 1987), 222–223; Ruina, interview.

12. See, e.g., J. David Singer, *Deterrence, Arms Control, and Disarmament: Toward a Synthesis in National Security Policy* (Lanham, Md., 1984; originally published in 1962), 131, 141–142.

sile defense in detail. The article reported that "it has openly been acknowledged in the US press that neither the US nor its allies" had yet developed an ABM system and that McNamara "once declared that the Pentagon did not have even reasonable prospects for the development of an effective antirocket defense."[13] (The article made no mention of McNamara's view of the strategic implications of ABMs, which was, in any case, still evolving.) The article cited approvingly the "exceedingly great attention" being paid by the Communist Party and Soviet government "to strengthening the defensive capabilities of our socialist motherland, including the development of effective means of combating aircraft and rockets."[14]

Soviet weapons technologists also followed the technical debates over ABM capabilities in the United States, including the dispute over Nike-X. The U.S. debates did not, however, affect Soviet commitment to building defenses at this point. Soviet political leaders did not yet acknowledge the legitimacy of concerns about arms-race stability, and many of their ABM designers never did so. The U.S. debates did, however, help highlight important technical shortcomings and challenges in Soviet ABM development.[15]

U.S. restraint on developing Nike-Zeus and ambivalence about Nike-X were interpreted in the Soviet Union during the Khrushchev years not as signaling an interest in mutual limitations on ABM but rather as realistic responses to the prevailing level of technology. This was the correct interpretation, as the broader political and strategic arguments against ABM were only beginning to gain currency within the U.S. government by the time Khrushchev was removed from office—and they had no visible impact on U.S. ABM developments or negotiating behavior.

The most authoritative document now available to researchers that reveals Soviet military views on ABM at the end of the Khrushchev period is a top-secret report prepared by Lt. Gen. P. Ivashutin, the head of military intelligence. Ivashutin commissioned the report, an overview of Soviet military views on nuclear war, for Marshal M. V. Zakharov, the former chief of the Soviet General Staff who was reappointed to that position following Khrushchev's ouster.[16] The document includes a detailed technical review of U.S. ABM programs. It reports that "U.S. military circles admit that resolution of the ABM problem is meeting colossal difficulties." The report gives a

13. [Col.] I. Zheltikov and [Col.] V. Igolkin, "Certain Tendencies in the Development of Aircraft and Antirocket Defense," *Voennaia mysl'*, 1964, no. 8:64. All citations from this journal, unless otherwise indicated, are from CIA translations available on microfiche.

14. Ibid., 64.

15. Kisun'ko, *Sekretnaia zona*, 474–475; Golubev et al., "Proshloe i nastoiashchee," 11–12.

16. Ivashutin, "Material o razvitii voennogo iskusstva v usloviiakh vedeniia raketno-iadernoi voiny po sovremennym predstavleniiam," prepared for Marshal M. V. Zakharov, with cover memorandum from Lt. Gen. P. Ivashutin, 28 August 1964. This document, from the Ministry of Defense archives, is now on deposit at the National Security Archives in Washington, D.C.

pessimistic prognosis for the capabilities of even the most advanced U.S. system, the planned Nike-X with its "Sprint" interceptor rockets, citing McNamara as its authority. The Nike-X system, which the report projected could be built toward the end of the decade, would still, however, "not solve the ABM problem."[17]

Rather than take heart from the U.S. failure to achieve reliable ballistic missile defenses, Ivashutin draws a more ominous implication—that "the most aggressively inclined military ideologues of imperialism," pessimistic about defending against Soviet rockets, would advocate instead preventive war or preemptive nuclear strikes against Soviet weapons to destroy them before they could be launched. Thus, rather than see the technical shortcomings of U.S. ABM developments as an opportunity to slacken Soviet efforts, Ivashutin finds a rationale to redouble them.[18]

Ivashutin's report contains a remarkably prescient discussion of the various countermeasures that could complicate the task of ballistic missile defense, including the use of false targets, difficult to distinguish from the actual missile warhead, radioelectronic interference, and the effect of high-altitude nuclear explosions on the ABM radar control systems.[19] Somewhat surprisingly, then, the report presents a rather upbeat picture of Soviet ABM capabilities. It cites foreign press accounts as admitting "that the Soviet Union significantly outstrips the USA in this field." It approvingly repeats an exaggerated claim—supposedly a quote from U.S. Senator Strom Thurmond—that "Russia's defense systems have achieved such a level where the Russians can destroy in the air our 'Polaris' rockets and even, possibly, our 'Minuteman' rockets. And we consider this weapon the most invulnerable." The report makes confident claims about the capabilities of various components of a Soviet ABM system, such as radars or interceptor rockets, as if they applied to the system as a whole. On radars, for example: "The Soviet Armed Forces dispose of battle complexes of various designations, including distant ones, capable of destroying practically all contemporary means of aerospace attack by the aggressor." Such optimistic but vague claims led Marshal Zakharov to fill the margins of his copy of the report with question marks and exclamation points.[20]

To the extent that military requirements and U.S. behavior drove Soviet ABM developments during the Khrushchev years, we can say the following. Soviet political and military leaders assumed that both sides would strive to develop and deploy defenses against nuclear attack. They evinced no awareness of the notion that pursuit of defenses would ultimately be counterproductive because it would stimulate an offensive arms race—a notion that,

17. Ibid., 348–349, 356–357.
18. Ibid., 348–349.
19. Ibid., 358–359, 428.
20. Ibid., 351–352.

in any case, was just emerging in the U.S. debate and had by no means achieved a consensus. The technical difficulties of the U.S. ABM programs, forthrightly admitted by McNamara's civilian science advisers, did not discourage Soviet weapons designers or military officials in their own pursuit of defenses. But alarmist claims from U.S. politicians about relative Soviet achievements probably gave Moscow's military and political leaders a false confidence about the capabilities of their own ABM system.

Economic Constraints

The prospect that building a national missile-defense system would entail enormous expense did not seem to hinder efforts at developing the relevant technology during the Khrushchev years. Designers of the Moscow ABM system, for example, received ample support from the Central Committee, which issued numerous decrees concerning development of the system. With the decrees in hand, as the designers later wrote, "it was possible to carry out the work, practically without thinking about costs."[21]

It is interesting to note that the U.S. Central Intelligence Agency, in its estimates of Soviet ABM programs at this time, also expressed little awareness of any economic constraints on Soviet progress. The limitations seemed entirely technological in nature.[22] Only in later years did the CIA's analysis reflect the economic concerns that were, by then, becoming part of the internal Soviet debate.[23]

The Transnational Scientists' Dialogue

Soviet debates about the merits of restrictions on ABM deployment were only just beginning when Khrushchev was removed from office in October 1964. Important antecedents to the transnational discussion of ABMs were already put in place during Khrushchev's tenure, however. The Communist Party leadership, for example, gave its permission for Soviet scientists to meet with Western counterparts under the auspices of Pugwash and related organizations. Some of the early meetings during which ABM was debated took place during Khrushchev's last year in office.

Scientists' Views of ABM

Aside from the specialized military press, most of the public discussions of ABM in the Soviet Union came from scientists who were participants in the

21. Golubev et al., "Proshloe i nastoiashchee," 13.

22. Central Intelligence Agency, "Soviet Military Capabilities and Policies, 1962–1967," NIE 11–4–63, 22 March 1963, p. 38.

23. Central Intelligence Agency, "Main Trends in Soviet Military Policy," NIE 11–4–65, 14 April 1965, p. 16.

international Pugwash movement. To what extent did these Soviet scientists call attention to the critique of ABM raised by their Western counterparts, and which issues did they choose to address?

Kapitsa's Curious Contradictions. The earliest comments on restricting defenses against nuclear weapons came in 1956 from Petr Kapitsa, perhaps the most internationally oriented of Soviet scientists; they were presented in response to an article by Bertrand Russell, a founder of the Pugwash movement, about the need to involve scientists in activity against the arms race.[24] Agreeing with Russell's general argument, Kapitsa proceeded to devote nearly half of his article to the issue of defense against nuclear weapons. His remarks coincided with the first public discussion of ballistic missile defense technologies in the USSR during the early years of the Soviet program,[25] although Kapitsa addressed not BMD per se but defense against nuclear weapons in general.

Unlike subsequent critiques, Kapitsa's did not emphasize the potential for an expensive offense-defense arms race (arms-race instability) or maintain that perfect defenses were impossible (the technical critique). On the contrary, he wrote that "the possibility of such a means being found cannot be denied." Indeed, Kapitsa himself had promoted the pursuit of strategic defenses to Soviet leaders Iosif Stalin and Georgii Malenkov in 1950 and to Nikita Khrushchev in 1954. Kapitsa's optimism about the technical prospects for defense against nuclear weapons contrasted sharply with the assessment of the leading figures in the Soviet atomic project who argued in 1954, in a classified report to the top leadership, that "defense against such weaponry is practically impossible."[26] As a later-generation Soviet critic of strategic defenses put it, Kapitsa's proposal for the use of high-intensity beam weapons "could now be described as an early precursor to SDI"—the equally optimistic Strategic Defense Initiative pursued by the Reagan administration in the 1980s.[27]

Thus, rather than make a technical critique of defenses, Kapitsa raised an early version—perhaps the earliest—of the crisis instability argument. Kapitsa argued that perfect defenses increase the risk of war if they are devel-

24. Peter Kapitza [Petr Kapitsa], "The Paramount Task," *New Times*, 1956, no. 39:10–11.

25. For examples of early Soviet writing on BMD, see G. I. Pokrovskii, *Science and Technology in Contemporary War*, trans. Raymond L. Garthoff (New York, 1959). This collection contains works published by Pokrovskii in 1956 and 1957.

26. I. V. Kurchatov et al., "Opasnosti atomnoi voiny i predlozhenie prezidenta Eizekhauera," Storage Center for Contemporary Documentation [Tsentr khraneniia sovremennoi dokumentatsii], fond 5, opis 30, delo 126, p. 40. This document is discussed in Yuri Smirnov and Vladislav Zubok, "Nuclear Weapons after Stalin's Death: Moscow Enters the H-Bomb Age," *Cold War International History Project Bulletin*, no. 4 (Fall 1994): 1, 14–18. I am grateful to Vlad Zubok for sharing his notes from this document with me.

27. P. L. Kapitsa, *Pis'ma o nauke, 1930–1980* (Moscow, 1989), 286–291, 294–295; Roald Sagdeev, *The Making of a Soviet Scientist* (New York, 1994), 95–96.

oped and deployed by a potentially aggressive state before others are able to do so: "If this is achieved by an aggressively-minded country, one that is sure it is protected against the consequences of nuclear weapons, it may decide more easily on unleashing atomic war." Although Kapitsa does not identify any particular country, he refers to "countries which are disposed to conduct their foreign policy 'from positions of strength,'" the slogan popularized by John Foster Dulles, President Eisenhower's secretary of state. To prevent a potential aggressor from developing perfect defenses, Kapitsa argued, future disarmament accords must "provide for obligatory exchange of information concerning experimental work" on defensive technologies.[28] Although Kapitsa's argument is not precisely the crisis-instability critique (which does not require that either side be a deliberate aggressor), he was the first to argue that deployment of defenses could contribute to the outbreak of war.

For several years after publication of Kapitsa's article, little public evidence of Soviet scientists' views of defense against nuclear weapons appeared.

The Anti-ABM Campaign Begins. Then, in 1964, several discussions about ABM took place between Soviet and Western scientists: at the Twelfth Pugwash Conference in Udaipur, India, at the end of January; at a meeting near Boston in June; and at the Thirteenth Pugwash Conference at Karlovy Vary, Czechoslovakia, in September. Articles about the meetings later appeared in the Soviet press, and they give some hint of Soviet scientists' views. So do the reminiscences of Western participants and the memoranda they wrote, recording their Soviet colleagues' remarks.

The initial reaction of the Soviet scientists to the Western analysis of ABM was, at best, skeptical. At the Twelfth Pugwash Conference, for example, Jack Ruina presented a critique of ABM, based on technical grounds, and detailing implications for arms-race stability and crisis stability. Ruina, the former Pentagon official and then professor at the Massachusetts Institute of Technology, proposed limiting ABM systems in an arms control accord.[29] The idea seemed so counterintuitive, that Mikhail Millionshchikov, the head of the Soviet delegation, asked Ruina if the interpreter had translated his remarks correctly: Did he really mean to propose limiting *defensive* weapons?[30] With the assistance of Murray Gell-Mann, Ruina prepared a written version of his remarks. After reading it, Millionshchikov told Ruina that the translation had been correct. He remarked that the paper had a peculiar logic to it, that he could see there was perhaps something to it, but that no government would survive if it told its people that it opposed building defenses.[31]

28. Kapitsa, "Paramount Task," 11.
29. Jack Ruina and Murray Gell-Mann, "Ballistic Missile Defense and the Arms Race," paper prepared for the Twelfth Pugwash Conference on Science and World Affairs, Udaipur, 27 January–1 February 1964.
30. York, *Making Weapons*, 223; Ruina, interview.
31. Ruina, interview.

That was as much as Millionshchikov and his colleagues were willing to concede to the American critique. In their public discussions of the Pugwash meetings they were even more circumspect. Articles in the Soviet press by participants in the international discussions give little indication that the Soviet scientists were persuaded by the arguments they heard. Millionshchikov, for example, as head of the Soviet Pugwash delegation from 1964, regularly published articles in both the Soviet popular and academic press following each Pugwash meeting. His report on the twelfth conference, published in the Academy of Sciences journal, made no mention whatsoever of discussions about ABM.[32] Nor did the article he published in *Izvestiia* on 2 October 1964, following the thirteenth conference.[33] Curiously, however, an article published on the same day in *Pravda*, which Millionshchikov coauthored with Lev Artsimovich and another Soviet Pugwash delegate, did mention the Western scientists' opposition to the deployment of "antirocket defense around population centers." The logic of the Western position was not spelled out, however, and the authors maintained that the proposal to provide for security "on the basis of fear" (i.e., the threat of retaliation) did not receive support at the conference.[34]

Between the twelfth and thirteenth Pugwash conferences, in June 1964, a smaller meeting of U.S. and Soviet scientists was held near Boston under the auspices of the American Academy of Arts and Sciences. The Soviet participants included Millionshchikov, L. I. Sedov, General N. A. Talenskii, V. S. Emel'ianov, and V. P. Pavlichenko.[35] Except for Sedov, all had attended the previous Pugwash meeting. Emel'ianov had written about it, without mentioning the ABM discussions.[36]

During both the large international Pugwash meetings and the smaller gatherings of only U.S. and Soviet participants the Americans deliberately set out to influence Soviet views on ABM. Before the June 1964 meeting, for example, Jeremy Stone wrote a paper called "Should the Soviet Union Procure an Urban Anti-Ballistic Missile System?"[37] He systematically developed the

32. M. D. Millionshchikov, "XII Paguoshskaiia konferentsiia," *Vestnik AN SSSR*, 1964, no. 5:104–106. The official statement from the conference did not mention the ABM discussions either. See J. Rotblat, *Scientists in the Quest for Peace: A History of the Pugwash Conferences* (Cambridge, Mass., 1972), app. 15, pp. 222–229.

33. M. D. Millionshchikov, "Nauka protiv iadernogo bezumiia: trinadtsataia Paguoshskaia konferentsiia," *Izvestiia*, 2 October 1964.

34. M. D. Millionshchikov, L. A. Artsimovich, and V. M. Khvostov, "Paguoshskii forum uchenykh," *Pravda*, 2 October 1964.

35. The U.S. participants included Donald Brennan, Paul Doty, James Fletcher, David Frisch, Henry Kissinger, George Kistiakowsky, Betty Lall, Frank Long, Isidore Rabi, Jack Ruina, Louis Sohn, Marshall Shulman, and Jerome Wiesner, not all of whom stayed through the entire eleven-day conference. See Duane Thorin, *The Pugwash Movement and U.S. Arms Policy* (New York, 1965), 8–9, citing the *Pugwash Newsletter* 2, 1 (July 1964).

36. V. Emelyanov [Emel'ianov], "Pugwash in India," *New Times*, 1964, no. 9:23–25.

37. Jeremy J. Stone, "Should the Soviet Union Procure an Urban Anti-Ballistic Missile System?" Hudson Institute Discussion Paper HI-301-DP, 15 November 1963. A revised version appeared as chapter 1 of his book, *Containing the Arms Race: Some Specific Proposals* (Cambridge, Mass., 1966).

case that Soviet security would benefit from restraint in deploying an ABM system: "The idea that it could be counterproductive, wasteful, and provocative to defend one's cities is a novel one but it must not be ignored. Defense is basically incompatible with mutual strategic deterrence and this fact must eventually be recognized." [38]

Stone recalls a rather hostile response from some of the senior Soviet scientists and military officials to his views on ABM. Trained as a mathematician, the twenty-eight-year old Stone had received his early education in arms control at the Hudson Institute under the expert tutelage of Herman Kahn and Donald Brennan. To his Soviet interlocutors, by contrast, much of the counterintuitive logic of arms control was completely unfamiliar. General Talenskii, for example, reacted to Stone's predictions of an American offensive buildup in response to a Soviet ABM with the charge that "this is an ultimatum!" [39] The reaction of most of the Soviet scientists at the meeting was more measured, but they did not rush to embrace Stone's position. The morning after the ABM discussion, Emel'ianov approached Stone and recounted a joke that he had heard from Henry Kissinger, one of the other American participants. Kissinger had told of the Texas sheriff who liked to beat up communists. When one of his victims protested that he was actually an *anti*communist, the sheriff replied, "I don't care what kind of communist you are. I hate them all." Emel'ianov told Stone he was just like that sheriff: "Missiles, anti-missiles, you hate them all." [40]

Back in Moscow writing about the Boston meeting for the Soviet weekly *New Times*, Emel'ianov remained unsympathetic to the Americans' position on ABM. His article took the form of a dialogue between himself and unnamed U.S. colleagues, and he devoted much of it to the discussions about ABM. Emel'ianov attributed the Americans' opposition to strategic defenses to their concern about excessive military spending. He mentioned none of the questions of crisis stability that had emerged in the American debate, and his only allusion to the interaction between offensive and defensive weapons also concerned military expenditures. He quotes his American interlocutor as arguing that "'if large numbers of antiballistic missiles are produced, we will have to perfect our [offensive] missiles, make them immune to anti-missiles. And if anti-missiles emerge from the laboratory stage . . . '—and here he paused, as if weighing his words—'if the whole thing is taken over by Big Business, arms spending will grow to monstrous proportions.'" [41] Emel'ianov criticizes his American counterpart not so much for the proposal to restrict defenses but for the view that deterrence by threat of nuclear retaliation is preferable to building defenses: "What do you propose," I asked, "to destroy the shield and leave the sword? That's not disarmament. What you suggest,

38. Stone, "Procure an Anti-Ballistic Missile System?" 14–15.
39. Jeremy Stone, interview by the author, 10 June 1991.
40. Jeremy Stone, interview by David Wright, Washington, D.C., 4 September 1989.
41. V. Emelyanov, "What Scientists Say," *New Times*, 1964, no. 35:9.

in effect, is to stop all work on means of defence. You will have a hard time getting other people to accept that."

Emel'ianov alludes to the technical critique of ABM by having the American scientist respond that "it's absolutely useless to produce means of defence—there is no defence against nuclear weapons." [42] As an alternative to banning ABM, Emel'ianov proposes "general and complete disarmament" as the ultimate objective and the official Soviet proposal for a minimum "nuclear umbrella" of offensive and defensive weapons as an intermediate goal. [43]

Absent the ideologically charged rhetoric about "Big Business," Emel'ianov's report of the June 1964 meeting accords fairly well with the Americans' contemporaneous account. [44] Emel'ianov did not, however, reveal the admission of his colleague, Academician Sedov, that "we can understand your arguments, but the possibilities of influencing decisions are very limited indeed." Sedov held out an intriguing suggestion, however—unreported by Emel'ianov but recorded by the Americans: "Sedov implied that if U.S. scientists were unanimous in advising against ABM deployment, the argument might be better received in Moscow. The snag, he implied, was that the Soviets knew that some of our scientists, particularly those in government, held a contrary view." [45] At this point, both the American and Soviet scientists were pessimistic that they could persuade the USSR to halt its ABM program.

Military Views

Western critics of ABM who hoped to influence Soviet policy expected to do so mainly by persuading leading scientists with access to the political leaders. It would certainly help, however, if they could also persuade some military officers to embrace the goal of an ABM ban. In other cases of transnational disarmament efforts, sympathetic military allies sometimes helped convince the political leadership of the merits of a particular proposal. In the case of the ABM debate during the Khrushchev era, a good candidate was Major General Nikolai Talenskii. Talenskii was a scholar-general, a former editor of *Military Thought*, who had retired from active service and was working as a liaison between the Ministry of Defense and the Academy of Sciences on matters of arms control and disarmament. [46] As Millionshchikov later told an American colleague who attended the general's funeral in Moscow, Talenskii was "our contact with the Defense Ministry." [47] Talenskii was an active

42. Ibid.
43. Ibid.
44. "Report on Informal Arms Control Meetings with the Soviets," American Academy of Arts and Sciences, Committee on International Studies of Arms Control, n.d. (between June 1964 and March 1965), document located by David Wright in the Academy's archives.
45. Ibid., section on "The Relation of Anti-Missile Systems to the Disarmament Process," 2.
46. Raymond L. Garthoff, "BMD and East-West Relations," in Carter and Schwartz, *Ballistic Missile Defense*, 292 n. 31.
47. Stone, interview by author.

member of the Soviet Pugwash delegation. He attended both 1964 Pugwash meetings and the intervening bilateral workshop near Boston. He would have been a valuable ally for the anti-ABM cause.

By all accounts, the Western scientists failed to bring General Talenskii over to their side. In addition to his strong reaction against Jeremy Stone's case for an ABM ban at the Boston meeting, Talenskii was outspoken in his support for a Soviet ABM system. In the autumn of 1964, he published an article for a broad international audience in which he explicitly endorsed Soviet efforts to develop ballistic missile defenses.[48] Along with Emel'ianov and the other Soviet Pugwashites, Talenskii also criticized the assumption of the American ABM opponents that mutual deterrence could serve as the foundation for stability and peace.

Talenskii's characterization of the Western critique leaves something to be desired, however. When he does tentatively concede a possible danger in ABM deployment, his argument is closer to Kapitsa's 1956 warning than to remarks he heard from his American colleagues: "If the effective anti-missile system is built by the side which adheres to an aggressive policy, a policy from positions of strength, this may well intensify the danger of an outbreak of war." He immediately adds, however, that "such a danger may also arise quite apart from the creation of any anti-missile defense." In any case, for Talenskii, the best remedy is for the "country which is a potential target for aggression" to deploy its own ABM system.[49]

Talenskii gives short shrift to several of the other critiques of ABM. He mentions briefly the excessive cost of the arms race, but without singling out ABM, and he proposes general and complete disarmament as the remedy. He describes the Western concerns about potential arms-race instability— the view that "construction of anti-missile defence systems may accelerate the arms race" by prompting the opposing side to build more offensive weapons—and he admits that "such a development is not at all ruled out." Yet he argues—prophetically, as it turned out—that a quantitative and qualitative offensive arms race could occur even in the absence of extensive ABM systems.[50]

Particularly interesting are Talenskii's remarks about counterforce. Some Western analysts would later argue that the Soviets agreed to limit ABMs in the early 1970s mainly in order to optimize their counterforce, damage-limitation capabilities.[51] Talenskii does not view counterforce as a plausible means of limiting damage to the civilian population. In his opinion, the potential victim of a counterforce attack could camouflage its retaliatory weapons, harden

48. [Maj. Gen.] N. Talensky [Talenskii], "Anti-Missile Systems and Disarmament," *International Affairs* (Moscow), 1964, no. 10:17.

49. Ibid.

50. Ibid., 18.

51. See, e.g., Stevens, "The Soviet BMD Program"; Yost, *Soviet Ballistic Missile Defense*, chap. 2; and Thomas W. Wolfe, *The SALT Experience* (Cambridge, Mass., 1979), 110–113.

them, or as a last resort, launch them on warning or under actual attack, thus thwarting the objectives of the enemy's counterforce strategy. According to Talenskii, a country intent on protecting its civilian population should defend them directly with ABMs, not count on destroying the enemy's offensive weapons in a first strike.[52] This is precisely the view that General Ivashutin expressed in his top-secret report for Marshal Zakharov.[53]

Not only does Talenskii favor ABM on strategic and moral grounds. He also admits no technical obstacles: "In our day, the human genius can do anything."[54] In this, he obviously differs from his Western interlocutors, but also from some fellow Soviet military observers as well. Numerous analyses published in the Soviet military press during the early years of the Brezhnev era—discussed in Chapter 10—were to reveal a sharp debate on the technical feasibility of ABM. There was no comparable debate at this time among military officers on the implications of ABM for arms-race or crisis stability or much concern expressed for the economic consequences of an ABM competition.

THE INFLUENCE OF THE TRANSNATIONAL SCIENTISTS

With the notable exception of Kapitsa, Western scientists expressed concerns about the destabilizing effects of ABM before their Soviet counterparts did—and long before Soviet military officials did. Western scientists deliberately sought to influence their Soviet colleagues in the expectation that they, in turn, might exert some influence on Soviet decision makers.[55] By the time Khrushchev was overthrown they still had relatively little to show for their efforts.

Official Soviet policy throughout the Khrushchev period consistently promoted the development of ABM systems. Interestingly, Khrushchev's own personal views on ABM turn out to have been rather more skeptical and certainly more sophisticated than his "fly in outer space" quip would indicate. Remarks Khrushchev made after his forced retirement in 1964 indicate, for example, that he was well aware of the technical shortcomings of ABM. In his tape-recorded reminiscences Khrushchev essentially reversed his previ-

52. Talenskii, "Anti-Missile Systems," 16.
53. Ivashutin, "Material o razvitii voennogo iskusstva," 348–349.
54. Ibid., 16.
55. The theoretical rationale for this approach was spelled out in detail by Jeremy J. Stone, *Strategic Persuasion: Arms Limitations through Dialogue* (New York, 1967). The issue of U.S. scientists as self-conscious agents of Soviet learning is a focus of David Wright's paper, "Scientists and Diplomacy in the 1960's: The Soviet American Defense Study Group," notes for a talk in Budapest, May 1990; and it was fairly explicit in the funding proposals and reports of the U.S. participants. See, e.g. Report by Chairman to Council, American Academy of Arts and Sciences Committee on International Studies of Arms Control, 11 May 1965 (from Paul Doty's personal file).

ous claims: "Well, now I consider that, if you take a rocket, it's almost invulnerable—theoretically it's possible to shoot down a rocket, and science permits this to be done, but in my time I came forward and said that we had created antiballistic missiles that could attack a fly. Well, this was just an expression. . . . I used it as a polemic, in order to sober up our opponent, [to show] that we, so to speak, also were armed with the means, means of rocket attack as well as means of defense."[56] But Khrushchev came to believe that such means could not guarantee defense against nuclear attack. "Theoretically it's possible to carry out the engagement of a rocket in space—that's to say that a rocket can destroy another rocket, if it's given a warhead. . . . But this isn't such an easy task. . . . And," he added, "the probability of [successful] attack is small. For this reason, if you launch a lot of rockets, then to destroy all the targets is not only hard, but impossible."[57]

Recent evidence suggests that Khrushchev's views were not simply the product of the hindsight he enjoyed while resting at his retirement dacha. In early 1963, the designers of the Moscow ABM system, led by G. B. Kisun'ko, prepared a film for Khrushchev demonstrating the successful interception of a missile warhead. The technique depended on "triangulation"—the use of six radars to guide each ABM interceptor to its target. Following the film, Khrushchev went up to Kisun'ko and, as the latter's colleagues recalled, said something along the following lines: "I congratulate you. You've created the world's first ABM system, and the film shows that well. But, you know, it seems to me that your system is too complicated. You remember the episode where the film shows many, many rays necessary to shoot down a single target? But what if there are a lot of them? Can't you think up something simpler?"[58] Khrushchev's remarks sent the designers back to the drawing board to work on a problem of which they were already aware. But it also foreshadowed a skepticism about the ability of defensive measures to overcome a determined attacker that would figure prominently in the decisions of Khrushchev's successors.

From whom did Khrushchev get these more realistic views about the prospects of successful ABM defense? Prime candidates include Soviet scientists who were involved in military research and development and with whom Khrushchev kept in close contact concerning advances in military technology. At one point he directed Academician M. A. Lavrent'ev to set up a council of scientific specialists to advise the government on technical matters, including presumably military ones, since Lavrent'ev had experience in the nuclear weapons field.[59] Khrushchev's son Sergei, a missile engineer, has

56. Khrushchev, transcript of tape-recorded reminiscences, Harriman Institute Library, Columbia University, 929.

57. Ibid.

58. Golubev et al., "Proshloe i nastoiashchee," 16.

59. N. Moiseev, "Zachem doroga, esli ona ne vedet k khramu?" in Iu. N. Afanas'ev, ed., *Inogo ne dano* (Moscow, 1988), 70. Brief mention of Lavrent'ev's military work is in Andrei Sakharov, *Memoirs* (New York, 1990), 160, 170.

written of his father's fascination with space and missile technology and of how he followed Soviet programs with great interest and held informal talks with weapons designers.[60] Sergei himself was in a good position to discuss technical matters of ABM defense with his father: he worked for a missile designer, V. N. Chelomei, who himself promoted an early version of space-based strategic defenses.[61]

The Soviet leader is also likely to have discussed ABM issues with Lev Artsimovich. Artsimovich admired Khrushchev for exposing Stalin's crimes and initiating the "thaw" in Soviet politics and culture, and he and his wife visited the former leader even after his forced retirement, when such actions entailed some political risk.[62] Yet, despite Artsimovich's prominent role in the Soviet Pugwash delegations, it is doubtful that the transnational discussions deserve much credit for Khrushchev's views—there was plenty of domestic expertise available on the technical shortcomings of ABM, the source of Khrushchev's misgivings about the system. On the strategic implications of an offense-defense competition, Artsimovich did not come out publicly until 1967 (see Chapter 10). Khrushchev, in any case, never articulated this critique of ABM. He never seemed to recognize that his goal of limiting the deployment of offensive missiles could be jeopardized if his public boasting about Soviet ABM capabilities ever came to fruition. Thus, the influence of transnational actors on Soviet ABM policy during the Khrushchev era was negligible.

60. Sergei Khrushchev, "Pensioner soiuznogo naznacheniia," part 3, *Ogonek*, 1988, no. 42 (October): 27; and his memoir, *Nikita Khrushchev: Krizisy i rakety*, 2 vols. (Moscow, 1994).
61. Khrushchev, *Krizisy i rakety*, 1:375, 488, 2:515–516; Kisun'ko, *Sekretnaia zona*.
62. Sergei Khrushchev, *Khrushchev on Khrushchev: An Inside Account of the Man and His Era*, ed. William Taubman (Boston, Mass. 1990), 337, 355–356.

PART III

The Brezhnev Era

[7]

Success, Stagnation, and Revival

From the beginning, we have conceived our project as part of a long-term educational effort, both for ourselves and the Soviets.

—PAUL DOTY, 1965

The ideas expressed in difficult meetings and confrontations with officials slowly had an impact on official thinking. "It's like water dripping on a stone," one Soviet official told me privately after a particularly disheartening and unpleasant meeting.

—MARY KALDOR, 1995

The "Brezhnev Era," as I characterize it, extended from Nikita Khrushchev's forced retirement in October 1964 until Mikhail Gorbachev came into office in March 1985. The first decade of the period witnessed the most impressive achievement of the transnational disarmament community—official U.S. and Soviet acceptance of the value of mutual limitations on antiballistic missile defenses and the ABM Treaty of 1972 that formalized that acceptance. By the beginning of the second decade of Brezhnev's rule—the mid-1970s—the transnational actors' successes had virtually put them out of business. Arms negotiations between the superpowers became a normal part of their relations and were handled by professional diplomats and politicians, working full-time, rather than by scientists and other amateurs.

By the end of the 1970s, however, neither side's expectations about détente had been fulfilled. The desire on the part of some Soviet leaders to use détente as an excuse for reducing Soviet military spending proved futile. Arms control, even at its most successful, had done little to restrain the arms race.[1] From the perspective of the U.S. government, attempts to use détente to impose a code of conduct on Soviet behavior in the Third World were equally discouraging.[2] Two events in December 1979 epitomized the dual disappointments of détente: the decision by the North Atlantic Treaty

1. For a strong contemporaneous statement of this view, see Alva Myrdal, *The Game of Disarmament: How the United States and Russia Run the Arms Race* (New York, 1978).

2. Raymond L. Garthoff, *Détente and Confrontation: American-Soviet Relations from Nixon to Reagan*, rev. ed. (Washington, D.C., 1994).

Organization to deploy a new generation of U.S. intermediate-range missiles in Europe, and the Soviet invasion of Afghanistan. The sharp deterioration of East-West relations inspired the transnational "amateurs" to reactivate their contacts.

TRANSNATIONALISM AND ARMS CONTROL

The Brezhnev era marked a high point in the activities of the transnational scientists movement. Pugwash convened some twenty-five conferences, workshops, and symposia in the five years between the end of Nikita Khrushchev's rule in October 1964 and the first session of the Strategic Arms Limitation Talks (SALT) in November 1969.[3] The early Brezhnev period also witnessed the most intense bilateral interchange between Soviet and U.S. scientists, as the Soviet-American Disarmament Study (SADS) group pursued the work begun during the last year of Khrushchev's tenure.[4]

From the early 1970s, Pugwash began to shift much of its activity from the realm of superpower arms control to other issues: environmental problems, economic development, food security, and, still in the area of disarmament, chemical and biological weapons.[5] Less than a decade later, however, Pugwash activists felt obliged to revive and accelerate their work on the East-West arms race, joined this time by a somewhat younger cohort, including social scientists and "peace researchers." Bilateral contacts between U.S. and Soviet scientists resumed in the early 1980s as well, and new links were forged, for example, between physicians who formed their own international movement, and between grassroots activists who sought, against formidable odds, to make common cause with Soviet-bloc counterparts. By the time Gorbachev came into office, the transnational disarmament movement was ready with a coherent set of proposals that the new Soviet leader found appealing.

The First Generation: Pugwash and SADS

The first-generation bilateral discussions between Soviet and U.S. scientists were conducted on the basis of formally similar organizational structures on each side. In the United States, Paul Doty and his colleagues had formed the Committee on International Studies of Arms Control under the auspices of the American Academy of Arts and Sciences. The Soviet participants, in turn,

3. J. Rotblat, "Appendix A, List of Pugwash Meetings, 1957–1992," *Pugwash Newsletter* 29, 4 (May 1992). For an overview of the Pugwash movement, see Metta Spencer, "'Political' Scientists," *Bulletin of the Atomic Scientists* 51, 4 (July/August 1995): 62–68.

4. On the origins of the SADS group, see Bernd W. Kubbig, "Communicators in the Cold War: The Pugwash Conferences, the U.S.-Soviet Study Group and the ABM Treaty," PRIF Reports No. 44, Peace Research Institute Frankfurt (Frankfurt am Main, 1996).

5. Rotblat, "Pugwash Meetings."

organized themselves into a USSR Academy of Sciences Commission on the Scientific Problems of Disarmament. It included the key participants in the U.S.-Soviet dialogue, such as Vasilii Emel'ianov, Lev Artsimovich, Petr Kapitsa, and Mikhail Millionshchikov.[6]

The U.S.-Soviet exchanges had barely begun when they were confronted with a major barrier. In the mid-1960s the United States undertook a serious escalation of its military activity in Vietnam. Within the Soviet Union, opponents of attempts at improving U.S.-Soviet relations and slowing the arms race seized on the U.S. intervention as evidence of aggressive intentions. They constantly used the Vietnam War to undermine efforts by their more moderate colleagues to seek rapprochement with the United States.[7] The actions of the United States in Vietnam, amplified by hawks within Soviet policymaking circles, threatened to sever the contacts that Soviet and U.S. scientists had worked so long to establish. It was one thing for Soviet scientists to participate in Pugwash conferences as the United States dropped bombs on the Soviet Union's allies in Indochina—at least the Soviet delegation could take advantage of the multinational forum to make propaganda against the U.S. actions.[8] It was another thing for the Soviet government to allow its scientists to meet privately with their U.S. counterparts to discuss arms control—tacitly indicating a willingness to disregard U.S. behavior. That the U.S. and Soviet members of the SADS group were able to overcome such an obstacle attests to their tenacity and seriousness of purpose.

There is little doubt, however, that the Vietnam War slowed down progress in the scientists' bilateral discussions of arms control. The Soviet scientists felt obliged to raise the issue before any other items on the agenda could be discussed, and clearly many of them were genuinely outraged by the U.S. behavior. Some meetings were dominated by discussion of Vietnam.[9] The Soviet scientists managed to continue meeting with their U.S. colleagues by

6. Betty Goetz Lall, "Notes on Trip to the Soviet Union, August 23–September 4, 1966," p. 3 (from Paul Doty's personal file).

7. Richard D. Anderson, Jr., *Public Politics in an Authoritarian State: Making Foreign Policy during the Brezhnev Years* (Ithaca, N.Y., 1993); James Richter, *Khrushchev's Double Bind: Domestic and International Constraints on Soviet Foreign Policy, 1953–1964* (Baltimore, Md., 1984).

8. Indeed, throughout this period the Vietnam War preoccupied the scientists involved in Pugwash, even when the subject was not on the agenda. Joseph Rotblat, *Scientists in the Quest for Peace: A History of the Pugwash Conferences* (Cambridge, Mass., 1972), 63–69.

9. R. N. Anreasian, "O vstreche Sovetskikh i inostrannykh uchastnikov Paguoshskogo dvizheniia v Parizhe, 16–18 iiunia 1967 g.," Papers of Mikhail D. Millionshchikov, f. 1713, op. 2, delo I.5.2, no. 195, Archive of the Academy of Sciences of the Russian Federation (hereafter ANRF); F. A. Long, memorandum, 30 August 1965, "Discussions with Soviet Scientists on the South Vietnam Problem, London, August 27 and 28, 1965," and G. B. Kistiakowsky, "Bipartite Meeting—Saturday Evening, August 28, 1965," 31 August 1965, both from Paul Doty's personal files. See also the following documents from the archives of the American Academy of Arts and Sciences, Committee on International Studies of Arms Control: Paul Doty, "Report of Visit of P. Doty and F. Long with Academicians Millionshchikov and Emelyanov in Moscow, June 10–11, 1965"; notes from Marshall Shulman, 29 October 1966; Frank Long, "Notes on Meeting in Moscow, May 31 and June 1, 1966"; Frank Long, "Notes on the Discussion with Millionshchikov, Tuesday, April 4, 1967"; Lall, "Notes on Trip."

trying to keep their discussions secret from opponents within the Soviet bureaucracy and by using Pugwash as an umbrella to cover the bilateral meetings. This technique sometimes backfired, however, as when Joseph Rotblat, Pugwash secretary-general, informed too many people about a forthcoming SADS meeting in July 1965, making Millionshchikov feel obliged to cancel it.[10]

As the following chapters reveal, both Pugwash and the bilateral Soviet-American workshop deserve considerable credit for substantial breakthroughs in U.S.-Soviet arms control in the late 1960s and early 1970s. Until recently the only available evaluations of the role of Pugwash came from Western participants and observers. Now with a partial opening of the Russian archives, we can get a view from the Soviet participants. In September 1972, Mikhail Millionshchikov, the chair of the Soviet Pugwash delegation, drafted a report to the ruling presidium of the Soviet Academy of Sciences in anticipation of the fifteenth anniversary of the Pugwash Movement. Millionshchikov clearly wanted to impress the Academy officials enough to encourage them to continue sponsoring the Soviet delegation. He wrote: "In fifteen years the participants of this movement have examined many important proposals having substantial significance for the resolution of problems of disarmament and the achievement of a reduction in international tensions. Several of these proposals later became subject of examination at the government level and were used in working out international agreements and treaties." Among the agreements that, in Millionshchikov's view, resulted from Pugwash proposals, he lists the nuclear nonproliferation treaty, the limited test ban treaty, international agreements banning the deployment of weapons of mass destruction on the ocean floor, the biological weapons convention, the ABM Treaty and SALT I.[11] Even accounting for hyperbole, Millionshchikov's list of what he considers Pugwash's accomplishments is impressive.

Perhaps more interesting is that Millionshchikov valued Pugwash—and particularly the bilateral Soviet-American meetings—for exactly the same reasons his U.S. colleagues did: the unofficial nature of the discussions, the importance of personal contacts, the common language and way of approaching problems that the Soviet and U.S. scientists seemed to share, and the prospect that insights and ideas from the discussions would reach governments: "The importance of the Pugwash meetings consists precisely in the fact that a dialogue takes place there between people who know the problems well and who can unofficially inform those government bodies which deal with these problems through state-to-state channels." He stressed the partici-

10. Kistiakowsky, "Bipartite Meeting," 3; and Kubbig, "Communicators in the Cold War," 30–31.

11. Mikhail Millionshchikov, "Proekt (dokladnyi zapiski) v Prezidium Akademii nauk SSSR ob itogakh 15-ti letnei deiatelnosti Paguoshskogo dvizheniia uchenykh," 24 September 1972, Millionshchikov papers, f. 1713, op. 2, delo I.5.2, no. 209, ANRF.

pation at past Pugwash meetings of U.S. presidential advisers such as George Kistiakowsky, Jerome Wiesner, Walt Rostow, and Henry Kissinger.[12]

By the end of 1969 the official SALT negotiations between the nuclear superpowers were already under way, and in 1972 the United States and the USSR signed the SALT I interim agreement on offensive nuclear forces and the Antiballistic Missile Treaty limiting defenses. Negotiations continued toward a SALT II Treaty, which was finally completed in 1979. The official arms control activity seemed to render the scientists' involvement superfluous. Henry Kissinger, for one, ended his brief association with Pugwash in favor of becoming a key figure in the U.S. arms negotiations, first as President Nixon's national security adviser and then as U.S. secretary of state.

The apparent successes of superpower arms control reduced the importance of Pugwash and the bilateral SADS group as well. When Millionshchikov died of cancer in 1973, the bilateral discussions lost one of their key promoters. At this point, Doty decreased his own involvement in SADS. He sent his colleague Michael Nacht to a final meeting of the SADS group in 1975 and then decided, as he put it, to "let it die."[13] Doty himself stayed interested in U.S.-Soviet relations, becoming chair of the arms control section of the Dartmouth Conference, but by and large the scientists ceded the subject of security policy to the diplomats and politicians.

The Second Generation: Scientists, Doctors, and Dissidents

Although transnational efforts to promote disarmament slackened in the 1970s as the United States and the USSR pursued formal negotiations on arms control, many of the networks remained in place. Many U.S. scientists, for example, maintained contacts with Soviet counterparts both professionally, while pursuing their scholarly research, and politically, when supporting colleagues such as Andrei Sakharov, Iurii Orlov, and others who were being persecuted as dissidents.[14] The deterioration of East-West relations in the late 1970s, the failure of the United States to ratify the SALT II Treaty, and especially the bellicose policies of the Reagan administration in the early 1980s revived the transnational linkages of the past and created new ones.

During the 1980s, the main actors on the Soviet side were scientists affiliated with various institutes of the USSR Academy of Sciences who formally organized themselves into the Committee of Soviet Scientists for Peace, Against the Nuclear Threat (hereafter the Committee of Soviet Scientists or CSS) in 1983, and members of the Soviet chapter of the International Physicians for the Prevention of Nuclear War (IPPNW), founded in 1980. Among the

12. Ibid., esp. 5–10.
13. Doty to Bernd Kubbig, cited in Kubbig, "Communicators in the Cold War," 44 n. 70; and in Doty, interview by David Wright, Cambridge, Mass., 17 July 1990.
14. Sakharov discusses the efforts of Sidney Drell, Kurt Gottfried, Jeremy Stone, and others in his *Memoirs*, trans. Richard Lourie (New York, 1990), and *Moscow and Beyond, 1986 to 1989*, trans. Antonina Bouis (New York, 1991).

many Western organizations active in transnational efforts, the most important for our cases were IPPNW, the Federation of American Scientists, the Union of Concerned Scientists, the Natural Resources Defense Council, and the National Academy of Sciences Committee on International Security and Arms Control (CISAC). The latter group, founded in 1979, was a direct descendant of the SADS workshops, although most of the participants on both sides were new.[15]

In December 1980, the Central Committee of the Soviet Communist Party officially approved contacts between the Soviet Academy of Sciences and CISAC. The Central Committee proposal was signed by the head of the science department and the deputy head of the international department.[16] Less than five years later the second official, Anatolii Cherniaev, became Mikhail Gorbachev's top aide for international affairs and a strong advocate of the "new thinking" on foreign policy.[17]

The preparations for the first meeting of Soviet scientists with U.S. members of CISAC in 1981 received high-level attention in Moscow. Given the state of U.S.-Soviet relations and the poor prospects for arms control under the Reagan administration, the Soviet government accorded the meeting quasi-official status. The same institutions that were involved in preparations for official arms control negotiations prepared detailed instructions for the Soviet delegation, running to some fifteen typed pages.[18]

THE PHYSICIANS' PRESCRIPTION

As David Holloway's work and the previous chapters indicated, Soviet physicists had since the 1940s enjoyed a certain degree of intellectual and political autonomy stemming from their involvement with nuclear weapons. Their privileged position enabled them to forge transnational links with Western colleagues and to share ideas about bringing the nuclear genie un-

15. Paul Doty had actually been invited to chair the new CISAC, but declined. Doty, interview.

16. "O predvaritel'nykh peregovorakh mezhdu Akademii nauk SSSR i Natsional'noi akademiei nauk SShA," No. St-241/9s, 16 December 1980. F. 89, op. 46, doc. 75, Storage Center for Contemporary Documentation [Tsentr khraneniia sovremennoi dokumentatsii] (hereafter TsKhSD).

17. The first official, Sergei Trapeznikov, was a notorious Stalinist and opponent of most reforms, internal and external. See A. S. Cherniaev, *Moia zhizn' i moe vremia* (Moscow, 1995), 241, 248–249; and Fedor Burlatsky, *Khrushchev and the First Russian Spring: The Era of Khrushchev through the Eyes of His Adviser*, trans. Daphne Skillen (New York, 1991), 238–239. Cherniaev was well suited to support the renewal of transnational contacts between scientists. His first published article was an obituary of Professor Frédéric Joliot-Curie, the famous French physicist and original signatory of the Russell-Einstein manifesto that founded the Pugwash movement; see Cherniaev, *Moia zhizn' i moe vremia*, 227.

18. Aleksandr G. Savel'yev and Nikolay N. Detinov, *The Big Five: Arms Control Decision-Making in the Soviet Union* (Westport, Conn., 1995), 71–72.

der control. The physicists' creation of nuclear weapons provided both the necessity and the opportunity to engage in transnational disarmament activities. The structure of the Soviet political system gave them access to the top leadership.

Starting in the 1970s another professional group began to play a similar role: medical doctors. In the United States, physicians had been active in the movement for a nuclear test ban in the early 1960s, prompted by concerns about the health consequences of nuclear testing and of nuclear war itself. The Physicians for Social Responsibility (PSR) was founded in Boston in 1961 and was reinvigorated at the end of the 1970s.[19] By December 1980 PSR had "gone transnational," when physicians from the United States and the Soviet Union met in Geneva to found the IPPNW, an organization that eventually came to include some two hundred thousand members in eighty countries and was awarded the Nobel Peace Prize in 1985. The award recognized the important contributions IPPNW had made in promoting a transnational dialogue on the threat of nuclear war.[20]

The Cardiologist Connection

In attempting to influence the arms race, and in particular Soviet policy, the physicians took advantage of an important "opportunity": the ill health of the Soviet Union's aging leaders. Much of IPPNW's success owes to the personal relationship between its original co-presidents, Bernard Lown and Evgenii Chazov, and Chazov's contacts with the top Soviet leadership.[21] Together they sought to influence the views of Soviet leaders on the dangers of nuclear war and to open up discussion of the issue to a wider Soviet public. Their efforts helped create a climate hospitable to the initiatives that Mikhail Gorbachev later pursued.

Dr. Bernard Lown, professor of cardiology at the Harvard School of Public Health, was the founding president of PSR. He first met Dr. Evgenii Chazov in 1966 at an international conference of cardiologists in India. Chazov was then, at age 38, already one of the USSR's leading cardiologists. A year after meeting Lown he was appointed director of the Fourth Main Administration of the USSR Ministry of Health, in charge of the "Kremlevka," the top

19. Helen M. Caldicott, "Introduction," in Ruth Adams and Susan Cullen, eds., *The Final Epidemic: Physicians and Scientists on Nuclear War* (Chicago, 1981), 1–3; Richard A. Knox, "MD Group's Aim Is the Prevention of N-War," *Boston Globe*, 7 July 1980.

20. Bernard Lown and E. I. Chazov, "Physician Responsibility in the Nuclear Age," *Journal of the American Medical Association* 274, 5 (2 August 1995): 416–419.

21. The information in this section comes from three main sources: Bernard Lown, interview by author, Brookline, Mass., 6 April 1994; Frank M. Castillo, "The International Physicians for the Prevention of Nuclear War: Transnational Midwife of World Peace," (Institute of International Peace Studies, University of Notre Dame, 1990); and Evgenii Chazov, *Zdorov'e i vlast'* (Moscow, 1992).

leadership's hospital in the Kremlin. He became Leonid Brezhnev's personal physician.

Lown and Chazov maintained close contact throughout the next decade. In 1972, at Chazov's initiative, Lown received an emergency call from the Soviet embassy in Washington to come see a patient in Moscow whose identity could not be revealed. It turned out to be the wife of a leading Politburo figure—and hard-line ideologist—Mikhail Suslov. Her cardiac problems were mainly the result of unwillingness to follow her doctors' plan for treating her diabetes, so Lown's expertise was not actually required. But Chazov saw Lown's visit as an opportunity to impress the Kremlin leaders with the goodwill and humanitarian instincts of his colleagues from the "imperialist camp"—one of many such opportunities he pursued in subsequent years. Lown took the occasion of a visit to Moscow to discuss with Soviet colleagues his research on sudden cardiac death. He later arranged for the provision to the USSR of advanced medical equipment, just coming onto the U.S. market.[22]

In 1979 Lown wrote to Chazov with a proposal to found an international movement of physicians modeled on PSR.[23] Chazov's initial answer was encouraging. He argued that the need for such an effort was apparent: the arms race was already exacting victims by diverting resources from health care to military uses. "Even if not in action, these weapons wound and kill," wrote Chazov.[24] By the time Lown next met him in Moscow in March 1980 Chazov had apparently got cold feet about the initiative. He accused his friend of being a Don Quixote, and expressed his own fear of jeopardizing his career and particularly the new cardiology center that he was establishing. Lown got angry and called Chazov an opportunist. Chazov stomped out of the meeting.[25]

The next day Chazov telephoned Lown to apologize. He told him about a conversation he had with his adult daughter when he returned home the night before. Chazov had asked his daughter, who was also a physician, whether she thought he was working too hard. When she answered yes, he said, "Well, an American doctor says I am not working hard enough." Chazov explained Lown's proposal to organize an international physicians movement to oppose the arms race, and his daughter urged him to participate—for the sake of his grandson.[26]

The Kremlin Doctor's Patients

When Soviet physicians attended the founding meeting of the international physicians' movement in Geneva in December 1980, most observers assumed

22. Chazov, *Zdorov'e i vlast'*, 100–101; Lown, interview.
23. This account is from my interview with Lown.
24. Chazov to Lown, 17 October 1979, reprinted in International Physicians for the Prevention of Nuclear War, *The Soviet Response to Medical Efforts for the Prevention of Nuclear War* (Boston, 1981), appendix A.
25. Lown, interview.
26. Lown, interview.

they were there at the behest of the Soviet government. A year earlier Soviet armed forces had invaded neighboring Afghanistan, driving one of the last nails into the coffin of superpower détente. Soviet leaders had good reason to try to demonstrate their country's interest in arms control and disarmament by sending a delegation to the physicians' meeting.

Even though official approval was required, Soviet involvement in IPPNW resulted mainly from Chazov's personal initiative. The Russian archives have yielded a couple of documents that highlight his role. In April 1980, for example, shortly after Lown's visit to Moscow, Chazov persuaded the Soviet minister of health to seek approval from the Central Committee for Soviet participation in the international physicians movement.[27] Subsequently, Chazov handled contacts with the communist authorities directly, in his own name. After the meeting in December 1980, for example, Chazov and his fellow delegates reported back to the Central Committee and described preparations for a follow-up meeting in March 1981.[28]

If the Soviet leadership had considered participation in IPPNW as mainly a propaganda opportunity, they would presumably have given Chazov and his colleagues consistent support. In fact, however, the top Soviet leaders' attitudes toward Chazov's work ranged from skeptical to hostile. A year after the founding of IPPNW Brezhnev himself expressed some ambivalence about the doctors' efforts. In a personal conversation with Chazov he first expressed the view—shared apparently by most of the leadership—that only Soviet military strength restrained the United States: "We're strong and that preserves peace," Brezhnev claimed. "But you're right," he continued. "Of course it's necessary to negotiate with the Americans, to do something about the missiles and nuclear bombs." He recalled Soviet attempts at negotiating strategic arms with the Nixon administration, but considered the prospects for dealing with Ronald Reagan and his advisers hopeless: "Your stories about the horrors of nuclear war don't affect them at all." Brezhnev also indicated that many in the Soviet leadership didn't appreciate the doctors' efforts (they "don't understand you"), but that he himself considered that "you are doing a good thing."[29]

In 1981, KGB chief Iurii Andropov asked Chazov to send him some of the information IPPNW had gathered on the consequences of nuclear war and the organization's statement of principles. Chazov had been on friendly terms with Andropov since the early 1970s and believed that the Soviet leader "understood that the nuclear arms race would lead to a dead end and ultimately ruin the country." But, as with Brezhnev, Andropov's appreciation of the doctors' efforts conflicted with his instinctive belief in peace through strength:

27. B. V. Petrovskii to the Central Committee, memorandum, 8 April 1980, F. 89, op. 46, doc. 55, TsKhSD.

28. E. I. Chazov, L. A. Il'in, and M. I. Kuzin to the Central Committee, memorandum, 17 December 1980, F. 89, op. 43, doc. 48, TsKhSD.

29. Chazov, Zdorov'e i vlast', 94.

"Why don't the Americans move first toward disarmament? Why are we the ones who have to start?" he asked Chazov. You have to consider that "they only talk to the strong." "But, in principle," he added, "you are right, and from a humanitarian perspective it is necessary to support your ideas."[30]

In 1981 Chazov prepared a speech to deliver at a session of the Supreme Soviet, presenting the views of the international physicians' movement on how to end the arms race. He was requested, as was customary at the time, to submit a copy of the speech ahead of time to the Central Committee. Chazov did not consider the speech to contain any "revolutionary" ideas, but "the style was unusual" in its lack of "any expressions such as 'American imperialism' and so forth." Boris Ponomarev, the hard-liner who headed the Central Committee's International Department, returned the speech with "corrections" that made it conform to what Chazov called "the traditional stupid style." Chazov telephoned Konstantin Chernenko, Brezhnev's close associate and fellow Politburo member, and told him that he would not deliver the speech in that form. Chernenko read the original speech and consulted with Mikhail Suslov, the Politburo ideologist, who objected strongly to it. Chernenko called Chazov back after a half hour, told him with some irritation of Suslov's reaction, but then gave him his blessing to do "as you consider necessary." So Chazov delivered his speech as written. Later, Andropov telephoned to tell him that after the session Brezhnev had walked out with his fellow Politburo members into the corridor and declared that "Chazov spoke best of all." Nobody interfered with Chazov's speeches anymore after that.[31]

According to Andrei Kokoshin, a major proponent of military reform during the Gorbachev era and later deputy defense minister in Boris Yeltsin's government, the work of the international physicians movement made a profound effect on the thinking of the top Soviet leaders. He mentions, in particular, the four most influential figures in the development of Soviet security policy during the Brezhnev era: Brezhnev himself; Andrei Gromyko, foreign minister; Andropov, KGB chief; and Dmitrii Ustinov, defense minister.[32] But Chazov's disarmament work made him some enemies within the Soviet establishment as well, although as a full Central Committee member since 1982 and personal physician to the Kremlin leaders, he was in a good position to defend himself. Chazov identified Suslov, Ponomarev, and senior Politburo member Andrei Kirilenko as particularly hostile, along with many officials in the military and even in the Foreign Ministry.[33] Kokoshin cites criticism from

30. Chazov, *Zdorov'e i vlast'*, 90.
31. Ibid., 92–93. Other sources confirm that Brezhnev did not think much of the highly orthodox phraseology in the speeches of Ponomarev and Suslov. He once described a Suslov speech as "boring . . . without a living word, or one thought that hasn't been said or written a thousand times." See Cherniaev, *Moia zhizn' i moe vremia*, 310.
32. A. A. Kokoshin, *Armiia i politika: Sovetskaia voenno-politicheskaia i voenno-strategicheskaia mysl', 1918–1991 gody* (Moscow, 1995), 163.
33. Chazov, *Zdorov'e i vlast'*, 94–95.

the Main Political Administration of the armed forces—the political "commissars"—that the doctors' descriptions of the consequences of nuclear war would "undermine the 'moral spirit'" of the troops, whose job it is to prepare for victory in war.[34] Bernard Lown remembered Leonid Zamiatin of the Central Committee apparatus and Aleksandr Bessmertnykh of the Foreign Ministry as unfriendly to IPPNW's efforts in the early 1980s.[35] At one point Lown was with Chazov in the Central Committee building in Moscow when another Central Committee member pulled him aside out of Chazov's earshot. "You have a very courageous colleague," he said, referring to Chazov. "But isn't he just supporting the official Soviet peace policy?" Lown asked, with feigned naiveté. "Doctor Lown," his interlocutor answered, "you are a lot smarter than that stupid remark suggests."[36]

In the 1980s, particularly after his organization's receipt of the Nobel Prize, Dr. Chazov was often asked by journalists how he could get away with promulgating a critique of the arms race and prescribing solutions to it that his government did not officially endorse. He was still struggling with the question years later when he wrote his memoirs. He recalled many instances when Brezhnev, Andropov, and Ustinov stressed the importance of maintaining "positions of strength" in relations with the United States, in order to prevent war and ensure the USSR's superpower status. At the same time, however, they recognized—perhaps not sufficiently or soon enough, however—the toll that high military spending exacted on the domestic economy.[37] Ultimately Chazov adduced two reasons the top leadership allowed him to speak out on the danger of nuclear war and to head a movement that implicitly criticized Soviet policies and programs (particularly the investment in civil defense and the reluctance to take meaningful unilateral initiatives of restraint): first, they depended on him for their health; and second, "inside, they agreed with the ideas that our movement fostered."[38]

Chazov is right to point to both factors. The Soviet leaders at some fundamental level agreed with IPPNW's diagnosis of nuclear war as unwinnable, yet they were reticent to express their views in a forthright and unqualified manner (although Brezhnev in his later years became more explicit—in part prompted by the physicians).[39] Moreover, many Soviet policies were inconsistent with the movement's views about the senselessness of striving to maintain "parity" at ever higher levels of nuclear weapons. Ideas about

34. Kokoshin, *Armiia i politika*, 163.
35. Lown, interview.
36. Ibid.
37. Chazov, *Zdorov'e i vlast'*, 90–91, 204–205.
38. Ibid., 92.
39. Fox Butterfield, "Brezhnev Replies to Doctors' Unit," *New York Times*, 2 May 1982. For overviews of Soviet leaders' statements about nuclear weapons, see David Holloway, *The Soviet Union and the Arms Race* (New Haven, Conn., 1983), esp. chap. 3.

peace through strength were incompatible with recognition of the redundant, "overkill" capacity of the superpower arsenals. Chazov's personal role and status were certainly crucial to his movement's success. The same is true for his Western colleagues who impressed the Soviet leadership with their nonideological approach and their many manifestations of goodwill in other areas—such as exchange of medical information and technology, and direct consultation on Soviet patients.

Nuclear Glasnost before Its Time

In the United States, the international physicians' movement and other transnational peace organizations were often accused of weakening the positions of the Western democracies while exerting no impact on Soviet policy. The gist of the argument was that Western freedom of the press allowed for full discussion of the threat of nuclear war—discussion which, in turn, might frighten the public into opposing military programs necessary for deterring potential Soviet aggression. The Soviet press, by contrast, was controlled. Any information about the arms race and nuclear war that could sow doubts among the Soviet citizenry about the wisdom of their leaders' policy would surely be censored. Typical was the comment of Milovan Djilas, the Yugoslav communist-leader-turned-dissident, quoted in a U.S. newspaper editorial: "No such accounts of [the] horror of nuclear war ever reach the Soviet public because the whole area of military planning is barred from discussion. This means that in the vital fields of psychological confrontation, the balance is strongly tilted in favor of Soviet interests."[40]

In early 1981 Bernard Lown visited the Soviet Union on behalf of IPPNW and brought along Carl Sagan, the Cornell University astronomer and host of a popular science program on television. In a meeting at the U.S. embassy in Moscow they were accused by Ambassador Arthur Hartman of "undermining democratic resolve" in the West and of receiving no coverage by the Soviet media. In fact, by that time, IPPNW had received at least as much coverage in the Soviet press as in the United States, including articles in major newspapers with millions of readers.[41] The articles reported accurately on the movement's objectives and activities. The newspapers often reprinted entire documents from IPPNW congresses without alteration.

Ambassador Hartman claimed to be unimpressed by this information, which was apparently news to him. He argued that only television mattered.

40. "What Good Is Nuclear Scare If Russian People Unaware?" *Omaha World-Herald*, 10 January 1981, reprinted in International Physicians for the Prevention of Nuclear War, *Soviet Response to Medical Efforts*, appendix C.

41. The following newspapers published articles and documents from IPPNW: *Pravda* (circulation over 10 million); *Izvestiia* (over 8 million); *Komsomol'skaia pravda* (10 million); *Literaturnaia gazeta* (over 2.5 million); *Meditsinskaia gazeta* (over 1 million); *Moskovskaia pravda* (10 million); and *Trud* (50 thousand). See the discussion in the introduction to *Soviet Response to Medical Efforts*; examples are reprinted and translated in appendix D.

"So, we'll get on TV," responded Lown and Sagan. Hartman was dubious. "I get on Soviet TV only once a year on the 4th of July and my speech needs to be approved 2 weeks in advance," he explained.[42]

When Lown returned to the United States, he visited Anatolii Dobrynin, the Soviet ambassador, in Washington. He asked Dobrynin about the possibility of getting coverage of IPPNW on Soviet TV. Dobrynin said that Chazov was the one who could do something. He advised Lown to write down what he had in mind; Dobrynin then sent Lown's request to Moscow by diplomatic pouch.[43] Chazov passed on the request to Gosteleradio, the state television company, and to the Communist Party Central Committee. Chazov believes that it was Andropov's personal intervention that allowed the project to go through. One June day in 1982, Soviet and foreign journalists were invited to the Ostankino television studio to participate in an open, uncensored discussion of the views of the international physicians movement. In Chazov's words: "In the course of the discussion, declarations resounded from the television screen that contradicted the official Soviet views on these problems at the time," as the physicians highlighted the futility of the arms race, the uselessness of civil defense, and the need for a nuclear test ban.[44] Over the next several years, Soviet television broadcast nine IPPNW congresses, as well as additional programs such as interviews with Chazov or discussions between Chazov and Sergei Kapitsa. Sergei, the son of Petr Kapitsa, was a noted physicist in his own right, and someone whose role in popularizing science for Soviet television audiences approximated that of Carl Sagan in the United States.

In addition to whatever effect they had on popular opinion, these broadcasts influenced the way some Soviet foreign-policy élites thought about the issue of nuclear war, according to interviews they gave to Western scholars years later.[45] The TV programs also brought Chazov under renewed criticism from the Soviet military. "You have made my life difficult," he complained to Lown.[46] Most important, the programs set a precedent for public discussion—*glasnost'*—on nuclear issues, well before Mikhail Gorbachev came into office and began using the term. Astute observers of the Soviet scene had already recognized some changes in public discussion of security policy even before Gorbachev—thanks in part to the efforts of the international physicians.[47] With Gorbachev's encouragement, nuclear glasnost would be expanded much further during the second half of the 1980s.

42. Lown, interview.

43. Ibid.

44. Chazov, *Zdorov'e i vlast'*, 95–96. For a contemporaneous U.S. report, see John F. Burns, "U.S. Doctors Debate A-War on Soviet TV," *New York Times*, 27 June 1982.

45. Steven Kull, *Burying Lenin: The Revolution in Soviet Ideology and Foreign Policy* (Boulder, Colo., 1992), 18.

46. Lown, interview.

47. Dusko Doder, "Soviet Public Debates Arms, Old Secrecy Wanes," *Washington Post*, 5 January 1985.

SCIENTISTS AS SECURITY POLICY ADVISERS

While the transnational physicians movement set the moral tone for new disarmament efforts in the early 1980s, a transnational coalition of scientists explored practical measures for slowing the arms race. The Soviet members formally constituted themselves as the Committee of Soviet Scientists for Peace, Against the Nuclear Threat in May 1983, but many of them had worked on issues related to arms control before and some had established contacts with like-minded scientists abroad—including members of the international physicians movement.

The Leading Figures

One of the key figures in the Soviet scientists' movement of the 1980s was Evgenii Velikhov, a nuclear and plasma physicist, head of the Kurchatov Institute of Atomic Energy and a vice president of the Soviet Academy of Sciences since 1977. His role was very much like Millionshchikov's a decade earlier. As an Academy official Velikhov was in a good position to organize research projects and conferences in the Soviet Union as well as maintain international contacts. With some background in military research and a particular expertise in lasers, he maintained a certain degree of credibility among those Soviet officials skeptical of efforts at disarmament.[48]

In 1982 Velikhov became head of the Soviet delegation to the U.S. National Academy's CISAC meetings. He took over in the wake of the death of Nikolai Inozemtsev, the previous head. Inozemtsev was a social scientist, director of the Institute for the World Economy and International Relations (IMEMO), and a person who played a major role in promoting East-West détente, owing to the great respect that Soviet leader Leonid Brezhnev had for him.[49]

When Velikhov took over the delegation, he wanted to involve more natural scientists. He invited Roald Sagdeev to join. Sagdeev, another prominent plasma physicist, directed the USSR's Space Research Institute, and was particularly active in discussions on the militarization of space. Sagdeev took over as chair of the Soviet CISAC delegation in 1986 and served until 1990. In 1987 he invited Andrei Sakharov to join the group and attend the October 1987 CISAC meeting in Vilnius, Lithuania.[50]

Several other scientists played particularly important roles in the early 1980s. Andrei Kokoshin was trained as an engineer at the Bauman Institute in

---

48. See, for example, E. P. Velikhov, ed., *Molecular Gas Lasers: Physics and Applications*, trans. S. Kittell (Moscow, 1981).

49. On the relationship between Brezhnev and Inozemtsev, and the latter's role in détente: A. S. Cherniaev, interview by author, Moscow, 7 June 1997. On IMEMO, see Jeffrey T. Checkel, *Ideas and International Political Change: Soviet/Russian Behavior and the End of the Cold War* (New Haven, Conn., 1997).

50. Roald Sagdeev, interview by author, College Park, Md., March 1994.

Moscow before pursuing a career in politics and history. He became deputy director of the Institute of the USA and Canada (ISKAN), headed by Georgii Arbatov. The son and grandson of military officers, Kokoshin served as an important link to reformers in the Soviet armed forces.[51] Aleksei Arbatov, son of the ISKAN director, worked as a political scientist at IMEMO and was a strong advocate of developing a cadre of knowledgeable civilian analysts competent to propose alternatives to official military policies formulated by the Soviet armed forces.

Arbatov and Kokoshin, as political scientists, had long worked on issues related to the arms race—particularly analyses of U.S. and NATO military policy.[52] Sagdeev and Velikhov were both students of Lev Artsimovich, a leading figure in the Soviet Academy of Sciences and a longtime Pugwash participant, but their arms control activities in the 1980s were not a direct result of their mentor's interests. As Sagdeev once observed, Artsimovich seemed confident that his generation would solve the problems of the arms race so that the younger generation would not have to be concerned about it. In 1971, however, Artsimovich did send Sagdeev in his place to a Pugwash meeting in Racine, Wisconsin, where the young scientist met several key U.S. arms control scientists of Artsimovich's generation, such as Franklin Long, Jack Ruina, and George Kistiakowsky. Sagdeev did not, however, resume work on arms control issues for more than a decade after that.[53]

Soviet arms control scientists had a number of ways of reaching top officials in charge of Soviet security policy. Velikhov, as an official of the Academy, was quite well connected. Sagdeev, when he headed the CISAC delegation, also developed many contacts. In fact, the delegations were required to submit drafts of papers and the proposed agenda for their U.S.-Soviet meetings to the Foreign Ministry, Central Committee, and the General Staff of the armed forces. Sagdeev recalls that he had no problems with the ministry or the Central Committee, but the General Staff kept returning paper drafts to him, arguing about the language. Finally, Sagdeev decided to invite the General Staff to add a member to the CISAC delegation to facilitate approval of drafts.[54]

The CISAC delegation was also obliged to send a summary (*otchet*) of each of its meetings to the Central Committee from the Washington embassy by *shifrofka*, or coded telegram, through Soviet ambassador Anatolii Dobrynin. Over the four years he headed the CISAC delegation, Sagdeev figures he

---

51. For more on Kokoshin's background, see Kimberly Marten Zisk, *Engaging the Enemy: Organization Theory and Soviet Military Innovation, 1955–1991* (Princeton, N.J., 1993), 126.

52. A particularly well informed example is Aleksei Arbatov, *Voenno-strategicheskii paritet i politika SShA* (Moscow, 1984).

53. Roald Sagdeev, interviews by author, Moscow, November 1990; Ann Arbor, Mich., May 1991; and College Park, Md., March 1994; and Evgenii Velikhov, interview by author, Moscow, November 1990 and July 1992.

54. Sagdeev, interview, March 1994.

signed a few dozen such *shifrofki*. He considered them the best way to get attention at the top.[55]

Nuclear Winter

Velikhov's first involvement in international arms control discussions came in 1982 when Soviet leader Leonid Brezhnev decided to send him to Rome to represent the USSR at a meeting called by the Papal Academy of Sciences to discuss the nuclear arms race.[56] As with many such transnational efforts, the idea for a meeting sponsored by the Vatican was first proposed by Leo Szilard in 1964, when he wrote a memorandum suggesting that the Pope host a discussion among scientists "whose Governments are at present not able to communicate with each other in a constructive fashion because of the existing political tensions."[57] That was certainly an apt characterization of the early 1980s, when the lack of constructive communication between the superpowers seemed especially dangerous, given what many scientists believed to be the increasing magnitude of the nuclear threat.

At the Rome meeting, Velikhov met, among other "important and interesting Western scientists," Victor Weisskopf, whose contacts with Soviet physicists dated to the 1930s. Thus, as with Sagdeev's visit to Racine a decade earlier, Velikhov became acquainted with the first generation of U.S. Pugwash scientists. As he later recalled, "Weisskopf made a great impression on me by his commitment to abolishing nuclear weapons. It's one thing when preachers say this must be done, but Weisskopf had worked on the Manhattan Project and lived through all of atomic history."[58]

At the time, the phenomenon of "nuclear winter"—the prospect that a large-scale nuclear war could ignite fires that would block out the sun and lead to dangerous climatic changes—was receiving considerable international attention. It became particularly associated with the work of astronomer Carl Sagan, who published an article in October 1983 in *Parade*, a mass-circulation magazine included as part of many U.S. Sunday newspapers.[59] Soviet scientists quickly became involved in the nuclear winter debate, with Velikhov at the forefront.

55. Ibid.
56. Evgenii Velikhov, "Chernobyl Remains on Our Mind," in Stephen F. Cohen and Katrina vanden Heuvel, eds., *Voices of Glasnost: Interviews with Gorbachev's Reformers* (New York, 1989), 160; Velikhov, interview, 29 July 1992.
57. The memorandum is quoted in Helen S. Hawkins, G. Allen Greb, and Gertrud Weiss Szilard, eds., *Toward a Livable World: Leo Szilard and the Crusade for Nuclear Arms Control* (Cambridge, Mass., 1987), 261.
58. Velikhov, "Chernobyl Remains on Our Mind," 160.
59. The first major study of the issue was P. J. Crutzen and J. W. Birks, "The Atmosphere After a Nuclear War: Twilight at Noon," *Ambio* 11, nos. 2–3 (1982): 114–125. Among Carl Sagan's efforts to promote the idea were "Nuclear Winter," *Parade* (Boston), 30 October 1983, 4–5, 7; and "Nuclear War and Climatic Catastrophe: Some Policy Implications," *Foreign Affairs* 62 (Winter 1983–84): 258–292.

Nuclear winter became the first major issue around which Velikhov rallied his Soviet colleagues in an effort to foster transnational scientific collaboration on arms control. Soviet scientists had for many years in fact developed models of related climatic phenomena. They began applying their models to nuclear winter, at first independently of Western scientists.[60] They circulated their research publications and shared their findings with Western colleagues, often in typescript.[61] With the formation of the Committee of Soviet Scientists, they obtained a vehicle for collaborative transnational research, joint sponsorship of conferences, and large-scale publication. Velikhov's role as an official of the Academy of Sciences was particularly important, as were Roald Sagdeev's long-standing professional relationship with Carl Sagan and the previous international contacts of the Soviet climate-studies community.[62]

Soviet work on nuclear winter was greeted with considerable skepticism in the West. Without tangible evidence of change in the military forces and nuclear strategy of the USSR—and nothing short of unilateral disarmament would satisfy some critics—one could easily argue that the scientists' work was merely an instrument of official propaganda.[63] Consequently, Velikhov and his colleagues sought out projects that could have more immediate impact and actually influence Soviet and U.S. policy. They found what they were looking for in early 1983, when Velikhov and Sagdeev traveled to Washington as members of a Soviet delegation meeting with CISAC.

Setting an Agenda

For Velikhov and Sagdeev, the 1983 meeting in Washington helped set the agenda for their subsequent activities in the arms control sphere. The Soviet-American discussions produced three main policy goals: (1) defend the ABM

60. An excellent analysis of the Soviet work and its political implications is Stephen Shenfield, "Nuclear Winter and the USSR," *Milennium: Journal of International Studies* 15, 2 (Summer 1986): 197–208.

61. V. V. Aleksandrov and G. L. Stenchikov, *On the Modelling of the Climatic Consequences of the Nuclear War* (Moscow, 1983), a booklet printed in seven hundred copies; statement by Sergei Kapitsa, prepared for a meeting in Washington, D.C., 8 December 1983, typescript; Committee of Soviet Scientists for Peace Against the Nuclear Threat, "Possible Climatic Consequences of Nuclear War and Some Natural Analogs: Scientific Investigation," Moscow, 1984, typescript.

62. For background materials and several of the studies, see Evgenii Velikhov, ed., *The Night After . . . : Climatic and Biological Consequences of a Nuclear War* (Moscow, 1985), and an expanded and updated Russian version, *Klimaticheskie i biologicheskie posledstviia iadernoi voiny* (Moscow, 1987). For Sagdeev's relationship with Sagan, see Sagan's forward to Sagdeev's autobiography: Roald Sagdeev, *The Making of a Soviet Scientist* (New York, 1994), ix–xi. Sagdeev contributed a chapter to Sagan's book on nuclear winter: See Paul Ehrlich, Carl Sagan, et al., *The Cold and the Dark: The World after Nuclear War* (New York, 1984). For a discussion of the Soviet climate-studies community, see Elizabeth Economy, "Negotiating the Terrain of Global Climate Change Policy in the Soviet Union and China" (Ph.D. diss., University of Michigan, 1994).

63. For an extreme view, see Leon Goure, "'Nuclear Winter' in Soviet Mirrors,'" *Strategic Review* (Summer 1985): 35–36; and the discussion in Shenfield, "Nuclear Winter and the USSR."

Treaty, (2) prevent deployment of weapons in space, including antisatellite weapons (ASAT), and (3) negotiate a comprehensive nuclear test ban.[64] These became high-priority objectives of the Committee of Soviet Scientists, when Velikhov founded it that same year, with Sagdeev and Kokoshin as his deputies.[65]

Through Evgenii Chazov, Velikhov and Sagdeev also met Bernard Lown and began to participate in activities of the international physicians movement and to publicize their appeals and conference documents.[66] Lown encouraged the Soviet scientists to form an organization to undertake policy research and public education on the arms race. "You need a think tank," he told Velikhov.[67] Velikhov himself was particularly impressed by the Federation of American Scientists and consciously used it as a model for the Soviet Scientists' Committee—much as his predecessor Mikhail Millionshchikov had established a Soviet counterpart to the American Academy's Committee on International Studies of Arms Control, the sponsor of the SADS group.[68]

TRANSNATIONALISM, EUROPEAN-STYLE

In addition to the U.S.-Soviet contacts, the 1980s witnessed a proliferation of transnational relations between various groups and individuals in Europe and the Soviet Union. These included élite-level contacts, as represented most notably by the Independent Commission on Disarmament and Security Issues, or the Palme Commission, as it was often called after its chair, the late Swedish prime minister Olof Palme. They also included attempts at forging a continent-wide European peace movement, as envisioned by the founders of the European Nuclear Disarmament movement.[69]

Although its impact did not become evident until Gorbachev came into office in 1985, the Palme Commission did much of its work during the late Brezhnev era. The Commission intended to do for the area of international security what the Brandt Commission on North-South relations had done for international economic development: present a thorough assessment of the

64. Velikhov, interview, 29 July 1992; Jeremy Stone, "FAS Visit to Moscow Initiates Star Wars Dialogue," *F.A.S. Public Interest Report* 36, 10 (December 1983).
65. Frank von Hippel, "The Committee of Soviet Scientists against the Nuclear Threat," *F.A.S. Public Interest Report* 37, 1 (January 1984).
66. Several documents are reprinted in Velikhov, *Night After*; and in Velikhov, *Klimaticheskie i biologicheskie posledstviia*.
67. Lown, interview.
68. Velikhov interview, 29 July 1992.
69. E. P. Thompson, *Protest and Survive* (London, 1980), a pamphlet put out by the Campaign for Nuclear Disarmament; E. P. Thompson and Dan Smith, eds., *Protest and Survive* (New York, 1981), a collection of essays; Thompson, *Beyond the Cold War* (New York, 1982); Thompson, *The Heavy Dancers* (New York, 1985). Jean Stead and Danielle Grünberg, *Moscow Independent Peace Group* (London, 1982).

current state of affairs and proposals to address it.[70] The Palme Commission's work began in 1980 and continued through the next two years of deteriorating U.S.-Soviet relations and increasing concerns about the risks of nuclear war. The Commission consisted, in addition to the chair, of sixteen prominent political figures from as many countries throughout the world. Former U.S. secretary of state Cyrus Vance participated, as did Academician Georgii Arbatov from the Soviet Union. Retired General Mikhail Mil'shtein, Arbatov's colleague at the Institute of the USA and Canada, served as an adviser.[71]

The Palme Commission took advantage of the fact that its leading members were former politicians and government officials. When the Commission convened in Moscow in June 1981, for example, Olof Palme met with Leonid Brezhnev.[72] During a plenary session, the Commission members held discussions with prominent representatives of the Soviet foreign and military establishments—Georgii Kornienko, Soviet first deputy foreign minister, and Marshal Sergei Akhromeev, first deputy chief of the General Staff.[73] Soviet authorities were already well aware of the Palme Commission's work. In addition to his original request to participate in the group, Arbatov had sent the Central Committee detailed reports after each session of the Commission's work. From these reports Brezhnev-era officials first heard such notions as "common security" that would form the basis for the subsequent Gorbachev reforms.[74]

The Palme Commission cooperated with other transnational efforts at slowing the arms race, including the scientists' movement and the International Physicians for the Prevention of Nuclear War. Evgenii Chazov, IPPNW's co-president, participated in the Moscow meeting in 1981. Then, at the third IPPNW conference in Amsterdam in 1983, Olof Palme chaired a session with fellow Commission members Egon Bahr and Georgii Arbatov. Evgenii Velikhov also attended.[75]

In his memoirs, Arbatov reveals that "the work in the Palme Commission began a very important stage in my life and exerted a major influence on my understanding of politics and international relations."[76] This is a rather extraordinary admission from the dean of Soviet academic specialists on the

70. Independent Commission on International Development Issues under the Chairmanship of Willy Brandt, *North-South: A Program for Survival* (Cambridge, Mass., 1980).

71. Independent Commission on Disarmament and Security Issues, *Common Security: A Blueprint for Survival* (New York, 1982).

72. "Ob itogakh besedy L. I. Brezhneva [12 iiunia] s predsedatelem Mezhdunarodnoi komissii po razoruzheniiu i bezopasnosti U. Pal'me," from the transcript of a Politburo session, 18 June 1981, F. 89, op. 42, doc. 44, TsKhSD.

73. Independent Commission on Disarmament, *Common Security*, 188–189.

74. G. Arbatov, "Otchet ob uchastii v zasedanii Mezhdunarodnoi komissii po razoruzheniiu i bezopasnosti ("Komissiia Pal'me") sostoiavsheisia v Vene v period s 13 po 15 dekabria 1980 g.," F. 89, op. 46, doc. 63, and other reports in the same folder, TsKhSD. "Common security" is discussed in the report on the eighth meeting of the Commission, 28 December 1981, 2–3.

75. Lown, interview.

76. G. A. Arbatov, *Zatianuvsheesia vyzdorovlenie (1953–1985 gg.): Svidetel'stvo sovremennika* (Moscow, 1991), 240.

United States and the director of the country's premier institute of foreign-policy studies. It indicates how influential transnational contacts could be, especially for a country as secretive and isolated as Brezhnev's Soviet Union. Although the Palme Commission began to change the views of leading members of the Soviet foreign-policy establishment already in the early 1980s, the real payoff came with Gorbachev's rise to power in 1985, when the "new thinking"—and, in particular, the notion of "common security" promoted by the Palme Commission—could be implemented in practice.

Independent Peace Groups and the Limits of Transnationalism

The Brezhnev era witnessed the emergence of key ideas that affected the course of Soviet foreign policy during the 1980s and ultimately contributed to the end of the Cold War. But, as Thomas Risse has put it, "ideas do not float freely."[77] The degree to which they are accepted and implemented depends on a country's domestic political structure and on the opportunities that arise. The success of ideas also depends on who is promoting them. This point is strikingly evident if we compare the official Soviet reception of the ideas of the international physicians movement, the transnational scientists, or the Palme Commission to reception of the same ideas promoted by independent citizens' peace groups and dissidents.

Brezhnev and his colleagues were willing to endorse arguments about the suicidal nature of nuclear war when put forward by certain people: their personal physician, on whom their health depended, and his Western colleagues, whose goodwill was evident in the professional medical assistance they provided to the USSR. The Soviet authorities gave a sympathetic hearing to Western Nobel laureate physicists who opposed the Reagan administration's military buildup. They allowed leading Soviet specialists on international relations to participate in a working group on the arms race chaired by a prominent social democratic politician from a country that had remained neutral in the Cold War and had promoted disarmament and détente. But they harassed and exiled their own Nobel laureate Andrei Sakharov when he dared to criticize Soviet military programs and the invasion of Afghanistan. And they brutally suppressed independent peace groups in the Soviet bloc, even if their disarmament proposals were identical to those of the Soviet government.

Different groups promoting essentially the same ideas were treated in sharply contrasting ways by the Soviet authorities. When the governments of Sweden and Finland, for example, put forward proposals for a Nordic

77. Thomas Risse-Kappen, "Ideas Do Not Float Freely: Transnational Coalitions, Domestic Structures, and the End of the Cold War," *International Organization* 48, 2 (Spring 1994): 185–214.

Nuclear-Weapon-Free Zone in 1981, the Soviet government responded respectfully. Indeed, Leonid Brezhnev, in an interview with a Finnish newspaper, raised the "possibility of considering some other measures applicable to our own territory in the region adjoining the nuclear-free zone in Northern Europe."[78] But when a group of thirty-eight citizens of the Soviet Baltic republics of Latvia, Lithuania, and Estonia wrote an open letter proposing that their countries be included in such a nuclear-free zone, the Soviet authorities reacted harshly. At least five of the activists were arrested and sentenced to prison terms of five to six years, plus internal exile.[79]

In a similar fashion, the Soviet government and its official Soviet Peace Committee appreciated the efforts of the European Nuclear Disarmament movement against the deployment of U.S. Pershing II and cruise missiles to Europe in the early 1980s. But END's criticism of Soviet SS-20 missiles was most unwelcome. Even more suspect were END's efforts to support independent peace activists in Eastern Europe and the USSR, such as Moscow's "Trust Group" and Hungary's "Peace Group for Dialogue."[80] The Hungarian authorities allowed the Dialogue group to exist for a time, according to Mary Kaldor, a prominent END leader, "because Western peace activists convinced Hungarian officials that the existence of an independent peace movement in the East would help in the campaign against new missile deployments." In 1984, however, once the United States succeeded in deploying its new missiles despite popular protests, the Hungarian government broke up the independent peace group.[81] Soviet authorities made no pretense of tolerating independent peace activists, even for the sake of promoting common objectives, such as a halt to U.S. missile deployments. When the Group to Establish Trust between the USSR and USA emerged in Moscow in 1982, appealing for a "dialogue in which average Soviet and American citizens are included on an equal footing with political figures," the government had its members arrested, beaten, committed to psychiatric hospitals, and expelled from the country.[82]

78. *Suomen Sosialdemokraatti*, 16 June 1981, quoted in Rein Taagepera, "Citizens' Peace Movement in the Soviet Baltic Republics," *Journal of Peace Research* 23, 2 (1986): 183–192.

79. Taagepera, "Citizens' Peace Movement."

80. Stead and Grünberg, *Moscow Independent Peace Group;* Ferenc Köszegi and E. P. Thompson, *The New Hungarian Peace Movement* (London, 1982). For documentation on relations between END and the official Soviet-bloc peace committees, see Dimitrios I. Roussopoulos, *The Coming of World War Three* (Montréal, 1986), 1:238–299.

81. Mary Kaldor, "Who Killed the Cold War?" *Bulletin of the Atomic Scientists* 51, 4 (July/ August 1995): 59.

82. Their misfortunes were reported at the time in an occasional newsletter, *Return Address: Moscow*, no. 1 (Septemter 1984), no. 2 (n.d.), no. 3 (February 1985); and in the Western press. See, for example, Serge Schmeman, "Soviet Blocks Pacifists' News Conference," *New York Times*, 2 November 1982; John F. Burns, "An Independent Disarmament Group is Harassed in Moscow," *New York Times*, 7 July 1982; " 'Peace March' Meets Soviet Barriers," *New York Times*, 22 July 1982; David Satter, "The Soviets Freeze a Peace Worker," *Wall Street Journal*, 13 August 1982; see also Stead and Grünberg, *Moscow Independent Peace Group*. The quotation comes from the group's "Appeal to the Governments and Publics of the USSR and the USA," Moscow, 4 June 1982, reprinted in *Return Address: Moscow*, no. 1 (September 1984): 1.

To conduct "dialogues" with Western peace activists, the Soviet government clearly preferred to choose its own representatives, namely, the official Soviet Peace Committee. The members were chosen less for their interest or expertise in matters related to the arms race than for the extent to which they could be seen as representative of a broad spectrum of Soviet society. Thus, a delegation sent to the United States in 1980 included the president of the Soviet Ice Hockey Federation, an editor of a women's magazine in Dagestan, a prominent musician and composer, and an archbishop of the Russian Orthodox Church.[83] There were exceptions, however. That same delegation included Andrei Kokoshin, who would emerge a couple of years later as a driving force behind Soviet military reforms. Indeed, the president of the Soviet Peace Committee at the time was Evgenii Fedorov, the physicist who had been a leading science official, Pugwash member, and active proponent of a test ban during the Khrushchev era.[84] Although often frustrating for their Western interlocutors from Europe and the United States, dialogue with these official Soviet representatives was not without some long-term impact—even if the process seemed at times "like water dripping on a stone."[85] The following chapters describe the influence of transnational relations on the Brezhnev-era policies concerning nuclear testing, conventional forces, and antiballistic missile systems.

83. "US Tour by Soviet Peace Committee Delegation Hailed as Success," *Peace and Solidarity* 2, 2 (July–August 1980): 1, the newletter of the U.S. Peace Council.

84. Fedorov led a delegation to the United States in January 1980, as guests of the American Friends Service Committee of Cambridge, Massachusetts, according to the program of their meeting, 8 January 1980. The AFSC had sent a delegation to the USSR in September 1979, as reported in its brochure, written by Everett Mendelsohn, *A Dialogue with the Soviets: Nuclear Weapons, Disarmament and Nuclear Energy* (Philadelphia, 1979).

85. Mary Kaldor, "Who Killed the Cold War?" *Bulletin of the Atomic Scientists* 51, 4 (July/August 1995): 59.

[8]

"Nothing More to Talk About": Nuclear Testing under Brezhnev

If an issue becomes subject to governmental negotiations, before there has been sufficient intellectual preparation through informal private discussions, the solutions proposed are likely to be rather pedestrian.

—Leo Szilard, 1960

Q: I remember the ban-the-bomb movement. Whatever happened to that?
Kistiakowsky: It was the partial test ban, that banned nuclear tests in the atmosphere, that destroyed it.

—Interview with George B. Kistiakowsky,
President Eisenhower's science adviser, 1981

The case of nuclear testing during the Brezhnev period lends support to arguments that the prospects for meaningful East-West arms control declined in the absence of popular pressure and coordinated transnational efforts.[1] A comprehensive nuclear test ban had been a key objective of the transnational disarmament movement since its inception in the mid-1950s. But interest in that goal waned in the wake of the Limited Test Ban Treaty, signed in Moscow in 1963, which eliminated the threat of radioactive fallout from nuclear tests. U.S. peace activists became preoccupied with the war in Vietnam. Meanwhile the superpowers seemed to be working to bring the nuclear arms race under control in the Strategic Arms Limitation Talks (SALT) that began in 1969.

The only measures relevant to nuclear testing negotiated during the Brezhnev era were the Threshold Test Ban Treaty of 1974 and the Peaceful Nuclear Explosions Treaty of 1976. The first limited underground tests on each side to 150 kilotons (about ten times the size of the bombs that destroyed Hiroshima and Nagasaki); the second banned PNEs of over 1.5 megatons and permitted observers from the other side to monitor any PNEs with an aggregate yield greater than 150 kilotons. These treaties certainly fit Leo Szilard's definition

1. Jeffrey W. Knopf, *Domestic Society and International Cooperation: The Impact of Protest on U.S. Arms Control Policy* (Cambridge, U.K., 1998).

of "pedestrian" solutions to the arms race, negotiated by officials taking an intellectually cautious and incremental approach to arms control. Glenn Seaborg, former chair of the Atomic Energy Commission, described the atmosphere in 1976 during hearings before the U.S. Senate Foreign Relations Committee in anticipation of ratification of the treaties: "The Threshold Treaty was repeatedly decried as a sham by those favoring a comprehensive test ban, on the basis that the 'ludicrously high' limit of 150 kilotons would have no adverse effect on the work of weapon designers."[2]

Nevertheless, despite the meager results of official negotiations, transnational activists devoted little effort to pursuing a comprehensive test ban until the early 1980s. At that point, the general resurgence of concern about nuclear war produced a revival of interest in the goal. The politics of the test ban in the late Brezhnev era suggests, however, that even if transnational relations were a necessary condition for disarmament—and the case of Khrushchev's troop reductions casts some doubt on this proposition—they were certainly not sufficient. Transnational appeals to Brezhnev, Andropov, and Chernenko fell on (sometimes literally) deaf ears. This chapter shows that transnational efforts, no matter how extensive, may be insufficient to produce a change in policy without the opportunity provided by receptive government leaders.

It should be acknowledged that the standard explanations for Soviet restraint, or lack of it, do not fare so badly in accounting for lack of progress toward a comprehensive test ban during the Brezhnev era. First, there were no obvious economic incentives to cease testing, although clearly the tests themselves were quite expensive for both sides. Second, the United States was not pursuing a comprehensive test ban at all, let alone "negotiating from strength." Thus arguments focusing on economic constraints and U.S. behavior would not expect major Soviet concessions on nuclear testing during this period.

As far as military requirements are concerned, however, one could make the case that Soviet interests would have been served by forestalling any new U.S. advances in nuclear weapons technology. Thus, the military requirements explanation might anticipate more Soviet interest in a comprehensive test ban than there actually was. The U.S. nuclear weapons laboratories during the 1970s were particularly taken with developing so-called mini-nukes, and a comprehensive test ban would have put a stop to them. But it is possible that the Soviet military authorities did not consider such weapons particularly threatening or worth putting constraints on Soviet nuclear testing.

In any event, the lack of interest in a comprehensive test ban during nearly two decades after the signing of the Moscow treaty seems overdetermined. It is certainly the case that the transnational disarmament movement did not

2. Glenn T. Seaborg with Benjamin S. Loeb, *Stemming the Tide: Arms Control in the Johnson Years* (Lexington, Mass., 1987), 232–233.

give the issue a high priority again until the early 1980s, when the Brezhnev era was drawing to a close.

"NOTHING MORE TO TALK ABOUT ON THE TECHNICAL SIDE"

Even the bilateral contacts between U.S. and Soviet scientists that would prove so valuable in discussions about limiting antiballistic missile systems contributed little to achieving a comprehensive test ban during the Brezhnev period. The U.S. participants in the Soviet-American Disarmament Study (SADS) group, for example, found their Soviet colleagues unwilling to pursue discussions about a test ban after Nikita Khrushchev—the USSR's leading proponent of a comprehensive ban—was removed from office in October 1964.

At a meeting with Soviet scientists in 1966, for example, Marshall Shulman, a SADS member and professional Sovietologist, asked whether it would be valuable to have small teams of one person from each side work on concrete technical problems of arms control. He specifically mentioned the idea that Professor Frank Long, another SADS participant and a chemistry professor at Cornell, might get together with Vasilii Emel'ianov or Lev Artsimovich, two leading SADS and Pugwash members, "to try to narrow the gap between the respective positions on the underground nuclear test ban." According to Shulman's notes of the meeting, Emel'ianov "replied that this would not be useful." He explained that at the recent Pugwash meeting in Sopot, Poland (September 1966), "Long and I were co-chairmen of the working group on this subject; we reached full agreement on it, and it only remains for the political people to decide to go ahead. There is nothing more to talk about on the technical side."[3]

Mikhail Millionshchikov, the leader of the Soviet SADS and Pugwash delegations, made a similar point in conversation with Paul Doty and Frank Long.[4] In fact, the main outstanding "technical" issue was really a political one—the question of on-site, "challenge" inspections—as subsequent discussions made clear. Western participants in transnational efforts at disarmament, visiting Moscow in late summer 1966, for example, found in their interviews with Soviet scientists and Foreign Ministry officials that the Soviet position on inspection had actually hardened. One official declared that the USSR "would not accept any inspection on its territory other than for general and complete disarmament."[5]

3. American Academy of Arts and Sciences, Committee on International Studies of Arms Control, notes from Marshall Shulman, 29 October 1966, p. 2.
4. Doty, "Doty-Long Visit to USSR, June 10 and 11, 1965" (draft), memorandum, 16 June 1965, p. 7.
5. Betty Goetz Lall, "Notes on Trip to the Soviet Union, August 23–September 4, 1966," pp. 2, 4, 6, 8, 14.

Brezhnev's government was clearly uninterested in retracing the faltering steps that Khrushchev had made toward compromise on on-site inspections. Nor did it see the scientists as a useful vehicle for bringing the two sides' positions closer together. It preferred instead to try to manipulate the U.S. delegation, however clumsy and transparent the effort appeared. At one meeting, for example, V. P. Pavlichenko, the Soviet delegation's KGB watchdog, told Betty Lall that she "should start a campaign in the U.S. to persuade people that inspection was not necessary for a test ban because the technical data showed one could not conduct a series of tests without some being detected."[6]

Thus a combination of factors led to a slackening of transnational efforts toward a comprehensive test ban for most of the Brezhnev period: the perception that the superpowers were serious about pursuing arms control and would resolve the main issues; a realization that technical disagreements were no longer the main barrier to a treaty; and a reluctance on the part of the Soviet scientists to pursue discussions of a complete ban on nuclear tests.

THE NEW TRANSNATIONALISM

Starting in the early 1980s, many disarmament groups began to focus their efforts on ending nuclear testing, especially by the United States and the Soviet Union. A number of groups advocated a comprehensive test ban as the first step toward a "nuclear freeze."[7] They adopted a wide range of approaches to influence U.S. policy—from lobbying by former top officials to civil disobedience by grassroots activists.

Direct Action and Direct Appeals

Some organizations were intent on pursuing a transnational strategy and sought to encourage popular opposition to nuclear testing in the USSR. Pressure on the Soviet Union to take the initiative in suspending nuclear tests converged from many directions.

Greenpeace: "We're Simply Not Going to Leave." The most visible proponent of transnational activism was Greenpeace, the organization whose very origins stem from opposition to nuclear testing. As its name indicates, the two main goals of Greenpeace since it began have been environmental protection and disarmament. The goals were combined in its first major action and in many subsequent ones. Greenpeace was founded in 1971 to protest a U.S. nu-

6. Ibid., 10.
7. David Cortright, *Peace Works: The Citizen's Role in Ending the Cold War* (Boulder, Colo., 1993), 209–210.

clear test, scheduled to be conducted underground on an uninhabited island in Alaska. The group opposed the test as a threat to both the environment and to peace. At the time, the administration of Richard Nixon justified the test as necessary for development of an antiballistic missile system and assured the public that the nuclear explosion would do no harm to the environment. James Schlesinger, then head of the Atomic Energy Commission responsible for building nuclear weapons, took his wife and two young daughters there to demonstrate his confidence in the test's safety.[8]

The Greenpeace protests failed to prevent the 1971 test. A quarter century later the organization produced evidence that the Alaskan test site was still leaking radioactive materials into the environment.[9] The emergence of Greenpeace indicated, nevertheless, that antinuclear activists were still willing to engage in direct action against nuclear testing, despite the signing of the Limited Test Ban Treaty.

Greenpeace is perhaps most famous for its daring attempts to interrupt nuclear test programs by sailing ships into test areas, and the tragic death of one of its crew when French commandos blew up the *Rainbow Warrior* in Auckland Harbor, New Zealand, in 1985. In fact, the precedents had already been set—both for audacious activism and harsh government response (although not as harsh as murder)—during the previous era of atmospheric nuclear testing. In April 1958 a group of protesters planned to sail their ship, the *Golden Rule*, into the U.S. nuclear test zone in the Pacific. U.S. officials arrested the crew in Hawaii, seized their vessel, and put them in jail for sixty days. Inspired by the crew's courage, an anthropologist named Earle Reynolds and his family sought to sail their boat, the *Phoenix*, into the restricted test area. The U.S. Coast Guard intercepted the vessel. Reynolds was brought to Hawaii, where he was put on trial and sentenced to jail for two years.[10]

In May 1982 Greenpeace set a new precedent by taking on the Soviet government. The organization sent a ship to Russia to protest Soviet nuclear testing. Crew members, including Daniel Ellsberg, the former Pentagon official turned peace activist, docked in Leningrad, after Soviet officials rushed through emergency visas (the ship had entered Soviet waters without permission). Ellsberg presented the group's demands for a halt in Soviet nuclear testing and announced: "We're simply not going to leave until we get an answer from Brezhnev. At least we won't leave voluntarily." Group members donned T-shirts saying "USSR Stop Nuclear Testing Now" and prepared to meet with members of the official Soviet Peace Committee, who at first refused to allow them to wear the shirts in Leningrad but later relented. When

8. Matthew L. Wald, "Radiation Leak Reported at Site of Nuclear Test," *New York Times*, 30 October 1996.

9. Ibid.

10. A description of these events is found in Martha J. Smith, "The Nuclear Testing Policies of the Eisenhower Administration, 1953–60" (Ph.D. diss., University of Toronto, 1997), 366–368. For more detail of the Reynolds case, see Earle Reynolds, *The Forbidden Voyage of the Phoenix into the AEC Prohibited Zone* (New York, 1961).

Greenpeace members began passing out leaflets and posting them on walls, they were asked to return to their ship. From the ship they released balloons with the same antinuclear message, and when they refused demands to stop, Soviet officials ordered two tugboats to tow them outside Soviet territorial waters.[11] Although they were not arrested nor murdered, the Greenpeace transnational activists were clearly not welcome in Brezhnev's Russia.

Letter to Chernenko. Reflecting the heterogeneity and diversity of the U.S. peace movement as a whole, the transnational campaign for a test ban included efforts by professional organizations and arms control lobbying groups to influence Soviet policy, as well as Greenpeace-style direct action aimed at influencing public opinion. The Washington-based Center for Defense Information directed its appeals to the very top, calling, in November 1984, for a halt to nuclear testing by 6 August 1985, the fortieth anniversary of the atomic bombing of Hiroshima.[12] Retired admirals Gene LaRocque and Eugene Carroll wrote to Soviet leader Konstantin Chernenko (and to U.S. President Ronald Reagan) proposing a mutual moratorium, but Chernenko died before he could respond. Only after Mikhail Gorbachev came into office did the appeal get a favorable response—but just from the Soviet side.

Doctors' Orders. The Physicians for Social Responsibility (PSR) also focused particular attention on the test ban issue in 1984 and 1985 during its public education efforts in the United States and in meetings with Soviet colleagues.[13] The International Physicians for the Prevention of Nuclear War (IPPNW) also came to advocate a test ban at the initiative of its U.S. chapter. Generally, according to its first U.S. president Dr. Bernard Lown, the international physicians movement sought to avoid "talking weapons" and refrained from discussing such issues as missile "throwweight" or the technical prospects for strategic defenses. Instead, the doctors emphasized the social and psychological effects of "nuclearizing" society, the costs of the arms race in diversion of resources from human needs, and, especially, the health and ecological consequences of nuclear weapons. But in 1983 the American doctors decided to pursue a particular arms control objective as a way of slowing the arms race, and they focused on a comprehensive test ban.[14]

Like many disarmament activists at the time, the doctors believed that a

11. This event is recounted in the *Arms Control Reporter* (Cambridge, Mass., 1982), 608.B.14, from Associated Press, *Boston Globe*, and *New York Times* reports. Although my citations are to the original paper version, the complete back files of the *Arms Control Reporter* are now available on CD from the Institute for Defense and Disarmament Studies (acr@idds.org).

12. *Defense Monitor* 13, 5 (1984); *Arms Control Reporter*, 608.B.50–51.

13. Jane Wales, "PSR in 1985: Keeping the Pressure On," and Jeffrey Patterson, "PSR and the CTB," *PSR Reports* 6, 1 (Winter 1985), 1, 6; Raoul Rosenberg, "PSR's CTB Campaign," *PSR Reports* 6, 2 (Spring 1985), 3; Michael McCally, "Letter from Moscow," *PSR Reports* 5, 2 (Summer 1984), 7.

14. Bernard Lown, interview by author, Brookline, Mass., 6 April 1994.

unilateral initiative of restraint might break the impasse in arms control efforts and lead to progress in slowing the arms race. At the Fourth World Congress of the IPPNW in Helsinki in June 1984, Bernard Lown made a speech advocating a unilateral nuclear test moratorium "by one or the other" of the superpowers. "If this step is matched," he argued, "additional steps are undertaken by the other superpower. The function of the physicians movement is to help mold a climate of world opinion to compel reciprocation."[15]

Lown and his colleagues doubted that the Reagan administration would take such an initiative, so they put their hopes on the Soviet government—even if Lown did not say so explicitly in his remarks to the Congress. The implications were clear to Evgenii Chazov, Lown's Soviet colleague and IPPNW co-president. Reluctant to put his government on the spot, Chazov urged Lown not to give his speech to the full plenum of the Congress. Lown, however, insisted on presenting his views to the plenum but agreed to speak at the morning session before some five hundred delegates rather than in the afternoon when representatives of the media would be present.[16]

During autumn 1984 Lown continued promoting the idea of a unilateral Soviet test moratorium. At that point he began traveling to the USSR several times a year. He lobbied Chazov on the issue to the point where his friend said he was sick of hearing about unilateral initiatives, to which Lown replied, "OK, glad you agree, who else should I talk to?"

With Chazov's help Lown then took his lobbying efforts to the Soviet Foreign Ministry. He received mixed responses to the idea of a unilateral Soviet test ban, with one official telling him he thought it was a "great idea, don't be discouraged." But Aleksandr Bessmertnykh, the head of the U.S. Department at the ministry (and later foreign minister at the end of the Gorbachev period), was particularly negative. He argued that if the Soviet Union undertook a unilateral ban, no one would hear about it. The *New York Times* would report with a small article explaining the ban as justified on military grounds, but big headlines would greet Soviet test resumption after the United States failed to reciprocate.[17] This turned out to be a prescient anticipation of how the U.S. media initially would react when Gorbachev announced a unilateral test ban in 1985, when he assumed power from the last Brezhnev-era leader, Konstantin Chernenko.

"I Won't Say That the Declaration Influenced Gorbachev . . . "

When the U.S. activists began to pursue a comprehensive test ban again in the early 1980s, they engaged a new generation of Soviet scientists. Probably

15. Bernard Lown, "The Urgency of a Unique Initiative" (address to the plenary session of the 4th World Congress of the IPPNW, Helsinki, 4 June 1984); copy courtesy of Dr. Lown.
16. Lown, interview.
17. Ibid.

the most important advocate of a test ban among the scientists was Evgenii Velikhov, vice president of the Soviet Academy of Sciences. Velikhov's participation in transnational disarmament activities began when he represented the USSR at a meeting of the Papal Academy of Sciences in 1982; it intensified the following year when he attended a meeting with U.S. scientists at National Academy of Sciences in Washington as the head of the Soviet delegation to the Committee on International Security and Arms Control. The goals proposed by his colleagues at that meeting helped set the agenda for his subsequent activities. The three main ones were to defend the ABM Treaty; prevent deployment of arms in space, including antisatellite weapons; and achieve a comprehensive nuclear test ban.[18] All three goals were related. Much of the discussion between U.S. and Soviet scientists on the need for a test ban had stressed the urgency of stopping the so-called third-generation nuclear explosives necessary for space-based strategic defenses.[19] Velikhov tried to take advantage of the Soviet military's apprehensions about Star Wars to sell the idea of a test ban, and he expressed enthusiasm about Lown's proposed initiative. But the idea of a unilateral moratorium was too radical for the Brezhnev-era leadership.[20]

Nevertheless, the ideas circulating within the transnational scientists movement were beginning to reach some reform-minded officials. In 1983, for example, Velikhov began working closely with Aleksandr Iakovlev, the former Soviet ambassador to Canada who became a key architect of perestroika. As Velikhov recalled years later, "He made a strong impression on me. He's the kind of person who writes his own speeches." They "developed a close relationship under Gorbachev, when the reforms were being worked out." Gorbachev himself Velikhov had first met in 1978. The physicist became one of Gorbachev's informal advisers on "issues having to do with national security and strategic defenses. He was interested in these questions even during the Brezhnev period."[21]

Velikhov has been reluctant to overstate his influence on Gorbachev's thinking about nuclear weapons. In later chapters we consider the evidence of his role in Soviet decisions on the test ban and strategic defenses during the Gorbachev period. In an interview in 1989, Velikhov did acknowledge one possible source of Gorbachev's antinuclearism. Speaking about the declaration he and Victor Weisskopf helped draft at the September 1982 meeting of the Papal Academy of Sciences, he said: "If you read it you'll see some of the ideas we now call the new thinking—the need for a nuclear-free world, the

18. Evgenii Velikhov, interview by author, Moscow, 29 July 1992.
19. Jeremy Stone, "FAS Visit to Moscow Initiates Star Wars Dialogue," *F.A.S. Public Interest Report* 36, 10 (December 1983).
20. Lown, interview; Velikhov, interview.
21. Evgenii Velikhov, "Chernobyl Remains on Our Mind," in Stephen F. Cohen and Katrina vanden Heuvel, eds., *Voices of Glasnost: Interviews with Gorbachev's Reformers* (New York, 1989), 160.

impossibility of nuclear superiority or of a defense against nuclear weapons. I won't say that the declaration influenced Gorbachev, but I know that he read it and reached his own conclusions. Compare that 1982 document with what Gorbachev said about nuclear weapons in 1986."[22]

Clearly the stage was set already in the early 1980s for the dramatic initiatives that Gorbachev would take in the second half of the decade. But Gorbachev himself—or someone quite like him—was a necessary "window of opportunity" for a policy entrepreneur such as Velikhov to promote the solutions that he and his transnational colleagues had worked out to deal with the arms race.

22. Velikhov, "Chernobyl Remains on Our Mind," 160. The document, drafted at the Vatican, 23–24 September 1982, is published as a "Declaration on Prevention of Nuclear War," in Evgenii Velikhov, ed., *The Night After . . . : Climatic and Biological Consequences of a Nuclear War* (Moscow, 1985), 155–157.

[9]

"A Train without a Locomotive":
Brezhnev's Army

We do not forget the big role which, as before, conventional types of armaments retain.

—LEONID BREZHNEV, 1965

[During the period of stagnation,] the marshals and generals, on the one hand, and the general designers from the military industry, on the other, received a totally free hand and went out of control.... Under the leadership ... of Brezhnev, Ustinov, and Grechko, they created an incredible military machine, in terms of its dimensions and cost (but it has surprised us more than once in recent years with its low level of effectiveness). What did we achieve, having created this giant? Above all, we managed in the 1970s, despite détente, to frighten the entire world and to rally against ourselves such a coalition of all the leading powers that nobody has had since probably the time of Napoleon.

—GEORGII ARBATOV, 1990

The Brezhnev era saw no progress in reducing conventional forces in Europe or reorienting them to favor defensive operations. On the contrary, the Soviet Army demonstrated its offensive nature with the invasion of Czechoslovakia in 1968 to crush the "Prague Spring" reform movement there. The years following the ouster of Nikita Khrushchev witnessed an enormous buildup of conventional forces in Europe on both sides. The dimensions of the Soviet buildup—in both quantitative and qualitative terms—were particularly striking. It coincided, ironically, with a set of multinational negotiations on reducing conventional armed forces, termed, in the West, the Mutual and Balanced Force Reductions or MBFR talks. The first part of this chapter considers how well explanations focusing on economic factors, military requirements, and U.S. behavior account for the lack of progress on conventional arms control.

The end of the Brezhnev era—the early 1980s—also witnessed the origins of a transnational community of civilian specialists interested in alternative means to resolve the security dilemma in Europe. The Soviet members of this community were ready, when the opportunity arose in the form of a new political leadership, to promote the new ideas with the direct assistance of their Western colleagues. The second part of this chapter describes the origins of this remarkable transnational community and the barriers it faced in the late Brezhnev interregnum.

Ambassador Jonathan Dean, who served as deputy head and then head of the U.S. team at the MBFR talks in Vienna, has referred to those negotiations as a "train without a locomotive." From the beginning of the negotiations in 1973, the parties to the MBFR talks disagreed over questions concerning the scope and objectives of the process and even basic data on the number of troops and weapons each side deployed. Dean argues that as the MBFR process lost momentum, "neither the Soviet Union nor the United States nor any Western European government took the initiative to get the train moving. The essential ingredient for a successful outcome—strong political interest by at least some of the participants—did not exist."[1]

Dean's train metaphor is useful in describing two other aspects of the Soviet army during the Brezhnev era. The buildup of Soviet conventional forces, and especially the mass production of armaments such as tanks and artillery, also resembled a train without a locomotive—heading downhill, building momentum and speed, but with no one at the wheel. Brezhnev and his colleagues largely gave the Soviet high command a free hand in directing the course of Soviet military posture toward war in Europe, even as they tried to reign in Soviet programs for strategic nuclear warfare.

In the early 1980s a small group of Soviet civilian and military reformers began to question the logic of Soviet conventional military strategy and to propose alternatives. The civilians forged links with a transnational community of advocates of "nonoffensive defense" and adopted many of their ideas. Until Mikhail Gorbachev came into office in 1985, however, this was a train without a conductor. By 1990, Gorbachev and his allies had brought the train to an unexpected destination: the reforms of the Soviet army provided the prerequisite for withdrawal of Soviet occupation forces from Eastern Europe and the peaceful overthrow of the Soviet-imposed regimes. Such a course was unthinkable in the Brezhnev era.

THE FAILURE OF CONVENTIONAL ARMS CONTROL

In accounting for the lack of progress in the MBFR talks the first explanation we encounter is the simplest: none of the participants desired it.[2] Although it would take only one side's opposition to ruin the prospects for a negotiated agreement, we know from the subsequent events of the late 1980s

1. Jonathan Dean, *Meeting Gorbachev's Challenge: How to Build Down the NATO–Warsaw Pact Confrontation* (New York, 1989), 101–104.
2. Dean, *Meeting Gorbachev's Challenge*, 101. See also John G. Kelliher, *The Negotiations on Mutual and Balanced Force Reductions* (New York, 1980); Coit D. Blacker, "The MBFR Experience," in Alexander L. George, Philip J. Farley, and Alexander Dallin, eds., *U.S.-Soviet Security Cooperation: Achievements, Failures, Lessons* (Oxford, U.K., 1988).

that one side's dramatic initiatives can also breathe new life into the negotiating process. Thus, even if U.S. lack of interest in mutual reductions in conventional forces would suffice to explain the failure of MBFR, we should also consider the Soviet position and why the Soviet side was unwilling to make the effort to enliven the negotiations. Identifying the reasons behind the lack of Soviet restraint in the sphere of conventional arms also provides an opportunity to evaluate the main factors we have examined as causes of Soviet restraint in other cases: military requirements, economic circumstances, and U.S. behavior.

Military Requirements

Most Western analysts would agree that the last thing the Soviet armed forces wanted in the 1970s was a reduction in their conventional military capability in Europe. The drastic unilateral reductions of the Khrushchev years had a demoralizing impact on the officer corps. The Soviet military rejected Khrushchev's emphasis on nuclear weapons and missiles at the expense of conventional forces as an unrealistic strategy for "one-variant" war.[3] Khrushchev's successors understood the military commanders' antipathy to political interference in what they considered their exclusive sphere of professional competence. Under the Brezhnev leadership the Soviet high command was given considerably more autonomy in matters of strategy, force planning, and budget than they had enjoyed during the Khrushchev period.[4] High on their list of priorities was a major buildup of conventional forces—a goal basically incompatible with the MBFR negotiations.

Most Western analysts would reconstruct the military rationale for the conventional military buildup as follows:[5] In the second half of the 1960s, the Soviet military began to recognize that U.S.-Soviet nuclear parity at the strate-

3. For an account of Soviet military thinking about nuclear war at the end of the Khrushchev period, see "Material o razvitii voennogo iskusstva v usloviiakh vedeniia raketno-iadernoi voiny po sovremennym predstavleniiam," prepared for Marshal M. V. Zakharov, with cover memorandum from Lt. Gen. P. Ivashutin, 28 August 1964. This document, from the Ministry of Defense archives, is now on deposit at the National Security Archives in Washington, D.C. When he received the document, Marshal Zakharov was in between tours as chief of the General Staff; he was serving as head of the military academy of the General Staff and became chief again in November 1964. Ivashutin was the chief of Soviet military intelligence.

4. For good overviews of these issues, see Thomas M. Nichols, *The Sacred Cause: Civil-Military Conflict over Soviet National Security, 1917–1992* (Ithaca, N.Y., 1993); Timothy J. Colton and Thane Gustafson, eds., *Soldiers and the Soviet State: Civil-Military Relations from Brezhnev to Gorbachev* (Princeton, N.J., 1990); and David Holloway, *The Soviet Union and the Arms Race* (New Haven, Conn., 1983).

5. The following discussion draws on Mary C. FitzGerald, "The Dilemma in Moscow's Defensive Force Posture," *Arms Control Today* 19, 9 (November 1989): 15–20; R. Hyland Phillips and Jeffrey I. Sands, "Reasonable Sufficiency and Soviet Conventional Defense," *International Security* 13, 2 (Fall 1988): 164–178; Phillip A. Petersen and Notra Trulock III, "A 'New' Soviet Military Doctrine: Origins and Implications," *Strategic Review* (Summer 1988): 9–24; and Jacques Sapir and Thierry Malleret, "La politique militaire soviétique: De la restructuration à la reforme" (paper presented to the 4th World Congress for Soviet and East European Studies, Harrogate, England, 21–26 July 1990).

gic level had created the possibility that a future war might begin and remain for some time at the conventional level. Both the new U.S. emphasis on conventional forces, which the Kennedy administration initiated in 1961, and NATO's formal adoption of "flexible response" in 1967 convinced Soviet officials that further attention to conventional capabilities was warranted. During the early 1970s, Soviet military doctrine accepted that the initial phase of a future war would probably be conventional. In order to prevent such a conflict from escalating to nuclear war, the Soviets decided to forswear their own first use of nuclear weapons and to seek to degrade U.S. and NATO nuclear capabilities by offensive air and missile attacks during the conventional phase.[6]

The Soviet emphasis on conventional operations contained a crucial offensive component. In addition to the efforts to disarm NATO nuclear forces by missile and air attacks, the Soviets envisioned high-speed, combined-arms offensives to seize NATO territory and forces. Soviet offensives would be carried out in waves, as succeeding echelons of forces were brought into the battle. Such offensives would also entail quick intermingling of Soviet and Western forces, thereby making nuclear use much less attractive for NATO. Furthermore, the introduction of "Operational Maneuver Groups," identified by Western analysts in the early 1980s, provided for even quicker and deeper offensive actions at the main axis of attack.[7]

In the mid-1980s a number of Western analysts began to doubt the military rationale behind the Soviet conventional buildup. They pointed out that the threat of large-scale Soviet offensives could actually bring about what they were ostensibly intended to prevent—NATO nuclear escalation.[8] Others claimed that the Soviet military leaders never considered "no first use" as anything but a propaganda slogan. Evidence from Warsaw Pact military exercises and documents indicates that the Soviet armed forces maintained contingency plans for use of nuclear weapons early in a European war if NATO initiated nuclear use, but they preferred to keep the conflict from escalating to that level.[9] What was the point of maintaining such a huge army if a war in Europe would one way or the other ignite a nuclear conflagration?

6. Dennis M. Gormley, "A New Dimension to Soviet Theater Strategy," *Orbis* 29, 3 (Fall 1985); Kerry L. Hines, "Soviet Short-Range Ballistic Missiles: Now a Conventional Deep-Strike Mission," *International Defense Review* 18, 12 (1985).

7. John G. Hines and Phillip A. Peterson, "The Warsaw Pact Strategic Offensive: The OMG in Context," *International Defense Review* 16, 10 (1983). For a discussion of historical antecedents to the OMG, see David R. Jones, *The Advanced Guard and Mobility in Russian and Soviet Military Thought and Practice*, SAFRA Papers No. 1 (Gulf Breeze, Fla., 1985).

8. For an important critique of the Soviet posture, see Richard Ned Lebow, "The Soviet Offensive in Europe: The Schlieffen Plan Revisited?" *International Security* 9, 4 (Spring 1985): 44–78.

9. Lothar Rühl, "Offensive Defence in the Warsaw Pact," *Survival* 33, 5 (September/October 1991): 442–450. See also Ghulam Dastagir Wardak, comp., *The Voroshilov Lectures: Materials from the Soviet General Staff Academy*, vol. 1 (Washington, D.C., 1989), especially the introduction by Raymond L. Garthoff.

Economic Constraints

Given the contradictions and uncertainty of identifying a coherent and persuasive military rationale for the Soviet emphasis on highly offensive conventional forces, some Western analysts came to favor more political explanations for Soviet behavior over the strategic military ones: the influence of a Soviet "military-industrial complex," the bureaucratic politics of the military services, or Brezhnev's desire for the high command's political support.[10] Behind these explanations lies the assumption that either (1) the Soviet economy was sufficiently robust to support an expensive military machine serving mainly parochial political interests or (2) Soviet political leaders were willing to countenance serious economic decline—or were motivated to ignore it—in order not to offend their military supporters. The first assumption posits that economic conditions were favorable for a major buildup. The second maintains that regardless of the state of the economy Soviet leaders were not interested in reducing military expenditures through arms control for fear of alienating the military command.

Brezhnev and the Military Industrialists. In fact Brezhnev does seem to have been concerned about the burden of military spending on the Soviet economy. His advisers have recounted many instances when he had to face down military opponents of his arms control policies, particularly Marshal Andrei Grechko, the defense minister during the early years of the strategic arms negotiations.[11] One example comes from the memoirs of Brezhnev's main foreign policy aide, Anatolii Aleksandrov-Agentov. He describes a stormy five-hour meeting that Brezhnev held with his top military officials and diplomats in early 1970 in order to persuade them to make the concessions necessary to achieve an arms agreement with the United States. The diplomats were willing, but the military resisted. Finally, Brezhnev turned to the officers and the military-industrial barons and exclaimed, "Well, good, we won't make any such concessions and there won't be an agreement. A further nuclear arms race will develop. And will you be able to give me here, as commander in chief of the armed forces, a firm guarantee that in the case of such a turn of events we will permanently overtake the United States and the correlation of forces between us will become more favorable for us than it is now?" No one was willing to make such a commitment. "Then what's the matter?" asked

10. Jack Snyder, "Limiting Offensive Conventional Forces: Soviet Proposals and Western Options," *International Security* 12, 4 (Spring 1988): 48–77.

11. Marshal Sergei Akhromeev describes Grechko as an "opponent of any kind of reductions in military expenditures." See S. F. Akhromeev and G. M. Kornienko, *Glazami marshala i diplomata* (Moscow, 1992), 22–23. See also G. A. Arbatov, *Zatianuvsheesia vyzdorovlenie (1953–1985 gg.): Svidetel'stvo sovremennika* (Moscow, 1991), 232–234; and A. S. Cherniaev, *Moia zhizn' i moe vremia* (Moscow, 1995), 317.

Brezhnev. "Why should we continue to exhaust our economy by continuously increasing military expenditures?"[12]

When Dmitrii Ustinov became defense minister in 1976, following Grechko's death, Brezhnev efforts to reign in military spending were complicated by several factors. Unlike Grechko, who was a career military officer, Ustinov was a civilian with long experience in the military-industrial sector. "Marshal" Ustinov was not well respected by the officer corps, no matter how often he dressed in a military uniform or how many medals he wore. Nevertheless, as a Party official with a reputation for intelligence and hard work, he could have been in a good position to bring military spending under control. But he had no interest in doing so. He was widely perceived by members of the Soviet foreign policy community as the standard-bearer of the Soviet "military-industrial complex." Moreover, Brezhnev and Ustinov were close friends. That made it all the more difficult for Brezhnev to economize in the military sphere against Ustinov's resistance.[13]

There is no doubt that Brezhnev was aware of the declining state of the Soviet economy. Plenty of information was available to him. In 1974, for example, each member of the Politburo and Central Committee received a packet of letters from citizens describing how difficult it was for them to obtain food and consumer goods.[14] The Politburo also received detailed reports about the dissatisfaction with economic conditions among Soviet allies in Eastern Europe.[15] But Brezhnev—especially as his health continued to deteriorate in the second half of the 1970s—could not muster the political will or energy to do anything about the Soviet economic decline, particularly if it meant challenging the military's sacred tradition of mass armies and tanks.

Declines in Growth, Labor Force, and Productivity. A second variant of the economic explanation for Soviet military reform focuses on demographic constraints. Indeed, one of the most plausible relationships between economic conditions and decisions on troop strength is the demographic one, especially in a country with such an enormous army as the Soviet Union. Thus, in trying to account for such developments as Gorbachev's unilateral con-

12. A. M. Aleksandrov-Agentov, *Ot Kollontai do Gorbacheva* (Moscow, 1994), 210–211; see also Aleksandr G. Savel'yev and Nikolay N. Detinov, *The Big Five: Arms Control Decision-Making in the Soviet Union* (Westport, Conn., 1995), 34–35.

13. Cherniaev, *Moia zhizn' i moe vremia*, 287, 306–309. For a description of Ustinov's style of work, see Grigorii Vasil'evich Kisun'ko, *Sekretnaia zona: Ispoved' general'nogo konstruktora* (Moscow, 1996), who at times wondered "does this person ever sleep?" (315). See also the characterization by Ustinov's personal physician, Evgenii Chazov, *Zdorov'e i vlast'* (Moscow, 1992), 204–205; and Anatoly Dobrynin, *In Confidence: Moscow's Ambassador to Six Cold War Presidents* (New York, 1995), 194.

14. Cherniaev quotes from several in *Moia zhizn' i moe vremia*, 327–328. He points out that the preparation of the packets was part of a plan to discredit Prime Minister Aleksei Kosygin and pin the blame on him for the poor state of the economy.

15. Ibid., 337.

Table 8. Working-Age Population in the USSR, 1950–95

Year	Midyear Population (× 1000)	Average Annual Increment	Growth Rate (per 1000)
1950	103,345	2,263	20.76
1955	114,658	960	8.20
1960	119,459	937	7.69
1965	124,142	1,726	13.44
1970	132,774	2,252	16.27
1975	144,035	2,087	13.99
1980	154,472	565	3.62
1985	157,295	591	3.72
1990	160,251	760	4.69
1995	164,053	1,713	10.17

Source: W. Ward Kingkade, "Estimates and Projections of the Population of the USSR, 1979–2025," Center for International Research, U.S. Bureau of the Census, Washington, D.C., CIR Staff Paper No. 33, December 1987, p. 6.

Note: Figures for 1990 and 1995 were projections.

ventional-force reductions in the late 1980s and the similar initiatives of the Khrushchev period, analysts have tried to identify a correlation between the availability of labor in the economy and Soviet decisions about the size of the armed forces. The data in Table 8 on the growth rate of the labor force do provide a meaningful context for understanding the large-scale unilateral demobilization of the Soviet army that Khrushchev undertook starting in the mid-1950s, as discussed in Chapter 5.

The data also show that demographic constraints relaxed considerably after Khrushchev's removal from office in 1964, allowing his successors to embark on a major increase in the size of the armed forces.[16] Subsequent Soviet behavior is less consistent with an explanation that focuses on demographic constraints. The Brezhnev era leadership increased military personnel by nearly nine hundred thousand troops during the two decades following Khrushchev's ouster. Growth in the labor force had already peaked by 1970, however, and it showed a precipitous decline after 1975. The growth rate of productivity of the civilian work force was sharply dropping as well, from 4.6 percent in 1960 to 1.4 percent in 1980 (see Table 9). Soviet security policy manifested little influence of these significant economic changes. On the basis of the demographic data, one would have expected the Soviets to pursue reductions in personnel more seriously at the MBFR talks that began in Vienna in 1973. They had plenty of notice of the impending shortfall in the labor market starting in the mid-1970s, because all of the new entrants into the la-

16. For a detailed analysis, see Steven W. Popper, *The Economic Cost of Soviet Military Manpower Requirements*, Rand Corporation, R-3659-AF (Santa Monica, Calif., 1989).

Table 9. Growth of Soviet Labor Force, Labor Productivity,
and Military Personnel, 1950–90

Year	Labor Force Growth (%)[a]	Productivity Growth (%)[a]	Military Personnel (× 1000)[b]
1950	2.0	—	4,600
1955	.8	4.6	5,800
1960	.8	4.6	3,973
1965	1.3	3.4	3,380
1970	1.6	3.2	3,535
1975	1.4	2.0	4,005
1980	.4	1.4	4,118
1985	.4	1.3	4,265
1990	.5	—	3,765
1995	1.0	—	—

Sources: For labor force growth, the source is W. Ward King-kade, "Demographic Trends in the Soviet Union," in U.S. Congress, Joint Economic Committee, Gorbachev's Economic Plans (Washington, D.C., 1987), 1:173. For productivity growth, Paul Gregory and Robert Stuart, Soviet Economic Structure and Performance, 3d ed. (New York, 1986), 331, 335, except for the 1985 figure, which is from Gur Ofer, Soviet Economic Growth (Santa Monica, Calif., 1988), 15. For military personnel, Stephen Rapawy, "Labor Force and Employment in the U.S.S.R.," in U.S. Congress, Gorbachev's Economic Plans, 194–195.
[a] Annual average of previous five years.
[b] Figures exclude internal security (MVD) and border troops (KGB).

bor force during that time had already been born. A straight economic-demographic explanation fails to account for the lack of serious Soviet pursuit of a conventional-force reductions in the late 1970s.

U.S. Behavior

Clearly Brezhnev and his colleagues had reason to resist undertaking serious reductions in conventional forces, regardless of economic conditions. It is probably true, as Georgii Arbatov has written, that Brezhnev "from the very beginning of his time in the leadership saw in the military a very important base of his power." It is an exaggeration, though, to argue that "for that reason he tried to give them everything that they asked for."[17] Brezhnev did seek to accommodate Soviet military commanders to the extent that he could, especially those in the traditional ground forces, in contrast to Khrushchev who had deliberately neglected and insulted them. But he required at

17. Arbatov, Zatianuvsheesia vyzdorovlenie, 232.

least some strategic rationale to justify the huge expenditures that the Defense Ministry requested. That is where U.S. behavior played a role.

The United States and its allies were reluctant to countenance major conventional reductions in Europe. In fact, the Nixon administration initially viewed MBFR as a means of preventing Congress from withdrawing U.S. forces from Europe. Nixon argued that efforts such as those by Senator Mike Mansfield to bring the troops home would undercut the U.S. bargaining position. Henry Kissinger, Nixon's secretary of state, revealed in his memoirs that the administration was not interested in genuine reductions but favored MBFR because it "saved our whole European defense structure from Congressional savaging."[18]

The United States did make one proposal in the early years of the MBFR negotiations that attracted favorable Soviet attention. In December 1975, NATO negotiators sought to gain Soviet support for unequal cuts in conventional forces (a reduction of 29,000 soldiers for NATO versus 68,000 for the Warsaw Pact) by offering to reduce the U.S. nuclear arsenal in Europe by 1,000 (out of about 7,000) nuclear warheads. Soviet negotiators characterized the proposal as "positive" but "inadequate."[19] In conversation with his advisers at the time, Brezhnev expressed interest in what he described as a trade of U.S. nuclear weapons for Soviet tanks. "From the security angle," he argued, "there are no obstacles. Neither the Americans nor the Germans will attack us after such an agreement. There is nothing to fear here. [But] there's another problem: our friends in the socialist countries will be against it. They need our tanks for another reason entirely."[20] In expressing concern that withdrawal of Soviet forces would undermine the regimes of Warsaw Pact allies, Brezhnev foreshadowed the link that Gorbachev would later deliberately pursue between conventional force reductions and "freedom of choice" for the countries of Eastern Europe.[21]

In 1977 some of Brezhnev's advisers, concerned that East-West détente could not be sustained without some tangible movement toward disarmament, attempted to gain the Soviet leader's support for some modest initiatives related to European security. In a draft of a speech they prepared for Brezhnev to deliver at a congress of the Young Communists' League, they included the announcement of a withdrawal of a thousand tanks from East Germany and an army corps from Czechoslovakia. Believing that Brezhnev had approved their draft, the advisers were surprised to learn that the an-

18. Quoted in Raymond L. Garthoff, *Détente and Confrontation: American-Soviet Relations from Nixon to Reagan*, rev. ed. (Washington, D.C., 1994), 132–134; and Blacker, "MBFR Experience." On the Soviet decision to undercut Mansfield's efforts, see Dobrynin, *In Confidence*, 146.

19. Blacker, "The MBFR Experience," 128.

20. Cherniaev, *Moia zhizn' i moe vremia*, 316–317.

21. On the Brezhnev leadership's concern that reducing Soviet troop levels would lead to instability in Eastern Europe, see Dobrynin, *In Confidence*, 146, 169.

nouncement of the initiatives had been left out of the speech. Apparently Gromyko and Suslov had removed it, and Brezhnev at that stage was too ill to notice one way or the other.[22]

The Soviet government did finally decide to make a minor gesture of unilateral restraint in October 1979, but by then East-West relations had deteriorated too much for it to make any difference. In a speech in East Berlin celebrating the fortieth anniversary of the German Democratic Republic, Brezhnev announced a unilateral withdrawal of a thousand Soviet tanks and twenty thousand troops from the country.[23] At this point the Soviet side was clearly motivated by U.S. behavior—namely, the impending NATO decision to deploy new U.S. cruise and Pershing II missiles to Western Europe. But Brezhnev's gesture failed to stop the NATO plans and did little to reinvigorate the MBFR talks. The United States did, however, appear to carry out its part of the bargain that it had proposed in 1975: it withdrew a thousand obsolete nuclear warheads to make way for the new ones.[24] Overall, however, U.S. negotiating behavior did not encourage Soviet interest in making major reductions in its conventional forces in Europe.

Beyond the negotiating table, U.S. and NATO policies reinforced Soviet reluctance to pursue conventional-force reductions. NATO's military strategy of flexible response, with its emphasis on enhanced capabilities for fighting a conventional war in Europe, made it unlikely that the Soviet side would consider reducing its own European forces to any great extent.[25] Certainly at the level of decisions on weapons procurement, the behavior of Soviet adversaries—most notably, the United States—appears to have been crucial in influencing Soviet policy.

Consider, for example, the case of aircraft intended mainly for use in conventional warfare. One analyst with the RAND corporation, who interviewed Soviet military officers and military-industrial personnel in the last days of the Soviet Union, detailed the "mounting evidence that both the formal issuance of military requirements for new Soviet combat aircraft and the actual design characteristics of those aircraft are directly responsive to development initiatives in the West." He cited conversations with Soviet engineers who claimed that "Soviet fighters have long been developed and deployed in reaction to U.S. aircraft." "One stated flatly that the Su-24, Su-25, Su-27, and MiG-29 were produced as direct Soviet 'answers' to the F-111, A-10, F-15, and

22. Cherniaev, *Moia zhizn' i moe vremia*, 384.

23. His speech was published in *Pravda*, 7 October 1979.

24. In fact, the United States described its withdrawal of the warheads as a unilateral move, in order to make the deployment of the new missiles more acceptable; it repudiated its earlier proposal to withdraw a thousand warheads as part of a troop-reduction agreement. At this point, the United States also wanted to call an end to the MBFR talks altogether, but its NATO allies objected. Dean, *Meeting Gorbachev's Challenge*, 102.

25. On Soviet reactions to flexible response, see Kimberly Marten Zisk, *Engaging the Enemy: Organization Theory and Soviet Military Innovation: 1955–1991* (Princeton, N.J., 1993), chap. 3.

F-16. 'Without the F-15,' he said, 'there would never have been a Su-27. Without the F-16, there would never have been a MiG-29.'"[26]

Perhaps it would be an exaggeration to argue, along the same lines, that without NATO's flexible response, there would never have been a Soviet conventional buildup. But NATO's policies certainly influenced the development of Soviet strategy for war in Europe and made it easy for the Soviet military and political leadership to reject conventional-arms control. In this respect, U.S. behavior hindered Soviet restraint.

ORIGINS OF THE TRANSNATIONAL DIALOGUE

Elements of the "new thinking" in Soviet security policy—especially the recognition that, as Gorbachev put it, one side cannot be secure at the expense of the other side's security[27]—date back at least to the 1960s. At that time, as later, many of the ideas were introduced into the Soviet debate by scholars familiar with the Western literature on international relations and security.[28] More immediate antecedents—that is, writings by people who influenced Gorbachev's thinking—appeared already in the early 1980s.[29] The impetus

26. Benjamin S. Lambeth, *From Farnborough to Kubinka: An American MiG-29 Experience*, RAND Corporation Report No. R-4000-RC (Santa Monica, Calif., 1991), 120. The same pattern appears to have been true with combat helicopters as well. See Lev Chaiko, *Helicopter Construction in the USSR* (Falls Church, Va., 1985), quoted in Lambeth, *From Farnborough to Kubinka*, 120. Elsewhere I have argued that the general pattern of Soviet weapons innovation was a reactive one: Matthew Evangelista, *Innovation and the Arms Race: How the United States and the Soviet Union Develop New Military Technologies* (Ithaca, N.Y., 1988). For a detailed discussion of how Soviet designers reacted to U.S. initiatives and drew on the experience of U.S. aircraft in Vietnam and the Middle East, see Judyth L. Twigg, "'To Fly and Fight': Norms, Institutions, and Fighter Aircraft Procurement in the United States, Russia, and Japan" (Ph.D. diss., Massachusetts Institute of Technology, 1994), chap. 6. Long before the end of the Soviet Union, U.S. intelligence analysts had recognized the extent to which Soviet weapons technology reacted to U.S. developments and had uncovered considerable evidence of Soviet efforts to acquire Western technology and incorporate it into its weapons. See *Soviet Acquisition of Militarily Significant Western Technology: An Update*, a report prepared by the U.S. Central Intelligence Agency (unacknowledged), September 1985. Soviet acquisition of radar technology for the U.S. F-14 and F-18 fighter aircraft is discussed on page 8.

27. M. S. Gorbachev, "Za bez"iadernyi mir, za gumanizm mezhdunarodnykh otnoshenii," *Literaturnaia gazeta*, 18 February 1987.

28. William Zimmerman, *Soviet Perspectives on International Relations, 1956–1967* (Princeton, N.J., 1969).

29. Fedor Burlatskii, "Filosofiia mira," *Voprosy filosofii*, 1982, no. 12:57–66; Aleksei Arbatov, *Voenno-strategicheskii paritet i politika SShA* (Moscow, 1984); Anatolii Gromyko and Vladimir Lomeiko, *Novoe myshlenie v iadernyi vek* (Moscow, 1984). For good secondary accounts that trace the development of the "new thinking," see Stephen Shenfield, *The Nuclear Predicament: Explorations in Soviet Ideology* (London, 1987); Patrick Litherland, *Gorbachev and Arms Control: Civilian Experts and Soviet Policy*, Peace Research Report No. 12 (Bradford, U.K., 1986); Allen Lynch, *The Soviet Study of International Relations* (Cambridge, U.K., 1987); Allen Lynch, *Gorbachev's International Outlook: Intellectual Origins and Political Consequences*, Institute for East-West Security Studies Occasional Paper No. 9 (Boulder, Colo., 1989); Scott R. Atkinson, *Soviet Defense Policy under Gorbachev: The Growing Civilian Influence*, Occasional Paper, Center for Naval Analyses, Alexandria, Va. (March 1990).

for such work came from the deterioration of East-West relations starting in the late 1970s, the stalemate in arms control, and the threatening prospect of a new, dangerous round in the arms race. Soviet scholars and scientists sought new ideas that could suggest a way out of the impasse and pursued transnational contacts with Western colleagues.

Common Security

The theme of "common security" received considerable attention in the early 1980s and, with the passing of the Brezhnev era, became especially influential in the thinking of Gorbachev and his foreign minister, Eduard Shevardnadze.[30]

The Palme Commission. Perhaps the most important route by which notions of common security entered the Soviet debate was through the Palme Commission, the Independent Commission on Disarmament and Security Issues, founded by Olof Palme, the late prime minister of Sweden. Georgii Arbatov, the leading Soviet participant, served as the main conduit for the Commission's ideas, through his reports back to the Central Committee and his conversations with Soviet leaders and their advisers.

One member of the Commission particularly impressed Arbatov: Egon Bahr. Bahr was a leading member of the West German Social Democratic Party. He had been interested in questions of conventional-force reductions at least since his service as head of the policy planning section of the West German Foreign Ministry in the government of Chancellor Willy Brandt.[31] He played a major role in developing the notion of common security. Not only does Arbatov acknowledge Bahr's influence on Soviet thinking about these issues: He calls him "one of the most outstanding political minds of our time."[32] Other Soviet officials held a similarly high opinion of Bahr.[33]

In his contributions to the Commission's discussions and in a special appendix to the report, Bahr emphasized the need to establish a balance in conventional forces in Europe (the implication being that Soviet forces were superior) as a prerequisite for creating a European nuclear-weapons-free zone. Coming from a staunch supporter of détente and disarmament, such views were taken more seriously by Soviet moderates than identical views proffered by Western hawks. Indeed Arbatov had previously considered Western

---

30. Eduard Shevardnadze, "Doklad E. A. Shevardnadze," *Vestnik Ministerstva Inostrannykh Del SSSR*, 1988, no. 15.

31. Jonathan Dean, *Watershed in Europe: Dismantling the East-West Military Confrontation* (Lexington, Mass., 1987), 102.

32. Arbatov, *Zatianuvsheesia vyzdorovlenie*, 192.

33. Valentin Falin, *Politische erinnerungen* (Munich, 1993); Cherniaev, *Moia zhizn' i moe vremia*, 348.

claims about a Soviet advantage in conventional forces as nothing but self-serving propaganda. Work on the Palme Commission changed his mind.[34] When the full text of the Palme Commission report was translated into Russian and published in Moscow, the analysis of the U.S.-Soviet balance made an especially big impression.

Arbatov and his colleagues tried to take advantage of the report's publication to promote its ideas about common security and its innovative solutions for slowing the arms race.[35] They continued to pursue transnational contacts with the Western advocates of common security, as when Arbatov traveled to the Netherlands to participate with Egon Bahr at the third annual conference of the International Physicians for the Prevention of Nuclear War in 1983. Olof Palme chaired their session.[36]

The efforts of Soviet reformers to promote the views of the Palme Commission failed to attract much sympathy within the sclerotic leadership of Brezhnev and his immediate successors. In 1982, for example, Georgii Arbatov sought unsuccessfully to interest the Soviet military establishment in the Commission's proposal to create a nuclear-free zone in central Europe. As he described in his memoirs, Arbatov appealed to Marshal Nikolai Ogarkov, chief of the General Staff, and Dmitrii Ustinov, the defense minister. Without even discussing the issue they gave him a categorical "no." Arbatov fared no better with the political leaders. When he asked Andropov for help, "he waved his hands at me: 'What, you want me to argue with Ustinov for your sake?'"[37]

Nonoffensive Defense

In addition to broad notions of common security and the links between conventional and nuclear disarmament, Soviet analysts also learned from their Western interlocutors about various proposals for alternative defense. Interest in nonoffensive defense among West European peace researchers dates back at least to the 1960s (and among some reformist West German military officers even earlier), but it attracted considerable interest in the early 1980s as concern about the risk of nuclear war in Europe increased.[38] Ideas

34. Arbatov made remarks to this effect during a conference at his institute in November 1990, which I attended.
35. Arbatov, *Zatianuvsheesia vyzdorovlenie*, 241. The Russian version was entitled *Bezopasnost' dlia vsekh: programma razoruzheniia* [Security for all: A program for disarmament] (Moscow, 1982). It was published in five thousand copies. See Raymond L. Garthoff, *The Great Transition: American-Soviet Relations and the End of the Cold War* (Washington, D.C., 1994), 595.
36. Bernard Lown, interview by author, Brookline, Mass., 6 April 1994.
37. Arbatov, *Zatianuvsheesia vyzdorovlenie*, 240. When the government of Sweden proposed that the Soviet Union embrace the Palme Commission's proposal for a nuclear-free zone, the Soviet government responded with a counterproposal for a broader zone that would mean the denuclearization of Germany—a prospect clearly unacceptable to NATO. See John W. Parker, *Kremlin in Transition: From Brezhnev to Chernenko, 1978–1985* (Boston, 1991), 1:224.
38. There is also a body of literature in U.S. international relations theory which explores the implications of the offense-defense balance and the "security dilemma," but it does not seem to have figured in the Soviet debate. The key work in this literature is Robert Jervis, "Cooperation under the Security Dilemma," *World Politics* 30, 2 (January 1978): 167–214.

about nonoffensive defense had little impact on Soviet policy until Gorbachev came into office, but transnational contacts during the Brezhnev era laid the groundwork for future policy influence.

German Origins of New Thinking. An important route for the introduction of ideas about nonoffensive defense into the Soviet debate was through West Germany. Starting in the 1970s, the Social Democratic Party of the Federal Republic (and, to a lesser extent, its British, Dutch, and Scandinavian counterparts) had held regular discussions with representatives of the ruling communist parties of East Germany and other Soviet-bloc states about questions of European security. Reports of these discussions, many of which focused on the concept of common security and alternative defense, made their way back to the USSR throughout the late Brezhnev period.[39]

German scholars were instrumental in deriving the military implications of common security, and their proposals for nonoffensive defense attracted the attention of Soviet diplomats and analysts. In the first half of the 1980s the West German Foreign Ministry sponsored seminars where prominent theorists of nonoffensive defense, such as Horst Afheldt and Lutz Unterseher, presented their views. The earliest meetings were held at the Evangelische Akademie in Loccum, West Germany. Diplomats were invited, including the negotiators from the talks on conventional forces in Vienna, some of whom regularly attended.[40] The seminars provided a direct route to Soviet officials involved in conventional arms control, but their impact revealed itself only with the arrival of a new foreign-policy leadership in Moscow in the second half of the 1980s.

The Copenhagen Connection. One of the preeminent European theorists of nonoffensive defense whose views influenced Soviet thinking was the late Danish physicist and professor of sociology Anders Boserup.[41] Boserup emphasized the importance of structuring conventional forces as "defense-dominant," thereby diminishing incentives for preemption in times of crisis. His analysis appears to have developed from two main sources. Boserup's notions of the offense-defense balance and its relation to crisis stability stem mainly from analogy to nuclear strategy. He was a longtime participant in the

39. Thomas Risse-Kappen, "Ideas Do Not Float Freely: Transnational Coalitions, Domestic Structures, and the End of the Cold War," *International Organization* 48, 2 (Spring 1994): 185–214; Stephan Kux, "Western Peace Research and Soviet Military Thought" (Department of Political Science, Columbia University, 20 April 1989).

40. Jonathan Dean, interview by author, Washington, D.C., 19 September 1994. A history of Unterseher's group and a list of its publications and public presentations are found in Ralph Ströber-Fassbender, *Die Studiengruppe Alternative Sicherheitspolitik: Eine Dokumentation* (Bonn, 1988). For Afheldt's views, see Horst Afheldt, *Defensive Verteidigung* (Reinbek, Federal Republic of Germany, 1983).

41. Boserup died suddenly of a heart attack at the age of fifty. For a brief biography, see the remarks made at his funeral by his friend Robert Neild, "Obituary: Anders Boserup (1940–1990)," in *Pugwash Newsletter* 28, 1 (July 1990): 96.

international Pugwash meetings, where such notions were frequently discussed, especially in the context of critiques of counterforce strategies and antiballistic missile systems.[42] Boserup developed his analysis of the strictly military dimensions of offense and defense from his reading of the Prussian military theorist Carl von Clausewitz.[43]

Boserup's ideas found their way into the Soviet debate by several routes. He was an active participant in the Pugwash movement and had expressed his views on nonoffensive defense at many conferences. In his statement to a 1981 conference in Alberta, Canada, Boserup stressed that "stability does not arise from an equality of force but from an inequality: the superiority of defensive over offensive capabilities."[44] At the next year's Pugwash meeting in Warsaw his colleague Robert Neild called attention to Boserup's 1981 statement and applied its insights in considerable detail to the problem of conventional forces in Europe.[45] In 1984 Boserup and Neild formed a special Pugwash workshop on conventional forces; by virtue of the participation of Soviet and other Warsaw-Pact scientists, it became, in Boserup's words, "the main forum for civilian-military, East-West discussions on nonoffensive defense."[46] By the time of the second convening of the workshop in 1985, at least one Soviet-bloc participant—a Hungarian scientist—had begun to apply the concepts of nonoffensive defense to analyzing the Warsaw Pact.[47]

Meanwhile, Boserup's ideas caught the attention of a Soviet diplomat who would later play an important role in promoting reformist ideas in the Gorbachev government. In May 1984, Lev Mendelevich, a Foreign Ministry official who had played a leading role in negotiating the Helsinki accords on European security in the mid-1970s, was appointed Soviet ambassador to Denmark.[48] According to a prominent Danish journalist with sources at the then-Soviet embassy in Copenhagen, Mendelevich took a great interest in work on nonoffensive defense being conducted in Germany and Denmark. He "ordered his staff to collect all the literature they could, apparently be-

42. Boserup was an editor of one of the Pugwash symposiums on the subject: C. F. Barnaby and A. Boserup, *Implications of Anti-Ballistic Missile Systems* (London, 1969).

43. Anders Boserup, conversation with author, July 1984. Boserup has published an essay on "State, Society, and War in Clausewitz" that is included in the Danish translation of *On War*: "Staten, Samfundet og Krigen hos Clausewitz," in C. von Clausewitz, *Om Krig*, vol. 3 (Copenhagen, 1986), cited in Bjorn Moller, *Non-Offensive Defence: Bibliography* (Copenhagen, 1987).

44. See, for example, A. Boserup, "Deterrence and Defence," in *Proceedings of the Thirty-First Pugwash Conference on Science and World Affairs*, Banff, Alberta, Canada, 28 August–2 September 1991, 111–113.

45. R. Neild, "Defence Policies as a Way to Disarmament," in *Proceedings of the Thirty-Second Pugwash Conference on Science and World Affairs*, Warsaw, Poland, 26–31 August 1982, 325–330.

46. Anders Boserup, "A Way to Undermine Hostility," *Bulletin of the Atomic Scientists* 44, 7 (September 1988): 19.

47. P. Deak, "The Possiblity of (and the Road Towards) a Military-Security System of Defensive Character from the Point of View of Military Science" (paper presented to the Pugwash Study Group on Conventional Forces in Europe, Second Workshop, Starnberg, Federal Republic of Germany, 1985), cited in Moller, *Non-Offensive Defence*, 90.

48. Parker, *Kremlin in Transition*, 1:377.

lieving that nonoffensive defense could provide a breakthrough for achieving conventional disarmament."[49] The possibility for such a breakthrough came only with the end of the Brezhnev era. In April 1986, as part of Gorbachev's restructuring of the Soviet foreign-policy bureaucracy, Mendelevich was appointed director of the Foreign Ministry's Evaluations and Planning Directorate. There he was able to bring some of the ideas of Boserup and others to bear on the question of conventional-force negotiations, one of the main issues with which he dealt.[50]

The Case of "Colonel X". Clearly, Soviet academic specialists and diplomats were familiar with Western European proposals on nonoffensive defense well before Gorbachev came into office, although they did not for the most part reveal their interest in open publications.[51] Some of them did, however, try to interest reformist elements of the Soviet military in the proposals—with limited success.

In 1983 and 1984, Stephen Shenfield, a British Sovietologist, conducted interviews with Colonel Viktor Girshfeld, retired, a researcher at the Institute of the World Economy and International Relations (IMEMO). Girshfeld expressed many of the views later associated with Gorbachev's new thinking and even coined the term "sufficient defense" (*dostatochnaia oborona*). Moreover, he endorsed not only a shift to emphasis on defense in the Soviet conventional-force posture but also a major unilateral conventional reduction, up to 50 percent over the next five to ten years. He spoke favorably of comparable initiatives launched by Nikita Khrushchev in the 1950s.[52]

The Girshfeld case suggests the complicated interaction between the reformers in the USSR and the West and their own political and military establishments. In addition to his work at IMEMO, Girshfeld was involved in the early 1980s with a group of military officers, some more senior than he, who favored a number of reforms in the Soviet military structure. Girshfeld became frustrated at the lack of attention such views received from the Soviet

49. Joergen Dragsdahl, "Are the Soviets Really Serious?" *Nuclear Times* (May/June 1988): 22–25; Lev Mendelevich, "Forty Years in the Diplomatic Service," *International Affairs* (Moscow), 1989, no. 6:67–76.

50. Mendelevich, "Forty Years," 75. See also Robert G. Herman, "Identity, Norms, and National Security: The Soviet Foreign Policy Revolution and the End of the Cold War," in Peter J. Katzenstein, ed., *The Culture of National Security: Norms and Identity in World Politics* (New York, 1996), 294.

51. Stephan Tiedtke, *Abschreckung und ihre Alternativen: Die sowjetische Sicht einer westlichen Debatte* (Heidelberg, 1986).

52. Stephen Shenfield, "The USSR: Viktor Girshfeld and the Concept of 'Sufficent Defence,'" *ADIU Report* 6, 1 (January/February 1984): 10. In the next two articles published from Shenfield's interviews, Girshfeld was given a pseudonym and the interviewer was left unidentified: "Colonel X's Warning: Our Mistakes Plus Your Hysteria," *Détente*, no. 1 (October 1984): 2–3; and "Colonel X's Peace Proposals," *Détente*, no. 2 (February 1985): 2–4; for a retrospective analysis, see Stephen Shenfield, "In Quest of Sufficient Defence," *Détente*, no. 11 (1988): 26–29.

political and military leadership. He suggested that Shenfield publish an article about his proposals that might be picked up by the mainstream Western press and then be noticed in the Soviet Union. That is precisely what happened. The *Observer*, a Sunday newspaper in London, reported on Shenfield's article in the *ADIU Report*, a small-circulation newsletter on peace research published at the University of Sussex. Back in Moscow, the *Observer* piece caught the attention of Kim Philby, the famous spy who kept an office at IMEMO and followed developments in the British press on behalf of the Institute. Philby translated and circulated the article within the Soviet political establishment, creating a scandal for Girshfeld, who had expected—but not clearly communicated to Shenfield—to be given a pseudonym (in subsequent interviews, Shenfield dubbed him "Colonel X"). At that point Girshfeld's views on "sufficient defense" received some attention from the higher-ups, and he justified his actions on the grounds that the Western media were the only source of new ideas that Soviet military and political officials took seriously.[53]

As it turned out, Girshfeld's ideas met with skepticism not only in the Soviet Union but among establishment Sovietologists in the West as well. Several years into Gorbachev's reformist program, one RAND Corporation analyst, for example, referred to Colonel X as an "alleged" former Army officer, "presumably in fact a representative of a Soviet intelligence service." The interviews with Shenfield, he argued, were part of a campaign of "planted rumors and private suggestions" about possible unilateral Soviet reductions, intended "to increase domestic popular pressures on Western governments to adopt a more forthcoming negotiating posture regarding Western reductions, and more generally to inhibit Western defense expenditures."[54] During the mid-1980s while most Sovietologists remained skeptical of the prospects for meaningful Soviet military reform, a few specialists such as Shenfield were already establishing the transnational contacts that would contribute to important reformist successes by the end of the decade.

Reformers in the Military. Within the Soviet Union as well, expectations of major reforms were hardly widespread. A few civilian analysts, however, recognized that not everyone in the Soviet armed forces was satisfied with the state of Soviet military strategy. They made efforts to forge links with reform-minded military officers and to find commonalities between their critiques of the Soviet military posture and the ideas about alternative security that were circulating in transnational discussions.

Andrei Kokoshin was probably the most influential civilian reformer who promoted the agenda of nonoffensive defense. As the son, grandson, and

---

53. Stephen Shenfield, letter to author, 18 January 1991.
54. Harry Gelman, *The Soviet Military Leadership and the Question of Soviet Deployment Retreats*, RAND Report R-3664-AF (Santa Monica, Calif., 1988).

nephew of military officers, Kokoshin had a strong interest in military history and good connections within the Soviet military establishment.[55] He was on good terms with several senior officers, such as General N. A. Lomov and A. I. Antonov, who had served in World War II (Antonov was chief of the General Staff) and later taught in the General Staff Academy. These "very well bred [kul'turnye] people," as Kokoshin recalled them in an interview, became in effect his tutors in matters of military history. From Lomov, for example, Kokoshin learned the true history of the disasters that befell Soviet forces after the German invasion of June 1941—disasters that Kokoshin later attributed to the USSR's neglect of defensive preparations. It was Lomov who, in 1974, introduced Kokoshin to the work of General A. A. Svechin, a leading Soviet military theorist of the 1920s, whom Stalin had arrested in the military purge of 1938. From the experience of the civil war and World War II, and the writings of "forgotten or half-forgotten" Red Army strategists, Kokoshin began to resurrect a tradition of legitimate Soviet interest and experience in defensive operations.[56]

At the same time, Kokoshin was probably the Soviet scholar most attracted to and involved in transnational discussions of nonoffensive defense. He was an active participant in Boserup's Pugwash group on conventional forces and followed the European debates closely. His views were particularly influenced by Unterseher's work. In the early 1980s Kokoshin, like Viktor Girshfeld, began to have discussions with military officers who were unhappy with the overly offensive character of Soviet military strategy. Reliance on Operational Maneuver Groups and plans for preemptive air attacks against NATO nuclear weapons "evoked particular dissatisfaction," he recalled.[57] But Kokoshin's reform-minded interlocutors were in no position to challenge the hierarchically established priorities of Soviet military strategy, still dominated at the time by Marshal Ogarkov.

At this point, in the early to mid-1980s, the interest of some military officers in reforming Soviet military strategy served mainly to encourage Kokoshin to pursue the topic and to take the views of Western proponents of alternative defense more seriously.

55. Andrei Kokoshin, interview by Bruce Parrott and author, Moscow, November 1990 (I am grateful to Bruce Parrott for allowing me to participate in this interview, which he had originally scheduled for himself). Kokoshin also discussed his background in an interview with Elena Agapova, "Nash chelovek v kongresse" [Our person in congress], Krasnaia zvezda, 15 September 1989, quoted in Zisk, Engaging the Enemy, 126–127.

56. The work was not published until Gorbachev's glasnost' policy made such discussions possible. Andrei Kokoshin, "Alexander Svechin: On War and Politics," International Affairs, November 1988, 118; A. A. Kokoshin and (General of the Army) V. N. Lobov, "Predvidenia (General Svechin ob evoliutsii voennogo iskusstva)," Znamia, no. 2 (February 1990): 170–182; Kokoshin and (Major General) Valentin V. Larionov, "Kurskaia bitva v svete sovremennoi oboronitel'noi doktriny" Mirovaia ekonomika i mezhdunarodnye otnosheniia, no. 8 (August 1987): 32–40.

57. Kokoshin, interview.

The story of conventional forces in the Brezhnev era resembles the case of nuclear testing examined in the last chapter. Efforts at arms control yielded no meaningful results. The lack of progress was partly a consequence of the overall stagnation in social, political, and economic life for which Gorbachev would later criticize his predecessors. But it was also the result of disinterest on the part of the United States in negotiating serious reductions in conventional forces. As with the case of nuclear testing, the stalemate in negotiations, combined with the dramatic deterioration of East-West relations, led to a burst of nongovernmental initiatives promoted by a transnational network. In the case of conventional forces, these initiatives ranged from broad theoretical innovations, such as "common security," to specific and highly technical proposals for defensive restructuring. The new ideas barely penetrated the upper echelons of the Soviet leadership during the Brezhnev era, but they eventually had a profound impact on the Gorbachev reforms.

[10]

"Not A Fool":
Brezhnev and the ABM Treaty

The idea that it could be counterproductive, wasteful, and provocative to defend one's cities is a novel one but it must not be ignored. Defense is basically incompatible with mutual strategic deterrence and this fact must eventually be recognized.

—Jeremy Stone, 1964

In order to come to the realization that in the nuclear-missile age the indisputable right of every country to defense . . . could be best accomplished by mutual rejection of antimissile defense of one's territory, it was necessary to study, to ponder, to weigh, to "turn the brain inside out," as it were. This was truly a powerful breakthrough of new thinking.

—Georgii Kornienko, 1992

Spanning two decades, the Brezhnev era encompassed most of the key developments in the history of U.S.-Soviet competition in ballistic missile defense systems. The first major superpower arms negotiations took place under Brezhnev's aegis, and in 1972 he personally signed its most significant result—the treaty limiting antiballistic missile (ABM) systems. Despite the treaty, but consistent with its provisions, Brezhnev approved a continuing research program into ABM technologies and the completion of the basic ABM system around Moscow.[1] In the last years of his life Brezhnev became aware of new efforts in the United States to develop ballistic missile defenses based on exotic new technologies.[2] His two immediate successors—the "Brezhnev

---

1. Grigorii Vasil'evich Kisun'ko, *Sekretnaia zona: Ispoved' general'nogo konstruktora* (Moscow, 1996), chaps. 19–21; O. V. Golubev, Ia. A. Kamenskii, M. G. Minasian, and B. D. Pupkov, "Proshloe i nastoiashchee Rossiiskikh sistem protivoraketnoi oborony (vzgliad iznutri)" (Moscow, 1992). Kisun'ko was the leader of the team that designed the Moscow system. The other authors were members of the team. I thank Sergei Khrushchev for sending me a copy of Kisun'ko's book and David Holloway for a copy of the Golubev paper.
2. Soviet proponents of ABM development called Brezhnev's attention to U.S. programs.

era" leaders Iurii Andropov and Konstantin Chernenko—had to deal with the consequences. The announcement by President Ronald Reagan of the Strategic Defense Initiative (SDI), soon dubbed "Star Wars" by its critics, threatened to undermine all that had been accomplished in the sphere of superpower arms control and unleash a new race in high-tech space weapons. Yet that race never happened.

This chapter and the next seek to explain this remarkable turn of events. How did the Soviet Union come to embrace limitations on strategic defenses and sign the ABM Treaty—the product, according to many analysts, of an intellectual revolution, a veritable "paradigm shift" in thinking about the nuclear dilemma? How did it react to the seemingly casual abandonment of that paradigm, signaled by the Reagan administration's pursuit of SDI? I argue that the role of transnational contacts between Soviet and Western scientists was crucial both in securing Soviet acceptance of ABM limitations and in preventing the development of a Soviet Star Wars in response to SDI.

BACKGROUND FOR THE ABM DEBATE

The case of ABM in the Brezhnev era is one of the strongest examples of transnational influence. At the same time, however, it is one of the most difficult to demonstrate. There are so many compelling explanations—all post hoc, to be sure—for why the Soviets would have agreed to limit ABM: economic constraints, technical difficulties, concern about likely U.S. responses to a vigorous Soviet ABM effort, pursuit of counterforce military advantages that U.S. ballistic missile defenses would hinder. If these explanations account well for Soviet policy decisions, then the efforts of Soviet scientists would appear superfluous. If, however, these explanations are indeterminate—if there was actually debate over how economic, technical, military, and political factors related to the question of ABM, then there may be greater scope for an explanation that emphasizes scientists' influence. In the absence of consensus on such questions as the economic costs or technical feasibility of ABM, or its implications for the strategic arms competition, scientists could have weighed in to influence the internal debate. They could have provided information or arguments—some, perhaps obtained through their transnational contacts—to one side or another.

I intend to make a stronger argument. In the case of ABM, the scientists were the first to make the case for limitations. They did so publicly at a time when official policy still supported widespread deployment and when the

---

They were also reported in the U.S. press at the time. See Richard Halloran, "U.S. to Increase Military Funds for Space Uses," *New York Times*, 29 September 1982; Philip M. Boffrey, "Pressures Are Increasing for Arms Race in Space," *New York Times*, 18 October 1982; William Broad, "Teller Briefs Reagan on Killer Lasers," *New York Times*, 18 October 1982.

Soviet government's attitude toward even the desirability of U.S.-Soviet strategic arms control was uncertain. The scientists argued in favor of an ABM Treaty as political leaders equivocated and military officials and weapons designers strenuously opposed arms control and promoted ABM.[3]

In this section I review the major events in ABM development and negotiation during the Brezhnev era to provide a context for Soviet views on the desirability of ABM limitations. Since some of the arguments concern the technical and economic viability of ABMs, it is important to identify what the U.S. and Soviet governments had decided about such issues on the basis of their behavior and the primary documentation that has become available. Because other arguments concern the arms race and the means for bringing it under control, it is also important to see how the timing of Soviet commentary corresponds to the tentative steps the sides were taking toward agreement on strategic arms talks.

Soviet and U.S. ABM Programs

By the time Khrushchev was deposed in October 1964, deployment of ABM defenses around Leningrad had ceased and work centered on Moscow's A-35 system. Work on A-35 apparently accelerated during 1966 and 1967, but only six of the eight complexes were under active construction. In 1968, construction on two of the six was halted, leaving a system of four complexes with a total of sixty-four missiles.[4] Despite the slowdown at the A-35 site, Soviet ABM work in general continued apace. In May 1968, the Communist Party Central Committee and the Council of Ministers issued a joint decree intended to accelerate the work on ABM defenses. The decree established a new Scientific-Thematic Center within the Vympel ("pennant") design bureau and led to the dispatch of a thousand technicians and engineers to work on ABM problems.[5]

It has been widely believed that the Moscow ABM system became operational in 1970 or 1971. In fact, however, according to a history of Soviet ABM developments, written by Soviet ABM designers, work on the Moscow ABM "dragged on to the end of the seventies." In their understated view, the signing of the 1972 ABM Treaty "also did not help to force the pace of work on the

---

3. My evidence supports much of the argument along these lines made by Emanuel Adler, "The Emergence of Cooperation: National Epistemic Communities and the International Evolution of the Idea of Nuclear Arms Control," *International Organization* 46, 1 (Winter 1992): 101–145.

4. Golubev et al., "Proshloe i nastoiashchee"; Sayre Stevens, "The Soviet BMD Program," in Ashton B. Carter and David N. Schwartz, eds., *Ballistic Missile Defense* (Washington, D.C., 1984), 182–220. Johan J. Holst, "Missile Defense, the Soviet Union, and the Arms Race," in Holst and William Schneider, Jr., eds., *Why ABM? Policy Issues in the Missile Defense Controversy* (New York, 1969), 145–186.

5. Golubev et al., "Proshloe i nastoiashchee," 18–19.

A-35 system." The Moscow system did not become operational until 1977—and even then with very limited capability and at enormous expense.[6]

At the time Brezhnev and his colleagues seized power in late 1964, the U.S. government had still not committed itself to deploying an ABM system. Secretary of Defense McNamara and his civilian scientists harbored serious misgivings about the technical capabilities of the proposed systems. They came, however, under strong pressure from the Army and its political and industrial allies to deploy an ABM. In the summer of 1966, for example, the Senate approved funds to procure ABM components—money that McNamara had not requested and refused to spend.[7] In January 1967, President Johnson finally felt obliged to request Congress to appropriate funds to procure an ABM, but he stated that he would defer the decision to deploy the system pending discussions with the Soviet Union on the possibility of strategic arms limitation talks (SALT).[8]

Unable to get a solid commitment from the Soviet government, Johnson instructed McNamara to announce in September 1967 the decision to deploy the "Sentinel" ABM system. Johnson allowed McNamara to chose whatever rationale he favored to justify the deployment. McNamara described Sentinel as a "thin" ABM system intended to defend some American cities against a possible future attack from China. In order to ward off a Soviet offensive buildup in response—the feared "arms-race instability"—McNamara emphasized that the system was not directed against the USSR.[9]

In June 1968, the Senate authorized funds for the construction of Sentinel. That autumn, when the administration revealed that the Sentinel system would entail missile deployments north of such major cities as Chicago and Boston, public concern, backed with scientific advice, spurred a major campaign against ABM.[10] In February 1969, the incoming Nixon administration suspended the Sentinel program for a month while it undertook a review of the strategic defense issue. In mid-March, Nixon announced a revised ABM policy: the "Safeguard" system, using existing technology from Sentinel, would be deployed to defend missile silos in the near term, and only later would it be broadened to include defense of cities.[11]

By this time, public opposition had found a reflection in Congress. Hearings were held in which ABM opponents and supporters debated the techni-

6. Ibid., 21.

7. John Newhouse, *Cold Dawn: The Story of SALT* (New York, 1973), 83.

8. Morton H. Halperin, "The Decision to Deploy the ABM: Bureaucratic and Domestic Politics in the Johnson Administration," *World Politics* 25, 1 (October 1972): 62–95.

9. Ibid.

10. Joel Primack and Frank von Hippel, *Advice and Dissent: Scientists in the Political Arena* (New York, 1974), chap. 13.

11. David N. Schwartz, "Past and Present: The Historical Legacy," in Carter and Schwartz, *Ballistic Missile Defense*, 341; Newhouse, *Cold Dawn*, 151–152; Anne Hessing Cahn, "Eggheads and Warheads: Scientists and the ABM" (Ph.D. diss., Massachusetts Institute of Technology, 1971).

cal and strategic merits of Safeguard. In August 1969, the proposal to fund deployment of the system passed by only one vote. The tie-breaking vote was cast by the vice president, Spiro Agnew.[12]

U.S.-Soviet Negotiations

The subject of negotiating limitations on ABM deployment was first broached by a U.S. official, William C. Foster, the director of the Arms Control and Disarmament Agency, in a discussion over lunch with Soviet ambassador Anatolii Dobrynin on 16 January 1964. Foster was evidently expressing his personal interest in the matter, without specific instructions from his government, and he continued to raise the issue from time to time in discussions with Dobrynin.[13] After one such discussion in January 1966, Dobrynin decided to interpret Foster's interest in ABM restrictions as an official probe. He reported back to Moscow and on 17 March 1966 replied to Foster that the Soviet government was interested in discussions on limiting both ABMs and offensive weapons. Foster informed Secretary of State Dean Rusk of Dobrynin's reply, and Rusk discussed the matter with Dobrynin the next day. Evidently, however, Rusk did not realize that the Soviet side was responding to what it took to be a U.S. initiative. Thus, both sides waited for the other to make the next move.[14]

In December 1966, Llewellyn Thompson, before departing to take up his position as U.S. ambassador to Moscow, met with Dobrynin to convey President Johnson's interest in discussions on ABM limitation. Dobrynin repeated the Soviet position that offensive and defensive weapons should be considered together. The formal Soviet response on 17 January 1967 linked this position to its long-standing proposals for "general and complete disarmament," usually a sign of Soviet ambivalence about meaningful negotiations. On 24 January, Johnson submitted his request to Congress for ABM funds but made deployment contingent on the outcome of arms talks with the Soviet Union.

When Prime Minister Aleksei Kosygin was asked about Soviet interest in limiting ABMs in London on 9 February 1967, he denied that defenses stimulated the arms race, but he did not state an official Soviet position on negotiations. Nevertheless, his remarks were interpreted by much of the Western press as a rejection of arms talks.[15] Curiously, a prominent reform-oriented Soviet journalist writing in *Pravda* a week later went beyond Kosygin's actual remarks to cite him as having expressed the Soviet government's readiness

---

12. Schwartz, "Past and Present," 341–342; Cahn, "Eggheads and Warheads."
13. Anatoly Dobrynin, *In Confidence: Moscow's Ambassador to Six Cold War Presidents* (New York, 1995), 149.
14. Raymond L. Garthoff, "BMD and East-West Relations," in Carter and Schwartz, *Ballistic Missile Defense*, 294–295.
15. Ibid., 295–296.

for "discussion of the question of the prevention of a further arms race both in the fields of offensive and defensive arms." [16] Unnamed Soviet authorities then informed a Western reporter that the article had been a mistake and that *Pravda* would soon publish a clarification of the Soviet position. No such article appeared. Rather, a week later, on 27 February, Kosygin wrote to President Johnson confirming Soviet interest in discussions of both offensive and defensive weapons. On 2 March, Johnson made a public announcement to that effect. [17]

In subsequent discussions with President Johnson and Secretary of Defense McNamara at Glassboro, New Jersey, in June 1967, Kosygin proved unwilling to embrace the logic of the American critique of ABM. He did not renege on Soviet expressions of interest in limiting both offensive and defensive systems, but he would not propose a specific time to begin negotiations. As McNamara recalls the meeting, he tried to impress upon Kosygin the concept of arms-race instability—that deployment of a Soviet ABM would force the United States to increase its offensive forces. McNamara implies that Kosygin found his remarks threatening: "The blood rushed to his face, he pounded on the table, and he said, 'Defense is moral; offense is immoral!' That was essentially the end of the discussion." [18]

In fact there was considerably more to the discussion. McNamara and Kosygin debated the merits of ABM for an hour over lunch. Marie Fehmer, one of the president's secretaries, had been taking notes from outside the dining room as McNamara began to speak. The defense secretary closed the door on her, apparently concerned that the Soviet delegation would feel constrained by her note taking. Fehmer then moved to the back stairs, where she could still hear the conversation, and compiled a detailed, verbatim account—occasionally interrupted by noise from the kitchen—of McNamara's presentation. It differs considerably from McNamara's subsequent recollections. [19]

McNamara tried to explain to Kosygin the concept of "cost-effectiveness at the margin" and why it would be counterproductive for the USSR to build ABM defenses. Kosygin was put off by McNamara's argument that the incremental cost of building one unit of offense would be less than the cost of building one unit of defense to defeat it. The Soviet leader could not understand why the Americans would build weapons to attack the USSR simply because they were cheaper than the ones necessary to defend themselves. [20]

16. F. Burlatskii, "Problemy obshchechelovecheskie," *Pravda*, 15 February 1967.

17. Garthoff, "BMD," 296–297.

18. Robert S. McNamara, *Blundering into Disaster: Surviving the First Century of the Nuclear Age* (New York, 1986), 57. For a similar account, based on an interview with McNamara, see Gregg Herken, *Counsels of War* (New York, 1985), 196–197.

19. Fehmer's notes are quoted at length in Glenn T. Seaborg with Benjamin S. Loeb, *Stemming the Tide: Arms Control in the Johnson Years* (Lexington, Mass., 1987), chap. 32. In presenting his version of this story, as with his versions of the Cuban missile crisis and the Vietnam War, McNamara was apparently unaware that the documentary record would reveal his casual attitude toward the truth.

20. Ibid., 426–428.

Kosygin's response resembles very much General Talenskii's heated reaction to Jeremy Stone's presentation of the same argument three years earlier in Boston (see Chapter 6).

One reason McNamara had trouble convincing Kosygin of the dangers of ABM is that he gave a poor presentation of his argument. As Anatolii Dobrynin, the Soviet ambassador who attended the luncheon, later recalled, McNamara had been expecting to meet alone with Kosygin and President Johnson. He hoped to impress the Soviet premier "with the latest American confidential scientific and military data demonstrating the essential futility of ABM systems." But Johnson neglected to invite McNamara to join them. He remembered his promise only when he noticed McNamara at lunch. At that point, with the full delegations from both sides present, Johnson asked McNamara to make his case. The defense secretary was unprepared and was concerned that many of the luncheon participants *on the U.S. side* did not have adequate security clearances to hear the information he intended to reveal to the leader of the enemy camp. "Confused, McNamara feverishly began to sort out his papers, trying to select the least secret charts and diagrams from his folder." As Dobrynin recalled, "because of his last-minute reorganization, his report proved disjointed, unconvincing, and uninteresting, and in fact Kosygin told me that night he was disappointed by it."[21] Judging by Marie Fehmer's notes, Dobrynin's characterization of McNamara's presentation is apt.

Whatever other reasons may explain the USSR's unpreparedness to enter into negotiations to limit ABMs in 1967, one reason was that the Soviet prime minister did not have a clear understanding of the rationale for doing so.

Not until June 1968 did the Soviet government formally announce its willingness to engage in talks on strategic offensive and defensive arms, in a speech by Foreign Minister Andrei Gromyko to the Supreme Soviet.[22] Ironically, by this time the planned U.S. opening position for the negotiations proposed not that both sides ban ABMs outright but merely that they deploy a "set and equivalent number" of systems—an earlier draft had suggested a number between a hundred and a thousand, the latter being the maximum anticipated for the Sentinel program.[23]

Owing to the Soviet invasion of Czechoslovakia in August 1968 and the change in U.S. administrations resulting from the November presidential elections, the negotiations did not begin until the following year. In June 1969 President Nixon announced U.S. readiness to begin talks. The next month, Gromyko again used a speech to the Supreme Soviet to express Soviet willingness to proceed. The talks did not get under way, however, until November.[24]

21. Dobrynin, *In Confidence*, 166.
22. Quoted in Garthoff, "BMD," 299–300.
23. Newhouse, *Cold Dawn*, 119–128.
24. Newhouse attributes the delay to Soviet preoccupation with the deteriorating situation with China; once talks were initiated on the Sino-Soviet border dispute, the Soviets were will-

THE EFFECT OF TRANSNATIONAL DISCUSSIONS

Long before the Soviet government had to make a decision on whether to negotiate strategic arms with the United States, and well before the U.S. government had decided to do so, Soviet and Western scientists began exploring the conceptual basis of East-West arms control. U.S. scientists agreed early on to focus on the merits of mutual restraints on antiballistic missile systems.

The Transnational Campaign for an ABM Ban

Western scientists' efforts to persuade their Soviet counterparts of the desirability of limiting ABMs took the form of the large, international Pugwash conferences; the smaller, bilateral meetings of the Soviet-American Disarmament Study group (SADS); and personal diplomacy. Several of the American scientists, such as Harvard's Paul Doty and Cornell's Franklin Long, were willing to travel to Moscow on short notice to organize future meetings of the scientists. Others, such as Betty Lall of the Committee on International Studies of Arms Control of the American Academy of Arts and Sciences, arranged longer visits to the USSR, sometimes at the invitation of the Soviet Academy of Sciences and sometimes privately. The Americans developed close personal relationships with Millionshchikov, Artsimovich, and others, spent time at their homes, got to know their families, and had ample time to pursue their discussions about arms control on an informal basis over dinner, drinks, and walks.[25]

Doty and the other organizers of the SADS workshops preferred to keep their discussions with Soviet counterparts small, informal, and unpublicized—in contrast to Pugwash. The Pugwash meetings were typically large, unwieldy, and less productive than they could be, with much attention focused on drafting a joint statement for publication at the meeting's end that would meet the approval of all the delegates. The American scientists were keen to maintain good contacts with U.S. officials and made a point of not undercutting the government's position on controversial issues such as the

---

ing to set a date with the United States. See Newhouse, *Cold Dawn*, 162–165. For Gromyko's speech, see Ministerstvo inostrannykh del SSSR, *Za mir i bezopasnost' narodov: Dokumenty vneshnei politiki SSSR, 1969 god* (Moscow, 1987), bk. 1, pp. 383–410.

25. These impressions draw on my discussions with Paul Doty and with documents from his personal files and from the archives of the Committee on International Studies of Arms Control of the American Academy of Arts and Sciences. I am grateful to David Wright for making copies of the latter documents available. See, for example, Paul Doty, "Report of Visit of P. Doty and F. Long with Academicians Millionshchikov and Emelyanov in Moscow, June 10–11, 1965"; Doty, "Doty-Long Visit to USSR, June 10 and 11, 1965" (draft), 16 June 1965; notes from Marshall Shulman, 29 October 1966; Frank Long, "Notes on Meeting in Moscow, May 31 and June 1, 1966"; Frank Long, "Notes on the Discussion with Millionshchikov, Tuesday, April 4, 1967"; Betty Goetz Lall, "Notes on Trip to the Soviet Union, August 23–September 4, 1966."

war in Vietnam or the ill-fated proposal for a multilateral force (MLF) of nuclear weapons to be shared by the European NATO allies.

By contrast to both the formal, structured Pugwash conferences and the informal, confidential SADS meetings, Jeremy Stone's efforts to promote an ABM ban were bold and unconventional. The son of the journalist I. F. Stone, to whom he dedicated his first book on arms control, Stone seems to have inherited much of his father's energy, determination, and chutzpah. The files of the SADS project contain several memoranda that Stone fired off to his senior colleagues at Harvard and MIT during the time when he and Morton Halperin served as assistants to the project. Stone's memos included forcefully argued and often quite creative proposals to engage the Soviets, but there is no evidence that they met with much positive response from the other members of the Cambridge arms control community.[26]

Stone seemed impatient with the status-conscious atmosphere at Harvard, and understandably so. When Soviet and American scientists met for their first series of bilateral arms control meetings in Boston in June 1964, protocol had directed Stone, in the shorthand of the memorandum reporting on the meeting, to sit "at side" rather than "at table," even during the session where his paper on ABM formed the main basis for the discussion.[27] Stone's own style and personality apparently contributed to the negative reaction of his senior colleagues. A person who in later years would claim credit for "inventing" the ABM Treaty, Stone was—even as a young postdoctoral research fellow—never known for excessive modesty or deference.

For whatever reasons, after leaving Cambridge in 1966 Stone subsequently undertook much of his anti-ABM activity independently of the American arms control establishment—and to good effect. From the summer of 1966 through the summer of 1970, Stone and his wife, B. J., took trips to the Soviet Union on tourist visas, spending up to a month at a time. B. J. had learned Russian, at Vasilii Emel'ianov's urging, and served as her husband's interpreter. Although traveling without any official status, the Stones made contact with many Soviet scientists and foreign-policy specialists. Jeremy Stone used to pass out pocket bomb-yield calculators to his Soviet contacts, so that they could figure out the destructive consequences of nuclear war for themselves and gain some understanding of the futility and counterproductive nature of ABM.[28]

26. See, e.g., Jeremy J. Stone, "Who's Complaining?" and "Talking about Talking," both from October 1965, copies from Paul Doty's personal files.

27. Paul Doty, "U.S.-USSR Joint Study Group on Disarmament," memorandum, 13 April 1964, in Doty's personal files. In a letter to Bernd Kubbig, Stone later recalled: "I definitely sat at the table when this paper was discussed; indeed, I presented it and, as I recall, this was my request in return for letting the Doty group use it." Quoted in Bernd W. Kubbig, "Communicators in the Cold War: The Pugwash Conferences, the U.S.-Soviet Study Group and the ABM Treaty," PRIF Reports No. 44, Peace Research Institute Frankfurt (Frankfurt am Main, 1996), 21 n. 37.

28. Jeremy Stone, interview by author, Washington, D.C., 10 June 1991.

Each summer in Moscow Stone gave speeches and seminars and even managed to publish an article in the weekly *Moscow News*. Initially he spoke at the House of Friendship (Dom druzhby) and the Institute of the World Economy and International Relations (IMEMO). After Georgii Arbatov founded the Institute of the USA (later renamed the Institute of the USA and Canada or ISKAN) in late 1967, he invited Stone to speak there as well. At Dom druzhby, Stone's talks were tape-recorded and attended by some well-dressed people who never introduced themselves. Stone later saw them at General Talenskii's funeral in Moscow.[29]

Before long the Stones' efforts had made an impression on the Soviet community of international-relations and disarmament specialists. When two Western guests of the Soviet Academy of Sciences met with a group of twenty-five members of IMEMO in late summer 1966 and argued for an ABM production cutoff, their Soviet hosts were already referring to the idea as Jeremy Stone's proposal.[30]

In 1968, London's Institute for Strategic Studies published Stone's monograph, *The Case against Missile Defences*, in its Adelphi Papers series.[31] Stone brought a copy to Moscow and had it translated into Russian for a hundred dollars; he managed to get it delivered to various Soviet officials, including Dmitrii Ustinov, then Central Committee secretary in charge of the military industry and later defense minister.[32] In addition to promoting the cause of arms control, Stone's efforts—including his outspoken support for dissidents and refuseniks (people denied permission to emigrate)—made him some enemies among Soviet hard-liners. Some Soviet officials even tried to discourage contact with Stone by warning his Soviet interlocutors that he was a CIA agent.[33]

Skeptics, Heretics and Converts: Scientists' Views of ABM

Despite the initially skeptical public reaction from Soviet scientists to Western arguments about ABM, the efforts of Western scientists—mavericks like Jeremy Stone as well as more established figures like Paul Doty—gradually changed some views. This has long been the view of Western scientists who participated in Pugwash and SADS, and it is confirmed by the new evidence from Russia.

Pugwash. Jack Ruina got the impression that his presentation of the technical and strategic arguments against ABM to the Twelfth Pugwash Conference

29. Jeremy Stone, interview by David Wright, 4 September 1989.
30. Lall, "Notes on Trip," 6–7.
31. Jeremy J. Stone, *The Case against Missile Defences*, Adelphi Paper No. 47 (London, 1968).
32. Stone, interview by author.
33. Sergei Khrushchev, *Khrushchev on Khrushchev*, trans. William Taubman (Boston, 1990), 270.

in India in January 1964 made sense to some of the Soviet delegates.[34] Joseph Rotblat, the secretary-general of Pugwash, also claims to have detected a change in the views of some Soviet scientists at that time. At the January conference, Millionshchikov, for example, espoused and appeared to believe in the Soviet government position supporting defenses. By the next Pugwash meeting, at Karlovy Vary, Czechoslovakia, in September 1964, Rotblat thought that Millionshchikov had come to appreciate the Americans' critique of ABM.[35] During the intervening period, Millionshchikov and his colleagues had participated in direct meetings with the American scientists at Boston, where much of discussion concerned ABM.

Millionshchikov, as a high-level official of the Soviet Academy and the Russian government, remained cautious about publicly expressing views that contradicted official policy. As late as April 1967, in a small dinner meeting with two American colleagues, Millionshchikov seemed obliged, when the topic of ABM came up, to "reiterate strongly that the desire for ABM was not simply one of Generals, but that it was inherently a desire of the Russian people," owing to the trauma of the German invasion during World War II.[36] Millionshchikov may have felt constrained to make such a statement by the presence at the meeting of V. P. Pavlichenko, the Soviet Academy's "aide for international affairs"—long considered by the American participants to be the government's watchdog over the Soviet scientists and the person who typically promoted the most orthodox views. Frank Long once referred to him as "the ubiquitous 'commissar,'" while Paul Doty said he had an "unpleasant superficiality" and a "greasy" manner.[37]

Other participants in the ABM discussions reinforce the impression that— for Millionshchikov, Emel'ianov, and others—conversion to the American position was not instantaneous. This is the view, for example, of Rudolf Peierls, a professor of physics at Oxford University, who attended the January 1964 Pugwash meeting. Contrary to Ruina's impression, he writes that "it seemed at the time that we failed to get the idea across" about the potentially destabilizing consequences of ABM deployment. Yet, argues Peierls, years later Millionshchikov "recalled this discussion and commented that we learned much from each other and that he passed the lesson on to his government."[38] Millionshchikov later told Jack Ruina as well that although at the

34. Jack Ruina, comments at a conference on "The Role of Scientists and Technology in the Making of Security Policy," University of Illinois at Champaign-Urbana, 28–29 October 1988; and Ruina, interview by David Wright, 6 July 1990.

35. Joseph Rotblat, conversation with author, en route from Kazakhstan to Moscow, 27 May 1990.

36. Long, "Notes on Discussion with Millionshchikov," 1–2; see also Doty, "Doty-Long Visit," 10.

37. F. A. Long, "Discussions with Soviet Scientists on the South Vietnam Problem, London, August 27 and 28, 1965," memorandum, 30 August 1965, from Paul Doty's personal files; and Doty, interview by David Wright, 17 July 1990.

38. Rudolf Peierls, Bird of Passage: Recollections of a Physicist (Princeton, N.J., 1985), 285.

time he had thought Ruina's ideas on ABM were peculiar, they had turned out to be right.[39]

Vasilii Emel'ianov, the Soviet Pugwash delegate who had expressed such skepticism about a ban on defenses in 1964, evidently came to accept the arguments about offense-defense interaction and strategic stability. In 1970 he wrote favorably of Pugwash demands for restrictions on ABM and multiple-warhead or MIRV (multiple, independently targetable reentry vehicles) technologies.[40] In later years he, like many of his American colleagues, accorded the transnational scientists an important role in making the ABM Treaty possible.[41]

Unlike Emel'ianov and Millionshchikov, Lev Artsimovich appears not to have needed lessons from his Western counterparts on the merits of an ABM ban. Joseph Rotblat sensed that Artsimovich was always skeptical of his government's rationale for ABM, even while his colleagues accepted it.[42] Bernard Feld has written that Artsimovich was one of the first Pugwash scientists to recognize the connection between offensive and defensive weapons—that defenses would have to be limited as a prerequisite for restraining the offensive arms race.[43] To those who knew him, these impressions that Artsimovich disagreed with his government's position would come as no surprise: he was renowned in Soviet scientific and political circles for his independence of mind.[44] As one high Foreign Ministry official put it, Artsimovich "showed no particular deference to the leadership" on anything.[45] A. D. Shveitser, who served for many years as a Soviet interpreter at Pugwash meetings, described him as "a man of unconventional and independent wisdom."[46]

"McNamara's Idea." In addition to the recollections of Western participants in Pugwash meetings, we look to the written accounts of Soviet scientists as one indicator of their understanding and acceptance of the critique of ABM. As we saw in Chapter 6, Soviet scientists' initial reaction to American pro-

39. Millionshchikov's comments came in response to Ruina's proposals for mutual curbs on anti-submarine warfare (ASW). Given the ABM experience, Millionshchikov thought Ruina's views on ASW should get a serious hearing. From Ruina, conversation with David Wright, 12 July 1990. In a 1972 report to the presidium of the Soviet Academy of Sciences on future tasks for the Pugwash movement Millionshchikov called particular attention to the ASW issue. See "Proekt (dokladnyi zapiski) v Prezidium Akademii nauk SSSR ob itogakh 15-ti letnei deiatelnosti Paguoshskogo dvizheniia uchenykh," 24 September 1972, Millionshchikov papers, f. 1713, op. 2, delo I.5.2, no. 209, Archive of the Academy of Sciences of the Russian Federation in Moscow (hereafter, ANRF), 4.

40. V. S. Emel'ianov, "XIX Paguoshskaia konferentsiia," *Vestnik AN SSSR*, 1970, no. 2:51–52.

41. V. S. Emel'ianov, "Bor'ba uchenykh za mir," *Voprosy filosofii*, 1974, no. 6:10.

42. Rotblat, conversation.

43. B. Feld, "Artsimovich and the Pugwash Movement," in *Reminiscences about Academician Lev Artsimovich* (Moscow, 1985), 84.

44. Roald Sagdeev, *The Making of a Soviet Scientist* (New York, 1994), 63–65, 139–143.

45. G. M. Kornienko, interview by author, Moscow, 28 July 1992.

46. Shveitser has written a wonderful memoir, *Glazami perevodchika* (Moscow, 1996), which he has translated as *An Interpreter Remembers* and made available on the World Wide Web at http://pages.prodigy.com/casanova/memoir.htm.

At a Pugwash meeting Mikhail Millionshchikov (left), vice-president of the Soviet Academy of Sciences and head of the Soviet Pugwash delegation, talks with Rudolf Peierls, a professor of physics at Oxford University. According to Peierls, Millionshchikov described how he had conveyed to Soviet government officials the Western critique of antiballistic missile systems, thus providing a foundation for the signing of the ABM Treaty in 1972. Photograph courtesy of Pugwash, used by permission.

posals for an ABM ban were cautious and pessimistic. Their published characterizations of the U.S. scientists' arguments were incomplete at best and often rather simplistic.

By far the most accurate and sympathetic account of the American critique of ABM came not from a military officer or a natural scientist but from Gennadii Gerasimov—a political analyst and journalist who later became a prominent spokesperson for the Soviet Foreign Ministry during the Gorbachev years. As early as 1965, Gerasimov, described by an American analyst as "one of the few Soviet civilian commentators knowledgeable about strategic matters" at that time, published an article that included all of the fundamental criticisms of ABM: technical infeasibility, crisis and arms-race instability, and expense.[47] More striking, Gerasimov based his critique on the same assumptions as the American opponents of ABM: namely, that secure, second-strike retaliatory forces provided an important measure of stability and should not be undermined by deployment of first-strike, counterforce capabilities or ABM defenses. He quoted at length top Pentagon officials such as Robert McNamara and his assistant John McNaughton on the theory of mutual deterrence, and admitted that "there is definite logic to such a theory." But he cautioned that "the balance of terror does not guarantee against war breaking out by accident or short-sighted miscalculation," and he cited with approval the observation of two prominent U.S. science advisers, Jerome Wiesner and Herbert York, that there was "no technical solution" to the arms race.[48]

By 1966, Gerasimov had explicitly endorsed the idea of a minimum deterrent force, at a time when both Soviet and U.S. arsenals had long since achieved "overkill": "The destructive power of nuclear weapons is so great that a definite and relatively small number of missiles is sufficient to meet any strategic military requirement."[49] This view was consistent, apparently, with Nikita Khrushchev's personal attitude toward nuclear weapons.[50] But public articulation of such views during the Brezhnev era was extremely rare and presumably risky.

When I asked Gerasimov at a reception in Moscow in November 1990 how he got away with expressing such unorthodox views about minimum deterrence and ABM restrictions in those days, he dismissively replied that "it was McNamara's idea, not mine."[51] While disappointingly uninformative about the internal politics of strategic discourse during the Brezhnev period, Gerasimov's remarks did highlight the American provenance of ideas about arms control.[52] By 1966, however, "McNamara's idea" about minimum deterrence for U.S. strategic nuclear forces had actually been abandoned in prac-

47. G. Gerasimov, "The First-Strike Theory," *International Affairs* (Moscow), 1965, no. 3:39–45. The characterization is from William Zimmerman, *Soviet Perspectives on International Relations, 1956–1967* (Princeton, N.J., 1969), 229.

48. Ibid. Gerasimov cites the article by Jerome Wiesner and Herbert F. York, "National Security and the Nuclear Test Ban," *Scientific American*, October 1964, 27–35.

49. G. Gerasimov, "Pentagonia, 1966," *International Affairs* (Moscow), 1966, no. 5:28.

50. Recall his remark that "missiles are not cucumbers, one cannot eat them and one does not require more than a certain number in order to ward off an attack." N. S. Khrushchev, *Pravda*, 29 May 1960.

51. Gennadii Gerasimov, conversation with author, Moscow, 12 November 1990.

52. Gerasimov might also have been implying that by presenting the ideas as McNamara's he could distance himself from them. His articles, nevertheless, did convey a strong sense of personal endorsement.

tice, and the following year McNamara would betray his own views on ABM restrictions by proposing the Sentinel system. But McNamara's critics in the Western scientific community continued actively to promote arms control ideas—and many of those ideas made their way into the Soviet debate.

In fact, it was in response to McNamara's announcement of the Sentinel deployment in September 1967 and his subsequent interview with *Life* magazine later that month that the Soviet popular press first began to pay attention to the ABM issue.[53] A *Pravda* report quoted at great length a *New York Times* editorial criticizing the decision as inconsistent with efforts to bring the arms race under control and likely to lead to the expenditure of enormous sums of money, as pro-ABM forces and the "military-industrial complex" push for expansion of the Sentinel system.[54] An *Izvestiia* article, written by the paper's correspondents at the United Nations in New York, also called attention to the potential expense of the Sentinel system, the pressure to deploy and expand it, and the risk that it would open "a new round of the arms race."[55] Thus, the economic critique and arguments about arms-race instability were first presented to a broad Soviet readership.

Sakharov's Role. By 1967, at least one prominent Soviet scientist—Andrei Sakharov—had come to appreciate the stabilizing role of mutual nuclear deterrence and to perceive ABM as a threat to that stability. Sakharov was never involved in the Pugwash movement or any informal contacts with Western scientists. He was a nuclear weapons designer, one of the key figures behind development of the Soviet H-bomb, and his work was considered too sensitive to allow him to travel abroad. Nevertheless, Sakharov was acquainted with Western views on such issues as nuclear testing and the ABM through his reading of the U.S. journals *Scientific American* and the *Bulletin of the Atomic Scientists*. Thus, he considered himself part of what I called in Chapter 3 the "tacit" transnational community of scientists.

Typically, though, Sakharov's opposition to ABM seems to have stemmed as much from his own study of the subject as from his awareness of the U.S. debate. In 1967, he decided to express his opposition publicly. He did so in an interview with Soviet journalist Ernst Henri (Semen Rostovskii). At the time, Sakharov still enjoyed official favor and had not yet broken with the Soviet regime or become a dissident. The interview with Henri was tape-recorded and intended to prepare a joint article for publication in *Literaturnaia gazeta*, a widely read weekly of culture and politics. The editors felt obliged to send the article for approval to Mikhail Suslov, Communist Party secretary for ideological matters. As Sakharov describes, somewhat obscurely, "Suslov found the manuscript interesting, but unsuitable for immediate publication since its

53. *Life*, 29 September 1967, 28a–28c.
54. Iu. Petrov, "Novyi tolchok gonke vooruzhenii?" *Pravda*, 24 September 1967, 4.
55. Iu. Barsukov and S. Zykov, "Kto v etom zainteresovan?" *Izvestiia*, 4 October 1967, 2.

ideas might be interpreted incorrectly."[56] The interview appeared only in *samizdat*, without Sakharov's knowledge or permission, in March 1967, in an unofficial, indeed, illegal collection edited by Roi Medvedev.[57]

In the interview Sakharov argued that both in the USSR and in the West science could make a major contribution to the maintenance of peace. When Henri asked for specifics, Sakharov raised the question of ABM: "Several of my colleagues and I have recently become especially interested in the problem of the so-called 'moratorium on anti-missile defense.'" In his memoirs, Sakharov reveals that both Soviet nuclear weapons laboratories had been studying ABMs and ways to counter them and that he had directly participated in the work: "In the course of many heated discussions, I, along with the majority of my colleagues reached two conclusions": (1) that an effective ABM system is technically impossible if the adversary has sufficient economic and technical resources to develop countermeasures; and (2) that ABM could upset the strategic balance, further stimulating the arms race.[58]

In his interview with Henri, Sakharov elaborated on both of these conclusions, going into considerable detail on the various technological countermeasures available for defeating an ABM system.[59] Yet this discussion of technical military issues was probably not the grounds for Suslov to reject the article. Similar discussions had already appeared in the Soviet military press, and more detailed ones would appear later that year.[60] More important probably was that by appearing to endorse an ABM moratorium, Sakharov was implicitly disagreeing with the Soviet government's position on ABMs—as well as the views of many pro-ABM Soviet scientists.[61] Sakharov specifically mentions Kosygin's remarks linking ABM limitations to the question of general and complete disarmament, and he complains of lack of coverage of the issue in the Soviet press. Admitting that the issue is controversial and difficult to discuss openly, he maintains that it is therefore "all the more important to begin this discussion." Ernst Henri apparently agreed, having already learned about the ABM issue sometime earlier from Paul Doty, when their mutual friend Petr Kapitsa invited the two of them to lunch at his *dacha* outside Moscow.[62] But Suslov evidently disagreed.

Although Sakharov was unable to publish his arguments against ABM in the Soviet press, he included many of them in his first *samizdat* essay, "Reflec-

56. Andrei Sakharov, *Memoirs* (New York, 1990), 276.
57. "Dialog mezhdu Ernstom Genri i A. D. Sakharovym," in R. Medvedev, ed., *Politicheskii dnevnik, 1964–1970* (Amsterdam, 1972), 197–205.
58. Sakharov, *Memoirs*, 267–268.
59. "Dialog mezhdu Genri i Sakharovym," 202–203.
60. See, e.g., [Col.] I. Zheltikov and [Col.] V. Igolkin, "Certain Tendencies in the Development of Aircraft and Antirocket Defense," *Voennaia mysl'*, 1964, no. 8:53–65 (all citations from this journal, unless otherwise indicated, are from CIA translations available on microfiche); and [Capt.] P. L. Sergeev, "Problems of Penetrating an Antimissile Defense," *Morskoi sbornik*, 1969, no. 9:91–96 (also a CIA translation).
61. Golubev et al., "Proshloe i nastoiashchee."
62. "Dialog mezhdu Genri i Sakharovym," 200; Paul Doty, letter to author, 5 July 1998.

tions on Progress, Coexistence, and Intellectual Freedom," which was widely circulated among the Soviet intelligentsia as well as abroad—and carefully scrutinized by the KGB.[63] Sakharov's arguments clearly resemble those of Western scientists who were critical of ABM. Indeed, his essay, which was initially copied and circulated in Moscow during May 1968,[64] cites the authoritative critique of ABM by Richard Garwin and Hans Bethe, published in *Scientific American* only two months earlier.[65]

The Turning Point: 1967. Whether prompted by discussions with Sakharov, with Western colleagues, or by some other motivation, Lev Artsimovich also publicly expressed his concerns about ABM in 1967. At the Seventeenth Pugwash Conference in Ronneby, Sweden, in September, Artsimovich described ABM systems as a new phase of escalation in the arms race and a threat to the "balance of power between the superpowers." He called particular attention to the stimulus that ABM would provide to the further development of strategic offensive weapons. He demonstrated concern about the implications of ABM for both crisis stability and arms-race stability, without drawing any particular attention to technical issues.[66]

Thus, Artsimovich—like Sakharov and, much earlier, Gerasimov—came out in opposition to ABMs at a time when the Soviet government was continuing its ABM deployment around Moscow and was still more than two years away from opening negotiations with the United States on ABM limitations. More striking was that Artsimovich's support for an ABM ban directly contradicted the presentation of another member of the Soviet Pugwash delegation, General A. A. Gryzlov. In his report at the Pugwash conference in Ronneby, Gryzlov, a career military officer with considerable experience in nuclear weapons matters, expressed firm opposition to an ABM ban or even simultaneous constraints on offensive and defensive weapons.[67]

Gryzlov's views were identical to those promoted by General Nikolai Talenskii three years earlier (see Chapter 6), suggesting that not much had changed in the Soviet military's evaluation of ABM. Like Talenskii, Gryzlov had contacts beyond the military itself. He served as liaison between the military (Ministry of Defense and General Staff) and the Soviet Foreign Ministry.[68] He was familiar with the Western critique of ABM but rejected it. He

63. Andrei D. Sakharov, *Progress, Coexistence, and Intellectual Freedom* (New York, 1968), 34–37.

64. Sakharov, *Memoirs*, 282–286.

65. Richard Garwin and Hans Bethe, "Anti-Ballistic-Missile Systems," *Scientific American*, March 1968, 21–31.

66. L. A. Artsimovich, "Novye idei v razoruzhenii," in *Vospominaniia ob akademike L. A. Artsimoviche*, 2d ed. (Moscow, 1988), 216–217.

67. In 1951, Gryzlov led a team of six officers from the General Staff to Turkestan to develop military exercises for training troops to fight under conditions of nuclear combat. See Vladimir Karpov, *Polkovodets* (Moscow, 1985), 522.

68. He later served on the Soviet SALT delegation in a minor role, from 1969 to 1971. See Garthoff, "BMD," 293–294 n. 38.

strongly opposed proposals for simultaneous freezing of defensive and offensive weapons: The danger, he argued, "lies in the arms race, in the development, perfection and stockpiling of offensive weapons but not defensive weapons."[69] At this point, he evidently did not acknowledge the link between ABM and an offensive arms race. Unlike the Western scientists—now joined by Artsimovich, Sakharov, and Gerasimov—military officers such as Gryzlov rejected concerns about arms-race stability.

The dispute within the Soviet Pugwash delegation apparently caught the attention of officials back in Moscow and helped contribute to a rethinking of the ABM issue.[70] Equally important, the September Pugwash conference was quickly followed up by a second meeting of the bilateral SADS group, where the American scientists were able to pursue their critique of ABM. The SADS meeting was held in Moscow in December 1967.[71] It was attended on the American side by some of the most prominent critics of ABM, including Paul Doty, Jerome Wiesner, Franklin Long, Jack Ruina, and George Rathjens, most of whom had worked on technical aspects of security policy in the Kennedy administration. Another U.S. participant, Henry A. Kissinger, later participated in the negotiation of the ABM Treaty.

On the Soviet side, the leading Soviet members of Pugwash were all in attendance—Millionshchikov, Artsimovich, and Emel'ianov, as well as Petr Kapitsa. The Soviet participants also included Academician A. M. Shchukin— a future member of the Soviet SALT delegation. Shchukin, a radar specialist who had worked at Moscow University's Department of General Physics under Artsimovich, had been skeptical of ABM since the original Soviet project was launched in 1953; at the time he reportedly described the task of "shooting a missile with a missile" as "stupid."[72] Nevertheless, he was an active participant in the development of Soviet ABM radars.

In his public comments at the December meeting Shchukin acknowledged that pursuing ABM is "extremely expensive," but he did not see how deployment of ABM would stimulate an offensive arms race. Defenses could be defeated by employing decoys, he argued, without increasing the destructive power of incoming missiles.[73] Shchukin's point was technically correct. He apparently did not understand, however, that U.S. weapons designers had already decided that if they were going to add extra things to the nose cone of a missile in order to overwhelm a Soviet ABM system, why not make those extra things nuclear explosives? Thus, the American scientists anticipated

69. A. A. Gryzlov, "The Freezing of Defensive Anti-Missile Systems" (paper presented to the 17th Pugwash Conference on Science and World Affairs, Ronneby, Sweden, 3–8 September 1967), 1.

70. Sergei Kapitsa, interview by David Wright, 11 September 1989.

71. A Soviet transcript of the December meeting is filed in the personal papers of M. D. Millionshchikov, "Zapis' besed sovetskikh i amerikanskikh uchenykh-uchastnikov Paguoshskogo dvizheniia, 28–30 dekabria 1967 g,"ANRF, fond 1713, opis' 2, delo I.5.2, no. 199.

72. Kisun'ko, Sekretnaia zona, 6.

73. Millionshchikov, "Zapis' besed sovetskikh i amerikanskikh uchenykh-uchastnikov," 8.

that ABM defenses would promote proliferation of multiple nuclear warheads on each side. Following the formal sessions, conducted somewhat ponderously in Russian or English with sequential translation, Jack Ruina held several direct discussions with Shchukin in French. He came away convinced that the Russian scientist had now grasped the basic critique of ABM on grounds of arms-race stability.[74]

At the December meeting the Americans for the first time met Georgii Arbatov, the leading Soviet specialist on the United States, who had just that month founded his Institute of the USA. Arbatov had been invited by Artsimovich and Millionshchikov to join the Soviet Pugwash delegation.[75] He soon became a major interpreter of the American scientists' critique of ABM for both the Soviet public and the top-level leadership.[76]

In private discussions between the formal sessions at the December meeting, some of the Soviet scientists told their American colleagues that "your message is being heard." Not only were they personally persuaded by the critique of ABM, but the argument was beginning to reach Soviet officials as well.[77] In fact, several government officials were present at the December 1967 meeting as "consultants" (konsul'tanty), but did not participate in the discussions. Among those who heard the American critique firsthand were General Gryzlov of the General Staff (who already knew it from Pugwash), O. A. Sokolov and M. P. Shelepin of the Foreign Ministry, and, perhaps most significantly, V. M. Karetnikov of the Military-Industrial Commission, a key organization responsible for the development and production of Soviet weapons.[78] In later years, several Soviet officials identified the December 1967 SADS meeting as having made a significant contribution toward shifting Soviet policy away from support for ABM and toward acceptance of the stabilizing function of mutual deterrence—or, in Raymond Garthoff's words, from the "Talenskii doctrine" to the "McNamara doctrine."[79]

Sources of Soviet Support for the ABM Treaty

How did the Soviet position move from active pursuit of ABM defenses at the end of the Khrushchev period, through skepticism of the merits of an

---

74. Roald Sagdeev, interview by author, College Park, Md., 31 March 1994 (on Shchukin's association with Artsimovich); Ruina, interview (on his conversations with Shchukin).

75. Artsimovich generally considered Soviet political scientists "absolutely stupid," but Arbatov was an exception. Roald Sagdeev recalls the first time he heard about Arbatov from his mentor Artsimovich: "I met this very bright guy. . . ." Sagdeev, interview.

76. Arbatov's institute submitted its first report on U.S.-Soviet relations to the government in April 1968. See G. A. Arbatov, *Zatianuvsheesia vyzdorovlenie (1953–1985 gg.): Svidetel'stvo sovremennika* (Moscow, 1991), 388–389.

77. Ruina, interview.

78. Millionshchikov, "Zapis' besed sovetskikh i amerikanskikh uchenykh-uchastnikov," 26.

79. Garthoff, "BMD," 298 n. 49.

ABM ban, to acceptance of a treaty effectively halting the competition in strategic defenses? This section reviews the main explanations given for Soviet acceptance of ABM limitations. It shows that there was no consensus on military, technical, economic, or political grounds for endorsing an ABM ban during the late 1960s—that political leaders were largely undecided and many prominent military figures and weapons designers directly opposed restrictions on ABM development. As we have seen, in May 1968 Soviet government and Communist Party officials approved an expansion and acceleration of the Soviet ABM program even as they neared a decision to participate in strategic arms talks with the United States. By that time Soviet scientists—who had been conducting bilateral "arms talks" with Americans for many years—had already made up their minds to support an ABM ban. Their activity was crucial to the origins of the ABM Treaty.

Military Requirements and Technological Possibilities

The early Brezhnev era, contrary to the Khrushchev period, witnessed a sharp debate among military analysts about strategic defense. It was reflected in the pages of *Military Thought*, the restricted-circulation journal published by the General Staff, and it focused mainly on the technical feasibility of ABM. As we recall from Chapter 6, the journal's former editor, Major General Nikolai Talenskii, had published an authoritative statement on the subject in a popular magazine in October 1964, the month Brezhnev and his co-conspirators ousted Khrushchev from office. General Talenskii offered a strong endorsement of ABM on strategic and moral grounds and expressed unbounded technical optimism: "In our day, the human genius can do anything."[80] As we saw, Talenskii's views coincided with the position of Soviet military intelligence, as expressed in a top-secret report prepared by General Ivashutin in August 1964. While detailing the extensive technical difficulties of the U.S. ABM program and outlining the possible countermeasures that could be deployed to complicate missile defense, Ivashutin voiced no doubts about the ultimate success of Soviet efforts.[81]

Other military analysts were less optimistic. In a review of U.S. developments, published in late 1965, for example, Lt. Col. V. Aleksandrov argued against ballistic missile defense on the basis of the American experience up to 1965: "Why hasn't the U.S., despite rather extensive scientific research and experimental design work in the field of antimissile defense, settled on some kind of definite plan for a system and begun actual construction of it?" His

---

80. [Maj. Gen.] N. Talensky [Talenskii], "Anti-Missile Systems and Disarmament," *International Affairs* (Moscow), 1964, no. 10:16.

81. [Lt. Gen.] P. Ivashutin, "Material o razvitii voennogo iskusstva v usloviiakh vedeniia raketno-iadernoi voiny po sovremennym predstavleniiam," prepared for Marshal M. V. Zakharov, with cover memorandum, 28 August 1964, esp. 347–359. See the discussion in Chapter 6.

answer: the ineffectiveness and high cost of BMD relative to offensive forces and the fact that extensive research into defenses has only "shown that the development and perfection of offensive means are more promising, cheaper, and simpler."[82] The next issue of the journal published a rebuttal from Lt. Gen. I. Zav'ialov, who argued that since a Soviet offensive (counter-force) missile attack could not assure the complete destruction of the enemy's nuclear forces, nationwide ABM defenses were necessary to counter any remaining weapons that were launched against the USSR.[83]

To some degree the debate about the effectiveness of ABM followed predictable bureaucratic lines, with officers of the Strategic Rocket Forces touting the invincibility of offensive missiles,[84] and leaders of the National Air Defense Forces (PVO Strany)—the service responsible for strategic defense—attesting to the reliability of BMD.[85] There was, however, a middle ground between these extreme claims. Perhaps not surprisingly, one of the most prominent examples of a relatively sober, balanced assessment of the technical possibilities for BMD and offensive countermeasures appeared in the journal of the Soviet Navy, an institution without a direct stake in the debate.[86]

General Surikov's Conversion. Interviews with retired Soviet General Staff officers indicate that some of them began to reconsider the technical feasibility of BMD starting in 1967. Major General Boris Trofimovich Surikov, for example, worked in the General Staff from 1963 on matters concerning nuclear weapons and BMD. He was one of the early Soviet ABM enthusiasts. Surikov claims to have drafted Prime Minister Kosygin's reply in January 1967 to President Johnson's invitation to engage in arms control negotiations on offensive and defensive forces as well as Kosygin's statement on ABM for the Glassboro summit the following June—both of which stressed the importance of limiting offensive forces while maintaining strong defenses. As Surikov put it, "I was very proud to see my words appear in *Pravda*."[87]

Yet Surikov came to view the prospects for successful BMD more pessimistically after 1967. As the United States began testing means of defeating

82. [Lt. Col.] V. Aleksandrov, "The Search for a Solution to the Problems of Antimissile Defense in the U.S.," *Voennaia mysl'*, 1965, no. 9, quoted in Bruce Parrott, *The Soviet Union and Ballistic Missile Defense* (Boulder, Colo., 1987), 29–30.

83. [Lt. Gen.]I. Zav'ialov, "An Answer to Opponents," *Voennaia mysl'*, 1965, no. 10, discussed in Parrott, *The Soviet Union and Ballistic Missile Defense*, 30.

84. For example, [Marshal] N. Krylov, "Raketnye voiska strategicheskogo naznacheniia," *Voenno-istoricheskii zhurnal*, 1967, no. 7:15–23.

85. For example, Army General P. F. Batitskii, commander of the PVO, interviewed on Moscow radio, 20 February 1967, quoted in Garthoff, "BMD," 295–296. For the bureaucratic-politics interpretation of Soviet policy in this area, see Stuart J. Kaufman, "Organizational Politics and Change in Soviet Military Policy," *World Politics* 46, 3 (April 1994): 355–382.

86. P. L. Sergeev, *Morskoi sbornik*, 1967, no. 9.

87. B. T. Surikov, interview, Moscow, 30 July 1992. Surikov made similar remarks to David Holloway, as conveyed to me in a letter of 30 November 1990. The claim of authorship of Kosygin's statements need not be taken at face value, but it does demonstrate the degree to which Surikov later changed his views.

defensive systems through the use of decoys, chaff, and other countermeasures, Soviet specialists recognized the limitations of ABM technology. Their own subsequent tests confirmed the effectiveness of countermeasures. When queried by General M. Povalii, deputy chief of the General Staff, about his views on the American proposal to ban ABM systems, Surikov said he favored it. Echoing Colonel Aleksandrov's point from *Military Thought*, Surikov argued that it cost more to build defensive systems than to build the offensive forces to overwhelm them.[88] In the U.S. jargon, Surikov and Aleksandrov were arguing that ABM was not cost-effective at the margin. Surikov eventually went on to serve as an adviser to the Soviet SALT delegation in drafting the ABM Treaty. In the 1980s, working with Evgenii Velikhov's Committee of Soviet Scientists, he became a prominent critic of new proposals for strategic defenses.[89]

Despite Surikov's conversion, the Soviet military remained divided on the merits of an ABM ban. The debate on the feasibility of BMD continued well into the 1970s, regardless, it seemed, of U.S. behavior. Even after the United States decided, for example, that the technical prospects for BMD were promising enough to pursue the Sentinel system with the Nike-X components, Soviet skeptics continued to promote the superiority and cost effectiveness of offensive systems. By the same token, subsequent U.S. willingness to embrace mutual restraints on ABM deployment—partly a reaction to technical realities—did little to quell the enthusiasm of some Soviet military officials for Moscow's pursuit of ABM technology. During 1968, the debate became tied to the broader controversy about whether the USSR should engage at all in strategic arms talks with the United States—especially as the United States escalated its war in Vietnam.[90]

As late as May 1972—the month the ABM Treaty was signed in Moscow— one author argued for the "steadily increasing role and importance of air defense, or more accurately, aerospace defense" against ballistic missiles as well as aircraft.[91] The most prominent advocate of ABM, not surprisingly, was Marshal P. F. Batitskii, head of the air and missile defense forces. Throughout the SALT negotiations and for years after the ABM Treaty was signed, Batitskii continued to press for pursuit of strategic defenses.[92]

Debates among Weapons Designers. Despite the technical problems with ABM defenses that convinced General Surikov and some other military of-

---

88. Surikov, interview.

89. Boris Surikov, *SDI: Key to Security or Disaster?* (Moscow, 1988).

90. Garthoff, "BMD," 298–300, esp. n. 53 for citations of the military views for and against ABM feasibility.

91. [Maj. Gen.] K. Provorov, "Missile and Space Offensive Weapons and the Problems of Countering Them," *Voennaia mysl'*, 1972, no. 5:119–125.

92. Kaufman, "Organizational Politics," 372; Garthoff, "BMD," 299–300. See also Golubev et al., "Proshloe i nastoiashchee," 22.

ficers by 1967 to favor a mutual ban on defenses, a strong community of weapons designers continued to advocate a vigorous program of ABM development. Throughout the late 1960s and into the early 1970s, secret debates raged within the Soviet weapons bureaucracy over the technical details and scope of the ABM program. They pitted leading weapons designers and their powerful political patrons against each other.[93]

One of the early leaders of the Soviet ABM effort was Grigorii Vasilievich Kisun'ko, a radar specialist, who became de facto director of the ABM program in 1954 at the age of 36.[94] During the Khrushchev period, Kisun'ko came into conflict with a prominent missile designer, V. N. Chelomei, over competing proposals for ABM interceptors. Kisun'ko favored nonnuclear warheads mounted on relatively small missiles. Chelomei promoted large-yield nuclear charges delivered by enormous rockets. Khrushchev, whose son Sergei worked in Chelomei's design bureau, favored Chelomei's approach. Kisun'ko subsequently came to explain all of the setbacks of his ABM projects as the result of politically motivated plots against him. His fortunes did seem to revive when Khrushchev was deposed in October 1964. Kisun'ko's design bureau, whose employees also included sons and daughters of prominent Soviet political figures, regained its former prominence and Kisun'ko himself was designated the main designer of the Soviet ABM system.[95] The volatile mix of political intrigue and technical debate surrounding ABM at this time was so compelling that a writer named Nikolai Gorbachev (no relation to the last Soviet leader) published a novel about it called *The Battle*. Its hero, an ABM designer named Umnov (the wise one), was a thinly disguised Kisun'ko, while the villain of the story represented Chelomei.[96]

Despite his newfound literary prominence and his liberation from Khrushchev's influence, Kisun'ko's plans for ABM defense continued to suffer setbacks. During the summer of 1967 a commission of military officers and civilian ABM specialists rejected his proposals for a territorial defense system called *Avrora*, which initially called for defending four European industrial centers: Moscow, Leningrad, Kiev, and Gor'kii. The critics argued that Kisun'ko's system took insufficient account of an opponent's likely use of countermeasures to overcome the defense.[97] Plans for extensive national

93. Kisun'ko, *Sekretnaia zona*. Sergei Khrushchev argues that Kisun'ko exaggerates the political reasons for his lack of support—that the issue was really the technical shortcomings of his ABM proposals. Sergei Khrushchev, telephone conversation with author, May 1997.

94. Golubev et al., "Proshloe i nastoiashchee," 8; G. V. Kisun'ko, interview by Stuart Kaufman, June 1992; Kisun'ko, *Sekretnaia zona*.

95. The sons of Dmitrii Ustinov and Mikhail Suslov, and the daughter of Lev Smirnov (head of the Military-Industrial Commission) all worked for Kisun'ko. Golubev et al., "Proshloe i nastoiashchee," 17–18.

96. The novel *Bitva*, by Nikolai Gorbachev, was published in several editions by various publishing houses of the Soviet Ministry of Defense.

97. Golubev et al., "Proshloe i nastoiashchee," 18–19; Kisun'ko, *Sekretnaia zona*, 474–475; Surikov, interview.

ABM defenses still circulated within the Soviet weapons community, but they were no longer associated with Kisun'ko's design bureau.

Gradually Kisun'ko began to lose control over development of the Moscow A-35 system as well. In May 1968, when the government decided to accelerate work on ABM, most of the resources went to found the new Scientific-Thematic Center under the leadership of A. G. Basistov. Supervision of the A-35 development was transferred from Kisun'ko to his deputy, I. D. Omel'-chenko. Starting in 1970, Basistov was put in charge of developing the "second-generation" A-35 system, before Kisun'ko's first-generation system ever became operational.[98]

Much of the debate among Soviet ABM designers and military officers has, in retrospect, a curiously insular quality. It often appears to have been carried out without heed to the conflicts raging in the United States over ABM or within the Soviet leadership about the merits of arms control. The designers focused so narrowly on the technical side of the issue—how to make strategic defenses work effectively—that they seemed genuinely surprised when the ABM Treaty was signed while there were so many promising (in their view) BMD technologies yet to explore.

The Strategic Case for ABM

The technical optimism of Soviet ABM designers aside, most Western analysts typically give pride of place to the military-technical reasons behind Soviet acceptance of the ABM Treaty. In addition, many accounts have offered strategic reasons for Soviet interest in ABM restrictions. In fact, the Western literature on the subject contains two diametrically opposed explanations, both based on military-strategic grounds. The first holds that the Soviet leaders came to accept the stabilizing role of mutual nuclear deterrence and to perceive ABM as a threat to strategic stability. The second holds that the Soviet leadership never accepted such a view of deterrence. Rather, Soviet political and military officials agreed to limit the competition in ABM systems because they expected that such a measure would give their side an advantage in pursuing a counterforce, "war-fighting" nuclear strategy.

Although the period after 1967 saw increasing sophistication in the military's discussions of technical matters related to ABM, there was little apparent appreciation for the Western critique of ABM on strategic grounds. The example of General Gryzlov is instructive. If military officials with exposure to the international scientific community and Western arguments about the arms race failed to recognize the potential hazards of an offense-defense competition, serving military officers and weapons designers with more limited experience were even less likely to do so. Thus, General Zav'ialov, in an au-

98. Golubev et al., "Proshloe i nastoiashchee," 20.

thoritative two-part article on Soviet military doctrine published in the daily *Red Star* in March 1967, presented the case for pursuing victory in nuclear war and for developing both offensive missiles and active defenses against nuclear attack.[99]

Following the U.S. decision, in September 1967, to deploy the Sentinel ABM system, Soviet military commentary continued to address the technical prospects for the system and began to mention the political controversy surrounding the decision, but without crediting concerns about arms-race stability and crisis stability.[100] In many respects, the Soviet military observers of the U.S. ABM debate resembled the author-participants of the inside histories of Soviet ABM developments. By focusing excessively on the technical debate they misread the nature of the U.S. critique of ABM.

By all appearances, the Soviet military came to recognize the implications of ABM for arms-race stability and crisis stability fairly late in the game, compared to the internationally oriented scientists. In May 1969, well after the Soviet government had formally announced its willingness to negotiate limitations on offensive and defensive arms, Major General Zemskov expressed concerns about crisis stability that Gennadii Gerasimov had described four years earlier and that Petr Kapitsa had voiced nine years before that: namely, that the stability of the "nuclear balance of power" could be disrupted either by a sharp increase in one side's offensive forces or by "the creation by one of the sides of highly effective means of protection from a nuclear attack of the enemy in conditions when the other side lags considerably in resolution of these missions."[101]

The most senior Soviet military officials waited until the ABM Treaty was signed to acknowledge concerns about arms-race stability. Thus, during the Supreme Soviet hearings on ratification of the treaty in September 1972, both Marshal Viktor Kulikov, chief of the General Staff, and Marshal Andrei Grechko, the defense minister, noted that the treaty would help prevent a competition between offensive and defensive arms.[102] Anticipating the inevitable, Grechko had already in 1971 ceased describing ballistic missile defense as one of the missions of the Air Defense Forces and did not even mention the Moscow ABM system as part of its arsenal.[103]

99. [Lt. Gen.] I. Zav'ialov, "O Sovetskoi voennoi doktrine," *Krasnaia zvezda*, 30 and 31 March 1967.
100. For example, [Col.] V. Bezzabotnov, "The U.S. Limited ABM System 'Sentinel,'" *Voennaia mysl'*, 1968, no. 5:69–75.
101. [Maj. Gen.] V. M. Zemskov, "Wars of the Modern Era," *Voennaia mysl'*, 1969, no. 5, quoted in David Holloway, *The Soviet Union and the Arms Race* (New Haven, Conn., 1983), 45. For Kapitsa's prescient views, see Chapter 6.
102. "Vazhnyi vklad v ukreplenie mira i bezopasnosti," *Pravda*, 30 September 1972, quoted in Parrott, *Soviet Union and Ballistic Missile Defense*, 28.
103. [Marshal] A. A. Grechko, *Na strazhe mira i stroitel'stva kommunizma* (Moscow, 1971), chap. 2.

The high command's reluctance publicly to embrace the logic of mutual deterrence has led some Western observers to argue that the Soviet military's acceptance of the ABM Treaty reflects more sinister motives. In this view, Soviet military leaders decided that a U.S.-Soviet competition in ABM defenses would hinder pursuit of a Soviet counterforce, damage-limiting strategy. Even limited U.S. defenses could disrupt the execution of a disarming Soviet first strike.[104] It would be better to seek to limit ABM on both sides.

One problem with this argument is that when the Soviet government appears to have decided to pursue strict negotiated limitations on ABM systems—during 1969, at the latest[105]—there is no evidence that the Soviet military had already agreed that such limitations would benefit Soviet strategy. Some Soviet strategists, to be sure, eventually revised their views on ballistic missile defense. Lieutenant General Zav'ialov, for example, who in 1967 had written so forcefully in favor of simultaneous pursuit of both offense and defense, appears to have changed his mind by late 1970. In an article for *Red Star*, he wrote that "nuclear weapons have established even more firmly the role of attack as the decisive form of military action and have made it necessary to accomplish even defensive tasks by active offensive measures."[106]

Other military writers, especially but not exclusively members of the Air Defense Forces, continued to insist on the need for defense against ballistic missile attack, even after the ABM Treaty was signed.[107] As late as 1976, the Soviet Ministry of Defense allowed publication of a book that criticized reliance on offensive retaliatory power as the sole basis of Soviet strategy: "If potential enemies possess weaponry for a mutual strike, then the side which first creates the means of defense against it receives a decisive advantage. The history of the development of military technology is full of examples in which a weapon that had seemed irresistible and intimidating after a certain time was opposed by sufficiently reliable means of defense."[108] At about the same time, PVO Strany supporters made a renewed effort to promote extensive ballistic missile defenses and to denigrate Soviet emphasis on the Strategic Rocket Forces.[109]

---

104. For sympathetic discussion of these arguments, see, among others: Wolfe, *The SALT Experience* (Cambridge, Mass., 1979), 110–113; David S. Yost, *Soviet Ballistic Missile Defense and the Western Alliance* (Cambridge, Mass., 1988); Stevens, "Soviet BMD Program."

105. Garthoff, "BMD," 312; Kornienko argues that by the beginning of 1970, the Soviet side had come to prefer a negotiated outcome somewhere between a limited deployment of ABM and a complete ban. G. M. Kornienko, *Kholodnaia voina: svidetel'stvo ee uchastnika* (Moscow, 1994), 141.

106. [Lt. Gen.] I. G. Zav'ialov, "Novoe oruzhie i voennoe iskusstvo," *Krasnaia zvezda*, 30 October 1970. It should be noted that the context suggests that the author is addressing mainly land combat, rather than intercontinental warfare, although he is not clear on the point.

107. See the sources cited in Garthoff, "BMD," 313.

108. V. M. Bondarenko, *Sovremennaia nauka i razvitie voennogo dela* (Moscow, 1976), quoted and discussed in Parrott, *Soviet Union and Ballistic Missile Defense*, 32–34.

109. [Marshal] G. V. Zimin et al., *Razvitie protivovozdushnoi oborony* (Moscow, 1976), discussed in Parrott, *Soviet Union and Ballistic Missile Defense*, 34–35.

There was no consensus within the Soviet military to welcome the ABM Treaty as a means of bolstering a counterforce strategy. Moreover, the implication that the Soviet military single-mindedly and exclusively sought to optimize counterforce, damage-limitation capabilities in its procurement of strategic weapons is not supported by other evidence, such as the evolution of Soviet missile guidance systems.[110] Even if much of the Soviet military continued to favor counterforce and the pursuit of "war-winning" strategies throughout the 1970s, the Soviet political leadership was far more skeptical.[111] The politicians directed their negotiators at SALT to stress the importance of preserving mutual deterrence and to denigrate the notion that nuclear war could be anything but suicidal.[112] These sentiments were closer to those embraced by the scientists who came out early in favor of an ABM ban than to those of the military who resisted SALT until the last moment.[113]

Economic Constraints

Concerns about the huge expense of a nationwide ballistic missile defense system undoubtedly helped persuade Soviet leaders to sign the ABM Treaty. One should not, however, assume that such an outcome was in any sense inevitable. The Brezhnev leadership squandered a fortune on an enormous buildup of conventional forces in Europe and on the border with China. If pursuit of strategic defenses had been of sufficient importance to Brezhnev and his colleagues, they could have diverted resources from other expensive military programs. Undoubtedly, they could also have squeezed the population further by cutting back on consumption.

In the Soviet debate over the ABM Treaty, opponents of ABM systems tended to emphasize the economic benefits of a ban. For supporters of ABM development, however, money was no object. They put forward proposals with unrealistic deadlines that were never met, mainly for their "mobilizing" potential. By "relying on them, it was possible to carry out work practically without thinking about expenses."[114] According to G. M. Kornienko, a high Soviet Foreign Ministry official involved in both the external and internal negotiations on ABM, the achievement of a consensus on this issue was not a simple matter. Some in the military resisted the ABM limitations, arguing that the United States wanted them only because the Soviet side was ahead. They were resistant to arguments about the economic costs of a race in defensive weapons: "So, let them build. We'll build, and we'll do it cheaper."[115] There

110. Donald MacKenzie, "The Soviet Union and Strategic Missile Guidance," *International Security* 13, 2 (Fall 1988): 5–54.

111. Holloway, *Soviet Union and the Arms Race*, chap. 3.

112. Gerard Smith, *Doubletalk: The Story of SALT I*, (Lanham, Md., 1985), 83.

113. For documentation of military resistance to SALT, see Samuel B. Payne, Jr., *The Soviet Union and SALT* (Cambridge, Mass., 1980).

114. Golubev et al., "Proshloe i nastoiashchee," 13.

115. Kornienko, interview.

was no consensus in Moscow on the economic necessity of the ABM Treaty or arms control in general.[116] Under such circumstances, Soviet scientists and others had an opportunity to bring to bear additional arguments.

U.S. Behavior

A common argument about the influence of U.S. behavior on Soviet policy toward the ABM Treaty holds that the U.S. decisions to deploy Sentinel, and later Safeguard, served as a "bargaining chip" to persuade the Soviet leadership to agree to limits on strategic defenses. There are various versions of this argument.

Some Western analysts have argued that the U.S. deployment decisions triggered some kind of reevaluation in Soviet military thinking about ABM. In particular, it is argued, Soviet military officials became more pessimistic about the effectiveness of their own ABM technology as they became more apprehensive about the stronger prospects for the U.S. system. This purported shift is difficult to document. Those officers who had played up the strengths of the U.S. system, even before any public deployment decisions were announced, continued to do so in order to make the case for the feasibility of BMD in general, and Soviet BMD in particular; they were typically affiliated with the Air Defense Forces. Some of those who denigrated the effectiveness of Soviet BMD also did so for parochial reasons, and regardless of the status of the U.S. ABM system: they wanted more resources for the Strategic Rocket Forces and, predictably, evinced no doubts about the ability of Soviet offensive missiles to penetrate an American ABM.[117]

Others, especially those associated with the General Staff such as General Surikov, came to believe that offensive weapons would always have the advantage over ABM. The U.S. announcements about Sentinel and Safeguard had no impact on their beliefs.[118] Furthermore, Soviet analysts at this point rarely described U.S. ABM defenses as a threat to the Soviet Union for which it would be worth making concessions at the negotiating table. They typically explained the U.S. decisions to go forward with ABM as the product of right-wing political pressure and the financial interest of the "military-industrial complex" to deploy systems even before they became technologically promising. One author claimed outright that "decisions to deploy the Sentinel system, followed by the Safeguard system, were made not so much from considerations of strategic expediency as to placate the arms manufacturers and 'hawks.'"[119]

116. Bruce Parrott, *Politics and Technology in the Soviet Union* (Cambridge, Mass., 1983), 192–202.

117. This is one of the main points in Kaufman, "Organizational Politics."

118. Surikov, interview. See also the sources listed in Garthoff, "BMD," 299 n. 53, and his discussion, 298–300; and Thomas W. Wolfe, *Soviet Power and Europe, 1945–1970* (Baltimore, Md., 1970), 439–441.

119. Provorov, "Missile and Space Offensive Weapons," 122; also Bezzabotnov, "Limited ABM System," 72–73.

Within the Soviet weapons establishment the Sentinel and Safeguard decisions did not stimulate any interest in mutual restraint on BMD systems. The fact that the U.S. government had made a decision to deploy an ABM system while the Soviet A-35 project was still under development led some critics of the Kisun'ko design bureau to claim that the United States "had solved the problem of territorial BMD against a massed nuclear-missile strike," whereas the USSR had failed to do so. Two studies undertaken in response to this charge revealed the weaknesses of the U.S. ABM system, but Kisun'ko was nevertheless replaced as head of the Soviet ABM program.[120] The point is, however, that the Soviet government in the wake of the Sentinel and Safeguard decisions did not abandon its pursuit of an ABM system or seize on the opportunity to negotiate it away. Rather, it reshuffled the leadership of Soviet ABM efforts and shifted attention to some other technological approaches besides the A-35. U.S. pursuit of Safeguard led some Soviet political leaders to push for adopting the same technical approaches to ABM as the United States developed for its ABM system—despite objections from Soviet weapons designers and military officials.[121] Kisun'ko later criticized the "safeguardization" of the Moscow ABM—the deployment of interceptor missiles with nuclear warheads—as "mining the capital with the goal of defending it."[122]

The influence of the U.S. deployment announcements on Soviet decision making was clearly more ambiguous than the bargaining-chip rationale suggests. Kornienko, who served as first deputy foreign minister under Andrei Gromyko and as the Foreign Ministry's representative in interdepartmental discussions of arms control, has acknowledged U.S. efforts to use Safeguard as a bargaining chip. But he also points out how unpopular the program was in the United States and how grassroots opposition managed to bring half of the U.S. Senate to oppose the system; it passed thanks only to the tie-breaking vote by Vice President Agnew. The close vote signaled the administration's weakness in the face of ABM opponents, not its victory over them. As *Newsweek* magazine reported on the vote at the time, "Not since Franklin Roosevelt's draft law cleared the House of Representatives by one vote in the summer of 1941 had a President been put to so stern a challenge by Congress on a major question of national defense."[123]

The Safeguard vote clearly influenced the prospects for an ABM Treaty on the U.S. side, thanks mainly to the mass protests that it provoked. In Kornienko's view, shared by U.S. observers as well, the unpopularity of the system and the close vote encouraged the U.S. administration to pursue

120. Kisun'ko, *Sekretnaia zona*, 474–475.

121. Kisun'ko, interview; [Lt. Gen.] M. S. Vinogradov, interview by Stuart Kaufman, July 1992; Golubev et al., "Proshloe i nastoiashchee," 19.

122. V. Abramov, "Den'gi na oborony," *Sovetskaia Rossiia*, 5 August 1990, 4 (an interview with Grigorii Kisun'ko). For a further critique of the Moscow ABM system, see Viktor Litovkin, "Den'gi na reformy u armii est'," *Izvestiia*, 11 March 1997, 5. I am grateful to Sergei Khrushchev for sending me a copy of this article.

123. Quoted in Paul Doty, "Science Advising and the ABM Debate," in Charles Frankel, ed., *Controversy and Decision: The Social Sciences and Public Policy* (New York, 1976), 186.

mutual limits with the USSR in expectation that the U.S. ABM might not be built anyhow.[124] As Herbert York put it, the one-vote margin of victory in the Senate "was so small that, in effect, this vote brought the plans for large-scale deployment to a halt."[125]

The popular opposition to Safeguard also reassured the Soviet leaders that restraints on ABM deployment would indeed be mutual, because U.S. citizens would see to it. At the 1964 SADS meeting in Boston, where the Americans had so strongly pressed the case for an ABM ban, Academician Leonid Sedov had suggested that without the unanimous opposition of U.S. scientists to ABM the chances were poor that Moscow would take the proposal seriously.[126] The scientists never did achieve a consensus in opposition to ABM, but it could well be that the widespread grassroots protests served as the functional equivalent, as far as the Soviet leaders were concerned.[127]

Indeed, V. P. Pavlichenko, the Soviet Academy of Sciences' main contact with Western scientists and the Pugwash movement, considered it a real victory that half the U.S. Senate opposed the ABM. In a handwritten letter to M. D. Millionshchikov, head of the Soviet Pugwash delegation, Pavlichenko wrote of his recent meeting in Boston with Jerome Wiesner, whom he described as leading the effort of the scientists who "rendered great assistance to the liberal Senators in their opposition the 'Safeguard' ABM." In a curious inversion of this chapter's main argument, Pavlichenko gave Soviet Pugwash members credit for defeating the American ABM: He praised Millionshchikov for "your significant role in exerting a corresponding influence on the American scientists."[128]

A previously top-secret report from Iurii Andropov, then head of the KGB, to Dmitrii Ustinov, the Central Committee official in charge of military matters, sheds further light on Safeguard as a bargaining chip. Written in April 1971, in the midst of the SALT negotiations, the report analyzes the U.S. position and the views of various bureaucratic actors. It admits that President Nixon was only "with difficulty able to get agreement" from Congress on funding Safeguard. Andropov anticipated that Nixon would prefer to expand Safeguard while limiting Soviet ABM deployments to the Moscow system, but that he would ultimately settle for limiting both sides to their one existing system.

124. Kornienko, *Kholodnaia voina*, 138. For a view close to Kornienko's about the implications of the close Safeguard vote, see Raymond L. Garthoff, *Détente and Confrontation: American-Soviet Relations from Nixon to Reagan*, rev. ed. (Washington, D.C., 1994), 150.
125. Herbert F. York, *Making Weapons, Talking Peace: A Physicist's Odyssey from Hiroshima to Geneva* (New York, 1987), 242.
126. American Academy of Arts and Sciences, Committee on International Studies of Arms Control, "Report on Informal Arms Control Meetings with the Soviets," section on "The Relation of Anti-Missile Systems to the Disarmament Process," n.d. (between June 1964 and March 1965), 2; document located by David Wright in the Academy's archives.
127. On the range of scientists' views, see Cahn, "Eggheads and Warheads."
128. V. P. Pavlichenko to M. D. Millionshchikov, n.d. (possibly summer 1969), in ANRF, fond 1713, opis' 3, ed. khr. 1.2, No. 193.

Thus, rather than serve as a bargaining chip to eliminate ABMs altogether, the Safeguard system allowed the USSR to maintain more strategic defenses—as a quid pro quo for Safeguard—than it otherwise would have done.[129] Former top Soviet officials have recently acknowledged—as some astute U.S. analysts had already recognized—that the USSR was by early 1970 seriously considering a total mutual ban on ABM systems. Presumably in the absence of U.S. interest in ballistic missile defenses, the USSR would have had no incentive to limit its own. But U.S. insistence on deploying Safeguard made the Soviet leaders adopt the more conservative position of maintaining the Moscow system rather than rejecting BMD altogether.[130]

THE RELATIVE INFLUENCE OF THE TRANSNATIONAL SCIENTISTS

The advent of glasnost and the end of the Soviet Union have provided some inside accounts of how Soviet leaders came to accept the ABM Treaty, as well as some documentary evidence such as Andropov's report to Ustinov. In addition to materials long available, but little used by Western scholars, the new evidence offers an opportunity to gauge the relative influence of the transnational community of ABM opponents on the Soviet debate.

Going Public with the ABM Critique

By 1968 most of the Soviet scientists engaged in the transnational dialogue on arms control had come to advocate an ABM ban. At that point they began to try to influence their government's position in three ways: (1) indirectly, by publishing articles advocating ABM restrictions and promoting the results of Pugwash discussions that dealt with the issue; (2) by mounting challenges—on technical, strategic, and economic grounds—to weapons systems that could undermine prospects for an ABM Treaty; and (3) by directly contacting key political leaders.

In April 1969, more than half a year before the opening of the SALT negotiations, not only the Soviet leadership but the broader Soviet public as well was able to learn in detail the American scientists' critique of ABM and MIRVs. Georgii Arbatov published an article in the mass-circulation government newspaper *Izvestiia* entitled "USA: The Great Missile Debates."[131] In it he presented a highly sympathetic account of the arguments of the U.S. anti-ABM campaigners, largely in the form of a review of a recent monograph by

129. Committee of State Security (KGB), 19 April 1971, Report no. 983-A, from Iu. V. Andropov to D. F. Ustinov, in Storage Center for Contemporary Documentation [Tsentr khraneniia sovremennoi dokumentatsii] (hereafter TsKhSD), fond 5, op. 63, d. 193, esp. pp. 35, 37–38.
130. Kornienko, *Kholodnaia voina*, 141; Kornienko, interview; Dobrynin, *In Confidence*, 213; Garthoff, "BMD."
131. Iu. Arbatov, "SShA: Bol'shie raketnye debaty," *Izvestiia*, 15 April 1969.

George Rathjens, an MIT professor and former Kennedy administration official. At about the same time Gennadii Gerasimov published an article in *Pravda Ukrainy* in which he pointed out the futility of ABM defenses, arguing that "investments in ABM can be neutralized by much smaller investments in additional offensive means"—precisely the argument whose significance Kosygin had found so difficult to grasp at Glassboro.[132] The following spring Arbatov's institute's journal published a detailed and balanced discussion of the arguments on both sides of the U.S. debate.[133] The author of the article was General V. V. Larionov, a professor at the General Staff Academy with close links to the academic foreign-policy *institutchiki*. Both Arbatov and Larionov made a point of naming the prominent opponents of ABM, including former presidential science advisers and Defense Department officials, stressing that this "loyal opposition" was motivated by concern that deployment of ABM and MIRVs would mark a "senseless and dangerous" escalation of the arms race. Contrary to the view put forward by some Soviet military writers and ABM designers, theirs was not simply a criticism of the technological capabilities of the present-generation ABM.[134]

According to Vasilii Emel'ianov—a relatively late convert to the cause of ABM limitations—the Pugwash conferences of 1968–69 provided important occasions for collaborative efforts to promote restrictions on strategic defenses.[135] Most important was the conference held in Sochi in the USSR in October 1969, less than a month before the opening of the first SALT negotiations. At a plenary session a panel discussion was organized to address the question of ABMs. It was chaired by Bernard Feld of the Massachusetts Institute of Technology and included George Rathjens and Georgii Arbatov. According to Joseph Rotblat, "in the ensuing debate, in which 14 discussants took part, all the ramifications and implications of the deployment of ABM's on the arms race, and their influence on the forthcoming SALT negotiations were brought to the fore from various angles."[136] The final communiqué from the conference directly advocated the limitation of both ABM and MIRV in the SALT negotiations and included the essence of the Western arms controllers' critique of counterforce offenses and ballistic missile defenses: the threat to crisis stability and arms-race stability, and the attendant waste of economic resources.[137] The underlying assumption of the scientists' concerns was the need to preserve the stability of mutual deterrence. Evidently the Soviet delegates had come a long way from their initial insistence on general

132. Gerasimov's article in *Pravda Ukrainy*, 23 March 1969, is quoted in Wolfe, *Soviet Power and Europe*, 439–440 n. 57.

133. V. V. Larionov, "Strategicheskie debaty," *SShA: ekonomika, politika, ideologiia*, 1970, no. 3:20–31.

134. For example, Bezzabotnov, "Limited ABM System," 72.

135. V. S. Emel'ianov, "Bor'ba uchenykh za mir," *Voprosy filosofii*, 1974, no. 6:10.

136. Joseph Rotblat, *Scientists in the Quest for Peace: A History of the Pugwash Conferences* (Cambridge, Mass., 1972), 77.

137. Ibid., 322–323.

and complete disarmament at the early Pugwash meetings to a willingness to accept deterrence as the foundation for arms control by the late 1960s.

Battling the Soviet Proponents of ABM

While attempting to educate the public about the merits of an ABM ban, Soviet scientists also fought a rearguard action against attempts by some of their colleagues to develop new BMD weapons. In 1969, the nuclear physicist and technological entrepreneur Gersh (Andrei) Budker attempted to persuade the Soviet military establishment to fund a project to develop space-based particle-beam accelerators to intercept missiles. His colleague Roald Sagdeev, a "second-generation" opponent of ABM systems, was at that point unaware of the strategic arguments against defenses. Nevertheless he questioned Budker about the morality of spending the state's "money before we have had a chance to even think seriously on the issue." Budker replied "it is moral to think of the protection of the sky above us, above our country."[138] In those years Budker did not hide his pro-ABM views even from American colleagues.[139]

But Budker was not a product of the Soviet "military-industrial complex," in the sense that Kisun'ko or Chelomei were. As director of the Institute of Physics in Novosibirsk, he directed most of his research toward civilian purposes, including lasers with medical applications. He maintained many contacts with Western colleagues and was widely admired by them.[140] Sagdeev considered Budker "a great scientist and generous caretaker." It was in this latter capacity that he sought, rather opportunistically, to attract military funding to his institute. As he tried to convince a skeptical Sagdeev: "After all, all these expenditures are but a drop in the sea of resources wasted for the military budget anyway." But Budker got even a smaller drop than he had requested. His proposal was reviewed by several academicians, including Lev Artsimovich, Boris Konstantinov, and Iulii Khariton, a leading figure in the Soviet nuclear weapons program. Their negative assessments managed to kill the project.[141] As Evgenii Velikhov—another second-generation critic of ABM defense—has written, "this debate vaccinated Soviet scientific opinion against the infectious ideas associated with directed-energy weaponry

138. Sagdeev, *Making of a Soviet Scientist*, 124.

139. Peter Auer, conversation with author, Ithaca, N.Y., 15 April 1989.

140. See A. N. Skrinskii, ed., *Akademik G.I. Budker: Ocherki vospominaniia* (Novosibirsk, 1988). See, for example, the contributions by Stanford Unversity's Wolfgang Panofsky. I am grateful to John Lepingwell and Roald Sagdeev for providing me some background information on Budker's work.

141. Sagdeev, *Making of a Soviet Scientist*, 123–125; Evgeny P. Velikhov, "Science and Scientists for a Nuclear-Weapon-Free World," *Physics Today*, November 1989, 32. This is a somewhat expanded and revised translation of Velikhov's article, "Nauka rabotaet na bez"iadernyi mir," *Mezhdunarodnaia zhizn'*, 1988, no 10:49–53; A. A. Kokoshin, *Armiia i politika: Sovetskaia voenno-politicheskaia i voenno-strategicheskaia mysl', 1918–1991 gody* (Moscow, 1995), 223.

and prepared the way for the discussion that followed President Reagan's March 1983 Star Wars speech."[142]

The Soviet Government Makes a Decision

Although Soviet scientists had been discussing the merits of an ABM ban with their transnational colleagues since 1964, the Soviet government did not give serious consideration to the subject until President Johnson raised the issue in his January 1967 letter to Prime Minister Aleksei Kosygin. During the previous year, Soviet ambassador Dobrynin had "sent Moscow numerous reports on ABM systems but received no formal reaction." The problem was, according to Dobrynin, that "there was no consensus within the government." Kosygin was still sticking by his view that defense was morally superior to offense, even in the nuclear age. Leaders of the military-industrial sector, such as Dmitrii Ustinov and Lev Smirnov, wanted to continue work on ABM. At the time Ustinov's son and Smirnov's daughter both worked for the Kisun'ko design bureau. According to Dobrynin, both officials "argued that the first Soviet ABM designs looked promising and the Soviet Union could fall behind the Americans if it allowed itself to become entangled in prolonged preliminary discussions" on arms control. Brezhnev, "who was familiar with defense and industrial problems" understood the technical argument "that ABM systems could be overwhelmed by increasing the number of offensive missiles," but he was not "willing to give up work on our ABM system entirely." As for the foreign minister, "Gromyko suggested what would amount to stalling by sticking to our well-known concept of demanding the whole loaf or nothing, 'universal and comprehensive disarmament.'"[143]

Once President Johnson formally proposed bilateral talks on reducing strategic weapons, officials from the Soviet Foreign Ministry, Defense Ministry, and the KGB met to prepare a report to the Politburo. It dealt only with the question whether or not to begin arms negotiations; it did not address any specific proposals.[144] When the negotiations got under way in 1969, however, a regular commission was formed to address all concrete questions related to arms control. It was chaired by Ustinov, and its members included Andropov, representing the KGB; Grechko for the military; Gromyko of the Foreign Ministry; Smirnov, head of the Military-Industrial Commission; Mstislav Keldysh, president of the Academy of Sciences; with Ivan Serbin, head of the Central Committee's military-industrial department as member-secretary.[145]

142. Velikhov, "Science and Scientists," 33.
143. Dobrynin, In Confidence, 150.
144. This account draws mainly on S. F. Akhromeev and G. M. Kornienko, Glazami marshala i diplomata (Moscow, 1992), esp. 37–41; Kornienko, Kholodnaia voina, chap. 6; Kornienko, interview; Surikov, interview; and notes from Stuart Kaufman's interviews with Kornienko, Surikov, Vinogradov, and Kisun'ko.
145. Aleksandr G. Savel'yev and Nikolay N. Detinov, The Big Five: Arms Control Decision-Making in the Soviet Union (Westport, Conn., 1995), 16; Akhromeev and Kornienko, Glazami, 37; notes of Kaufman interview with Kornienko, July 1992.

The commission's reports to the Politburo were prepared by the various members' deputies, including Georgii Kornienko for the Foreign Ministry, and they always presented a consensus view. Difficulties sometimes arose in getting Marshal Grechko's acquiescence to the group's position. He was extremely hostile to arms control and suspicious of its proponents—even to the point of accusing Kornienko of being a U.S. agent for his support of an ABM ban. Only KGB chief Andropov was able to reassure Grechko on Kornienko's behalf. Grechko's obstinacy was such that Ustinov would sometimes have to speak to Brezhnev and request that his close friend intercede with the Marshal to get him to cooperate.[146]

The first specific item addressed by the arms control commission when it formed in 1969 was the question of ABM. According to Kornienko, the path from those first discussions to the ABM Treaty itself was "very thorny."[147] Ustinov, as chair of the commission, was the key figure to convince of the merits of an ABM ban. He came into the discussion with a favorable attitude toward strategic defenses—he had long been the patron of ABM designer Kisun'ko—and skepticism about the value of limiting them.

Ultimately the top political leaders, General Secretary Leonid Brezhnev and Prime Minister Aleksei Kosygin, signed on to the goal of ABM restrictions. The strongest evidence that the transnational scientists played a role in gaining Soviet acceptance of the ABM Treaty would show some link between their efforts and a change in the views of the top leaders. Although much of the relevant Russian archival material on this question remains closed, a considerable amount of circumstantial evidence points to such a link.

Who Had Kosygin's Ear? Kosygin—despite his remarks in London and at Glassboro in 1967—did eventually come to appreciate the value of limiting ABMs, and it is likely that the arguments the Soviet scientists discussed with their Western counterparts made a difference. There are a number of ways that scientists' arguments about ABM reached Kosygin during the period 1967–68, when the Soviet government was debating whether to pursue limitations on offensive and defensive systems. Both Artsimovich and Millionshchikov were close to Kosygin.[148] In discussions with Western colleagues they revealed a great deal of respect for the prime minister, as many reform-oriented intellectuals did in those days and since. As Paul Doty reported, "There seemed to be a spontaneous confidence in Kosygin."[149]

Millionshchikov, in particular, had direct access to Kosygin, through his official duties as vice president of the Soviet Academy of Sciences, and, for a time, as chair of the Supreme Soviet of the Russian Republic. Nominally

---

146. Akhromeev and Kornienko, *Glazami*, 40–41; Kornienko, interview by Kaufman, July 1992.
147. Akhromeev and Kornienko, *Glazami*, 40.
148. Kapitsa, interview.
149. Doty, "Report of Visit," 3.

a high political office, the position was in practice mainly ceremonial. It did, however, bring him into contact with influential political leaders, to whom, as he later confided to a Western colleague, he did in fact appeal concerning ABM.[150]

We know of one concrete instance when Millionshchikov met with Kosygin and had ABM very much on his mind. Following the SADS meeting in Moscow in late December 1967—a key turning point in the transnational ABM debate—the Soviet scientists invited their U.S. colleagues to a New Year's Eve party. Millionshchikov, however, did not attend. He had an invitation to Prime Minister Kosygin's party instead.[151]

Another likely channel through which arguments in favor of an ABM ban reached Kosygin was the State Committee on Science and Technology. Its chair was Academician Vladimir Kirillin, a powerful figure in the Soviet science establishment, a vice president of the Academy, and a deputy prime minister under Kosygin. Kirillin became the head of the Soviet Pugwash delegation in 1963 and was instrumental in securing official approval for Soviet participation in the SADS workshops.[152] He was well acquainted with Artsimovich, Millionshchikov, and other Soviet scientists involved in the ABM debate. Kirillin had also met with Andrei Sakharov in the spring of 1967 at the time when Sakharov was preoccupied with the ABM question.[153] There is little doubt that Kirillin discussed with Kosygin the views that Artsimovich, Sakharov, and others were developing on ABM. He also had contacts within the Soviet military industry who pursued research on ABM technologies.[154]

A more direct link between the Pugwash arguments and Kosygin came through his own family. Kosygin's daughter, Dr. Liudmila Gvishiani, was a historian who spoke good English and who was briefly affiliated with Arbatov's institute. She attended the 1969 meeting in Sochi where Rathjens and Arbatov discussed the rationale for ABM limitations, and the next two meetings as well.[155] She also had accompanied her father to Glassboro and may have learned something of his difficulty in understanding McNamara's arguments there.[156] Kosygin's son-in-law, Liudmila's husband, was Dzherman Gvishiani, Kirillin's deputy at the State Committee on Science and Technology, and a person well placed to inform the prime minister about the merits of an ABM

150. Peierls, *Bird of Passage*, 285.
151. Ruina, interview.
152. See, especially, Kirillin to the Central Committee, 16 September 1963, letter contained in the materials from protocol no. 96, Secretariat session of 4 April 1964, no. 186g., "On the participation of Soviet scientists in the work of the joint Soviet-American group for the study of problems of disarmament and international security," TsKhSD. Kirillin mentions the Central Committee's decision of 22 August 1961 (no. P-342/36) granting the Soviet Pugwash Committee permission to participate for one year in such a study group. See also Rotblat, *Quest for Peace*, 57.
153. Sakharov, *Memoirs*, 275.
154. Sagdeev, *Making of a Soviet Scientist*, 136–139.
155. Rotblat, *Quest for Peace*, 329.
156. Seaborg, *Stemming the Tide*, 429.

ban. Gvishiani had served as host to Jerome Wiesner on a visit to the USSR and was undoubtedly acquainted with the views of one of the most prominent, earliest, and staunchest U.S. opponents of ABM.[157]

Kosygin and the other Soviet leaders had another direct link to the arguments of the U.S. critics of ABM, one that they respected perhaps more than the scientists: the Committee on State Security (KGB). We now know for certain what many U.S. Pugwash participants always suspected—that V. P. Pavlichenko, the Academy of Sciences official who organized the day-to-day work of the Soviet Pugwash committee and became a strategic arms negotiator in the 1980s, was also an agent in the first chief directorate of the KGB.[158] Although Pavlichenko's correspondence with Mikhail Millionshchikov, the head of the Soviet Pugwash delegation in the early 1970s, is available in the archive of the Academy of Sciences, his reports to the KGB about Pugwash meetings are still classified.

We know, however, from some materials that have been released, that the KGB kept the top Soviet leadership well informed about such East-West contacts. In May 1961, for example, Norman Cousins, the sponsor of the Dartmouth Conferences, organized a Soviet-American meeting in the Crimea. Among the participants were Harvard's Paul Doty; the former State Department official Robert Bowie; Shepard Stone, the Ford Foundation representative who was working with Doty to obtain funding for the SADS workshops; Evgenii Fedorov, a leading Soviet participant in the test ban negotiations, who was also involved in discussions leading to Soviet approval of the SADS exchanges; and at least one KGB informant.[159] The KGB's report, with verbatim quotations from conversations with U.S. participants, was on Nikita Khrushchev's desk within the week. A second report, from another Soviet participant, was sent to the Foreign Ministry.[160] On occasion, Soviet participants in international exchanges would report back in person to the Soviet leaders, as Georgii Arbatov did to Brezhnev on his return from a Dartmouth Conference meeting in 1980.[161] With such efficient and timely reporting on Pugwash and other unofficial East-West contacts, there is no doubt that top Soviet leaders were aware of the views of U.S. opponents of ABM.

157. Walter C. Clemens, Jr., "Jerome B. Wiesner, 1915–1994," *Bulletin of the Atomic Scientists* 51, 1 (January/February 1995): 10. For background on Gvishiani's other transnational activities, see Clemens, *Can Russia Change? The USSR Confronts Global Interdependence* (London, 1990), 147–153.

158. Savel'yev and Detinov, *Big Five*, 12.

159. The Crimea meeting, and some of its participants, are mentioned in the chronology of the activities of the Soviet-American Disarmament Study (SADS) group, compiled by Anne Cahn and located in the archives of the American Academy of Arts and Sciences, Cambridge, Mass. I am grateful to David Wright for providing me a copy of this useful document.

160. The reports are cited in Aleksandr Fursenko and Timothy Naftali, *"One Hell of a Gamble": Khrushchev, Castro, and Kennedy, 1958–1964* (New York, 1997), 126–127.

161. Arbatov wanted Brezhnev to know how damaging the Soviet invasion of Afghanistan had been to East-West relations. Arbatov, *Zatianuvsheesia vyzdorovlenie*, 231.

Faced with such evidence from his scientists' transnational contacts, Kosygin persisted in trying to understand the sources of U.S. concerns about strategic defense. He even went as far as to contact Robert McNamara in November 1968, while the recently resigned defense secretary was visiting Moscow as a tourist. They discussed prospects for the SALT negotiations, the opening of which had been delayed by the Soviet invasion of Czechoslovakia a few months earlier, and McNamara had one more opportunity to present the logic of the ABM critique. By this time Kosygin seems to have got it. The day after Kosygin's meeting with McNamara, the Soviet ambassador to the United Nations announced that the USSR was prepared "without delay to undertake a serious exchange of views" on strategic arms control.[162] By the end of 1968 a confidential exchange of documents between the U.S. and Soviet governments had led to agreement on the objectives for the forthcoming talks—including "stable mutual strategic deterrence"—and a recognition of the "integral relationship" between offensive and defensive systems.[163] These agreed objectives reflected the essence of American concerns about ABM.

Brezhnev's Motives and Influences. In determining the Soviet position on arms negotiations, Leonid Brezhnev's attitude toward ABM was probably even more important than Kosygin's. Some observers, such as Georgii Kornienko, maintain that Brezhnev never fully understood the critique of ABM, but embraced the ABM Treaty for political reasons.[164] Clearly Brezhnev had political motives for favoring arms control. He chose to make it the centerpiece of his effort to strengthen his authority in the foreign-policy realm and thereby increase his stature in domestic politics.[165] He deliberately sought to deflect credit and attention from Kosygin to himself, for example by having his aides let President Nixon's staff know that correspondence concerning arms control should be addressed to him as general secretary rather than to Kosygin as prime minister.[166] Yet there is no reason to believe that Brezhnev did not understand the strategic rationale behind an ABM ban. As Georgii Arbatov—who sent memos and briefed Brezhnev on arms control many times—put it, Brezhnev was "not a fool."[167] He was capable of assimilating large amounts of information, handled himself well during negotiations (at least until his health deteriorated in the mid-1970s), and, according to his top

162. Newhouse, *Cold Dawn*, 135–136.
163. Ibid., 137–138; and Garthoff, "BMD," 301, for the quotations from the still classified documents.
164. Akhromeev and Kornienko, *Glazami*, 40–41.
165. This argument, made by, among others, Richard D. Anderson, Jr., *Public Politics in an Authoritarian State: Making Foreign Policy during the Brezhnev Years* (Ithaca, N.Y., 1993) is supported by memoir accounts from Brezhnev's advisers. See, for example, A. S. Cherniaev, *Moia zhizn' i moe vremia* (Moscow, 1995), 290, 299.
166. Kornienko, *Kholodnaia voina*, 142; Dobrynin, *In Confidence*, 134, 177, 228.
167. Arbatov, interview by author, Cambridge, Mass., 18 May 1995.

foreign-policy aide, was directly involved in the planning of the 1972 Moscow summit meeting where the ABM Treaty was signed.[168]

Perhaps the greatest influence on Brezhnev's thinking about ABM was Mstislav Keldysh, president of the Soviet Academy of Sciences. Although not a direct participant in the transnational discussions on arms control, Keldysh played a crucial role in making them possible. As head of the Academy, Keldysh, along with his deputy Kirillin, was responsible for putting together the list of Soviet participants at Pugwash meetings and bilateral U.S.-Soviet workshops.[169] They reported back to him and undoubtedly contributed to his understanding of issues of international security, such as the ABM debate. He in turn brought those views to bear in high-level discussions, evidently to good effect. For Brezhnev, according to his personal physician Evgenii Chazov, Keldysh "was the indisputable authority in the area of science and technology."[170] Keldysh took advantage of that authority when he helped formulate Soviet policy toward ABM. In his colleague Georgii Kornienko's words, "I am convinced that only thanks to Academician M. V. Keldysh, whose opinion Brezhnev and Ustinov closely heeded, was the top political leadership convinced of the idea of a ban on a widescale ABM system."[171]

Summary: Scientists and the ABM Treaty

In a 1972 draft report to the top officials of the Soviet Academy of Science, written just months before his death, Academician Mikhail Millionshchikov accorded the Pugwash movement considerable credit for the first successes of U.S.-Soviet arms control. "Already in 1965," he wrote,

> at a meeting in the framework of the Pugwash movement of scientists of the USA and Soviet Union, there was a detailed examination of the problem of antimissile weaponry. Possible paths to agreement on the limitations of further development of strategic weaponry and antimissile technology were discussed. The clarification of points of view on these problems allowed for better understanding of the conceptions of both sides, which turned out to be useful for working out subsequent bilateral government agreements and treaties between the USSR and USA on the limitation of systems of antimissile defense

---

168. A. M. Aleksandrov-Agentov, *Ot Kollontai do Gorbacheva* (Moscow, 1994), 217–218. See also Cherniaev, *Moia zhizn' i moe vremia*, esp. chaps. 8–9.

169. See, e.g., Keldysh to Central Committee, 29 November 1963 and 13 May 1964, proposing names for the forthcoming SADS meeting in Boston, and the decree approving the delegation, "O komandirovanii Sovetskikh uchenykh v SShA," contained in the materials from the Twenty-second Convocation of the Central Committee of the Communist Party of the Soviet Union, protocol no. 96, Secretariat session of 4 April 1964, no. 186g., "On the participation of Soviet scientists in the work of the joint Soviet-American group for the study of problems of disarmament and international security," TsKhSD.

170. Evgenii Chazov, *Zdorov'e i vlast'* (Moscow, 1992), 102.

171. Akhromeev and Kornienko, *Glazami*, 40–41.

and the interim agreement on several measures in the area of limitations of strategic offensive weapons [SALT I].[172]

Millionshchikov's evaluation of the collaboration between U.S. and Soviet scientists on the ABM issue coincides with the evidence presented in this chapter. Indeed much of his attitude about the value of the scientists' dialogue, and the very words he used to describe it, are a direct reflection of the views of his U.S. colleagues.[173] Discussions between Soviet and Western scientists contributed to the change in official Soviet policy from promotion of ABM defenses to support for their limitation. People such as Artsimovich, Gerasimov, Millionshchikov, and Sakharov came out in favor of ABM limitations before the Soviet government even agreed to pursue bilateral arms control negotiations. The scientists presented their views to Soviet leaders—views that contrasted with some strongly voiced opinions within the Soviet military command and among Soviet weapons designers. Yet the civilian scientists' concern about arms-race stability and their acceptance of mutual deterrence ultimately found expression in their government's decision to limit ABMs and strategic offensive arms.

172. "Proekt (dokladnyi zapiski) v Prezidium Akademii nauk SSSR ob itogakh 15-ti letnei deiatelnosti Paguoshskogo dvizheniia uchenykh," 24 September 1972, Millionshchikov papers, ANRF, f. 1713, op. 2, delo I.5.2, no. 209.

173. Millionshchikov's 1972 report, for example, contains wording and sentiments quite similar to those in a four-page, single-spaced letter from Jeremy Stone to Donald Brennan of 25 August 1965 on the "importance of a continuing dialogue" between Soviet and U.S. scientists. A copy of the memo was found in Correspondence of M.D. Millionshchikov, ANRF, fond 1713, opis' 2, delo I.5.2.2, no. 412.

[11]

The "Reckless Star Wars Scheme": A New Challenge

Velikhov told me that the reason he decided to organize the Committee of Soviet Scientists [in 1983] was to educate a new generation of Soviet scientists, including himself, about nuclear arms control and to reopen the US-Soviet dialogue on strategic defense with the roles reversed. Now it would be the Soviet scientists who would try to convince the US government, with US scientists as intermediaries, that the pursuit of ballistic missile defenses would be counterproductive.

—FRANK VON HIPPEL, 1989

In a most ironic twist, a "study" by Soviet scientists written in 1983—actually a propaganda effort designed to undermine Western support for SDI—adopted the many "countermeasures and responses" dreamed up by American opponents of SDI and then fed them back to Western readers as original Soviet analysis.

—STEPHEN MEYER, 1985

The ABM Treaty put no restrictions on the research of ballistic missile defense technologies, as long as they did not lead to the development, testing, or deployment of new ABM systems or their components. The treaty itself allowed for the maintenance and upgrading of one limited ABM system in each country. The USSR kept the Moscow A-35 system operational and occasionally improved various components of it. The United States built a system to defend against an attack on its base of intercontinental ballistic missiles near Grand Forks, North Dakota, but soon closed it down as an ineffective waste of money. Both sides actively pursued research into various forms of BMD technology, within the limits of the treaty.

Thus, when President Reagan announced his intention to develop a space-based ballistic missile defense (BMD) system in March 1983, he took most observers, including top officials in his own administration, by surprise. Senator Edward Kennedy criticized the program as a "reckless Star Wars scheme," after the popular movie of that name.[1] Kennedy correctly perceived SDI as

1. See Katherine Magraw, "Weapons Brokers and Policy Entrepreneurs: Congress and the

a repudiation of the legacy of the ABM Treaty and the U.S. commitment to stable mutual deterrence. A popular campaign against Star Wars was launched, with many of the scientists and diplomats whose efforts had produced the ABM Treaty leading the way in an attempt to preserve it.[2]

Many scientists in the Soviet Union criticized Reagan's Star Wars proposal as well. Their anti-SDI campaign was interpreted by some in the West as mainly a propaganda effort intended to undermine U.S. military programs but with no impact on Soviet ones. This critique of the Soviet scientists' intentions is familiar from the other cases we have examined, perhaps most notably the test ban debate during the Khrushchev era. But as in that case, it is not hard to demonstrate that the Soviet scientists who criticized U.S. military programs were as much concerned about halting dangerous military developments in their own country as they were in influencing the internal U.S. debate. They also recognized, as their critics frequently did not, that the two activities were interrelated. With SDI, as with the test ban and other arms control issues, Soviet proponents of disarmament faced a "battle on two fronts." This chapter chronicles the first two years of the battle, from Reagan's SDI speech in March 1983 to Mikhail Gorbachev's advent to power in March 1985. It is a story of tremendous activity by the transnational disarmament community and considerable success. The scientists' greatest achievements, however, came during the Gorbachev years, the subject of the next section of the book.

THE ANTI-SDI VACCINATIONS

Although Reagan's Star Wars speech came as a surprise to Soviet as well as U.S. audiences, in several respects Soviet scientists, through their previous "combat experience," were prepared for it. Soviet scientists had engaged the battle at home because the Soviet military establishment had continued to pursue a vigorous program of research into defense-related technologies, within the framework of the ABM Treaty. As usual, the Soviet proponents of the new military programs received "reinforcements" from their counterparts on the U.S. side. Evgenii Velikhov has called particular attention to the campaign of General George Keegan in the late 1970s on behalf of a U.S. strategic defense effort. Keegan was chief of intelligence in the U.S. Air Force and a briefer for the 1976 "Team B" study that challenged U.S. Central Intel-

---

Strategic Policy Community During the Reagan Era" (Ph.D. diss., Massachusetts Institute of Technology, June 1992), 278.

2. Thomas Longstreth, John Pike, John Rhinelander, *Impact of U.S. and Soviet Ballistic Missile Defense Programs on the ABM Treaty* (Washington, D.C., 1985); John Tirman, ed., *The Fallacy of Star Wars* (New York, 1983); E. P. Thompson, ed., *Star Wars* (New York, 1985). For an account of the anti-SDI campaign, see Magraw, "Weapons Brokers," chap. 5.

ligence Agency estimates of Soviet military capabilities.[3] Keegan claimed that the USSR was testing nuclear-powered beam weapons for missile defense at its test range near Semipalatinsk. The claim turned out to be false, but it made the Soviet weapons community suspect that the United States was interested in such programs. Soviet weapons designers then sought to promote their own BMD research on the basis of the argument that "the Americans are doing it."[4]

The Soviet Union had particularly good information on the nature of the U.S. BMD research program. Much of the literature on the basic lines of technological development was public knowledge or could be discovered through close scrutiny of the annual military budgets approved by Congress. In addition, the Soviets learned a fair amount of additional information through espionage. In the mid-1980s the CIA revealed that an electronics engineer named James Harper, a U.S. citizen, had worked for the Polish intelligence services. Harper had access to information from the Ballistic Missile Advanced Technology Center at Systems Control Inc., a high-technology firm in California. According to the CIA, Harper "provided dozens of documents on potential U.S. ballistic missile defense programs" to the Polish secret service and presumably to Soviet intelligence as well.[5]

In 1979 or 1980, well before Reagan's Star Wars speech, "the idea of effective missile defenses received fresh impetus in the USSR," according to Velikhov. Academician V. N. Chelomei "proposed the creation of a space-based defense using interceptor missiles, a concept very similar to the U.S. first-phase scheme that the Reagan Administration proposed during its last year."[6] Chelomei was the same missile designer who had competed unsuccessfully with Grigorii Kisun'ko to design an ABM system in the early 1960s. As Lev Artsimovich once told his "favorite student" Roald Sagdeev, Chelomei liked to call himself "the most expensive man" in the Soviet Union because of the size of his institute's budget for military research.[7] But in the late 1970s Chelomei ran afoul of Dmitrii Ustinov, the defense minister, and

3. See Anne Cahn and John Prados, "Team B: The Trillion Dollar Experiment," *Bulletin of the Atomic Scientists* 49 (April 1993): 22–31; and Matthew Evangelista, "Second-Guessing the Experts: Citizen Groups and the CIA's Estimates of Soviet Military Policy," *International History Review* 19, 3 (August 1997).

4. Evgenii Velikhov, interview by author, Moscow, 29 July 1992.

5. *Soviet Acquisition of Militarily Significant Western Technology: An Update*, a report prepared by the U.S. Central Intelligence Agency (unacknowledged), September 1985, table 4, p. 20.

6. Evgenii Velikhov, "Science and Scientists for a Nuclear-Weapon-Free World," *Physics Today* (November 1989): 32–36 (an expanded version of a speech Velikhov delivered at a "Scientific-Practical Conference" of the Soviet Foreign Ministry, the original of which was published as "Nauka rabotaet na bez"iadernyi mir," *Mezhdunarodnaia zhizn'*, 1988, no. 10:49–53); Velikhov, interview.

7. A. M. Prokhorov refers to Sagdeev as Artsimovich's favorite student in his essay, "Vo glave otdeleniia," in *Vospominaniia ob akademike L. A. Artsimoviche*, 2d ed. (Moscow, 1988), 75. Artsimovich's comment about Chelomei comes from Roald Sagdeev, *The Making of a Soviet Scientist* (New York, 1994), 202.

lost many of his contracts. In proposing a system of ABM defenses, Chelomei avoided Ustinov and wrote directly to Brezhnev. In Sagdeev's words, Chelomei's "Star Wars" proposal marked the weapons designer's "last desperate attempt to regain his power and role in the Soviet military-industrial complex."[8]

Brezhnev set up a commission to review Chelomei's proposal. It was chaired by General Vitalii Shabanov, a deputy defense minister, and included Velikhov and Iulii Khariton, whose critical assessments helped defeat previous ABM proposals. Brezhnev accepted the Shabanov committee's recommendation to reject Chelomei's project.[9]

For Velikhov and his colleagues, the defeat of the challenge posed by the Chelomei proposal served as a second "vaccination" against the ABM "disease," following by a decade the unsuccessful attempt by Gersh Budker to promote a similar effort (see Chapter 10). The experience "enabled us to respond to Reagan's speech rapidly and energetically."[10]

The initial response consisted of a meeting that Velikhov organized at the Academy of Sciences within a month of Reagan's speech. Attendance was voluntary; the meeting was open to any members who wanted to discuss the issue. Velikhov later wrote that the "discussion was not an easy one—because of secrecy restrictions and the absence of a government position on the matter, we could not express all the arguments."[11] Moreover, even in 1983, many of the scientists were not familiar with the basic concept of nuclear deterrence—that "offense is good, defense is bad"—and found it difficult at first to accept. But, as Velikhov put it, "physicists understand quantum mechanics." They soon grasped the logic of the Star Wars critique.[12]

One reason that Velikhov did not find an immediately receptive audience at the Academy meeting is that Soviet scientists who opposed the arms race were undergoing a generational change between the signing of the ABM Treaty in 1972 and the emergence of SDI in 1983. Artsimovich and Millionshchikov had both died in 1973. Some members of the older generation were still alive: Andrei Sakharov, for example, became an outspoken dissident and lost his job in nuclear weapons research in the late 1960s, but remained committed to arms control. Iulii Khariton, a leading nuclear weapon designer, was never part of the transnational scientists movement (even the "tacit" one), but from time to time took positions that helped bolster their cause. But by and large a younger generation had to educate itself in order to oppose the new round of the arms race threatened by the Reagan administration's military buildup and hostility to arms control. The leaders of the new genera-

---

8. Sagdeev, *Making of a Soviet Scientist*, 209–211.
9. A. A. Kokoshin, *Armiia i politika: Sovetskaia voenno-politicheskaia i voenno-strategicheskaia mysl', 1918–1991 gody* (Moscow, 1995), 223.
10. Velikhov, "Science and Scientists," 33.
11. Ibid., 33.
12. Velikhov, interview.

tion included two of Artsimovich's most promising students—Velikhov and Sagdeev—joined by political scientists, mainly protégés of Georgii Arbatov, such as his son Aleksei and the deputy director of his institute, Andrei Kokoshin. They quickly focused their attention on the dangers posed by an arms race in space weaponry, including SDI.

THE INITIAL SOVIET RESPONSE TO STAR WARS

By historical precedent one would have expected the Soviet reaction to the U.S. pursuit of strategic defenses to include both a short-term effort to counter the new U.S. program and a longer-term attempt to develop analogous systems. Most Western observers anticipated that response.[13] Iurii Andropov, the Soviet leader at the time of Reagan's Star Wars speech in March 1983, had argued precisely in those terms just a few months earlier. He maintained that the Reagan administration's arms buildup would not force the Soviet Union to make "unilateral concessions" and that the USSR would match every U.S. development.[14] His first reaction to Reagan's speech was consistent with the long-standing Soviet approach: "Should this conception be converted into reality, this would actually open the floodgates of a runaway arms race of all types of strategic arms, both offensive and defensive."[15]

The ASAT Moratorium

Despite Andropov's commitment not to make unilateral concessions, the USSR did precisely that within months of Reagan's Star Wars speech. On 18 August 1983, Andropov met with nine U.S. senators in the Kremlin and pledged a unilateral Soviet moratorium on the testing of antisatellite (ASAT) weapons. Members of the Senate and the House of Representatives had been working on legislation calling for a joint U.S.-Soviet moratorium, so Andropov's action strengthened their case considerably.[16]

Evgenii Velikhov and his transnational allies in the United States deserve credit for persuading the Soviet leadership to impose the unilateral ASAT moratorium. In March 1983, Velikhov and Sagdeev had just returned from Washington, where they had taken part in discussions with members of the U.S. National Academy of Sciences Committee on International Security and

13. Stephen M. Meyer, "Soviet Strategic Programmes and the US SDI," *Survival* 27, 6 (November–December 1985); David Holloway, "The Strategic Defense Initiative and the Soviet Union," *Daedalus* 114, 3 (Summer 1985): 257–278; Matthew Evangelista, *Innovation and the Arms Race: How the United States and the Soviet Union Develop New Military Technologies* (Ithaca, N.Y., 1988), 258–261.

14. "Doklad tovarishcha Iu.V. Andropova," *Pravda*, 22 December 1982.

15. Iurii Andropov, interview, *Pravda*, 26 March 1983.

16. *The Arms Control Reporter* (Cambridge, Mass., 1983), 573.B.15–18; Magraw, "Weapons Brokers," 303.

Arms Control. A ban on ASAT testing was one of the goals the group sought to implement. Velikhov proposed the idea to Marshal Sergei Akhromeev, then deputy chief of the General Staff, and later to Ustinov, the defense minister.[17] In May 1983, the Union of Concerned Scientists presented a draft treaty limiting antisatellite weapons—the work mainly of Kurt Gottfried of Cornell University and Richard Garwin of IBM corporation.[18] Velikhov had met Garwin at the Washington meeting and had discussed proposals for ASAT limitations with him. He supported the UCS proposals, many of which ultimately became incorporated in a draft treaty submitted by the USSR to the United Nations in early 1984.[19]

A Soviet Star Wars?

Despite the restraint that the USSR exercised in the related field of anti-satellite weapons, the initial Soviet response to the Reagan Strategic Defense Initiative was of a very different character. It suggested that the USSR would respond vigorously with development of defensive as well as offensive systems, including space-based defenses. Senior military leaders made numerous warnings along those lines.[20] Velikhov, Sagdeev, and their colleagues feared that the constituency within the Soviet scientific-military-industrial sector that favored pursuit of strategic defenses would be bolstered by the Reagan administration's SDI program. Thus, they were the first to argue against copying the U.S. initiative, just months after Reagan's speech—and they did so in direct contradiction to the impression that top Soviet military and political officials were trying to convey. The scientists argued on the basis of their understanding of the dangerous implications of mutual strategic defense as they were worked out by the transnational community of Soviet and Western scientists during the 1960s. And they did so well before Mikhail Gorbachev came into office and began articulating his "new thinking" in foreign policy.

In 1983 Velikhov, Sagdeev, and Kokoshin were already presenting some of the key ideas to Soviet and Western audiences—not to copy Star Wars but to

17. Velikhov, interview; Velikhov, "Science and Scientists," 33–34. See also Marshal Akhromeev's discussion of Ustinov's reaction to SDI, in S. F. Akhromeev and G. M. Kornienko, *Glazami marshala i diplomata* (Moscow, 1992), 19–20.

18. *Arms Control Reporter*, 573.C.3–6.

19. Excerpts of statement by Igor Iakovlev at the UN Symposium on Preventing the Arms Race in Outer Space, 26 January 1984, quoted in the *Arms Control Reporter* (1984), 574.D.5. For the text of the Soviet draft treaty, see 574.D.1–3.

20. See, for example, the remarks by the chief of the General Staff, Marshal Sergei Akhromeev, "Dogovor po PRO—pregrada na puti gonki strategicheskikh vooruzhenii," *Pravda*, 4 June 1985; and the discussion in Mary C. FitzGerald, *Soviet Views on SDI*, Carl Beck Papers No. 601, Center for Russian and East European Studies, University of Pittsburgh, May 1987, 39–40. See also Don Oberdorfer, "Military Response Planned to 'Star Wars,' Soviet Says," *Washington Post*, 8 March 1985.

pursue arms control and, if necessary, build cheap countermeasures to SDI.[21] These recommendations for an "asymmetric response" to Star Wars were incorporated in a report issued by the newly created Committee of Soviet Scientists and distributed internally and abroad.[22]

At that time and later, the writings of Velikhov and his colleagues were interpreted by some in the West as part of a government-orchestrated propaganda campaign to defeat the American SDI program while the USSR continued its own military programs unhindered.[23] The Soviet scientists' campaign was, however, directed primarily at Soviet military and political leaders, to persuade them not to fall for American attempts to undermine the Soviet economy through an expensive and counterproductive arms race.[24] That goal would be served by bolstering the efforts of American opponents of Star Wars, but that was not an end in itself. In addition to reducing the risk of nuclear war, the Soviet scientists were keenly interested in the demilitarization and democratization of their own society—goals they saw as closely linked.[25] Once Gorbachev came into office they were able to pursue both goals with great determination. But in the first half of the 1980s, the prospects

21. See, e.g., the following interviews: with Velikhov, *Los Angeles Times*, 24 July 1983, reprinted in Robert Scheer, *With Enough Shovels: Reagan, Bush, and Nuclear War* (New York, 1983), 298–304; with Velikhov, *Sovetskaia Rossiia*, 21 April 1985; with Sagdeev, *Sotsialisticheskaia industriia*, 9 February 1986. Also Jeremy Stone, "FAS Visit to Moscow Initiates Star Wars Dialogue," *F.A.S. Public Interest Report* 36, 10 (December 1983): 3; and Frank von Hippel, "Arms Control Physics: The New Soviet Connection," *Physics Today*, November 1989, 40.

22. *Strategicheskie i mezhdunarodno-politicheskie posledstviia sozdaniia kosmicheckoi protivoraketnoi sistemy s ispol'zovaniem oruzhiia napravlennoi peredachi energii* (Moscow, 1984). In 1986 a revised version of the report was published in several languages and attracted considerable attention abroad: E. P. Velikhov, R. Z. Sagdeev, A. A. Kokoshin, eds., *Kosmicheskoe oruzhie: dilemma bezopasnosti*; English translation published as *Weaponry in Space: The Dilemma of Security* (Moscow, 1986).

23. For example, Benjamin S. Lambeth, "Soviet Perspectives on the SDI," in Samuel F. Wells, Jr., and Robert S. Litwak, eds., *Strategic Defenses and Soviet-American Relations* (Cambridge, Mass., 1987). For a similar interpretation of another initiative of the transnational scientists' organizations, see Leon Gouré, "'Nuclear Winter' in Soviet Mirrors,'" *Strategic Review* (Summer 1985): 35–36.

24. This is also a point that Georgii Arbatov emphasized. He criticized the Soviet propaganda campaign against SDI—after the fact—as having played into the Americans' hands by encouraging the Soviet side to develop costly and unnecessary responses. See G. A. Arbatov, *Zatianuvsheesia vyzdorovlenie (1953–1985 gg.): Svidetel'stvo sovremennika* (Moscow, 1991): 206, 348. Sagdeev expressed similar views in Roald Sagdeev, interviews by author, Moscow, November 1990, Ann Arbor, May 1991, and College Park, April 1994; and in Sagdeev, *Making of a Soviet Scientist*. See also Strobe Talbott, *The Master of the Game: Paul Nitze and the Nuclear Peace* (New York, 1988), 360–361.

25. Andrei Sakharov is, of course, the most famous proponent of these views, but they were evident in the statements and actions of other Soviet scientists, including prominent members of the Committee on Soviet Scientists, such as Roald Sagdeev. See, e.g., Irwin Goodwin, "Soviet Scientists Tell It Like It Is, Urging Reforms of Research Institutes," *Physics Today* (September 1988): 97–98: "Perestroika and the Scientific Intelligentsia," summary of talk by Roald Sagdeev, Kennan Institute for Advanced Russian Studies, Washington, D.C., 16 November 1988; Roald Sagdeev, "Science is a Party to Political Decisions," transcript of a speech delivered at a conference of the Soviet Foreign Ministry, published in *International Affairs* (Moscow), 1988, no. 11:26–28.

for success even of their campaign for an asymmetric response to SDI were uncertain—let alone their more ambitious hopes for internal reform.

PEACE THROUGH STRENGTH AND THE "GRAND COMPROMISE"

In the wake of the demise of the Soviet Union, a number of observers, including various officials who served in the administrations of Ronald Reagan and George Bush, have accorded SDI a leading role in ending the Cold War. One argument is that SDI served as a bargaining chip to induce the Soviets to agree to deep reductions in their arsenal of strategic nuclear missiles—something that they had pointedly refused to do when President Jimmy Carter proposed it in March 1977.[26] The notion of such a "grand compromise" apparently motivated some Reagan administration officials, such as Paul Nitze and Robert McFarlane, to back SDI, even though they had doubts about its technical feasibility. Another argument holds that in attempting to match the U.S. strategic defense program, the USSR undermined its economy, leading inexorably to its downfall. This view is most typically associated with Reagan's defense secretary Caspar Weinberger, who claims to have adopted it as a deliberate strategy. Finally, some observers believe that the fear of an inability to compete in the areas of advanced technology represented by the Star Wars program led the USSR to pursue a more moderate course in foreign policy, perhaps with the goal of bolstering its economic prospects through greater integration into the world economy.

Reactions to Star Wars before Gorbachev

The first, most obvious point to make in regard to these notions is that none of the conjectured Soviet responses to Star Wars had occurred before Gorbachev came into office, even though Reagan's SDI speech was delivered two years earlier. The USSR made no major concessions of any sort in arms control negotiations and did not adopt a conciliatory foreign policy. If anything, it became more hostile. Although the Soviet government announced in 1984 an increase of almost 12 percent in its published military budget (representing only part of the actual spending), the marginal impact on the Soviet economy was insignificant. The announcement, in Raymond Garthoff's view, "was primarily a political sign to the West and to the Soviet people."[27] Even this increase, he points out, "remained far below the Soviet rate of buildup before 1976"—when the military budget was constrained not to grow any faster

26. On Soviet reactions to the Carter proposal, see G. M. Kornienko, *Kholodnaia voina: svidetel'stvo ee uchastnika* (Moscow, 1994), 172–177.
27. Raymond L. Garthoff, *The Great Transition: American-Soviet Relations and the End of the Cold War* (Washington, D.C., 1994), 189.

than the overall, sluggish rate for the economy as a whole—"and far below the rate of the American buildup from 1980 on." [28]

Some fascinating insights into the reactions of Gorbachev's predecessors to the Reagan policies of "peace through strength" are found in a declassified transcript of a Politburo meeting held on 31 May 1983, just two months after Reagan's Star Wars speech. [29] The meeting was ostensibly intended to determine the appropriate reaction to the planned deployment of new U.S. cruise and Pershing II missiles in Europe later that autumn, but the discussion covered a range of other U.S. policies, including, briefly, space weapons. The scheduled deployment of the missiles was months away, and European peace activists were regularly organizing mass demonstrations against them. Nevertheless, every member of the Politburo who participated in the discussion voiced a firm conviction that the missiles would be deployed despite the protests. This fact undermines arguments, common at the time and since, that the Soviet side was counting on the peace movement to prevent the deployment and only got serious about arms control once the weapons were in place.

It is true that the Politburo in the early 1980s had trouble advancing arms control proposals that could lead to an agreement. But the problem lay mainly in a failure of imagination and excessive caution, not in any sense of optimism that the Reagan buildup could be halted without Soviet concessions. Even assuming the missile deployment as a fait accompli, for example, the Soviet leaders could hardly think of anything worth changing in their approach to arms control. Iurii Andropov, chairing the session, asked early on whether there was a point in even continuing any arms negotiations with the United States after the deployment. (In the event, the Soviets broke off all negotiations for over a year.) Andrei Gromyko, the foreign minister, thought that it would not be useful to continue them in the current form. "It's necessary to introduce something fresher," he argued. But the best he could come up with was a proposal to unite the talks on intermediate-range nuclear forces (including Pershing II, cruise, and Soviet SS-20 missiles) with the talks on strategic nuclear weapons ("and tactical nuclear weapons," added Andropov). Gromyko offered no changes in the Soviet negotiating position, let alone unilateral reductions of the sort that Gorbachev would later carry out. He neglected even to mention any negotiations to forestall strategic defense weapons such as SDI. [30]

Ustinov, the defense minister, flatly declared that "everything that we are doing in relation to defense we should continue doing. All of the missiles that we've planned should be delivered, all of the airplanes put in those places

28. Ibid., 506.
29. The transcript is located in F. 89, op. 42, d. 53, Storage Center for Contemporary Documentation, Moscow.
30. Ibid., 5.

where we've designated." So much for a conciliatory response to "peace through strength." Ustinov did, however, make a suggestion for arms control. The exchange that followed between Ustinov and Gromyko indicates just how out of touch some of the leaders responsible for Soviet security policy were. Ustinov started by suggesting that the Soviet Union propose that both sides reduce their missiles by 50 percent.

> Gromyko: "Reduce what?"
> Ustinov: "We could reduce all the missiles."
> Gromyko: "We have proposed that."
> Ustinov: "Yes, proposed, but we have to make the proposal again."[31]

That was the extent of the discussion on arms control.

Ustinov then jumped to a subject that clearly interested him more: "We need to set up a space command, as in the USA."[32] Such, apparently, was his reaction to U.S. interest in space-based defense systems. The meeting concluded with a comment by the junior member of the Politburo, Mikhail Gorbachev: "I fully support the proposals, including on the military line."[33]

Evidently Reagan's SDI project made little impact on Gorbachev's predecessors except to encourage them to emulate some aspects of it. Even so, they did not increase their spending on strategic defenses—already rather high if one includes a broad definition of the category—enough to make any difference in the state of the Soviet economy.

SDI and Soviet Reform

If SDI were to lead to the kind of reforms that Gorbachev ultimately pursued—including deep reductions of the nuclear arsenal, economic revitalization, reconciliation with the West, and integration into the international economy—one would expect that it would have been welcomed by Soviet reformers. In fact none of the Soviet proponents of reforms viewed Star Wars as advancing their cause.

Consider the case of Roald Sagdeev, former head of the Soviet Space Research Institute and a leading proponent of arms control. He maintained that SDI had "absolutely zero influence" on the origins or course of Soviet reforms.[34] Sagdeev was particularly critical of the argument that a fraudulent test of an SDI interceptor missile in June 1984 "helped persuade the Soviets to spend tens of billions of dollars to counter the American effort to develop a space-based shield."[35] The test, which entailed putting a beacon on the target

---

31. Ibid, 7.
32. Ibid., 9.
33. Ibid., 12.
34. Roald Sagdeev, interview by author, College Park, Md., 31 March 1994.
35. Tim Weiner, "Lies and Rigged 'Star Wars' Test Fooled the Kremlin, and Congress," *New York Times*, 18 August 1994.

Left to right: Roald Sagdeev, a leading Soviet opponent of strategic defenses, with U.S. activists Jeremy Stone and Thomas Cochran. Photo courtesy of Tom Cochran.

and a receiver on the interceptor, evidently fooled the U.S. Congress into spending billions on the Star Wars program, but to think that it fooled Soviet military experts, argued Sagdeev, is "naive." Sagdeev, who closely followed developments in strategic defense from Moscow at the time, said the 1984 test was hardly noticed. He pointed out that the Soviet Union achieved the successful interception of a warhead by an ABM defense missile—without fraud—already in March 1961. Therefore for the United States to achieve the same result twenty-three years later was meaningless.[36] This is an argument that pro-ABM scientists in Russia made as well—even though one might expect them to have seized on any evidence of alleged U.S. success to promote an acceleration of their own programs.[37]

U.S. Intentions and Behavior

Regardless of the triumphal retrospective accounts of the influence of SDI on Soviet reforms, is there any evidence that the U.S. government actually expected Star Wars to have such an impact on the USSR? Did anyone really expect Star Wars to turn the Soviet Union into a peaceful, democratic, capitalist

36. Sagdeev, interview, March 1994.
37. G. V. Kisun'ko, *Sekretnaia zona: Ispoved' general'nogo konstruktora* (Moscow, 1996), 5–6.

country? Did anyone think SDI would lead to the disintegration of the Soviet empire? Did anyone even anticipate major concessions on arms control of the sort that Gorbachev eventually initiated?

For one thing, there was no single U.S. government view on any of these questions. President Reagan had very different expectations about the impact of SDI on the USSR than, for example, his advisers Nitze and McFarlane did. They hoped to use the threat of SDI as a bargaining chip to induce Soviet concessions in the arms negotiations. In particular, they hoped for a "grand compromise"—a reduction in the most powerful Soviet offensive missiles in return for some restraints on U.S. pursuit of SDI.[38] As McFarlane claimed ten years after Reagan's Star Wars speech, "I believed that if we played our cards right with Congress and the allies, we wouldn't have to build this system— the Soviets would come our way on arms control."[39] President Reagan, by contrast, rejected any consideration of SDI as a bargaining chip.[40] He expected to be able to convince the Soviet Union, especially after Gorbachev took over in 1985, to agree to mutual reduction of offensive forces, and cooperative pursuit of defenses; he even offered to "share" U.S. BMD technology.[41]

Moreover, Reagan claimed to believe, along with the major promoters of strategic defenses such as the High Frontiers organization, that—if it bargained at all—the United States was not negotiating from a position of strength. They argued that the Soviet Union already possessed an effective ballistic missile defense system around Moscow, and had the "break-out" potential to expand it quickly. In their view, there was no question of the USSR *reacting* to U.S. BMD development by making concessions on arms control: the Russians had already taken the initiative in strategic defense.[42] As Reagan complained about Soviet initiatives during the year before Gorbachev came into office, "the Soviets were demanding that we halt work on the SDI just as we were beginning to get indications from our scientists that it might work"—presumably the fake test of June 1984 —"and at a time when the Soviets had missile defense weapons that in some cases were more sophisticated than ours."[43]

In September 1983, six months after Reagan's Star Wars speech, the CIA issued a classified report on "Possible Soviet Responses to the US Strategic Defense Initiative." The analysis thoroughly discredited Reagan's expectations and was not very hopeful about those of Nitze and McFarlane either. It predicted that the USSR would continue "to try to prevent development and

38. Talbott, *Master of the Game*, chap. 11.

39. Robert McFarlane, "Consider What Star Wars Accomplished," *New York Times*, 24 August 1993.

40. Garthoff, *Great Transition*, 226; Ronald Reagan, *An American Life* (New York, 1992), 548, 608, 665–666; Lou Cannon, *Ronald Reagan: The Role of a Lifetime* (New York, 1991), 326–327.

41. Don Oberdorfer, *The Turn: From the Cold War to a New Era* (New York, 1992), 145, 149, 204.

42. For a summary of the views, see William J. Broad, *Teller's War: The Top-Secret Story behind the Star Wars Deception* (New York, 1992), esp. 114–115.

43. Reagan, *American Life*, 602–603.

eventual deployment of US defensive systems." It suggested that the Soviets might "offer publicly" to make "concessions of interest to the United States in return for a negotiated ban or limitations on BMD development." It was more likely, however, that "Moscow would be very reluctant to offer the kind of offensive forces concessions the United States is looking for, probably preferring to take its chances on thwarting US BMD plans by other means." The report discussed a wide range of political-propaganda and military-technical responses that the USSR could make to SDI, but argued that the Soviets "will be reluctant to divert scarce assets to expensive technological efforts." Rather, they "will try to cope with deployment of US advanced technology BMD with the least possible change to their planned programs."[44]

The report stressed the difficult economic choices the Soviet leaders would have to make in order to pursue a "crash" program in response to SDI, and it expressed doubt that they would decide to do so. Finally, the report addressed the interaction between U.S. behavior and the domestic Soviet debate over the appropriate response to SDI: "Soviet directed energy programs already have important internal Soviet advocates, and support for them will be enhanced by aggressive US pursuit of directed energy weapons."[45] This turned out to be a remarkably accurate prediction.

By the time Mikhail Gorbachev came into office in March 1985 none of the Reagan administration's expectations for the SDI's impact on the USSR had come true. There was no massive, economy-busting increase in Soviet military spending, no concessions on arms control, and no interest in "sharing" SDI with the United States. Instead, Soviet opponents of an arms race in space, and their transnational allies, had their hands full keeping the Soviet Union's Star Wars "boosters" from trying to match the U.S. program. The task would preoccupy them for the rest of the decade.

44. Central Intelligence Agency, "Possible Soviet Responses to the US Strategic Defense Initiative," NIC M 83–10017, 12 September 1983, 1–3.
45. Ibid.

PART IV

The Gorbachev Era

[12]

Transnational Renaissance

The informal and lively dialogue of [foreign] politicians, scientists and cultural personalities is an imperative. The meetings with such people not only enrich one's theory and philosophy, but have also influenced the political moves and decisions that had to be taken in recent years.

—MIKHAIL GORBACHEV, 1987

Glasnost has uncovered a range of informal social organizations which are supported by Westerners. There is a tendency to diminish the Party and state influence on the spiritual life of the people. . . . This all has a negative, criminal effect on the people.

—VIKTOR CHEBRIKOV, 1987

On 25 September 1990 the *New York Times* published a photograph on its front page intended to symbolize the end of the Cold War. It shows General Petr Lushev, then Soviet commander of the Warsaw Pact, and Rainer Eppelmann, the last defense minister of the German Democratic Republic, exchanging copies of an agreement on the complete withdrawal of Soviet troops from East German territory in anticipation of the unification of East and West Germany. Before assuming his ministerial post, Eppelmann was well known as a Protestant minister, a pacifist, and one of the leading figures in the independent East German peace movement that emerged in the early 1980s. The movement was part of a transnational community of peace and human rights activists who sought to forge bonds across the Iron Curtain in order to bring it down—and along with it the Cold War and nuclear arms race that it represented.

British and West German church-affiliated peace activists first met with their East German counterparts in 1981. The next year, Pastor Eppelmann and Robert Havemann, a prominent dissident writer, circulated the "Berlin Appeal," calling for nuclear disarmament and withdrawal of U.S. and Soviet troops from Germany. Western peace groups continued to pursue contacts with Eppelmann and other East German activists, including Bärbel Bohley and Ulrike Poppe; these two members of a small women's peace group in East Berlin went on to found, respectively, New Forum and Democracy Now, the

This front-page *New York Times* photo of 25 September 1990 shows General Petr Lushev, then Soviet commander of the Warsaw Pact, and Rainer Eppelmann, the last defense minister of the German Democratic Republic, exchanging copies of an agreement on the complete withdrawal of Soviet troops from East German territory in anticipation of German unification. The *Times* did not see fit to inform its readers that Eppelmann, a Protestant minister, had been one of the leading figures in the independent East German peace movement. Photo by Michael Probst, Reuters/Archive Photos, used by permission.

organizations most responsible for mobilizing popular support for the peaceful overthrow of the East German communist regime in the autumn of 1989. Pastor Eppelmann, as defense and disarmament minister of the new noncommunist government, helped achieve one of the main goals that he had advocated as a peace activist eight years earlier: the end of the Soviet military occupation of east-central Europe, one of the preeminent causes and symbols of the Cold War.[1]

1. E. P. Thompson, "History Turns on a New Hinge," *The Nation*, 29 January 1990, 117–122; David Cortright, *Peace Works: The Citizen's Role in Ending the Cold War* (Boulder, Colo., 1993), 212–215; Patricia Chilton, "Mechanics of Change: Social Movements, Transnational Coalitions, and the Transformation Processes in Eastern Europe," in Thomas Risse-Kappen, ed., *Bringing Transnational Relations Back In: Non-State Actors, Domestic Structures and International Institutions* (Cambridge, U.K., 1996); Mary Kaldor, "Who Killed the Cold War?" *Bulletin of the Atomic Scientists* 51, 4 (July/August 1995): 57–60.

The irony of a peace activist serving as a defense minister and overseeing the withdrawal of the largest army in Europe was lost on most *New York Times* readers. The newspaper provided no details of Pastor Eppelmann's background. Yet Eppelmann was far from the only member of the transnational disarmament community to emerge in a position of responsibility in the post–Cold War world. Jiří Dienstbier had worked with the British historian and activist E. P. Thompson to forge links between Charter 77, the organization of Czechoslovak human rights activists, and the European Nuclear Disarmament movement; he became the first foreign minister of postcommunist Czechoslovakia. Andrei Kokoshin of Moscow's Institute of the USA and Canada was a key figure in East-West discussions of alternative security during the 1980s. In April 1992 he was appointed first deputy defense minister in Boris Yeltsin's government. On the Western side, many former transnational activists also assumed positions of responsibility within their respective governments, including in the United States when the Clinton administration came into office in January 1993.

The Gorbachev era was the heyday of East-West transnational activity on behalf of international peace and human rights. Thus, it might seem surprising that these people and their stories are so little known. Indeed, transnational relations have figured hardly at all in most explanations for the end of the Cold War, despite the fact that two of the most prominent transnational organizations received the Nobel Peace Prize for their efforts in that regard: the International Physicians for the Prevention of Nuclear War in 1985, and the Pugwash Movement in 1995. Mikhail Gorbachev, the focus of much of the transnational disarmament movement's activity, and in some respect its patron, was the 1990 Nobel laureate. At least among a small group in Oslo, transnational activists received their due, but in the broader public debate about how the Cold War ended they are barely visible.[2]

In one sense it is not so surprising that a "transnational explanation" for the end of the Cold War has not emerged as a major contender. Besides the theoretical reasons, discussed in Chapter 2, for not expecting transnational influence on security policy and on Soviet-type states, there are already several compelling alternative explanations for why the Cold War ended. The purpose of this chapter is to review those explanations, to point up their shortcomings, to indicate where they might be complemented or contradicted by an account that gives transnational relations a significant role.

2. This is despite the efforts of scholars such as David S. Meyer, Gloria Duffy, Jeffrey W. Knopf, Metta Spencer, Emanuel Adler, and others cited in previous chapters. It is worth pointing out that the activists themselves had developed a theoretical foundation for their work long before political scientists recognized what they had done. For early articulations of the strategy of forging transnational alliances of human rights and peace activists, see E. P. Thompson, "Détente and Dissent," and other essays in Ken Coates, ed., *Détente and Socialist Democracy: A Discussion with Roy Medvedev* (Nottingham, U.K., 1975); E. P. Thompson, *Beyond the Cold War* (New York, 1982); and George Konrad, *Antipolitics* (New York, 1984).

Thus this chapter differs from those that introduced transnational relations in the Khrushchev and Brezhnev eras in that it does not spend much time discussing the actors themselves. In fact, those transnational disarmament activists who came to prominence after 1985 are essentially the same people who appeared in the late Brezhnev period: there is no need to reintroduce them here.[3] Rather, we should consider what circumstances peculiar to the Gorbachev period offered them a greater role in influencing Soviet security policy than ever before.

COMPETING EXPLANATIONS FOR THE END OF THE COLD WAR

We have already encountered versions of the main explanations for why the Cold War ended. They are the same ones that observers used to account for previous periods or initiatives of moderation in Soviet security policy since the Khrushchev era: economic constraints, U.S. behavior, and changing Soviet military requirements. In each of the three Gorbachev-era chapters that follow, I address these explanations directly in order to account for developments in the areas of nuclear testing, conventional forces, and ballistic missile defense. Here it is worth taking a general look at the explanations and, in particular, how they interrelate.

Ronald Reagan: Architect of Perestroika?

The main characteristic that all of the conventional explanations share is an assumption that one can identify a common, consensual Soviet position regarding economic constraints, U.S. behavior, and military requirements. If there were great differences of opinion among Soviet leaders about the nature of the problems facing the country and vastly divergent solutions proposed to deal with them, then the standard explanations would prove inadequate. Take, for example, the notion, put forward by many supporters of U.S. President Ronald Reagan, that Reagan was the "architect of perestroika,"[4] that he was somehow responsible for the Soviet reforms undertaken by Gorbachev. The explanation seems to assume that any group of Soviet leaders less physically debilitated than Gorbachev's predecessors would have responded more or less in the same fashion as he did to U.S. policies of "peace through strength." This explanation locates the sources of Soviet change not in the domestic political and economic situation but in the external environ-

3. I do not address in any detail the transnational human rights activists. On that subject, see, in particular, Daniel C. Thomas, "Human Rights Norms and the Rise of Opposition to Communist Rule in Eastern Europe and the Soviet Union," paper prepared for the SSRC/MacArthur Foundation Workshop, "Catalysts of Change: Non-State Actors, International Social Norms and State Behavior in New Issue-Areas," Cornell University, 27–29 September 1996.
4. Robert MacFarlane, "Reagan: Architect of Perestroika," *Daily Telegraph* (London), 11 August 1988, cited in Michael Cox, "Whatever Happened to the 'Second' Cold War? Soviet-American Relations: 1980–1988," *Review of International Studies* 16 (1990): 164.

ment—or at least it argues that U.S. behavior played a crucial role in exacerbating internal Soviet problems, which, in turn led to major changes in Soviet domestic and foreign policy. Sometimes the Reagan position even implies that Gorbachev was selected as the new Soviet leader in March 1985 specifically in order to address the challenge posed by the assertive U.S. policy, that in electing Gorbachev as general secretary his colleagues were deliberately choosing a course that would lead to an improvement in relations with the United States via Soviet concessions.

The end of the Soviet Union has produced enough new evidence to refute this latter interpretation conclusively. The new information includes diaries of Politburo members and their aides, interviews, and the transcript of the Politburo meeting at which Gorbachev was elected top Soviet leader. Even before such information became available, astute students of traditional Kremlinological sources had argued that Gorbachev was not elected in order to carry out revolutionary changes in Soviet foreign policy, but rather to return Soviet policy to the status quo ante of the mid-1970s, before the invasion of Afghanistan and the confrontational policies of the Reagan administration had soured relations. Bruce Parrott, for example, made the most persuasive case that Gorbachev was selected to return Soviet policy to its prior emphasis on a dual-track approach: on the one hand, détente and arms control, on the other, a strong defense.[5]

All of the new evidence supports the view that in matters of foreign policy, Gorbachev sought to portray himself as the candidate who represented continuity rather than dramatic change. It seems clear, for example, that among his main patrons as he made his way up into the ranks of the top Communist Party leadership were Iurii Andropov, the former KGB chief who became general secretary on Leonid Brezhnev's death in November 1982, and Dmitrii Ustinov, the defense minister. The "nominating speech" proposing to elect Gorbachev general secretary at the Politburo meeting of 11 March 1985 was given by Andrei Gromyko, the foreign minister. He promised that Gorbachev would treat defense, in the stock Soviet cliché, as "the holy of holies."[6] Along with Brezhnev, these three figures—Andropov, Ustinov, and Gromyko—dominated Soviet foreign policy in the decade preceding Gorbachev's rise to power. It is hardly likely that they would knowingly have supported someone who deliberately intended to repudiate their legacy in order to end the Cold War.[7] During the first Politburo meeting following his selection as general secretary, Gorbachev declared that "there is no need to change our foreign policy; it has gained authority and needs only to be activated." A month

5. Bruce Parrott, "Soviet National Security under Gorbachev," *Problems of Communism* 37, 6 (1988): 1–36.

6. A. S. Cherniaev, *Shest' let s Gorbachevym: po dnevnikovym zapisiam* (Moscow: 1993), 30.

7. On Ustinov's role in supporting Gorbachev, see Mikhail Gorbachev, *Zhizn' i reformy* (Moscow, 1995), 1:248, 252, 259, 266; Vorotnikov, *A bylo tak* (Moscow, 1995); Vadim Medvedev, *V Komande Gorbacheva: Vzgliad iznutri* (Moscow, 1994), 17; Yegor Ligachev, *Inside Gorbachev's Kremlin* (New York, 1993); On Andropov: Gorbachev, *Zhizn' i reformy*, 1:22, 148, 248, 266; Nikolai Ryzhkov, *Perestroika: Istoriia predatel'stv* (Moscow, 1992), 8, 33, 85, 361–363, 373–374.

later, at a meeting of the Central Committee plenum, he again "affirmed the basic direction of foreign-policy activity."[8] Gorbachev himself acknowledges in his memoirs that his early foreign policy stayed essentially within the bounds of the existing framework.[9]

The Burden of Military Spending

A related explanation for Gorbachev's policies suggests that they were a reaction not only to the overall assertive character of U.S. policy but specifically to the high levels of military spending occasioned by the arms race with the United States. In this view, one of Gorbachev's first priorities was to reduce the military burden on the Soviet economy by concessions in arms negotiations and by retrenching on Soviet global commitments—particularly by ending the Soviet war in Afghanistan. Those who credit the Reagan administration with initiating the Gorbachev revolution point to the major U.S. arms buildup that preceded Gorbachev's coming to power and U.S. aid for anti-Soviet guerrilla movements in the Third World.

Soviet policy toward the Third World is beyond the scope of this book. It does seem apparent, however, that the Soviet leaders were not particularly preoccupied with the cost of their commitments there. The war in Afghanistan is another story: Gorbachev and his reformist advisers came into power expecting to end it, for political as much as economic reasons; but even if they faced little opposition to the idea among the conservatives and the military, it still took nearly four years to get the troops out.[10]

As for the arms race, the evidence on relative U.S. and Soviet military spending produces a picture more complicated than the one described by proponents of "peace through strength." During the period 1979–84, the height of the Reagan buildup (which actually began under his predecessor, Jimmy Carter), the United States increased its military spending in real terms by 36 percent, according to estimates of the U.S. Central Intelligence Agency. By comparison, the Soviet Union increased its military spending by only 11 percent during the same period—hardly a dramatic reaction.[11] By the time Gorbachev came into office, the Reagan buildup was essentially over. Even so, Soviet military spending was not reduced until 1988.

We must also consider when the Soviet leadership came to agree that the economy was in sufficiently dire straits to necessitate reducing military

8. Vorotnikov, *A bylo tak*, 60, 64.

9. Gorbachev, *Zhizn' i reformy*, 1:271.

10. Cherniaev, *Shest' let*, 37–39, 57–59; Sarah Mendelson, *Changing Course: Ideas, Politics, and the Soviet Withdrawal from Afghanistan* (Princeton, N.J., 1998).

11. James Noren and Laurie Kurtzweg, "The Soviet Economy Unravels: 1985–1991," in Joint Economic Committee, U.S. Congress, *The Former Soviet Union in Transition*, (Washington, D.C., 1993), 1:19 n. 17. For a thorough analysis of the relationship between Soviet and U.S. military spending, see Fred Chernoff, "Ending the Cold War: The Soviet Retreat and the U.S. Military Buildup," *International Affairs* 67, 1 (1991): 111–126.

spending. The "peace through strength" argument assumes that there was some consensus on this point. In fact, as Gorbachev points out in his memoirs, no one in the leadership believed that there was a systemic crisis in the Soviet economy in the mid-1980s.[12] Even though he himself was more sensitive to the impact of military spending—largely because his values oriented him to favor consumer welfare over an aggressive military stance—he admits an unwillingness at first to challenge the existing priorities.[13] His original approach, consistent with that of his predecessors, was that Soviet economic problems would be solved by a combination of discipline and new technology. The expectation that his economic reforms would represent essentially a continuation of the "Andropov line" is undoubtedly what attracted such leading officials of the "younger" generation as Egor' Ligachev and Nikolai Ryzhkov—also Andropov protégés—to support Gorbachev.[14]

Much as Gorbachev's challenge to the existing political and economic structure of the USSR emerged gradually, so did his assault on the "holy of holies."[15] Gorbachev raised the issue of military spending from time to time in the Politburo during discussions of arms control negotiations in 1986 and 1987.[16] But it was only in 1988 that he made a serious effort to emphasize the effect of the arms race on the Soviet economy in discussions with the top leadership, in order to make the case for cutting military spending.[17]

Among reformist leaders Eduard Shevardnadze, the foreign minister, was the most outspoken critic of the militarized Soviet economy. In August 1988, he made the case for a conciliatory Soviet foreign policy that would undermine the arms race and relieve the burden of military spending: "We have agreed that war cannot be a rational means of politics. But couldn't the arms race be such a means? However paradoxical it seems—it can. Yes, the arms race can exhaust and bleed the opponent dry, with the goal of undermining its very economic and social base."[18]

By the time Gorbachev and Shevardnadze launched their attack on Soviet military spending, the government's own contradictory and ill-conceived attempts at economic reform had done far more damage to the Soviet economy than whatever marginal increase in military spending Reagan's policies had

12. Gorbachev, *Zhizn' i reformy*, 1:208, 247.
13. Gorbachev, *Zhizn' i reformy*, 1:271.
14. Ligachev, *Inside Gorbachev's Kremlin*; Ryzhkov, *Perestroika*. In an interview conducted by Michael McFaul and Sergei Markov on 14 October 1992, Ryzhkov emphasized the origins of reform in the study groups of younger scholars and officials sponsored by Andropov. It is recorded as tape #36, box 2, Hoover Institution Library, Stanford, California.
15. Gorbachev used the expression himself in a Politburo meeting in November 1985 when he argued for maintaining a strong defense. See Vorotnikov, *A bylo tak*, 79.
16. Cherniaev, *Shest' let*, 146.
17. Cherniaev, *Shest' let*, 253–254; Vorotnikov, *A bylo tak*, 215. See especially the minutes of the Politburo meeting of 27 December 1988, reprinted in *Istochnik*, 1993, nos. 5–6:130–147, esp. 134, 144–145.
18. "Doklad E. A. Shevardnadze," *Vestnik Ministerstva Inostrannykh Del SSSR*, 15 August 1988, 36.

occasioned. It was because of the dire state of the economy in late 1988, not in early 1985 (when Gorbachev was elected), that the Soviet leaders agreed to cuts in military spending and unilateral initiatives of restraint.[19]

By this time, far from pursuing peace through strength, Reagan had declared an end to the Cold War, repudiating his previous characterization of the Soviet Union as an "evil empire" as belonging to "another time, another era."[20] It was Reagan's new conciliatory stance that allowed Gorbachev to reduce Soviet military spending, not his earlier hard line. Writing about Gorbachev in his memoirs, Ronald Reagan recognized this point himself: "I might have helped him see that the Soviet Union had less to fear from the West than he thought, and that the Soviet empire in Eastern Europe wasn't needed for the security of the Soviet Union."[21] Anatolii Dobrynin, the former Soviet ambassador to Washington, made an even stronger case about Reagan's change of heart: "if the president had not abandoned his hostile stance toward the Soviet Union for a more constructive one during his second term, Gorbachev would not have been able to launch his reforms and his 'new thinking.'"[22]

Despite Reagan's newfound sensitivity to Soviet security interests, the concern that George Bush, Reagan's successor, would slow down the process of U.S.-Soviet reconciliation gave Gorbachev a further argument for increasing the pace of unilateral Soviet initiatives: "We need the conditions that we've created with our initiatives to strengthen and move this process forward," he told his colleagues.[23]

Even so, not all of them were convinced. Hard-liners in the KGB and the military-industrial sector denied to the end that any concessions were necessary in negotiations with the West or that military spending posed an excessive burden on the Soviet economy. Ultimately some of them expressed their dissatisfaction with Gorbachev's policies—domestic and foreign—by attempting to overthrow him in a coup in August 1991. Take, for example, Vladimir Kriuchkov, the head of the KGB from 1988 and a leading coup plotter. He never reconciled himself to any of the foreign policy initiatives of the Gorbachev period and, in memoirs published in 1996, was extremely critical of Shevardnadze.[24]

Even at the time, a number of Soviet leaders criticized Shevardnadze (and, indirectly, Gorbachev) for creating "another Munich" in the negotiations that led to the reunification of Germany and the withdrawal of Soviet troops

19. Vorotnikov, *A bylo tak*, 223. Gorbachev's reforms were also the victim of a sharp downturn in the world price of oil, a major Soviet export and source of foreign-currency revenue.
20. Don Oberdorfer, *The Turn: From the Cold War to a New Era* (New York, 1992), 299.
21. Ronald Reagan, *An American Life* (New York, 1992), 708.
22. Anatoly Dobrynin, *In Confidence: Moscow's Ambassador to Six Cold War Presidents* (New York, 1995), 611.
23. Minutes of the Politburo meeting of 27 December 1988, 133.
24. Vladimir Kriuchkov, *Lichnoe delo* (Moscow, 1996), 1:312–319.

from Eastern Europe.[25] Such harsh attacks by the "so-called patriots and the military-industrial complex," and Gorbachev's unwillingness to do anything about it, led one prescient journalist to predict in November 1990 that Shevardnadze "could even be on the way out."[26] Shevardnadze announced his surprise resignation from the Foreign Ministry just a month later, and warned, with similar prescience, of a coming dictatorship.

In late 1990 and early 1991 Oleg Baklanov, head of the Central Committee commission on military policy, emerged as a serious critic of the entire course of Soviet security policy. He and his fellow commission members expressed "alarm" and "anxiety" about the state of Soviet defenses, criticized disarmament agreements for destroying the parity between U.S. and Soviet forces, and urged the Foreign Ministry's arms control negotiators to show more "responsibility" for "maintaining the defense capability of the country."[27]

The views of Baklanov, the top official in charge of military-industrial matters in the late Gorbachev period, are particularly relevant to the issue of military spending. As late as November 1990, at an international forum in Moscow on conversion of military production to civilian uses, he expressed his contempt for critics of excessive arms production. Present at the conference were a number of leading Soviet economists, such as Stanislav Shatalin, who had been hard at work trying to discover and publicize the true extent and consequences of the Soviet military burden. In his comments to the conference, V. S. Avduevskii, chair of the Supreme Soviet committee on economic conversion, and a scientist with extensive background in military research, acknowledged that his committee was unable to obtain reliable figures on Soviet military spending, but he estimated that the machine-building sector alone was 70 percent devoted to military production. Other economists had estimated that by some definitions, more than half of the Soviet economy was connected to military industry. In the face of such arguments, and as his fellow Soviet participants groaned and rolled their eyes, Baklanov brazenly stated that the military absorbed merely 7–8 percent of state resources— a figure lower even than official Soviet statistics. To add insult to injury, Baklanov argued that rather than enjoy a "peace dividend," the Soviet government would need to spend billions of rubles more to retrain and relocate

25. The reference to Munich was made by Egor' Ligachev in *Pravda*, 7 February 1990. See the discussion in John Van Oudenaren, *The Role of Shevardnadze and the Ministry of Foreign Affairs in the Making of Soviet Defense and Arms Control Policy*, RAND Report R-3898-USDP (Santa Monica, Calif., 1990).

26. Maxim Sokolov, "An Escape for the Desert Rat?" *Commersant* (Moscow), English edition, 5 November 1990, 11.

27. O. Baklanov, "Ob itogakh obsuzhdeniia v komissii TsK KPSS po voennoi politiki partii khoda razrabotki kontseptsii voennoi reformy i perspektiv razvitiia Vooruzhennykh Sil SSSR," 8 January 1991, reporting on a meeting of 12 December 1990. See also "Ob itogakh obsuzhdeniia v komissii TsK KPSS po voennoi politiki khoda peregovorov po sokrashcheniiu vooruzhenii," 6 February 1991. F. 89, index 21, doc. 63, Storage Center for Contemporary Documentation [Tsentr khraneniia sovremennoi dokumentatsii].

military workers if it were to carry out a program of conversion.[28] In retrospect—given how much he had to lose from the Gorbachev reforms—it is not surprising that "big Oleg," as he was known in military-industrial circles, became a major figure behind the August 1991 coup.

Apparently by 1988 enough of his fellow political leaders accepted Gorbachev's arguments about the effect of arms spending on the economy to allow him to cut the military budget. Either that or they were overwhelmed by a combination of Gorbachev's tactical skills and the legacy of deference to the top leader. In any case, a few holdouts, such as Kriuchkov and Baklanov, actively opposed the reformist line until the end. They did their best to wreck implementation of such reforms as arms control and conversion of the military sector, intended to reduce the burden of Soviet military spending. Their example should make us cautious about assuming a straightforward relationship between high military spending and Gorbachev's foreign-policy reforms.

Relative Decline as an Impetus to Reform

As an alternative to explanations that emphasize the absolute burden of military spending, some theorists of international relations have proposed an explanation for Gorbachev's reforms that focuses on comparative economic performance.[29] They emphasize the realist notion of "defensive positionality"—that states in the international system seek to maintain their relative positions of power vis-à-vis other states. In this view, the long-term decline of Soviet power relative to its international rivals is what drove the reforms.

The explanation has some problems of timing: Why did the USSR initiate reforms in the mid-1980s rather than a decade or more earlier? It fails to acknowledge that alternative courses of action were open—"muddling through" or pursuing limited Andropov-style reforms that the majority of the leadership favored. One also wonders why this explanation, apparently grounded in traditional realist theory, represents power as economic growth and technological prowess while downplaying standard realist indicators of nuclear and conventional military force. By these latter criteria the Soviet Union remained strong until the end. It undoubtedly makes sense to take into account changing perceptions of power—why Soviet leaders might, for example, come to consider a computer-literate population more important to

28. From my notes from the conference held in Moscow, 12–15 November 1990. For background on "big Oleg," see Roald Sagdeev, *The Making of a Soviet Scientist* (New York, 1994).

29. For example, Kenneth Oye's chapter in Richard Ned Lebow and Thomas Risse-Kappen, eds., *International Relations Theory and the End of the Cold War* (New York: Columbia University Press, 1995); and William C. Wohlforth, "Realism and the End of the Cold War," *International Security* 19, 3 (Winter 1994/95). For a critique of the realist position, see Richard Ned Lebow, "The Long Peace, the End of the Cold War, and the Failure of Realism," in "Symposium: The End of the Cold War and Theories of International Relations," *International Organization* 48, 2 (Spring 1994): 249–277.

security than a force of nuclear missiles. But such considerations would take us far from traditional realism into the realm of ideas and domestic political debates—as some students of the Gorbachev reforms have done rather successfully.[30] If the Soviet leaders during the Gorbachev years were open to new interpretations of power and security—as some of them clearly were—then one would not be surprised to find transnational actors trying to influence those interpretations too.[31]

In fact, however, most Soviet political and military leaders do not seem to have been preoccupied or dissatisfied with the USSR's international standing. The political élite, by definition, lived better than everyone else, in rather insular conditions, and had little sense of the relatively low level of material welfare in Soviet society at large compared to the industrialized West. They seem to have had little interest and limited ability to make the kind of comparisons that international-relations theory assumes they made. Their occasional attempts to do so illustrate the general problem. In criticizing Soviet proponents of market reforms, for example, Ligachev complained that "they often refer to capitalist countries" as the examples to emulate. In his view, however, "only a small number of the Western countries are thriving" and mainly because "capitalists pump superprofits out of poorly developed countries by using cheap work forces and raw materials."[32]

At a Politburo meeting in May 1985, two months after Gorbachev became general secretary, N. A. Tikhonov, the head of the Soviet Council of Ministers, and a member of the Brezhnev generation, presented a report on "The Basic Direction of Socio-Economic Development for 1986–1990 and to the Year 2000." Tikhonov argued that the current five-year plan would be fulfilled and the goal for the year 2000 would be to reach "the level of industrial production of the USA." Younger members of the Politburo found the exercise a bit surrealistic. Vitalii Vorotnikov, for example, commented sarcastically in his diary: "Again the idea to catch up and overtake?!"—a reference to the discredited economic forecasts and "hare-brained schemes" of Nikita Khrushchev. At the meeting, Vorotnikov pointed out, accurately, that "it is difficult to compare the level of development attained by our society with other countries." More significantly, he acknowledged that "we don't have the comparable figures even for the Politburo."[33] It is generally understood now that

---

30. On the impact of norms and ideas in the Soviet foreign and military reforms, see especially Jeffrey T. Checkel, *Ideas and International Political Change: Soviet/Russian Behavior and the End of the Cold War* (New Haven, Conn., 1997); and Robert G. Herman, "Identity, Norms, and National Security: The Soviet Foreign Policy Revolution and the End of the Cold War," in Peter J. Katzenstein, ed., *The Culture of National Security: Norms and Identity in World Politics* (New York, 1996), 271–316; Janice Gross Stein, "Political Learning by Doing: Gorbachev as Uncommitted Thinker and Motivated Learner," *International Organization* 48, 2 (Spring 1994): 155–183.

31. Thomas Risse-Kappen, "Ideas Do Not Float Freely: Transnational Coalitions, Domestic Structures, and the End of the Cold War," *International Organization* 48, 2 (Spring 1994): 185–214.

32. Ligachev, *Inside Gorbachev's Kremlin*, 320–321.

33. Vorotnikov, *A bylo tak*, 66–67.

even the top Soviet political leaders were unable to get any realistic sense of the relative burden of Soviet military spending—so tightly held was the information and so mysteriously budgeted were the funds—even though this is presumably one of the indicators most relevant to theories of "defensive positionality."[34]

Soviet military officials were certainly attentive to relative levels of Western and Soviet military power, including the implications of advanced technology, but they seem by and large to have remained satisfied with Soviet accomplishments. At least they were not willing to give up the high priority accorded to military research and production in the Soviet budget in the near term to gamble that a long-term effort to reform the civilian economy would eventually put the Soviet military in a stronger position.[35]

"Why Do We Live Worse Than Other Developed Countries?"

Still, we should not completely abandon explanations that focus on the relative levels of economic performance. Even though most Soviet leaders were not particularly interested in the issue, and most military officials focused mainly on their parochial concerns, Gorbachev himself seems personally to have cared a great deal about how his country compared to the rest of the world. In contrast to most other Soviet leaders, Gorbachev, even in his early career, traveled abroad quite a lot—not only on official trips but for tourism as well, and often accompanied by his wife, Raisa Maksimovna. They traveled not only within the Soviet bloc but to Western Europe too. Because some of these trips were private ones, they were not reported in the Soviet press and, therefore, not known to Western intelligence analysts, who otherwise kept good track of the foreign travels of Soviet officials. Only with the publication of Gorbachev's memoirs in 1995 did we learn, for example, that he and Raisa had visited Italy in 1971 and took a three-week driving tour of France in 1977, covering some five thousand kilometers.[36]

On official business during the 1970s Gorbachev traveled to Belgium, West Germany, Italy, and France, in addition to the countries of the Soviet bloc. While in Belgium with a Communist Party delegation in 1972, he and some colleagues took a day trip to visit the Netherlands. Gorbachev marveled at the way people took care of their homes and gardens: "I thought, oh, we are so far from that, if we could attain it at all." Crossing the border from Bel-

---

34. Gorbachev, *Zhizn' i reformy*, 1:319, 334.

35. S. F. Akhromeev and G. M. Kornienko, *Glazami marshala i diplomata* (Moscow, 1992), 12–13; Judyth L. Twigg, "'To Fly and Fight': Norms, Institutions, and Fighter Aircraft Procurement in the United States, Russia, and Japan" (Ph.D. diss., Massachusetts Institute of Technology, 1994), chap. 6; Matthew Evangelista, "Economic Reform and Military Technology in Soviet Security Policy," *Harriman Institute Forum* 2, 1 (January 1989).

36. Gorbachev, *Zhizn' i reformy*, 1:155–169. For a list of Gorbachev's travels known in the West, see Alexander G. Rahr, *A Biographic Directory of 100 Leading Soviet Officials*, 3d ed. (Munich, 1986), 74.

gium to Holland, the Soviet officials were surprised that no one checked their passports: "in general no one was visible," except at the foreign-currency exchange office. "It isn't hard to guess our reaction," Gorbachev recalled: "Damned decadent capitalism. They don't even have borders."[37]

Gorbachev was curious about how people lived outside the Soviet Union, and what he discovered made a deep impression. He was constantly comparing his country to others. The Soviet system of public transportation seemed better, he thought, and education and medical care were distributed more fairly. "But as far as the functioning of civil society and the political system was concerned, our a priori trust in the superiority of socialist over bourgeois democracy was somewhat shaken." Gorbachev reported that the most important conclusion he drew from his travels, and the one that stayed with him longest, was that people outside the USSR lived in better, more secure material conditions. "Why," he wondered, "do we live worse than other developed countries?"[38]

The early chapters of Gorbachev's memoirs also depict the modest circumstances of his early life, even after he became a Party official in Stavropol'. Unlike many of his contemporaries, he never forgot the everyday difficulties of making ends meet—even things like how to arrange child care for their baby daughter when both he and Raisa were working.[39]

The impetus to Gorbachev's reforms, once he had the opportunity to implement them, does seem to have stemmed from his curiosity about other countries, combined with his determination that people in the Soviet Union—a country enormously rich in natural resources and with a highly educated population—should live as well as people in the West. One of his first projects, when he became Communist Party secretary for agriculture in 1978, was to commission a study of grain production in the USSR and Western Europe. This sort of interest in comparative economic indicators differs from what realist theories anticipate because it is focused less on matters of military security than on people's material well-being.[40]

It is likely that Gorbachev's foreign contacts influenced his values concerning the relative importance of military spending versus consumer welfare as well as the role that the Soviet Union should play in international affairs. In law school at Moscow State University in the early 1950s Gorbachev's roommate was a Czech student named Zdeněk Mlynář. Although young communists, both students were rather liberally inclined. Mlynar went on to become one of the leaders of the ill-fated Prague Spring reform movement in 1967–68.[41] Through his friend, Gorbachev managed to get an impression of

---

37. Gorbachev, *Zhizn' i reformy*, 1:165.
38. Ibid.
39. Ibid., 88–89.
40. Ibid., 183–184.
41. For his firsthand account of the events, see Zdeněk Mlynář, *Night Frost in Prague: The End of Humane Socialism* (London, 1980).

"socialism with a human face" that differed considerably from the official Soviet propaganda that justified military intervention in August 1968. Sent on a delegation to Prague and Bratislava in November 1969, Gorbachev again witnessed the contrast between the official Soviet interpretation and the events on the ground. He was clearly troubled by his conversations with Czech and Slovak reform communists who were outspokenly hostile to the Soviet occupation authorities and rejected every justification for the crackdown.[42]

His upbringing, his natural curiosity about the outside world, and his foreign contacts, both at home and abroad, go a long way toward explaining why Gorbachev personally favored a demilitarization of Soviet domestic and foreign policy. He seems to have shared many of these values with the person he appointed foreign minister, Eduard Shevardnadze.[43] These traits and experiences of Gorbachev and Shevardnadze make understandable their offer of "freedom of choice" to the countries allied with the Soviet Union in Eastern Europe and also help account for their openness to international and transnational sources of ideas for the reforms that they wanted to carry out.

TRANSNATIONAL OPPORTUNITIES

There is no doubt that Gorbachev himself came into office with the intention of reducing the military burden on the Soviet economy. But the idea of demilitarizing the economy and seeking a reconciliation with the West was far from a consensus position in the Soviet leadership. The story of Gorbachev's foreign-policy reforms is essentially the story of his efforts to persuade, cajole, or ignore opponents of the initiatives he launched to end the Cold War. For even if his fellow leaders came to agree with Gorbachev's goal of stemming the relative decline of the Soviet Union, they did not always accept his proposals or understand how he came up with them. Many of them could, for example, see the economic sense of cutting military spending and reducing the armed forces. But why was it necessary to reorient the army toward "nonoffensive defense" and offer political freedom to countries located in a crucial buffer zone? Perhaps they came to be persuaded that the U.S. Strategic Defense Initiative was not such a threat after all. By why agree to cut in half the arsenal of powerful SS-18 missiles that offered the best hedge against the prospect that "Star Wars" might amount to something? The most economical means of counteracting SDI was to do nothing: the existing force of multiwarhead missiles was the best, most cost-effective countermeasure available to deal with a potential U.S. defense. Why maintain a unilateral moratorium on Soviet nuclear testing, while the United States used its test

42. Gorbachev, *Zhizn' i reformy*, 1:157–159.
43. Eduard Shevardnadze, *Moi vybor: v zashchitu demokratii i svobody* (Moscow, 1991).

program to develop precisely the kinds of weapons that could make SDI come to fruition? It is not clear why these particular initiatives—at the heart of Gorbachev's security policy—would be considered necessary or even desirable if the goal were simply to reverse the Soviet decline.

Existing explanations for the end of the Cold War are unable to answer these questions, because they neglect the role of transnational relations in influencing Gorbachev's reforms. Why these particular initiatives, and where they came from, is the story I tell in the next three chapters of this book.

[13]

"Silence Reigned on Our Nuclear Test Ranges":
Gorbachev and the Moratorium

There was a fundamental asymmetry between East and West during that era that no amount of moral relativistic argument could ever balance. To wit, would-be saviors had at least some chance of influencing policy in the West, where there was open and free debate. They had absolutely no chance of doing that in the Soviet Union, as the house arrest of physicist Andrei Sakharov made clear. So the criticism of nuclear testing and the like usually was directed at the policy makers of the West, not those of the East.

—GEORGE MELLOAN, 1995

There were both proponents and opponents of the moratorium in the Soviet Union and the voices of the latter became louder with each American test.

—VITALII GOLDANSKII, 1988

One of the first foreign-policy initiatives that Mikhail Gorbachev undertook when he became General Secretary in 1985 was to announce a unilateral moratorium on Soviet nuclear testing to take effect on 6 August 1985, the fortieth anniversary of the U.S. atomic bombing of Hiroshima. The moratorium was intended to continue only until the end of the year—or indefinitely if the United States ceased its nuclear testing as well. Despite U.S. refusal to join the Soviet test moratorium, however, the USSR extended its unilateral ban several times. Moreover, for the first time ever it allowed on-site monitoring of the ban by a team of Soviet and Western scientists. This dramatic departure from previous policy marked an important precedent and opened possibilities for further measures of intrusive, on-site verification of future arms accords. The role of transnational actors was crucial in bringing about these initiatives. Yet a key goal of the transnational disarmament movement—a comprehensive multilateral ban on nuclear tests—remained unachieved during the Gorbachev years.

Explaining the Unilateral Moratorium

Military Requirements

When the Soviet unilateral moratorium was announced at the end of July 1985, U.S. government officials argued that it was merely a propaganda ploy, that the USSR had conducted a "significant acceleration" of tests in recent weeks and could refrain from testing without harming its nuclear weapons modernization: "Clearly, this was designed to put the Soviet Union in a position not to need to test over the next five months, and to break out on an accelerated schedule . . . without real costs to Soviet programs." A "senior administration official" charged that such Soviet gestures as the unilateral moratorium "are self-serving and designed to lock in areas of Soviet advantage."[1] Secretary of State George Shultz maintained that it was not in the U.S. "interest to stop our testing program under such circumstances," and he expressed doubts about Soviet sincerity: "History has shown when they feel the need to test, they'll break out of it with a bang."[2] Even before the USSR had formally announced its unilateral ban, the U.S. State department issued a statement expressing concerns about the ability to monitor a halt in nuclear testing. On 17 April 1985, the department claimed that the U.S. government was "deeply concerned about the desirability of an uninspected testing moratorium and the verifiability of restraints on nuclear tests."[3]

Here then were the main elements of a military-requirements explanation—that the Soviet test ban was an attempt to lock in military advantages that had been achieved by accelerating tests in the period before the moratorium and that the USSR could gain further advantages by continuing to test secretly. The implication was that the Soviet military supported the moratorium in the hope that the United States would follow suit and that a U.S. test moratorium would hinder the development of new U.S. weapons. It would not be surprising if the Soviet military were concerned about the testing of such weapons. It was generally becoming clear, for example, despite the Reagan administration's emphasis on the Strategic Defense Initiative's "antinuclear" character, that developing a new generation of nuclear explosives was essential for key SDI components—particularly nuclear-powered lasers.[4]

In fact, however, the Soviet military's position ranged from skepticism to outright opposition to the unilateral moratorium. Marshal Sergei Akhromeev, then chief of the Soviet General Staff, reports in his memoirs his doubts about Gorbachev's rationale for the unilateral ban: "It was assumed that a full

---

1. David Hoffman in the *Washington Post*, 30 July 1985, quoted in *Arms Control Reporter* (Brookline, Mass., 1985), 608.B.66.
2. Ibid.
3. Don Oberdorfer in the *Washington Post*, 18 April 1985, quoted in *Arms Control Reporter*, 608.B.62.
4. William J. Broad, *Teller's War: The Top-Secret Story behind the Star Wars Deception* (New York, 1992).

cessation of nuclear weapons testing could serve as a powerful impulse to halting the race in nuclear—and indirectly—space weapons. However, this noble intention didn't have a chance of success in view of the simple, firm, negative position of the USA regarding the full cessation of nuclear explosions." As it turned out, argued Akhromeev, the United States was committed to continue nuclear testing "to improve and create new types of nuclear weaponry and for developing some components of a space-based ABM system."[5] Therefore the Soviet moratorium would retard only the Soviet testing program, not the U.S. one.

Georgii Kornienko, a senior Foreign Ministry official and close colleague of Akhromeev, later reported that Soviet military officials had warned the political leaders that a unilateral moratorium would give the United States an advantage in SDI-related research, but their warning had come too late to influence the decision.[6] Despite the warnings, in January 1986 Gorbachev announced an extension of the moratorium for another three months. Later he described the extension as "a major step which involved a certain risk for us because the development of space technology and new types of nuclear weapons, such as nuclear-pumped lasers, continued."[7] On 28 February 1986, Kornienko held a press conference to announce that the Soviet moratorium would be lifted at the end of March; he expressed doubts about "whether we can indefinitely postpone our program of testing and development," given the Reagan administration's claim that "as long as nuclear weapons exist, the United States will continue testing."[8]

Opposition to the test ban was mounting not only within the military but among the Foreign Ministry's old guard as well. Officials of the Soviet nuclear weapons complex also denounced the moratorium—first behind the scenes but later publicly—as "actual unilateral nuclear disarmament."[9] The transnational disarmament coalition sought to counter the main objections to the moratorium—particularly the military's concerns that the United States was testing nuclear explosives for lasers. Eduard Shevardnadze's reformist advisers and like-minded scientists assembled data from various Western sources to cast doubt on the military effectiveness or feasibility of such weapons.[10] Their arguments worked. In mid-March Gorbachev again announced that the moratorium would continue.[11]

5. S. F. Akhromeev and G. M. Kornienko, *Glazami marshala i diplomata* (Moscow, 1992), 56.

6. Ibid., 95–96.

7. Mikhail Gorbachev, *Perestroika i novoe myshlenie dlia nashei strany i dlia vsego mira* (Moscow, 1987), 240–241.

8. *Arms Control Reporter*, 608.B.77, 80–81.

9. One of the most outspoken was Viktor Mikhailov, who rose to the post of minister of nuclear energy under Boris Yeltsin. The quote comes from his article, "Pochemu dolzhny molchhat' iadernye poligony strany?" *Pravda*, 24 October 1990, reprinted with much other evidence of his views, in V. N. Mikhailov, *Ia—"Iastreb"* (Moscow, 1993).

10. Aleksei Arbatov, interview by author, Cambridge, Mass., 18 August 1993.

11. *Arms Control Reporter*, 608.B.82.

Just after Gorbachev's announcement the Reagan administration revealed that satellite photographs had indicated Soviet preparations to resume testing. "They have been involved in making preparations for follow-on testing from the very beginning" of the moratorium, one official argued. "It says to me that they regard testing as a continuing requirement. They know we won't stop testing. They want testing to go on and to pin the blame on us." [12] In other words, the Soviet moratorium was purely a propaganda gesture.

In April 1986 the Soviet government announced that it was free from its unilateral commitment to refrain from testing, but a month later Gorbachev extended the moratorium again, until 6 August 1986—making it a full year's duration.[13] At that point, Marshal Akhromeev publicly complained that the Soviet initiative had harmed the country's security—on "the military side, this is a serious matter"—but "as yet it is tolerable to accept a certain degree of detriment." [14] On 18 August, Gorbachev announced a further extension until 1 January 1987, observing that the United States had conducted eighteen nuclear tests, three of them unannounced but detected by the Soviet side, since the Soviet moratorium began and expressing hope that the United States would finally join the ban. The White House responded with the clearest rejection of the initiative yet: "A nuclear test ban is not in the security interests of the United States, our friends, or our allies." [15] That latter claim was soon challenged by Hans-Dietrich Genscher, the West German foreign minister, who said that his government "would be happy if an agreement on a comprehensive test ban could be reached" at the forthcoming summit meeting in Iceland; he described the Soviet extension as "a useful step" toward that goal.[16]

Throughout the course of the moratorium the Soviet government sought to convince the United States to join it. Gorbachev made one last push at the summit meeting in Reykjavik in October 1986. The United States remained intransigent. A month later, Marshal Akhromeev again spoke out, complaining that "it is not easy for us to observe our moratorium for 18 months, but we understand the need for it as a political measure and we are unanimous on this score"—a claim belied by his subsequent memoir account.[17] Three

12. Michael Gordon in the *New York Times*, 18 March 1986, quoted in *Arms Control Reporter*, 608.B.84.

13. *Arms Control Reporter*, 608.B.92, 96. The April 1986 announcement is reprinted as "From the Statement by the Soviet Government, 12 April 1986," Document No. 92, in Valentin Falin, ed., *The Last Nuclear Explosion: A Historical Survey* (Moscow, 1986), 220–221. The May announcement is "From Mikhail Gorbachev's Speech on Soviet Television, 14 May 1986," in ibid., 221.

14. Press conference broadcast on Moscow television, 25 August 1986, reported in *Arms Control Reporter*, 608.B.107.

15. Michael Gordon in the *New York Times*, 19 August 1986, quoted in *Arms Control Reporter*, 608.B.106.

16. Karen DeYoung in the *Washington Post*, 20 August 1986, quoted in *Arms Control Reporter*, 608.B.106.

17. Akhromeev's interview with the German magazine *Stern*, quoted in *Izvestiia*, 27 November 1986.

weeks later the Soviet government announced that it would resume testing following the first U.S. test of 1987.[18] After two U.S. tests in the first half of February, a Soviet Defense Ministry official announced the resumption of Soviet testing with an explosion at the test range near Semipalatinsk on 26 February 1987. He claimed that the USSR did "not plan to compete with the United States in the frequency of tests" but that it was necessary to understand the kinds of weapons the United States was developing for use in the Strategic Defense Initiative so as to counter, rather than imitate, them.[19]

It is clear, then, that military concerns influenced decisions about the Soviet test moratorium. The Soviet military did not want the United States to gain an advantage in developing nuclear-powered "Star Wars" weapons. Gorbachev's answer was to try to achieve a mutual halt on the development of such weapons by initiating a unilateral Soviet test moratorium and convincing the United States to join. Top Soviet military and nuclear industry officials evidently always considered such a gesture dubious and risky. The unilateral moratorium—and more obviously its many extensions—cannot be understood primarily as a response to Soviet military requirements. The ultimate effect was to slow the modernization of Soviet nuclear weapons and to delay Soviet understanding of the nuclear aspects of Star Wars.

Economic Constraints

The Soviet test ban is also difficult to explain on the basis of economic constraints. Undoubtedly the country would save money from discontinuing nuclear testing. Although we do not know for certain the cost of the Soviet test program, one Soviet source suggested that the cost of an underground test, including the device being exploded, averaged about 30 million rubles.[20] This estimate would be comparable to the cost of U.S. tests. In the United States during the same time period of the late 1980s, each nuclear test ranged in cost from $30 million to $60 million.[21] Even though that amount of money was enormous in absolute terms, it was relatively small compared to the overall Soviet (or U.S.) military budget and the savings that could be obtained by other disarmament measures—such as major reductions in forces. Moreover, maintaining the test range in a state of readiness to resume testing was quite costly in itself, even if no tests were conducted, as Soviet military officials often pointed out to Soviet supporters of the ban.[22]

18. *Arms Control Reporter*, 608.B.124.
19. TASS statement, 26 February 1987, quoted in *Arms Control Reporter*, 608.B.130–131.
20. Nevada-Semipalatinsk Movement, "Brief Information on Semipalatinsk Test Site" (Alma Ata, Kazakhstan, 1989), 1.
21. Robert S. Norris and William M. Arkin, "Nuclear Notebook," *Bulletin of the Atomic Scientists* 49 (April 1993): 49.
22. General Nikolai Chervov made such remarks to Roald Sagdeev, for example. Sagdeev, interview by author, College Park, Md., 31 March 1994.

U.S. Behavior

As for the role of U.S. behavior, one cannot argue that the United States was pursuing a policy of "negotiation from strength" that in turn induced Soviet restraint. On the contrary, the United States had withdrawn from negotiations with the USSR on a comprehensive test ban in 1982 and had rejected the idea of a complete halt to testing as anything but a very long-term goal. The United States was not negotiating from strength because it was not negotiating at all. The Soviet initiative put the United States government in an awkward position because it thrust the comprehensive test ban back onto the arms control agenda. It was with evident relief that U.S. officials received the news of the resumption of Soviet testing.

THE TRANSNATIONAL CONNECTION

Conventional explanations find the Soviet Union's decision to undertake a unilateral halt to its nuclear tests something of a mystery. Certainly a test moratorium was within the standard repertoire of Soviet disarmament initiatives, dating back to the Khrushchev period. Perhaps some Soviet officials judged the Khrushchev experience a successful precedent, having led eventually to the Limited Test Ban Treaty. Others, however, might have remembered the opprobrium that greeted the Soviet nuclear tests of September 1961; they signaled the end of Soviet participation in the trilateral moratorium that began in 1958 and the betrayal of the coalition of transnational disarmament activists and nonaligned countries that had advocated a test ban. Whatever parallels Soviet officials drew to the Khrushchev-era test moratorium, one fact clearly distinguished the situation of 1985 from that of a quarter century earlier: The Reagan administration, unlike its predecessors, did not even pretend to be interested in a comprehensive test ban treaty.

An explanation for the Soviet test moratorium must account for why reform-oriented Soviet leaders, such as Gorbachev and Shevardnadze, although intent on improving East-West relations, would undertake an initiative that the U.S. government plainly did not want. Part of the answer is that they expected the USSR to gain a propaganda advantage from the moratorium by proving its willingness to show restraint in the nuclear arms race, even—and perhaps especially—if the United States refused to go along. In addition, at least Gorbachev and Shevardnadze believed that their gesture would bolster the opponents of the Reagan administration's military policies—both within the United States and abroad—and that perhaps the advocates of a nuclear test ban would, with evidence of continued Soviet restraint, be able to persuade the United States to join the moratorium.

Where did the Soviet leaders hear these arguments? They heard them from precisely the actors who saw themselves playing such a key role in the campaign for a comprehensive test ban: the transnational disarmament community and the nonaligned movement. These groups promoted the initial unilateral halt to Soviet nuclear testing and were instrumental in securing the several extensions of the moratorium.

"You Have Succeeded"

The revival of transnational activity promoting the peace movement's long-standing goal of a comprehensive nuclear test ban began already under the Brezhnev regime. It coincided with heightened concern about nuclear war following the NATO decision to deploy new U.S. missiles to Europe, the Soviet invasion of Afghanistan, the U.S. failure to ratify the SALT II strategic arms treaty, and the overall worsening of East-West relations. Although the main focus of the U.S. peace movement, starting in 1981, was a "nuclear freeze"—a mutual halt in the production and deployment of new nuclear weapons—many organizations saw a comprehensive test ban as a valuable first step toward that goal.[23] Their strategies varied widely, including public education, discussions among professionals such as physicians and scientists, high-level lobbying, and direct action and civil disobedience—even in the Soviet Union, as demonstrated by Greenpeace's uninvited voyage to Leningrad in 1982 (discussed in Chapter 8).

Transnational approaches were prominent at every level, as groups sought to convince the Soviet Union to take the initiative in achieving a comprehensive test ban. A number of efforts launched in the early 1980s bore fruit only after Mikhail Gorbachev came into office. In November 1984, for example, retired admirals Gene LaRocque and Eugene Carroll, directors of the Center for Defense Information, had written to Soviet leader Konstantin Chernenko and U.S. President Ronald Reagan proposing a mutual moratorium to begin on 6 August 1985.[24] Chernenko's death prevented his response, but in April 1985 the two admirals were invited to the Soviet embassy in Washington. There Ambassador Anatolii Dobrynin presented them a letter from Mikhail Gorbachev, Chernenko's successor, indicating that the Soviet leadership was giving the moratorium "serious consideration." They wrote to Gorbachev to encourage him to pursue the test ban.[25]

In the meantime, some Soviet scientists and officials, influenced by their international contacts, began lobbying their government to halt testing. Tair Tairov, then secretary-general of the Soviet-backed World Peace Council, cabled Moscow in 1985 to urge a unilateral moratorium. He was initially re-

23. David Cortright, *Peace Works: The Citizen's Role in Ending the Cold War* (Boulder, Colo., 1993), 209–210.
24. *Defense Monitor* 13, 5 (1984); *Arms Control Reporter*, 608.B.50–51.
25. Cortright, *Peace Works*, 209–210.

buked by officials from the Soviet Peace Committee, but he continued to press for a ban.[26] Tairov and the other Soviet interlocutors were encouraged to promote a unilateral Soviet ban by the expectation that Western publics would pressure the United States to reciprocate.

The International Physicians for the Prevention of Nuclear War (IPPNW) were especially influential in promoting a Soviet test moratorium. In early 1985, before Gorbachev came into office, the U.S. branch of the movement hosted an exchange from a Soviet delegation led by Evgenii Chazov. Chazov and his colleagues traveled to Los Angeles, Chicago, and Philadelphia. By the end of the trip, according to his host, Bernard Lown, Chazov came to agree that IPPNW should advocate a unilateral initiative by one of the sides. Lown and his U.S. colleagues had persuaded their Soviet counterparts that if the Soviet side halted its nuclear tests, U.S. activists would be able to convince their government to reciprocate—the same argument that Tairov was hearing from his international colleagues at the World Peace Council.[27]

Evgenii Velikhov, vice president of the Soviet Academy of Sciences, was encouraged by the advent of Gorbachev to redouble his efforts to achieve a test ban—one of the goals to which he and his transnational allies in the United States had committed themselves in 1983.[28] Velikhov seized a new opportunity to promote a traditional arms control goal—the comprehensive test ban—by using the Soviet military's concerns about the implications of U.S. nuclear testing for Star Wars research. Although the military leaders saw some merit in a mutual ban that would hinder U.S. SDI-related experiments, they were too cautious to advocate a unilateral Soviet moratorium.

Yet Gorbachev was convinced by Velikhov's arguments and the apparent popular Western support represented by his transnational contacts. In late April 1985, several of Gorbachev's reformist advisers, including Velikhov and Georgii Arbatov, held a small party for Bernard Lown, who was visiting Moscow to promote IPPNW's proposal for a test ban. Velikhov took Lown aside and told him that his efforts had paid off: "You have succeeded," said Velikhov. Gorbachev had agreed to a unilateral moratorium.[29] The USSR formally announced its moratorium on 29 July.

The Test Ban Continues

The transnational disarmament movement deserves credit not only for the initial idea of the Soviet moratorium but especially for its continuation in the face of the U.S. refusal to join. As Gorbachev himself wrote, the many extensions of the unilateral Soviet moratorium were "the result of a serious study

26. Ibid., 209.
27. Bernard Lown, interview by author, Brookline, Mass., 6 April 1994.
28. Evgenii Velikhov, interview by author, 29 July 1992; Jeremy Stone, "FAS Visit to Moscow Initiates Star Wars Dialogue," *F.A.S. Public Interest Report* 36, 10 (December 1983).
29. Lown, interview.

Drs. Bernard Lown (far right) and Evgenii Chazov of the International Physicians for the Prevention of Nuclear War meet with Soviet leader Mikhail Gorbachev in December 1985. Lown managed to persuade Gorbachev to continue the unilateral nuclear test moratorium and reverse a Politburo decision to end it. Photo courtesy of Bernard Lown.

of numerous appeals to the Soviet leadership from various circles of foreign intellectuals." He called particular attention to a meeting in November 1985, which Velikhov organized, where a delegation of Nobel laureates stressed "the significance of banning nuclear tests and the danger of militarizing space."[30]

Later that fall, Dr. Lown met for three hours with Gorbachev in the Kremlin. He too urged the Soviet leader not to end the moratorium. In fact by that time, according to Anatolii Cherniaev, Gorbachev's top aide for foreign policy, the Politburo had already approved the resumption of Soviet nuclear tests and the preparation of the relevant "propaganda provisions" to deal with the consequences. Cherniaev and his friend Georgii Arbatov coauthored a "private memo" to Gorbachev, reminding him of the need to maintain the support of Lown and the International Physicians. From Washington, Soviet ambassador Anatolii Dobrynin sent Gorbachev a telegram with a similar message.[31] These efforts were not coordinated in any formal sense, but they are typical of the way the transnational network linking Western supporters of disarmament and Soviet reformers worked. And in this case it worked well. On 15 January 1986, in a major statement announcing a program for nuclear disarmament by the year 2000, Gorbachev pledged to extend the unilateral moratorium another three months.[32]

30. Gorbachev, *Perestroika i novoe myshlenie*, 157–158; Velikhov, interview.

31. A. S. Cherniaev, *Shest' let s Gorbachevym: po dnevnikovym zapisiam* (Moscow, 1993), 62.

32. *Zaiavlenie General'nogo sekretariia TsK KPSS M.S. Gorbacheva, 15 ianvaria 1986 goda* (Moscow, 1986). For a discussion of the proposals, see Matthew Evangelista, "The New Soviet Approach to Security," *World Policy Journal* 3, 1 (Fall 1986).

Gorbachev managed to achieve the test ban extension in a characteristically clever way. Rather than conduct a full Politburo discussion of nuclear testing, he had four of his colleagues (led by Shevardnadze, the foreign minister) present the overall disarmament plan for approval the day before it was scheduled to be published. Moreover, Gorbachev himself did not even attend the meeting—he was on vacation. The extension of the unilateral moratorium was folded into an ambitious list of bilateral and multilateral measures. In traditional fashion, the Politburo members gave a blanket approval of their leader's decision. Nevertheless, two of the more conservative members could not resist some critical remarks, ostensibly about how decisions used to be made "in the past." As Vitalii Vorotnikov reconstructed the discussion from notes he took at the meeting, Andrei Gromyko and Egor' Ligachev mentioned that during the Brezhnev era "decisions were often taken without agreement by members of the Politburo. There was a lot of voluntarism and posturing. Three or four people plus Brezhnev made the decisions. A range of questions were generally outside the Politburo's control."[33] There is little doubt that these reminiscences were a thinly veiled criticism of the form and content of Gorbachev's disarmament initiatives.

The Chernobyl Effect

After Kornienko's February 1986 press conference and the government's announcement in April that it was free of its commitment to a unilateral test moratorium, Gorbachev came under increasing pressure from transnational organizations and countries in the nonaligned movement not to resume testing. Their efforts were bolstered by an unexpected and tragic "policy window"—the explosion at the Chernobyl nuclear power plant near Kiev on 26 April 1986. The Chernobyl disaster reinforced Gorbachev's already strong antinuclear sentiments and helped convince him to extend the moratorium and redouble his efforts to get the United States to join.

The "Chernobyl effect" on Gorbachev was so evident that even Ronald Reagan recognized it. When the two leaders met at Reykjavik in October 1986, just half a year later, Reagan wondered if Chernobyl might be "behind Gorbachev's new eagerness to discuss abolishing nuclear weapons."[34] Secretary of State George Shultz was also "struck by how deeply affected Gorbachev appeared to be by the Chernobyl accident" as late as May 1988, when he and Reagan and their spouses spent an evening at the Gorbachevs' dacha at the conclusion of a summit meeting in Moscow: "It was obvious from that evening that Chernobyl has left a strong anti-nuclear streak in Gorbachev's thinking."[35] This interpretation has been confirmed by Gorbachev's

---

33. V. I. Vorotnikov, *A bylo tak . . . Iz dnevnika chlena Politburo TsK KPSS* (Moscow, 1995), 83–84.

34. Ronald Reagan, *An American Life* (New York, 1990), 676.

35. Shultz to Reagan, memorandum, reprinted in Reagan, *American Life*, 710–711.

top foreign-policy aides, although they point out that Gorbachev's antinuclearism was present even before the Chernobyl disaster.[36]

In a television address on 14 May 1986, Gorbachev argued that "the accident at Chernobyl showed again what an abyss will open if nuclear war befalls mankind. . . . For inherent in the nuclear arsenals stockpiled are thousands upon thousands of disasters far more horrible than the Chernobyl one." He then pledged to extend the Soviet moratorium until August and urged President Reagan to meet with him "in the capital of any European state that will be prepared to accept us, or, say, Hiroshima, and to agree on a ban on nuclear testing."[37] The two leaders eventually met in Reykjavik, Iceland, in October. Even though Reagan recognized the sincerity of Gorbachev's antinuclear sentiment, he refused to join the moratorium.

Chernobyl served as an important policy window for Gorbachev because it had a sobering effect even on those who were ambivalent about his antinuclear initiatives. Marshal Akhromeev, for example, wrote about the accident in his memoirs in 1990: Even after five years "I cannot recall it without a feeling of spiritual pain and anxiety. Its first day is imprinted in my memory like the start of the war with fascist Germany on 22 June 1941." Akhromeev saw Chernobyl as a turning point in popular Soviet thinking about nuclear power: "After Chernobyl the nuclear danger for our people ceased to be something abstract. It became tangible, concrete. People began to regard all problems connected with nuclear weapons much differently."[38] A similar transformation seems to have affected members of the Soviet foreign-policy élite as well.[39] Under the circumstances it would have been very difficult for Akhromeev to make a case for resuming Soviet nuclear tests during the summer of 1986, especially when one of the key supporters of the moratorium—Evgenii Velikhov—was also one of the heroes of Chernobyl, who risked his life coping with the catastrophe.[40]

"We Were Supported by Outstanding Scientists"

In the wake of the Chernobyl disaster, transnational groups kept the pressure on Gorbachev not to resume testing. On several occasions the leaders

36. See, for example, the comments by Aleksandr Bessmertnykh, then deputy foreign minister, and Anatolii Cherniaev, Gorbachev's personal foreign-policy aide, in William C. Wohlforth, ed., *Witnesses to the End of the Cold War* (Baltimore, Md., 1996), 33, 37; also Aleksei Arbatov, interview by author, Cambridge, Mass., 18 August 1993.

37. "From the Speech on Soviet Television," 14 May 1986, in Mikhail Gorbachev, *The Moratorium: Selected Speeches and Statements by the General Secretary of the CPSU Central Committee on the Problem of Ending Nuclear Tests* (Moscow, 1986), 116–117.

38. Akhromeev and Kornienko, *Glazami*, 98–99.

39. See Steven Kull, *Burying Lenin: The Revolution in Soviet Ideology and Foreign Policy* (Boulder, Colo., 1992), 18, based on his interviews.

40. Evgenii Velikhov, "Chernobyl Remains on Our Mind," in Stephen F. Cohen and Katrina vanden Heuvel, eds., *Voices of Glasnost: Interviews with Gorbachev's Reformers* (New York, 1989), 157–173.

of Argentina, India, Mexico, Tanzania, Sweden, and Greece—the so-called Delhi Six—wrote to urge him to maintain the unilateral moratorium and to offer their assistance in helping to monitor a test ban.[41] In June 1986 the International Physicians issued an appeal to both the United States and the Soviet Union to join in a mutual moratorium and resume negotiations toward a comprehensive test ban; they also formally endorsed the efforts of the Delhi Six.[42]

Some of the strongest and most effective arguments for prolonging the unilateral ban came in July 1986 at a meeting in Moscow between Gorbachev and a group of Western and Soviet scientists, including Thomas Cochran of the Natural Resources Defense Council (a U.S. environmental organization based in Washington, D.C.), Frank von Hippel of Princeton and the Federation of American Scientists, and Joseph Rotblat of Pugwash, as well as Velikhov, Roald Sagdeev, Evgenii Chazov, Georgii Arbatov, and others on the Soviet side. The scientists, who had just participated in a forum on nuclear testing, summarized for Gorbachev their reasons for urging a continued moratorium, despite U.S. unwillingness to go along.[43] Von Hippel made the essential point that "the introduction of new nuclear weapons cannot change the fact that both the Soviet Union and the United States have the ability to destroy each other many times." Thus, despite the Soviet military's concerns about possible U.S. advances from continued nuclear testing, the fundamental nuclear stalemate would remain unchanged.

Recognizing Soviet concerns about the connection between nuclear testing and SDI research, von Hippel called attention to the widespread skepticism and opposition within the U.S. scientific community to Star Wars and the fact that the majority of physicists at leading U.S. universities had signed a pledge not to accept funds to work on SDI.[44] He and other participants stressed the important effect of the Soviet moratorium on public opinion, arguing that the Soviet initiative had already improved the international climate and enhanced the prospects for disarmament. Von Hippel also noted that continuing the Soviet moratorium was a prerequisite for any success the U.S. Congress might have in reducing budgetary allocations for U.S. testing. Finally,

41. Gorbachev's reply of 3 May 1986 is reprinted in Mikhail Gorbachev, *For a Nuclear-Free World* (Moscow, 1987), 91–94.

42. "From an Appeal of the Sixth Congress of International Physicians for the Prevention of Nuclear War to the General Secretary of the CPSU Central Committee and the President of the United States, 1 June 1986," Document No. 97 , 224–226; and "From a Message from International Physicians for the Prevention of Nuclear War to the Six Leaders of the Five Continent Peace Initiative," Document No. 101, 228–229, both in Falin, *Last Nuclear Explosion*.

43. "Vstrecha M. S. Gorbacheva s predstaviteliami mezhdunarodnogo foruma uchenykh za prekrashchenie iadernykh ispytanii," *Pravda*, 15 July 1986.

44. The pledge campaign was organized by physics graduate students Lisbeth Gronlund and David Wright at Cornell University, who coordinated their efforts with students at the University of Illinois. See the discussion in Cortright, *Peace Works*, 184–186. For their efforts Gronlund and her colleagues were later nominated for a Nobel Peace Prize by twenty-four members of the U.S. House of Representatives.

the scientists described the recent collaboration between U.S. and Soviet scientists to set up seismic monitoring equipment in the USSR and reported their conclusion that a comprehensive test ban could be successfully verified using seismic technology.[45]

On 18 August 1986, Gorbachev announced on Soviet television that he was prolonging the unilateral test moratorium yet again until January 1987. He acknowledged the appeals of the Delhi Six and "messages from politicians and public figures, from individuals and organizations of many countries, including the United States." He stressed the importance of the transnational efforts of the scientists: "We were supported by outstanding scientists— physicists and physicians—who understand better than anyone else the dangers inherent in the atom. I saw for myself at a recent meeting in Moscow that our moratorium had inspired scientific workers from various countries to take vigorous action on the nuclear issue."[46]

Perhaps most indicative of the influence of the transnational coalition of scientists was the fact that Gorbachev's arguments in defense of prolonging the unreciprocated moratorium took on an increasing sophistication, reflecting the information he had received from his science advisers and their Western colleagues. For example, as U.S. complaints about the difficulty of verifying a nuclear ban appeared increasingly unjustified, the Reagan administration began to focus on the need for nuclear tests to maintain the safety and reliability of the existing arsenal. President Reagan himself seems to have been particularly persuaded of this rationale.[47] Gorbachev was better informed. As he explained in an interview:

> Experts prove very convincingly that nuclear explosions are not needed to ensure that the existing nuclear weapons remain reliable. Other methods not requiring nuclear blasts can be used to control reliability just as effectively, notably less expensively, and much more safely at that. Long-standing practice also shows that the reliability of nuclear weapons can be assured without conducting explosions and by limiting oneself to checks of non-nuclear components of bombs and warheads. Since 1974 the USA and USSR have not conducted tests with a yield of over 150 kilotons, in compliance with the existing treaty. Meanwhile, weapons with yields over that "threshold" comprise 70 percent of the nuclear arsenal in the USA, and our percentage is no less. This means that we both believe in the reliability of weapons without explosions![48]

Gorbachev made similar arguments in personal correspondence with Reagan, but to no effect.[49]

45. "Vstrecha M. S. Gorbacheva."

46. "Statement by the General Secretary of the CPSU Central Committee on Soviet Television, 18 August 1986," in Gorbachev, *Nuclear-Free World*, 151–160.

47. Reagan, *American Life*, 660–661.

48. Interview published in the Soviet press as "Otvety M. S. Gorbacheva na voprosy glavnogo redaktora gazety 'Rude pravo' tovarishcha Zdeneka Gorzheni," *Krasnaia zvezda*, 9 September 1986, 1, and other newspapers.

49. See, e.g., his letter of 16 September 1986, reprinted in Reagan, *American Life*, 671–672.

The success of transnational contacts was often enhanced by the personal rapport that developed between the participants as they spent time at each other's homes and met their families. Here the daughter of Evgenii Velikhov entertains their guests in October 1986. *Left to right*: Frank von Hippel, Mikhail Gokhberg, Andrei Kokoshin, Velikhov, and Christopher Paine. Photo courtesy of Tom Cochran.

The Test Ban Ends

The United States ultimately refused to go along with the Soviet moratorium. On 14 December 1986 the Politburo approved a proposal to resume testing following the first U.S. nuclear test of the new year, but to continue or resume the moratorium if the United States ever joined it. The proposal to resume testing has been declassified, and it gives some insight into the Soviet government's thinking about the issue. The main reason given for test resumption, not surprisingly, was the harm to national security posed by the twenty-three tests carried out by the United States during the period of the unilateral Soviet moratorium, and particularly the relevance of the U.S. tests to development of the SDI. At the same time, however, the decision echoed the arguments of Western supporters of the test ban that "despite the decision of the USA not to join our unilateral moratorium, the moratorium had great significance in the political sphere." At the very least it yielded a certain propaganda value in discrediting the "theory of equal responsibility of the superpowers" for continuing the arms race.[50]

In approving the test resumption, the Politburo also decided to notify various countries in advance, through Soviet ambassadors, of the decision. The most detailed instructions were issued to those ambassadors who had to present the Soviet decision to the members of the Delhi Six. The leaders of these countries—among the most prominent international supporters of the test ban—were told that despite the test resumption the Soviet moratorium had achieved a number of benefits, including demonstration that verification of a test ban could no longer be considered a serious barrier to a comprehensive test ban treaty.[51] The Soviet government reiterated its readiness to reimpose the moratorium at any point that the United States halted its nuclear tests.

Much as Khrushchev had done a quarter century earlier, when he decided to break a Soviet test moratorium, Gorbachev sought to reassure his transnational allies. In June 1987 he met with the members of the IPPNW executive committee and told the doctors that he admired "both your movement and your work. . . . We take into account the activities of your movement in shaping our foreign policy." He particularly praised the organization's role in putting "worthy ideas" into the political arena.[52]

50. "Zapiska L. N. Zaikova, V. M. Chebrikova, E. A. Shevardnadze, S. L. Sokolova, A. F. Dobrynina, Iu. D. Masliukova i L. D. Riabeva v TsK KPSS o vozobnovlenii Sovetskim Soiuzom iadernykh ispytanil, esli SShA ikh prodolzhat v 1987 g.," 8 December 1986, approved by the Politburo on 14 December, in F. 89, list 18, doc. 109, Center for the Storage of Contemporary Documentation, Moscow.

51. Ibid. On other political benefits of the moratorium, see Jeffrey W. Knopf, "Soviet Public Diplomacy and U.S. Policymaking on Arms Control: The Case of Gorbachev's Nuclear Testing Moratorium" (paper presented at the annual meeting of the International Studies Association, London, 28 March–1 April 1989).

52. Excerpts from notes taken at the meeting on 2 June 1987, quoted in Bernard Lown and E. I. Chazov, "Physician Responsibility in the Nuclear Age," *Journal of the American Medical Association* 274, 5 (2 August 1995): 418.

Despite the worthiness of the transnational disarmament movement's ideas, the United States kept testing nuclear weapons, exploding two devices in early February 1987. The USSR resumed its nuclear test program later that month. Thus, the transnational disarmament coalition failed at this point to achieve its primary goal of a comprehensive test ban treaty. Nevertheless, the scientists were notably successful in other areas—particularly, as the Politburo acknowledged when it decided to resume testing—in addressing the problem of verification.

ON-SITE MONITORING: "WE ARE AS SURPRISED AS ANYONE"

It was a transnational coalition of American and Soviet scientists, rather than an official interstate organization, that successfully conducted the first on-site verification of Soviet arms control measures. In 1986 the Natural Resources Defense Council (NRDC) pursued a joint project with the Soviet Academy of Sciences (SAS) to install seismic monitoring equipment to verify the unilateral Soviet test moratorium.[53] As one observer described, the "NRDC accomplished what the United States government had, since the Eisenhower administration, tried and failed to achieve: it put American scientists on Soviet soil with types of equipment that could help to verify Soviet compliance with limitations on nuclear testing."[54] That effort set a precedent for cooperative verification measures and eliminated the most potent U.S. criticism of a comprehensive test ban—the supposed impossibility of achieving reliable verification.

There is a straightforward explanation for Soviet acceptance of on-site inspection that does not require any appeal to the role of transnational actors. The United States had, after all, since the beginning of discussions with the Soviet Union about disarmament in the 1940s, stressed the importance of verification. It had always been a stumbling block in negotiations on a test ban. Furthermore, the Reagan administration had highlighted the issue of test ban verification by accusing the USSR of violating the 1974 treaty limiting underground tests to less than 150 kilotons. It should have been apparent to any Soviet leader that willingness to accept on-site monitoring was a prerequisite for a comprehensive U.S.-Soviet test ban.

Although the basic premise of this explanation is sound—that the United States sought to focus Soviet attention on the issue of verification—it does not account for why or how the USSR agreed to allow on-site monitoring of its unilateral test moratorium. In fact, the apparent U.S. preoccupation with verification turned out to be something of a red herring. Close examination of

53. Natural Resources Defense Council, *Annual Report 1986–87* (Washington, D.C., 1987), 29–30.
54. Philip G. Schrag, *Listening for the Bomb: A Study in Nuclear Arms Control Verification Policy* (Boulder, Colo., 1989), 7.

the relevant data convinced most seismologists that the USSR had not, for example, violated the 1974 treaty—despite the fact that the United States had never even ratified it. In April 1986 the U.S. Central Intelligence Agency acknowledged that it had systematically overestimated the yields of Soviet nuclear tests.[55] If U.S. officials were so concerned about verification of a test ban, one might have expected them to propose ways of carrying it out. But that would presumably have entailed Soviet verification of a U.S. test ban as well. The Reagan administration did not want to stop U.S. nuclear testing. The United States was willing to allow Soviet observers to evaluate its favored new method for measuring the yields of nuclear explosions, but only on the condition that U.S. tests would continue.[56]

Once the NRDC project demonstrated the verifiability of a test ban, the Reagan administration was obliged to fall back on other excuses for continued testing—such as the need to explode nuclear warheads in order to insure their reliability and safety. Some officials insisted that even on-site inspection had not solved the problem of Soviet cheating, that the Soviets might now test new nuclear weapons in outer space, where it would be difficult for the United States to verify them. According to one particularly original argument, "they could go beyond Mars" to test a nuclear weapon, "in which case we'd have to go beyond Mars to measure it."[57] Most analysts found such arguments for rejecting a test ban of dubious merit.

Despite the Reagan administration's putative concerns about verification, it was a civilian, transnational, nongovernmental initiative—not a state-to-state agreement—that provided the motivation and the means for verifying the Soviet test ban. The idea for a nongovernmental group to monitor the Soviet nuclear test site seems to have had several independent sources in the United States, the Soviet Union, and elsewhere. In September 1985, Frank von Hippel met Evgenii Velikhov at a conference in Copenhagen, where they discussed their common arms control objectives. In considering ways to alleviate U.S. concerns about test ban verification, Velikhov suggested that the Soviet Union might be willing to allow an outside group to establish a seismic monitoring system in the country.

Later that month, Jack Evernden visited Moscow on behalf of the U.S. Geological Survey (a government agency) to propose an experimental network of eighteen seismic monitoring stations. He met with M. A. Sadovskii, director of the Institute of the Physics of the Earth. Sadovskii was a onetime Pugwash participant and consultant to the Soviet nuclear testing program. His institute

---

55. Don Oberdorfer, "New CIA Calculations Cast Doubt on Test Ban Violations by Soviets," *Washington Post*, 3 April 1986.

56. For a discussion of the so-called CORRTEX system, see Schrag, *Listening for the Bomb*, 14, 28–29. The acronym stands for Continuous Reflectometry for Radius versus Time Experiments.

57. Paul Brown of Lawrence Livermore Laboratory, quoted in the *Washington Post*, 24 June 1986, in *Arms Control Reporter*, 608.B.99.2.

had provided technical support of Soviet diplomats during the test ban negotiations of the late 1950s. He was sympathetic to Evernden's proposal, but he was willing to endorse the program of joint seismic research only on condition that the United States join the Soviet test moratorium. With official government channels blocked, Evernden became open to nongovernmental initiatives.[58]

The core proposal for joint U.S.-Soviet experiments in seismic monitoring originated with staff members of the NRDC. The organization had been producing a series of Nuclear Weapons Databooks with information on the nuclear establishments of all the nuclear powers, starting with the United States. Researchers found that although the United States historically had announced and published lists of its nuclear tests, it also kept many tests secret—a practice that the Reagan administration particularly favored. Some of the tests were of too low a yield for the seismic monitors of the U.S. Geological Survey to record. One member of the Databook project jokingly suggested that the NRDC set up its own monitors near the Nevada test site. As Philip Schrag reports, "the idea remained only a joke because it seemed somehow unpatriotic for NRDC unilaterally to release information which the U.S. government was, for some reason, keeping secret." Inspired by the suggestion of a journalist friend, the NRDC senior scientist Thomas Cochran then suggested monitoring Soviet tests as well.[59]

Cochran became the driving force behind the seismic monitoring project. In early 1986 he drafted letters to Ronald Reagan and Mikhail Gorbachev requesting permission for a team of "U.S. and Soviet seismologists, other scientists, and technicians who are not affiliated with the nuclear weapons programs" to set up a system of seismic stations in each country.[60] Discouraged by a Soviet embassy official in Washington, Cochran never sent the letters. Gorbachev, he was told, was unlikely to accept a plan for verification which included no commitment to a halt in U.S. testing—the same argument that hindered the Evernden-Sadovskii project.[61]

At this point, Jeremy Stone of the FAS suggested that the NRDC work with the Soviet Academy of Sciences as he and Frank von Hippel had done on other issues. He invited Cochran to attend a meeting with representatives of the Soviet Academy in Virginia in March 1986. The Soviet delegation, led by

58. *Arms Control Reporter*, 608.B.99.1–99.2; on the role of Sadovskii's institute, see documents in the Archive of the Foreign Policy of the Russian Federation [Arkhiv Vneshnei Politiki Rossiiskoi Federatsii], Fond: Otdel mezhdunarodnykh organizatsii, op. 4, por. 24, papka 60, delo 194/III-a, "Bor'ba za zapreshchenie ispytanii atomnogo i vodorodnogo oruzhiia," 24 March 1958–30 October 1958, especially the information sent to S. K. Tsarapkin, 27 June 1958.

59. Schrag, *Listening for the Bomb*, 11–12; Thomas Cochran, telephone interview by author, 14 April 1998.

60. Undated letters from Natural Resources Defense Council files, quoted in Schrag, *Listening for the Bomb*, 12.

61. Thomas Cochran, interview by Philip Schrag, in Schrag, *Listening for the Bomb*, 12.

Roald Sagdeev and Andrei Kokoshin, was quite receptive to the idea of a nongovernmental seismic monitoring experiment.

In April 1986 von Hippel was in Moscow accompanying a delegation from the Parliamentarians for Global Action to meet with Shevardnadze; they urged the Soviet government to maintain its moratorium on testing in order to give Western activists time to influence their own governments to go along. The Parliamentarians group, led by Aaron Tovish, was promoting what came to be known as the Five-Continent Peace Initiative, a proposal to support a comprehensive test ban by, among other things, developing a worldwide system of seismic monitoring stations.[62] The Soviet foreign minister received the delegation politely, but von Hippel was not sure that anything had been accomplished. He proposed meeting with Velikhov.[63]

Velikhov proved a crucial ally of the seismic monitoring project. He made good use of his personal relationship with Gorbachev, his influential position as vice president of the Academy of Sciences, and his familiarity with the United States to promote the project within the Soviet leadership. The explosion at the Chernobyl nuclear reactor later that month provided a catastrophic but useful policy window for promoting the seismic monitoring agreement, as it had done for the extension of the moratorium. Moscow faced sharp criticism for the delay in notifying other countries of the accident—particularly those in the path of the radioactive plume that contaminated a vast area from Belarus to Lapland. Some glasnost on the nuclear weapons test ban might compensate for lack of it in the sphere of civilian nuclear power.

As a first step Velikhov organized a workshop in Moscow on seismic verification for the end of May 1986—less than a month after the Chernobyl disaster. The participants included Thomas Cochran and Adrian DeWind of the NRDC; Aaron Tovish of Parliamentarians for Global Action; Jack Evernden of the U.S. Geological Survey; Christopher Paine, a leading congressional staff expert on arms control; and Charles Archambeau, a seismologist from the University of Colorado. Observers from India and Sweden—key supporters of the test ban initiative—also attended. The two-day workshop resulted in Soviet approval of Cochran's proposal for a joint seismic experiment under the sponsorship of the NRDC and the Soviet Academy. The project led to a new cooperation between the various groups and individuals. Archambeau, for example, who had originally worked with the Parliamentarians for Global Action, became a technical adviser to the NRDC project, helping put together a team of seismologists led by Jon Berger of the Scripps Institution of Oceanography in California. The Soviet participants were directed by Mikhail Gokhberg of Sadovskii's Institute of Physics of the Earth. As the main

62. For background on Tovish and the Parliamentarians, see Philip G. Schrag, *Global Action: Nuclear Test Ban Diplomacy at the End of the Cold War* (Boulder, Colo., 1992), chap. 2.

63. Frank von Hippel, "Arms Control Physics: The New Soviet Connection," *Physics Today* (November 1989): 39–46.

progenitor of the project, and its overall scientific director, Cochran coordinated his efforts with Velikhov and Gokhberg in the USSR and worked with Jacob Scherr, an NRDC attorney, in attempting to elicit enough cooperation from the Reagan administration to make the project succeed.

On the Soviet side, the hierarchical, centralized nature of the system paved the way for implementation of the joint seismic agreement, but the road was not always smooth. At the May workshop in Moscow, Velikhov had insisted on writing into the joint agreement a commitment to begin work before the end of June, "if possible." He evidently wanted to show some progress in seismic verification before the unilateral Soviet test moratorium was scheduled to end on 6 August. An NRDC team was quickly assembled and flew to Moscow at the beginning of July. In the meantime some Soviet officials, such as Anatolii Dobrynin, the former ambassador to the United States who had just been appointed to head the Central Committee's International Department, began to get cold feet. But Velikhov had the support of Gorbachev, the Soviet leadership's most ardent proponent of the test ban, and had, in effect, already pulled off a fait accompli by welcoming the U.S. scientists to Moscow. "What are we supposed to do now," he responded to Dobrynin, "send them home?" The team flew to Kazakhstan on 6 July, set up some rudimentary equipment, and took its first seismic readings—of earthquakes—on its first day at the site. From a discouraging start with Soviet embassy bureaucrats to a successful agreement brokered by Gorbachev's science adviser, Cochran's NRDC project had come a long way. "Nobody gave us any hope of pulling this off," Cochran commented. "We are as surprised as anyone."[64]

Implementation of the NRDC project on the U.S. side provides a striking contrast. The cooperation required of the U.S. government in the monitoring scheme was fairly modest—the granting of export licenses, visas for visiting Soviet scientists, and permission for setting up seismic stations on U.S. territory. Although at the highest levels most U.S. officials were unenthusiastic about the NRDC-SAS project, their views seemed to have little effect on how the various aspects of the project were handled. The decentralization of the U.S. system meant that many decisions were taken by middle- or low-level bureaucrats following standard operating procedures and adhering to statutory regulations. The result was that some potentially controversial questions—on the export of sensitive technologies needed for seismic monitoring—went rather smoothly, whereas other seemingly routine matters—issuing visas—ran into trouble. The contrast between the domestic structures of the United States and the USSR seems to account for the differences.[65]

The success of the NRDC seismic monitoring effort and the repeated extensions of the Soviet test moratorium took the Reagan administration

64. Schrag, *Listening for the Bomb*, 12–14; Cochran, interview by author; Cochran, quoted in *Arms Control Reporter*, 608.B.98.
65. See Schrag, *Listening for the Bomb*.

In July 1986 the first on-site verification of a Soviet arms control initiative was carried out by a nongovernmental group. Tom Cochran of the Natural Resources Defense Council (standing second from right) negotiated the agreement that brought a team of seismologists to set up equipment to verify the unilateral Soviet test moratorium. The team was led by Jon Berger of the Scripps Institution of Oceanography in California (seated in front of Cochran). Photo courtesy of Tom Cochran.

by surprise. U.S. officials—and much of the conventional political-science analysis—had been dismissive of the Soviet scientists, viewing them as nothing but propagandists for the Soviet regime. That Soviet scientists would sponsor a project of on-site verification to undermine the secrecy of the Soviet nuclear establishment was beyond their comprehension. When Christopher Paine informed assistant secretary of defense Richard Perle of the NRDC project in the summer of 1986, the influential Pentagon official was astounded. "Do you mean to tell me there are U.S. scientists going around setting up a seismic monitoring system in the Soviet Union and I don't know about it?" he sputtered.[66]

Perle had been busy trying to disrupt the budding collaboration between the U.S. Geological Survey and Soviet scientists at Sadovskii's Institute. He was blindsided by the NRDC agreement. It was a sweet moment for Paine, though. As a congressional staffer and later at the NRDC, he devoted much of his career to nuclear disarmament. The seismic monitoring agreement marked a major step on the way to the goal he shared with the broad community of transnational disarmament activists: a comprehensive nuclear test ban.

TRANSNATIONAL LIMITATIONS

Both the Soviet reformers and their transnational allies sought an end to nuclear testing in the United States as well as in the Soviet Union. U.S. proponents of a test ban had argued all along, in trying to persuade the Soviet side to undertake a unilateral initiative, that a serious gesture of Soviet restraint would strengthen their efforts to get the U.S. side to reciprocate. Once the Soviet Union launched its unilateral test moratorium, the head of the official Soviet Peace Committee lost no time in reminding the U.S. activists of their promise: "As you may remember, many peace movements in the West called upon the USSR to discontinue nuclear tests unilaterally." You "wrote to us that if such bold steps were undertaken," then you "would make the American Administration follow the example. . . . Now, it would seem to me that the peace movements in the West should keep their word."[67]

In reality, the U.S. activists had little hope of persuading the Reagan administration to halt U.S. tests. They focused their attention instead on Congress. This was an alternative route to a U.S. cessation of tests—one consistent with the logic of transnational politics.[68] Sophisticated Soviet observers

---

66. Christopher Paine, interview by author, Arlington, Va., 2 April 1994.

67. Letter of 22 August 1985, quoted in *Arms Control Reporter*, 608.B.70–71.

68. See, e.g., Margaret Keck and Kathryn Sikkink, *Activists beyond Borders: Advocacy Networks in International Politics* (Ithaca, N.Y., 1998); and Jeffrey W. Knopf, "Beyond Two-Level Games: Domestic-International Interaction in the Intermediate-Range Nuclear Forces Negotiations," *International Organization* 47, 4 (Autumn 1993): 599–628.

Evgenii Velikhov and Tom Cochran inspect the seismic monitoring equipment near Kara-
ganda, autumn 1987. Photo by Igor Mikhalev, courtesy of Tom Cochran.

of the U.S. scene, such as Aleksei Arbatov, Andrei Kokoshin, and some officials in the Foreign Ministry, recognized the potentially important role for Congress. In internal Soviet debates they made the same argument for prolonging the moratorium as their U.S. allies did: The more the Soviet Union showed restraint in the face of the Reagan administration's intransigence, the more likely Congress could be persuaded to use its power of the purse to limit funding for nuclear tests.[69] A precedent had already been set in restrictions placed by Congress on U.S. military programs that would violate SALT II— the strategic arms treaty that the Reagan administration had criticized and refused to submit for ratification.[70]

During much of the period of the Soviet unilateral moratorium, congressional staffers sympathetic to the transnational movement for a test ban were busy promoting legislation that would limit U.S. nuclear testing and force reciprocation of the Soviet initiative. In fact, Christopher Paine, the person most active in drafting the legislation, was also a key figure in the transnational negotiations with Soviet scientists that led to the NRDC monitoring agreement. In 1986, as a member of Representative Edward Markey's staff, Paine had led the successful effort to get the House of Representatives to pass a test ban amendment. In 1987 Paine joined the staff of Senator Edward Kennedy of Massachusetts as his main aide for disarmament issues "with the purpose of repeating the success in the Senate."[71] In coordinating U.S. legislative initiatives with Soviet test ban policy, Paine worked with several Soviet scientists and officials, including Andrei Kokoshin, Evgenii Velikhov, Evgenii Primakov, then director of the Institute of the World Economy and International Relations (and later Russian foreign minister and prime minister), and Vitalii Churkin, second secretary at the Soviet embassy in Washington.[72]

The Soviet resumption of tests in February 1987 was something of a setback for the proponents of legislated U.S. test restrictions, but their efforts nevertheless continued. By September 1987, Paine and his colleagues were anticipating a vote in the Senate to eliminate funds for any U.S. nuclear tests above one kiloton yield for a period of two years. The prospects for success looked good. Then, just days before the scheduled Senate vote, during a visit to Washington, Shevardnadze made a key concession to the Reagan administration's position on nuclear testing. The Soviet official agreed to set aside his country's goal of negotiations toward a comprehensive test ban and engage

69. Arbatov, interview. For a well informed analysis of the role of Congress, see A. A. Kokoshin and Iu. A. Ivanov, eds. *Kongress SShA i problemy vneshnei i voennoi politiki* (Moscow, 1989).

70. Robert T. Huber, *Soviet Perceptions of the U.S. Congress: The Impact on Superpower Relations* (Boulder, Colo., 1989), 108–109.

71. For an excellent account of these events, see Katherine Magraw, "Weapons Brokers and Policy Entrepreneurs: Congress and the Strategic Policy Community During the Reagan Era" (Ph.D. diss., Massachusetts Institute of Technology, 1992), chap. 4. The quote is from 257.

72. Paine, interview.

instead in discussions with the United States about additional measures of verification of the existing, unratified treaties, such as the Threshold Test Ban Treaty—which most experts outside the Reagan administration believed was already adequately verified.[73] In Thomas Cochran's words, the Soviet démarche "cut the legs off" the attempts by the transnational disarmament coalition to halt U.S. tests. Unwilling to undermine the president's bargaining position in the forthcoming test-verification talks, the Senate rejected the nuclear testing amendment by a vote of 61 to 36.[74]

Thus, the Soviet government snatched defeat out of the jaws of victory. It betrayed its transnational allies in the United States and its own disarmament agenda in the interest of improving state-to-state relations with the Reagan administration.

In retrospect, Gorbachev chose to look on the bright side. "Did it turn out that our moratorium was useless?" he wondered. "I don't think so." Gorbachev credited the unilateral Soviet moratorium—that fact that "silence reigned on our nuclear test ranges" from August 1985 to February 1987—with pushing the United States toward formal negotiations: "We can congratulate ourselves and everyone for getting the issue moving."[75] By the end of 1987 the Soviet government was even more intent on developing a working relationship with the Reagan administration, even if it meant sometimes undermining its transnational supporters. In key respects the strategy paid off. In December 1987 the two sides signed the treaty on Intermediate-Range Nuclear Forces—the first agreement that entailed substantial reductions in the superpowers' nuclear arsenals. Agreements on strategic weapons and conventional forces would follow.

The transnational coalition of disarmament activists played a major role in making these agreements possible. By urging the Soviet Union to prolong its unilateral test moratorium despite U.S. refusal to reciprocate, scientists and physicians such as Lown, von Hippel, Velikhov, and Chazov helped demonstrate the USSR's genuine interest in ending the arms race. By establishing a system of seismic verification of the Soviet moratorium, the scientists and activists of the NRDC and Soviet Academy of Scientists set an important precedent for on-site monitoring of all of the arms accords that followed. Ironically, it was the immediate goal of the transnational disarmament coalition—a comprehensive test ban—that had to wait until 1996 to be achieved. But the close call in the autumn of 1987, when the Senate nearly forced U.S. reciprocation of the Soviet test moratorium, suggests that there was even more potential in the transnational disarmament strategies than was realized at the time.

73. Raymond L. Garthoff, *The Great Transition: American-Soviet Relations and the End of the Cold War* (Washington, D.C., 1994), 319, 329; Christopher Paine, "Nuclear Test Restriction Fails to Pass Senate: Victim of Weapons Lab Lobbying Campaign; New US-Soviet Agenda for Test Ban Talks," *F.A.S. Public Interest Report* 40, 9 (November 1987): 1–4.

74. Quoted in *Arms Control Reporter*, 608.B.148.

75. Gorbachev, *Perestroika i novoe myshlenie*, 242.

[14]

"We Are Not Floating above Reality": Gorbachev's Revolution in European Security Policy

The mass of letters that come to me from citizens, and, just recently, my meeting at the Palace of Youth, compel us finally to think seriously about the question that the young communists put to me at that meeting: "Why do we need such a large army?"
—MIKHAIL GORBACHEV, 1988

Gorbachev didn't understand the army, he overturned our entire policy in Eastern Europe, a policy that was based on the presence there of the most powerful group of our troops. He didn't discuss with the military in the necessary manner the question of what happens if the Warsaw Pact collapses. Sergei Fedorovich [Akhromeev] tried to change Gorbachev's relationship to the army. He tried to persuade [him]: ... "Without a powerful army, 'new thinking' won't be worth anything to anybody." It was all useless. Gorbachev was listening to other people.
—TAMARA VASIL'EVNA AKHROMEEVA, 1995

In the second half of the 1980s, the USSR announced a revision of its military doctrine to emphasize defensive operations, implemented a unilateral reduction of a half-million troops and their equipment, and renounced military intervention in neighboring countries in favor of an emphasis on "freedom of choice" and "common security." These key steps toward ending the Cold War cannot be fully understood without taking into account transnational relations.

COMPETING EXPLANATIONS

As in the past, the main explanations for these Soviet initiatives focused on military, economic, and political factors. Western analysts described the troop reductions as consistent with new military requirements for a "leaner, meaner" high-technology army; some portrayed them as motivated by severe economic pressures; others viewed them as conciliatory reactions to a hard-line U.S. policy of "negotiation from strength." Each of the explanations has some degree of plausibility, but they are in no sense determining, nor are they sufficient to understand the nature and timing of the Gorbachev initiatives.

The key to the success of Gorbachev's disarmament strategy for Europe was a transnational coalition of Soviet and Western supporters of alternative security and "nonoffensive defense." To promote their ideas, these support-ers took advantage of the policy windows opened by a Soviet economic de-cline and a period of uncertainty and transition in Soviet military strategy. They did so against considerable resistance from the military high command and conservative members of the political leadership. Their success owes much to a Soviet domestic structure that offered them the backing of a power-ful general secretary working within a context that still encouraged deference to the top leader's wishes and discouraged open opposition.

Military Requirements: Arms Control as Military Policy?

In the first years of the Gorbachev period, a number of Western analysts in-terpreted Soviet disarmament initiatives as driven by changes in military requirements. This was a common interpretation, for example, of the decis-ion to accept the American "zero-option" proposal and eliminate the en-tire force of SS-20 missiles. A number of analysts found the treaty reducing intermediate-range nuclear forces (INF) and proposals for deep reductions in strategic nuclear weapons explicable in terms of Soviet military require-ments. They argued that "Gorbachev's call for radical arms control can be justified within current Soviet military doctrine," owing to a new Soviet emphasis on conventional operations.[1] They maintained that "Gorbachev and the Soviet military are now in agreement on an arms control and nu-clear weapons development program."[2] The most extreme interpretation de-scribed Soviet interest in nuclear disarmament as evidence of a desire to "make Europe safe for conventional war."[3]

Soviet interest in measures of conventional disarmament weakened expla-nations for Soviet arms control policy that focused exclusively on the Soviet military's purported desire to shift resources from nuclear to conventional forces. A number of analysts sought, nevertheless, to explain the changes in Soviet military policy—the announcement of a shift to a force posture of nonoffensive defense as well as the unilateral reductions—as consistent with the military's analysis of its requirements. Their explanations had a certain ad hoc quality about them, however. In fact few Western analysts predicted ei-

1. Mary C. FitzGerald, "The Strategic Revolution behind Soviet Arms Control," *Arms Control Today* 17, 5 (June 1987): 16–19.
2. George G. Weickhardt, "The Military Consensus behind Soviet Arms Control Proposals," *Arms Control Today* 17, 7 (September 1987): 24.
3. This was the view put forward by Zbigniew Brzezinski, among others.

ther unilateral reductions or any meaningful defensive restructuring.[4] On the contrary, most analysts argued that Soviet military requirements in the 1990s and beyond would entail "incredibly demanding new offensive depths and frontages" and unprecedented "scale and speed of offensive operations."[5] Accounting for the declaratory shift from offense to defense required them to amend their explanations to a considerable extent.

NATO's Technological Challenge. In the early 1980s, NATO and the United States began to introduce concepts for employing long-range, advanced conventional munitions for deep attacks into the rear of Warsaw Pact territories. The various programs went by names such as AirLand [*sic*] Battle and Follow-On Forces Attack (FOFA). They were oriented toward deep interdiction of Soviet forces, especially those in the second and third echelons.[6] Most analysts of Soviet military policy expected that the Soviets would react to these Western initiatives by further increasing the offensive nature of their own forces, and the early Soviet responses did bear out these predictions.[7] Then, in 1986, Mikhail Gorbachev announced at the Twenty-seventh Congress of the Soviet Communist Party that henceforth Soviet military doctrine would be based on "reasonable sufficiency," and that Soviet conventional forces should be structured so as to defeat an invasion but not to carry out large-scale offensive action.[8] In December 1988, Gorbachev bolstered these words with deeds, when he announced at the United Nations that 500,000 Soviet troops would be unilaterally demobilized and that 10,000 tanks, 8,500 artillery pieces, and 800 combat aircraft and other equipment oriented toward offensive action would be withdrawn from Europe.[9] The Soviet government

4. A representative selection of the common wisdom is found in *General Secretary Mikhail Gorbachev and the Soviet Military: Assessing His Impact and the Potential for Future Changes*, Report of the Defense Policy Panel of the Committee on Armed Services, House of Representatives, 100th Congress, 2d Session, 13 September 1988 (Washington, D.C., 1988). For an excellent early assessment, see Raymond L. Garthoff, "The Gorbachev Proposal and Prospects for Arms Control," *Arms Control Today* 16, 1 (January–February 1986); for an analysis that did anticipate unilateral initiatives, see Matthew Evangelista, "The New Soviet Approach to Security," *World Policy Journal* 3, 1 (Fall 1986).
5. William E. Odom, "Soviet Force Posture: Dilemmas and Directions," *Problems of Communism* 34 (July–August 1985): 7.
6. An early brief for the new technologies was *Strengthening Conventional Deterrence in Europe: Proposals for the 1980s*, Report of the European Security Study (New York, 1983); for a critical review of the proposals, see Matthew Evangelista, "Offense or Defense: A Tale of Two Commissions," *World Policy Journal* 1, 1 (Fall 1983).
7. John G. Hines, Phillip A. Petersen, and Notra Trulock III, "Soviet Military Theory from 1945–2000: Implications for NATO," *Washington Quarterly* 9, 4 (Fall 1986): 117–137; Michael J. Sterling, *Soviet Reactions to NATO's Emerging Technologies for Deep Attack*, Rand Note N-2294-AF, RAND Corporation (Santa Monica, Calif., 1985); Odom, "Soviet Force Posture."
8. M. S. Gorbachev, *Politicheskii doklad Tsentral'nogo Komiteta KPSS XXVII s"ezdu Kommunisticheskoi partii Sovetskogo Soiuza, 25 fevralia 1986 goda* (Moscow, 1986).
9. Bill Keller, "Gorbachev Vows Major Military Cutback and a 'Clearly Defensive' Stand in Europe," *New York Times*, 8 December 1988. The text of Gorbachev's address is on p. 6.

subsequently announced a 14.2 percent decrease in its military budget and a 40 percent cut in tank production.

In the wake of Gorbachev's initiatives, numerous Western analysts sought to explain them as the product of changing military requirements. In this view, NATO's introduction of advanced conventional weaponry, and Soviet analysis of the implications of the new technologies, forced a rethinking of Soviet strategy that ultimately led to a new emphasis on defense.[10] Western analysts typically combined this interpretation with the earlier description of the Soviet shift from nuclear to conventional emphasis, suggesting a long-term trend that predated Gorbachev's initiatives. As one analyst put it, "few Westerners realize that new military technologies—first nuclear and then conventional—compelled Soviet force planners to reevaluate the role of the defense long before the arrival of Gorbachev."[11]

In the view of Soviet military theorists, the new conventional technologies, like nuclear weapons before them, blurred the distinction between offense and defense. Long-range, highly accurate, conventional munitions created new vulnerabilities for the attacker, which in turn required new attention to defending the attacking forces. As Major General I. N. Vorob'ev wrote in the military daily, *Red Star*, in 1984, the greater vulnerability of Soviet troops to long-range attack generated "increased requirements for ensuring the survivability and reliable protection of subunits, for skillful utilization of the natural features of the local terrain, for carefully prepared field defenses, for the implementation of camouflage measures, and for misleading the opponents regarding the true location of the subunits."[12] Western analysts who focused on the views of such Soviet military writers claimed to find the origins of the new Soviet defensive doctrine in the change in military requirements precipitated by NATO's introduction of new conventional weapons technologies.

Soviet military requirements were certainly influenced by perceptions of changes in NATO and U.S. military strategy and weaponry. But it strains credibility to make the case that Soviet military leaders decided on a program of defensive restructuring, let alone unilateral disarmament, mainly as a reaction to technological change. For one thing, the implications of the new technologies for warfare were not obvious and were in some respects contradictory. Russian archival materials reveal that the Soviet side was grappling with this issue many years before any official changes in NATO doctrine were announced. In December 1975, for example, Iurii Andropov, head of the KGB,

---

10. *General Secretary Mikhail Gorbachev*, esp. 12–13.

11. Mary FitzGerald, "The Dilemma in Moscow's Defensive Force Posture," *Arms Control Today* 19, 9 (November 1989): 15; for a similar argument, see Jacques Sapir and Thierry Malleret, "La politique militaire Sovietique: de la restructuration à la reforme" (paper presented to the 4th World Congress for Soviet and East European Studies, Harrogate, England, 21–26 July 1990).

12. Quoted in FitzGerald, " Dilemma," 17.

submitted a report to the Central Committee presenting an overview of the impact of the introduction of new, highly accurate conventional weapons, such as laser-guided bombs and rockets, into U.S. and NATO forces. Andropov reported the claims of Western experts that such weapons would lessen the likelihood of nuclear escalation by the Western side because they would bolster NATO's defensive capabilities even against a numerically superior offensive force. He also summarized the argument that the new weapons would threaten some of the most expensive heavy tanks and aircraft on the Soviet side and would promote a shift to cheaper, lighter tanks and armored personnel carriers, as well as unpiloted aircraft, such as cruise missiles. The KGB chief did not draw any conclusions or make any recommendations based on this analysis. A plausible conclusion, though, might have been that the Soviet armed forces should stop investing in the sorts of tanks and aircraft that would be rendered ineffective by the new technologies. Yet they continued to do so.

Nor did the analysis of the new technologies reassure the Soviet side about the prospects of nuclear war. Despite the claims of Western experts that the new weapons would "lower the nuclear threshold," Andropov's report pointed out, correctly, that NATO planned to provide low-yield nuclear warheads for the new, highly accurate "conventional" weapons. In the KGB's assessment such dual-use capability would help "simplify the procedure for making a decision on military use of tactical nuclear weapons."[13] It would be difficult for the Soviet side to anticipate when NATO might escalate to nuclear use.

Not surprisingly, the Soviet high command reacted to the NATO changes by hedging its bets. It sought to develop comparable advanced-technology conventional weapons, but it also continued mass production of expensive heavy tanks and aircraft. It dealt with the threat of nuclear escalation by striving to develop the capability for preemption and disruption of a NATO nuclear attack, but it maintained a vast arsenal of its own tactical nuclear weapons as well.

The Civilian Alternative. Such military plans were inconsistent with the thrust of Gorbachev's disarmament initiatives—without even taking into consideration the Soviet withdrawal from Eastern Europe. The demands of Marshal Nikolai Ogarkov, chief of the Soviet General Staff from 1977 to 1984, for immediate increases in military spending for research, development, and production of advanced conventional weapons went unheeded even by

13. "O Vozmozhnykh politicheskikh i voennykh posledstviiakh sozdaniia i rasprostraneniia tochnogo takticheskogo oruzhiia," report from Iurii Andropov, head of the KGB, to the Central Committee, 14 December 1975, in F. 89, op. 37, doc. 30, Storage Center for Contemporary Documentation [Tsentr khraneniia sovremennoi dokumentatsii] (hereafter TsKhSD), Moscow.

Gorbachev's predecessors.[14] The subsequent economies introduced into Soviet military programs—such as the 14.2 percent reduction in military spending and the 19.5 percent decrease in arms production for 1989—could hardly satisfy the military's requirements for a crucial shift to high-tech weaponry.

What the Gorbachev leadership and its academic advisers had in mind by "reasonable sufficiency" and "nonoffensive defense" differed considerably from the military's analysis of what was necessary to meet the challenge of new technologies. In short, the military wanted better tactical defenses in an overall strategy that remained offensive, or at least retained the ability for theater-wide counteroffensives.[15] The civilians, by contrast, wanted sharp restrictions on offensive capabilities, some going as far as to favor what the German proponents of alternative defense called *strukturelle Nichtangriffsfähigkeit*—the structural inability to attack.[16] Eventually it became difficult to reconcile the civilian plans for nonoffensive defense and other major military reforms with the professional military's preferences for robust counteroffensive capabilities and immediate production of advanced-technology weapons, as many analysts belatedly admitted.[17] Finally, prominent Soviet military officials consistently and publicly opposed unilateral Soviet initiatives of restraint and were not happy when Gorbachev cut the army.[18]

If the civilian notions of military reform differed markedly from those of the military, one must ask where the civilian proposals came from. The military-requirements explanation presumably does not tell the whole story.

14. For an insider's account of how Ogarkov lost his job as chief of the General Staff, see V. I. Vorotnikov, *A bylo tak . . . Iz dnevnika chlena Politburo TsK KPSS* (Moscow, 1995), 45–48. For background, see Coit D. Blacker, *Hostage to Revolution: Gorbachev and Soviet Security Policy, 1985–1991* (New York, 1993), 47–51; Thomas M. Nichols, *The Sacred Cause: Civil-Military Conflict over Soviet National Security, 1917–1992* (Ithaca, N.Y., 1993), 119–124; Bruce Parrott, "Political Change and Civil-Military Relations," in Timothy J. Colton and Thane Gustafson, eds., *Soldiers and the Soviet State: Civil-Military Relations from Brezhnev to Gorbachev* (Princeton, N.J., 1990), 65–70.

15. Lothar Rühl, "Offensive Defence in the Warsaw Pact," *Survival* 33, 5 (September/October 1991): 442–450; Raymond L. Garthoff, *Deterrence and the Revolution in Soviet Military Doctrine* (Washington, D.C., 1990), 159–174.

16. For reviews of the various proposals, see Karsten D. Voigt, "Konventionelle Stabilisierung und strukturelle Nichtangriffsfähigkeit: Ein systematsicher Vergleich verschiedener Konzepte," *Aus Politik und Zeitgeschichte* 18 (29 April 1988): 21–34; and Jonathan Dean, *Meeting Gorbachev's Challenge: How to Build Down the NATO-Warsaw Pact Confrontation* (New York, 1989), chap. 4.

17. William E. Odom, "The Soviet Military in Transition," *Problems of Communism* 39, 3 (May–June 1990); FitzGerald, " Dilemma"; R. Hyland Phillips and Jeffrey I. Sands, "Reasonable Sufficiency and Soviet Conventional Defense," *International Security* 13, 2 (Fall 1988): 164–178; Phillip A. Petersen and Notra Trulock III, "A 'New' Soviet Military Doctrine: Origins and Implications," *Strategic Review* (Summer 1988): 9–24.

18. For representative military critiques, see (Lt. Gen., res.) E. Volkov, "Ne raz"iasniaet, a zatumanivaet," *Krasnaia zvezda*, 28 September 1989; (Maj. Gen.) G. Kirilenko, "Legko li byt' oborone dostatochnoi?" *Krasnaia zvezda*, 21 March 1990; (Maj. Gen.) Iu. Liubimov, "O dostatochnosti oborony i nedostatke kompetentnosti," *Kommunist vooruzhennykh sil*, 1989, no. 16:21–26; (Gen.) M. A. Moiseev, "Eshche raz o prestizhe armii," *Kommunist vooruzhennykh sil*, 1989, no. 13:3–14.

Economic Constraints

Soviet advocates of military reform clearly benefited from their leaders' concern about economic decline in the 1980s. But the relationship between the economy and the moderation in Soviet military policy was hardly the direct, almost mechanistic one that many Western observers have depicted. Rather, the economic situation provided a "window" for Soviet policy entrepreneurs and their transnational allies to promote their reformist solutions.

Some accounts describe Soviet moderation in the late 1980s—and, particularly, the conventional-force reductions—as the inevitable result of economic crisis. Within this general economic explanation, one can distinguish three variants. The first focuses on declining growth rates, the second on demographic constraints, and the third on the inability of the Soviet economy to compete in the sphere of advanced technologies.

Economics and Demographics. Our discussion in previous chapters indicated that the first two explanations—overall decline of economic growth and demographic pressures—should have applied more to the Brezhnev era than to Gorbachev. The greatest and most rapid declines in Soviet growth took place in the decade of the 1970s—long before Gorbachev launched perestroika. The economy actually saw some improvement during the early period of Gorbachev's tenure (as well as during the Andropov interregnum). The Brezhnev era witnessed the demographic trends that we would most expect to influence the size of the armed forces—decline in the growth of the labor force from 1975 (it began to pick up again in the early 1980s), and a sharp drop in labor productivity. Yet Brezhnev's major buildup of conventional forces (including an addition of nearly nine hundred thousand soldiers from the Khrushchev-era level) was the opposite of what an emphasis on demographic factors would expect.

One might be tempted to salvage the economic/demographic explanation for Soviet moderation by describing Gorbachev's December 1988 announcement as a delayed response to the demographic situation. In fact, however, even as the cuts were being implemented, labor-force growth began an upswing. Moreover, Gorbachev understood that as a consequence of his economic reforms the demobilized soldiers would be entering not a taut, inefficient, full-employment economy, but one characterized by unemployment and a deteriorating social safety net. These soldiers would not be the welcome "inputs" for extensive growth that they might have been in past decades under the old Soviet economic order.

The Breathing-Space Explanation. At the core of the third common economic explanation for Soviet disarmament initiatives, the "breathing-space" argument, is the notion that the Soviet military supported Gorbachev's reforms in the expectation that a reinvigorated economy would provide a firm foundation for the development of advanced military technologies in the future.

Several Western analysts who typically favored explanations for Soviet change that focused on military requirements shifted to the breathing-space argument when they saw the extent to which many of Gorbachev's initiatives ran contrary to short-term military interests. "Beginning in the early 1980s," they argued, "the Soviet military has demonstrated concern over the magnitude of the stagnation in the Soviet economy, and in particular the absence of the production technologies and processes requisite to mass-producing the weapons systems of the future. The military understands full well the industrial base needed for future military-technical development. . . . [I]t needs the benefits of economic reconstruction [*perestroika*]."[19]

Not only did such analysts argue that the military supported perestroika for the sake of its future weapons needs, they implied that economic reform itself was driven by military concerns rather than by any interest in improving the overall economic welfare of Soviet citizens. The Soviet leadership, they argued, decided "to revitalize the economy as a whole in order to support future defense requirements. Rather than seeing this decision as a choice between guns or butter, it might be more useful to pose the choices as between guns now or guns later."[20] The breathing-space argument bears similarities to attempts by scholars in the realist tradition of international relations theory to account for Soviet retrenchment as a rational response to internal economic decline.

The validity of the breathing-space argument would be bolstered if we could find some degree of consensus on the long-term goals of perestroika between the military and the Party leaders who initiated the reforms. In fact, a wide range of divergent views was represented in the Soviet debate on national security in the mid- to late 1980s. On the civilian side, the reformers were never prepared to sacrifice the future benefits of economic reform for the sake of providing the military with their desired high-tech weaponry. Instead, civilian reformers—and indeed, the population at large—grew increasingly bold in expressing views quite hostile to the military.[21] We now know that the top reformist leaders—Gorbachev, Shevardnadze, and Aleksandr Iakovlev, most notably—shared these views in private. They were determined to limit the military's dominance of the economy—the source, as they eventually came to believe, of much of the country's economic woes.

19. Petersen and Trulock, "'New' Soviet Military Doctrine," 18, 20.
20. Hines, Petersen, and Trulock, "Soviet Military Theory," 129–130.
21. Two relatively early criticisms of the military's pernicious effect on Soviet technology policy are A. Dobrynin, "Za bez"iadernyi mir, navstrechu XXI veku," *Kommunist*, 1986, no. 9:18–31; and L. Feoktistov, "Gonka vooruzhenii, voina i nauchno-tekhnicheskii progress nesovmestimy!" *Kommunist*, 1986, no. 15:97–106. For a sharp attack on military priorities by an erstwhile regime stalwart, see Georgii Arbatov, "Armiia dlia strany ili strana dlia armii?" *Ogonek*, 1990, no. 5:4. Such harsh criticisms led some analysts at the time to fear a backlash from the military: see Jack Snyder and Andrei Kortunov, "French Syndrome on Soviet Soil?" *New Times*, no. 44 (1989): 18–20.

In a discussion of the economic situation at a Politburo meeting in the spring of 1987, Gorbachev alluded to popular concern about military spending: "people say we're littering the defense industry with money." In a February 1988 Politburo session, he warned: "It's now clear that without a significant cut in military expenditures we won't resolve the problems of perestroika."[22] Both Shevardnadze and Gorbachev took pains to emphasize their support for qualitative improvements in the armed forces (not only the quality of weapons but also of personnel), but they also made clear their unwillingness to pay for them. They were determined to end the military's priority access to Soviet economic resources.[23] The civilian reformers' main goal for economic reform was neither "guns now" nor "guns later," but fewer guns indefinitely.

Within the military, support for perestroika, and particularly for major reductions in forces and military expenditure, was far less widespread than the breathing-space argument requires. Indeed, few in the Soviet military appear to have explicitly adopted such reformist views. Moreover, no senior commander expressed the requisite combination of alarm at U.S. military-technological advances and support for restraint in Soviet military spending.

Early in the Gorbachev era, some Western analysts identified a couple of key articles in the Soviet military press as indicating the high command's support of near-term restraint for the sake of longer-term technological advances.[24] A closer look at these sources suggests that they were at best ambiguous, and more often advocated traditional military preferences. A case in point was an article in the *Military-Historical Journal* by Colonel V. A. Zubkov. The author invokes Lenin's views on the importance of the economy for the state's defense and selectively quotes Gorbachev, but in such a way as to support the traditional goals of the Soviet military: an emphasis on heavy industry, transport, the "creation of large-scale reserves" of fuel and stocks of weapons. He quotes Lenin's injunction that the USSR should not permit "the slightest weakening in the task of equipping the Red Army with 100% of its needs." This hardly sounds like a new thinker's desire to impose restraints on Soviet military spending.

Nor does Zubkov evince the concerns about the USSR's ability to compete with U.S. high-tech weapons that supposedly underlay the Soviet military's support for perestroika: He claims that the Soviet Union's present "level of development of science and technology permits [it] successfully to resolve the most complicated technical tasks and in a short time to create any kind of

22. A. S. Cherniaev, *Shest' let s Gorbachevym: po dnevnikovym zapisiam* (Moscow, 1993), 146, 253.

23. Cherniaev, *Shest' let*, 253–254; Eduard Shevardnadze, "Doklad E. A. Shevardnadze," *Vestnik Ministerstva Inostrannykh Del SSSR*, 1988, no. 15:35–36; Shevardnadze, *Moi vybor: v zashchitu demokratii i svobody* (Moscow, 1991), 252–253.

24. Stephen M. Meyer, "The Sources and Prospects of Gorbachev's New Political Thinking on Security," *International Security* 13, 2 (1988): 124–163.

weapon on which the aggressors stake their hopes."[25] An editorial in the same journal, intended to endorse the resolutions of the Twenty-seventh Party Congress—the one at which Gorbachev announced the new doctrine of "reasonable sufficiency"—repeated some of the rhetoric of Gorbachev's reform proposals but waxed far more enthusiastic about according the military its traditional high priority in access to resources and technology.[26]

Were senior Soviet military commanders concerned enough about falling behind the United States in military technology to support unilateral restraint? Certainly users of Soviet military equipment in the armed forces were often dissatisfied with its quality, particularly with the way the Soviet economic system affected the design and production of weapons. There was less concern, however, about the level of technology per se.[27] The conventional weapons that Soviet design bureaus produced—advanced fighter aircraft, for example—typically compared favorably to their U.S. counterparts, although they normally appeared some years after the U.S. weapons and were usually designed as specific responses to them.[28] Soviet designers were proud of their accomplishments and took offense at any suggestion that their U.S. counterparts were better.[29] Some went to the point of arguing that "Soviet designers are superior because they produce superior quality products under harsh conditions."[30] Both designers and users of Soviet military technology undoubtedly favored reforms and rationalization of the economic system, but that is different from the breathing-space argument, which hinges on concerns about lagging technology and willingness to implement unilateral restraint.

25. V. A. Zubkov, "Zabota KPSS ob ukreplenii ekonomicheskikh osnov voennoi moshchi sotsialisticheskogo gosudarstva" *Voenno-istoricheskii zhurnal*, 1986, no. 3:3–8.

26. "XXVII s"ezd KPSS o dal'neishem ukreplenii oboronosposobnosti strany i povyshenii boevoi gotovnosti Vooruzhennykh Sil," *Voenno-istoricheskii zhurnal*, 1986, no. 4:3–12.

27. Judyth L. Twigg, "'To Fly and Fight': Norms, Institutions, and Fighter Aircraft Procurement in the United States, Russia, and Japan" (Ph.D. diss., Massachusetts Institute of Technology, 1994), chap. 6.

28. Ibid. See also Benjamin S. Lambeth, *From Farnborough to Kubinka: An American MiG-29 Experience*, RAND Corporation Report No. R-4000-RC (Santa Monica, Calif., 1991). Kim Zisk has suggested that aircraft, as a relatively successful branch of Soviet miltary production, might not be representative of the quality of Soviet military technology overall, and that officers concerned about procurement of high-tech, computer-based conventional weapons, for example, might have been more worried about the level of Soviet technology than my account allows. Still, I find no evidence of army officers who, motivated to address such concerns, became advocates of unilateral concessions and restraint of the sort that Gorbachev favored. Moreover, representatives of other branches of military technology have expressed comparable self-confidence. A leading official in the nuclear field, for example, has claimed that the "military-industrial complex" (his expression) was "the only complex in the country working on the level of the best world standards, both in machine building and instrument making." V. N. Mikhailov, *Ia—"Iastreb"* (Moscow, 1993), 70.

29. Comments by German Zagainov, director of TsAGI (the leading Soviet aircraft design institute), at an informal seminar at the University of Michigan, November 1989.

30. A former MiG designer, quoted in Twigg, "'To Fly,'" 412.

Pride in Soviet military technology was common at the most senior levels in the military—and not only from conservatives who sought to deny the need for reform. Even such a staunch supporter of reform as Marshal Evgenii Shaposhnikov objected to any implication that the products of Soviet military aircraft technology, for example, were in any way inferior to their U.S. counterparts.[31] Shaposhnikov was the head of the Soviet Air Forces at the time of the attempted coup against Mikhail Gorbachev in August 1991. He was the only member of the military high command unambiguously to support Gorbachev and thus became, for the last few months of its existence, defense minister of the Soviet Union. When asked specifically whether U.S. military-technological advances induced the Soviet military to support perestroika and Gorbachev in the interest of a breathing space, he replied with a joke: "What do militarists and generals' wives have in common? A common enemy: disarmament and détente." In other words, most military officers were more concerned about the negative effects of Gorbachev's policies on their own careers—lower military budgets leading to loss of their jobs—than to any long-term benefits to Soviet military technology sometime in the distant future.[32]

The World according to Marshal Akhromeev. If there is any military officer who could be credited with views compatible with the breathing-space argument it should be Marshal Sergei Akhromeev. Akhromeev served as chief of the General Staff from 1984 through 1988 and then as Gorbachev's personal military adviser until 1991. He was an active participant in many of the key arms control negotiations of the Gorbachev era. Western observers have attributed to Akhromeev what many had believed, mistakenly, about his predecessor Marshal Ogarkov, for whom Akhromeev had served as first deputy chief of the General Staff—namely, that he became a supporter of perestroika out of his concern for a Soviet lag in advanced-technology weapons for fighting a conventional war in Europe.[33] This view seems supported by the reminiscences of a former Soviet official who knew Akhromeev well. According to Valentin Falin, a Communist Party specialist on Germany, it was Akhromeev "who had alarmed the General Staff with regard to NATO plans to force the

31. Evgenii Ivanovich Shaposhnikov, informal discussion, Kennedy School of Government, Harvard University, Cambridge, Mass., 18 October 1994. It must be noted that Shaposhnikov at this time was serving as the head of the Russian arms export company, so he was in the business of extolling the virtues of Russian military technology. On the other hand, he knew that his interlocutors—Randall Forsberg, Joanna Spear, Andrew Peach, and myself—were not potential customers but rather critics of arms exports. His pride in Soviet achievements—particularly the Su-27 aircraft—seemed quite genuine.

32. Ibid.

33. Dale Herspring, *The Soviet High Command, 1967–1989: Personalities and Politics* (Princeton, N.J., 1990). For a critique, see Matthew Evangelista, "New Politics in the Soviet Union," *American Political Science Review* 85, 4 (December 1991).

Soviet Union into an even more exhausting arms race in the high-tech conventional area. The Marshal's opinion was: It can't go on as it used to be!"[34]

In fact, however, the preponderance of evidence suggests that Akhromeev was not so much alarmed by the gap between Soviet and U.S. military technology. To the extent that it did concern him, he did not see the kind of radical reforms that Gorbachev and Shevardnadze initiated as offering any solution. Contrary to those who would portray him as a natural advocate of defensive restructuring, for example, Akhromeev initially showed no interest in revising the legacy of ambitious offensive operations that he inherited from Ogarkov. In April 1985, Akhromeev made a point of persuading the new general secretary, Mikhail Gorbachev—who in the marshal's view "had a definitely skeptical attitude toward generals and admirals"—that Ogarkov's offensive innovations were justified.[35]

Akhromeev voiced many opinions inconsistent with key assumptions of the breathing-space explanation. In his memoirs, completed in the first half of 1991, he expressed pride—rather than alarm—in the accomplishments of Soviet military technology. He claimed that during the 1960s and 1970s, "the defense branches of industry were outfitted with the latest equipment and technology. The combat readiness and military capability of the Soviet armed forces were fully satisfactory." Even if he became more pessimistic about the relative military situation in the 1980s, Akhromeev did not view perestroika primarily as a means to improve Soviet military technology. On the contrary, he indicated his concern that the priority traditionally given to Soviet military research came at the expense of other branches of the economy, such as agriculture and medicine.[36]

Akhromeev's initial support for perestroika, like that of such leading political figures as Egor' Ligachev and Nikolai Ryzhkov, was based on a general recognition of the need for reform of the economy and the Communist Party, not on narrow parochial views or instrumentalist thinking about how economic reform would benefit military technology.[37] Shaposhnikov's motivations were similar.[38] In the realm of security policy, Akhromeev became a crucial, early supporter of moderate reforms, including some defensive restructuring of conventional forces. Yet he eventually came to oppose the direction of the reforms—particularly the emphasis on unilateral initiatives and civilian interference in military matters—and he ultimately regretted his support for perestroika itself.[39] He committed suicide in the wake of the

34. Valentin Falin, *Politische erinnerungen* (Munich, 1993), 477. I thank Thomas Risse for help with my translation of this comment.

35. S. F. Akhromeev and G. M. Kornienko, *Glazami marshala i diplomata* (Moscow, 1992), 65–67.

36. Ibid., 12–13.

37. Ibid., 33.

38. Shaposhnikov, seminar.

39. Akhromeev and Kornienko, *Glazami*, 319; Akhromeev reveals a strong animus against the civilian reformers, esp. on 290–291.

failed coup against Gorbachev in August 1991. Marshal Shaposhnikov, by contrast, was the highest military officer to side with the democrats during the coup, and he went on to become a key figure in the transition of the Soviet Union into the Commonwealth of Independent States.

Given his intense skepticism about Gorbachev's initiatives in the restructuring and unilateral reduction of conventional forces, it is curious that Akhromeev, in his posthumous memoirs coauthored with Georgii Kornienko, describes the origins of those initiatives as if they were exclusively of military provenance. Akhromeev and Kornienko, for example, give the Soviet General Staff the main credit for the initiative that led to broadening the talks on conventional-force reductions to include Soviet territory. According to their account, the General Staff decided in 1983 that the talks on Mutual and Balanced Force Reductions (MBFR) could not succeed if limited geographically to the territory of central Europe. After two years of study, the military decided that "it was necessary to carry out the negotiations on reductions in armed force in Europe as a whole—from the Atlantic to the Urals." This initiative, they argue, came "not from someone above or beside, but from the General Staff itself." The idea was proposed to the government by the Ministry of Defense in early 1986 and became part of the official Soviet position in April.[40] One wonders why it took the Soviet military sixteen years—from the start of the MBFR negotiations in 1973—to decide on the new formula. In fact the proposal to expand the territory covered by the negotiations was one long advocated by the NATO powers.[41] As for the slogan itself—"from the Atlantic to the Urals"—it was initially coined by French president Charles de Gaulle and popularized by the European Nuclear Disarmament movement starting in the late 1970s, long before the Soviet General Staff began to reconsider its position on the negotiations.[42]

A closer look at Akhromeev's own words, complemented by other sources, suggests that he did not play such a key role in initiating the reforms that ended the Cold War in Europe, but, on the contrary, was frozen out of many discussions. In the summer of 1987 Akhromeev and the new defense minister Dmitrii Iazov sent Gorbachev a report outlining their views on Soviet policy toward Eastern Europe and European security. They included a request that he "examine along with the military the aggravation of the situation and the problems that had arisen." Gorbachev read the report and examined the situation, writes Akhromeev, "but without us, and, as I understood, that was no accident." Gorbachev's style was to address "the most significant military-political problems with the military step by step, without straining relations with them, where that was possible," but basically keeping them in the dark

---

40. Ibid., 96–97.

41. Jonathan Dean, interview by author, Washington, D.C., 19 September 1994.

42. Dean, *Meeting Gorbachev's Challenge*, 109. Gorbachev associates the slogan with de Gaulle in his memoirs, *Zhizn' i reformy*, vol. 2 (Moscow, 1995), 194.

about his overall views.[43] This was true, in fact, of Gorbachev's approach to his more conservative colleagues in the political leadership (such as Ligachev and Ryzhkov) as well.[44] "Not once in my memory," wrote Akhromeev, "did M. S. Gorbachev thoroughly discuss with the military leadership the military-political situation in Europe and perspectives on its development during 1986–1988." Only "in relation to concrete decisions already taken did the military introduce proposals concerning the armed forces."[45]

Akhromeev reports that Gorbachev repeatedly insisted that the military give up its monopoly on analysis of security affairs: "We value your opinion as professionals, as theoreticians and practitioners of military affairs," argued Gorbachev. "But you, as the interested parties, try to arrange things so that the problem gets resolved the way you propose. Let's listen to the opinions of others, including politicians and scholars." Akhromeev agreed "in principle," but he sincerely believed that the military "as the people responsible for the country's defense, were the most competent in these matters."[46]

Akhromeev suggests that Gorbachev knew what kind of reaction he would receive from the military if he forthrightly revealed his proposals for reductions, retrenchment, and restructuring. Gorbachev's policy would have been revealed as a radical break with "the entire understanding by the military leadership of the essence of the country's defense capability in Europe." Withdrawal from Eastern Europe meant giving up "that which had been won at a cost of enormous amounts of blood and millions of lives."[47] In an interview conducted four years after the marshal's death, his widow Tamara Vasil'evna summarized the sources of her husband's resistance to Gorbachev's reforms: "Sergei Fedorovich [Akhromeev] understood that Gorbachev's policy would lead to the breakup of the Warsaw Pact, the whole system of security in Europe. He considered his participation in the creation [of that system] his life's work. . . . Having left the General Staff, he couldn't work as Gorbachev's adviser for very long. He wrote several letters of resignation."[48]

The Role of the Economy in Perspective. There is no doubt that the desire to improve the Soviet economy lay behind all of Gorbachev's security policy initiatives, including the unilateral reduction in conventional forces. Other leaders, however, including those in the military, were initially more sanguine about the state of the economy and less motivated to challenge existing

43. Akhromeev and Kornienko, *Glazami*, 69.
44. Vorotnikov, *A bylo tak*, 41, 192–193; Vadim Medvedev, *V Komande Gorbacheva: Vzgliad iznutri* (Moscow, 1994), 72; Yegor Ligachev, *Inside Gorbachev's Kremlin* (New York, 1993).
45. Akhromeev and Kornienko, *Glazami*, 70–71.
46. Ibid., 72.
47. Ibid., 70–71.
48. Tamara Vasil'evna Akhromeeva, "Ia nikogda ne poveriu, chto on ukhodil na smert'. . . ," *Sovershenno sekretno*, 1995, no. 7:16–17.

priorities. It was only after the perestroika reforms began undermining the basis for the old command-administrative economy in 1988 that the military leaders and Gorbachev's more conservative political colleagues came around to accepting the necessity for major unilateral cuts in military forces and spending—because the weakened economy could no longer sustain the burden.[49] Even so, they never signed on to the broader implications of the posture of "nonoffensive defense" and common security—that the Soviet Union renounce the use of its military forces to impose its political system on neighboring countries in Eastern Europe, and that those countries would be given "freedom of choice," including the choice of disbanding the Warsaw Pact and requesting Soviet troops to leave their territory.

It is clear, then, that by 1988 economic conditions helped convince Soviet skeptics of the need to reduce conventional forces—even, if necessary, unilaterally. Less plausible, though, are the arguments that demographic constraints dictated the changes or that the "new thinking" was simply the product of the military's advocacy of a breathing space during which the Soviet economy could gear up to develop advanced-technology conventional weapons. Given the range of views on the state of the Soviet economy, the level of Soviet technology, and the nature of the military threat to the USSR, economic conditions served to bolster the arguments of the reformers, but they did not dictate any particular outcome. Nor do economic factors explain in any way the adoption of "nonoffensive defense" and "reasonable sufficiency" as the new orientation for a reduced Soviet military. The same indeterminacy of outcome is true of explanations that focus on U.S. behavior.

U.S. Behavior

Many analysts have sought to account for the retrenchment and restructuring of Soviet conventional forces by arguing that U.S. behavior induced Soviet restraint. In particular, proponents of this explanation argue that "negotiation from strength" encouraged Soviet concessions.[50] One can look not only at U.S. negotiating behavior but also at U.S. military programs for evidence that the United States contributed to the changes in Soviet policy. For the case of the conventional-force reductions and restructuring, the U.S. military programs appear to have had more influence than U.S. negotiating tactics, but neither constitutes an entirely satisfactory or sufficient explanation for Soviet behavior.

49. By the beginning of 1988, Akhromeev argues, he and his colleagues in the General Staff "began to realize the necessity and the possibility" of "unilateral reductions of our armed forces"—even though they had not yet received a specific assignment to study them and did not propose any initiatives on their own. Akhromeev and Kornienko, *Glazami*, 72–73.

50. For a typical account that gives Ronald Reagan credit for the rise of Gorbachev and the change in Soviet policy, see John Lewis Gaddis, "Hanging Tough Paid Off," *Bulletin of the Atomic Scientists* 45, 1 (January 1989): 11–14. For a contrasting view that emphasizes internal Soviet changes and their effect on U.S. policy, see Gail W. Lapidus and Alexander Dallin, "The Pacification of Ronald Reagan," ibid., 14–17.

It is difficult to argue that the United States, in the negotiations on conventional forces that preceded Gorbachev's 1988 announcement of a unilateral troop reduction, bargained from strength. On the contrary, throughout the fifteen years of MBFR negotiations in Vienna the United States insisted that the Soviet Union was superior in most important indices of conventional military power (even though anyone could see that the Soviet forces suffered one fundamental weakness: their main task was military occupation of an involuntary alliance of potentially hostile neighbors). One of the main stumbling blocks in the negotiations themselves was the question of the degree of numerical disparity between NATO and Warsaw Pact forces; the Soviets would not present sufficient data to convince the West that its estimates were too high.

Outside of the negotiating room, one could argue, U.S. behavior did have an impact on subsequent Soviet decisions for restraint. Particularly worth mentioning in this context are the U.S. deployment of cruise and Pershing II missiles and NATO's adoption of the Follow-On Forces Attack program for developing advanced-technology conventional weapons. Soviet military theorists closely followed these initiatives and pondered their implications for Soviet military strategy. The Pershing II, with its reportedly high accuracy and short flight time, appeared especially threatening to the command and control of Soviet conventional operations. The new technologies associated with FOFA were claimed to blur the distinction between offense and defense, but, in any case, to portend problems for Soviet offensive operations. The eventual outcome of these U.S. and NATO initiatives—unilateral reductions in the Soviet armed forces and a commitment to restructure them in a defensive orientation—cannot, however, be understood strictly in terms of a rational response to external stimuli. Like much else in Soviet policy, the outcome was indeterminate. It was the result of an internal debate, in which participants from all sides cited the Western initiatives to bolster their case.

The initial Soviet response to the hard-line policies of the Reagan administration—the deployment of new missiles in Europe, the offensive orientation in NATO strategy, and the technological challenge represented not only by FOFA but especially by the Strategic Defense Initiative—was anything but conciliatory.[51] Soviet policy hardened, as Moscow broke off arms negotiations in the wake of the Pershing II and cruise missile deployments in late 1983, and the military's demands for more resources to compete in the technological arms race became increasingly strident.[52] There was nothing inevitable about the shift to a more conciliatory Soviet policy starting in 1985.

It was only as Gorbachev consolidated power that civilian reformers began

51. For the close analysis of the internal debates, see Bruce Parrott, "Soviet National Security under Gorbachev," *Problems of Communism* 37, 6 (1988): 1–36.

52. See, for example, the booklet by the former chief of the Soviet General Staff Marshal Nikolai Ogarkov, *Istoriia uchit bditel'nosti* (Moscow, 1985), and the discussion in Parrott, "Soviet National Security."

to reinterpret the actions of NATO and the United States, and to draw attention to the increasingly deleterious effects of high Soviet military spending. At that point the possibility for unilateral Soviet restraint arose. In these efforts, the Soviet reformers received important help from like-minded individuals and groups in the West. It was not the Soviet military or Gorbachev's conservative Politburo colleagues but the transnational disarmament community that provided the Soviet leader with ideas for initiatives that would have the greatest impact on the West. "He knew from all of these contacts what he had to do," according to Ambassador Jonathan Dean, for many years the senior U.S. negotiator on conventional forces in Europe.[53]

TRANSNATIONAL NETWORKS AND CONVENTIONAL FORCES

Despite the superficial similarity between the Soviet military's revived interest in defensive operations in the 1980s and Gorbachev's rhetoric about nonoffensive defense, the latter was not simply a consequence of the former. Gorbachev's interest in defense stemmed more from the influence of his civilian advisers, who, in turn, drew their inspiration from foreign analysts working on concepts of alternative security. The foreigners—mainly Western European peace researchers—and the Soviet civilian reformers were tacit members of a transnational network that advocated reform of Soviet and Western military postures to reduce Cold War tensions in Europe and lower the risk of war. Through multiple channels, described in Chapter 9, Western views about alternative defense and common security made their way into the Soviet debate. The civilian reformers took advantage of similarities between the transnational proposals and some military analysts' reevaluation of defense whenever they could. Here the role of Andrei Kokoshin and his reform-minded colleagues in the armed forces was especially important.[54] But the most significant accomplishment of the civilian reformers consisted not in convincing the military high command to embrace the concepts of common security and nonoffensive defense—they never did so. Rather it was in convincing key political leaders of the wisdom of their reformist ideas that the transnational disarmament activists exerted influence on Soviet security policy and contributed to the end of the Cold War.

Social Democracy and Common Security

The first change occurred in the overall conceptualization of the Soviet security dilemma. Soviet reformers came to recognize that many Soviet actions

---

53. Dean, interview.
54. On the military reformers, see Eugene B. Rumer, *The End of a Monolith: The Politics of Military Reform in the Soviet Armed Forces*, RAND Corporation report R-3993-USDP (Santa Monica, Calif., 1990); and Kimberly Marten Zisk, *Engaging the Enemy: Organization Theory and Soviet Military Innovation: 1955–1991* (Princeton, N.J., 1993), 161–164.

appeared threatening to the West, even if they were motivated by defensive concerns. They noticed, for example, that even those in the West who were sensitive to Soviet security interests—for example, members of European peace movements—remained sharply critical of Soviet weapons deployments and military activity beyond Soviet borders, not to mention the Soviet Union's treatment of its own independent peace activists.[55] In this respect the fact that European public opinion opposed Soviet SS-20 missiles as well as U.S. cruise and Pershing II missiles may have had as much influence on the subsequent course of events as the actual deployment of new U.S. weapons in Europe.[56] By the same token, the new offense-oriented NATO strategies and proposed weapons in themselves would not have produced the shift in the Soviet military posture that took place in the late 1980s without the influence of alternative proposals for nonoffensive defense that were developed in the European peace research community years before.

Quite early, Gorbachev's reformist advisers managed to get the new general secretary's endorsement of the fundamentals of common security, as outlined in the 1982 Palme Commission report on disarmament. Given Gorbachev's recognition that something was seriously wrong with Soviet foreign policy, and his relatively open mind, it is not surprising that he would be sympathetic to common security.[57] The Russian translation of the Palme Commission report was published shortly after the English version in 1982, and many Soviet scholars and diplomats were familiar with its basic message. Gorbachev heard about the commission's work directly from its leading Soviet representative, Georgii Arbatov.[58] Moreover Soviet political leaders and diplomats heard variants on that message repeated constantly in their contacts with European officials and scholars. As Thomas Risse points out, "by the time Gorbachev came into power, common security was one of the mainstream foreign policy concepts in Europe."[59]

Gorbachev himself had a certain affinity for the Western European social democrats. He felt that he could communicate more openly with them than with the "bourgeois" representatives of Western governments.[60] Moreover, he remarked on the similarity of their views on "the topical issues of interna-

55. See, for example, the following essays by E. P. Thompson in his collection, *The Heavy Dancers* (New York, 1985): "The Soviet 'Peace Offensive,'" 13–20; "The Soviet Union: Détente and Dissent," 121–134; and "Acting as Free Persons," 255–294; and Jean Stead and Danielle Grünberg, *Moscow Independent Peace Group* (London, 1982).

56. Cherniaev, *Shest' let*, 107; Mikhail Gorbachev, *Zhizn' i reformy*, 2:58–59. The universal condemnation of the Soviet invasion of Afghanistan had a similar impact on official Soviet thinking about what was necessary to bring the "peace-loving forces" of the world to adopt a more supportive attitude toward Soviet foreign policy. See A. S. Cherniaev, *Moia zhizn' i moe vremia* (Moscow, 1995), chap. 10.

57. Janice Gross Stein, "Political Learning by Doing: Gorbachev as Uncommitted Thinker and Motivated Learner," *International Organization* 48, 2 (Spring 1994): 155–183.

58. A. S. Cherniaev, interview by author, Moscow, 5 June 1997.

59. Thomas Risse-Kappen, "Ideas Do Not Float Freely: Transnational Coalitions, Domestic Structures, and the End of the Cold War," *International Organization* 48, 2 (Spring 1994): 197.

60. Gorbachev, *Zhizn' i reformy*, 2:210, 483–484; Cherniaev, *Shest' let*, 102.

tional security and disarmament."[61] Gorbachev's advisers—who also often found it easier to deal with the social democrats than with even the "friends" in the international communist movement—sought to achieve their leader's endorsement of the whole package of views associated with common security. They relied on symbolic as well as practical means. When Olof Palme was assassinated in March 1986, for example, Arbatov and Gorbachev's foreign-policy aide Anatolii Cherniaev convinced Gorbachev to instruct the delegates to the Twenty-seventh Congress of the Soviet Communist Party to observe a moment of silence in Palme's honor. This was "an unprecedented thing," according to Cherniaev, because Palme, as a social democrat, was, in traditional Soviet thinking, considered an "ideological opponent" of communism.[62] By publicly honoring Palme, Gorbachev also paved the way for acceptance of his ideas.[63]

Peace Research and Nonoffensive Defense

In addition to broad notions of common security and the links between conventional and nuclear disarmament, Soviet analysts also learned from their Western interlocutors about various proposals for alternative defense. Interest in nonoffensive defense among Western European peace researchers dates at least back to the 1960s, but it attracted considerable interest in the early 1980s as concern about the risk of nuclear war in Europe increased. As described in Chapter 8, Soviet academic specialists were familiar with Western European projects on nonoffensive defense well before Gorbachev came into office. Again, the Palme Commission deserves considerable credit. As Andrei Kokoshin has written, the commission's report was "largely instrumental in providing a favorable climate for such projects," although that climate did not really emerge until three years after the report's publication—coincident with Gorbachev's rise to power.[64]

As soon as Gorbachev opened the "policy window" and signaled his interest in a new direction for Soviet foreign policy, the proponents of alternative security began promoting their ideas.

Kokoshin and the Military Reformers. Consider, for example, Andrei Kokoshin's work in support of nonoffensive defense. Within months of Gorbachev's advent to power Kokoshin published a favorable discussion of the

---

61. M. S. Gorbachev, *Perestroika i novoe myshlenie dlia nashei strany i dlia vsego mira* (Moscow, 1987), 217.
62. Cherniaev, *Shest' let*, 66. Later Cherniaev remarked with some amusement that the person chairing the meeting that honored Palme was Viktor Chebrikov, the KGB chief. Cherniaev, interview. On relations with the social democrats and the "friends," see Cherniaev, *Moia zhizn'*, 239, 304; and G. A. Arbatov, *Zatianuvsheesia vyzdorovlenie (1953–1985 gg.): Svidetel'stvo sovremennika* (Moscow, 1991), 213–214.
63. In his memoirs, Gorbachev reports that he was deeply shaken by the news of Palme's murder: Gorbachev, *Zhizn' i reformy*, 2:210.
64. Andrei Kokoshin, "Defense Is Best for Stability," *New Times*, no. 33 (1988), 18–19.

subject in the journal of the USSR Academy of Sciences Institute of the USA and Canada.[65] Particularly significant was the context of Kokoshin's remarks. His article addressed the so-called Rogers Plan (named after then NATO commander General Bernard Rogers) for reorienting NATO strategy to stress attacks against Soviet second- and third-echelon forces (Follow-On Forces Attack). Kokoshin contrasted official NATO plans for a more offense-oriented conventional posture to alternative ideas for nonoffensive defense. He summarized the main points of the Western critiques of FOFA, including the suggestion that probable Soviet countermeasures would, along with the new NATO strategy itself, contribute to a further destabilization of the situation in Europe.[66] Thus, at a time when many U.S. analysts predicted with equanimity that the Soviets would respond to initiatives such as FOFA and Air-Land Battle with a renewed emphasis on the offense—and Soviet military writers stressed that offense and defense were becoming indistinguishable—Kokoshin emphasized the need for both sides to adopt more defensive postures.

In his 1985 article, Kokoshin wrote favorably of Soviet unilateral initiatives to reduce the military threat in Europe. Although the example he cited—the withdrawal of twenty thousand Soviet troops from East Germany in 1979–80—had been dismissed by the West at the time as insignificant, for a Soviet scholar publicly to advocate unilateralism in 1985 was unusual. Kokoshin concluded his article on an optimistic and controversial note: he argued that the activities of the peace movement in Europe (despite its failure to stop the deployment of new U.S. missiles), and the development of new ideas about alternative security, improved the prospects for preventing war—and this at a time when there was no sign yet from the United States that the West would contribute to an improvement in the international climate, and when top military and political figures in the Soviet Union expressed considerable distrust of Western intentions.[67]

During the next three years, Kokoshin actively promoted proposals for nonoffensive defense with sophisticated historical and theoretical analyses, several of them coauthored with retired General V. V. Larionov.[68] He also served as an informal adviser to the government on conventional-force nego-

65. A. A. Kokoshin, "'Plan Rodzhersa,' al'ternativnye kontseptsii oborony i bezopasnost' v Evrope," *SShA: ekonomika, politika, ideologiia*, 1985, no. 9:3–14. I am grateful to Kimberly Zisk for calling my attention to this article.

66. See ibid., esp., 10.

67. Kokoshin, "'Plan Rodzhersa,'" 14.

68. Andrei A. Kokoshin, "Razvitie voennogo dela i sokrashchenie vooruzhennykh sil i obychnykh vooruzhenii," *Mirovaia ekonomika i mezhdunarodnye otnosheniia* [World economy and international relations], 1988, no. 1:20–32; Andrei A. Kokoshin and Valentin V. Larionov, "Protivostoianie sil obshchego naznacheniia v kontekste obespecheniia strategicheskoi stabil'nosti," *Mirovaia ekonomika i mezhdunarodnye otnosheniia*, 1988, no.6:23–30; Kokoshin and Larionov, "Kurskaia bitva v svete sovremennoi oboronitel'noi doktriny," *Mirovaia ekonomika i mezhdunarodnye otnosheniia*, 1988, no. 8:32–40; Kokoshin and Larionov, *Predotvrashchenie voiny: Doktriny, konsteptsii, perspektivy* (Moscow, 1990).

tiations. He contributed, for example, to the formulation of important declarations by the Soviet Union and its allies in the Warsaw Treaty Organization (WTO) issued in Budapest in 1986 and in Berlin in 1987.[69] The Berlin declaration of May 1987 described Soviet military doctrine as "subordinated to the task of preventing war, nuclear and conventional."[70] Kokoshin later described the significance of this document in a study of Soviet military strategy that was published in 1995 during his tenure as Russia's first deputy minister of defense. He calls particular attention to the Berlin declaration's proposal for "reduction in Europe of armed forces and conventional weapons to the level at which neither side, in guaranteeing its own defense, will have the means for sudden attack on another country or for the deployment of offensive operations in general."[71]

In addition to their contribution to such broad statements of policy, civilian reformers increasingly sought to play a more active role in the technical and strategic analysis of military affairs. They were particularly intent on challenging the Soviet military's monopoly of expertise in the area of conventional forces. For as Kokoshin pointed out, Soviet military strategists, even in the wake of the Berlin declaration, were inclined to argue that as long as their country's overall military-political orientation was defensive, there was nothing wrong with a military strategy that followed the motto "The best defense is a good offense." Even when pressed by political authorities, the high command resisted making meaningful changes in military operations to stress the defense. As Dmitrii Iazov, the Soviet defense minister, argued in 1987, "it is impossible using only defense to destroy the aggressor. For that reason, after repelling an attack the troops and naval forces should be ready to carry out a decisive offensive. The transition to it will take the form of a counteroffensive."[72]

Kokoshin argued that Soviet military theorists and leaders were late in facing the fact that it was "abnormal" to have "the political part of military doctrine bear a defensive character, but the military part an offensive one."[73] The civilian reformers stepped into the breach to try to reshape the military component of Soviet conventional-force posture toward Europe.

IMEMO *and the Nuclear-Conventional Nexus.* One early product of those efforts was *Disarmament and Security 1986,* a yearbook produced at the Institute of the World Economy and International Relations (IMEMO) by a team led by

69. Zisk, *Engaging the Enemy,* 161–164.

70. For an assessment of the declaration, see ibid. and Raymond L. Garthoff, "New Thinking in Soviet Military Doctrine," *Washington Quarterly* 11, 3 (Summer 1988): 137. The argument that Kokoshin contributed to the declaration is found in Eberhard Schneider, "Soviet Foreign-Policy Think Tanks," *Washington Quarterly* 11, 2 (Spring 1988): 154.

71. A. A. Kokoshin, *Armiia i politika: Sovetskaia voenno-politicheskaia i voenno-strategicheskaia mysl', 1918–1991 gody* (Moscow, 1995), 230–231.

72. D. T. Iazov, *Na strazhe mira i sotsializma* (Moscow, 1987), 33, quoted in ibid., 233.

73. Kokoshin, *Armiia i politika,* 232.

Aleksei Arbatov and including Kokoshin. It was modeled on the publications of the Stockholm International Peace Research Institute and the International Institute for Strategic Studies in London. The chapters on European security clearly show the influence of transnational discussions and in many respects mark a sharp break from traditional Soviet thinking as well as the contemporary views of the Soviet Ministry of Defense. The authors anticipated, and helped to promote, several official Soviet initiatives on conventional forces.

The IMEMO analysis of European security formed a framework for advancing new Soviet proposals and concessions. As their predecessors did during the ABM debates of the 1960s, these Soviet analysts adopted the language and concepts of the Western strategic discourse. In the jargon of the time they wrote of various "levels" of conflict, from the strategic nuclear level, through the tactical nuclear level, down to the level of the conventional military balance in Europe. In the U.S. debate, hawkish analysts often used this framework to complain that the Soviet achievement of "parity" with the United States at the strategic nuclear level had made disparities at the lower levels dangerous, at least when the disparities favored the Soviet side. Such analysts typically prescribed a U.S. military buildup to compensate. The IMEMO authors took a different tack. Although they acknowledged that the USSR enjoyed certain advantages (still somewhat rare in the official Soviet discourse of the time), they stressed the need to anticipate and avoid a conventional arms race.[74]

The IMEMO authors argued that major conventional arms limitations were a prerequisite for reducing nuclear weapons, especially at the tactical or battlefield level.[75] This argument resembles the emphasis that Egon Bahr, Randall Forsberg, and others had put on the need to understand the links between nuclear weapons and deterrence of conventional war.[76] Although the argument was often made in the West as a way of rationalizing a continuing nuclear arms race, Arbatov and his colleagues used it as Forsberg had done—as a way of understanding the barriers to nuclear disarmament in order to overcome them. Such arguments made a profound effect on Eduard Shevardnadze, who came into his job as foreign minister in July 1985 with no experience or background in security affairs.[77]

The IMEMO chapter on conventional forces contained the seeds of much of subsequent Soviet proposals and unilateral initiatives. At the same time, it called attention to developments that were preoccupying the Soviet military, but it interpreted them to enhance the prospects for a disarmament agree-

---

74. *Disarmament and Security 1986*, Yearbook of IMEMO, USSR Academy of Sciences (Moscow, 1987), 1:190–191.

75. Ibid., 196.

76. See, e.g., Randall Forsberg, "Parallel Cuts in Nuclear and Conventional Forces," *Bulletin of the Atomic Scientists* (August 1985): 152–156.

77. Shevardnadze, *Moi vybor*, 166–167.

ment. For example, the authors wrote, as Soviet military theorists had done, of the impact of new technologies in eroding "the traditional boundaries between offensive and defensive operations." But they used this point to emphasize the urgency of coming to a conventional-force agreement while it was still possible to determine the criteria for a force posture of "sufficient defense."[78] The arms agreement they advocated would focus on the forces most suitable for offensive operations and lead to disproportionate reductions on the Soviet side. At the time the authors were writing, Gorbachev had proposed that each side reduce the types of forces in which it had superiority, but without particular regard for the nature of the weapons. From the standpoint of theories of nonoffensive defense, however, it makes no sense to eliminate all asymmetries; rather, one should eliminate only those that favor the offense over the defense. The IMEMO authors presented a favorable review of Western concepts of nonoffensive defense in order to draw the conclusion that reduction of offensive systems should be accorded priority.[79] Many of the systems they mentioned—such as heavy artillery, armored formations, and bridge-crossing equipment—figured prominently in the unilateral Soviet reductions that were announced in December 1988.[80]

In their discussion of the history and status of conventional-force negotiations (the MBFR talks in Vienna), the authors were pessimistic that any meaningful reductions would take place. Even if there were instant agreement on either side's proposals, the cuts envisioned were mainly symbolic. Thus, at the same time the authors discuss the "tremendous economic importance" of implementing major conventional reductions, they assess the prospects for achieving such cuts under the old format as quite bleak.[81] The implications, then, are clear—even if not made quite explicit. To achieve substantial economic benefit from conventional disarmament, either the Soviet Union must revise its negotiating position dramatically in order to get the West to agree to a treaty, or it must carry out reductions unilaterally. In the event, Gorbachev chose to do both, making precisely the same sort of argument to his potentially skeptical Politburo colleagues: why should we hold the economic benefits from disarmament hostage to negotiations with the United States?

Here it is worth noting that the IMEMO authors' stress on the economic burden of the arms race and the economic advantages of disarmament predate the Soviet government's decision to reduce the military budget in 1988. Perhaps encouraged by the apparent success of their ventures into military

---

78. *Disarmament and Security 1986*, 1: 202–206.
79. For an analysis that takes this position to its logical conclusion—a "zero option" for tanks—see Vitaly Shlykov, "'Strong is the Armour . . . ': Tank Asymmetry and Real Security," *International Affairs*, 1988, no. 12:37–48. This article, too, was written before Gorbachev's announcement of unilateral cutbacks.
80. *Disarmament and Security 1986*, 1:218–224.
81. Ibid., 210–218.

analysis, Arbatov and his colleagues continued to promote unilateral restructuring of Soviet conventional and nuclear forces on the basis of their assessment of "reasonable sufficiency."[82] In doing so, they provoked the wrath of some members of the Soviet armed forces—including General Mikhail Moiseev, Akhromeev's successor as chief of the General Staff—who challenged their competence and otherwise expressed displeasure at the civilians' interference in the military's domain.[83]

Transnational Influence on Soviet Proposals. By 1987, the Soviet military was already fighting a rearguard action in its attempts to restrict civilian influence on military policy. Top Soviet leaders such as Gorbachev, Shevardnadze, and Iakovlev had welcomed not only the views of Soviet civilians but of international experts as well. On 4 February 1987, for example, in a speech in Munich, Egon Bahr drew on his work in the Palme Commission to propose a corridor along the border between West Germany and Czechoslovakia and East Germany free of offensive weapons. Less than two weeks later, addressing an international peace forum in Moscow, Gorbachev "submitted an almost identical plan."[84]

Members of the Pugwash movement played particularly important roles in attracting Gorbachev's interest in defensive restructuring of conventional forces. Pugwash was well respected in the Soviet Union for its work on the nuclear arms race. Its involvement in the area of alternative conventional defense gave the subject a certain credibility within the governments of the USSR and its allies.[85] In February 1987, at the suggestion of Frank von Hippel of the Federation of American Scientists, Evgenii Velikhov invited three key theorists of alternative defense, Anders Boserup, Robert Neild, and Albrecht von Mueller—all members of the Pugwash Study Group on Conventional Forces in Europe—to attend the international forum on disarmament in Moscow, where Gorbachev presented the proposal based on Bahr's work.[86] The Pugwash experts wanted the Soviet Union to go further and commit to defensive restructuring to reduce Soviet offensive capabilities. Von Hippel promoted these ideas in his own address to the forum participants, who included Gorbachev and other senior Soviet officials.[87]

Boserup, Neild, and von Mueller made a favorable impression on their So-

82. For subsequent proposals, see: Aleksei Arbatov, "Parity and Reasonable Sufficiency," *International Affairs*, 1988, no. 10; Aleksei Arbatov, "How Much Defence Is Sufficient?" *International Affairs*, 1989, no. 4.

83. Moiseev, "Eshche raz o prestizhe armii."

84. Stephan Kux, "Western Peace Research and Soviet Military Thought" (Department of Political Science, Columbia University, 20 April 1989), 10.

85. Vitalii Goldanskii, quoted in the *F.A.S. Public Interest Report* 40, 8 (October 1987): 9.

86. The following discussion draws on Frank von Hippel, interview by author, Princeton, N.J., 2 May 1991.

87. Frank von Hippel, "A U.S. Scientist Addresses Gorbachev," *Bulletin of the Atomic Scientists* 43, 4 (May 1987): 12–13.

viet hosts, and they were invited back two months later, in April 1987. This time they met with Andrei Kokoshin and Lev Mendelevich. Mendelevich, then director of the Foreign Ministry's Evaluations and Planning Directorate, knew Boserup from his previous job as Soviet ambassador to Denmark (see Chapter 9). Kokoshin and Mendelevich urged their Western visitors to write a letter to Gorbachev. In the meantime Boserup was offered the opportunity to present his proposals to a wider Soviet audience by publishing an article in a Soviet journal that was becoming a major forum for debates on security policy and disarmament.[88]

In October 1987, Boserup, Neild, von Mueller, and von Hippel wrote to Gorbachev to present both the underlying theory behind nonoffensive defense and some specific proposals for the upcoming talks in Vienna. They particularly stressed the link between restructuring and nuclear disarmament: "Reductions of the current forces without changes in their composition would preserve their offensive structure and the associated fears of aggression and therefore would perpetuate the justification for relying on nuclear weapons in Europe." They tried to encourage and reassure Gorbachev about the need for disproportionate cuts on the Soviet side: "Although the reductions required to reach equality will be unequal, the security of both sides will be increased." Gorbachev replied three weeks later, writing that the scientists' analysis was "very close to our understanding of the problem." In fact, he had fully embraced the concept of "nonoffensive defense," arguing that both sides should have no "more military strength and armaments than is necessary for their reliable defense" and that their armed forces should be "structured in such a way that they will provide all that is needed for the repulsion of any possible aggression but could not be used for offensive purposes." Gorbachev assured the Pugwash experts that in the course of preparing for the forthcoming negotiations "we will pay great attention to the concrete ideas laid out in the memorandum attached to your letter."[89]

In April 1988 the Soviet Foreign Ministry commissioned a working group from IMEMO to formulate a proposal for conventional-force reductions, drawing on transnational ideas for nonoffensive defense. Representatives from the Defense Ministry were invited to participate, but they declined.[90] In July 1988, Gorbachev instructed the General Staff to carry out its own study of a major cut in conventional forces.[91] It examined the possibility of reductions in the range of 300,000 to 700,000 soldiers.[92]

---

88. Anders Boserup, "Road to Trust: Non-Aggressive Defense," *XX Century and Peace*, no. 8 (August 1987), cited in Kux, "Western Peace Research," 10. On the importance of the journal to internal debates: Gennadii Koloskov of IMEMO, interview by author, Ann Arbor, Mich., 19 October 1990.

89. Both the letter to Gorbachev of 10 October 1987 and his reply of 16 November 1987 are reprinted in *F.A.S. Public Interest Report* 41, 2 (February 1988), 14–15.

90. Koloskov, interview.

91. Don Oberdorfer, *The Turn: From the Cold War to a New Era* (New York, 1992), 319.

92. Akhromeev and Kornienko, *Glazami*, 212.

Members of the IMEMO group favored more radical, unilateral cuts—on the order of a million troops. They were emboldened by the surprising success of the INF Treaty, which required far more reductions of missiles on the Soviet side than on the U.S. side, as well as intrusive on-site inspections, but which, nevertheless, was ratified by the Supreme Soviet (parliament).[93] The treaty set a precedent in another respect. Two leading Western arms control specialists, Bahr and von Hippel, were invited to testify to the Supreme Soviet in support of its ratification.[94] Both were advocates of conventional-force reductions, and both took the occasion of their visit to reassert the connection between nuclear disarmament and the need for defensive restructuring.

The summer and autumn of 1988 was a particularly active time for promotion of Western ideas on defensive restructuring. During the summer, just as the General Staff was beginning its work analyzing the possibility of reductions, the IMEMO group presented a memorandum of its proposals to Shevardnadze and Iakovlev. In September 1988, Randall Forsberg, director of the Boston-based Institute for Defense and Disarmament Studies (IDDS) and two of her colleagues—Frank von Hippel and retired U.S. ambassador Jonathan Dean—held a joint seminar on conventional-force reductions with IMEMO experts in Moscow and met with military advisers to the Central Committee.[95] Forsberg was especially interested in promoting the ideas of the Study Group on Alternative Security Policy (Studiengruppe Alternative Sicherheitspolitik), founded in West Germany in 1980 by Lutz Unterseher.[96] Unterseher's work became particularly influential in Kokoshin's thinking about defense.[97] Forsberg, a founder of the Nuclear Freeze movement and a major theorist of alternative security policy, was well respected in the community of Soviet academic specialists on military policy, many of whom she had known since at least the early 1980s.[98]

In its September meetings, the members of Forsberg's delegation encouraged the Soviet side to take some unilateral initiatives to improve the atmo-

93. Aleksei Arbatov, interview by author, Washington D.C., 10 June 1991.

94. TASS report, 24 March 1988, cited in Kux, "Western Peace Research," 10.

95. Other U.S. participants included William Miller, president of the American Committee on U.S.-Soviet Relations; Stanley Resor, former U.S. secretary of the Army and head of the U.S. delegation to the MBFR talks from 1973 to 1978; Edward Warner III of the RAND Corporation. "Joint US-Soviet Seminar on Conventional Arms Reduction in Europe," *Defense and Disarmament Alternatives* 2, 1 (January 1989): 4.

96. A history of the group and a list of its publications and public presentations are found in Ralph Ströber-Fassbender, *Die Studiengruppe Alternative Sicherheitspolitik: Eine Dokumentation* (Bonn, 1988).

97. Andrei Kokoshin, conversation with author, June 1990. For another Soviet analyst's views on Western work on nonoffensive defense, see "Alternative Defense in the Soviet Union: A Discussion with Alexei Arbatov," Institute for Defense and Disarmament Studies (Brookline, Mass., 4 November 1987), transcript.

98. Randall Forsberg, "The Prospects for Arms Control and Disarmament: A View from Moscow," and "Randall Forsberg Visit to Moscow, 8–18 December 1981: List of Organizations and People Visited," Institute for Defense and Disarmament Studies (Brookline, Mass., n.d. [early 1982]).

sphere and build political momentum for the upcoming negotiations on conventional forces. They specifically proposed a unilateral reduction of one thousand tanks, a rather modest suggestion compared to what Gorbachev ultimately announced. Nevertheless, their Soviet colleagues were cautious and unreceptive to the idea of a unilateral initiative. They did, however, readily agree that any future reductions should emphasize offensive weapons and entail defensive restructuring.[99]

In October 1988 Anders Boserup was in Moscow again to discuss conventional-force issues with high-ranking officials from the Foreign Ministry and the Central Committee and with academic analysts, including Aleksei Arbatov and Sergei Karaganov.[100] Among the senior Soviet participants were veteran arms negotiator Oleg Grinevskii; Lieutenant General Viktor Starodubov, an arms control expert in the Central Committee's International Department; and Vladimir Shustov, head of the Foreign Ministry's Scientific Coordination Center and an outspoken proponent of transnational efforts to develop new concepts for security policy.[101] Shustov later credited the civilian analysts with playing an important role in the actual negotiations that produced the Treaty on Conventional Forces in Europe in November 1990.[102]

GORBACHEV AT THE UNITED NATIONS: A TRANSNATIONAL VICTORY

Even as Gorbachev's policy of glasnost and "new thinking" on foreign policy was slowly expanded to encompass military affairs in 1987, the number of Soviet analysts willing publicly to advocate unilateral disarmament could be counted on the fingers of one hand.[103] They faced harsh criticism from the "old thinkers" in the army.[104] Foreign activists and specialists were understandably more forthcoming with proposals for unilateral Soviet disarmament—and promises to persuade their governments to reciprocate. Even though such promises were rarely fulfilled (Western governments turned out to be less susceptible to transnational influence than the Soviet one), Gorbachev still valued the proposals. As he wrote to Frank von Hippel and

---

99. "Joint US-Soviet Seminar," 4–10; von Hippel, interview.
100. "Report on Moscow IGCC Conference, 2–8 October 1988," *Defense and Disarmament Alternatives* 2, 1 (January 1989): 10.
101. Vladimir Shustov, "Diplomacy and Science," *International Affairs*, 1990, no. 4:13–23.
102. Vladimir Shustov, comments at a meeting in Moscow, 12 November 1990, from my notes, and ibid., 21. Jonathan Dean, in my interview with him, also called attention to Shustov's interest in involving transnational organizations in the problem of conventional arms control.
103. The key statement was by Vitaly Zhurkin, Sergei Karaganov, and Andrei Kortunov, "Reasonable sufficiency—or how to break the vicious circle," *New Times*, no. 40 (1987): 13–15.
104. General Ivan Tret'iak, "Reliable Defense, First and Foremost," *Moscow News*, 1988, no. 8:12. For an overview of the state of debate on this and related issues, see Thomas Nichols and Theodore Krasik, "Civil-Military Relations under Gorbachev: The Struggle over National Security," in William C. Green and Theodore Krasik, eds., *Gorbachev and His Generals: The Reform of Soviet Military Doctrine* (Boulder, Colo., 1990).

his colleagues in November 1987, "I want to underline again that we attach great significance to the active participation of learned people in seeking solutions to what are the most pressing military-political and international problems."[105]

Thus, Gorbachev's announcement of a substantial unilateral reduction of Soviet conventional forces, delivered in a speech to the United Nations in December 1988, marked a clear victory for the transnational alliance of supporters of alternative security. Gorbachev began his address with a statement that received relatively little attention at the time compared to his announcement of the unilateral cuts. He stated that "the use or threat of force no longer can or must be an instrument of foreign policy." With clear reference to past Soviet policies toward Eastern Europe, he claimed that "all of us, and primarily the stronger of us, must exercise self-restraint and totally rule out an outward-oriented use of force." He then asked whether this view might "be a little too romantic"—a criticism he had heard from some skeptics "both in our own country and from some of our Western partners." But Gorbachev insisted: "I am convinced that we are not floating above reality."[106]

The transnational disarmament community cannot take credit for Gorbachev's pledge not to intervene militarily in Eastern Europe. His commitment to "the principle of freedom of choice," as he put it in his UN speech, was deeply held and widely shared among his civilian advisers. For most of them the 1968 Soviet invasion of Czechoslovakia to overthrow "socialism with a human face" had been a painful humiliation.[107] The transnational proponents of nonoffensive defense made an important contribution to solidifying Gorbachev's pledge of nonintervention. The unilateral reductions and restructuring that they advocated limited the threat of Soviet attack. In combination with Gorbachev's commitment to "freedom of choice," they set in motion demands from the Warsaw Pact allies for further reductions and ultimately withdrawal of Soviet troops.

It was this limitation of Soviet options for controlling the situation in Eastern Europe that seemed most troubling to the military and conservative political opponents of Gorbachev's reforms.[108] Tamara Akhromeeva was right when she claimed that Gorbachev had ignored her husband's warning that "without a powerful army, 'new thinking' won't be worth anything to anybody." At that point, Marshal Akhromeev ceased to influence the So-

105. Gorbachev to von Hippel, 16 November 1987, reprinted in *F.A.S. Public Interest Report* 41, 2 (February 1988): 15.

106. *New York Times*, 8 December 1988.

107. Cherniaev, *Moia zhizn'*, 264–266; Georgii Shakhnazarov, *Tsena svobody: Reformatsiia Gorbacheva glazami ego pomoshchnika* (Moscow, 1993), 104–106. Shakhnazarov argues that Gorbachev did not come to that realization easily, but Gorbachev's account of his visit to Czechoslovakia in the wake of the Soviet invasion describes an awkward and difficult experience. See Gorbachev, *Zhizn' i reformy*, 1:157–159.

108. Akhromeev and Kornienko, *Glazami*, 65; Falin, *Politische erinnerungen*, 488–489.

viet leader's views on European security. "Gorbachev was listening to other people."[109]

The Politburo Accepts a Fait Accompli

Of course Gorbachev needed the General Staff to implement his proposed restructuring and reductions. As Akhromeev later explained, the military's proposals came only in response "to concrete decisions already taken" by Gorbachev and his allies.[110] Specifically, on 9 November 1988 the Soviet defense council, chaired by Gorbachev, instructed the Defense Ministry to work out a plan for the withdrawal of Soviet troops from Eastern Europe.[111] Thus the military's participation in planning the reductions came long after IMEMO and the Foreign Ministry had persuaded Gorbachev of the merits of a large-scale unilateral withdrawal, combined with a shift to a clearly defensive posture. Finally, armed with the IMEMO-Foreign Ministry proposals and the General Staff's implementation plan, Gorbachev was ready to seek formal approval from his fellow political leaders to launch his unilateral initiative, virtually at the last minute. Anatolii Dobrynin captures well the flavor of the decision process: "Before going to the UN General Assembly in New York in 1988," he recalled, "Gorbachev urgently pushed through the Politburo a bold unilateral reduction of our armed forces by half a million men."[112] To get some idea of the scope of the reduction, consider that the NATO proposals throughout the course of the MBFR negotiations had advocated a Soviet cut of between thirty and seventy thousand, with some compensating Western reductions.[113]

Dobrynin's recollection of Gorbachev's method of "pushing through" the unilateral reduction suggests that there was no consensus in the Kremlin on what to do about the burden of military spending, how to carry out military reforms, or what positions to take in disarmament negotiations. Dobrynin had been invited back to Moscow from his position as ambassador to the United States in March 1986 and put in charge of the Communist Party Central Committee's International Department; but he soon found that he had little to do. Gorbachev was systematically reducing the role of the Party in Soviet life and arrogating control of foreign policy to himself and Shevardnadze. As Dobrynin put it, "when Shevardnadze became foreign minister, fewer papers were presented or discussed. Gorbachev clearly strove to avoid

109. Akhromeeva, "Ia nikogda ne poveriu," 16–17.
110. Akhromeev and Kornienko, *Glazami*, 70–71.
111. Politburo meeting, minutes, 27 December 1988, located in Fond 89, op. 42, doc. 24, TsKhSD, and published in *Istochnik*, 1993, nos. 5–6:130–147.
112. Anatoly Dobrynin, *In Confidence: Moscow's Ambassador to Six Cold War Presidents* (New York, 1995), 626.
113. Richard A. Falkenrath, *Shaping Europe's Military Order: The Origins and Consequences of the CFE Treaty* (Cambridge, Mass., 1995), 24–25.

Politburo guidelines and directives and sought a free hand in dealing with foreign heads of state. Ultimately, with Shevardnadze's help, Gorbachev reached his goal. In fact if not in form, he single-handedly devised the foreign policy of the country and implemented it as well."[114]

Without such centralization of foreign policy, it is unlikely that Gorbachev's initiatives would have succeeded. The resistance from the military and the conservative politicians was strong. In 1991, a senior Foreign Ministry official who worked with Shevardnadze in arranging studies of conventional-force reductions acknowledged that "the unilateral cutbacks were the most difficult issue the diplomats had ever faced with the military, even more touchy than the problems of nuclear arms reductions." In describing the views of senior military officials, Shevardnadze's aide said that for them "nuclear war was really foreign, and they accepted the logic of the cuts. But tanks were something very real, and that was different."[115]

In the wake of Gorbachev's UN speech, the Politburo gave a pro forma endorsement of the disarmament initiative. But Shevardnadze was worried that despite the seemingly unanimous support for the unilateral reductions, opponents would sabotage the initiative at the implementation stage. Shevardnadze was particularly upset about efforts by the Defense Ministry to reinterpret Gorbachev's policy of defensive restructuring to fit its own views and interests.

At the Politburo meeting he expressed his concerns in the bluntest manner. The military's position "directly contradicts what was said from the tribune" by Gorbachev at the UN. "I have in mind the formulation of the Defense Ministry that the troops remaining on the territory of the socialist countries after the reductions will be given a 'large'—and, I stress—'large' defensive 'tendency' (*napravelennost'*). These are only words, but they have principled significance. Comrade Gorbachev spoke of giving these forces a different, exclusively (*odnoznachno*) defensive *structure*." The difference between the two formulations, argued Shevardnadze, was "large and important," especially given that the West would be following every subsequent move the Soviets took. Now the Defense Ministry "is proposing to speak not about structure but about some abstract tendency." Shevardnadze insisted that the reductions be carried out exactly in the spirit that Gorbachev intended, with maximum openness and publicity (*glasnost'*), both toward the West and toward the new Soviet Congress of People's Deputies that was intended for the first time to submit the Soviet military budget to democratic scrutiny.[116]

Shevardnadze had good reason to be concerned. In his response to the foreign minister's accusations, Iazov, the defense minister, explained that the army planned to bring about the "defensive tendency" simply by with-

114. Dobrynin, *In Confidence*, 623.
115. Oberdorfer, *Turn*, 319.
116. Politburo meeting, minutes, 137–138.

drawing ten thousand tanks, as Gorbachev announced at the UN. Tank regiments would be removed from the larger tank divisions deployed with the Group of Soviet Forces in Germany, but within those divisions the motorized rifle regiments—with considerable offensive potential themselves—would remain. After describing in these quite general terms the existing structure and the proposed changes, Iazov asked, "Is it worth showing our whole structure just because we want glasnost?" He conceded only that "what it's possible to show, we'll show, but it's not necessary to reveal everything to them."[117] By "them," Iazov meant not only, or even primarily, the countries of the NATO alliance; after all, the structure of Soviet military forces was publicly well known in the West, and any changes to it would be immediately apparent to Western intelligence services and governments. Iazov was more concerned about revealing information to people on the *Soviet* side—especially the skeptical parliamentary deputies responsible for funding the Soviet military machine.[118] Clearly the gap between the reform-minded Shevardnadze and the conservative Iazov was enormous.

Transnational Public Relations

Fortunately for the Gorbachev-Shevardnadze reforms, Soviet members of the transnational disarmament coalition did not rest on their laurels in the wake of the December 1988 UN speech. In a classic technique from the theory of transnational politics, they sought first to persuade Western audiences to interpret the Soviet initiatives in a positive fashion. Then they called attention to the positive response from the West in order to bolster the prospects within the USSR for successfully implementing the initiatives.

Andrei Kokoshin's efforts in this regard were by far the most imaginative and effective. First Kokoshin invited Les Aspin, chair of the Committee on Armed Services of the U.S. House of Representatives, to visit the Institute of the USA and Canada in Moscow for a briefing on Soviet thinking about military reform and especially conventional-force restructuring. In a return visit to the United States in March 1989, Aspin invited Kokoshin to participate in an extraordinary hearing before his committee, where the Soviet analyst's presentation of the details of the Soviet unilateral reductions, the new emphasis on defense, and his analysis of civil-military relations in the USSR were very well received.[119] Then, in October 1989, Aspin returned to the Soviet Union, this time as a guest of the Supreme Soviet's Committee on Defense

---

117. Ibid., 143–144.

118. Iazov's remarks came in the context of an explicit discussion of what the deputies should be told.

119. House Committee on Armed Services, Defense Policy Panel, *Gorbachev's Force Reductions and the Restructuring of Soviet Forces*, 101st Cong., 1st Session, 1989 (Washington, D.C., 1989), 1–50.

and State Security. He visited military facilities in the USSR and in East Germany to assess the progress of the unilateral cuts and of military glasnost in general. He received considerable media attention—virtually all favorable—in both countries, as well as in the United States.[120] If nothing else, Kokoshin's contacts with Aspin helped to counter the "enemy image" of the hard-liners in both countries and made it easier for him to promote the transnational agenda for Soviet military reform.

In the 1980s, economic conditions, U.S. behavior, and changes in the military's perceptions of Soviet security requirements all contributed to a rethinking of Soviet security policy. The change in Soviet policy represented by the new thinking—and in particular the unilateral reduction of conventional forces and the adoption of the goal of nonoffensive defense—were not in any sense determined by such factors, however. In many respects, for example, the conclusions that civilian reformers drew were very different from those of the military.

In December 1988 Gorbachev announced unilateral reductions that only a minority of Soviet civilians had been willing publicly to support as well as a reorientation of the structure of Soviet military forces to exclude the ability for a large-scale attack—without making these actions contingent on Western reciprocation. The important point is that the civilian reformers involved in transnational discussions on alternative security were early advocates of views that eventually became official Soviet policy, whereas the military officials in the General Staff came to accept the idea of unilateral initiatives very late and very reluctantly. The civilians prevailed in influencing government policy at least in part because they successfully forged transnational alliances and appealed to information, ideas, and norms developed by and with their Western counterparts.

The effects of Gorbachev's reforms for Russia and Europe were profound. A leading Soviet diplomat characterized them accurately, if somewhat critically, as follows: "The Soviet Union that Gorbachev inherited in 1985 was a global power, perhaps somewhat tarnished in that image, but still strong and united and one of the world's two superpowers. But in just three years, from 1989 to 1991, the political frontiers of the European continent were effectively rolled eastward from the center of Europe to the Russian borders of 1653."[121] Whether expanding European borders eastward means welcoming Russia into Europe or pushing it further away is still a matter of some dispute. Hence the conflicting evaluations among Russians of the wisdom of the Gorbachev-Shevardnadze revolution. It is presumably less contentious, though, that the

120. See, e.g., V. Kocherov, "L. Espin: 'My khotim nachat' dialog,'" *Krasnaia zvezda*, 10 August 1989; "Parlamentariengruppe aus den USA in Truppenteil der NVA," *Neues Deutschland*, 8 August 1989; Michael R. Gordon, "Congress Inspects a Soviet Pullback," *New York Times*, 9 August 1989.

121. Dobrynin, *In Confidence*, 615.

transnational disarmament proposals that contributed to the reshaping of Europe's boundaries also helped eliminate the danger of a major East-West war erupting there. The possible outbreak of such a war had posed the risk of nuclear devastation for some four decades. The benefits of that revolutionary change should not be underestimated.

[15]

"If There Were No Nuclear Missiles": Gorbachev's Answer to Star Wars

You should see that if both sides go ahead with disarmament, there can be no Star Wars. Disarmament in and of itself might be the answer to Star Wars.
— JEREMY STONE, 1985

As I suggested in Geneva, if there were no nuclear missiles, then there might also be no need for defenses against them.
— RONALD REAGAN, 1986

As the myths grew, one of them was that I had proposed the idea to produce a bargaining chip for use in getting the Soviets to reduce their weaponry. I've had to tell the Soviet leaders a hundred times that the SDI is not a bargaining chip.
— RONALD REAGAN, 1990

During the Gorbachev years, the main achievements of the transnational disarmament community in the realm of antiballistic missile systems were to shape the Soviet Union's response to the Strategic Defense Initiative, to undermine the threat to the ABM Treaty posed by the Soviet government's own questionable adherence to it, and to promote deep reductions in strategic nuclear weapons despite the continued U.S. pursuit of Star Wars. To argue that the transnational community influenced these Soviet policies, one must argue counterfactually that the decisions of the policymakers would have been different were it not for its activities. Otherwise such factors as economic conditions, military requirements, and U.S. behavior would be sufficient to account for Soviet actions.

THE SOVIET RESPONSE TO "STAR WARS"

On 23 March 1983, President Ronald Reagan issued an appeal to the "scientific community in our country, those who gave us nuclear weapons, to turn their great talents now to the cause of mankind and world peace, to give us the means of rendering these nuclear weapons impotent and obsolete."[1] Although many U.S. scientists heeded the call, and welcomed the vast sums of money that became available to support research into strategic defense technologies, others—including most of the surviving participants in the original Manhattan Project—adopted an extremely negative attitude toward the goals of the Strategic Defense Initiative.

By the time Mikhail Gorbachev came into office in March 1985, a number of U.S. scientists had been working for two years with their Soviet colleagues in a transnational effort to defeat the Star Wars challenge to nuclear arms control and disarmament. I argue that the position adopted by the Soviet government—not to respond "in kind" to Star Wars, but to develop relatively inexpensive countermeasures—cannot be understood without considering the role of these transnational actors. Their advocacy of an "asymmetric response" was a genuinely new policy idea that broke with long-standing Soviet military practice of imitating U.S. technological innovations.[2]

More striking is the fact that the Soviet government chose not to rely on the cheapest countermeasure of them all—the existing force of multiple-warhead intercontinental missiles. Instead it embraced deep cuts in its most potent force of SS-18 missiles during the first Strategic Arms Reduction Talks (START I). The pursuit of arms reductions despite Star Wars was the result of the strong normative commitments of Gorbachev and Shevardnadze to nuclear disarmament. Their attitude toward nuclear weapons was shaped in part by their interaction with the transnational disarmament movement, particularly its representatives among Soviet and Western scientists and physicians.

The task that the Soviet Committee of Scientists faced, as its leading members later described it, was to prevent the proponents of offensive and defensive responses to Star Wars from spending the Soviet economy into the ground and further destabilizing the nuclear standoff. With that goal in mind, Gorbachev in late 1985 appointed Evgenii Velikhov science director of a committee set up to develop measures for counteracting SDI. In his colleague Roald Sagdeev's words, Velikhov acted as something of a "Kamikaze." He alienated some pro-disarmament scientists by his association with military technologists on the committee. On the other hand the military technical people, who hoped the committee would give them everything they wanted to respond to Star Wars, were wary of Velikhov for his role in the transnational disarmament movement.[3]

Given what U.S. analysts were predicting for Soviet responses to SDI, the

1. Quoted in Sidney D. Drell, Philip J. Farley, and David Holloway, *The Reagan Strategic Defense Initiative: A Technical, Political, and Arms Control Assessment* (Cambridge, Mass., 1985), 1.
2. Matthew Evangelista, *Innovation and the Arms Race: How the United States and the Soviet Union Develop New Military Technologies* (Ithaca, N.Y., 1988).
3. Roald Sagdeev, interview by author, College Park, Md., 31 March 1994.

pro-disarmament scientists had the most to worry about. Western observers anticipated that in the immediate future simply maintaining the current Soviet strategic missile force with thousands of nuclear warheads provided the cheapest countermeasure to Star Wars. Beyond that the Soviets could deploy more real or "dummy" warheads on existing missiles in order to overwhelm a U.S. defense. To foil American plans for "boost-phase intercept" of Soviet missiles as they are launching, the USSR could produce large numbers of unarmed rocket boosters to saturate that layer of the Star Wars defense. In the somewhat longer term, the Soviets could develop fast-burn boosters that would launch missiles before the U.S. interceptors had time to respond; they could emphasize evading U.S. radars with low-flying cruise missiles and "stealth" technologies. Finally, many analysts predicted that the Soviets would directly emulate an American SDI by deploying both ground- and space-based antimissile defenses.[4]

The actual Soviet response to SDI varied over time. Initially, Soviet leaders, including Mikhail Gorbachev in his early months in office, threatened to respond with offensive countermeasures and a defensive system of their own if SDI went ahead. Eventually, however, Gorbachev came to emphasize political means of dealing with SDI. His perestroika and new thinking in foreign policy helped to reduce the perception of a Soviet threat and undermined support for SDI within the United States. Finally, assured that nothing threatening would come of SDI, he agreed to substantial reductions in offensive nuclear forces (U.S. reductions were part of the deal as well), in the course of the START negotiations, without any U.S. commitment to forswear SDI or continue to abide by the ABM Treaty. The Soviet commitment to major reductions served further to undermine U.S. domestic support for SDI.

Soviet scientists, such as Velikhov, Sagdeev, and Kokoshin, influenced this course of events in two ways. First, through their contacts in the United States, they kept Gorbachev and his advisers up to date on the state of opposition to SDI, for example, in Congress.[5] Second, through the initiatives they promoted on the Soviet side, Velikhov and his colleagues helped to diminish the mistrust that hindered progress in arms control.

4. Stephen M. Meyer, "Soviet Strategic Programmes and the US SDI," *Survival* 27, 6 (November-December 1985): 274–292; David Holloway, "The Strategic Defense Initiative and the Soviet Union," *Daedalus* 114, 3 (Summer 1985): 257–278; *Soviet Strategic Defense Programs*, report released by the U.S. Departments of Defense and State, October 1985; see also Paul H. Nitze, "SDI: The Soviet Program," United States Department of State, Current Policy No. 717, July 1985; and Sayre Stevens, "The Soviet BMD Program," in Ashton B. Carter and David N. Schwartz, eds., *Ballistic Missile Defense* (Washington, D.C., 1984), 182–220. For a comprehensive review of Soviet defense capabilities during the early Gorbachev years, see Mark N. Kramer, "Air Defense Forces (VPVO)," in David R. Jones, ed., *Soviet Armed Forces Review Annual, 1987–88*, vol. 11 (Gulf Breeze, Fla., 1989), 105–161.

5. Katherine Magraw, "Weapons Brokers and Policy Entrepreneurs: Congress and the Strategic Policy Community During the Reagan Era" (Ph.D. diss., Massachusetts Institute of Technology, 1992), chap. 5.

The Krasnoiarsk Gambit

A key event in lowering the level of U.S. mistrust was getting the Soviet leadership to acknowledge that the giant phased-array radar near Krasnoiarsk in Siberia constituted a violation of the ABM Treaty. The United States government had accused the USSR of violating the terms of the treaty, even while the United States itself sought to weaken or do away with it altogether. But calling attention to U.S. hypocrisy rarely gained the Soviets much in the U.S. domestic debate on arms control, and in this case the accusation of a treaty violation was correct. The Krasnoiarsk radar constituted a violation because of its location. By the terms of the treaty such an installation could only be constructed on the periphery of the country and facing outward.

Evidently, the Soviet military had developed plans to build the radar to comply with the treaty but found that it would cost several times as much money to do so as to build it further inland.[6] Knowing that the radar would be in technical violation of the treaty, the Defense Ministry, Foreign Ministry, KGB, and ultimately the Politburo nevertheless advocated building it near Krasnoiarsk.[7] When the United States first noticed construction of the complex in 1983, it accused the Soviets not only of violating the treaty but of planning to break out of the treaty's restraints and deploy a comprehensive strategic defense with the Krasnoiarsk radar as part of a "battle management" system.[8] Perhaps influenced by the spuriousness of the latter claim, the Soviet leadership decided to reject all of the U.S. criticisms. Rather than admit that the radar was intended to provide early warning of possible launches of new U.S. Trident missiles, they claimed that it was intended for the purely civilian purpose of tracking objects in space.

The contribution of the Soviet scientists to resolving the Krasnoiarsk issue entailed lifting the veil of secrecy on the complex itself. Velikhov was persuaded of the deleterious effects of Soviet secrecy mainly by his American colleagues. Bernard Lown, co-chair of the International Physicians for the Prevention of Nuclear War, used to speak of the U.S. military buildup and Russian secrecy as "two sides of the same coin," and eventually Velikhov came to agree.[9] Urged on by transnational colleagues such as Christopher Paine, an arms control expert on Senator Edward Kennedy's staff, and Thomas Cochran of the Natural Resources Defense Council, Velikhov, Kokoshin, and the other Soviet scientists persistently sought to push forward

---

6. Raymond L. Garthoff, "Case of the Wandering Radar," *Bulletin of the Atomic Scientists* 47, 6 (July/August 1991): 7–9. Georgii Kornienko (former first deputy foreign minister), interview by author, Moscow, 28 July 1992; Aleksei Arbatov, interview by author, Cambridge, Mass., 18 August 1993.

7. Kornienko, interview.

8. *Arms Control Reporter* (Cambridge, Mass., 1983), 603.B.17.

9. Bernard Lown, interview by author, Brookline, Mass., 6 April 1994; Evgenii Velikhov, interview by author, Moscow, 29 July 1992.

Christopher Paine, an arms control expert then on Senator Edward Kennedy's staff, in front of the Krasnoiarsk radar, September 1987. Photo courtesy of Tom Cochran.

the boundaries of military *glasnost'*—and Krasnoiarsk was an obvious place to start.

In September 1987, Cochran and Paine arranged for a U.S. congressional delegation to visit the Soviet Union to observe a test of the NRDC seismic monitoring system (using a chemical explosive device rather than a nuclear weapon). Velikhov managed to convince Gorbachev to let the group visit the Krasnoiarsk site as well. The Americans, accompanied by Velikhov, Koko-shin, and Aleksei Arbatov, as well as Soviet military officials, were allowed to photograph the complex extensively. As Chris Paine recalled, the "officers did not look happy" about it, but the approval came from the very top, so they had no choice.[10] Experts in the U.S. delegation dismissed the Pentagon's claim that the Krasnoiarsk radar would be useful for "battle management" as part of a nationwide ballistic missile defense system, but they also found Soviet claims of a space-tracking role for the radar implausible. In their view the radar was best suited for early warning of a missile attack—which, as we now know, was its original intention—although they were not particularly impressed with its capabilities even in this area.[11]

Not until October 1989 did the Soviet Union, at Shevardnadze's insistence, admit that construction of the Krasnoiarsk radar violated the ABM Treaty.[12] Shevardnadze claimed that he had been deceived about the true nature of the radar and that it had taken four years to learn the truth. One of Shevardnadze's more prominent former colleagues in the Foreign Ministry charges, however, that the foreign minister was informed of the status of Krasnoiarsk as a likely violation as early as September 1985.[13] If the charge is true, then we should not understand the transnational actors involved in exposing the Krasnoiarsk violation as "teachers of norms" (for example, about the value of openness).[14] Indeed, Shevardnadze himself had long argued eloquently about the pernicious effects of secrecy and deception on international security.[15] Instead, the transnational actors should be seen as part of a clever political gambit to embarrass and discredit the "old thinkers" in the Soviet security establishment and pave the way for more progress on disarmament.

Eventually the Soviets agreed to dismantle the facility. The work of the U.S.-Soviet disarmament coalition contributed to this important turning point in U.S. perceptions of Soviet intentions. Moreover, it set a precedent for considering inspections of suspected treaty violations an acceptable means of resolving disputes, rather than an infringement on national sovereignty, as the previous Soviet view held.

The role of transnational actors in opening up Soviet military facilities (Krasnoiarsk and the laser research laboratories) to inspection is fairly apparent from the public activities of members of the international physicians movement, the Natural Resources Defense Council, the Federation of American Scientists, and the Soviet Committee of Scientists. Certainly the goal of fostering trust in order to broaden the possibilities for arms control was not

10. Christopher Paine, interview by author, Arlington, Va., 2 April 1994.

11. William J. Broad, "Inside a Key Russian Radar Site: Tour Raises Questions on Treaty," *New York Times*, 7 September 1987; Thomas J. Downey, Bob Carr, and Jim Moody, "Report from Krasnoyarsk," *Bulletin of the Atomic Scientists* 43, 9 (November 1987): 11–14.

12. *Arms Control Reporter*, 603.B.182.

13. S. F. Akhromeev and G. M. Kornienko, *Glazami marshala i diplomata* (Moscow, 1992), 255–256. Kornienko claims to have briefed Shevardnadze himself.

14. On this concept, see Martha Finnemore, *National Interests in International Society* (Ithaca, N.Y., 1996).

15. For example, "Doklad E. A. Shevardnadze," *Vestnik Ministerstva Inostrannykh Del SSSR*, 1988, no. 15:27–46.

held exclusively by the transnational disarmament coalition—but its members were the ones who promoted concrete initiatives within the Soviet government that would make the biggest impression on the United States.

The only alternative explanation for Soviet behavior of which I am aware is Paul Nitze's argument that the change in Soviet policy came about because the "Soviet Union apparently had decided it had more to learn from on-site inspection than we did." [16] Nitze's only "evidence" for this argument is his observation that *American* military officials evinced considerable reluctance to allow Soviet inspectors into U.S. facilities once the Soviets had accepted the principle of on-site inspection. This is typical of Nitze's style of argument. In fact, Soviet military officials—and, indeed, members of the public at large—remained extremely wary of allowing the West access to Soviet military sites, even as part of accepted measures for implementing arms accords such as the treaty reducing intermediate-range nuclear forces, regardless of what Soviet inspectors got to see on the other side.[17] But with the inspection of Krasnoiarsk and the laser research facilities Nitze's argument does not even apply. The Soviet concessions were *unilateral* and *unconditional*. They entailed no Soviet inspection of U.S. sites at all.

Unlinking Star Wars

The ultimate accomplishment of the transnational actors consisted of "unlinking" the Strategic Defense Initiative from arms control. Previously the Soviet government had tenaciously insisted that no arms treaties could be signed without a U.S. commitment to abide by its existing treaty obligations, maintain limitations on ABM systems, and forswear SDI. Gorbachev put forward this position most forcefully at the Reykjavik summit in October 1986, when he presented a "package" of arms control concessions, all contingent on U.S. restraint on Star Wars.[18] The intercession of prominent Soviet scientists such as Sagdeev, Velikhov, and Andrei Sakharov, working with their American colleagues and sympathetic aides to Gorbachev and Shevardnadze, helped convince the Soviet leadership to sign two major arms accords, without insisting on any U.S. commitments regarding the ABM Treaty or SDI. The timing of the transnational actors' policy advocacy, and the fact that major figures in the Soviet security establishment opposed any Soviet concessions on SDI, suggest an important role for the transnational efforts.

Andrei Sakharov was the first and most outspoken internal Soviet critic of the linkage between SDI and arms control. He addressed the issue at his first

16. Paul N. Nitze, *From Hiroshima to Glasnost* (New York, 1989), 442.
17. For some evidence, see Matthew Evangelista, "Soviet Policy toward Strategic Arms Control," in Bruce Parrott, ed., *The Dynamics of Soviet Defense Policy* (Washington, D.C., 1990), esp. 293–296.
18. Michael Mandelbaum and Strobe Talbott, *Reagan and Gorbachev* (New York, 1987), chap. 5.

impromptu press conference at the Iaroslavl train station, on his return to Moscow from internal exile in Gor'kii in December 1986. He repeated his argument in mid-February 1987 at an international disarmament forum in Moscow to which Velikhov had invited him, and which Gorbachev also attended. Before the opening of the forum, Sakharov met with Frank von Hippel and Jeremy Stone from the Federation of American Scientists, who shared his critique of the SDI linkage. All three spoke at the forum, and their speeches were widely disseminated in the Soviet media. Moreover, Stone and von Hippel sat at Gorbachev's table at the forum's concluding banquet, where they had further opportunity to advocate their positions.[19] Gorbachev was also able to learn through another route about arguments made during the earlier strategy session between Sakharov, Stone, and von Hippel: the KGB had secretly recorded the meeting in Sakharov's apartment, and Viktor Chebrikov, the KGB chief, had personally sent Gorbachev a partial transcript of the discussion.[20]

Less than two weeks after the Moscow forum, Gorbachev announced the unlinking of Star Wars from the negotiations on intermediate-range nuclear forces (INF) in Europe, and the INF Treaty was signed by the end of the year.[21] As he later explained, his discussions with foreign and Soviet intellectuals at the forum "made a big impression. I discussed the results of the congress with my colleagues in the Politburo. And we decided to make a major new compromise—to untie the Reykjavik package, detaching from it the problem of intermediate-range missiles in Europe."[22] Even as he paved the way for an INF Treaty, Gorbachev reiterated Soviet opposition to unlinking SDI from a possible START agreement.[23] Finally, after a vigorous campaign by the Soviet scientists and their U.S. counterparts, working in tandem with Shevardnadze, Gorbachev relented in late 1989. As Michael Beschloss and Strobe Talbott observed, now "the Soviet Union would be willing to sign and implement a START treaty without a separate accord limiting space-based defenses."[24] The details of the treaty took another year and a half to negotiate, but the main stumbling block was removed by December 1989, in accordance with the prescription of the transnational disarmament community.

19. Andrei Sakharov, *Moscow and Beyond, 1986 to 1989*, trans. by Antonina Bouis (New York, 1991), 21–24; Strobe Talbott, *The Master of the Game: Paul Nitze and the Nuclear Peace* (New York, 1988), 360–361.

20. V. M. Chebrikov to M. S. Gorbachev, memorandum, 23 February 1987, F. 89, op. 18, d. 114, Storage Center for Contemporary Documentation, Moscow.

21. *Arms Control Reporter*, 403.B.426.

22. M. S. Gorbachev, *Perestroika i novoe myshlenie dlia nashei strany i dlia vsego mira* (Moscow, 1987), 157–158.

23. *Arms Control Reporter*, 403.B.434.

24. Michael Beschloss and Strobe Talbott, *At the Highest Levels: The Inside Story of the End of the Cold War* (Boston, 1993), 117–119. Sagdeev at this point served as an informal adviser reporting directly to Shevardnadze (Sagdeev, interview).

Frank von Hippel (left) and Andrei Sakharov discuss arms control at Sakharov's Moscow apartment in February 1987. One conversation, which included Jeremy Stone, focused on the need to pursue nuclear disarmament as a means of undermining U.S. support for the Strategic Defense Initiative. The KGB taped this discussion and sent a transcript to Mikhail Gorbachev on 23 February. Three days later the Politburo agreed to "untie the package" that linked reductions of the Soviet SS-20 missiles to U.S. restraint on SDI. Photo by Jeremy Stone, courtesy of Frank von Hippel.

Alternative Explanations

The explanations typically offered to counter arguments about the influence of transnational actors on Soviet security policy could be applied to SDI as well. They tend to rely on the notion that the Soviet government, primarily for military or economic reasons, already intended to pursue the policies advocated by transnational actors; therefore transnational relations were irrelevant or transnational actors merely served as instruments of Soviet policy.

Economic Constraints. There is no denying that economic concerns motivated much of the change in Soviet security policy, including Soviet opposition to SDI, especially after Gorbachev came into office. The Soviet economic crisis constituted a "policy window" through which transnational policy entrepreneurs could promote their solutions. But the content of those solutions often depended on the transnational actors themselves.

Not all of the relevant officials involved in the Soviet response to Star Wars were equally concerned about the implications for the economy, however. Defense Minister Dmitrii Iazov, who came into office in May 1987, two years into Gorbachev's term, seemed relatively complacent. In a book published in 1988, Iazov called attention to "attempts by imperialist reaction [i.e., the United States] to attain military superiority over the USSR, including with the help of SDI to exhaust it economically." But he then goes on to quote Gorbachev to make the point that the Soviet economy is sufficiently strong to meet the challenge of SDI without any grave economic consequences: "Only a blind person does not see that our possibilities to support a strong defense and simultaneously resolve social and other tasks have repeatedly grown."[25]

Even if Gorbachev and his political colleagues were uniformly convinced of the economic necessity of avoiding an arms race in Star Wars defenses, they needed the arguments and expertise of the transnational scientists to use against skeptics in the armed forces and military industry. In private conversations with the military high command, Gorbachev did stress both the economic constraints on Soviet security policy and the need for military officials to take into account the views of the scientists.[26]

Economic constraints do not tell the whole story of the Soviet reaction to Star Wars, however. Indeed, some of the Soviet initiatives, far from saving money, were actually quite expensive. They demonstrate that the Soviet leaders' commitment to disarmament and improvement of East-West relations extended beyond narrow economic objectives. Dismantling the Krasnoiarsk radar, for example, was something that Gorbachev was loath to do, both for what it meant in abandoning the "sunk costs" of having built it and for the immediate expense of taking apart such an enormous structure—"on the scale of the Egyptian pyramids," as Shevardnadze described it.[27] Gorbachev had initially tried to save face and avoid conflict with the Soviet military over how to pay for dismantling the radar by proposing an alternative: the Soviet government would, instead, transfer control of the station to the Soviet Academy of Sciences for use as an international space research center.[28] But his scientists told Gorbachev in effect that they had no use for such a monstrosity; they persuaded him to agree to U.S. demands to tear it down in the interest of improving the international climate and furthering the prospects for meaningful disarmament—despite the cost.

25. D. T. Iazov, *Verny Otchizne* (Moscow, 1988), 350.
26. Akhromeev and Kornienko, *Glazami*, esp. 71–73.
27. Don Oberdorfer, *The Turn: From the Cold War to a New Era* (New York, 1992), 374.
28. Proposed in Gorbachev's speech at the United Nations, printed in the *New York Times*, 8 December 1988, 6.

Military Requirements. The argument that the Soviet armed forces, for their own military reasons, supported an asymmetric or even no response to SDI is unpersuasive. Even while Gorbachev was arguing against imitating SDI, his top military leaders were threatening "to adopt retaliatory measures in both offensive and other spheres, not excluding defensive arms, and including space-based ones."[29] Certainly many Soviet military leaders appreciated the strategic benefits of constraining a race in defensive systems and therefore supported the ABM Treaty. Yet the top military leadership—as well as prominent Foreign Ministry officials—were adamantly opposed to concluding arms agreements with the United States in the absence of a U.S. commitment not to go forward with SDI. Marshal Akhromeev contemplated resigning over the way Gorbachev and Shevardnadze handled the INF negotiations.[30] He and Kornienko, the deputy foreign minister, were certainly not alone in the Foreign and Defense Ministries in steadfastly opposing the decision to sign the START Treaty without securing limitations on SDI.[31]

Without the transnational scientists' efforts, it is highly unlikely that Gorbachev and Shevardnadze would have been able to muster sufficient support to negotiate strategic arms reductions.

U.S. Behavior. The explanation that U.S. behavior persuaded the Soviet Union to sign disarmament treaties focuses on the notion of "negotiation from strength" and SDI as a "bargaining chip." Paul Nitze, the State Department's leading arms control negotiator, and Robert McFarlane, the president's national security adviser, were the main proponents of such an approach in the Reagan administration. One key problem, however, with the Nitze-McFarlane idea of a "grand compromise," with SDI as a bargaining chip, was that the progenitor of Star Wars—President Reagan—seemed unwilling to give it up. At the summit meeting in Geneva in 1985 and again in a letter to Gorbachev of February 1986, Reagan did admit that "if there were no nuclear missiles, then there might also be no need for defenses against them."[32] But in the same book where he quoted that letter he also wrote: "I've had to tell the Soviet leaders a hundred times that the SDI is not a bargaining

29. Marshal Sergei Akhromeev, chief of the General Staff, in *Pravda*, 19 October 1985. See also the remarks of Marshal Sergei Sokolov, defense minister, in *Krasnaia zvezda*, 5 May 1985, and numerous other quotations cited in Mary C. FitzGerald, *Soviet Views on SDI*, Carl Beck Papers No. 601, Center for Russian and East European Studies, University of Pittsburgh (Pittsburgh, 1987).

30. Akhromeev and Kornienko, *Glazami*, 109.

31. Akhromeev claimed that Shevardnadze was prepared to "unlink" START from SDI as early as December 1987, whereas he and the first deputy foreign minister, Georgii Kornienko, insisted that the United States forswear pursuit of defenses. See Akhromeev and Kornienko, *Glazami*, 142, 192. In Roald Sagdeev's view, Akhromeev's commitment to the link between START and Star Wars did not mean that he favored development of a Soviet SDI. Rather, he was a "tough guy," a tough negotiator. Sagdeev, interview.

32. Ronald Reagan, *An American Life* (New York, 1992), 657.

chip. . . . One day a madman could come along and make the missiles and blackmail all of us—but not if we have a defense against them."[33]

It is doubtful that Reagan would have been willing to give up SDI under any conditions. In the event, it was the tacit collaboration between the transnational disarmament movement, Gorbachev's arms negotiators, and the U.S. Congress that rendered Star Wars "impotent and obsolete."

Grand Compromise: The Transnational Version

Bargaining-chip arguments do not typically accord a role to transnational actors because they adopt the unitary-actor assumption—that any Soviet leadership group would respond to U.S. pressure with concessions. The case of the "grand compromise" is, however, a striking exception. The version that persuaded Gorbachev to agree to strategic arms reductions was not the one associated with Nitze and McFarlane. They had argued that the United States would "cash in" its bargaining chip by agreeing to slow the momentum of its Star Wars project, and, in return, the Soviet side would reduce its long-range strategic missiles. Instead, the Soviets adopted an approach that Jeremy Stone of the Federation of American Scientists had been promoting to his transnational colleagues in the Soviet Union for years.

At a conference in Moscow in April 1985, just a month after Gorbachev came into office, Stone made the case to an audience of forty scientists:

> You people are saying that if we go ahead with Star Wars, there can be no disarmament. I agree, but you should turn it around. You should see that if both sides go ahead with disarmament, there can be no Star Wars. Disarmament in and of itself might be the answer to Star Wars. With offensive reductions underway, there would be no political support for Star Wars [in the United States]. On the other hand, if there are no offensive reductions in prospect, there will be all the more support for Star Wars. You need political restraints, not further legal assurances concerning the ABM treaty.[34]

It was an ingenious suggestion—not surprising from the person who two decades earlier launched the seemingly quixotic but ultimately successful campaign to persuade the Soviet Union to forsake defenses against nuclear attack in favor of an ABM treaty.

Thus, Soviet nuclear disarmament was not a response to Star Wars, as McFarlane and others would have it. It was a goal that Soviet reformers pursued despite Star Wars. Their successful achievement of the START Treaty,

---

33. Ibid., 548.
34. Quoted in Talbott, *Master of the Game*, 261.

which entailed deep reductions in both sides' arsenals, then undermined the SDI program to such an extent that the prospect of a U.S. "space shield" faded into irrelevance. In 1990, the U.S. Congress passed legislation cutting the SDI budget by a quarter from the previous year and reorienting research away from any programs that would promote early deployment of a strategic defense system.[35]

"STAR WARS" IN PERSPECTIVE

Within the group of Soviet participants in the debates over SDI, ranging from establishment figures in the Foreign Ministry to "young Turks" in the academic institutes, there is virtual consensus that the Star Wars program did not aid Soviet reform or promote arms control.

Aleksei Arbatov, a strong proponent of military reform throughout his years at the Institute of the World Economy and International Relations (IMEMO) and his service as a deputy in the Russian Duma, has perhaps put it best: "SDI was always detrimental to our efforts."[36] Andrei Kortunov of the Institute of the USA and Canada, a pioneer of military glasnost during the Gorbachev years, agrees that SDI "made it more difficult for proponents of military reform."[37] Before his death in 1989, Andrei Sakharov, perhaps the foremost proponent of political reform and arms control, also criticized SDI's impact. "The claim that the existence of the SDI program has spurred the USSR to disarmament negotiations" was, in his view, "wrong. On the contrary, the SDI program is impeding those negotiations."[38]

Only one Soviet official with real inside knowledge of the Gorbachev government's attitude toward SDI has publicly expressed views that could be interpreted as endorsing the argument that Star Wars improved the prospects for arms control.[39] According to Aleksandr Bessmertnykh, who served as deputy foreign minister from 1986 to 1990, "in a certain way, the SDI pronouncement might have brought us closer to solutions in arms control, because we realized that we were really approaching a very dangerous situation."[40] At the same time, however, even Bessmertnykh admits that "the arms buildup under President Reagan caused great difficulties" for Gorbachev and

35. Magraw, "Weapons Brokers," 344.
36. Aleksei Arbatov, interview by author, Washington D.C., 10 June 1991.
37. Andrei Kortunov, conversation with author, Cambridge, Mass., 21 September 1996.
38. Sakharov, *Moscow and Beyond*, 21–22.
39. Several officials who had *no* direct knowledge of Gorbachev's policymaking, such as Vladimir Lukin and Sergei Stankevich, have been cited by Robert McFarlane as supporters of his arguments. Sagdeev, interview.
40. Comments in William C. Wohlforth, ed., *Witnesses to the End of the Cold War* (Baltimore, Md., 1996), 33.

that SDI led "to a tug-of-war inside the Soviet bureaucracy, with the military wanting to build missiles to counter 'star wars' and the enemies of the cold war seeking to use the threat of another upward spiral in the arms race to push their plans for arms curbs."[41] "So SDI's impact went both ways," he suggests. The people in the Foreign Ministry "believed that we should use this situation to go further with arms control," whereas "the people who dealt with defense used SDI as an argument for increasing the production of offensive weapons."[42]

One prominent American Sovietologist has argued that SDI's importance lay not so much in its relationship to arms control but to Gorbachev's overall program of reform. His views resemble those of the "Reagan-as-architect-of-perestroika" school discussed in Chapter 12. According to Jerry Hough, SDI was a "godsend for the Soviet leadership" because it bolstered arguments for economic reform.[43] To overcome conservative opposition and secure support for reforms, Gorbachev "needed to emphasize the dangerous consequences of technological backwardness." Star Wars, according to this analysis, "was the perfect symbol of the technological danger," so Gorbachev sought to play up the threat.[44]

Georgii Kornienko, a key promoter of the ABM Treaty who served as first deputy foreign minister under Andrei Gromyko, has dismissed this proposition as "far-fetched" (*nadumannyi*).[45] Gorbachev's top foreign-policy aide Anatolii Cherniaev, whose liberal views put him on the opposite side of many debates from Kornienko, nevertheless agrees on this point: "*Perestroika* was the result of internal demands, analysis of the internal situation in the Soviet Union, not pressure from Ronald Reagan or SDI." Much of Gorbachev's criticism of SDI was directed to an internal audience within the Soviet military-industrial establishment, in an effort to prevent an expensive and dangerous Soviet response.[46] Gorbachev "felt that the deployment of SDI would create a very difficult situation for him because he would have to do something. There would certainly be a backlash in the Soviet Union. He wanted to avoid the kind of atmosphere that would create that backlash."[47]

Nevertheless, according to Gorbachev's reformist colleague Aleksandr

---

41. Paul Lewis, "View from the Cold War's Trenches: Ex-Foes Trade Stories," *New York Times*, 1 March 1993, reporting on a conference at Princeton University. Also, "Experts Examine the End of the Cold War," *WWS Newsletter* (Woodrow Wilson School, Princeton) 16, 2 (Summer 1993).

42. Comments in Wohlforth, *Witnesses*, 34–35.

43. Jerry F. Hough, "Soviet Interpretation and Response," in *Arms Control and the Strategic Defense Initiative: Three Perspectives*, Occasional Paper 36, Stanley Foundation (Arlington, Va., 1985), 11.

44. Jerry Hough, *Russia and the West: Gorbachev and the Politics of Reform*, 2d ed.(New York, 1990), 231.

45. Kornienko, interview.

46. A. S. Cherniaev, interview by author, Moscow, 5 June 1997.

47. A. S. Cherniaev's comments in Wohlforth, *Witnesses*, 39.

Iakovlev "Star Wars was exploited by [Soviet] hardliners to complicate Gorbachev's attempt to end the Cold War." It did not serve to promote reform.[48] In fact, the Soviet critics of Star Wars eventually realized that if they wanted to forestall an expensive Soviet response, it was better to play down the SDI threat than call attention to it.[49]

Gorbachev himself addressed the link between Star Wars and his campaign for economic reform quite early in his administration. In a July 1986 meeting with Soviet and foreign scientists, for example, Gorbachev devoted a large portion of his remarks, subsequently printed in *Pravda*, to this very question. He argued that "it is said that SDI is the path to the development of science, to new heights of scientific-technological progress." "But is it true," he asked, "that we can't move science and technology, all the components of scientific knowledge, including the creation of new materials, radioelectronics, mathematics and so forth by carrying out peaceful projects?" He then went into great detail, listing the advances that had been achieved through international scientific cooperation in such areas as space exploration, concluding that the "argument that science and technology can be developed only with the help of an arms race is an absurd argument."[50]

One problem with the assertion that Star Wars benefited the proponents of Soviet technological revitalization is that they did not need to be persuaded. Long before SDI, reformers had been making the case that the USSR needed to join the "third industrial revolution" of microchips and information technology—but their goal was civilian, not military, development.[51] It is telling that Evgenii Velikhov, one of the leading Soviet critics of SDI, was also one of the best informed about the country's technological backwardness. As director of the Department of Information Science, Computer Technology, and Automation at the Soviet Academy of Sciences, he instituted a program in the early 1980s to expand access to computers in Soviet society.[52] Like most reformers, Velikhov saw potential Soviet overreaction to SDI as threatening to drain resources from such civilian technology initiatives rather than bolster them.

Unlike reformers such as Velikhov, the groups that opposed market-oriented reforms were generally complacent about the state of Soviet technology, and SDI did not shake that complacency. Within the armed forces, for example, "Marshal Akhromeev and his people never attributed much to

48. Aleksandr Iakovlev, quoted in Richard Ned Lebow and Janice Gross Stein, "Reagan and the Russians," *Atlantic Monthly*, February 1994, 36.

49. Roald Z. Sagdeev, *The Making of a Soviet Scientist* (New York, 1994), 273.

50. *Pravda*, 15 July 1986.

51. Fedor Burlatskii, "Filosofiia mira," *Voprosy filosofii*, 1982, no. 12:57–66; Oberdorfer, *Turn*, 215.

52. E. P. Velikhov, "Personal'nye EVM—segodniashniaia praktika i perspektivy," *Vestnik Akademii nauk SSSR*, 1984, no. 8:3–9.

SDI's technical prospects," according to Roald Sagdeev. Nor did SDI as a symbol of overall U.S. technological prowess make Soviet military-technical people lose any sleep at night. "They were confident of their accomplishments," says Sagdeev.[53]

Even the moderate, Andropov-style reformers, such as Egor' Ligachev and Nikolai Ryzhkov, did not interpret SDI as a stimulus to market reforms and democratization, the ultimate aim of Gorbachev's perestroika. Ligachev, in fact, characterized SDI not as an exemplar of the benefits of a free-market democracy, but as quite the opposite. "It is well known from history," he wrote, "that a planned economy is advantageous in concentrating vast forces and resources in the resolution of key national problems. . . . In the United States, for example, two of the most impressive examples of this type are the state programs for the development of the high-tech industry: NASA and SDI, the Strategic Defense Initiative."[54]

Gorbachev and his advisers viewed Star Wars not as a godsend but as an American attempt to wreck the Soviet economy by forcing the USSR to compete in areas of advanced technology where it was weak compared to the United States.[55] Yet because of the efforts of the transnational coalition of scientists, proponents of an expensive program of responses to SDI were defeated. As Anatolii Dobrynin explained, "the Soviet response to Star Wars caused only an acceptable small rise in defense spending." He correctly points out that "the troubles in our economy were the result of our own internal contradictions of autarky, low investment, and lack of innovation."[56]

Contrary to the claims of the proponents of "peace through strength," SDI did not serve as a bargaining chip because it was never cashed in: the United States never made any commitment not to go ahead with the program.[57] Rather, it was the American people and their elected representatives who realized the absurdity of building strategic defenses against a country they no longer considered an enemy—indeed a country whose leader they rated more favorably than their own. Although Ronald Reagan felt vindicated by the transformation of Soviet policy that Gorbachev brought about, things did not really turn out as he expected either. Reagan got only part of what he wanted—some nuclear disarmament in the form of a START treaty—but nothing came of his dream of an SDI "space shield." Gorbachev got all of what he wanted out of arms control—nuclear disarmament and the

53. Sagdeev, interview.

54. Yegor Ligachev, *Inside Gorbachev's Kremlin* (New York, 1993), 315.

55. See *Mikhail Gorbachev's Answers to Questions Put by l'Humanité* (Moscow, 1986), 19; and *Mikhail Gorbachev's Answers to Questions Put by Time Magazine* (Moscow, 1986), 17.

56. Anatoly Dobrynin, *In Confidence: Moscow's Ambassador to Six Cold War Presidents* (New York, 1995), 611.

57. Fred Greenstein and William Wohlforth, eds., *Retrospective on the Cold War* (Princeton, N.J., 1994), 10–11.

confident expectation that SDI would die a natural death. Alas, it was something of a Pyrrhic victory: the financial savings of foregoing a competition in defenses were unable to compensate for the serious economic, social, and political problems of the Soviet system that perestroika had exposed and exacerbated.

PART V

The Post-Soviet Era

[16]

The Paradox Of State Strength

We tried to create a new reality by the old methods, sending out directives from above. Well, directives, whether statutes or decrees, are accepted for implementation only by a community that is connected with the command center either by a unity of interests or by bonds of obedience and fear. When these are absent, the directive does not work.

—EDUARD SHEVARDNADZE, 1991

Dealing with the Soviet military reminds me of the old Russian anecdote about the two brothers who went bear hunting. At one point Dmitrii calls to his brother: "Ivan, Ivan, I've caught the bear!" "Bring him here then," Ivan calls back. "I can't," yells his brother. "He won't let me go."

—ALEKSEI ARBATOV, 1991

The end of the Soviet era preceded the end of the Soviet Union. When Mikhail Gorbachev introduced competitive elections to a functioning parliament, when he abolished the Communist Party's political monopoly, when his policies of glasnost and democratization eliminated censorship and encouraged political activity of all sorts, and when he made even security policy subject to the scrutiny and influence of ordinary citizens, he ushered in a new, "post-Soviet" system. The implications for transnational activity, as for so much else, were profound.

I have argued that the peculiar domestic structure of the Soviet Union— highly centralized, secretive, and authoritarian—made it difficult for transnational actors to gain access to foreign-policy decision makers. If a transnational organization managed nevertheless to get the attention of the top leadership, and its policy proposals found a welcome hearing, they could be implemented effectively even against the opposition of well-entrenched bureaucracies. Transnational actors took advantage of policy windows, such as Soviet economic constraints, U.S. behavior, and the Soviet armed forces' assessments of their own military requirements, but these factors rarely influenced policy in a straightforward or predictable way. Within the Soviet foreign-policy community there were nearly always alternative assessments of the problems facing the USSR and competing solutions for how to deal with them. The success of transnational actors in getting their preferred policies accepted and implemented depended in part on the quality of their arguments and information. But more important, I argue, was the structure of the Soviet system, which allowed the leadership to promote policies even in the absence of a large coalition to support them.

The post-Soviet era offers an opportunity to evaluate this structural argument. The reforms that Gorbachev instituted undermined the main characteristics of the Soviet system that had served to benefit transnational actors. Under conditions of increasing democracy and freedom of speech and the press, and in the absence of a powerful Communist Party, the conditions affecting transnational organizations dramatically changed during the period 1989–90. Contacts between Soviet and foreign groups and individuals became commonplace, and Soviet newspapers published a wide range of policy proposals for dealing with any number of domestic and international issues. At the same time, the decline of the Communist Party led to a reassertion of the interests of established bureaucracies, especially in the realm of national security.

A structural explanation for the success of transnational actors during the early Gorbachev years would anticipate possible changes in the late Gorbachev period and the Yeltsin administration that followed. In particular, the transnational groups would lose their privileged access to the top leader and would have to compete with the traditional security institutions for influence. If those institutions preferred policies that differed from the ones favored by the transnational disarmament groups, one could expect reversals or setbacks in the earlier policy successes. That is essentially the story of this chapter.

As I described in the previous three chapters, before the end of 1989, when most of the major changes in Soviet domestic structure had been accomplished, a transnational coalition of U.S. and Soviet supporters of arms control (mainly scientists) achieved considerable success in influencing Soviet security policy on nuclear testing, conventional forces, and strategic defenses, as well as several other issues. After 1989 the traditional institutions of the Soviet military-industrial sector came close to reversing many of the prior achievements: they sought to secure the government's commitment to a renewal of nuclear testing; they nearly thwarted negotiation and implementation of the Treaty on Conventional Forces in Europe (CFE); and they tried to revive interest in developing strategic-defense weapons. Major changes in U.S. policy, initiated under the Clinton administration, helped prevent the pro-military forces from gaining the upper hand on nuclear testing and ballistic-missile defense. The new administration's skepticism about strategic defenses and its agreement (albeit, reluctant) to abide by Congress's demand for a halt in nuclear testing appear to have helped tip the balance in Russia in favor of the transnational opponents of Star Wars and new nuclear weapons.

The situation with conventional forces was more complicated. The liberation of eastern Europe from Russian occupation seemed secure, but the conceptual innovations of the 1980s—common security and nonoffensive defense—fared much worse. During the early 1990s Russian armed forces intervened militarily in many areas of the former Soviet Union and in December 1994 launched a devastating war against the separatist republic of Chechnya that cost tens of thousands of lives. In all of these cases, the U.S. government kept a low profile, apparently more interested in Boris Yeltsin's political survival than in bolstering the norms of nonintervention that had helped end the Cold War. The war in Chechnya was a clear defeat for the transnational network of foreign and Russian human rights and peace activists. Under the new domestic structural conditions, and without U.S. support, they were no match for the so-called power ministries of the Russian national-security establishment.

INTERNATIONAL CHANGE

To identify domestic politics as the source of changes in Soviet and Russian security policy in the early 1990s may seem strange indeed, given the magnitude of the international changes that took place during that period. The loss of the USSR's Eastern European buffer zone starting in 1989, and the breakup of the country itself at the end of 1991, signaled the demise of "bipolarity," the key structural attribute of the Cold War international system. The domestic structural changes in the USSR that marked the end of the Soviet era coincided with—or, many would argue, produced—this major structural change in the international environment and led to a transformation of U.S.-Russian relations. One might expect that such international changes would account for the near reversals of Soviet/Russian policy toward ABM, nuclear testing, and conventional forces.

In fact, despite the dramatic international changes, on all three of these issues the signals that Russian policymakers read to interpret the international environment, namely the behavior of the relevant international actors, stayed remarkably constant. In particular, as late as January 1993 the *objectives* of both the United States government and the transnational groups vis-à-vis the ABM treaty and nuclear testing remained the same, even as the Soviet Union changed fundamentally and then disintegrated: The U.S. government, under the Bush administration, wanted to abolish or at least to amend the ABM treaty and to pursue a new generation of ballistic missile defenses. The transnational organizations still wanted to preserve and strengthen the treaty and prevent the development of new weapons. The Bush administration rejected any halt in nuclear testing, even though both Russia and France had ceased their tests by the spring of 1992 and called on other countries to join their moratoria. The transnational groups continued to pursue a comprehensive test ban treaty and supported unilateral moratoria as well. On the issue of conventional forces in Europe, the U.S. government and the transnational groups agreed. Both wanted to see the provisions of the CFE Treaty carried out, regardless of the disintegration of the Warsaw Pact and the USSR. The United States, however, was more forthcoming than the transnational peace groups on the revisions of the treaty demanded by Russia's power ministries. They wanted the treaty to allow for redeployment of Russian military forces in the southern part of the country, where the war in Chechnya was fought, and they eventually got their way.

The external "inputs" to the Soviet policy process regarding strategic defenses, nuclear testing, and conventional forces remained similar even as the international system underwent profound changes in the late 1980s and early 1990s. Even so, one might argue that this broader transformation nonetheless affected Soviet/Russian behavior toward transnational relations. According to the prevailing wisdom, however, the international changes should have influenced behavior in the *opposite direction* from what a domestic-structure approach anticipates. The end of the Cold War and the rapprochement between Russia and the United States alleviated the security dilemma for both countries and diminished the "fear of mutual exploitation" that Jack Snyder has identified as a barrier to the formation of transnational security coalitions. Thus, skeptics of transnationalism would expect the prospects for transnational influence on Soviet/Russian policy to have improved after 1989, whereas the domestic-structure approach would expect them to have declined. The three case studies in this chapter provide a test of the competing expectations.

TRANSFORMATION OF THE SOVIET DOMESTIC STRUCTURE

During the decade of the 1980s the domestic structure of the Soviet Union changed dramatically. Thanks mainly to the reforms initiated by Mikhail Gorbachev, Russia was transformed from a highly centralized, authoritarian state dominated by the Communist Party into a state with weakened central control, quasi-corporatist policy networks, and an active civil society (see Table 10). I and many other observers associate the changes primarily with the election of a functioning parliament in 1989 and the diminishing influence of the Communist Party from that point on.[1]

Although the changes were momentous, many of them unfolded gradually. Consider, for example, such key dimensions of the old Soviet structure as secrecy, Communist Party domination, and centralization. *Glasnost'* grad-

1. Mikhail Gorbachev, *Zhizn' i reformy* (Moscow, 1995), 1:434, 466; V. I. Vorotnikov, *A bylo tak ... Iz dnevnika chlena Politbiuro TsK KPSS* (Moscow, 1995), 300; Vadim Medvedev, *V Komande Gorbacheva: Vzgliad iznutri* (Moscow, 1994), 165; Nikolai Ryzhkov, *Perestroika: Istoriia predatel'stv* (Moscow, 1992), 283; Anatoly Dobrynin, *In Confidence: Moscow's Ambassador to Six Cold War Presidents* (New York, 1995), 626.

Table 10. Change in Soviet Domestic Structure

	Pre-1989	Post-1989
Political Institutions	Centralized	Incipient separation of powers
Society	Weak, passive	Strong, assertive
Policy Networks	Party-state dominated	Quasi-corporatist

ually diminished the degree of secrecy enshrouding all aspects of Soviet life, including security policy—as, indeed, its architects intended.[2] The Communist Party's monopoly on political power was undermined bit by bit, with the emergence of "informal" political groups in 1987, the introduction in 1989 of an elected parliament, the transfer of ultimate power from the Party's general secretary to the country's president, the founding of alternative political parties, the constitutional amendment revoking the Party's monopoly position, and, finally, the banning of the Party in the wake of the failed coup by hardliners against Gorbachev in August 1991. The centralized aspect of the Soviet domestic structure changed both gradually—with the growing fissiparous tendencies in the independence-minded republics—and dramatically, with the breakup of the Union at the end of 1991.

The Components of Domestic Structure

So far we have not had to focus on a detailed definition of the Soviet domestic structure in order to make the case that the Soviet system provided unusual opportunities to certain transnational actors compared to countries with very different domestic structures, such as the United States. But to make the case that a change in the Soviet domestic structure led to a change in the influence of transnational actors, we need to devote attention to the specific components of the structure that changed.

The most specific, yet widely applicable, definition of domestic structure proposed so far focuses on three components: political institutions, society, and policy networks.[3] The nature of the *political institutions* concerns the degree of their centralization and concentration, particularly of executive power. The *structure of society* has to do with its degree of polarization, the strength of social organization, and the extent to which societal pressure can be mobilized. Finally, we consider the nature of the coalition-building processes in the *policy networks* linking state and society.

2. Aleksandr N. Iakovlev, "Dostizhenie kachestvenno novogo sostoianiia Sovetskogo obshchestva i obshchestvennye nauki," *Kommunist*, 1987, no. 8; Eduard Shevardnadze, "Doklad E. A. Shevardnadze," *Vestnik Ministerstva Inostrannykh Del SSSR*, 1988, no. 15; Eduard Shevardnadze, *Moi vybor: v zashchitu demokratii i svobody* (Moscow, 1991).

3. Thomas Risse-Kappen, "Public Opinion, Domestic Structure, and Foreign Policy in Liberal Democracies," *World Politics* 43, 4 (July 1991): 485–486. His definition draws on Peter Katzenstein, ed., *Between Power and Plenty: The Foreign Economic Policies of Advanced Industrial States* (Madison, Wisc., 1978).

There are three main types of policy networks. In countries with centralized political institutions but polarized societies and weak social organizations, the policy network is typically state dominated. Here coalition building takes place among political élites and tends to exclude societal actors and ignore public opinion. By contrast, in countries characterized by a high degree of societal mobilization but weak state structures, we would expect coalition building to take place among societal actors and government policymaking to include a significant role for public opinion. Finally, in countries with political institutions and social organizations of comparable strength, policy networks are likely to be characterized by corporatist bargaining between political and societal actors, resulting in middle-of-the-road policies that broadly reflect public opinion.

This framework has proved quite useful in accounting for differences in the foreign policies of the United States, France, Germany, and Japan, and—in the realm of transnational relations—for the different degrees of receptivity to transnational influence among very different types of states and a range of issues.[4] How well does it describe the Soviet domestic changes?

Political Institutions. The old Soviet system was highly centralized, with power concentrated in the hands of the Communist Party, and in particular its Politburo and General Secretary. Legislation was mainly enacted by decree—typically joint decrees of the Council of Ministers and the Party's Central Committee.[5]

In 1989 quasi-competitive elections were held to fill many of the seats in a new Congress of People's Deputies (although some were reserved for Party-controlled organizations).[6] The Congress was enjoined to elect a Supreme Soviet to function as a genuine legislature. During the same time, Gorbachev managed to remove most of his conservative opponents from the Politburo, while simultaneously reducing the role of that body and its leader, the General Secretary (himself). He introduced the role of president and was elected to that office by more than 95 percent of the delegates to the Congress of People's Deputies. Over the course of the next year, the Congress and the Supreme Soviet strove to eclipse the Communist Party's Central Committee as the country's most important deliberative and legislative bodies. Meanwhile

---

4. Thomas Bisse-Kappen, "Ideas Do Not Float Freely: Transnational Coalitions, Domestic Structures, and the End of the Cold War," *International Organization* 48, 2 (Spring 1994): 185–214; and Risse-Kappen, ed., *Bringing Transnational Relations Back In: Non-State Actors, Domestic Structures and International Institutions* (Cambridge, U.K., 1995); Rodger A. Payne, "Nonprofit Environmental Organizations in World Politics: Domestic Structure and Transnational Relations," *Policy Studies Review* 14, nos. 1–2 (Spring/Summer 1995): 171–182.

5. For a thorough discussion of the old system, see Jerry Hough and Merle Fainsod, *How the Soviet Union is Governed* (Cambridge, Mass., 1979).

6. The events discussed in this section are summarized in a useful "Chronology of Noteworthy Events, March 11, 1985–July 11, 1991," in Ed A. Hewett and Victor H. Winston, eds., *Milestones in Glasnost and Perestroyka: Politics and People* (Washington, D.C., 1991), 499–536.

Gorbachev sought to shift policymaking authority from the Party to the new government, establishing a (short-lived) Presidential Council to fulfill some of the functions previously reserved for the old Politburo. Gorbachev's desire for a strong presidency in the French mold often conflicted with the preference on the part of many Supreme Soviet deputies for a strong parliamentary system with reliable checks and balances. The new competition between the executive and legislative branches fatally weakened the centralized, Party-dominated state and left a legacy of policy fragmentation and incoherence that outlived the USSR itself.

A key turning point in the transition from the old domestic structure to the new one came with the repeal of Article 6 of the Soviet Constitution in February 1990. That article had provided the legal guarantee for the Communist Party's monopoly on political power. Although the Party remained a powerful institution, it now had to face increasingly organized opposition and eventually alternative political parties. The Party was discredited by the failed coup of August 1991 and outlawed shortly thereafter—leaving, as Georgii Arbatov points out, "a power vacuum and a completely disorganized political process."[7] With the disintegration of the Soviet Union, the emerging political system in Russia was characterized by chaos and uncertainty. Some of its elements resembled systems of interest-group pluralism, others suggested a variant of corporatism, and dominating all aspects of politics was the legacy of Soviet bureaucratic inertia.

Structure of Society. Under the old Soviet system, society played a limited and indirect role in policymaking. Censorship, control of information, and the repressive apparatus of the security agencies insured passivity and conformity, even though beneath the surface Soviet society reflected the widest possible divergence of views. One might even describe Soviet society as "polarized," say between the "friends and foes of change," as a prominent Sovietologist put it.[8] It probably makes more sense, however, to retain the old terminology of Soviet studies and consider Soviet society, at the risk of some exaggeration, as "atomized" and passive. Certainly independent social organizations were weak or nonexistent, although official policy-oriented research institutes sometimes appeared to exert significant influence, especially at early stages of policymaking.

The reemergence of Soviet civil society became evident already in the first year of Gorbachev's tenure in office (he was elected general secretary in March 1985), and a growing movement of "informal" groups was quite active by 1987.[9] By the end of the decade hundreds of self-defined political parties

7. Georgii Arbatov, *The System: An Insider's Life in Soviet Politics* (New York, 1992), 351.
8. Stephen Cohen, "The Friends and Foes of Change," in Alexander Dallin and Gail Lapidus, eds., *The Soviet System in Crisis* (Boulder, Colo., 1991), chap. 6.
9. A. V. Gromov and O. S. Kuzin, *Neformaly: Kto est'kto?* (Moscow, 1990); M. Steven Fish, *Democracy from Scratch: Opposition and Regime in the New Russian Revolution* (Princeton, N.J., 1995); Vyacheslav Igrunov, "Public Movements: From Protest to Political Self-Consciousness," and Andrei Fadin, "Emerging Political Institutions: From Informals to Multiparty Democracy,"

were competing for influence in a functioning legislature.[10] Vibrant print and broadcast media raised the quality and diversity of political discourse and contributed to an informed and attentive citizenry.[11] All of these developments stemmed from Gorbachev's policy of *glasnost'*, which gave voice to the range of political views encompassed by Soviet society and allowed groups access to information as a tool for organizing their political activity.

Policy Networks. The correspondence that Risse-Kappen identified between weak social organizations and state-dominated policy networks fits the Soviet case, although here one should speak of *party*-state domination rather than simply state domination. Under the old Soviet system, coalition building by and large excluded societal actors and was influenced only indirectly and weakly by public opinion.

Characterizing the post-reform policy networks in the Soviet Union and post-Soviet Russia is somewhat difficult. The party-state-dominated policy network is certainly a thing of the past, but it is not clear what has replaced it. The Communist Party, as the official governing party, was abolished, but many state institutions remained strong, including several economic ministries, the defense and foreign ministries, and the successors to the KGB. At the same time social organizations remained active, and some of them acquired considerable political influence. At first it was not easy to identify the various organizations' political constituencies, as a remark by the Russian neofascist politician Vladimir Zhirinovskii (head of the misnamed Liberal Democratic Party) suggested in 1990: "My program? It is like everybody else's: *perestroika*, free market, and democracy!"[12] Gradually, however, somewhat distinct political programs emerged, and in some cases one could begin to identify genuine constituencies. These organizations were engaged in a bargaining process with state institutions, such that the post-Soviet system of policy networks that evolved in the last years of Gorbachev's tenure can probably be considered a form of corporatism.[13] One must qualify such a characterization, however, in two respects: first, by acknowledging that most "corporate" entities were still in the process of trying to determine where their interests lay and were far from homogeneous; and second, by recognizing the presence of grassroots social movements—active especially on nationalist

---

both in Brad Roberts and Nina Belyaeva, eds., *After Perestroika: Democracy in the Soviet Union* (Washington, D.C., 1991).

10. Vladimir Pribylovskii, *Dictionary of Political Parties and Organizations in Russia* (Washington, D.C., 1992); Vera Tolz, *The USSR's Emerging Multiparty System* (New York, 1990).

11. For a useful overview, see Jamey Gambrell, "Moscow: The Front Page," *New York Review of Books*, 8 October 1992.

12. Pribylovskii, *Dictionary of Political Parties*, ix. Zhirinovskii and his colleagues drafted the LDP program in December 1989 and held the party's first congress the following March. See Michael McFaul and Sergei Markov, *The Troubled Birth of Russian Democracy: Parties, Personalities, and Programs* (Stanford, Calif., 1993), 247.

13. Michael McFaul, "State Power, Institutional Change, and the Politics of Privatization in Russia," *World Politics* 47, 2 (January 1995): 210–243.

and ecological issues—that resisted corporatist forms of representation in favor of direct appeals to the government.

Expectations about the Impact of Domestic Structure

So long as the USSR functioned as a strong, hierarchical, centralized state, transnational actors often had direct access to the top—to the general secretary of the Communist Party. With the weakening of the party-state apparatus, as we saw happening in 1989–90, we should expect a decentralization and fragmentation of the policy process. With the removal of the Communist Party's political monopoly, more actors would participate in policymaking, including in the security sphere.[14] We should also expect the military and the weapons laboratories to find more opportunities to express their views and potentially to influence policy, once Gorbachev could no longer implement Party discipline and societal resources became available to groups espousing views contrary to the government's policy. The transnational coalition would remain active, but it would no longer have the preferential access to the top, mainly because the system would no longer be as centralized and hierarchical as it was. My expectation for the post-Soviet period is that transnational relations would flourish but their impact would be diffuse and uncertain. As Risse-Kappen hypothesized, transnational actors would have multiple channels to raise their demands, but given the fragmentation of the political process and frequently shifting policy coalitions, their impact on policies could be short-lived. Societal organizations would be too weak to serve as reliable allies for transnational groups, and sympathetic government agencies would face opponents within the bureaucracy.[15]

The introduction of a functioning legislature in 1989 provided a new forum for discussion of security issues and legitimated the role of new actors in Soviet foreign policy. The transition to a market economy made enterprises, including those in the military sector, more dependent on their own resources and eager to find international partners and customers. These structural attributes of the new Soviet system that gradually emerged out of Gorbachev's reforms had a noticeable impact on the behavior of transnational coalitions.

THE TEETER-TOTTER OF NUCLEAR TESTING

The fate of nuclear testing in the Soviet Union from 1989 to 1993 depended on the relative strengths of the proponents and opponents of a unilateral Soviet moratorium. The transnational coalition of scientists no longer played a

14. The USSR Supreme Soviet's Committee on Defense and State Security was a case in point. See G. Sturua, "Komitet po voprosam oborony i gosudarstvennoi bezopasnosti: pervye mesiatsy raboty," *Mirovaia ekonomika i mezhdunarodnye otnosheniia*, 1990, no. 1:79–85.

15. Risse-Kappen, "Bringing Transnational Relations Back In."

key role in influencing Soviet policy. On the one hand, they were eclipsed by a mass movement of antinuclear activists who enjoyed considerable success in disrupting the Soviet nuclear test program. On the other hand, the transnational disarmament coalition helped give rise, and then gave way, to a competing transnational group of weapons designers who opposed even a bilateral test ban and who exerted substantial influence on the government of Boris Yeltsin. The politics of the test ban debate reveal the post-Soviet domestic structure as an unusual mix of societal activism and corporatist bargaining.

The original unilateral nuclear test moratorium initiated by Gorbachev lasted from August 1985 until February 1987. The resumption of testing should not be understood as the main indication of the weakening of the transnational coalition's influence on Soviet policy. As Chapter 13 explains, advocates of the unilateral moratorium had always promoted it as a means of getting the United States to stop testing—most likely through the efforts of the U.S. side of the coalition to convince Congress to legislate a U.S. halt.[16] Those efforts failed, and the United States continued to pursue a vigorous program of nuclear testing.[17]

In the absence of U.S. restraint, it was only a matter of time before Gorbachev would heed the counsel of his military officials and resume Soviet tests. Given the similarity between Gorbachev's behavior and that of his predecessor Nikita Khrushchev, who also failed in his efforts to use a test moratorium to achieve a comprehensive test ban twenty-five years earlier, we should not look to structural changes as the impetus to the Soviet resumption of tests.

Test-Ban Opponents Speak Up

For the most part the structural changes came later. Soviet military objections to the test moratorium in 1985 and 1986 were rather subdued—as one would expect, given the role of Party discipline and restrictions on public discussion of security policy associated with the old domestic structure. What changed with the expansion of glasnost and especially with the transformation of the Supreme Soviet into a medium of public debate was the ability of test ban opponents to promote their views openly. In July 1989, for example, the Soviet defense minister responded to demands from parliamentary deputies to revive the moratorium by arguing that the "USSR's unilateral suspension of nuclear weapons upgrading could cause the existing parity in this

16. Interviews by author with Aleksei Arbatov, 18 August 1993; with Evgenii Velikhov, 29 July 1992; with Christopher Paine, 28 October 1988; with Frank von Hippel, 24 April 1992.
17. Christopher E. Paine, "Nuclear Test Restriction Fails to Pass Senate: Victim of Weapons Lab Lobbying Campaign; New U.S.-Soviet Agenda for Test Ban Talks," *F.A.S. Public Interest Report* 40, 9 (November 1987).

sphere to be upset and lead to catastrophic, unpredictable consequences."[18] Such hyperbolic defense of military prerogatives would have been considered a major breach of Party discipline just a couple of years earlier.[19]

Not only did military officers began to express their views about nuclear testing in the new conditions of glasnost and parliamentary debate. Workers from towns whose very existence had recently been secret—the employees of the Soviet military-industrial complex—began to voice their concerns about imminent unemployment if the nuclear test sites were closed.[20] The deputy minister of nuclear power and industry published a long article in *Pravda* in October 1990 making the case for further nuclear tests by warning that "our country's unilateral nuclear disarmament paves the way to a U.S. monopoly."[21] The director of the nuclear weapons laboratory at Arzamas-16 (the previously anonymous "installation," where Andrei Sakharov worked on nuclear weapons from 1950 to 1968),[22] argued that the Soviet nuclear arsenal must be developed "dynamically" in order to keep up with the United States: "I recall that when we asked the Japanese how far behind them we were in electronics, the answer was given, 'forever.' . . . If we fall behind the Americans it will be simply impossible to catch up."[23]

The Nevada-Semipalatinsk Movement

Ranged in opposition to the increasingly outspoken proponents of Soviet nuclear testing was an unprecedented, large, and effective mass movement. The emergence of a popular grassroots movement against nuclear testing was both a consequence of the changing Soviet domestic structure and a catalyst for further change—namely the disintegration of the multiethnic state.

In 1989, an antinuclear group called "Nevada" was formed in Kazakhstan to protest nuclear testing at the main Soviet test site near Semipalatinsk.[24] The

18. *Krasnaia zvezda*, 21 July 1989, quoted in *Arms Control Reporter* (Cambridge, Mass., 1989), 608.B.181.

19. Other deputies, mainly military officers, also supported the continuation of testing, in the absence of U.S. agreement to a mutual ban. See, e.g., the remarks of Col. N. S. Petrushenko in *Krasnaia zvezda*, 29 November 1989, quoted in *Arms Control Reporter*, 608.B.188; and of retired chief of the General Staff Marshal Sergei Akhromeev on Moscow television, 9 October 1990, quoted in *Arms Control Reporter*, 608.B.204–205.

20. *Krasnaia zvezda*, 4 January 1990, quoted in *Arms Control Reporter*, 608.B.196.

21. V. Mikhailov, "Why Should the Country's Nuclear Test Sites Remain Silent?" *Pravda*, 24 October 1990, translation of the Foreign Broadcast Information Service, in *Daily Report: Soviet Union*, FBIS-SOV-90-207, 1–3.

22. Andrei Sakharov, *Memoirs* (New York, 1990); see David Holloway's review in *Bulletin of the Atomic Scientists* 47, 6 (July/August 1991): 37–38.

23. *Krasnaia zvezda*, 25 December 1990, quoted in *Arms Control Reporter*, 608.B.208–209.

24. My main sources on the Nevada movement include: Peter Zheutlin, "Nevada, USSR," *Bulletin of the Atomic Scientists*, March 1990, 10–12; Ian Mather, "Life and Death under a Cloud in Radiation City," *The European*, 1–3 June 1990; various issues of the movement's newspaper, *Izbiratel'*; S. Erzhanov, "Krepnet golos razuma," *Vecherniaia Alma-Ata*, 25 May 1990; "O Budushchem mira—s trevogoi i bol'iu," *Kazakhstanskaia Pravda*, 26 May 1990; Olzhas Suleimenov, "Semipalatinsk-Nevada as viewed by a people's deputy of the USSR," interview by Iurii Dmitriev, *Moscow News*, 24–31 December 1989, 15; Daniel Young, "Thousands in

movement was transnational in its very conception: the name was chosen to attract the attention of grassroots antinuclear activists ("downwinders") working to shut down the U.S. test site in Nevada, and links between the two groups were quickly formed.[25]

The Nevada movement was founded by the renowned Kazakh poet Olzhas Suleimenov. In early 1989 Suleimenov was beginning his campaign for a seat in the newly created Congress of People's Deputies. He had scheduled an appearance on local television for 26 February when he learned that two underground nuclear tests at the Semipalatinsk test range earlier in the month had vented radioactive or other toxic materials into the atmosphere. He scrapped his original campaign speech and discussed the accidents instead. He called on all concerned citizens of Kazakhstan to meet at the Writers' Union hall in Alma Ata two days later. Five thousand people showed up at what turned out to be the founding meeting of the Nevada-Semipalatinsk movement. Among other demands, the movement called for the closing of the Semipalatinsk test site, an environmental cleanup program, and an end to secrecy concerning the fate of Soviet victims of radiation. Eventually over a million signatures were gathered in support of the petition.

Suleimenov handily won election to the Congress of People's Deputies and then to the USSR Supreme Soviet. He became a prominent spokesperson for antinuclear and environmental issues throughout the Soviet Union, but he particularly tapped into the anti-Moscow sentiment of the citizens of his native Kazakhstan (about half of whom are ethnic Russians). As the efforts of the transnational network of scientists began to reach the limits of its effectiveness, the volatile mix of environmentalism, antinuclearism, and nationalism propelled the Nevada-Semipalatinsk movement into a central role in the struggle over Soviet nuclear testing. A mass demonstration on 6 August 1989 (Hiroshima Day) drew fifty thousand people. Another twenty thousand assembled to greet several hundred international delegates to a Congress on Nuclear Testing in Alma Ata in May 1990, and thousands more met the delegates when they visited the city of Semipalatinsk, the village of Karaul near the test site, and even a roadside rest area in between.[26] The movement had such widespread support that Suleimenov could credibly threaten to call the

Alma-Ata Demand Test Ban," *PSR Reports* 10, 2 (Summer 1990); *Vital Signs* [IPPNW newsletter] 3, 1 (March 1990) and 3, 2 (August 1990); Peter Zheutlin, "Kazakhstan: Life and Death in the Shadow of the Mushroom Cloud," *Los Angeles Times*, 1 April 1990.

25. Students of social movements, such as my colleague Sidney Tarrow, might disagree with my calling Nevada-Semipalatinsk a *transnational social movement*, which he defines as "sustained interactions with opponents—national or nonnational—by connected networks of challengers organized across national boundaries." If the contacts between the Nevada movement and the U.S. movement of "downwinders" were temporary or episodic rather than sustained, Tarrow would prefer to speak of "transnational political exchange" or "cross-border diffusion." See his *Power in Movement: Social Movements and Contentious Politics*, 2d ed. (Cambridge, U.K., 1998), 184–188.

26. *PSR Reports* (Summer 1990); and personal observation.

In May 1990 some ten thousand demonstrators from around the world met at Alma Ata and Karaul in Kazakhstan to protest against nuclear testing and demand a comprehensive test ban. Photo © James Lerager.

coal miners of Kazakhstan—one of the main coal-producing regions of the USSR—out to strike if the movement's demands were not met. In fact, closing the Semipalatinsk test site topped the list of the miners' demands when they threatened strikes in the summer of 1990.[27]

The Nevada movement was a clear example of an effective use of transnational symbols, allies, and resources—at least in its impact on Soviet policy. It received little attention, however, in the United States and had no impact on U.S. plans for nuclear testing. Members of the transnational test ban coalition tried to come up with ways to tap the power of the grassroots Kazakh movement to influence U.S. policy. Evgenii Velikhov at one point jokingly suggested flying a hundred thousand Kazakhs to Washington, D.C., on Aeroflot, with or without visas, to demonstrate at the White House. Thomas Cochran of the Natural Resources Defense Council (NRDC) proposed flying them directly to the Nevada test site to bolster the cause of their weaker U.S. counterparts.[28]

To influence Soviet policy the Nevada-Semipalatinsk movement required no such fanciful schemes. The impact was direct and powerful. An official in the Soviet foreign ministry admitted in early 1990 that the movement was responsible for forcing the Soviet military to cancel eleven of its eighteen scheduled nuclear tests for 1989.[29] In early 1990 the Soviet government promised to conduct only twenty-seven more tests at Semipalatinsk and then close the site in 1993, but that was not soon enough for the grassroots activists.[30] Ultimately the nuclear debate became caught up in the power struggle between "the center" (the Soviet government, ministerial, and Party apparatus in Moscow) and the republics. In December 1990, the Kazakhstan parliament banned nuclear weapons testing on the republic's territory.

Although Nevada-Semipalatinsk was a self-consciously international and transnational effort, its appeal rested to considerable measure on the anti-Moscow sentiment that so prevailed throughout the Soviet Union in its last years. In May 1990, for example, participants at an international test ban congress in Kazakhstan traveled to Karaul, the village nearest the test range, to join local victims of the Soviet nuclear complex in a demonstration. One of the speakers, a local Kazakh man, issued a strong indictment of the historical role of the Russians in his country: "The Russians have never cared about Kazakhstan. The only reason they developed the region was because they were fleeing the Germans [in 1941] and had to have someplace where they could build up their strength to fight again." Concerned about the volatile nature of his comments, the Soviet interpreter chose to "translate" his remarks

---

27. "Soviet Miners Speak," interviews by William Mandel, *The Station Relay* 5, 1–5 (1989–1991), 28; Peter Rutland, "Labor Unrest Movements in 1989 and 1990," *Soviet Economy* 6, 4 (1990), reprinted in Hewett and Winston, *Milestones*, 287–325.
28. Thomas Cochran, interview by author, 22 May 1990.
29. Zheutlin, "Nevada, USSR," 11.
30. "Soviet Union to Close Testing Site," *Arms Control Today*, April 1990, 31.

Near the Kazakh village of Karaul in May 1990, Olzhas Suleimenov (right), founder of the Nevada-Semipalatinsk movement, and Bernard Lown, of the International Physicians for the Prevention of Nuclear War, dedicate a monument to victims of nuclear testing and of the atomic bombings of Hiroshima and Nagasaki. Photo © James Lerager.

as follows: "We are against the threat of nuclear war! We must fight to abolish all nuclear testing!" Since the man had spoken in Russian rather than Kazakh, the interpreter had only managed to spare the non-Russian speakers among the foreign participants. The Russians in attendance—at least some of whom probably shared the Kazakhs' antipathy to the government in Moscow—heard him loud and clear.[31]

The grassroots movement against Soviet nuclear testing represented more than a manifestation of center-regional conflict, although that aspect was certainly important. The atmosphere of glasnost and the demise of Communist Party discipline led to public disagreements about the appropriate Soviet test ban policy, even within official Soviet organizations. At the test ban congress in May 1990, for example, Lev Semeiko, a retired military officer affiliated with the Institute of the USA and Canada, expressed the official Soviet policy of the time that a test moratorium would have to be mutual—that the USSR would not resume its test ban without U.S. reciprocation. His remarks prompted a representative of the Soviet Peace Committee—heretofore a

31. Personal observation, Karaul, 27 May 1990.

mouthpiece of government policy—to declare that the Committee's official position favored the reimplementation of a unilateral Soviet moratorium.[32]

Elite-Mass Linkages in the Test Ban Movement

On 21 May 1990, officials of the International Physicians for the Prevention of Nuclear War met with Eduard Shevardnadze, the foreign minister, to urge the Soviet Union to resume its unilateral moratorium on nuclear testing. Shevardnadze replied that the USSR was ready to resume the moratorium if the strength of popular opposition to testing could be demonstrated.[33] This criterion marked an important change from the previous Soviet position—requiring a U.S. halt in testing as a condition of resumption of the Soviet ban—and was evidently intended to encourage the efforts of the IPPNW and the Nevada-Semipalatinsk mass movement.

Anticipating the unavailability of the Semipalatinsk test site (every test there was being met with mass protest demonstrations), Soviet military officials had long been planning to move nuclear testing to the second and little used Novaia Zemlia site near the Arctic Circle. The grassroots activists were always one step ahead of them, however. From the very beginning of the Nevada movement, Suleimenov and his followers had expressed solidarity with the peoples of the north and with the Pacific islanders of Mururoa, site of French nuclear testing. Members of the Nevada-Semipalatinsk-Mururoa movement, as it was renamed at the May congress, demanded a global test ban, not simply the shifting of nuclear tests away from their "backyard."[34]

Domestic opposition to nuclear testing at Novaia Zemlia from local residents as well as deputies of the USSR Supreme Soviet was reinforced by international criticism of the plans to resume testing there. Finland, Norway, Sweden, Denmark, and Iceland all expressed concern. Greenpeace launched a campaign to interfere with the tests, sending a ship that was intercepted by the KGB but welcomed by local residents. A couple of weeks earlier the Soviet coast guard had seized a Norwegian ship with a crew of environmentalists who were trying to test for radioactivity in the area of the test range.[35]

Despite such widespread domestic and international opposition, the Soviet military authorities managed to conduct a nuclear test, unannounced, on 24 October 1990—their first in over a year, and, as it turned out, their last. Further plans for tests at Semipalatinsk and Novaia Zemlia were canceled

---

32. Personal observation, Alma-Ata, 25 May 1990.
33. Bernard Lown, comments at conference in Alma-Ata, 22 May 1990.
34. In 1995, the movement directed its attention to Chinese nuclear testing as well. See Bruce Pannier, "Kazakhstan's Anti-Nuclear Marchers Stopped before Chinese Border," *OMRI Daily Digest*, 1995, no. 153, pt. 1 (8 August) (electronic version).
35. Shannon Fagan, "Target Novaya Zemlya: Journey into the Soviet Nuclear Testing Zone," *Greenpeace Magazine*, January/February 1991, 13–16; *Arms Control Reporter*, 608.B.204–205.

owing to popular opposition at the grassroots level and within the Soviet parliament.[36] In the wake of the failed coup in August 1991, the president of Kazakhstan closed the Semipalatinsk range.[37] Bowing to the inevitable, Mikhail Gorbachev declared a year-long moratorium on Soviet nuclear testing starting in early October 1991. Three weeks later, Boris Yeltsin banned nuclear tests on Russian territory for a year and specifically decreed that the Novaia Zemlia archipelago no longer be used as a nuclear test range.[38]

At the end of 1991 Kazakhstan became an independent country, and, as the Soviet Union disintegrated, it gained sovereign control over the Semipalatinsk test range. The Soviet nuclear weapons left on its territory made Kazakhstan de facto the world's fourth most powerful nuclear state. Yet the country's government and citizens chose nuclear disarmament. The nuclear weapons were dismantled and sent back to Russia, and the nuclear test range remained silent.

The Countercoalition: Transnational and Pronuclear

Despite the seemingly decisive victory of the antinuclear movement in shutting down the Soviet Union's two main test ranges and reinstating the unilateral test moratorium, the proponents of nuclear testing showed no sign of conceding. In February 1992, barely a month after the breakup of the Soviet Union, the Russian deputy minister for nuclear energy and industry began arguing for a resumption of nuclear tests following the end of Yeltsin's moratorium in October 1992. The official, Viktor Mikhailov, expressed concern about the potential "degradation" of the country's scientific expertise. He argued that "it is better for everyone to agree on a limited number of tests instead of a complete ban, because otherwise we might lose the level of [expertise] we now possess."[39]

The arguments of the Russian proponents of nuclear testing sound remarkably similar to those of their American counterparts—and not by coincidence. During the late 1980s Soviet advocates of nuclear testing were able to forge transnational alliances with U.S. opponents of a test ban. They did so in some measure by taking advantage of the successful efforts of the protest-ban coalition to get nuclear testing and particularly verification back on the official Soviet-American arms control agenda.

By demonstrating the feasibility of seismic verification and threatening to legislate an end to testing through congressional action, the test ban coalition

---

36. I. Sichka, "We Blast without Warning," *Komsomol'skaia Pravda*, 26 October 1990; "Resolution Adopted on Novaya Zemlya Nuclear Test," TASS report, 31 October 1990; "Arkhangelsk Leadership Protests Nuclear Tests," TASS report, 31 October 1990; all translations from the Foreign Broadcast Information Service, in *Daily Report: Soviet Union*, FBIS-SOV-90-210, 30 October 1990.

37. *Arms Control Reporter*, 608.B.208, 216.

38. *Arms Control Reporter*, 608.B.220–221.

39. *Washington Post*, 5 February 1992, cited in *Arms Control Reporter*, 608.B.225.

managed to get the Reagan administration to reverse its objection to a comprehensive test ban in principle. The administration agreed to undertake to negotiate a series of steps gradually limiting the number and size of tests, with the long-term goal of a total cessation. President Bush subsequently reneged on this commitment, but the Clinton administration resumed negotiations on a comprehensive test ban and finally achieved it in 1996.[40]

Test ban verification became a natural focus of official U.S.-Soviet negotiations and a rallying point for Soviet and U.S. weapons designers. This is a not a surprising outcome, given the progress in seismic monitoring of nuclear testing that the joint project between the NRDC and the Soviet Academy of Sciences had achieved, combined with the Reagan and Bush administrations' preoccupation with Soviet cheating. The coalition of American and Soviet test ban proponents had actually paved the way for such negotiations by bringing U.S. and Soviet weapons designers together for the first time to discuss verification at a conference in Moscow. The weaponeers got along remarkably well and seemed to sympathize with each other's desire to continue testing—much to the dismay of the conference organizers.[41] One thing that both sides could agree upon was that "joint efforts were needed to upgrade verification methods."[42] In the view of the weapons scientists, joint efforts at evaluating verification methods required continued nuclear explosions so that there would be something on which to base the evaluations. This approach coincides exactly with the one favored by the Reagan and Bush administrations. First with some reluctance, and then with increasing enthusiasm, Russian weapons scientists began observing U.S. nuclear tests in Nevada. In March 1992, twenty-three Russians were on hand to observe the first U.S. nuclear test of that year.[43] On their return home, they argued that carrying out the Russian-American agreements on verification required further nuclear tests. As one observer complained at the time, thanks to the new transnational contacts between Russian and U.S. bomb makers, "Russian officials simply adopt the U.S. nuclear establishment's arguments for continued testing and translate them into Russian."[44]

Corporatist Bargaining on Nuclear Testing

The Russian nuclear testing lobby seemed to have achieved considerable success in influencing President Boris Yeltsin—thanks largely, it seems, to the efforts of Viktor Mikhailov. Mikhailov's entire career had been devoted to the

---

40. On the Bush administration policy, see *Arms Control Reporter*, 608.B.191, citing various press reports from January 1990.
41. Discussions with Frank von Hippel of the FAS, Thomas Cochran of the NRDC, and Steve Fetter of the University of Maryland, in Moscow, Alma Ata, and Semipalatinsk, 22–25 May 1990.
42. TASS report, 29 May 1990, cited in *Arms Control Reporter*, 608.B.199.
43. *Arms Control Reporter*, 608.B.227.
44. George Perkovich, "Weapons Complexes v. Democracy," *Bulletin of the Atomic Scientists* 48, 5 (June 1992): 17.

design and building of nuclear weapons.[45] In 1986 Mikhailov had participated, albeit incognito, in the negotiations led by the NRDC to monitor the Soviet nuclear test moratorium.[46]

In January 1992, Mikhailov became first deputy head of the newly independent Russia's Ministry of Nuclear Energy and Industry. He immediately issued an invitation to President Yeltsin to visit the top-secret nuclear weapons laboratory at Arzamas-16. Mikhailov was searching for ways to keep his operations going, and he needed Yeltsin's support. Rather than close the Novaia Zemlia test range, Mikhailov proposed using it to conduct tests of "peaceful nuclear explosions." He suggested using the site as a disposal center to get rid of toxic materials such as the chemical and nuclear weapons that had to be destroyed because of arms control treaties. The idea would be to blow them up with nuclear explosives. Mikhailov apparently had a direct financial stake in such operations. His ministry was collaborating with a Russian company to sell disposal services to any interested customers. The company was founded by weapons scientists at Arzamas-16 and originally funded by the Soviet Military-Industrial Commission, which financed some of the projects of the Ministry of Nuclear Energy as well.[47] The arrangement mixed private and state economic activities in a way that was becoming increasingly common in Russia in the early 1990s.

During a long, vodka-inspired discussion, Mikhailov had considerable success persuading Yeltsin of the merits of his proposals. Mikhailov presented three "treaties" for the president's signature: (1) to resume nuclear testing at Novaia Zemlia after the expiration of the one-year moratorium, thereafter conducting 3–4 tests per year; (2) to maintain the formerly closed nuclear research and test sites, such as Arzamas-16, under the central government's jurisdiction, in order to protect them from hardships of economic reform and from the interference of local authorities who might prefer to convert them to civilian activities; and (3) Mikhailov's own promotion to minister. Yeltsin signed all three.[48]

The Russian president's subsequent actions give this story the ring of truth. First, in February 1992, the month after his meeting with Mikhailov, Yeltsin instructed the Ministry of Nuclear Energy and the joint high command of the armed forces of the Commonwealth of Independent States "to continue in 1992 the necessary work involved in preparing tunnels and wells for conducting underground nuclear tests on Novaia Zemlia at a rate of two to four per year, if the declared moratorium expires."[49] Second, Yeltsin signed a decree transferring Novaia Zemlia from the USSR Defense Ministry's Sixth State

45. V. N. Mikhailov, *Ia—"Iastreb"* (Moscow, 1993).
46. Christopher Paine, interview by author, Arlington, Va., 2 April 1994.
47. *Arms Control Reporter*, 605.B.120–122, an extensive summary of an investigation conducted by Canadian researchers.
48. Von Hippel, interview. Von Hippel's source for this story was a high-level official of the Russian Foreign Ministry.
49. *Arms Control Reporter*, 608.B.226, citing *Nezavisimaia gazeta*, 24 March 1992, and the Russian television news program *Vesti* of 3 March 1992.

The Post-Soviet Era

Central Test Site to the Russian Federation's control.[50] Finally, Mikhailov was promoted from first deputy to minister for nuclear energy. He became increasingly outspoken about the need to continue nuclear tests, relying on standard nostrums about "the need to maintain the country's defense sufficiency" as well as the newer arguments learned from his transnational allies in the United States: nuclear testing must continue in order to ensure proper verification of nuclear testing in compliance with current treaties.[51]

Alternative Explanations

A possible alternative explanation for the shifts in Soviet policy on nuclear testing—one that does not emphasize the change in domestic structure— might focus instead on the nature of the Russian-American relationship. From the late 1980s two trends seemed to coincide—a weakening in Russia's economic and political situation and an improvement in Russian-American relations. The United States, especially during the Bush administration, consistently made promises to help the Soviet economy, promises that were contingent on Soviet willingness to pursue policies congenial to the United States.[52] By this argument, the Russian government saw no reason to push for a comprehensive test ban that the United States opposed or even to maintain its own moratorium, because the United States would continue testing with or without the Russians. Only when U.S. policy changed under the Clinton administration toward support for a test ban would the Russians decide not to resume testing. This explanation has much to recommend it, although it gives insignificant attention to the pressures on President Yeltsin from both the grassroots antinuclear activists and the nuclear establishment. Despite the important role of the United States, Russian testing policy often hinged on the delicate internal balance of pro- and antinuclear forces—a balance that emerged as a result of the change from a highly centralized, hierarchical domestic structure to a fragmented and fluid one.

THE ARMY ON THE OFFENSIVE

The case of conventional forces in Europe is the one we would most expect to see affected by the transformation of the international environment starting in late 1989. The opening of the Berlin Wall on 9 November 1989—a year to the day since Gorbachev had ordered the Soviet Defense Ministry to draw up plans for withdrawal of Soviet troops from eastern Europe—was quickly

50. Ibid.
51. *Rossiiskaia gazeta*, quoted in *Arms Control Reporter*, 608.B.233–234.
52. Michael Beschloss and Strobe Talbott, *At the Highest Levels: The Inside Story of the End of the Cold War* (Boston, 1993).

followed by the formation of noncommunist government throughout the region. Less than a year later, on 3 October 1990, the Federal Republic of Germany absorbed the East German *Länder*, and the German Democratic Republic ceased to exist. The combination of these events ended the bipolar, Cold War division of Europe. The negotiations on Conventional Forces in Europe (CFE), initiated in the context of a confrontation between two alliances, NATO and the Warsaw Pact, were completed under entirely different circumstances. Far more than in the other two issues discussed in this chapter—nuclear testing and strategic defense—the profound international changes bore directly on the substance of the negotiations on conventional forces.

It is all the more remarkable, then, that the behavior of the other parties with which the Soviet government negotiated did not change. As the most comprehensive study of the negotiations describes, "only in Moscow was there even the slightest interest in revising the CFE Treaty to accommodate the continuing process of historical change. Every other party to the agreement was committed to the goal of having the CFE Treaty enter into force, and be implemented, exactly as it had been negotiated."[53] Thus, although the signals that Russian policymakers received from the West on the issue of conventional forces remained unchanged, Russia's own behavior changed dramatically—in part as a result of the major structural transformation in Russian domestic politics.

Glasnost for the Opponents of Reform

A key turning point for debates on the Soviet armed forces, and military reform in general, came with elections to the new Congress of People's Deputies in 1989. The electoral campaign marked a new stage in the expansion of glasnost into the security realm, with a wide range of proposals advanced and debated: shifting from a conscript to a professional-militia army, an end to the stationing of recruits outside their native areas, and, in general, a vast reduction in the claims of defense on the Soviet economy.[54] As the new atmosphere gave reformers opportunities to criticize the existing state of affairs, it also gave conservatives a chance to defend the status quo and even undermine the reforms already accomplished.

The reaction among the conservatives to the changes in eastern Europe was harsh, and blame was placed squarely on Gorbachev, Shevardnadze, Iakovlev, and their "new thinking" in foreign policy. In early 1990, a prominent journalist, a favorite of the military hard-liners, wrote: "The sentimental theory of 'our common European home' has brought about the collapse of

---

53. Richard A. Falkenrath, *Shaping Europe's Military Order: The Origins and Consequences of the CFE Treaty* (Cambridge, Mass., 1995), 146.
54. Eugene B. Rumer, *The End of a Monolith: The Politics of Military Reform in the Soviet Armed Forces*, RAND report R-3993-USDP (Santa Monica, Calif., 1990); Steven L. Solnick, *Stealing the State: Control and Collapse in Soviet Institutions* (Cambridge, Mass., 1998), chap. 6.

Eastern Europe's communist parties, a change in the state structures, and imminent reunification of the two Germanys. . . . As the color and contours of Europe's political map are changing, the bones of Russian infantrymen stir in their unknown graves."[55]

More worrying to Shevardnadze than the sniping of journalists was the rank insubordination among his own staff. V. I. Brovikov, the Soviet ambassador to Poland, who had to sit by and watch as the communist government there was replaced in August 1989, later minced no words in criticizing his boss. He complained that the West "while heaping praise on us, is crowing over the collapse of the 'colossus with feet of clay' and the demise of Communism and world socialism. Yet we are trying to present all this as a dizzying success for perestroika and the new thinking in international affairs."[56] The reference to Shevardnadze's upbeat assessment of the changes in eastern Europe was unmistakable.

Even Foreign Ministry officials loyal to the reformist orientation found their work undermined by the new political situation. The consequences were evident in the negotiations on conventional forces. At one point, Oleg Grinevskii, the head of the Soviet delegation to the CFE talks, reported back to Gorbachev that the military members of the Soviet delegation seemed to have their own instructions from the Ministry of Defense. They appeared to be deliberately sabotaging the negotiations.[57] But Gorbachev, who had taken a "turn to the right" during the autumn of 1990 in an attempt to bolster his political position, was reluctant to rein in the military leaders. Soviet Foreign Ministry representatives at the CFE negotiations privately complained to their U.S. counterparts "that they had become mouthpieces for the Defense Ministry back in Moscow."[58] It was under these circumstances that Shevardnadze announced his resignation as Soviet foreign minister at the end of December 1990.

The CFE Treaty under Assault

Gorbachev and his allies deliberately undermined the Communist Party's control over Soviet political life and sought to decentralize and democratize the process of decision making. One consequence was an unprecedented assertion of autonomy on the part of the Soviet Ministry of Defense, reflected in the military's approach to the CFE Treaty.

---

55. Aleksandr Prokhanov, "Tragediia," *Literaturnaia Rossiia*, 5 January 1990, quoted in John Van Oudenaren, *The Role of Shevardnadze and the Ministry of Foreign Affairs in the Making of Soviet Defense and Arms Control Policy*, RAND Report R-3898-USDP (Santa Monica, Calif., 1990), 57.
56. *Pravda*, 7 February 1990, quoted in Van Oudenaren, *Role of Shevardnadze*, 57.
57. A. S. Cherniaev (Gorbachev's aide for foreign policy), interview by author, Moscow, 5 June 1997.
58. Beschloss and Talbott, *Highest Levels*, 363.

Starting in mid-1990, Soviet military officials undertook three initiatives intended either to undermine the treaty itself or to reinterpret it to serve better their conception of Soviet interests.[59] First, in the weeks prior to the signing of the treaty in November 1990, the Soviet military moved enormous stocks of weapons and equipment out of the "Atlantic-to-the-Urals" area covered by the treaty, thereby reducing the amount liable for reduction. The equipment was transferred to locations east of the Ural Mountains on such a massive scale that the effort reportedly tied up the rail transport system and exacerbated the distribution of food supplies throughout the country.[60]

Second, Soviet negotiators, relying on data supplied by their military representatives, provided figures for the amount of equipment subject to reduction that were much lower than Western assessments. Third, and most serious, the Soviet military reassigned three ground-forces divisions from the army to the navy in order to escape treaty limitations and claimed that four "naval infantry" or marine regiments were also exempt. As one analyst has observed, these actions threatened to open "a massive loophole in the treaty's numerical limits: the Soviets claimed, in essence, that a unit could be exempted from CFE limitation simply by giving the navy titular authority over it."[61]

Through these actions, the military expressed its main objection to the CFE Treaty—that it covered only the areas of conventional ground forces where the USSR held advantages, but left completely untouched the conventional naval forces, in which the United States was vastly superior. As General Mikhail Moiseev, the chief of the Soviet General Staff, reportedly complained to one U.S. politician, "your side has steadfastly refused to deal with naval armaments in arms control. We have been disappointed, and we have had to take appropriate measures."[62]

It seems certain that these initiatives were taken by the Soviet military without the knowledge of the civilian authorities. Soviet negotiators apparently learned for the first time of the magnitude of the withdrawal of equipment from Europe from their Western counterparts in September 1990. Then, in a discussion with U.S. secretary of state James Baker in early December, Soviet foreign minister Shevardnadze was shown evidence from satellite photography that convinced him that the Soviet military had indeed underreported the amount of Soviet equipment in the area covered by the treaty. Shevardnadze described his position in a 1991 interview: "The transfer of huge quantities of equipment to areas beyond the Urals created an awkward situation in our relations with partners. . . . I as Foreign Minister was

59. This discussion draws mainly on Falkenrath, *Shaping Europe's Military Order*, chap. 4.
60. *Sovetskaia Rossiia*, 9 January 1991, cited in Harry Gelman, *The Rise and Fall of National Security Decisionmaking in the Former USSR*, RAND Report R-4200-A (Santa Monica, Calif., 1992), 39.
61. Falkenrath, *Shaping Europe's Military Order*, 132.
62. Beschloss and Talbott, *Highest Levels*, 363.

presented with a fait accompli."[63] As one observer has pointed out, "there is some reason to believe that this embarrassing revelation—or, more precisely, his indignation at having been lied to by his own military—contributed to Shevardnadze's decision to resign two weeks later."[64]

The Soviet military's challenges to implementation of the CFE Treaty were resisted by the Bush administration. It insisted that Gorbachev reassert control over the arms control process and carry out Soviet obligations. Some measure of compromise was entailed in securing Soviet compliance with the treaty. The Soviet side was allowed, for example, to reassign its three ground divisions to the navy, but only if a commensurate amount of equipment were removed from other units in the region. Although the CFE Treaty was signed in November 1990, the compromise agreement on implementation was not worked out until June 1991. The entire episode demonstrated the extent to which the domestic structural changes in the Soviet Union had allowed for a resurgence of influence by the traditional institutions of national security and how, under the new circumstances, the United States could play a key role in tipping the balance back in favor of the civilian authorities.

Alternative Explanations

The main rival explanation to a domestic structural one would focus on the changing strategic environment facing the Russian military. This explanation is not particularly relevant for the three initiatives taken in mid-1990 that challenged the CFE Treaty. They were of little military significance; their importance lay rather in the threat they posed to civilian control of the negotiating process and the extent to which they expressed the military's unhappiness with the terms of the treaty—particularly the lack of limitations on naval forces.

There is, however, one issue related to the CFE Treaty that apparently involved strategic considerations. This was the problem of the so-called flank zone. The original CFE Treaty had allowed the greatest number of forces to remain in the central region of Europe, where the two alliances had traditionally faced off. In the northern and southern "flanks," forces were subject to much greater limitations, and the overall ceilings were shared among members of the alliances. When the Soviet Union broke up in 1991, Russia was obliged to share its quota of troop deployments in the southern region of the limitation zone with several new countries: Moldova, Georgia, Armenia, and Azerbaijan. The number of forces the Russian army could deploy in the volatile North Caucasus region was severely constrained. Yeltsin's government sought revision of the CFE flank limits to accommodate larger deployments in that region.[65]

63. "Eduard Shevardnadze's Choice," *International Affairs*, 1991, no. 11:4.
64. Falkenrath, *Shaping Europe's Military Order*, 130 n. 33.
65. Ibid., 231–239.

Even this strategic argument is, however, related to the post-Soviet change in domestic structure. One of the reasons the Russian army sought greater flexibility for deployment of its forces is because it frequently engaged them in military interventions within Russia and outside Russia's borders in the former republics of the Soviet Union—most disastrously in Chechnya from 1994 to 1996. Many observers believe that in several of these cases the Russian military "operated independently with only very loose, or in some cases no, control from the president." [66] Such a situation would have been inconceivable under the old Soviet system of centralized control and Communist Party discipline.

THE STAR WARS SEDUCTION

The situation with antiballistic missile systems from 1989 on resembled that of conventional forces and military reform in general. As glasnost flourished and the Communist Party's monopoly on truth diminished, new voices were heard in the Soviet discussions about strategic defenses. Gorbachev was no longer able to impose the "party line" opposing SDI.

Soviet Star Warriors

One of the first to speak out in favor of developing Soviet ballistic missile defenses was not a military official but a senior scientist at the Institute for Space Research. The institute's former director, Roald Sagdeev, was a prominent opponent of Star Wars, yet he was not inclined to impose his views on his subordinates, particularly in the new atmosphere. Viktor Etkin, chief of applied space physics at the institute argued in *Pravda* in favor of limited defenses against accidental nuclear launches and terrorist attacks: "such a limited system including ground- and space-based positions for combating non-massed missile launches is within the bounds of feasible technical solutions." [67]

Conducted in parallel with, and reinforcing, the efforts of some Soviet scientists to promote strategic defenses was an official U.S. government campaign to sell the Soviets on the merits of Star Wars. The U.S. invited Soviet officials to visit the nuclear weapons laboratory at Los Alamos in February 1990 to inspect the Beam Experiment Aboard Rocket (BEAR); the project was intended to demonstrate the feasibility of creating a weapon employing

---

66. F. Stephen Larrabee and Theodore W. Karasik, *Foreign and Security Policy Decisionmaking under Yeltsin* (Santa Monica, Calif., 1997), 13. For a detailed review of Russian interventions, see Fiona Hill and Pamela Jewett, *Back in the USSR: Russia's Intervention in the Internal Affairs of the Former Soviet Republics and the Implications for United States Policy toward Russia* (Cambridge, Mass., 1994).

67. *Pravda*, 20 July 1989, quoted in *Arms Control Reporter*, 575.B.370.

Frank von Hippel (right) and Christopher Paine (head reflected above von Hippel) inspect a Soviet laser at Sary Shagan, September 1987. Two years later, the Bush administration invited Soviet scientists to visit U.S. laser facilities in an effort to interest them in joint work on strategic defenses. Photo courtesy of Tom Cochran.

neutral particle beams.[68] Ironically, BEAR had evidently benefited considerably from published Soviet research on laser technology in the late 1960s.[69] The U.S. government also arranged a visit to a facility of TRW, a private military corporation in San Juan Capistrano, California, in order to view the company's Alpha laser project. The Bush administration evidently "hoped the visit would lead to Soviet understanding and eventual acceptance of U.S. proposals in the Defense and Space Talks" in Geneva to weaken the ABM Treaty and allow development of space-based defenses.[70]

The U.S. invitations were in some sense offered in reciprocation for the visits of U.S. citizens to secret Soviet military sites to investigate Soviet progress in laser and particle-beam technology. In August 1989, for example, a U.S. congressional delegation visited a branch of the Kurchatov Institute, headed by Velikhov, to inspect its gas laser equipment.[71] The initial precedent for

68. *Arms Control Reporter*, 575.B.375, 392.
69. Soviet research, according to Colonel Thomas Meyer, head of SDIO's directed energy program, "enabled the U.S. to shrink the machinery enough to loft it into space." *Arms Control Reporter*, 575.B.369.
70. *Arms Control Reporter*, 575.B.375.
71. Michael R. Gordon, "U.S. Visitors See Soviet Laser Firing," *New York Times*, 17 August 1989; Frank von Hippel, "Visit to a Laser Facility at the Soviet ABM Test Site," *Physics Today*, November 1989, 34–35; Frank von Hippel and Thomas B. Cochran, "The Myth of the Soviet 'Killer' Laser," *New York Times*, 19 August 1989; *Arms Control Reporter*, 575.B.373.

such visits, of course, was the NRDC seismic monitoring project, which paved the way for contacts between representatives of the Soviet military-research community and its U.S. counterpart. In effect, these visits by military officers to the research facilities of "the enemy" helped forge an alternative transnational linkage—one that little by little came to play an active role in thwarting the efforts of the original transnational network of disarmament proponents.

This transnational countercoalition even had its own "tacit" variant, as U.S. officials and other proponents of SDI took every opportunity to promote the views of Soviet supporters of strategic defenses, often calling attention to articles in the Soviet military press that would otherwise have gone unremarked.[72]

Gorbachev and Yeltsin on the Defensive

In July 1990 Gorbachev cautiously proposed to the Group of Seven industrialized countries the "development of joint ABM early warning systems to prevent unauthorized or terrorist operated launches of ballistic missiles."[73] President George Bush responded in September by agreeing to cooperative efforts on early warning, but he also called upon the USSR to permit the limited deployment of nonnuclear defenses. The U.S. secretary of defense pursued the matter a few days later, remarking that in the USSR "there are signs that there are people in positions of responsibility who are willing to entertain the notion of discussing defenses for the first time. . . . I think there's a growing awareness on the part of the Soviets of their vulnerability to ballistic missile attack from someplace besides the United States."[74] At the same time, an official in the SDI office made clear that Gorbachev's proposal for collaboration on early warning did not go far enough: "If we were to cooperate with them, it would have to be in the context of missile defenses. It wouldn't be early warning for the sake of early warning."[75] White House officials echoed that view.[76] Within a few days Gorbachev had conceded, stating that "we are ready to discuss the U.S. proposals on non-nuclear anti-missile defense systems. We propose to the U.S. side that the possibility of creating joint systems to avert nuclear missile strikes with ground- and space-based elements also be examined."[77]

---

72. In November 1990, for example, Keith Payne of the National Institute for Space Policy cited an article in the Soviet journal *Voennaia Mysl'* to argue that the USSR was becoming more accepting of strategic defenses. *Arms Control Reporter*, 575.B.399.

73. *Arms Control Reporter*, 575.B.403.

74. Ibid.

75. Ibid., 575.B.405.

76. Matthew Bunn, "The ABM Talks: The More Things Change . . . ," *Arms Control Today* 22, 7 (September 1992): 19.

77. *Arms Control Reporter*, 575.B.405.

Under pressure from domestic supporters of strategic defenses, and with few instruments available to control the debate, Boris Yeltsin allowed officials of his government to go even further in proposing joint efforts with the United States. In October 1991, several Soviet military officials, who simultaneously served on the Russian republic's State Committee on Defense, attended a meeting in Washington to discuss ballistic missile defense. They argued that, owing to Russia's relatively greater vulnerability to potentially hostile Third World countries, "our interest in joint work on ABM systems is obvious." During the same month several articles in mass-circulation newspapers and specialist journals promoted the idea of ABM defenses for Russia.[78] The new transnational coalition of U.S. and Russian proponents of ballistic missile defenses was established.[79] It continued well into the Clinton administration to promote amendment of the ABM Treaty, if not its complete abandonment, to allow at least the development of so-called theater ballistic missile defense systems.

Alternative Explanations

Both Gorbachev and Yeltsin had other reasons, besides pressure from transnational actors, for reconsidering the blanket Soviet condemnation of ballistic missile defense systems that could undermine the ABM Treaty. As the various Soviet republics bordering Russia asserted their claims of sovereignty and independence, they put at risk the integrity of the Soviet early warning system against missile attack. Thus, one can understand Gorbachev's proposals to cooperate with the United States in developing a joint system of early warning.

No doubt there is also some basis to Russian concerns about missile attacks by terrorists or aggressors from the Third World. In a sense though, these rationales mainly provided an opening for policy entrepreneurs—both in Russia and the United States—who wanted to promote the development of major strategic defense systems in any case. Those who have maintained a principled opposition to widespread strategic defenses had no trouble proposing alternative means to limit the threat of ballistic missile attacks (e.g., measures to stem the proliferation of missile and nuclear technology) and suggesting collaboration in early warning while maintaining a commitment to the ABM Treaty. Aleksei Arbatov, the academic military reformer who became a leading liberal member of the Russian Duma, is an outstanding example. But under the new domestic structural conditions, Arbatov's voice was only one of many, and it was often drowned out by those representing the Russian military-industrial sector. Nor did Arbatov's transnational allies enjoy any of the privileges that Gorbachev and Shevardnadze accorded them

78. Ibid., 575.B.405.
79. Fred C. Iklé, "Comrades in Arms," *New York Times*, 13 December 1991.

in the 1980s. One telling aspect of the change was evident to Christopher Paine, the disarmament expert who had been traveling frequently to Russia since the mid-1980s on behalf of the Federation of American Scientists, the NRDC, and U.S. senators and representatives. Commenting on what had changed since the end of the Soviet era, he said "Now we have to go through customs like everybody else . . . it's not special anymore."[80]

THE FATE OF THE TRANSNATIONAL NETWORKS

The opening up of the Soviet system made it possible for transnational contacts to flourish. Paradoxically, however, the new circumstances meant that the particular transnational network of disarmament proponents that was so influential in the early Gorbachev years now had to compete with groups advocating very different policies—and many of them now had their own transnational allies. To the extent that transnational contacts give domestic groups more resources to influence their government, the new pro-military groups were often much better endowed than their predecessors. The public interest groups, peace activists, and university professors who made up the Western side of the transnational disarmament network typically did not dispose of the kind of resources available to, say, the Strategic Defense Initiative Office, the U.S. government weapons laboratories, or TRW Corporation.

Russian Policy Reversals

As a consequence in part of the disproportionate resources of the competing transnational actors, the old disarmament coalition often saw its prior achievements reversed. In May 1988, for example, in one of many such collaborative arms control initiatives, the Federation of American Scientists (FAS) and the Committee of Soviet Scientists jointly proposed a ban on nuclear reactors in earth orbit. The document was signed in Washington by Frank von Hippel on behalf of the FAS and Roald Sagdeev for the Soviet committee.[81] Back in the USSR, the Soviet space-reactor community responded with newspaper articles promoting the importance of nuclear reactors in space and criticizing Sagdeev. Subsequently a Soviet delegation attended the annual U.S. space-reactor conference in Albuquerque and offered their reactors for sale. Their most enthusiastic customer was the SDI office of the Pentagon.[82] The leader of the Soviet delegation, Academician Nikolai N. Ponomarev-Stepnoi, was asked at the meeting about Sagdeev's opposition to

80. Paine, interview.
81. *F.A.S. Public Interest Report* 41, 9 (November 1988).
82. William J. Broad, "U.S. Moves to Bar Americans Buying Soviet Technology," *New York Times*, 1 March 1992.

nuclear reactors in earth orbit. He said that he had met with Sagdeev before leaving Moscow and that Sagdeev "told me his opinion and I told him mine. And we were both so glad that we could tell each other our own opinion in our own country finally."[83] The scientist's coy remark illuminates the larger reality—that the structural changes induced by glasnost, democratization, and market reforms, although supported and promoted by the transnational disarmament network, were a mixed blessing as far as its policy preferences were concerned.

In some cases, the change in domestic structure seems to have contributed to a change in the policy preferences of actors themselves. Thus, Evgenii Velikhov, a hero of the transnational scientists' movement, became a much more ambiguous figure in the new conditions. He, too, began promoting the sale of nuclear space reactors to the U.S. government—the Topaz model was developed at his Kurchatov Institute—even though the organization he founded (the Committee of Soviet Scientists) favored banning them.[84] In his efforts to find employment for scientists and international investment for enterprises of the former Soviet military-industrial sector, Velikhov developed extensive contacts with representatives of U.S. military contractors. He also appeared to have modified his opposition to ballistic missile defenses. In the summer of 1992, he invited Edward Teller and Lowell Wood of the Lawrence Livermore nuclear weapons laboratory for their first visit to Russia, ostensibly to discuss proposals for a global monitoring system to warn against missile attacks.[85] But Teller and Wood were well known as the most ardent proponents of Star Wars missile defenses,[86] and they no doubt hoped to persuade Velikhov of the merits of such systems and of the benefits of collaborating with U.S. military technologists.

The New Importance of U.S. Policy

When Bill Clinton became president in 1993, he initiated some policies that served to weaken the influence of the new transnational lobbies promoting nuclear testing and strategic defense. Clinton was more sympathetic than his predecessors to the views of transnational disarmament activists, some of whom even took jobs in his administration.

In the realm of nuclear testing, the U.S. Congress had by the end of the Bush administration done what test ban proponents had long hoped it would do: it imposed a moratorium on the U.S. nuclear test program as long as Russia

83. Frank von Hippel, "Arms Control Physics: The New Soviet Connection," *Physics Today,* November 1989, 44.

84. Bunn, "ABM Talks," 23; Maxim Tarasenko, "Twinkle, Twinkle Little Topaz," *Bulletin of the Atomic Scientists* 49, 6 (July/August 1993): 11–13.

85. Velikhov, interview.

86. William J. Broad, *Teller's War: The Top-Secret Story behind the Star Wars Deception* (New York, 1992).

refrained from testing. The Clinton administration's decision to abide by the congressional ban clearly undercut the Russian advocates of a test resumption. Clinton's reversal of the Reagan and Bush policy owes a great deal to the efforts of members of the U.S. side of the transnational disarmament network, particularly Christopher Paine and Thomas Cochran of the NRDC and Frank von Hippel of the Federation of American Scientists. Their influence on U.S. policy grew as that of their counterparts in Russia declined.[87] President Yeltsin welcomed the move and agreed to maintain the Russian moratorium.[88] Eventually Clinton threw his weight behind efforts to negotiate a comprehensive ban on nuclear testing, although the U.S. weapons laboratories extracted a high price for their rather tepid support: an annual budget of some four billion dollars for nuclear "stockpile maintenance"—more than the amount spent each year on nuclear weapons development and testing at the height of the Cold War.[89] In the face of such U.S. ambivalence about its commitment to nuclear weapons technology, it is not surprising that the head of Russia's nuclear complex vowed to continue his country's nuclear weapons development program as well, despite the test ban.[90]

Clinton's initial approach to the 1972 ABM Treaty bolstered the position of the opponents of strategic defenses both in the United States and in Russia. In July 1993, his administration came out in support of the "narrow" or "traditional" interpretation that the treaty "prohibits the development, testing and deployment of sea-based, air-based, space-based and mobile land-based ABM systems and components without regard to the technology utilized."[91] In early 1993 then Secretary of Defense Les Aspin declared the "Star Wars era" over. Some Russian reformers expressed confidence that the lobby for strategic defenses in Russia had been seriously weakened.[92] Step by step, however, the administration began to reverse course. It created a Ballistic Missile Defense Program as a successor agency to the SDI Office and requested $3.8 billion to fund it—the same amount that Congress had appropriated for SDI in the last year of the Bush administration. It pursued research on theater missile defenses, and, finally, in January 1999, came out explicitly in favor of strategic defense of the continental United States.[93] The administration pushed the Russian government to agree to amend the ABM Treaty in

87. See *NRDC News* 15, 3 (Fall 1993): 49; Douglas Jehl, *New York Times*, 1 July 1993; Mary McGrory, "O'Leary's Energy Is Felt," *Washington Post*, 14 December 1993.

88. *Arms Control Reporter*, 608.B.267.

89. Christopher Paine, "The Comprehensive Test Ban in the Current Nuclear Context," in Matthew McKinzie, ed., *The Comprehensive Test Ban: Issues and Answers*, Cornell University Peace Studies Program Occasional Paper No. 21 (Ithaca, N.Y., 1997), chap. 5.

90. Doug Clarke, "Mikhailov: Russia Developing New Nuclear Weapons," *OMRI Daily Digest*, 1996, no. 47, pt. 1 (6 March) (electronic version).

91. Thomas L. Friedman, "U.S. Formally Rejects 'Star Wars' in ABM Treaty," *New York Times*, 15 July 1993.

92. Ibid.; Aleksei Arbatov, interview.

93. Michael Wines, "Russia Is Silent, but Unhappy, About U. S. Proposal on Missiles," *New York Times*, 22 January 1999.

a way that critics feared could render it irrelevant as a barrier to a future arms race in offensive and defensive systems.[94]

Whereas the Clinton administration's policies on nuclear testing and strategic defenses initially helped undermine the position of Russian militarists, its approach to conventional-force issues had the opposite effect. Following the example set by the Bush administration, Clinton had little to say about the use of the Russian army to intervene in the nominally independent countries of the "near abroad."[95] Both administrations were more interested in Boris Yeltsin's political survival, regardless of the mistakes and crimes he committed, than in standing up for international legality or morality.

This was most evident in the Clinton administration's (non)response to the Russian army's invasion of Chechnya in late 1994. Although legally governments have the right to use force to put down armed rebellions on their territory, Russia broke a number of international and domestic laws (including, apparently, its own new Constitution) during the Chechen war. In undertaking its military operation Russia violated the provisions established by the Conference on Security and Cooperation in Europe for prior notification of large troop movements. Yet the U.S. government did not challenge the Russian action. The actual conduct of the war—mass air attacks against civilians, massacres of noncombatants, and the like—produced even more violations of international norms and laws. Again, U.S. officials offered few criticisms. According to President Clinton, Russia's attack on Chechnya was simply an "internal matter." The U.S. secretary of state insisted that "Russia is operating in a democratic context" and therefore the U.S. should "not rush to judgment."[96] Much as Clinton's efforts in support of a test ban and in opposition to Star Wars bolstered the Russian members of the transnational disarmament movement, his silence on Chechnya undermined those in Russia who sought to appeal to international humanitarian norms to stop the war.

Finally, in its desire to expand NATO to include former allies of the Soviet Union, the Clinton administration conceded to the position of those in the Russian government who had hindered implementation of the CFE Treaty.[97] In return for Russian willingness to look the other way as Poland, Hungary, and the Czech Republic were offered NATO membership, the Clinton administration supported a revision of the CFE Treaty. Henceforth Russia would be free to deploy additional troops in the unstable area of the North Caucasus, making more likely a resort to military means to resolve disputes there.

94. Doug Clarke, "Senior Officer Lauds Presidents' Stand on ABM Treaty," *OMRI Daily Digest*, 1995, no. 91, pt. 1 (11 May) (electronic version); "Star Wars, the Sequel," *New York Times*, 14 May 1996.
95. Hill and Jewett, *Back in the USSR*.
96. Elaine Sciolino, "Administration Sees No Choice but to Support Yeltsin," *New York Times*, 7 January 1995.
97. Michael Mihalka, "CFE Flank Limits Open for Discussion," *OMRI Daily Digest*, 1995, no. 91, pt. 1 (11 May) (electronic version).

Developments in these three areas—nuclear testing, conventional forces, and strategic defense—reinforce the impression that changes in the Soviet/Russian domestic structure have exerted an important influence on the prospects for transnational actors to advance their policy goals. Under the old, highly centralized, hierarchical structure, Soviet scientists and arms control advocates were able to persuade Mikhail Gorbachev to implement initiatives of unilateral restraint in nuclear testing and strategic defenses, despite obvious U.S. intention to pursue such programs vigorously. With their Western allies they convinced the Soviet government to implement a unilateral reduction and restructuring of Soviet conventional forces.

Under the new, post-1989 domestic structure, without a strong, centralized political authority backing them, the scientists and disarmament activists found it difficult to compete with Russian proponents of nuclear testing and ballistic missile defense—many of them lodged in the still powerful institutions of the former Soviet military-industrial sector. Only after major changes in U.S. policy in 1993 did the political balance shift in favor of Russian transnational supporters of arms control and restraint. The one area in which the U.S. government declined to get involved—conventional forces—saw the greatest setbacks: violations of treaty provisions, military interventions of various types, and a brutal and unnecessary war.

[17]

Power, Persuasion, and Norms

Science has played a major role in the arms race. Yet science was the first to speak out authoritatively against this folly and to look for a way out. Here we have to give credit to the joint efforts of Soviet and American scientists. . . . I am referring to the development of the basic principles of such concepts as international security and strategic stability. Without a serious and objective approach to defining stability and mutual security, without a scientific analysis taking into account all factors—political, scientific, military, technical, and political-military—it is impossible to make the right decisions on cardinal issues, nuclear and conventional arms reductions.

—MIKHAIL GORBACHEV, 1990

We do not claim to have invented all the ideas of the new thinking. Some of them originated years ago outside the Soviet Union with people such as Albert Einstein, Bertrand Russell, and Olof Palme.

—GEORGII ARBATOV, 1989

In December 1987, Mikhail Gorbachev attended a reception at the White House where he met the pianist Van Cliburn. Gorbachev and his Russian colleagues remembered how in 1958 Cliburn, then a young and unknown American virtuoso, had created a sensation in Moscow by winning the top prize in the first international Tchaikovsky piano competition. After meeting Gorbachev, Cliburn sat down at the piano and performed the popular Russian ballad "Moscow Evenings." The moment was poignant. The song had been composed thirty years earlier for the 1957 Festival of Youth. Held in Moscow, the event represented a watershed for Gorbachev and his generation: their first informal contacts with foreigners, their first experience of transnational culture.[1]

The mid-1950s were a formative period for Gorbachev's political as well as cultural views. In 1955, as a young law student, he met Jawaharlal Nehru, the prime minister of India, at a reception at Moscow University. Nehru's message of world peace, his plea to set aside ideological differences, and his prin-

1. Mikhail Gorbachev, *Zhizn' i reformy* (Moscow, 1995), 2:66.

cipled stand against nuclear weapons made a profound effect on Gorbachev. Three decades later, in November 1986, Gorbachev traveled to India to meet the newly elected prime minister—and Nehru's grandson—Rajiv Gandhi. There they signed the Delhi Declaration on nuclear disarmament and non-violence—a document that Gorbachev considered so significant that years later he included it as an appendix to his memoirs.[2]

Nineteen fifty-five was also the year that Albert Einstein and Bertrand Russell issued their antinuclear manifesto calling on humankind to face the threat of atomic weapons by adopting a "new way of thinking." Thirty years later, Gorbachev would embrace the slogan "new thinking" to symbolize the profound changes in Soviet foreign policy that he hoped to undertake.

Nineteen fifty-seven was the year that a transnational movement of scientists, inspired by the Russell-Einstein Manifesto, met for the first time in Pugwash, Nova Scotia, to discuss ways to end the arms race. Thirty years later, Gorbachev traveled to Washington to sign the Treaty on Intermediate-Range Nuclear Forces—the occasion for the White House reception where he met Van Cliburn. As the first U.S.-Soviet agreement that entailed substantial nuclear disarmament, the INF Treaty offered a hopeful step toward a world free from the nuclear threat. Gorbachev later sent a signed copy of the treaty to Dr. Bernard Lown, the Harvard cardiologist and founder of another key transnational disarmament organization, the International Physicians for the Prevention of Nuclear War. On the back, he wrote a note: "Dear Bernard! I want to thank you for your enormous contribution to preventing nuclear war. Without it and other powerful anti-nuclear initiatives, it is unlikely that this Treaty would have come about. I wish you all the best. Mikhail Gorbachev."[3]

The late 1980s marked the high point of transnational antinuclear activism, and the results were impressive: the signing of the INF Treaty, followed by agreements on substantial reductions of strategic nuclear weapons, broad international support for the Delhi Declaration and the Five-Continent Test Ban Initiative, and Soviet unilateral restraint that led to the peaceful demise of the Cold War military standoff in Europe. The explosion of transnational cultural, political, and economic contacts seemed to portend the dawning of the new era that Gorbachev's generation of "children of the sixties" had awaited so long, after catching their first glimpse of it during Khrushchev's "thaw."

Conventional explanations for the end of the Cold War leave little room for such influences on Soviet behavior as Gorbachev's affinity for transnational cultural and political contacts, his deep-rooted antipathy to nuclear weapons, his respect for India as the leader of the nonaligned movement and advocate

2. Ibid., 629–632.
3. Gorbachev literally wrote, "I want to express (*vyrazit'*) to you the enormous contribution. . . ." In his hurry to inscribe the treaty he evidently left out the word "thanks" (*blagodarnost'*).

have the right to withdraw from this Treaty if it decides that extraordinary events related to the subject matter of this Treaty have jeopardized its supreme interests. It shall give notice of its decision to withdraw to the other Party six months prior to withdrawal from this Treaty. Such notice shall include a statement of the extraordinary events the notifying Party regards as having jeopardized its supreme interests.

Article XVI

Each Party may propose amendments to this Treaty. Agreed amendments shall enter into force in accordance with the procedures set forth in Article XVII governing the entry into force of this Treaty.

Article XVII

1. This Treaty, including the Memorandum of Understanding and Protocols, which form an integral part thereof, shall be subject to ratification in accordance with the constitutional procedures of each Party. This Treaty shall enter into force on the date of the exchange of instruments of ratification.

2. This Treaty shall be registered pursuant to article 102 of the Charter of the United Nations.

DONE at Washington on December 8, 1987, in two copies, each in the English and Russian languages, both texts being equally authentic.

FOR THE UNITED STATES OF AMERICA:

FOR THE UNION SOVIET SOCIALIST REPUBLICS:

President of the United States of America

General Secretary of the Central Committee of the CPSU

The signature page of the 1987 treaty eliminating intermediate-range nuclear forces. Mikhail Gorbachev presented a copy to Dr. Bernard Lown, the Harvard cardiologist and founder of the International Physicians for the Prevention of Nuclear War. On it he wrote: "Dear Bernard! I want to thank you for your enormous contribution to preventing nuclear war. Without it and other powerful anti-nuclear initiatives, it is unlikely that this Treaty would have come about. I wish you all the best. Mikhail Gorbachev." Copy courtesy of Bernard Lown.

of nuclear disarmament, and the memories that he and many of his generation shared of the reformist hopes of the Khrushchev era. Instead, most explanations, following realist theories of international relations, focus on more tangible material factors: the balance of military power, Soviet economic constraints, and U.S. behavior.

Gorbachev and his colleagues were undoubtedly motivated by economic concerns, but, contrary to realist expectations, their concern was as much for the overall well-being of the Soviet Union and its citizens as for narrow considerations of military capability. The reformers benefited from the perception of economic crisis—it gave a sense of urgency to their efforts—but the economic situation did not determine the nature of Gorbachev's initiatives. Economic conditions have always been poorly correlated with periods of Soviet retrenchment or moderation. The most antagonistic Soviet policies toward the outside world were pursued by Stalin in the early postwar period at a time when the Soviet economy was in ruins. By contrast, a sense of economic optimism during the late 1950s had emboldened Stalin's successors to launch a number of conciliatory initiatives and unilateral gestures of restraint, such as Khrushchev's troop reductions and the moratorium on nuclear testing. The economic decline of the late Brezhnev era produced little in the way of moderation of foreign and security policy, whereas the early Gorbachev years, which saw an initial improvement in economic performance, also witnessed the onset of the reformist "new thinking." Finally, during the mid-1990s, Boris Yeltsin's Russia suffered years of negative growth rates and severe contraction of its industrial base. Yet its foreign-policy orientation was in many respects less congenial to the United States than the one endorsed by Gorbachev and Shevardnadze and later criticized by Yeltsin's advisers as naive "romanticism." Moreover, thanks to his war against Chechnya, Yeltsin bears responsibility for more Russian deaths than occurred in all of the military actions of his postwar Soviet predecessors put together—including the war in Afghanistan.

THEORETICAL IMPLICATIONS

The case studies in this book have suggested that explanations that rely heavily on shifts in the balance of power and other material constraints of the international system, to the exclusion of ideas, norms, and domestic politics, are unlikely to provide a good understanding of international change. In the case of the Cold War and the Soviet-American arms race, such explanations have failed to recognize the role that transnational networks of supporters of arms control and disarmament have played in moderating the East-West competition by taming the Russian bear. Transnational activists, working in tandem with Soviet reformers, provided many of the ideas that enabled

Mikhail Gorbachev to overcome internal opposition to the conciliatory policies that brought the Cold War to a peaceful end.

It seems surprising that foreign citizens, engaged in transnational networks, should have been able to influence such an authoritarian and insular state as the Soviet Union. The concept of domestic structure contributed much to explaining how this happened: how a state that would normally be impervious to external influences would, once the ideas promoted by a transnational network caught the attention of the top leadership, be able to carry out the relevant policies even against internal opposition. Domestic structure also helps explain the seemingly paradoxical finding that a more democratic post-Soviet Russia has proved more resistant to transnational influence. Particularly in the area of security policy, powerful institutions that had been held in check by the Communist Party's political monopoly have emerged to pursue their interests even to the point of war.

What does the emphasis on domestic structure add to our present understanding of the role of transnational networks as promoters of new ideas? Many scholars have argued that new ideas are much more likely to be adopted and implemented as policy if they become associated with bureaucracies that have past experience with similar policies or if they become embedded in powerful institutions that can promote new policies. As Peter Haas and Emanuel Adler argue, for example, "new ideas and policies, once institutionalized, can gain the status of orthodoxy."[4] What is surprising about the Soviet case is how unnecessary institutionalization appears to have been for the success of the ideas promoted by transnational actors. Once Gorbachev, Khrushchev, or even Brezhnev embraced a particular idea, he could often effect its implementation even against strong institutional resistance from the security establishment. This was particularly so in Khrushchev and Gorbachev's policies on nuclear testing and conventional-force reductions, Brezhnev's support for the ABM Treaty, and Gorbachev's pursuit of arms-reduction treaties in the absence of U.S. restraints on Star Wars.

This is not to argue that institutions are irrelevant to the Soviet case. On the contrary, Soviet institutions mattered a great deal. But it was the overall *system* of institutions—in other words, the domestic structure—that mattered most. The high centralization of the system and the enormous power and authority concentrated in the Politburo and in the person of the general secretary are the main characteristics that fostered the promotion of innovations— once a sympathetic leader came to power. The support of the general secretary allowed policy entrepreneurs to prevail against strong institutional opposition.

4. Emanuel Adler and Peter M. Haas, "Conclusion: Epistemic Communities, World Order, and the Creation of a Reflective Research Program," *International Organization* 46, 1 (Winter 1992): 384–385.

Eduard Shevardnadze was the most striking example of an entrepreneur who used Gorbachev's support to substitute for lack of institutional backing for his policies. As Strobe Talbott and Michael Beschloss observe, in the course of arms negotiations with the United States Shevardnadze grew increasingly "frustrated with the reflexive tendency of the [Soviet] Defense Ministry and the General Staff to block almost any modification of the Soviet negotiating position." Yet the foreign minister "found that he could deliberately exceed his authority by short-circuiting the decision-making process in Moscow and bypassing the generals."[5] This was precisely how Shevardnadze rammed through the transnationally sponsored idea of ignoring Star Wars and committing the USSR to major reductions in the START Treaty at the end of 1989. The resentment from Marshal Akhromeev and the "old thinkers" in Shevardnadze's own ministry to the foreign minister's manipulation of the system was intense.[6]

As long as Shevardnadze had the support of his friend Gorbachev, in a system where support of a strong general secretary counts for a lot, he could afford to offend some people in the interest of promoting innovative policies. After 1989, however, the new Soviet domestic structure required more deference to other governmental and societal actors—including, for example, deputies in the new parliament and institutions no longer bound by Communist Party discipline. Moreover, Soviet institutions, like those anywhere, always had some capacity to hinder or distort policies at the implementation stage. As central authority waned, the military made increasing use of that capacity, especially in areas where they possessed unique capabilities—such as the formulation of operational military doctrine to conform to the principles of "new thinking" or the physical destruction of weapons as dictated by an arms agreement. With the military and its allies openly opposing him, and Gorbachev under the new domestic structure either unable or unwilling to support him, Shevardnadze resigned as foreign minister at the end of 1990, as Chapter 14 recounts.

Boris Yeltsin's Russia inherited the same new structural constraints, and they limited his ability to pursue the ideas of the transnational disarmament network. In some cases he was unable even to secure fulfillment of prior Soviet arms control obligations, such as the destruction of former Soviet nuclear weapons on Ukrainian territory as stipulated by the START Treaty. The independence of Ukraine and the other former republics marked the extreme point of decentralization of the old Soviet system.

Another expectation from the literature on ideas that the Soviet cases fail to bear out is the notion that transnational ideas would serve as "coalitional

5. Michael Beschloss and Strobe Talbott, *At the Highest Levels: The Inside Story of the End of the Cold War* (Boston, 1993), 118.
6. S. F. Akhromeev and G. M. Kornienko, *Glazami marshala i diplomata* (Moscow, 1992), 79–80, 93, 142, 192.

glue"—that they would help political factions to identify their common interests, suggest new possibilities for coalition building, and, as John Ikenberry puts it, define "a 'middle ground' between old political divisions."[7] This was certainly a reasonable expectation. Indeed many contemporary analysts interpreted the Gorbachev security policy innovations as serving the interests of both the civilian reformers and the military. To some extent, policy entrepreneurs such as Evgenii Velikhov did seek to tailor their proposals to address the concerns of the Soviet military. The military leaders were worried about U.S. nuclear tests that might produce a Star Wars breakthrough. How about challenging the United States to reciprocate a unilateral test moratorium? Why not open the Soviet test range to on-site monitoring, to alleviate U.S. doubts about verification? If the military were genuinely worried about Star Wars why not sign onto the most cost-effective way of defeating it—with relatively inexpensive countermeasures, with the existing force of offensive missiles, or even with a START-reduced missile force? Andrei Kokoshin and Aleksei Arbatov took a similar approach in seeking to promote initiatives such as nonoffensive defense. They tried to make their proposals appeal to existing concerns within the military itself about Soviet strategy.

We now know—thanks in part to Marshal Akhromeev's memoirs, but also to considerable evidence available at the time as well—that Soviet military officials were very wary of the transnational initiatives. Yet, when Soviet policy entrepreneurs managed to create the *appearance* of common interests, when their proposals seemed ostensibly to address the military's concerns and objectively to serve Soviet security interests, they were often able to convince Gorbachev that enough support existed to merit launching a new initiative. Rather than speak of their ideas as coalitional glue, then, a more appropriate metaphor might be coalitional Velcro. The coalitions were ephemeral and pulled apart as soon as the divergence of interests between the military and the reformers became apparent—for example, as members of the transnational network sought to extend the unilateral Soviet test moratorium indefinitely, regardless of what the United States did, or as they promoted such notions as "asymmetric response" and "unilateral restraint" from the status of occasional tactic to universal principle.[8] Nevertheless, as long as the Soviet domestic structure remained highly centralized, with power heavily concentrated in the general secretary, forming large "winning

7. G. John Ikenberry, "A World Economy Restored: Expert Consensus and the Anglo-American Postwar Settlement," *International Organization* 46, 1 (Winter 1992): 289–321; Peter A. Hall, ed., *The Political Power of Economic Ideas* (Princeton, N.J., 1989); Judith Goldstein and Robert O. Keohane, "Ideas and Foreign Policy: An Analytical Framework," in Goldstein and Keohane, eds., *Ideas and Foreign Policy: Beliefs, Institutions, and Political Change* (Ithaca, N.Y., 1993), 17–18.
8. See, especially, Vitalii Zhurkin, Sergei Kortunov, and Andrei Kortunov, "Reasonable Sufficiency—or How to Break the Vicious Circle," *New Times*, 12 October 1987.

coalitions"—whether with glue or Velcro—need not have been a major function of transnational actors or their ideas.

BEYOND DOMESTIC STRUCTURE

Gorbachev was able to carry out his revolutionary changes in Soviet security policy, many of them influenced by the ideas of a transnational community of disarmament activists, largely because of the peculiar structure of Soviet domestic politics. The centralization of power and the communist tradition of deference to the authority of the top leader allowed for transnational proposals to be implemented even against the wishes of major institutional actors in the national security sector. With the change in domestic structure starting in 1989 and continuing into the post-Soviet era, transnational actors lost the advantages they had enjoyed under the Soviet system. One is left then with the question, What relevance does the experience of transnational networks during the Soviet period hold for the future?

It should be apparent that the finding that "strong states" are most effective at implementing policies that originate with transnational networks may not be particularly relevant to many contemporary international problems. Soviet-style domestic structures have become an endangered species in the current climate that opposes a strong role for government and favors privatization of everything. Moreover, most of the issues that affect people's security do not fit the state-centric model of East-West conflict during the Cold War. Many observers predict that ethnic or nationalist conflicts of the kind represented by the tragedies of Bosnia and Rwanda are likely to dominate the security agenda of the future.

States experiencing such internal conflict are by definition not strong. If they cannot maintain civil peace on their territory, they are unlikely to be able to implement proposals for conflict resolution offered by transnational networks when those proposals run counter to the interests of other powerful parties to the conflict. Structurally, the situation of ethnic or nationalist conflict most resembles the cases where a weak state faces strong societal forces. Under those circumstances, as our examination of post-1989 Russia illustrated, transnational organizations are obliged to compete with other societal and governmental actors for influence on policymakers—and they are typically at a disadvantage in terms of resources and bureaucratic wherewithal.

Although the structural attributes of likely cases of future conflict differ from what we observed in the Cold War, we still might gain some useful insights by examining the strategies that transnational organizations pursued. Here I review three strategies that appeared frequently in the preceding chapters: providing ideas and information to reformist allies, coordinating policy initiatives to influence the parties to the conflict, and appealing to international norms that resonate in the domestic context.

Provision of Information and Ideas

In the realm of strategy, one of the most straightforward ways that transnational networks helped Soviet reformers in their efforts to end the Cold War was by providing information and ideas. As we saw in Chapters 9 and 14, for example, the theme of "common security" that came to figure so prominently in the thinking of Gorbachev and Shevardnadze was first transmitted to the Soviet Union through a transnational organization: the Independent Commission on Disarmament and Security Issues, or the Palme Commission. The European members of the Palme Commission, particularly West Germany's Egon Bahr, helped persuade its Soviet members of the importance of viewing the provision of security as a common endeavor. They in turn conveyed the new approach to the reformist political leadership, who adopted it as official policy.

When the opportunity arose, under Gorbachev, to debate competing proposals for Soviet security policy openly, the reformers continued to rely on their Western colleagues for information and ideas. The data for analyses of the conventional balance (Chapter 14) or the technical and economic prospects for a "Star Wars" missile defense (Chapters 11 and 15) typically came from Western members of transnational organizations.

Transnational Policy Coordination

Transnational actors in the Soviet Union and the United States tried to coordinate their actions to influence the behavior of their governments. Such efforts were common during the test ban debates of the 1950s (Chapter 4), and they were an explicit objective of the Western scientists who sought to persuade the Soviet government to embrace restrictions on ABM systems in the 1960s (Chapters 6 and 10). Gorbachev's first disarmament initiative—the unilateral cessation of Soviet nuclear tests implemented on 6 August 1985—was a clear product of such transnational policy coordination. As Chapter 8 described, U.S. organizations such as the Center for Defense Information and IPPNW had been pressing the Soviet Union since 1984 to halt its nuclear tests, in the expectation that the U.S. arms control community would then urge the U.S. government to reciprocate. Under Gorbachev, the Soviet leadership was convinced by the arguments of Soviet reformers, and the apparent popular Western support represented by their transnational contacts, that the Soviet initiative would lead to a comprehensive test ban. This turned out to be a false hope. The Reagan administration remained recalcitrant, continuing to test its nuclear weapons even as Gorbachev extended the unilateral moratorium—against considerable internal opposition—for over a year and a half.

Considerable evidence, presented in Chapter 13, attests to the influence of transnational contacts in promoting the test ban. At key junctures in the internal Soviet debate on the test ban, Gorbachev's advisers reminded him of the need to maintain the support of Dr. Lown and the International Physicians, for example. Such arguments helped Gorbachev and Shevardnadze persuade more skeptical members of the leadership to prolong the moratorium.

As the opportunities for contact expanded during the Gorbachev years, policy entrepreneurs on both sides of the East-West divide increasingly tried to coordinate their efforts. Chapter 13 recounted how legislative aides to U.S. senators and representatives, for example, sought to time votes on congressional restrictions on spending for nuclear testing to correspond with announcements of Soviet unilateral initiatives. Promoters of a test ban within the Federation of American Scientists and the Natural Resources Defense Council worked with Soviet colleagues to produce a major breakthrough: nongovernmental on-site seismic monitoring of the Soviet test moratorium. This successful project pushed forward the pace of military glasnost in the USSR, paving the way for intrusive verification measures in future arms-reduction treaties, and it undercut U.S. opposition to a test ban stemming from concerns about Soviet cheating.

In addition to coordination of specific policy initiatives, the transnational network of U.S. and Soviet disarmament supporters also worked together to create an overall atmosphere conducive to restraint on each side. In order for Gorbachev to succeed in cutting back Soviet military programs and military spending, he had to make a plausible case that the United States did not pose a serious threat to Soviet security. As Anatolii Cherniaev, his top foreign-policy aide, put it in a memo, "both our military estimates and our military spending as well must be built" on the premise that "there will be no war."[9] Here a more tacit form of East-West cooperation played a role. As the Nuclear Freeze movement sought to persuade Ronald Reagan that he had to tone down his harsh rhetoric about the Soviet Union and careless comments about nuclear war, Soviet reformers pushed initiatives that would diminish the "enemy image" of the USSR in Reagan's eyes. Gorbachev considered it a major achievement when, at the Geneva summit meeting in October 1985, he persuaded Reagan to declare that "a nuclear war can never be won and must never be fought"—a statement that contradicted some well-publicized remarks by Caspar Weinberger, the U.S. secretary of defense. Such a declaration on Reagan's part gave Gorbachev considerable room to maneuver among Politburo colleagues skeptical of U.S. intentions.[10] The warming of U.S.-Soviet relations would not have been possible had Reagan not been pushed

9. A. S. Cherniaev, *Shest' let s Gorbachevym: po dnevnikovym zapisiam* (Moscow, 1993), 106–107.
10. Gorbachev, *Zhizn' i reformy*, 2:20–21.

by the U.S. peace movement to address the threat of nuclear war. He did it in his own way, by seeking to develop a personal rapport with Soviet leaders: "I had come to realize there were people in the Kremlin who had a genuine fear of the United States. I wanted to convince Gorbachev that we wanted peace and they had nothing to fear from us."[11]

American transnational activists, while trying to constrain U.S. military programs, also considered it important to persuade the Soviet government that the United States did not pose a threat so grave that Soviet unilateral restraint or even negotiated settlements would be dangerous. Much attention in this regard was focused on the Strategic Defense Initiative (SDI). As Chapter 15 recounts, U.S. and Soviet members of the transnational scientists' movement all considered "Star Wars" a dangerous waste of money, but they did not want it to stand in the way of negotiating deep reductions in nuclear forces. The Americans kept their Soviet colleagues apprised of the fate of SDI in congressional deliberations, the astronomical cost estimates, and the technical critiques. They managed to persuade Gorbachev, sometimes in direct discussion, that the Soviet Union should "unlink" the signing of a strategic weapons reduction treaty from U.S. pursuit of SDI. Star Wars, they argued, would eventually fade away, especially if the Soviet Union continued to pursue its reformist course in defense and disarmament, not to mention internal democratization.

The Appeal to Norms

One less tangible way that transnational organizations proved useful to domestic reformers was as representatives of international norms that were resonant in the domestic culture, even among opponents of reform. In the USSR, given the searing memory of the Nazi invasion, there was a universal normative commitment to both a strong defense and the preservation of peace. Typically, the former was understood to produce the latter. But because of the USSR's self-perception as a country that was forced to develop its atomic weapons in response to a U.S. nuclear threat, there was also a rhetorical commitment to the goal of nuclear disarmament. Finally, despite the patently offensive capabilities of Soviet conventional and nuclear forces, Soviet officials—civilian and military alike—consistently felt obligated to stress their country's strictly defensive intentions.

Western transnational actors and their Soviet counterparts took advantage of this normative context to promote their policy reforms. They sought to persuade Soviet military officials and members of the national security bureaucracy that even major initiatives of Soviet unilateral restraint were consistent

---

11. Ronald Reagan, *An American Life* (New York, 1990), 12. This is a major theme of part 6 of his autobiography, 545–723.

with a commitment to nuclear disarmament and peace that represented an unassailable normative consensus in Soviet society. That the norms favoring peace and disarmament could in fact be in tension with the norms promoting "strong defense" created an additional task for the transnational actors. They were obliged either to persuade Soviet skeptics that the West did not pose such a military threat that unilateral reforms would be unsound, or to foster Western responses to Soviet initiatives that would lead to bilateral or multilateral restraint and therefore entail fewer risks for the Soviet side. Typically they tried to do both, as, for example, when they played down the threat of Star Wars and when they urged the U.S. government to reciprocate the Soviet cessation of nuclear testing.

A brief review of two examples from the Gorbachev period illustrates how transnational actors attempted to invoke norms to influence their opponents. Two of the policies advocated by military reformers and their transnational contacts were radical reductions in nuclear weapons (Chapter 15) and defensive restructuring of conventional forces (Chapter 14). The reformers were encouraged when Gorbachev gave a major address in January 1986 proposing a multistage process of nuclear disarmament by the year 2000. The proposal included concessions on a number of issues that had deadlocked negotiations between the Reagan administration and Gorbachev's predecessors. Although this speech included reference to the importance of reducing conventional forces as well, the real achievement in this sphere came nearly three years later with Gorbachev's December 1988 address to the United Nations, where he committed the USSR to a unilateral reduction of five hundred thousand troops and a substantial number of tanks and other weapons. Thus, as Chapter 14 described, the concepts of "nonoffensive defense" and "common security" promised to be carried out in practice—with potentially profound implications for Soviet relations toward its allies in Eastern Europe, the targets of actual Soviet military offensives in the past.

Gorbachev's nuclear disarmament program was not popular in the military, particularly when it entailed unilateral concessions on nuclear forces in Europe, a willingness to proceed with reductions despite U.S. insistence on pursuing SDI, and intrusive provisions for verification. Yet the normative commitment to nuclear disarmament was so strong in Soviet discourse on security policy that even "old thinkers" within the Soviet national security bureaucracy perceived some benefit in associating themselves with Gorbachev's initiatives. In his memoir, Marshal Sergei Akhromeev, former chief of the Soviet General Staff, claimed that the January 1986 proposal for nuclear disarmament in fifteen years resulted from studies he commissioned in the General Staff.[12] His coauthor, Georgii Kornienko, a stalwart of the old system as first deputy to Foreign Minister Andrei Gromyko for many years, agreed, as

12. Akhromeev and Kornienko, *Glazami*, 86–89.

did their colleague from the international department of the Communist Party apparatus, Valentin Falin.[13]

As with nuclear disarmament, Soviet military officials also sought to embrace "nonoffensive defense" as their own initiative. In 1989, a military journal published recently declassified Soviet war plans of the late 1940s that demonstrated a Soviet intention to go on the defensive, rather than the offensive, in the event of war in central Europe.[14] By ignoring the intervening shift to a highly offensive strategy, the editors sought to imply that defense had always been the main Soviet orientation and therefore reforms were unnecessary. Civilian reformers, including prominent members of transnational networks such as Andrei Kokoshin, perceived an opportunity in such rationalizations. As Chapters 9 and 14 describe, they encouraged their military colleagues to resurrect the history of Soviet military strategists who had emphasized defensive operations and to highlight defense as a Soviet military tradition, for example, by publishing studies of the use of defensive strategies at key junctures during World War II. As we saw in Chapter 15, Marshal Akhromeev took credit for other Soviet concessions in the realm of conventional arms control—namely, the willingness to include Soviet territory for the first time in proposals for conventional-force reductions.

Akhromeev's claim of Soviet military paternity for Gorbachev's disarmament brainchild is about as plausible as that of the Coca-Cola executive who maintained that the popular environmental-movement slogan "think globally and act locally" was really "created by the Coca-Cola company through our franchises and local bottlers."[15] There is little evidence to support the view that the military was the source of Soviet disarmament initiatives. Mikhail Gorbachev, in his own memoir, is unequivocal on this point: "The Ministry of Defense, knowing well how hard it was for the country to endure [the costs of] the arms race, did not once in all the years of my activity in Moscow put forward a proposal to reduce the armed forces or the production of weapons."[16] Other insider accounts reinforce this point. In regard to Akhromeev's work on the proposal for nuclear disarmament by the year 2000, for example, these accounts suggest that the officials in the Ministry of Defense were motivated mainly by fear that "Gorbachev and his 'team' might unilaterally try to change the Soviet position" on arms control. Therefore they hurried to put forward their own proposal for complete nuclear dis-

13. Ibid., 88–90; Valentin Falin, *Politische erinnerungen* (Munich, 1993), 469–470.

14. "Plan komandirskikh zaniatii po operativno-takticheskoi podgotovke v polevom upravlenii gruppy Sovetskikh okkupatsionnykh voisk v Germanii na 1948 god," *Voenno-istoricheskii zhurnal*, 1988, no. 8:24–26. For an excellent discussion of these materials, see Gilberto Villahermosa, "Stalin's Postwar Army Reappraised: Déja Vu All Over Again," *Soviet Observer* 2, 1 (September 1990): 1–5; see also Matthew Evangelista, "The 'Soviet Threat': Intentions, Capabilities, and Context," *Diplomatic History* 22, 3 (Summer 1998): 439–449.

15. Ira Herbert, former president of Coca-Cola North America, quoted in John Palattella, "The Producers," *Lingua Franca* 6, 7 (November 1996): 26.

16. Gorbachev, *Zhizn' i reformy*, 2:13.

armament, expecting that "such a declaration hardly could lead to any practical results in the foreseeable future, or affect, in any form, the ongoing negotiations." [17]

Like the civilian reformers who used Soviet military claims to a defensive tradition to promote their agenda for reform, Gorbachev himself was pleased to get the rhetorical support of the Soviet skeptics, and he used it to his advantage. Whenever possible he would make Marshal Akhromeev, for example, represent the Soviet position in a given negotiation, so that he would share responsibility for the concessions made by the Soviet side. Gorbachev would often give Akhromeev the task of defending the resulting agreement in public, before the Soviet parliament, for example, as that body evolved into an instrument of genuine democratic deliberation.

One conclusion that can be drawn, then, is that Soviet reformers used international norms conveyed by transnational actors—what Kathryn Sikkink calls the "power of principled ideas"—in an instrumental fashion to promote their agenda. [18] They did not always have an easy time of it, and they were not always successful. Attempting to find common ground with the military, the reformers sometimes risked becoming co-opted. Aleksei Arbatov's anecdote about the two bear-hunting brothers, quoted at the head of the preceding chapter, captures the point well. Military conservatives during the perestroika era sometimes sought to appropriate the language of reform ("defense sufficiency," for example) to hide their inaction or resistance. More often though, the language of the reformers, and the normative implications it contained, did seem to pose constraints on what the military was able to do. [19]

Perhaps most striking, though, is that these norms—of nuclear disarmament, common security, and nonoffensive defense—continued to exert an influence on the people who ultimately came to oppose Gorbachev's reforms. Akhromeev, Kornienko, and Falin were far from the most hostile opponents of the "new thinking." Yet they all came to consider Gorbachev in effect a traitor to Soviet interests. (Akhromeev, although not an active supporter of the attempted coup against him in August 1991, nevertheless committed suicide when it failed.) Yet even after knowing where the reforms were to lead—the withdrawal of Soviet power from Europe, nuclear disarmament in the face of a persistent U.S. interest in strategic defenses, and, ultimately, the breakup of the Soviet Union—people such as Falin, Akhromeev, and Kornienko nevertheless sought to associate themselves with the *norms* underlying those reforms.

In addition to appealing to norms that already enjoyed popular acceptance

17. Aleksandr G. Savel'yev and Nikolay N. Detinov, *The Big Five: Arms Control Decision-Making in the Soviet Union* (Westport, Conn., 1995), 92–93.
18. Kathryn Sikkink, "The Power of Principled Ideas: Human Rights Policies in the United States and Western Europe," in Goldstein and Keohane, *Ideas and Foreign Policy*, 139–170.
19. On the constraining effects of language, see Albert S. Yee, "The Causal Effects of Ideas on Politics," *International Organization* 50, 1 (Winter 1996): 69–108.

in the Soviet context, Soviet reformers and their transnational allies sometimes sought to propagate new norms. One particularly interesting example
concerns the notion of "asymmetric response." Soviet and Western scientists
originally developed the concept as a way of advocating a Soviet refusal to
copy the Reagan administration's SDI program or allow it to hinder progress
in nuclear disarmament. Emboldened by their apparent success in convincing Gorbachev to embrace their approach to Star Wars, and encouraged by
the precedent of unequal Soviet reductions established by the INF Treaty, the
reformers pushed further. Now they advocated asymmetrical responses to a
broad range of military threats, in effect enshrining a new general principle
of Soviet security policy; they criticized strict adherence to parity in favor of
"reasonable sufficiency"; and they promoted unilateral gestures of restraint
explicitly modeled on the Khrushchev troop reductions.[20] They began to
downplay the value of the military instrument altogether and to stress that
economic strength in itself makes the biggest contribution to security. They
implied that if the U.S. goal were to bankrupt the USSR with an arms race,
then the less the Soviets spent on the military the better. Nikita Khrushchev
had once expressed such radical sentiments to a small circle of the Soviet
leadership.[21] During the Gorbachev era they finally received public expression, particularly in Shevardnadze's speeches.

For more than four decades analysts of Soviet security have sought to explain
Soviet behavior with reference to material factors such as economic conditions, military requirements, and the actions of Soviet adversaries. In investigating a dozen cases spanning four decades I have found these explanations
inadequate. Undoubtedly concern for domestic political and economic reform was the driving force behind Gorbachev's foreign-policy initiatives. But
his level of concern and awareness about the internal situation, which differed considerably from that of his predecessors and many of his contemporaries, cannot be understood on the basis of material factors alone. The solutions Gorbachev embraced in pursuit of foreign-policy reform cannot be
explained without acknowledging the normative commitments that he
shared with his advisers and with their transnational colleagues: to nuclear
disarmament and to integration of the Soviet Union as a "normal country"
into the international political and economic community.

The case studies in this book suggest an important role for norms, ideas,
and nongovernmental and transnational actors in a country (the Soviet
Union) and an issue area (security policy) where one would least expect it.
Although some of the success of transnational actors owes to the peculiar na-

20. Aleksei Arbatov, "Parity and Reasonable Sufficiency," *International Affairs*, 1988,
no. 10:75–87; and Arbatov, "How Much Defence is Sufficient?" *International Affairs*, 1989,
no. 4:31–44; Zhurkin, Karaganov, and Kortunov, "Reasonable Sufficiency."
21. Vladislav M. Zubok, "Khrushchev's 1960 Troop Cut: New Russian Evidence," *Cold War
International History Project Bulletin*, nos. 8–9 (Winter 1996/97): 416–420.

ture of the Soviet domestic structure, other aspects of their efforts are more widely applicable—particularly their strategic use of norms, ideas, and information. With good reason these issues, and related ones, have become the subject of much promising research on the role of transnational relations, advocacy networks, and norms in international relations.[22]

This book's emphasis on the importance of broadening the approach to security beyond considerations of material power holds implications for public policy as well as theory. Much of U.S. policy toward the Soviet Union during the Cold War was driven by the assumption that the USSR would respond to superior U.S. military and economic power with conciliation and restraint. The peaceful end of the Cold War has led many observers to conclude that U.S. policies of containment and deterrence did indeed work as they were intended to do. In fact, however, the evidence from this book supports an alternative argument: that much of U.S. policy served to prolong the Cold War.[23] In fact there were many opportunities during the Khrushchev era and even the Brezhnev era to wind down the nuclear arms race. That it ultimately took the dramatic reforms of Mikhail Gorbachev to end the Cold War is less a tribute to the success of a U.S. policy of "staying the course" than to the persistent inability of U.S. policymakers to recognize and seize earlier opportunities for change.

Nor was the long U.S. commitment to containment without cost or risk. The Soviet Union was not the only participant in the Cold War to suffer from excessive militarization of its economy and society.[24] Moreover, there was no guarantee that the conflict would end peacefully. On more than one occasion the U.S.-Soviet antagonism threatened to escalate to nuclear war.[25] In fact, at the height of the Reagan administration's confrontational approach to the Soviet Union, in the early 1980s, Soviet leaders launched "the largest peacetime intelligence operation in Soviet history" in an effort to discover U.S. plans for a surprise nuclear first strike. In November 1983 some Soviet intelligence

22. In addition to the work cited above, some important recent contributions include: Andrew P. Cortell and James W. Davis, Jr., "How Do International Institutions Matter? The Domestic Impact of International Rules and Norms," *International Studies Quarterly* 40, 4 (December 1996): 451–478; Jeffrey Checkel, "Norms, Institutions, and National Identity in Contemporary Europe," *International Studies Quarterly* 43, 1 (March 1999); Martha Finnemore, *National Interests in International Society* (Ithaca, N.Y., 1996); Peter J. Katzenstein, *Cultural Norms and National Security: Police and Military in Postwar Japan* (Ithaca, N.Y., 1996); and Richard Price, "Reversing the Gunsights: Transnational Civil Society Targets Land Mines," *International Organization* 52, 3 (Summer 1998): 613–644.

23. On this and several other points mentioned here see Richard Ned Lebow and Janice Stein, *We All Lost the Cold War* (Princeton, N.J., 1994).

24. Eugene Rochberg-Halton, "Cold War's Victims Deserve a Memorial," *New York Times*, 10 March 1990; and Christopher Lasch, "The Costs of Our Cold War Victory," *New York Times*, 13 July 1990; Cynthia Enloe, *The Morning After: Sexual Politics at the End of the Cold War* (Berkeley, 1993).

25. On the history of potentially disastrous nuclear accidents, see Scott Sagan, *Limits of Safety: Organizations, Accidents, and Nuclear Weapons* (Princeton, N.J., 1993); on two of the most dangerous crises, see Lebow and Stein, *We All Lost*.

officials feared that a NATO military exercise, intended to practice procedures for release of nuclear weapons, would turn into a real attack; at one point Moscow sent emergency telegrams to its intelligence officers abroad mistakenly reporting an alert at U.S. bases.[26] The danger inherent in such a situation would be even greater if what some experts claim is true—that the Soviet Union deployed a "doomsday machine," a computerized system that would order the automatic launch of thousands of nuclear weapons if it received evidence that the command authorities had been killed.[27] Clearly the Cold War could have ended in nuclear disaster rather than peaceful reconciliation.

U.S. intelligence officials soon figured out what had happened during the tense days of November 1983, and they informed President Reagan. As he recalls in his memoirs, "I began to realize that many Soviet officials feared us not only as adversaries but as potential aggressors who might hurl nuclear weapons at them in a first strike; because of this, and perhaps because of a sense of insecurity and paranoia with roots reaching back to the invasions of Russia by Napoleon and Hitler, they had aimed a huge arsenal of nuclear weapons at us."[28] Ronald Reagan's belated recognition of the security dilemma that faced the Soviet Union led him to adopt a more conciliatory approach during his second term and made him receptive to the policy initiatives that Gorbachev introduced. It was Reagan's change of heart rather than his earlier bellicose policies that opened the window for Soviet reformers and their transnational allies to bring in the new thinking that brought down the Cold War.

The transnational networks that have sought since the 1950s to tame the Russian bear by promoting disarmament and respect for human rights were ultimately successful. The political-military division of Europe ended, the Soviet regime fell, the testing of new nuclear weapons ceased, and many of the old ones were dismantled. Post-Soviet Russia has proved something of a disappointment, however. Although Russia's military budget is only a fraction of what the Soviet Union used to spend, it is still more than the country needs or can afford.[29] Focusing on the state's domestic structure helps account for why Russian policies have tended to reflect far less the goals of the transnational peace activists than the interests of the traditional national-security

26. Christopher Andrew and Oleg Gordievsky, *Comrade Kriuchkov's Instructions: Top Secret Files on KGB Foreign Operations, 1975–1985* (Stanford, Calif., 1993), chap. 5; Ben B. Fischer, "A Cold War Conundrum: The 1983 Soviet War Scare," U.S. Central Intelligence Agency, Center for the Study of Intelligence report CSI 97–10002 (Washington, D.C., 1997). I thank Mark Kramer for sending me a copy of this report.

27. Bruce G. Blair, "Russia's Doomsday Machine," and William J. Broad, "Russia Has Computerized Nuclear 'Doomsday' Machine, U.S. Expert Says," both in *New York Times*, 8 October 1993.

28. Reagan, *American Life*, 588–589.

29. Viktor Litovkin, "Den'gi na reformy u armii est'," *Izvestiia*, 11 March 1997, 5. I thank Sergei Khrushchev for calling this article to my attention.

bureaucracies. As the domestic structure of Russia has become decentralized and fragmented, the state's instruments for implementing policies that threaten powerful interests have atrophied. The United States has been reluctant to step into the void. It has used its potential leverage somewhat sparingly—and not at all in the case of the brutal war against Chechnya, where the silence of U.S. leaders in the face of Russian war crimes undermined Russia's own advocates of peace and human rights.

Western proponents of disarmament had always hoped that the changes in Soviet policy would have a salutary effect on the United States as well—in both its domestic and foreign policy. In this respect, they were also disappointed. In levels of military spending, for example, the United States has not cut back to much below its Cold War average, after subtracting the costs of the hot wars in Korea and Vietnam, and the country still maintains an enormous national-security apparatus. Rather than use the end of the Cold War as an opportunity for widespread demilitarization of international relations, the U.S. government has promoted arms sales throughout the world, including in the former Soviet bloc and in regions such as Latin America where states face a relatively benign security environment and can little afford to divert resources from pressing domestic needs.

Working on the assumption that it was U.S. military and economic superiority that won the Cold War, the United States has pursued security policies—such as expansion of NATO into Eastern Europe—that Moscow opposes, in the expectation that Russia will remain too weak to do anything about it. More attention to the nonmaterial, normative, and domestic political influences on the end of the Cold War might have made U.S. policymakers more sensitive to the risks of that approach. Creating a new division of Europe with Russia outside the "club" reinforces those elements of Russian society that promote a Russian identity distinct from the transnational cultural, economic, and political society that Gorbachev worked so hard to join. Policymakers should heed the lessons of transnational relations during the Cold War and not squander the opportunity to cultivate a peaceful and democratic Russia as a full member of the international community.

Index

Index

Boserup, Anders, 187–188, 191, 312–313, 315
Bowie, Robert, 229
Brandt, Willy, 161 n.70, 185
Brandt Commission, 160
BRAVO test, 47, 51–52. *See also* Bikini Atoll
Breathing-space explanation, 14, 295–300, 303
Brennan, Donald, 36, 135
Brezhnev, Leonid, 20, 65, 72, 122, 150, 152–153, 156, 158, 163, 166, 181–183, 226–227, 229–231, 253; and Chelomei, 236; and economic decline, 295; and Greenpeace, 169; and IPPNW, 151; and military industrialists, 178–179; and Palme, 161
British Atomic Scientists' Association, 31
Brovikov, V. I., 362
Budker, Gersh (Andrei), 225, 236
Bulganin, Nikolai, 54–55, 106; and Eisenhower, 110
Bulletin of the Atomic Scientists, 28, 39–40, 84, 207
Bundeswehr, 115
Bundy, McGeorge, 43
Bush, George, 256, 358, 367; administration, 343, 360, 364, 366, 370–372

Campaign for Nuclear Disarmament, 56
Camp David, 68
Carroll, Eugene, 170, 270
Carter, Jimmy, 240
Center for Defense Information, 170, 270, 382
Central Committee of the Communist Party of the Soviet Union, 33–34, 37–38, 57–59, 63–64, 97–98, 100–101, 106, 108, 127, 131, 148, 151–153, 155, 157, 161, 179, 195, 222, 226, 314–315; closed letter to armed forces, (1960), 101, (1957), 108; commission on military policy (1990–91), 257–258; International Department, 152, 283, 315, 317; joint decrees with Council of Ministers, 346; reduced role in Soviet policy, 317. *See also* Communist Party of the Soviet Union
Central Intelligence Agency (CIA), 50, 67, 131, 202, 234–235, 254, 280; "Possible Soviet Responses to the US Strategic Defense Initiative" report, 244; Team B Study, 234, 235 n.3
Centralization, 344, 378
Charter 77, 251
Chazov, Evgenii, 5, 149, 151, 153, 155, 160–161, 171, 231, 271, **272**, 275, 288
Chebrikov, Viktor, 249, 307 n.62, 329
Chechnya, 11, 343; invasion of, 372; war in, 344, 365, 377, 391
Chelomei, V. N., 140, 215, 225, 235–236
Chernenko, Konstantin, 15, 20, 152, 166, 170–171, 194, 270
Cherniaev, Anatolii, 148, 272, 307, 335, 383
Chernobyl nuclear accident, 274, 282; effect on Gorbachev's test moratorium, 273

China: as justification for ABM, 196
Churchill, Winston, 30
Churkin, Vitalii, 287
CIA. *See* Central Intelligence Agency
CIS. *See* Commonwealth of Independent States
CISAC. *See* National Academy of Sciences: Committee on International Security and Arms Control
Civil defense, 128, 153, 155
Civil disobedience, 168, 270
Civil society, 39, 347
Clausewitz, Carl von, 188
Cliburn, Van: meets Gorbachev, 375; wins Tchaikovsky piano competition, 374
Clinton, William, 9, 370, 372; administration of, 251, 342, 358, 360, 368, 371–372
Coalitional glue, 379–381
Coalitional Velcro, 380
Coalition-building, 345, 348, 380
Coalition politics, 380–381
Cochran, Thomas, **243**, 275, 281–283, **284**, **286**, 288, 325–326, 354, 371
Cockcroft, James, 29
Cold War: explanations for end, 252–262; and SDI, 240
Colonel X. *See* Girshfeld, Viktor
Committee for a SANE Nuclear Policy, 47, 56, 85, 88
Committee for Non-Violent Action, 56
Committee of Soviet Scientists for Peace, Against the Nuclear Threat (CSS), 147, 156, 159–160, 214, 233, 239, 323, 327, 369–370
Committee on International Studies of Arms Control, 38, 144, 160, 200; meeting in Boston (1964), 134–135
Committee on State Security. *See* KGB
Common security, 11, 161–162, 185–187, 192, 289, 303, 305–307, 343, 382, 385, 387
Commonwealth of Independent States (CIS), 301, 359
Communist Party of the Soviet Union (CPSU), 11, 47, 61–62, 99, 129, 261, 342, 346; abolished, 348; anti-Party group (1957), 41, 97; approves expansion of Soviet ABM program, 212; discipline, 350–351, 355, 365, 379; domination of, 344–345, 378; general secretary's role, 15, 346, 349, 378–380; International Department, 386; need for reform in, 300; political monopoly ended, 341, 347, 349, 365; 27th Congress of (1986), 291, 298, 307. *See also* Central Committee of the Communist Party of the Soviet Union
Comprehensive nuclear test ban, 67, 82, 160, 166, 168, 170–172, 267, 270, 275, 288, 350, 360, 371, 382–383; attempted congressional amendment (1987), 287; treaty, 45, 278–279,

Index

Index

IDDS. *See* Institute for Defense and Disarmament Studies

Ideas as source of policy change, 377–379, 381–382, 387, 389

IISS. *See* International Institute for Strategic Studies

Ikenberry, G. John, 380

IMEMO. *See* Institute of the World Economy and International Relations

Independent Commission on Disarmament and Security Issues (Palme Commission), 160–162, 185–186, 307, 312, 382; report (1982), 306

India, 47, 67, 282, 375; Delhi Six, 275

INF. *See* Intermediate-Range Nuclear Forces

Inozemtsev, Nikolai, 156

Inspection, 327; aerial, 117, 119; non-intrusive, 81. *See also* On-site inspection

Installation, the, 54. *See also* Arzamas-16

Institute for Defense and Disarmament Studies (IDDS), 314

Institute of History, 38

Institute of Physics (Novosibirsk), 225

Institute of the Physics of the Earth, 280, 282, 285

Institute of Space Research, 156, 242, 365

Institute of the USA and Canada (ISKAN), 157, 161, 202, 211, 228, 251, 308, 319

Institute of the World Economy and International Relations (IMEMO), 38, 156–157, 189–190, 202, 309–312; proposal for conventional force reductions, 313–314

Institutions, 378; political, 345; Soviet, 379

Interdepartmental Arms Control Commission (Soviet), 226–227

Intermediate-Range Nuclear Forces (INF), 144, 241, 290; negotiations, 332; Treaty, 288, 314, 328–329, 375, **376**, 388

International change as source of policy, 343–344, 360–361

International Democratic Federation of Women, 63

International Forum for a Nuclear-Free World, for Survival of Humanity (Moscow, February 1987), 312, 329

International Forum of Scientists for an End to Nuclear Tests (Moscow, July 1986), 275–276

International Institute for Strategic Studies (IISS), 202, 310

International Physicians for the Prevention of Nuclear War (IPPNW), 5, 147–149, 154, 161, 170, 271–272, 275, 325, 355, 375–376, 382–383; conference in Amsterdam (1983), 161, 186; and Gorbachev, 278; Nobel Peace Prize, 251; and Shevardnadze, 356; Soviet involvement in, 151; Soviet resistance to, 153; Fourth World Congress in Helsinki (June 1984), 171

IPPNW. *See* International Physicians for the Prevention of Nuclear War

ISKAN. *See* Institute of the USA and Canada

Ivashutin, P., 129–130; report to Zakharov, 138, 212

Izvestiia, 34, 103, 134, 207, 223

Japan, 47–48, 57, 350

Johnson, Lyndon B., 196–197, 199, 213; and Kosygin, 198, 226

Joint Chiefs of Staff, U.S., 85

Kádár, János, 103

Kahn, Herman, 135

Kaldor, Mary, 143, 163

Kapitsa, Petr, 27, 30–31, 132–133, 137–138, 145, 155, 208, 210, 217

Kapitsa, Sergei, 155

Karaganov, Sergei, 315

Karaul, 51, 352–355

Karetnikov, V. M., 211

Karlovy Vary, 133

Kazakhstan, 9, 109, 351–353; gains independence, 357; nuclear test site, 51

Keegan, George, 234–235

Keldysh, Mstislav, 38, 226, 231

Kennan, George, 14–15, 28, 121

Kennedy, Edward, 325–326; on SDI, 233, 287

Kennedy, John F., 70, 74, 77, 79, 81–82, 85, 87; administration, 34, 37, 42–44, 78, 88, 114, 120–121, 128, 210

Kennedy, Robert, 78–79

KGB, 80, 99, 168, 209, 222, 226, 229, 256, 292–293, 325, 348, 356; and Sakharov, 329–330

Khariton, Iulii, 72–73, 83, 225, 236

Khrushchev, Nikita, 20–21, 25, 36, 40, 42–45, 50, 52, 62, 64–65, 71, 73–75, 77–79, 81, 85, 88, 96–97, 100, 132, 229, 259, 269, 278, 350; and Chelomei, 215; and Eisenhower, 92, 119; emphasis on nuclear weapons, 176, 206; missile diplomacy, 122; new military doctrine, 102; ousted from power, 32, 39, 138; speech of January 1960, 100; and Szilard, 35; television interview, 41; thaw, 375; troop reductions, 388; visits New York, 35

Khrushchev, Sergei, 54–56, 65–67, 73–74, 79, 81–82, 87–88, 103–104, 139–140; and Chelomei, 215

Khrushcheva, Nina Petrovna, 76

Killian, James, 55

Kirilenko, Andrei, 152

Kirillin, Vladimir, 37–38, 228, 231

Kissinger, Henry A., 135, 147, 182, 210

Kistiakowsky, George B., 38, 147, 157, 165

Kisun'ko, Grigorii Vasilievich, 123, 139, 215–216, 221, 225, 227, 235; design bureau, 226

Index

MLF. *See* Multilateral force
Mlynar, Zdenek, 261
Moiseev, Mikhail, 312, 363
Molotov, Viacheslav, 47, 49–50, 112–113, 115
Moratorium on nuclear tests, 46, 51; trilateral, 60–72, 269; unilateral Soviet, 53–60, 171, 264–288. *See also* Nuclear testing
Moscow Agreement, 77, 80–86. *See also* Limited Test Ban Treaty
"Moscow Evenings," 374
Moscow News, 202
Moscow State University, 26, 76, 261, 374
Moscow system (ABM), 126, 196, 217, 222–223. *See also* A-35 system
Moscow Treaty. *See* Moscow Agreement
Multilateral force (MLF), 201
Multiple, independently targetable reentry vehicle. *See* MIRV
Mururoa: nuclear test site, 356
Mutual and Balanced Force Reduction talks (MBFR), 174–176, 180, 183, 301, 304, 311, 317

Nacht, Michael, 147
Nagasaki, 31, 165, 355
NASA, 337
National Academy of Sciences, 172; Committee on International Security and Arms Control (CISAC), 148, 156–157, 159, 237–238; meeting in Vilnius, 156
National Aeronautics and Space Administration. *See* NASA
National Air Defense Forces. *See* PVO Strany
Nationalism, 352
National Security Council, 111, 118
NATO, 11–12, 17, 67, 112, 114, 118, 184, 305, 319; advanced conventional weaponry, 291–293; and CFE, 361; deploys U.S. missiles in Western Europe, 143–144, 183, 270; expansion of, 372, 391; flexible response, 177; force structure, 122; military policy, 157; and MBFR, 301, 317; and MLF, 201; nuclearization, 113, 115; offense-oriented conventional posture, 308; and Warsaw Pact, 304
Natural Resources Defense Council (NRDC), 148, 275, 279–281, 288, 325, 327, 359, 369, 383; in Kazakhstan, 283, 285; Nuclear Weapons Databooks, 281; seismic monitoring system, 326, 358, 367
Nazi Germany, 5, 47, 127; invades USSR, 384
Negotiation from strength, 14, 48, 50, 54, 87, 110–113, 133, 137, 153, 166, 244, 269, 290, 303, 332
Nehru, Jawaharlal, 26, 31, 374; on nuclear test moratorium, 41, 47–48, 50, 75
Neild, Robert, 188; and alternative defense, 312–313
Nesmeianov, A. N., 64

Nevada-Semipalatinsk movement, 9, 351–352, **353**, 354–356
Nevada test site, 83 n.151, 352, 354, 358
New Delhi, 32
New Forum, 249
Newsweek, 221
New Thinking in Soviet foreign policy, 3–4, 20, 148, 162, 172, 184, 189, 193, 238, 289, 303, 315–316, 320, 324, 361–362, 374–375, 377, 379, 387, 390; German origins of, 187. *See also* Gorbachev, Mikhail
New Times (Soviet weekly), 135
New York Times, 3–5, 48, 82, 115, 171, 207, 249–251
New Zealand, 169
Nike: air-defense missile program, 127; Nike-X, 128–130, 214; Nike-Zeus, 127–129
Nitze, Paul, 240, 244, 328, 332–333
Nixon, Richard M., 70, 147, 199, 222; administration of, 151, 169, 196, 230; and MBFR, 182
Nobel Committee, 3–5
Nobel laureates, 162, 272
Nobel Peace Prize, 3–5, 149, 153, 251, 275 n.44
No first use, 177
Nonaligned countries, 74, 76, 269; meeting in Belgrade, 75; movement of, 47, 50, 270, 273
Nonoffensive defense, 11, 121–122, 175, 186–191, 262, 290, 294, 303, 305–308, 311, 313, 316, 320, 343, 385, 386–387. *See also* Alternative defense; Defensive restructuring
Nordic Nuclear-Weapon-Free Zone, 162–163; and Soviet Baltic states, 163
Norms, 7–8, 327, 377, 385, 387–388; humanitarian, 372; international, 384, 387; strategic use of, 384–389
Norstad, Lauris, 119
North Atlantic Treaty Organization. *See* NATO
Novaia Zemlia: test site, 356–357, 359
Nova Scotia, 32
NRDC. *See* Natural Resources Defense Council
Nuclear deterrence, 104, 236; foundation for arms control, 225; minimum, 118, 122, 206; mutual, 207, 211, 216, 218–219, 224, 230, 232, 234
Nuclear disarmament. *See* Disarmament
Nuclear escalation, 293
Nuclear freeze, 168, 270; movement, 314, 383
Nuclear-free zones, 10. *See also* Europe; Nordic Nuclear-Weapon Free Zone
Nuclear Nonproliferation Treaty, 146
Nuclear parity, 176, 310, 350
Nuclear reactors: proposed ban from orbit, 369–370
Nuclear testing, 9, 31, 34, 45–89, 165–173, 192, 264–288, 349–360, 385; ban, 155, 264, 342–343; congressional ban, 371; cost of Soviet program, 268; legislated restrictions, 287;

Index

Index

anti-Semitic campaign of, 28; death of, 111; post-Stalin thaw, 25, 31, 140
Starodubov, Viktor, 315
START I, 323–324, 329, 380; Treaty, 332–334, 337, 379
Star Wars. *See* Strategic Defense Initiative (SDI)
Stassen, Harold, 111, 116–117
Stockholm International Peace Research Institute (SIPRI), 310
Stone, B. J., 201
Stone, I. F., 201
Stone, Jeremy, 134–135, 136 n.47, 137, 147 n.14, 193, 199, 201, **243**, 281, 322, 329–330, 333; *The Case Against Missile Defences*, 202; support for dissidents, 202
Stone, Shepard, 229
Stowe, Vermont (Pugwash meeting), 34, 74
Strategic Arms Limitation Talks (SALT), 144, 165, 196, 210, 214, 219, 222–224, 230
Strategic Arms Reductions Talks (START I), 323–324, 329, 380; Treaty, 332–334, 337, 379
Strategic Defense Initiative (SDI), 10, 132, 194, 233–234, 237, 241, 262–263, 265, 268, 335, 337, 342, 379–380, 384; asymmetric response to, 239–240, 323, 332; economic effect on Soviet Union, 331, 337, 388; emergence of, 236, 278; fraudulent test (June 1984), 242–244; grand compromise, 244, 332–334; nuclear-powered weapons, 268; Office, 367, 369, 371; proponents of, 370; research, 266, 271, 275; role in ending Cold War, 240; sharing, 245; Soviet response to, 304, 322, 365; as a threat, 385; U.S. universities pledge not to accept funds for work on, 275; unlinking from arms control, 328–330, 384. *See also* ABM Treaty; Anti-ballistic missile defenses; Strategic defenses
Strategic defenses, 9–10; space-based, 172, 194, 237–238, 242, 266; talks on, 199; technical prospects for, 170. *See also* ABM Treaty; Anti-ballistic missile defenses; Strategic Defense Initiative (SDI)
Strategic Rocket Forces, 102–103, 213, 218, 220
Strukturelle Nichtangriffsfähigkeit, 294
Study Group on Alternative Security Policy (Studiengruppe Alternative Sicherheitspolitik), 314
Suez, 120
Sufficient defense, 189–190, 311, 387. *See also* Reasonable sufficiency
Suleimenov, Olzhas, 352, **355**, 356
Summit meetings: Geneva (July 1955), 92, 113–119; Geneva (1985), 332, 383; Moscow (1972), 231, 273; Moscow (July 1986), 275–276; Reykjavik (October 1986), 267, 273–274, 328–329. *See also* Geneva; *entries for various treaties*
Supreme Soviet, 53, 64, 101, 152, 199, 217, 227, 314, 346–347, 350, 352, 356–357, 379, 387;

Committee on Defense and State Security, 319–320; Committee on Economic Conversion, 257
Surikov, Boris Trofimovich, 213–214, 220
Suslov, Mikhail, 34, 53, 150, 152, 183, 207–208, 215 n.95
Svechin, A. A., 191
Sweden, 162, 282; Delhi Six, 275
Szilard, Leo, 27, 43–44, 85, 165; and Khrushchev, 35; proposal for direct US-Soviet dialogue, 33, 41; proposal for meeting at the Vatican, 158; and Stalin, 28–29, 41–42; and Topchiev, 36; *Voice of the Dolphins*, 42, 84

Tairov, Tair, 270–271
Talbott, Strobe, 329, 379
Talenskii, N. A., 134–137, 199, 209, 212; attends Pugwash meetings, 137; funeral, 202; Talenskii Doctrine, 211
Tamm, Igor', 61
Tanzania: Delhi Six, 275
Tarrow, Sidney, 352 n.25
Team B Study, 234, 235 n.3
Teller, Edward, 84, 370
Thermonuclear weapons, 31; "clean," 84; 50-megaton Soviet test (1961), 72–74. *See also* Hydrogen bomb
Thomas, Norman, 62
Thompson, E. P., 251
Thompson, Llewellyn, 197
Threshold test ban, 69; Treaty (1974), 68, 165–166, 279–280, 288
Thurmond, Strom, 130
Tiedtke, Jutta, 109
Tikhonov, N. A., 259
Tokyo, 57
Topaz nuclear space reactor, 370
Topchiev, Aleksandr, 31–32, 34; death, 37; and Rotblat, 64; and Szilard, 36
Tovish, Aaron, 282
Treaty on Conventional Forces in Europe. *See* Conventional Forces in Europe (CFE) Treaty
Trust Group (Moscow), 163
Tsarapkin, Semen, 61, 63–64
Transnational influence: practice, 20–21; strategies, 381–383; theory, 18–19
Transnationalism: tacit, 39, 82–83, 88, 207, 367
Transnational norms, 84
Transnational relations: definition, 6; theory, 16–19
Tret'iak, Ivan, 98
Trident missiles, 325
Troop reductions, 74, 122; in Czechoslovakia, 182; demographic considerations, 106; in Germany, 110, 182, 308; Gorbachev's unilateral reductions, 180; high cost of maintaining troops abroad, 109; in Hungary, 110; Khrushchev and, 101, 180, 388; negative reaction of army, 98; unilateral, 176, 317; in U.S., 114; U.S. behavior, 110. *See also*